NZMANN · JOHN M LYONS · RODNEY BRADFO

N · RANDALL A THOMPSON · GEORGE F McDA

V PART IDGE · TONY G POWELL · JOSE M QUESN

RU ALFRED V SCHOFIELD · ANTHONY R SIG

GL M · DALE A MORROW · MARTHELL TRAYLO

WIM ERLY · MICHAEL E ADAMS · ERNEST J BAY

BURK RICHARD A CHAMBERS · J

VIS VEN J DAWSON · COLOMBO P DELTER

L LOW · BRUCE J FEDLER · JOHN W GEOR

AYES TRISTAN W HAYES · RAYMOND J MAZYC

SON Jr · GARY F JOHNSTON · HAROLD J KISSIN

TORRES · JERRY LEE MARCUM · JAMES E MARLO

UNDELL · FRANK J McMANUS · FREDRICK E NI

DOMINICK POLLASTRO · MICHAEL W POUSSO

RANGE Jr · JAMES P RAWLINS · STEVEN J REICHAR

ALD L RONDO · ALBERT E ROSE · JUAN O SANCH

MANS Jr · GEORGE A YARBROUGH · LARRY D SM

SONGNE · BILLIE G STICKLAND · FRANK A SAY

RRY H ALLEN · MICHAEL R BARTELL · ROB

NING · WILLIAM E BRUSTER · DEWAYNE T W

DECKER · JOHN F DOWNEY Jr · RAYMOND

MAN · JOE A GALVEZ · PEDRO GALLARD

HAYS · ROBERT L JANOWITZ · AARON G

M MAESTAS · JAMES R McCOY · CHESTER

THE Sixties CHRONICLE

CONSULTANT
David Farber, Ph.D.

WRITERS
Peter Braunstein, M.A.
Phillip Carpenter, Ph.D.
Anthony O. Edmonds, Ph.D.
David Farber, Ph.D.
Michael S. Foley, Ph.D.
Robert A. Rodriguez
Jeffrey C. Sanders, Ph.D.
Bradley G. Shreve, M.A.

FOREWORD
Walter Cronkite

PREFACE
Tom Hayden

LEGACY

Publisher & CEO
Louis Weber

Editor-in-Chief
David J. Hogan

Editor
David Aretha

Associate Editor
Jeremy Weber

Art Director
James Slate

Creative Director
Marissa Conner

Acquisitions Editor
Victoria Smith

Acquisitions Project Assistant
Michael Staples

Director of Acquisitions & Visual Resources
Doug Brooks

Associate Director of Acquisitions
Susan Barbee

Production Editor
Valerie A. Iglar-Mobley

Production Director
Steven Grundt

Electronic Publishing Specialist
Ron Gad

Visual Resources Specialist
Matthew Schwarz

Legacy Logo Designer
James Schlottman

Assistant to the Publisher
Renee G. Haring

Editorial Assistants
Shavahn Dorris
Kathline Jones
Nicholas Myers

Publications Coordinator
Julie Greene

Director, Pre-Press
David Darian

Pre-Press Coordinator
Laura Schmidt

Imaging Development Manager
Paul Fromberg

Imaging Specialists
Sara Allen
Melissa Hamilton

Director of Purchasing
Rocky Wu

Manufacturing Manager
Kent Keutzer

Legal Adviser
Dorothy Weber

Legacy Publishing is a division of Publications International, Ltd.

Manufactured in China.

8 7 6 5 4 3 2 1

ISBN: 1-4127-1009-X

Library of Congress Control Number: 2004109277

Contributors

Foreword

Walter Cronkite began his career as a journalist by hosting small radio shows and writing for newspapers. In 1939 he joined United Press to cover World War II, during which he went ashore on D-Day, parachuted with the 101st Airborne, and flew on bombing missions over Germany. He joined CBS in 1950, hosting the historical series *You Are There* and the documentary series *Twentieth Century*. In 1962 he moved into the *CBS Evening News* anchor position, which he held until his retirement in 1981. Mr. Cronkite was one of the first to report the assassination of President John F. Kennedy in 1963, and in 1969 he covered the Apollo 11 mission for 27 hours of its 30-hour journey. In a 1972 poll, respondents named Mr. Cronkite "the most trusted man in America." Since his retirement in 1981, Mr. Cronkite has hosted documentaries for PBS, the Discovery Channel, and the Learning Channel, in addition to writing pieces for newspapers and other publications. Throughout his career, which spans more than 60 years, he has gained the respect of not only the American public, but of politicians and leaders worldwide.

Preface

Tom Hayden teaches at Occidental College in Los Angeles and is the author of 11 books, most recently *Street Wars and Rebel*. He served in the California legislature from 1982 to 2000, and chaired its committees on higher education, labor, and natural resources. In the early 1960s, he was a student editor, Freedom Rider in Georgia, president of Students for a Democratic Society, and author of the Port Huron Statement. A foremost opponent of the Vietnam War, he was indicted and eventually acquitted of all charges in the Chicago Conspiracy trial of 1969–70. Based in Culver City, California, he continues to participate in and write about antiwar and social justice movements.

Consultant

David Farber, Ph.D., (consultant and essayist) is a professor of history at Temple University. He has authored several books, including *The Age of Great Dreams: America in the 1960s, Chicago '68,* and *Sloan Rules: Alfred P. Sloan and the Triumph of General Motors,* for which he was awarded the 2002 Herbert Hoover Prize by the Herbert Hoover Library Association for the best book on any topic in American history. In addition, the book *The Columbia Guide to America in the 1960s,* which he coauthored with his wife, Beth Bailey, won the 2001 Choice Outstanding Academic Book. Dr. Farber also has contributed to a book series entitled *Counter Cultures,* and has delivered numerous presentations and lectures on the 1960s, including "The Politics of Liberalism in the United States During the Sixties Era," "The Civil Rights Movement in the United States," "The Monterey Pop Festival: From Memory to History," and "The Sixties From a Twenty-First Century Perspective."

Primary Authors

Anthony O. Edmonds, Ph.D., (captions author) is a professor of history at Ball State University. He teaches courses on the Vietnam War, recent U.S. history, American values, and the impact of popular culture on conceptions of history. He is the author of the book *The War in Vietnam* and has contributed to many other books, including *War and American Pop Culture, The Vietnam War on Campus: Other Voices, More Distant Drums,* and *Silhouettes on the Shade.* Dr. Edmonds currently serves on the editorial board for the Popular Culture Association/American Culture Association Internet Network. In addition, he has served as editor for *Proceedings* for the Indiana Academy of Social Sciences, and has served on the editorial board for *Forum.*

Michael S. Foley, Ph.D., (sidebars author) is an assistant professor of history at the College of Staten Island, City University of New York. He is the author of the book *Confronting the War Machine: Draft Resistance During the Vietnam War,* and has contributed to such publications as *A Companion to the Vietnam War, The New Left Revisited,* and *Peace & Change: A Journal of Peace Research.* He also has conducted presentations for public and academic audiences, including "Draft Resistance During the Vietnam War" and "Confronting the War Machine."

Robert A. Rodriguez (sidebars and captions author) is a freelance writer and researcher. He is author of the book *The 1950s Most Wanted,* which covers history and pop culture of the decade, and is currently working on books about the Beatles and Buddy Holly.

Jeffrey C. Sanders, Ph.D., (sidebars and captions author) is the author of the book *McClellan Park: The Life and Death of an Urban Greenspace.* He also has contributed to *The Columbia Guide to America in the 1960s* and *Environmental Atlas of the United States and Canada.*

Bradley G. Shreve, M.A., (sidebars author) is the author of many biographical articles. He wrote the article "The U.S., the USSR, and Space Exploration, 1957–1963" for the *International Journal on World Peace.* He is currently a graduate teaching assistant and a Ph.D. candidate at the University of New Mexico.

Additional Writers

Peter Braunstein, M.A., (sidebars contributor) is a freelance writer who has contributed articles to *Culturefront, Village Voice,* and *American Heritage.* He also was the coeditor of the anthology *Imagine Nation: The American Counterculture of the 1960s and 1970s.* He holds a masters of arts in American history, with a concentration in post-World War II cultural history.

Phillip Carpenter, Ph.D., (captions contributor) is a researcher at the University of Illinois and a columnist for the *History News Network.* He has contributed dozens of articles and essays to *The Octopus, The History Resource Center: United States,* and *TomPaine.com.* He also served as a researcher for The Learning Channel documentary *The Pentagon.*

Jo Ellen Warner (captions contributor) is the former policy director for the Seattle Office for Civil Rights. As a freelance writer, she has contributed to *Civil Rights Chronicle: The African-American Struggle for Freedom, The Seattle Medium* (a weekly African-American newspaper), and *The Seattle Post-Intelligencer.*

Gary West (timeline contributor) is the founder and editor of *Pop History Now!,* an online publication that features events in history, news, politics, sports, movies, music, and fashion from the end of World War II through the 1990s. He also contributes weekly to WestwoodOne Oldies in California with his radio segment "This Week in History."

Factual Verification

Barbara Cross has contributed to a variety of titles as a researcher, fact checker, and editor on topics such as history, biology, and other sciences.

Regina J. Montgomery is a research editor and writer. She served as associate producer and assistant director for *For My People,* a televised community news and talk show in Detroit. She recently was named to the Wall of Tolerance in Montgomery, Alabama.

Christy M. Nadalin is a documentary television producer, freelance writer, and editorial researcher whose clients have included the National Geographic Society, the Discovery Channel, A&E Television Networks, and Time–Life Books.

Index by Ina Gravitz

Acknowledgments can be found on page 479.

Contents

Both candidates in the U.S. presidential race were born in the 20th century—a first. Good looks and charisma win the day as Massachusetts Senator John F. Kennedy narrowly defeats Vice President Richard Nixon. JFK brings with him a glamorous, young wife and a vigorous commitment to an active federal government and social change. Cuba tilts farther to the left under Fidel Castro, and numerous European colonies in Africa become independent nations.

A JFK–CIA plan to foment revolution in Cuba with a ragtag beachhead assault at the Bay of Pigs goes humiliatingly wrong, handing Cuba and the Soviet Union a significant propaganda victory. U.S. prestige suffers another blow when Soviet cosmonaut Yuri Gagarin becomes the first human in space. But shortly after, American astronaut Alan Shepard completes a similar journey. The Cold War heats up in Europe when Communists erect a wall to imprison East Berliners within their sector of the city.

Soviet missiles in Cuba become a major test of the Kennedy Administration. The world teeters close to nuclear war until Soviet Premier Nikita Khrushchev blinks, and orders the missiles removed. Astronaut John Glenn is the first American to orbit the Earth, and in the American South, a young black man named James Meredith risks his life to enroll at the University of Mississippi.

The American civil rights movement, led by the charismatic Martin Luther King, Jr., galvanizes African-Americans and sympathetic whites. Progress is made in the face of white hatred, but not without the tragic sacrifice of four girls in a church in Alabama. In November, the world is stunned when President Kennedy is shot and killed in Dallas. Rangy, blunt-talking Texan Lyndon Johnson assumes the presidency.

1964 170

Rock 'n' roll enters a new era and youth culture is irrevocably altered when the Beatles make a triumphant arrival in America. A commission on the assassination of President Kennedy issues the *Warren Commission Report,* concluding that Lee Harvey Oswald acted alone. In Mississippi during "Freedom Summer," three young civil rights workers are murdered and secretly buried by white racists.

1965 212

American troop levels and casualties increase dramatically in Vietnam. At home, the antiwar movement expands, and grows increasingly outspoken. In a momentous year for the civil rights movement, the fiery Malcolm X is murdered, the Voting Rights Act of 1965 is passed, racially motivated riots tear through Los Angeles and Chicago, and thousands of marchers accompany Martin Luther King, Jr., from Selma, Alabama, to the state capitol in Montgomery.

1966 254

The National Organization of Women is founded by Betty Friedan and others to ensure equal opportunity in education, employment, and business. Huey Newton and Bobby Seale establish the Black Panther Party, and civil rights activist James Meredith is sniper-shot and wounded in Mississippi. In China, Mao Tse-tung launches the violently hardline-Communist Cultural Revolution.

1967 296

San Francisco's "Summer of Love" brings youth culture to a highly publicized apex, but all is not mellow. Antiwar fervor is increasing, and drug use is on the rise. Detroit and other cities are rocked by racial violence, and three American astronauts die in a launchpad fire. In the Middle East, Israel launches a preemptive strike and triumphs against its Arab neighbors in the Six-Day War.

1968 346

Martin Luther King, Jr., and leading presidential candidate Bobby Kennedy are felled by assassins' bullets. President Johnson, wearied by the Vietnam War and urban riots, announces he will not seek reelection. Outside the Democratic convention in Chicago, protest dissolves into open warfare between activists and police. Richard Nixon wins the presidency. In Czechoslovakia, a move toward liberalized socialism is brutally quashed when Soviet tanks roll into Prague.

1969 400

While Michael Collins orbits overhead, Apollo 11 astronauts Neil Armstrong and Buzz Aldrin walk on the moon. Some 400,000 young people gather at the Woodstock Music and Art Fair in rural New York. In Los Angeles, followers of career criminal Charles Manson carry out grisly multiple murders. President Nixon begins to reduce U.S. ground troops in Vietnam, and Massachusetts Senator Ted Kennedy leaves the scene of a car accident in which a young campaign worker is drowned.

Epilogue 448

Index 454

Foreword

THE SIXTIES—the incredible decade. There were great scientific advances, there were assassinations, and there were sometimes bloody demonstrations that brought African-Americans their long-delayed civil rights. Women organized and demonstrated and won federal protection against sexual discrimination. And we had a war that split the American people.

If there was anything that united the American people, it was their grief over the senseless murder of John Fitzgerald Kennedy—handsome, charismatic, and the youngest man ever elected president.

Every American and hundreds of thousands of people around the globe remember exactly where they were when the shocking news came across their radios and television sets.

I reported the tragic news from our CBS news headquarters. I almost lost my composure when I had to confirm that the President had died in Dallas's Parkland Hospital. I think my near breaking point came with a vignette of memory from Kennedy's inaugural day. I was in CBS's open camera car, which had drawn the straw that put us immediately ahead of the new President and his wife as they departed the Capitol for the parade down Pennsylvania Avenue to the White House.

The weather had blessed his big day. The blizzard that had raged the night before had given way to a bright and sunny, if cold, day. The Kennedys were in an open limousine during a time before terrorism forced dignitaries into closed and armored cars.

I waved to them from my post a few yards ahead of them. They waved back with the happy smiles of eloping

lovers. It was that image that my memory uncovered just as I had to make the announcement that the official word had come: "President Kennedy died at one o'clock Central Standard Time, some 38 minutes ago."

Kennedy's assassination was one of four that put an indelible mark of shame on the decade of the Sixties. Medgar Evers, one of the courageous pioneers who had led his people in their successful battle to win racial equality with whites, was murdered in 1963. Robert F. Kennedy, while running for president, met the same fate as his older brother in June 1968.

The fourth great leader to fall from an assassin's bullet was Martin Luther King, Jr., the black preacher who, from the steps of Washington's Lincoln Memorial, delivered one of the greatest orations of modern times. "I have a dream," he said, and the words echoed around the world among people everywhere who yearned for freedom from despotism.

Behind King as he spoke was that great statue of a seated Lincoln, and this observer could almost swear that he saw a satisfied smile on the face of the great emancipator. King had the magic touch, and you could sense the beating hearts of that crowd of more than 250,000, mostly African-Americans, as they took King's words as the promise that he would lead them to the equality so long deserved but always postponed.

Of course they were right, but the equality they sought would come only after blood was spilled as they gathered to demonstrate in some southern communities where law enforcement officers met them with billy clubs and fire hoses. Television coverage of those beatings, and the bombing of a black church in Birmingham, Alabama, that took the lives of four girls attending Sunday school, inflamed the sensitivities of most Americans and virtually guaranteed government action to respect the civil rights of all minorities.

The triumph was assured from an unexpected quarter. Lyndon Johnson, before he was picked as Kennedy's vice president, was a U.S. senator from Texas, and he used his considerable power in Congress to help his southern friends defend racial segregation. But with Kennedy's assassination, he abandoned his sectionalism and, recognizing his new responsibility to all the people, pushed through Congress the civil rights laws that, enforced by federal authority, finally, in the 1960s, extended to all our people the freedoms Abraham Lincoln had promised a century before.

Women, too, contributed to the Sixties' revolutionary turmoil by launching a movement to ban sex discrimination in the workplace. With marches and demonstrations by thousands of supporters, they won the battle. However, as with racial matters, 40 years later perfection in achieving equality is yet to be realized.

Another important advancement was the development of the birth control pill. It liberated women from male dominance and made a great contribution to their independence in today's world.

Back in the 1960s, I agreed in principle with women's demands, but some gave me a little trouble. For instance, they decided that, since men did not indicate by their form of address whether they were married or not, it was somehow demeaning that women had to reveal their marital status with the *Miss* or *Mrs.* label. So they invented *Ms.* as suitably equivalent to the male's *Mr.* As one whose journalistic chores required frequent mention of women, I faced with my fellow broadcasters the problem of how to pronounce *Ms.* We finally settled on *Mizz,* which, to my mind, despite common usage is still rather inelegant.

I learned the hard way of the sensibilities of the women activists. I thought highly of most of the leaders of the movement and thus was disturbed when one of them took offense at some broadcast comment of mine. I invited her to lunch to try to set things right.

It went well until she chose to have a postprandial cigarette. I unthinkingly did what a gentleman should do: I held a match for her cigarette. She exploded with invective. My gentlemanly gesture, she pointed out, showed my disrespect for her equal right to light her own cigarette.

Well, I squared that somehow and we left the restaurant. As we began to walk to a cab rank, I danced around her to take the outside position, which I always had observed as another of those gentlemanly gestures at which I considered myself quite adroit. She almost screamed at me: "You don't get it at all, do you? You still think you have to protect the little woman. Well forget it!" And away she strode.

Perhaps an even more significant example of the decade's turbulence was the 1968 Democratic convention in Chicago. A few thousand young people camped out in Grant Park to demonstrate their objection to the Vietnam War. Many were sincere, but their number was peppered with hooligans. Mayor Richard J. Daley's police reacted with an excess of force. They bloodied many a young demonstrator, and the demonstrations turned into full-scale riots. The police officers' tear gas filled the lobby of the Democratic headquarters hotel, and the Democratic delegates' weeping eyes symbolized the sad state of their party.

Foreword

Daley's police even invaded the convention hall itself, and they dared pummel and manhandle reporters they encountered on the convention floor. Television coverage of the unseemly disorder helped defeat the Democratic nominee, Hubert Humphrey, and paved the way for Richard Nixon to become the 37th president of the United States.

For the ultimate turmoil of the Sixties there was, of course, the Vietnam War. It divided this country as had nothing since the Civil War a century before. In one particular way, the division perhaps was even deeper than back in the 1860s.

The Civil War was a sectional war between North and South, and where one lived pretty well determined his or her view of the conflict. In contrast, the split on Vietnam was on ideological grounds. Households were divided and friendships were destroyed, as people either supported or detested the U.S. attempt to try to save a corner of Southeast Asia from the Communists, who were taking over Vietnam's neighboring states.

Not unlike Iraq today, opponents of the American presence occasionally bombed restaurants and other gathering places of American soldiers. I was somewhat nervous about these episodes as I flew for the first time into the beleaguered country aboard a Vietnam Airlines plane. But when I saw the beautiful, smiling, Vietnamese hostess, my fears abated—until she handed me the English-language Hong Kong paper. The banner headline shouted from the front page the news that some Vietnam air hostesses were suspected of conspiring with the bomb planters. I kept a sharp eye on the hostess on that ride to Saigon. Come to think of it, I might have paid her that attention anyway.

Despite all the turmoil of the Sixties, the decade ended on a resounding note of triumph. I maintain that of all the incredible technical and scientific developments of the 20th century, July 20, 1969, the date of our landing on the moon, will be remembered by schoolchildren 500 years from now.

How can I be so sure of that? Well, think of it: The date today's schoolchildren most likely remember is October 12, 1492, the day Columbus landed on this continent and proved that there was a whole other world across the seas from Europe.

That was 500 years ago. Five hundred years from now there is every likelihood that human beings will be living on other planets and cities built in space. Surely they will memorize the date when humans first broke free from the earthly environment and set in motion the space age that paved the way for their habitat among the stars.

Yes, it was a formidable decade that warrants Dickens's oft-quoted description of another era: It was the best of times, and the worst of times.

Walter Cronkite

Walter Cronkite

Preface

L IKE A GREAT RIVER, the Sixties arose from mysterious forces at the margins. Its streams flowed into a movement, and its flows rechanneled the mainstream, leaving meanings to be explored for generations to come.

I experienced the Sixties in all the passion, the hope and bitterness, the action and reaction, from beginning to end. In 1960 I was a budding student editor who dreamt of escaping our first suburbs to become an adventurous foreign correspondent. I took notes next to Martin Luther King, Jr., on a picket line that year, feeling foolish at being merely a writer, and again next to John F. Kennedy that fall when he proposed the Peace Corps on the steps of the University of Michigan Student Union.

Still ambitious, I published my first article on the new student movement in *Mademoiselle* magazine the next year. But that fall I was beaten in Mississippi, and I spent my 22nd birthday in 1961 in jail as a Freedom Rider in Albany, Georgia. That same year I drafted the Port Huron Statement of Students for a Democratic Society (SDS). By decade's end, I was a revolutionary on trial in Chicago for protests at the 1968 Democratic convention. The FBI had ordered that I be "neutralized" as a "prime objective" of their counter-intelligence program. My Irish-American, ex-Marine, accountant father disowned me for 16 years.

At age 64, although I've led several additional lives—husband of Jane Fonda for 16 years, father of three, state legislator for 18 years, author of 11 books—the Sixties remain the neighborhood I represent. For years I was uncomfortable with this identity, wanting to move on, to be judged for who I was in the present. I learned, however, that few could let it rest.

I came to realize that for some, the entire era of the Sixties needed to be purged from American consciousness. Justice Robert Bork was one of many conservatives who found that the Port Huron Statement's call for "participatory democracy" was "ominous." Lynne Cheney, wife of Vice President Dick Cheney, blamed the Sixties' "political correctness" for causing more 17-year-olds to know the name of Harriet Tubman (83.8 percent) than to know that George Washington commanded the Revolutionary Army.

The Sixties was a seismic event, an upheaval along political, economic, and cultural fault lines from fissures that remain inscrutable. No historian or futurist predicted that four black students at North Carolina A&T College in Greensboro, North Carolina, would "sit in" at a segregated lunch counter. This was evidence of things not yet seen. Suddenly, thousands of young people took direct action to destroy the walls of segregation after more than 300 years of white dominance. Their action was central to the Sixties theory of participatory democracy. As Henry David Thoreau had urged long before, "Cast your whole vote, not a strip of paper merely, but your whole influence. A minority is powerless while it conforms to the majority…but it is irresistible when it clogs by its whole weight."

Such inspirational action birthed the Sixties. Americans elected a youthful president. Students and women came alive, farmworkers stood up, shaggy-haired musicians became subversive, and "the pill" became available. An ice age was over.

The Sixties were global. Thousands embraced, and many gave their lives for, a liberation theology that sanc-

Preface

tified the poor. Their spirit was echoed by Baptist Reverend Martin Luther King, Jr., in his "Letter from Birmingham Jail," and became manifest on the streets of Prague in 1968. Revolutions in Vietnam and Cuba confounded the American superiority complex. The emergence of 20 independent African nations in 1960 galvanized African-Americans across the ocean. Revolts by youth in Czechoslovakia, South Korea, Japan, Mexico, Germany, France, Northern Ireland—the list was like a roll call of the United Nations—created a "generation of '68."

Today's Western leaders directly shaped by the Sixties include a former Vietnam draft opponent, President Bill Clinton; a former German revolutionary, Joschka Fischer, now his country's foreign minister; a former Marxist radical, Jorge Castenada, who became Mexico's foreign minister; and many other influentials across the globe. While such leaders are the pragmatic wing of our generation, they still are deeply mistrusted by conservatives for their youthful radicalism.

There were at least two Sixties, the utopian period from 1960 to 1964 when all things seemed possible, and the bloody denouement between the beginning of Vietnam and the fall of Richard Nixon, a period in which America descended into civil war. More than 200 race riots occurred from the time of the Watts uprising in August 1965 to King's murder in April 1968. From January 1969 to April 1970, more than 5,000 bombings took place on American soil. California Governor Ronald Reagan, speaking for countless flustered parent voters, declared in 1970, "These students seek disruption....If it takes a bloodbath, let's get it over with."

Then came the killings at Kent State and Jackson State, the gradual end of the greater bloodbath in Vietnam, the timely opening of the system to its left-outs, and the sudden vanishing of the Sixties.

We will never cease to wonder what might have happened without the assassinations of John F. Kennedy, Robert F. Kennedy, Martin Luther King, Malcolm X, and Medgar Evers. We were plunged, as writer Jack Newfield said in sadness, into being might-have-beens.

The achievements of the Sixties became forgotten as they blended into the expectations of everyday life: Voting rights for southern African-Americans. Equal opportunity measures for women and minorities. The 18-year-old vote. The end of military conscription. The toppling of presidents. The War Powers Act. The end of the FBI's spying on activists. Amnesty for draft resisters. Consumer protection. Laws to ensure clean air and water. Occupational health and safety. The first Earth Day. The birth of the gay-lesbian movement. A new generation of investigative journalists.

As times changed, conservatives and liberals had choices to make. For conservatives, the choice was between damage control (from supporting segregation to voting for Martin Luther King's holiday) and a new, sophisticated resistance to the reforms of the Sixties (blaming hip-hop for moral degeneracy, or claiming that Dr. King, in advocating a color-blind America, would have opposed affirmative action).

For many liberals, the choice was between running from their radical past and seeing the past as a prelude to passionate stirrings against global injustice, symbolized by the 1999 Seattle confrontations and the 2003 global anti-Iraq demonstrations.

The Sixties will remain with us as a new generation ponders what to do about racism and poverty, and about liberty, in a time of terror. *The Sixties Chronicle* should help us grapple with the magnificent complexity of the current era, offering alternatives to either nostalgia or amnesia.

Tom Hayden

Introduction

EVERY DECADE IS RICH with incident, but the 1960s were particularly dramatic. Consider: a still-expanding post-World War II economy and a divisive war in Vietnam; continued antagonism between the United States and the Soviet Union; emergence of a vocally iconoclastic, international youth culture; sea changes in music, film, television, theater, art, and literature; racial and gender activism; the collision of American affluence and poverty; startling advances in science and technology that culminated in a moon landing; assassinations of beloved American leaders; and a newly adversarial relationship between Washington and the press. All of this and much more defined the decade.

To encapsulate those 10 years, 1960 to 1969, within the pages of a single volume has been a daunting but pleasurable challenge. Although the Sixties have receded into history, the period remains very much alive, and continues to inform much of our social and political discourse. When the period is carefully reconsidered, it comes to life almost palpably.

The Sixties Chronicle is a lively time capsule, a portable archive that can be held in one's hands. It is your single-volume guide to 120 of the most momentous months in the history of America and the world. Arranged for ease of use as well as learning and pleasure, the book will stir discussion as well as nostalgia.

Within each of the 10 chapters, you'll find scores of provocative images that are the book's visual centerpieces. The pictures were selected after the editors scoured traditional photo archives as well as private collections. Many thousands of images were reviewed as the assortment was winnowed to the best and most significant.

The images are described in colorful, extended captions written by Sixties historians. Lively and engaging as well as authoritative, these captions give life to the faces, places, and events you will see.

A detailed and useful timeline of events runs consecutively on the book's left-side pages, bringing you the dates and quick facts about events great, odd, and amusing. Additionally, each year's timeline concludes with a list of new and notable books, television programs, songs, movies, and theatrical productions.

Events, personalities, organizations, and pertinent issues that require special explication are covered in detailed, illustrated sidebars. In addition, distinctive sidebars with a "you are there" feel feature the first-person accounts of people who witnessed and participated in important events.

A Prologue describes America and the world from 1945 to 1959; an Epilogue discusses ways in which the Sixties echo today.

Two specially commissioned pieces, a Foreword by Walter Cronkite and a Preface by Tom Hayden, include insights from men who witnessed the decade from unique vantage points, and who had profound impacts upon it.

A detailed index guides you to whatever about the 1960s you may be searching for, from the Student Nonviolent Coordinating Committee to the Wham-O toy company; from John F. Kennedy to *The Munsters*.

Written with expertise and energy by skilled academics, and meticulously fact-checked, *The Sixties Chronicle* will propel every reader on a journey—sometimes dark, sometimes ecstatically bright—across an amazing period that helped make us what we are today.

Prologue

The Baby Boom and Cold War Culture

"The Sixties" started long before John F. Kennedy set up shop in the White House or those four young black men in Greensboro, North Carolina, politely asked the waitress at the all-white lunch counter for a cup of coffee. Before the Beatles rocked Shea Stadium, the Sixties was taking root in the most unexpected places. Before there was long hair and the "generation gap" and the terrible war, what would become the Sixties was being born in the hearts of millions. The era was conceived in the prosperous victory culture that blessed the United States after so many years of sacrifice. It also was born in the struggles for racial justice as well as in the wrenching fears of Cold War apocalypse.

The seeds of the Sixties were planted shortly after the United States and its allies defeated Nazi Germany and Japan, thus saving Europe and Asia from rules of terror. The joy of those victories, and the relief of the millions of men who came home alive in 1945, was indelibly captured in the iconic photograph of a young sailor and a young woman kissing exuberantly in one of the many welcome-home parades held all over the nation. The United States had awakened from its isolationist stance and—in the words of Britain's wartime leader, Winston Churchill—come to the rescue of the Old World. Americans were proud of what they had accomplished both on the battlefield and on the home front, where they had worked around the clock to create an unmatchable "arsenal of democracy."

Unlike almost all the other participants involved in World War II, Americans could celebrate their victory in towns and cities that were untouched by wartime devastation. Europeans and Asians were not so fortunate. So many

> "In our nation, work and wealth abound. Our population grows. Commerce crowds our rivers and rails, our skies, harbors, and highways. Our soil is fertile, our agriculture productive. The air rings with the song of our industry; rolling mills and blast furnaces, dynamos, dams, and assembly lines; the chorus of America the bountiful."
>
> —President Dwight Eisenhower, January 20, 1957

A typical postwar American family takes a stroll through their planned suburban community, Levittown, New York. Economically prosperous, Americans delighted in affordable housing and near full employment. This postwar confidence in the American economy led to a tremendous surge in birthrates, which made way for a new Baby Boomer generation that would take center stage in the 1960s.

Prologue

of their communities had been torn apart by battle. Tokyo had been fire-bombed. Berlin was an archaeological ruin. London had been pulverized by bombs and rocket fire. Dozens of Italy's ancient towns were in rubble. Stalingrad was a wasteland. And few wanted to dwell on what had happened to Hiroshima and Nagasaki.

But when American soldiers and sailors came home, they found a golden land. New York was bursting with commerce and creativity. Detroit had developed into an economic mecca for poor black and white Southerners. Los Angeles had become one of the world's great industrial centers, pulling in Mexican-Americans from all over the Southwest and small-town white Midwesterners looking for fresh starts. The same story of economic growth, population boom, and exuberant metropolitan zest could be told about numerous cities throughout the United States.

While Russians, Europeans, and many Asians could only begin to rebuild their cities, societies, and national spirits, Americans celebrated and happily turned their wartime economic success into peacetime prosperity. While not all Americans shared equally in the postwar riches, between 1945 and 1960 the median family income in the United States nearly doubled. That rising tide meant that record numbers of Americans became homeowners, car owners, and proud possessors of washers, dryers, electric ranges, and television sets.

The Barry Sisters singing duo (*standing*) and Beverly Lawrence feign shock while reading about Alfred Kinsey's 1953 report on female sexuality. In postwar America, most American women seemed happy in their roles as housewives and mothers. By the 1960s, women's feelings of discontent with such roles would rise to the surface.

Population statistics demonstrated the different realities of the postwar world. In the Soviet Union, Germany, Japan, England, France, and all the other countries that saw the carnage of war on their own soil, national birthrates remained stagnant—an indication that people were loath to commit to an uncertain future. In the United States, however, birthrates exploded. What came to be called the "baby boom" began with a rush in 1946 and did not let up for nearly two decades.

In the postwar years, almost half of all American women married before they were 20 to men just slightly older. In some ways, this rush to early marriage marked a turn away from the greater autonomy enjoyed by women and the increased sexual experimentation that had characterized the preceding three decades. After so many years of war and economic difficulties, a great majority of Americans, it seemed, simply wanted to enjoy the security of marriage. They actively embraced highly regimented gender roles in which married women threw themselves into housework and motherhood, while men took advantage of a strong job market to earn a "family wage." Despite the apparent bliss, popular movies such as *Rebel Without a Cause* (1955), with its portrait of highly dysfunctional, sexually repressed, postwar suburban families—and bestsellers such as *The Organization Man* (1956), a dreary portrait of workplace conformity—suggested that not all men and women had found happiness in postwar American society.

Whatever the psychological forces or tensions, the young postwar newlyweds—confident, at least, of their economic prospects—began having babies, an average of 3.2 children per family. At the height of the boom, in 1957, the rate reached 3.8 babies per household. With those early marriages and big families came a home-buying spree and a run on furniture, appliances, and autos, not to mention diapers and baby food.

Those new families, looking for independence and greater living space—often helped through the generosity of the GI Bill, which provided veterans with the means to become homeowners—began to move to new, relatively inexpensive suburban developments, which soon ringed America's cities. All that building and buying added zip to an already expanding U.S. economy. The government got into the act in 1956 by approving billions of dollars to create a national highway system, making it easier to transport goods and creating unlimited travel possibilities.

The Baby Boomers lived like no other generation before them. Given postwar American prosperity, the nation was able to serve their various needs through each step of their generational progression. Schools, for example, were built in record numbers. And because the nation was doing so well economically, large numbers of young people were urged by parents, educators, and experts of every stripe to continue their education, at the very least through high school. As late as 1940, less than half of all American students made their way to high school graduation. By the early 1960s, nearly three in four graduated high school and the number of college admissions soared.

As a result of all that additional schooling, the Baby Boomers remained happily immersed in their own youth culture, outside the demands of a full-time job or family responsibilities, longer than any group of young people the world had ever before seen. And because so many of their parents had an unprecedented amount of disposable income to lavish upon them, these young people became prime targets of advertisers. Baby Boomers were the

A fiery plume rises from the Nevada Desert on April 15, 1955, during the testing of a 22-kiloton nuclear device. For years, hundreds of nuclear bombs were detonated at the Nevada test site. Although reassuring Americans of their country's military might, the testing poisoned much of Nevada and Utah, and helped fuel the Cold War between the U.S. and the USSR.

Beatnick poet Dick Woods chats with Eddy Slaton at the Gaslight Coffeehouse in New York's Greenwich Village. By the mid-1950s, writers, artists, and musicians converged in the West Village to talk philosophy, art, and jazz. Culturally influential, the beats provided inspiration for a wide range of artists in the 1960s.

Prologue

Johnny Gray, 15, of Little Rock, Arkansas, points his finger at one of two white boys who had tried to force his sister off the sidewalk. The confrontation turned into a fistfight, with Gray chasing the white boys down the block. By the late 1950s, the struggle for civil rights was beginning to move at full force as African-Americans became increasingly less intimidated.

first generation to be raised on television. Network broadcasts began in 1947, and by 1960 almost 90 percent of all households owned at least one TV set. Barbie dolls, introduced in the late 1950s and heavily advertised on children's television shows, became the constant companion of tens of millions of baby-boom girls. Moreover, the postwar introduction of inexpensive vinyl records and cheap hi-fi stereo systems created a massive music industry geared toward young people.

American society had to respond to the Boomers' sheer mass. In 1964, 17-year-olds made up the single largest age segment in the nation, and by 1965 fully 41 percent of all Americans were under 20. This postwar baby-boom generation—well fed, well educated, and accustomed to a societal focus on their every need and want—would, ironically, become a roaring engine of social change in the 1960s. Their parents, scarred by the dark days of the Great Depression and the deep sacrifices of the war years, would struggle to understand the risk-taking enthusiasm and cocky self-assurance of so many of the Baby Boomers. Here was the making of a "generation gap," and it too would mark the era that was to come.

If postwar prosperity and the baby boom it engendered set the stage for the Sixties era, so too did the struggles of those Americans who were unable to fully share in the 1950s "happy days." For African-Americans in particular, the 1950s was a time of hope and optimism but also a period of struggle. The modern civil rights movement that would gain its greatest victories in the 1960s was born during World War II and the postwar years.

During the 1940s and '50s, black Southerners saw new opportunities that would change their individual lives as well as the nation's racial politics. Simply stated, wartime labor shortages and then the postwar economic

British troops guard suspected Mau Mau rebels during an early-1950s uprising in Kenya. Many European nations saw the sun set on their empires throughout the decade as unrest stirred among the colonies. Amid Cold War anxieties, some nations sought to keep Communist influence at bay by providing their former holdings with economic support and development.

boom created a plethora of new jobs in America's industrial centers. California shipbuilders and airplane factories, Detroit manufacturers, Chicago-area steelworks, and New Jersey chemical and munitions plants all needed workers. They were willing—or in some cases were pushed by the federal government—to hire black workers.

From 1940 to 1960, more than four million black citizens moved out of the South to start new lives. Because these migrants could vote in their new northern and western communities, more and more politicians—often for pragmatic electoral reasons—began to address issues of racial justice. In 1948 President Harry Truman, locked in a tight presidential race, was told by his campaign strategist that he had to court black northern voters if he hoped to win. So he did. Black votes in Illinois, Missouri, and other midwestern and northeastern states greatly contributed to Truman's upset victory in 1948.

President Truman supported African-American civil rights for reasons beyond electoral votes. In 1947 Truman was informed by Secretary of State Dean Acheson that American racism, especially southern Jim Crow segregation, was being used against the United States by clever Soviet propagandists. The hearts and minds of people throughout the decolonizing nations of Africa and Asia, repulsed by America's disregard for its own citizens of color, were being lost to the USSR. Truman responded by creating a national commission to investigate civil rights abuses, and he called for moderate civil rights legislation.

This concern for America's image in the world, following so soon after the Allied war against the racist ideology of the Nazis, made many white Americans rethink their notions of race. Racism became a far more pressing issue for many of America's more thoughtful citizens. These kinds of concerns were noted by the Supreme Court in 1954, when the nine justices unanimously ruled in *Brown v. Board of Education* that racially "separate but equal" schools went against core constitutional principles of equality and justice for all.

Led by activists in the National Association for the Advancement of Colored People (NAACP) and other outspoken advocates for racial justice, small-scale political actions began to break out in increasing numbers throughout the nation. The most famous of these actions took place in Montgomery, Alabama, in 1955 when a member of the local NAACP chapter, Rosa Parks, refused to give up her seat for a white man on a segregated bus. Almost to a person, black Montgomerians, inspired by the charismatic leadership of a 26-year-old minister named Martin Luther King, Jr., boycotted city buses until the system was desegregated a year later. Thus, the first victory of the modern civil rights movement was achieved.

Similarly, President Dwight Eisenhower was forced to respond to the outpouring of racism that greeted the 1957 attempt to integrate a high school in Little Rock, Arkansas, in compliance with the Supreme Court's 1954 *Brown* ruling. To protect nine black children from the wrath of white mobs, the Pres-

Prior to being sworn in as his country's prime minister, 32-year-old revolutionary leader Fidel Castro emphatically addresses the Cuban people. Leading the resistance against the seven-year military rule of Fulgencio Batista, Castro and his 10,000-man guerrilla force deposed Batista into exile on January 1, 1959. Castro's growing alliance with the Soviets and an antagonistic relationship with the United States set the stage for what would culminate in the Bay of Pigs invasion and the Cuban Missile Crisis.

Prologue

ident had to call in the 101st Airborne to provide security. Well before the Greensboro sit-in of 1960, then, the battle for racial justice in the United States was well underway.

As noted, this battle was, in a way, just a small piece of a larger international struggle. In the years after World War II, people of color all over the world fought for freedom against their white dominators. In Indochina and Algeria, French imperialists sought to wipe out, by whatever means necessary, local freedom-fighters who demanded the right of national self-determination. Similar uprisings broke out in sub-Saharan Africa against the Belgians and the British. In 1959 revolutionary forces, led by Fidel Castro, overthrew an American-supported Cuban dictatorship. Castro called for racial justice, economic equality, and true independence for the small island nation that lay just 90 miles south of Florida.

The French garrison at Dien Bien Phu, in northwestern Vietnam, was established late in 1953 to protect Laos, a member of the French Union, from incursions by Vietnamese nationalists led by Ho Chi Minh. Poor intelligence subjected the French positions to ceaseless artillery fire, and the base fell on May 7, 1954. French Indochina was shattered, and Vietnam was bisected into North and South.

Castro, like so many of the other revolutionaries of the era, equated capitalism with such imperial nations as the United States, England, and France. Those countries had long controlled societies in Africa, Asia, and Latin America—either directly through political and military means or indirectly through economic might. Castro, like the leaders of Vietnam, Algeria, and almost every other new revolutionary regime, declared himself an opponent of capitalist exploitation and a champion of an egalitarian economic system. American political elites looked on with horror as many of those fighting for national liberation declared themselves Communists and looked for help from the Soviet Union.

President Eisenhower responded to the 1954 defeat of the French at the hands of the Vietnamese, led by the Communist Ho Chi Minh, by seeking to provide Vietnam—and then, he hoped, other new nations—with an American-style system of government and economics. In the mid-1950s, to prevent a Communist "domino effect" in Southeast Asia, the United States government, inspired by postwar optimism and a Cold War sense of duty, began a nation-building experiment in the southern part of Vietnam. This relatively small, somewhat cavalier intervention, made in response to the widespread anti-capitalist, anti-western fervor that accompanied postwar decolonization, would become, a decade later, something quite different.

The Cold War and the possibility that the United States and the Soviet Union would destroy one another via an exchange of nuclear weapons served as a counterpoint to America's domestic prosperity. Almost as soon as World War II had ended, the Soviet Union and the United States, onetime allies against the Nazis, had become locked in enmity. The Soviets, seeking security against future attack, refused to remove their troops from Eastern Europe, bringing an "Iron Curtain" down on Poland, Hungary, Romania, eastern Germany, and many other nations. The United States, fearful of Soviet plans for expansion, repulsed by Communist totalitarianism, and then further threatened by the 1949 Communist victory in China, instigated a massive military buildup to contain international communism.

By the early 1950s, both the United States and the Soviets had begun an enormous buildup of nuclear weapons. This weapons race became even more frightening for Americans when the Soviets moved ahead of the United States in the development of long-range missiles. In 1957 the Soviets used a powerful rocket to launch a satellite, Sputnik, into orbit. It was an impressive scientific achievement, but for Americans it seemed to indicate a dangerous "missile gap." In response, the Eisenhower Administration pledged more rapid progress in the race to win the Cold War in outer space.

Even while Americans relished their new push-button, all-electric kitchens and gyrated to the latest hit from Elvis, a figurative mushroom cloud hung over their heads. Schoolchildren, living in idyllic suburban subdivisions, regularly prepared for a Soviet long-range missile attack by learning how to "duck and cover." The Baby Boomers were the first American generation to grow up knowing that they could be the last generation on Earth.

Before the 1960s had officially begun, many of the challenges and opportunities that would give shape to the era were in place. African-Americans had begun to lay the framework for a rights revolution. The Cold War calculus that would turn Vietnam into a battleground between American troops and Communist forces was a strategic orthodoxy. The prosperity that would produce a new age of consumption without any clear limits had become an integral aspect of the "American Dream." And watching all of these changes from the idealistic standpoint of youth were tens of millions of Baby Boomers eager to shape the history they were inheriting.

Armed Hungarian freedom-fighters patrol the streets of Budapest during the 1956 revolution. Hungary became the first of the Eastern Bloc countries to chafe at the poor conditions typical of Soviet rule. The revolt was brutally suppressed, and exacerbated ideological tensions between NATO nations and members of the Warsaw Pact.

An Italian man is awed by a model of Russia's Sputnik, the world's first satellite, on display in a Rome department store. About the size of a basketball and weighing approximately 183 pounds, the satellite orbited the Earth on its elliptical path in just 98 minutes. The success of Sputnik ushered in a new era of space exploration and marked the beginning of an ongoing "space race" between the United States and the USSR.

1960

JFK and a New Generation of Leadership

O N July 15, 1960, Massachusetts Senator John Fitzgerald Kennedy stepped up to the podium at the Los Angeles Coliseum to accept the Democratic Party nomination for president of the United States. The campaign for the nomination had been hard fought, and Kennedy was exhausted.

In the heavy Boston accent that comedians would have a field day imitating, John F. Kennedy made his opening bid to lead the nation: "We are not here to curse the darkness, but to light the candle that can guide us through that darkness to a safe and sane future.... Today our concern must be with that future. For the world is changing. The old era is ending. The old ways will not do.... Too many Americans have lost their way, their will, and their sense of historic purpose. It is time, in short, for a new generation of leadership— new men to cope with new problems and new opportunities."

Kennedy offered the people of the United States a challenge: "We stand today on the edge of a new frontier—the frontier of the 1960s, a frontier of unknown opportunities and perils, a frontier of unfulfilled hopes and threats." It was a bold speech and a prophetic look forward to a decade that would, as Kennedy predicted, create an extraordinary new generation of leadership.

John Kennedy was just 43 years old when he announced his "rendezvous with destiny." During World War II he had not been a commanding general like the man he meant to replace, President Dwight D. Eisenhower. Kennedy had done his part as commander of PT 109, a small "patrol torpedo" boat. After his boat was rammed and sunk by a Japanese destroyer, he courageously

"In the decade that lies ahead—in the challenging revolutionary Sixties—the American presidency will demand more than ringing manifestos issued from the rear of the battle. It will demand that the President place himself in the very thick of the fight, that he care passionately about the fate of the people he leads, that he be willing to serve them, at the risk of incurring their momentary displeasure."

—Senator John F. Kennedy (D–MA), January 14, 1960

By October 1960 American voters were gearing up for what was going to be one of the closest elections in U.S. history. Here, Democratic candidate John F. Kennedy—with his wife, Jacqueline, seated nearby—speaks in front of City Hall in New York City.

helped his surviving men swim to a small islet. The extraordinary press and praise for his actions stemmed largely from the high visibility of his father, as Kennedy self-mockingly acknowledged (at least in private). Joseph Kennedy was an immensely rich political power broker who served as ambassador to England during the war. Regardless, young John Kennedy was well positioned in all ways to begin a meteoric political career at war's end.

Just like the Republican he would face in the 1960 presidential election, Kennedy ran for Congress in 1946. He won, and then just six years later he ran for Senate. He won that election, too. Pushed by his father and by his own extraordinary ambition, Kennedy set his sights on the presidency. After eight years of Eisenhower, Kennedy believed that 1960 was his year to run.

The Republican candidate Kennedy faced was one of the wiliest American politicians of the 20th century: Richard Nixon. In 1960, though, Kennedy and Nixon were much alike. Both men were born in the 20th century—a first for rival presidential candidates. And both politicians emphasized foreign policy, particularly the need to wage a successful war against the threat of Soviet Communist expansion. Each man, within his respective party, raced easily to the presidential nomination. But whereas Kennedy had made his lightning-quick moves backed by his father's money and power—and through his own extraordinary good looks, magnetic charm, and sophisticated intelligence—Nixon had done it the old-fashioned way.

Born to a lower-middle-class family in Southern California, Nixon had fought his way to the top, going for the political jugular in his campaigns for office. He had made a national name for himself by attacking his political opponents as Communist sympathizers or appeasers. He once accused a high-ranking State Department official, Alger Hiss, of being a Soviet spy, and during his 1960 presidential campaign—at the height of the Cold War—he emphasized the importance of his experience. In addition to his time in the House and Senate, Nixon had served two terms as Eisenhower's vice president. But experience alone was then, as now, no sure ticket to the White House.

On September 26, Nixon and Kennedy squared off in the nation's first televised presidential debate. Seventy million Americans watched the two men display impressive knowledge of world affairs and domestic policies. On the issues, each man held his own. But in less tangible ways, John Kennedy trounced his opponent. On television, Nixon came off as a haggard, bullying presence more concerned with browbeating Kennedy than with offering the nation leadership. Kennedy—tanned, smartly dressed, and at ease—impressed

The first of four televised presidential debates, held in Chicago on September 26, 1960, revealed a perspiring Richard Nixon, who at times came across as nervous and combative. Meanwhile, Senator John F. Kennedy sported a tan and appeared fresh and confident. The debates marked a transition in which television replaced newspapers as the most important communications medium in American politics.

a majority of viewers as a natural-born leader. Polls showed that most people who heard the debate on radio believed that Nixon had won the contest, but a large majority of those who watched the debate on television considered Kennedy the easy winner.

Kennedy did indeed win the presidential election that November, but far from easily. He beat Nixon by just 118,574 votes, 34,226,731 to 34,108,157. Two major voting blocs pushed Kennedy ahead. Catholics turned out to vote for JFK in huge numbers. Kennedy was just the second Catholic to run for the presidency. The first, Al Smith, had been trounced in 1928, and anti-Catholic prejudice had played a major role in his defeat.

Kennedy confronted anti-Catholic biases throughout his campaign. In West Virginia, an overwhelmingly Protestant state, Kennedy put the matter bluntly: "Nobody asked me if I was a Catholic when I joined the United States Navy. Nobody asked my brother if he was Catholic or Protestant before he climbed into an American bomber plane to fly his last mission." While Kennedy was the first man to win the presidency with a minority of the Protestant vote, he did prove that a Catholic could be president. And his compelling campaign rhetoric helped to further diminish the power of an old prejudice that had for too long been a part of American life.

As the threat of a nuclear attack loomed, the Civil Defense Administration distributed pamphlets, built public fallout shelters, and called for mandatory classes in schools that would teach survival techniques. This poster signified to those in rural communities just how far-reaching a nuclear blast could be.

African-Americans were making a difference in 1960. Their support of presidential candidate John F. Kennedy led to his election, while black sit-ins in numerous southern cities, including this one in Nashville, led to the desegregation of drugstore lunch counters.

The second voting bloc critical to Kennedy's victory was the African-American electorate. A remarkable incident helped mobilize the black vote for Kennedy. In October 1960 civil rights leader Martin Luther King, Jr., was convicted of a bogus traffic violation and sentenced to hard labor in Georgia. His wife, Coretta Scott King, feared that her husband would be killed in prison and reached out to Kennedy for assistance. Kennedy phoned her, offering his sympathy and help. His brother and campaign manager, Robert F. Kennedy, followed up by calling the judge who had thrown King into jail. King was subsequently released.

Word of the Kennedy brothers' actions impressed African-Americans, and black voters enthusiastically turned out for Kennedy on election day, ensuring his victory in several crucial swing states. Here was a sign of the new kind of leadership Kennedy had promised in his speeches.

Kennedy's victory in the 1960 presidential election marked, as the new president later declared in his inaugural address, the passing of the torch "to a new generation of Americans." With his glamorous and beautiful wife, Jacqueline, at his side, Kennedy for many Americans would represent the optimistic hopes the nation held as the 1960s began. But Kennedy was far from alone in offering new leadership to the American people.

Months before the 1960 election, a wave of sit-ins challenged the traditional power of the segregated South. These sit-ins were driven by hundreds and then thousands of African-American grassroots activists, many of them students who were not even old enough to vote. The sit-in movement promised to upend the system of racial oppression that had stained American claims to international leadership and poisoned life within the United States.

Similarly, from across the political spectrum, small numbers of white young people were beginning to challenge the political conventional wisdom their elders had bequeathed them. On the right, the Young Americans for Freedom organized in 1960 to combat what they saw as the creeping power

On May 13, 1960, more than 200 demonstrators gathered at City Hall in San Francisco to protest a House Un-American Activities Committee (HUAC) hearing of students alleged to be Communists. After a dousing from fire hoses failed to disperse the group, many of the protesters were thrown down stairs, dragged, or beaten with clubs.

of Big Government. They began agitating for a society more dedicated to principles of individualism and liberty.

On the left in 1960, hundreds of students in Berkeley, California, shocked their peers and university officials by brazenly challenging the anti-Communist dogma that had ruled in the United States for nearly 15 years. When the House Un-American Activities Committee (HUAC) went to the Bay Area to hunt for Communists, students picketed the hearings and mocked the committee with shouts of derision. These students demanded that American political life open itself to new ideas and to greater participation in decision-making by the American people themselves. New leadership, they insisted, need not come only from presidents and members of Congress.

The promise of new leadership was, in 1960, not only an American concern. Much of Africa was undergoing a rapid and often violent process of

While embroiled in a civil war for the reunification of Vietnam, North Vietnamese Communist leader Ho Chi Minh (*left*) dines with Chinese Premier Chou En-Lai. In 1960 Communist Vietcong guerrillas were killing several hundred South Vietnamese each month.

decolonization that cried out for courageous leaders. One of the most vibrant of these new leaders, the Congo's Patrice Lumumba, was assassinated just as Kennedy assumed the presidency, creating a crisis for the new American administration.

Asia, too, roiled as countries struggled to overthrow their colonial rulers and create independent nations. While the American government focused on the violent civil war taking place in 1960 in the former French colony of Laos, even greater troubles brewed for American interests within Vietnam. The United States had vigorously supported the creation and maintenance of an independent South Vietnam ruled by the aristocratic Ngo Dinh Diem. In the north of Vietnam, Ho Chi Minh, the Communist revolutionary hero who had led the forces that defeated the French imperialists and gained Vietnam its independence, planned to unify the country under his leadership. In 1960 he helped create the National Liberation Front in South Vietnam. It aimed to overthrow the American-backed Diem regime. Few Americans outside the government were aware of this Vietnamese struggle for national leadership. Soon enough, they would be.

In 1960 Americans did follow the world-threatening Cold War struggle between the Soviet Union and the United States. The premier of the USSR, Nikita Khrushchev, was himself a new-generation leader. He had replaced the diabolic, murderous Joseph Stalin in 1953. An earthy man (he was raised on a farm) and prone to red-faced public tirades, Khrushchev was a hard-line Communist who promised to figuratively "bury" the United States. With their growing nuclear arsenals, the Soviet Union and the U.S. were engaged in an arms race of terrifying proportions. In 1960 the American people had to face, on a daily basis, the possibility of a nuclear war that would kill them all. This possibility, not surprisingly, was President Kennedy's gravest concern.

In running for the presidency, John Kennedy had promised the American people a new generation of leadership. In the 1960s, he and many others who sought to lead the nation would face challenges, both domestic and international, that would demand sacrifices few could have imagined.

Soviet Premier Nikita Khrushchev (*right*) and Cuban dictator Fidel Castro embrace as they meet for the first time, at the United Nations Building in New York on September 20, 1960. Having been spurned by the Eisenhower Administration, Castro aligned his country with the USSR—a relationship that would lead to the Cuban Missile Crisis in 1962.

1960: Membership in the United Nations increases from 82 to 99. All but one of the new members are African states. • Throughout the South, black activists stage "wade-ins" to desegregate public beaches and "kneel-ins" in whites-only churches. *See* February 1, 1960. • Thousands of Cuban refugees arrive in Miami, overwhelming immigration and refugee personnel. • The Daughters of Bilitis, a lesbian organization, holds its first national conference, in San Francisco. • The Framingham Heart Study reports that cigarette smoking increases the risk of heart disease.

1960: New York City developers and city officials propose a World Trade Center to be built in lower Manhattan. • Red Chinese and Formosan fighter jets battle over possession of Quemoy and other offshore islands. • Digital Equipment Corp. introduces the PDP-1, the first commercial computer with keyboard input and a CRT monitor to display entered material. The unit is fully transistorized. • Following rival Royal Crown Cola, Coca-Cola becomes available in cans in certain areas. • Comedian Bob Newhart's *The Button Down Mind* begins a trend of best-selling albums by comedians.

Early 1960: Conducting Navy-sponsored experiments, Dr. John C. Lilly determines that dolphins have very high IQs—perhaps equal to humans. He says dolphins can talk to each other, mimic humans' words, and come to each other's assistance in moments of distress.

January 4: After 116 days and millions of dollars of losses, the longest steel strike in U.S. history ends. • French existential novelist Albert Camus, 46, dies in a one-car crash near Sens, France.

January 7: President Dwight Eisenhower announces a $200 million government surplus and says he will submit a balanced $79.8 billion budget for fiscal 1961.

In 1958 NASA established Project Mercury. Its goals: place a manned spacecraft in orbit around the Earth, observe human performance in space flight, and recover the crafts (all of which it would achieve). America's first astronauts were (*top, left to right*) Alan Shepard, Jr., Virgil "Gus" Grissom, and L. Gordon Cooper, Jr., as well as (*bottom, left to right*) Walter Schirra, Donald K. "Deke" Slayton, John Glenn, and Malcolm Scott Carpenter. Each man survived a screening process that was both physically and psychologically difficult. According to NASA, perhaps the most unnerving events were a series of demanding interviews. The seven chosen (out of 508 originally screened) became American heroes, replete with what writer Tom Wolfe called "the right stuff."

In the Albert Camus novel *The Plague,* a French doctor, Rieux, tries to combat an outbreak of bubonic plague in North Africa against impossible odds. As Camus puts it, "Rieux believed himself to be on the right road—in fighting against creation as he found it." Camus was a major French existentialist in the late 1940s and 1950s. His novels, plays, and essays focus on the importance of individual moral commitment in the face of a universe without purpose. His insights, wrote William Chafe, helped "provide the intellectual milieu" of the late 1950s and early 1960s. Camus died in a car crash on January 4, 1960.

A billboard on the Miami waterfront in early 1960 welcomes Americans to vacation in Cuba. Fidel Castro's rebel forces had overthrown Cuban dictator Fulgencio Batista in January 1959, bringing, in Castro's view, "freedom" to Cuba. Skeptical from the onset of the Castro-led revolution, the Eisenhower Administration grew increasingly hostile as the new Cuban regime became more oppressive. Cuban "show trials," which sent many to their deaths, were "like something out of Kafka in Spanish," wrote historian Geoffrey Perret. The administration worried even more about Cuban appropriation of American businesses and Castro's burgeoning relationship with the Soviet Union.

Going Ballistic

BY 1960 THE PROSPECT of imminent nuclear war frightened many Americans. Public officials warned of a growing "missile gap" between the Soviet Union and the United States, and Soviet Premier Nikita Khrushchev famously declared that Soviet missiles rolled off the assembly line like sausages.

Consequently, in the late 1950s, the U.S. Air Force and Army successfully developed two Intermediate Range Ballistic Missiles (IRBMs), the Jupiter and the Thor. These liquid-fueled rockets could deliver nuclear warheads over a range of 1,500 and 2,000 miles, respectively, to their targets. Since these ranges were not sufficient to launch the IRBMs from the United States, the Thors were deployed in the United Kingdom in late 1959; Jupiters were deployed in Italy and Turkey in 1960.

About the same time John F. Kennedy entered the White House, the United States successfully tested two Intercontinental Ballistic Missiles (ICBMs): the Titan II, with a range of 5,500 miles, and the Minuteman, with a range of 6,300 miles. Unlike the IRBMs, which were launched above ground and were, thus, vulnerable to attack, the ICBMs were dispersed in more than 1,000 underground silos across America. The missile gap had been closed, but the anxiety persisted.

In this series of test photographs, a U.S. Army Hawk surface-to-air missile destroys an Honest John missile on January 29, 1960. This was the first known "kill" of one supersonic missile by another. The Hawk program began in 1952, and the missile was declared operationally capable by 1959. From the Soviet point of view, a successful anti-missile missile gave the United States potential first-strike capability. Theoretically, the U.S. could launch a nuclear attack on the USSR under the assumption that Hawk missiles could destroy incoming Soviet ones. Ironically, the Hawk's success helped intensify the arms race between the two nations.

1960

January 11: The United States lodges a formal protest over the Cuban government's seizure of U.S. property in Cuba. • Georgia Governor S. Ernest Vandiver, Jr., threatens to withhold state funding from any school that attempts to integrate.

January 20: Students for a Democratic Society holds its first meeting, in Ann Arbor, Michigan. The group's aim is to build a "left" movement within universities and to spread its influence across American society.

January 22: Some 17,000 employees of the Industrial Union of Marine and Shipbuilding Workers strike at Bethlehem Steel shipyards. They will not return to work for five months.

January 24: Insurrection against French rule breaks out in Algiers, Algeria. A state of siege is declared. *See* July 3, 1962.

January 29: A U.S. test at White Sands, New Mexico, marks the first known destruction of a ballistic missile in flight. In the test, an Honest John missile is tracked and destroyed by a Hawk missile about 1.5 miles above ground.

February 1: North Carolina A&T students Ezell Blair, Jr., Joseph McNeil, David Richmond, and Franklin McCain stage a sit-in of a whites-only lunch counter at Woolworth in Greensboro, North Carolina. The publicity given to the demonstration will spark sit-ins in more than 50 cities over the next two months.

February 13: France successfully test-detonates a plutonium bomb in the French Sahara. • Cuba signs a five-year trade agreement with the USSR.

February 18: The House Armed Services Committee orders an immediate review of all U.S. military training manuals after learning that an Air Force manual claims Communist infiltration of U.S. churches. • The Winter Olympic Games open in Squaw Valley, California.

In 1960 French workers set up test dummies in the Sahara Desert to check the effect of a nuclear blast. By then, France, Britain, the United States, and the Soviet Union had successfully tested nuclear weapons. Nuclear proliferation became a major concern in the 1960s. France hoped to develop a nuclear capability independent of NATO and the U.S. The close friendship between British Prime Minister Harold Macmillan and American President Dwight Eisenhower rankled French President Charles de Gaulle. Moreover, the French leader was not convinced that the U.S. would defend Europe against a Soviet attack if that meant a potential nuclear attack on America.

Sitting Down to Take a Stand

I WAS FROM NORTH CAROLINA but I had lived in New York and when I went back down there to school I realized the transition, the difference in public accommodations....It seemed to me that people in Alabama, where they had the Montgomery bus boycott, were at least trying to do something about it. The people in Little Rock, with the trouble at Central High School, were trying to do something. And we weren't.

I had heard people talk about demanding service but no one had ever done it. You either ate in Negro areas or you took a sandwich out. So I decided to see if we could do it.

—JOSEPH MCNEIL, NORTH CAROLINA AT&T STUDENT WHO HELPED LAUNCH THE FIRST SIT-IN IN GREENSBORO ON FEBRUARY 1, 1960

A worker at a Nashville restaurant refuses to let sit-in demonstrators through the door. Though sit-ins were successful in Nashville and other cities, the strategy often was met with stiff resistance. Angry whites looking for a showdown provided a striking contrast to the sit-in protesters. Dressed in their Sunday best, protesters adhered to a strict code, maintaining decorum despite the indignities inflicted by ardent racists. The sit-ins, along with national boycotts of certain chains, put economic pressure on department stores and restaurants and helped make segregated lunch counters a thing of the past.

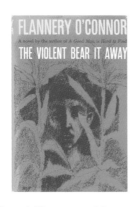

In Flannery O'Connor's southern Gothic novel, *The Violent Bear It Away* (1960), a young man struggles with the burden of being a prophet. The story features religious fanatics, mad prophets, and the drowning of an idiot child during baptism. O'Connor was one of America's most revered writers, in part because of her ability to combine the comic with the tragic and the southern weird. Most critics consider her short story collection, *A Good Man Is Hard to Find,* her greatest work. But *Bear It Away* also reflects her ability, in the words of one critic, to be a "grotesque amalgam of Jonathan Edwards, Charles Brockden Brown, Edgar Allan Poe, and William Faulkner."

The Sit-In Movement

FED UP WITH SEGREGATED facilities in the South—such as restaurants, restrooms, motels, and department store lunch counters—four freshmen from North Carolina A&T College decided to take action. On February 1, 1960, Joseph McNeil, Ezell Blair, Franklin McCain, and David Richmond entered the F. W. Woolworth in Greensboro. After buying school supplies and toothpaste, the four strolled purposefully to the "whites only" lunch counter and seated themselves.

Reasoned one of the students, "Since we buy books and papers in the other part of the store, we believe we should get served in this part." There was little chance of that, although at least they were not summarily thrown out. Drawing scant attention, the four students sat in dignified silence, leaving only when the facility closed. The next day, about two dozen sit-in protesters arrived at the store.

Once the press caught wind of the drama, the pressure was on. Curly Harris, manager of the Greensboro Woolworth, met the attention coolly. "They can just sit there," he said. "It's nothing to me." Unwittingly, Harris's measured response validated the effectiveness of the protest, igniting a sit-in movement that exploded throughout dozens of cities. By July, the Greensboro Woolworth succumbed to the inevitable. Harris even allowed his black employees to become the first served at the newly integrated diner.

At lunch counters in other cities, protesters encountered hostile reactions from outraged white patrons. Sit-in demonstrators were assaulted with verbal abuse, hot coffee, lit cigarettes, and worse. Invariably, it was the young protesters who ended up arrested for "creating a disturbance." Nevertheless, by fall 1961 the movement could claim substantial victories among many targeted cities.

A sit-in at the Greensboro Woolworth, February 2, 1960

1960

February 27: In Nashville, 81 protesters are arrested for disorderly conduct in a nonviolent demonstration against segregated stores. *See* May 9, 1960.

February 28: The U.S. hockey team wins a gold medal at the Olympic Games in Squaw Valley, California.

February 29: Eighteen southern Democratic senators begin a 125-hour, 31-minute filibuster against proposed U.S. civil rights legislation. *See* May 6, 1960. ● In Chicago, Hugh Hefner opens his first Playboy Club with a complete staff of Playboy Bunny waitresses.

March: President Eisenhower agrees to a CIA proposal to train Cuban exiles to subvert Fidel Castro.

Early March: Approximately 628,000 acres, 437,000 of them along the Missouri River, are flooded in Missouri because of heavy snowfall and rapid thaw.

March 4: A munitions ship explodes at dock in Havana, Cuba, killing 75. Cuban leader Fidel Castro blames the United States.

March 8: Alfred Hitchcock's frightening film *Psycho* is released in the United States. Hitchcock decrees that theaters are to seat no patrons after the film begins.

March 9: Hundreds of black students stage a peaceful protest against segregation in front of the former Confederate capitol building in Montgomery, Alabama. The next day, nine Alabama State students connected with the protest will be expelled.

March 11: The U.S. launches the Pioneer 5 space probe from Cape Canaveral, Florida, for orbit around the sun.

March 15: Police in Orangeburg, South Carolina, arrest more than 350 African-Americans participating in sit-in demonstrations. ● Julian Bond and the newly formed Committee on Appeal for Human Rights holds its first sit-in, in Atlanta.

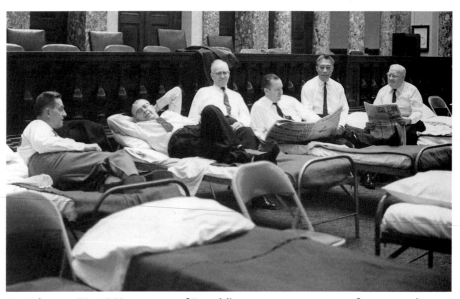

On February 29, 1960, a group of Republican senators prepares for a marathon session concerning the civil rights bill. Liberal Democrats and some Republicans pushed for the act to help fight racial discrimination. However, southern senators mounted a continuous 125-hour filibuster, which helped defeat certain provisions. The watered-down Civil Rights Act of 1960 did include penalties for people who tried to deny citizens their right to vote or register to vote.

Hugh Hefner sits at his typewriter, backed by a group of Playboy Bunnies, at the first Playboy Club, which opened in Chicago on February 29, 1960. Hefner had founded *Playboy* magazine in 1953, targeting males in the 21- to 45-year-old age group. Featuring cartoons, interviews, short fiction, Hefner's "Playboy Philosophy," and—most crucially—half-naked female "Playmates" posing provocatively, it became immensely successful. The private Playboy clubs offered relaxation for its members, who were waited on by Playboy Bunnies. Hef's enterprises represented a liberalization of American attitudes toward sex.

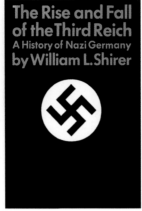

The Rise and Fall of the Third Reich
A History of Nazi Germany
by William L. Shirer

WILLIAM L. SHIRER

Former CBS radio reporter William Shirer won multiple awards for his study of Nazi Germany, *The Rise and Fall of the Third Reich* (1960). Shirer, who had covered Germany and World War II as a journalist, made use of numerous captured German documents, testimony at the Nuremberg trials, and his own reportage to create this gargantuan work of more than 1,000 pages. Because it is so well written and passionate in its moral outrage, *Rise and Fall* became a hugely popular book, with the original edition exceeding three million copies. At the time, however, some professional historians were critical of the book, partly because Shirer was not a trained academic.

Elvis Presley holds a news conference on March 1, 1960, the day before he is to be discharged from the U.S. Army, in which he had served for two years. The King of Rock 'n' Roll recovered quickly from his absence from the pop music scene. In 1960 he recorded three No. 1 singles—"Stuck on You," "It's Now or Never," and "Are You Lonesome Tonight." His style in 1960 and after was less "rebellious [and] sensuous" and more "mainstream, easy listening," according to writer Roy Arthur Swanson. Even Frank Sinatra, who once had referred to rock singers such as Presley as "cretinous goons," hosted a 1960 television special with Elvis.

In Somerville, Tennessee, on March 2, 1960, about 170 African-Americans and an estimated 106 whites braved icy roads to register to vote (*pictured*). Blacks stood in one line, whites another. By the time the office closed, 76 of the whites (about 70 percent) and 70 of the blacks (about 40 percent) had been registered. Southern whites used all kinds of tricks to keep African-Americans from registering to vote, including poll taxes and extremely difficult tests about government. In one town, blacks needed to guess how many jellybeans were in a jar as a "test" to see if they were qualified voters.

March 16: San Antonio, Texas, becomes the first major southern city to integrate its lunch counters.

March 21: Sixty-nine black South Africans demonstrating in Sharpeville (near Johannesburg) against mandatory passes are killed in clashes with police, who employ armored cars and automatic weapons. More than 150 demonstrators are injured. *See* March 29, 1960.

March 29: Blacks in Capetown and Vereeniging, South Africa, initiate a general strike. *See* March 30, 1960.

March 30: The South African government declares a state of emergency in 122 of the nation's magisterial districts. The decree will not be lifted for five months. *See* April 9, 1960.

April: South Vietnamese President Ngo Dinh Diem receives a petition advocating reforms for his rigid and increasingly corrupt government. Diem responds by closing several opposition newspapers and having journalists and others arrested. • Che Guevara's handbook on guerrilla tactics is published. • John Coltrane forms his own quartet. He is known for his "way-out" jazz interpretations in and around Greenwich Village in New York City.

April 9: South African Prime Minister H. F. Verwoerd is seriously wounded when he is shot twice in the head by a British-born Transvaal farmer.

April 14: The Montreal Canadiens win their NHL-record fifth consecutive Stanley Cup with a 4–0 win over the Toronto Maple Leafs.

April 15: College students in Raleigh, North Carolina, establish the Student Nonviolent Coordinating Committee (SNCC), which will take an active role in student sit-ins, Freedom Rides, marches, and voter registration.

April 17: In his Easter message to the world, Pope John XXIII cites racial intolerance and Communist persecution of the Church as evils that diminish the holiday.

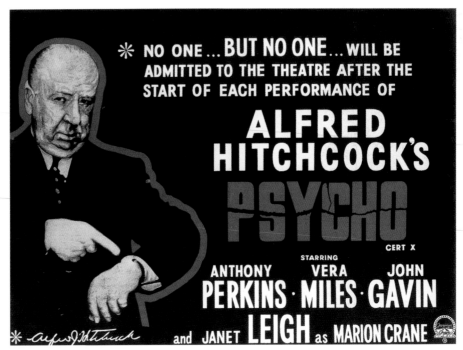

This British poster promotes Alfred Hitchcock's classic 1960 film Psycho. *Hitchcock stresses punctuality because of the plot twists in the early scenes. The film focuses on an embezzler (played by Janet Leigh) who is gruesomely murdered while she showers in the creepy Bates Motel. We think the killer is a woman, but it turns out to be the psychotic owner of the motel (played by Anthony Perkins), a momma's boy who keeps his long-dead mother's corpse in a rocking chair and dresses like her when he kills. Critic Roger Ebert opined that the film "connects directly with our fears: Our fears that we might impulsively commit a crime, our fears of the police, our fears of becoming the victim of a madman, and of course our fears of disappointing our mothers."*

In this 1960 political cartoon, "Herblock" (Herbert L. Block) criticizes the wasteful spending of middle- and upper-class Americans and the woefully inadequate federal spending on public needs—including defense. The noted *Washington Post* cartoonist skewers not only Middle Americans but also the Eisenhower Administration for its parsimony and obsession with balanced federal budgets. During the presidential campaign that year, John F. Kennedy also criticized Ike's reluctance to fund social programs.

On March 21, 1960, South African police opened fire on black demonstrators in Sharpeville in the Transvaal, killing 69 people and injuring 180. The protesters, organized by the nationalist Pan-African Congress, were voicing their opposition to the pass system, an especially odious aspect of South African apartheid. Under that system of legalized separation, black South Africans (who comprised a majority of the population) were forced to carry passes that allowed them to move from their segregated living areas. The massacre likely was a panic reaction by undisciplined police rather than a planned government response. The shooting was condemned worldwide and became a major symbol of violent white oppression for black-nationalist movements in South Africa.

Pictured is the unfinished skyline of Brasilia, which became Brazil's official capital on April 20, 1960. This remarkable city earned worldwide fame because it was planned from the ground up. The seed was planted by successful presidential candidate Juscelino Kubitschek in 1955, when he promised to build a new federal capital in the country's central plateau. Designed to resemble a bird and carefully organized to reflect Brazil's modernizing culture, Brasilia became an architectural wonder. However, numerous instances of political and economic turmoil slowed the building process significantly. Most of the city's main structures would not be completed until the 1980s.

On April 19, 1960, television disk jockey Dick Clark testifies before a congressional committee investigating charges of bribery in the music business. In this "payola scandal," as it was called, Clark (the star of ABC's *American Bandstand*) and Alan Freed (who coined the term "rock 'n' roll") were accused of accepting payoffs from music companies for giving air time to selected songs. Freed ultimately pleaded guilty to commercial bribery. Clark, insisting on his innocence, was never charged, although ABC did force him to sell his interests in various parts of the music business. The network wanted Clark to maintain his squeaky-clean image.

April 24: Dr. Albert Sabin's polio vaccine is distributed throughout the U.S. Unlike Dr. Salk's version, Sabin's is taken orally, reduces viral spread, and does not require additional booster treatments. • Attempts to integrate beaches in Biloxi, Mississippi, lead to a race riot.

April 29: TV personality and record producer Dick Clark testifies before the U.S. House Subcommittee on Legislative Oversight that he never accepted "payola" from record companies for playing their records.

May: Black trade unionist A. Philip Randolph helps establish the Negro American Labor Council to challenge discrimination in hiring and promotion. • Dr. Theodore H. Maiman of Hughes Aircraft develops the laser (Light Amplification by Stimulated Emission of Radiation) in a company research project.

May 1: An American U-2 spy plane is shot down by the Soviets near Sverdlovsk. Pilot Francis Gary Powers is captured. *See* August 17, 1960.

May 2: Convicted "Red Light" rapist Caryl Chessman is executed at San Quentin Prison in California following eight stays of execution since his conviction in 1948.

May 4: Actress Lucille Ball divorces husband Desi Arnaz.

May 6: President Dwight Eisenhower signs the Civil Rights Act of 1960, which is intended to remove barriers for southern black citizens who try to vote.

May 7: The USSR and Cuba resume diplomatic relations for the first time since 1952.

May 9: The U.S. government pledges to defend any ally attacked by Soviet missiles. • Several stores in Nashville decide to desegregate their lunch counters. • The U.S. submarine *Triton* completes an 84-day underwater voyage around the world.

Civil rights leader Martin Luther King, Jr., examines a burned cross in front of his Atlanta home in April 1960. Clearly meant as a warning by opponents of integration, this symbol of the Ku Klux Klan failed to deter King. He and his organization, the Southern Christian Leadership Conference (SCLC), continued to preach nonviolence in the face of growing white resistance to the civil rights movement. In 1960 King offered moral support and advice to the burgeoning sit-in movement, and was arrested and sentenced to jail during an Atlanta sit-in in October. King was released through the personal intervention of John F. Kennedy and Robert Kennedy during the 1960 presidential campaign.

On May 13, 1960, San Francisco police arrested demonstrators protesting a meeting of the House Committee on Un-American Activities (HUAC) at City Hall. The protest was organized by members of SLATE, a liberal student political organization at the University of California at Berkeley. Since 1958, SLATE had been running candidates for student government posts while supporting civil rights and a ban on nuclear testing. Tom Hayden, a student at the University of Michigan, visited Berkeley in 1960 and helped form VOICE—similar to SLATE—at his university. Thus, college student dissent was percolating in 1960. Sociologist Todd Gitlin asserts that with such events as the anti-HUAC demonstrations, "the Fifties expired" and a new age was born.

The U-2 Affair

ON MAY 1, 1960, as he prepared for a Paris summit meeting with Soviet Premier Nikita Khrushchev, President Dwight Eisenhower learned that an American U-2 spy plane had disappeared somewhere over the Soviet Union. The CIA pilot, Francis Gary Powers, was missing. This event, though seemingly minor compared with the major confrontations of the Cold War, would dash Eisenhower's peace prospects at the summit.

When Khrushchev denounced the United States for its "aggressive provocation" in sending a "bandit flight" over the USSR,

Francis Gary Powers (*right*)

Eisenhower initiated a cover-up. At the time, Eisenhower felt certain that the plane had been destroyed and that Powers had perished. He also believed that although the Soviets knew such flights had been going on for years, they never would risk the humiliation of acknowledging their inability to stop them. Therefore, Eisenhower denied that he had authorized the flights, hoping that the Soviets would let the crisis blow over. Ike's plan, however, blew up in his face.

As it turned out, Powers ejected from the plane and the Soviets apprehended him. Parts of the plane survived, along with the rolls of film Powers had taken during the flight. Khrushchev thus had the evidence he needed to prove that America was spying, and he announced that Powers would be tried for espionage. When they met in Paris in mid-May, Khrushchev demanded that Eisenhower publicly apologize for the U-2 incident, promise that the flights would stop, and punish those involved. Eisenhower replied that he already had stopped the flights, but he refused to go any further. Khrushchev stormed out of the meetings, and the summit collapsed.

Meanwhile, the Soviets convicted Powers of espionage and sent him to prison. On February 10, 1962, they traded him to the United States for one of their own captured spies.

> *"The Soviet Army at present possesses such weapons and such firepower as has never been possessed by any army before. . . . Should any madman provoke an attack on our state, or other Socialist states, we should be able literally to wipe off the face of the Earth the country or countries which had attacked us."*
>
> —SOVIET PREMIER NIKITA KHRUSHCHEV, JANUARY 15, 1960

During the pace lap of the 1960 Indianapolis 500, a privately owned and constructed scaffold collapsed. Approximately 125 people, who paid $5 to $10 for these infield seats, fell to the ground. Two died and 40 were injured. Such structures were banned from future races. Ironically, from 1957 through 1961 at Indy, 1960 was the only year in which a race car driver did not die.

May 11: The FDA approves the contraceptive pill. It will go on sale in December.

May 12: Frank Sinatra features Elvis Presley on his ABC-TV variety special. It is Elvis's first TV appearance since his March 2 Army discharge. The show is the biggest TV special in several years, scoring a 41.5 Media-trend rating.

May 13: Busloads of students from the University of California–Berkeley demonstrate against the House Un-American Activities Committee in San Francisco, the site of HUAC hearings.

May 14: Several hundred supporters and opponents of Premier Fidel Castro clash in front of the Cuban consulate on the east side of Manhattan. Eighteen people are arrested.

May 16: Former boxer turned song-writer/producer Berry Gordy founds Motown Records in Detroit.

May 21–June: Earthquakes, volcanoes, and tidal waves rip through Chile, killing as many as 10,000 people. *See* May 23, 1960.

May 23: A tsunami resulting from Chilean earthquakes hits the Hawaiian port city of Hilo, killing 61 people. • Israeli Prime Minister David Ben-Gurion reports that Israeli agents have captured fugitive Nazi war criminal Adolf Eichmann in Argentina. *See* April 11, 1961.

May 30: A temporary grandstand constructed at the Indianapolis 500 collapses, killing two people and injuring several dozen.

June 10: A U.S. Marine helicopter lands at Tokyo Airport to rescue White House Press Secretary James Hagerty and U.S. Ambassador to Japan Douglas MacArthur II from mobs protesting a proposed visit to Japan by President Eisenhower. The visit will be canceled.

Citizens of Conception, Chile, react as a major earthquake hits the country on May 21, 1960. At 9.5 on the Richter Scale, it was one of the most powerful earthquakes ever recorded. Up to 10,000 people died in Chile, while tidal waves associated with the quake killed 231 people in Hawaii, Japan, and the Philippines.

The film *Saturday Night and Sunday Morning* was based on the novel of the same name by Alan Sillitoe. The author was a member of a group of young British writers dubbed the "Angry Young Men." Prominent from the mid-1950s into the early '60s, Sillitoe, novelist John Braine, and playwright John Osborne focused on the working class's disillusionment with the established institutions of English society. Their sentiments might best be summed up by a letter Osborne wrote to a British newspaper. He titled it, "Damn You, England."

Masses of young Chinese women march with submachine guns in Peking in 1960. They celebrated "Youth and Vigor Day," one of several Chinese militant demonstrations in a year that also featured an "anti-American week" in June. In part, these demonstrations illustrated Communist China's commitment to national defense and support of wars of liberation in former western colonies, such as Vietnam. But in 1960, China also was experiencing the utter economic failure of Mao Tse-tung's "Great Leap Forward," an attempt to jump-start a stagnant socialist economy. With massive food shortages and starvation rampant, demonstrations aimed at such alleged "foreign devils" as the United States served to divert attention from domestic ills.

Eyeglasses without side bars, as well as closely coiffed hairstyles, became fashionable in 1960. Bouffant hairdos also were popular. In clothing, DuPont Corporation introduced Lycra, the first of the spandex fabrics. Males were not ignored, as Pierre Cardin introduced his first major collection of men's clothing, prompting many raised eyebrows from fellow couturiers.

In June 1960, Japanese demonstrators protest the impending visit of U.S. President Dwight D. Eisenhower to Japan, while also voicing their opposition to stationing American U-2 spy planes in their country. Japanese Prime Minister Kishi Nobusuke had recently negotiated a revision of the 1951 Peace Treaty, one that was favorable to Japan. However, many Japanese leftists and students bristled at continued U.S. influence in their country. The turmoil forced the Japanese to ask Ike to postpone his trip—a postponement that became permanent.

June 13: In Greenwich Village, Gerde's Folk City begins open-mike hootenannies on Monday nights. Other village nightspots will begin their own hootenannies, and Greenwich Village will quickly become the place for aspiring folk singers.

June 14: At the Manila airport, President Eisenhower gets a rousing welcome from nearly two million Filipinos.

June 18: Golfer Arnold Palmer storms from seven strokes behind in the final round to win the U.S. Open at Cherry Hills Country Club in Denver.

June 19: Freedomland USA, an East Coast counterpart to Disneyland, opens on 200 acres in the East Bronx, New York. Approximately 25,000 people visit on the first day.

June 20: Boxer Floyd Patterson knocks out Ingemar Johansson, becoming the first man to regain the heavyweight crown.

Spring–summer: Nationalists riot in British-controlled Northern and Southern Rhodesia.

Summer: United Arab Republic President Gamal Abdul Nasser says he looks forward to the day when Iran will be free of the U.S.-backed Shah "and Zionism."

June 21: In a speech in Bucharest, Romania, Soviet Premier Nikita Khrushchev says Lenin's notion of inevitable war between communism and capitalism is no longer valid.

June 30: The Democratic Republic of Congo (formerly the Belgian Congo) attains independence from Belgium.

July 4: The new 50-star flag is officially flown in the United States for the first time.

July 5: The most extensive exhibit ever of works by Pablo Picasso opens at the Tate Gallery in London.

In the film *The Apartment,* Bud Baxter (played by Jack Lemmon) chats with Fran Kubelik (Shirley MacLaine), an elevator operator for the insurance company for which he works as a clerk. This 1960 tragicomedy, directed by Billy Wilder, won five Academy Awards, including best picture and best director. The film focuses on Bud, who lends out his apartment to company executives for adulterous sexual encounters. The central tension comes when he discovers that his boss (Fred McMurray) is taking Fran, whom Bud has befriended, to his apartment for trysts. *The Apartment,* wrote critic Tim Dirk, is a "bleak assessment of corporate America, big business and capitalism, success, and the work ethic" in America during this time period.

Golfer Arnold Palmer celebrates after sinking the putt that clinched the U.S. Open championship on June 18, 1960. Going into the final round at Denver's tough Cherry Hills course, Palmer trailed leader Mike Souchak by seven strokes. When a friend, reporter Bob Drum, told Palmer he was too far back to win, Arnie answered, "The hell I am!" He proceeded to shoot a 65 to win the tournament, thanks partly to a 325-yard drive on the par-4 1st hole. The victory helped fuel the legend of Palmer as a fierce competitor who could charge from behind to win championships. An All-American hero, Palmer was cheered on by his legion of followers, known as "Arnie's Army."

African Independence

ON SEPTEMBER 15, 1960, an editorial in the Angolan newspaper *La Voix de la Nation* declared that "the torrent of the African liberation movement is irresistible, and it can neither be stopped nor channeled." The editors of the paper summed up the situation quite succinctly: In 1960 alone, 17 African nations gained independence from their European colonial overseers, including Nigeria, Senegal, Niger, Ivory Coast, Cameroon, Somalia, and Madagascar. While the United Kingdom, Italy, and Belgium each wrangled with decolonization, France was hit the hardest, losing nearly all of its African colonies.

The independence movement was driven by the rise of Pan-Africanism. Inspired by successes in India and other Asian nations, African nationalist leaders such as Kwame Nkrumah and Mangaliso Sobukwe claimed "Africa for Africans." Some of the new independent African nations successfully installed democratic governments, but others saw the rise of despotic autocracies.

In the Belgian Congo, anticolonial sentiments ran especially high. After independence was declared on June 30, 1960, the nation's army mutinied—killing more than 25 people. Moreover, the mineral-rich province of Katanga seceded in July, triggering a civil war and necessitating the involvement of UN troops. Not until Joseph Mobutu assumed power in 1965 did the Democratic Republic of the Congo achieve political stability.

A Congolese citizen celebrates his country's independence by removing a portrait of King Boudouin of Belgium at the Leopoldville Airport. Belgium granted independence to its largest colony on June 30, 1960. The Congo quickly descended into near chaos, as competing political groups struggled for power. Within a week of independence, an army mutiny occurred and the mineral-rich Katanga province seceded from Prime Minister Patrice Lumumba's central government—with the support of Belgian troops and American complicity. Such were the perils of decolonization. Troubles in the Congo would rage throughout the early 1960s.

Scientist Dr. Theodore Maiman examines the ruby used to create the first operable laser beam, which he perfected in 1960. The laser, which is an acronym for Light Amplification by Stimulated Emission of Radiation, initially was feared by some Americans, who considered it a possible weapon. But most people eventually realized the laser's enormous practical value. Early on, laser technology recorded the distance from the Earth to the moon. In subsequent years, it was used for such diverse purposes as retina surgery, tattoo removal, and supermarket price scanning.

Nigeria's "Miss Independence," Rosemary Anieze

July 11: Accords are signed granting independence to the African nations of Dahomey, Ivory Coast, Niger, and Upper Volta.

July 12: Ohio Art introduces the Etch-A-Sketch drawing toy.

July 13: Massachusetts Senator John F. Kennedy is nominated as the presidential candidate on the first ballot at the 1960 Democratic National Convention in Los Angeles. *See* July 14, 1960.

July 14: Texas Senator Lyndon Johnson is named Democratic vice presidential candidate by acclamation in Los Angeles. • The UN Security Council votes to send UN troops to the Congo to quell military mutiny and protect resident Europeans.

July 16: Jane Goodall, 26, heads to Tanzania to become the first person to study chimpanzees in their natural habitat.

July 20: The first successful launch of a Polaris missile from a submerged submarine, the USS *George Washington,* is carried out. The missile has a range of about 1,000 nautical miles. • Sirimavo Bandaranaike is elected prime minister of Ceylon, becoming the first female premier of a modern parliamentary government.

July 27: At the Republican National Convention in Chicago, Vice President Richard Nixon is named his party's nominee by acclamation. *See* July 28, 1960.

July 28: Henry Cabot Lodge, a U.S. delegate to the UN, is nominated for vice president at the Republican National Convention in Chicago.

July 31: Nation of Islam leader Elijah Muhammed calls for the establishment of an all-black state.

August: The U.S. Air Force announces the readiness of the first SAC missile squadron, at Francis E. Warren Air Force Base in Wyoming.

Senator John F. Kennedy and his wife, Jacqueline, sail on their boat in Nantucket Sound off the coast of Massachusetts. This July 1960 photograph captures much of the Kennedy appeal to many Americans. JFK was young (43), handsome, athletic, and married to a beautiful, talented woman, thus providing a clear contrast to Dwight Eisenhower, who turned 70 in October 1960. We now know that Kennedy, far from being full of "vigah" (as he pronounced it), suffered from several debilitating illnesses. He was in constant pain and was on a complex regimen of drugs.

Supporters of John F. Kennedy cheer their candidate as he is nominated for president at the 1960 Democratic National Convention. The young Catholic senator had won 10 Democratic primaries, with his most notable victories coming over Hubert Humphrey in Wisconsin and West Virginia. Lyndon Johnson, a well-connected senator from Texas, hoped to sway enough delegates at the convention to win the nomination. Kennedy, though, won on the first ballot on July 13. The next day, attempting to heal rifts within the party, he named Johnson as his running mate.

Nikita Khrushchev

EW WORLD LEADERS in the 1960s exasperated American presidents as much as Soviet Premier Nikita Khrushchev. Although Khrushchev had sought the 1960 Paris summit with Dwight Eisenhower and welcomed the 1961 summit with John F. Kennedy, both meetings ended with Khrushchev threatening war. Against the backdrop of tensions in Berlin, Southeast Asia, and especially Cuba, such breakdowns in relations between the United States and the Soviet Union did not bode well for a peaceful future.

Born to a peasant family in 1894, Khrushchev joined the Communist Party in 1918. A supporter of Joseph Stalin, he rose steadily through the party ranks to become a secretary of the Central Committee in 1949. After Stalin's death in 1953, Khrushchev emerged as the most powerful member of the collective leadership.

In 1956 Khrushchev gave a "secret speech" to the Twentieth Congress of the Communist Party. In it, he attacked Stalin's totalitarian policies and the "cult of personality" Stalin had created. This speech soon became public. At the same conference, Khrushchev first began to speak of "peaceful coexistence" with the United States. In 1958 he was named premier.

Under Khrushchev's leadership, the Soviet space and nuclear weapons programs flourished, convincing many American policy makers that the United States lagged behind in both areas. In addition, Khrushchev confronted the Americans over the status of West Berlin—first in 1958 and again in 1961, when he approved the Berlin Wall's construction—and attempted to place nuclear weapons in Cuba in 1962. Such actions added up to a pattern of unpredictability that kept American leaders off balance.

But Khrushchev also could be reasonable. In 1963, for example, following the resolution of the Cuban Missile Crisis, he signed the Nuclear Test Ban Treaty and agreed to establish a hotline between Washington and Moscow. The direct phone line would help defuse any crisis before it escalated.

Students at the University of Nicaragua hang the U.S. ambassador in effigy and trample an American flag as they demonstrate against the United States' influence in their country. The U.S. supported the Nicaraguan strongman dictator, Luis Somoza Debayle, the second in a line of three authoritarian leaders from the Somoza family. Somoza's government was loudly anti-Communist, and in 1959 it was among the first Latin American nations to condemn Fidel Castro's Communist-influenced revolution in Cuba. Many Nicaraguans who lived in poverty or were leftist sympathizers condemned the U.S. for assisting the Somozas.

1960

August 4: An experimental U.S. rocket plane, the X-15, achieves the fastest manned flight to date: 2,196 mph. *See* August 12, 1960.

August 12: The X-15 rocket plane is piloted by Major Robert M. White to 136,500 feet—the highest altitude yet achieved by man. • The Beatles, a new rock 'n' roll band in Liverpool, England, hire Pete Best as their drummer.

August 15: The Congo attains independence from France.

August 17: A "show trial" of downed U.S. U-2 spy plane pilot Francis Gary Powers begins in Moscow. Powers is convicted. *See* February 10, 1962.

August 25–September 11: The Summer Olympic Games are held in Rome. Wilma Rudolph of Clarksville, Tennessee, wins gold medals in the 100-meter dash, 200-meter dash, and 400-meter relay. Also at the Games, Cassius Clay of Louisville, Kentucky, scores a 5–0 decision over Poland's Zbigniew Pietrzykowski, winning boxing's light-heavyweight gold medal.

August 29: Jordanian Prime Minister Hazza Majali is assassinated by a bomb that explodes in his office in Amman. Ten other people are killed. Jordan variously accuses the United Arab Republic and Syria of perpetrating the attack.

August 29–September 14: Hurricane Donna, a Category 4 storm, pounds the Bahamas and the U.S. East Coast from Florida to New York with peak wind gusts of 175 mph. The death toll is approximately 350, including 50 in the U.S.

September: William F. Buckley, Jr., cofounds Young Americans for Freedom (YAF) to challenge Communist thought on college/university campuses throughout the world. • "The Twist," by Chubby Checker, hits the top of the charts. The song begins a new dance fad, with twist clubs popping up in most major cities.

The first submarine-launched Polaris test missile is fired on July 20, 1960, off the Florida coast. This sea-to-surface weapon, with a range of 1,000 nautical miles, greatly expanded the United States' capability to deliver nuclear weapons to their targets, since submarines could operate virtually undetected off the coasts of hostile nations. The arrival of the Polaris spurred the USSR to try to upgrade its own nuclear program.

Strelka and Belka were the fourth and fifth dogs sent into space by the Soviets—and the first to return alive. Launched on August 19, 1960—along with 40 mice, two rats, and multiple plants—the dogs orbited the Earth 18 times. At this point, the American space program seemed to be significantly behind the Soviets'. Democratic presidential nominee John F. Kennedy used such events to bolster his claim that a substantial "missile gap" existed between the U.S. and the USSR.

Pictured is an artist's recreation of the head of the earliest known human. Fossil remains of the 600,000-year-old skull of "East Africa man" were discovered by renowned British anthropologist Richard Leakey and his wife, Mary, in the Olduvai Gorge in Tanganyika. The findings were publicly announced in the September 1960 issue of *National Geographic* magazine. Mary Leakey actually discovered the initial evidence. Richard, groggy with a headache, heard her yell, "I've got him! I've got him!" What she found were two huge teeth. Richard reported that "magically, my headache departed."

American track standout Wilma Rudolph displays the three gold medals she won at the 1960 Rome Olympics. Rudolph finished first in the 100- and 200-meter dashes and anchored America's gold-winning 400-meter relay team. In a period of great turmoil over civil rights for African-Americans, Rudolph became emblematic of black accomplishment. Her performance paralleled that of Cassius Clay, the African-American boxer who won the light-heavyweight gold medal in Rome.

Singer Chubby Checker does "The Twist," a dance and song that were all the rage in the early 1960s. Black singer Hank Ballard originally recorded the song in 1957. For the television show *American Bandstand,* host Dick Clark convinced the virtually unknown Checker to cover the song, which became an instant hit. The dance craze, which involved partners standing apart while twisting, was seen by many as an uninhibited challenge to traditional moral codes.

This painting of a harmonious, rural landscape was created by folk painter "Grandma Moses" (born Anna Mary Robertson). Grandma Moses reached her 100th birthday on September 7, 1960. Although she was never a favorite with critics, reproductions of her paintings—especially in the form of greeting cards— were wildly popular during the two decades after World War II. According to absolutearts.com, Grandma Moses's "message of hope provided a welcome antidote to the anxieties of the Cold War era."

Mead Johnson's weight control product Metrecal was introduced in 1959. Metrecal's liquid version became immensely popular in 1960, as millions of Americans jumped on the weight-loss bandwagon. In 1961 Jean Nidetch, taking advantage of the growing interest in dieting, started Weight Watchers. In addition, exceptionally thin models, who began emerging in the 1950s, appeared more frequently, culminating with the barely visible Twiggy in 1966.

1960

September 1–12: The Pennsylvania Railroad, America's largest, is struck by 15,000 members of the Transport Workers Union over work rules and job security.

September 5–6: American Rafer Johnson wins the decathlon with an Olympic-record 8,392 points.

September 9: The eight-team American Football League, a rival to the NFL, begins play. The AFL consists of the Boston Patriots, Buffalo Bills, Houston Oilers, New York Titans, Dallas Texans, Denver Broncos, Los Angeles Chargers, and Oakland Raiders.

September 24: The USS *Enterprise,* the first U.S. atomic-powered aircraft carrier, is christened and launched in Newport News, Virginia.

September 25: Etiquette adviser Emily Post dies.

September 26: At the UN, Fidel Castro delivers a 4½-hour speech directed against U.S. policies. • Senator John Kennedy and Vice President Richard Nixon meet in Chicago for the first of four nationally broadcast, 60-minute presidential debates. *See* October 7, 1960.

September 28: Boston Red Sox slugger Ted Williams plays his last big-league game and homers in his final at-bat.

September 30: *The Flintstones,* the first animated cartoon on prime-time television, premieres on ABC.

October: The Southern Education Reporting Service announces that there are 766 desegregated school districts among 2,838 biracial districts in 17 southern states and Washington, D.C. • Some radio stations refuse to play "Tell Laura I Love Her" by Ray Peterson because of its death storyline. • *An Evening with Nichols and May,* with comic monologuists Mike Nichols and Elaine May, debuts on Broadway.

"The magnificent seven" ride on in the 1960 film of the same name. John Sturges directed this remake of Japanese director Akira Kurosawa's classic *The Seven Samurai,* moving this tale of honor to the West. In the remake, poor Mexican villagers assemble seven gunfighters to protect their homes against greedy bandits. A strong cast—led by Yul Brynner, Steve McQueen, and Eli Wallach—and a stirring score by famed Hollywood composer Elmer Bernstein helped make *The Magnificent Seven* a popular hit.

The USS *Enterprise,* the world's first aircraft carrier powered by nuclear reactors, was launched on September 24, 1960. Its enormous range and flexibility unnerved the USSR and contributed to the growing arms race. Still in service in the 2000s, the carrier would launch air attacks against Al-Qaeda terrorist camps and Taliban military installations.

Boston Red Sox legend Ted Williams crosses home plate after his last at-bat as a major-leaguer. In what seemed to many an act of divine intervention, one of the greatest hitters in history blasted a home run with his final swing. He retired with two American League MVP Awards, six batting titles, a career batting average of .344, and 521 home runs. He might have topped 700 homers had he not served as a pilot in World War II and Korea.

The main characters in *The Flintstones*, Wilma and Fred Flintstone (*top*) and neighbors Barney and Betty Rubble (*bottom*), watch themselves on TV. This popular ABC cartoon show premiered on September 30, 1960, and ran in a Friday evening time slot until 1966. (NBC picked it up in the late 1960s.) The first prime-time animated cartoon series, *The Flintstones* was produced by Hanna–Barbera, and was patterned after the sitcom *The Honeymooners*, with Fred just as bombastic as the Jackie Gleason character Ralph Kramden. Billed as a "modern Stone Age family," the Flintstones powered their car with their feet and used animals as household items—such as a bumblebee inside a clamshell for Fred's electric shaver.

Young Americans for Freedom

STUDENT ACTIVISM in the Sixties was not the monopoly of the liberal Left. A case in point was the Young Americans for Freedom (YAF), a conservative student group founded in 1960. The YAF was the brainchild of two icons of conservative thought, William F. Buckley, Jr., and Barry Goldwater, the latter having just published the Resurgent Right's "manifesto," *The Conscience of a Conservative.*

In September 1960 Buckley convened the student arm of his conservative network at his estate in Sharon, Connecticut. The Young Americans for Freedom was born. Its leaders issued a mandate known as the Sharon State-ment. It also launched a magazine, *New Guard,* that took aim at what YAFers deemed the left-leaning National Student Association (NSA), which it accused of "brainwashing" students into being soft on communism.

Among YAF's *bete noires* were President John F. Kennedy, the Peace Corps (which it considered a waste of taxpayer money), and, of course, liberal student organizations. By the

William F. Buckley, Jr.

end of the decade, the YAF boasted some 60,000 members and 500 chapters nationwide—as well as sponsors that included John Wayne and Ronald Reagan.

October 5: Nervous heads at NORAD receive a missile-attack message from the early-warning system in Thule, Greenland. A fault in the computer system had removed two zeros from the radar's ranging components. The radar actually was detecting a reflection from the moon, 250,000 miles away.

October 7: Presidential candidates John Kennedy and Richard Nixon meet in Washington, D.C., for the second of four nationally broadcast debates. *See* October 13, 1960.

October 12: Soviet Premier Nikita Khrushchev waves his right shoe and bangs it on the desk in a noisy UN session. Khrushchev was responding to a statement by a member of the Philippine delegation. • A teenage, right-wing political zealot stabs to death Inejiro Asanuma, chairman of Japan's Socialist Party.

October 13: Presidential candidates John Kennedy and Richard Nixon meet for the third of four nationally broadcast debates. The debate is telecast in a unique split-screen format, with Nixon speaking from Los Angeles and Kennedy from New York. *See* October 21, 1960. • The Pittsburgh Pirates defeat the New York Yankees 10–9 in the decisive Game 7 of the World Series on a game-ending home run by Bill Mazeroski.

October 17: Woolworth, Kress, W. T. Grant, and McCrory–McLellan variety stores announce the integration of lunch counters in more than 100 southern cities. • Quiz show winner Charles Van Doren and 13 others are arrested in New York on charges of second-degree perjury in testimony relating to rigged television quiz shows. • Baseball's National League grants franchises to New York and Houston. *See* October 25, 1960.

October 20: The U.S. bans all exports to Cuba except food and medicine. ➤

Two University of California–Berkeley students ignore the screening of *Operation Abolition,* a 1960 film that painted demonstrators as Communist-inspired radicals. It was produced by a private company shortly after Berkeley students and others had protested HUAC hearings in San Francisco. Incensed by distortions in the "documentary," the American Civil Liberties Union produced a film in response, titled *Operation Correction.* The two films contributed to the polarization of conservatives and liberals in the early 1960s.

This massive UNIVAC, typical of computer technology in 1960, required two people to use it successfully. However, less-cumbersome units were on the horizon. In 1959 the DEC PDP-1, the precursor of the modern minicomputer, sold for $120,000. Early computer hackers at Massachusetts Institute of Technology used the smaller version of the UNIVAC to write the first computerized video game, Space War!

"It was not so much what the candidates said, however, but how they looked. . . . [O]n camera Nixon's skin was transparent and unattractive. His jowls seemed to hang heavily. He sweat enough so that the Lazy Shave that had been applied to mask his heavy stubble began to run."

—Author Charles Kenney, *John F. Kennedy: The Presidential Portfolio*

The Kennedy–Nixon Debates

Though leading in the presidential race in September 1960, Vice President Richard Nixon had yet to seal the deal with voters. Renowned for his verbal jousting and fondness for confrontation, he saw the upcoming series of television appearances with Senator John F. Kennedy (D–MA) as his key to victory. For his part, Kennedy correctly noted that as the perceived underdog, he had far more to gain from the exposure and thoroughly prepped himself for the first of the candidates' four debates, on September 26. Nixon, however, was confident that his debating skills alone would carry the day.

The two candidates arrived in Chicago a study in contrasts. Sickly and underweight, Nixon had been running himself ragged in recent days. Moreover, a knee injury incurred weeks earlier had led to an infection that sidelined him for two weeks. Kennedy, meanwhile, sported a Hollywood tan thanks to a recent swing through Califor-

The last debate, October 21

nia. Proximity to this charismatic upstart seemed to accentuate Nixon's worst traits, making him look like a joyless scold.

Troubles continued for Nixon. Upon arrival at the studio, he banged his injured knee while exiting his car. In great pain, he compounded his troubles by refusing the offer of stage makeup, instead applying some drugstore "Lazy Shave" to his infamous five o'clock shadow. The magnitude of the error did not escape Chicago Mayor Richard Daley, who remarked, "My God! They've embalmed him before he even died."

Beneath the hot studio lights, audiences saw a calm and cool Kennedy address the camera directly, while his opponent sweated, fidgeted, and looked decidedly uncomfortable. Though radio listeners scored Nixon the winner, television viewers overwhelmingly gave the victory to Kennedy. The resulting buzz gave JFK much-needed momentum going into the election, while Nixon's shot at a knockout blow failed. Said an aide, "Dick didn't lose this election; Dick *blew* this election."

You wouldn't call it a gang. Just Danny Ocean and his 11 pals – the night they blew all the lights in Las Vegas!...

In the 1960 film *Ocean's 11,* the main character assembles a group of criminals who attempt to pull off simultaneous robberies of Las Vegas casinos. The four male leads—Frank Sinatra, Dean Martin, Sammy Davis, Jr., and Peter Lawford—were known as the "Rat Pack" during the late 1950s and early '60s. The Pack became famous for hanging around Las Vegas casinos at which they often headlined, staging loud parties, womanizing, and consuming large amounts of alcohol. The Rat Pack could be regarded as the last gasp of "cocktail culture" before a more youth-oriented culture emerged in the mid-1960s.

1960

Don Knotts (Deputy Barney Fife, *left*) and Andy Griffith (Sheriff Andy Taylor, *right*) starred in the immensely popular *The Andy Griffith Show,* which ran from 1960 to 1968. The show never placed lower than seventh in the Nielsen Ratings and ranked first in its final year. Its popularity derived from its charming small-town setting in the fictional Mayberry, North Carolina, and the genuinely funny, lovable characters— including Andy's freckle-faced son, Opie (Ron Howard). The relationship between the homespun but wise Andy and the bumbling Fife was at the heart of the show. During a turbulent decade, *The Andy Griffith Show* provided an oasis of nice people and simple values.

Inejiro Asanuma, chairman of the Japanese Socialist Party, is stabbed to death at a political debate in Tokyo on October 12, 1960. The assassin, Otoya Yamaguchi, was a 17-year-old member of an extreme nationalist, pro-emperor party. Although anti-Americanism was common in Japan in the early 1960s, this murder had more to do with internal Japanese politics than with opposition to the United States. Both Asanuma and his killer, for example, opposed the U.S.-Japan Security Treaty, a 1951 pact that formed a strong alliance between the two countries. Before Yamaguchi hanged himself in prison, he scrawled in toothpaste on his cell wall, "May His Majesty the Emperor live for 10,000 generations."

Pittsburgh Pirates second baseman Bill Mazeroski rounds third after belting a ninth-inning home run in Game 7 of the 1960 World Series against the New York Yankees. Many baseball historians rank the series finale as the most dramatic game in history. The Yankees scored two runs in the eighth to go up 7–4, but Pittsburgh rallied in the bottom of the eighth to take a 9–7 lead. New York tied it in the ninth, 9–9, before Mazeroski ended the drama with a solo blast. He was the only player in the 20th century to club a game-ending homer in Game 7 of the World Series.

Marilyn Monroe and Clark Gable appear in this 1960 still from *The Misfits*, a film that itself was deeply troubled. It brought together the clashing egos of its stars, which also included Montgomery Clift and Eli Wallach, as well as its director (John Huston) and screenwriter (Arthur Miller, Monroe's husband). The story focuses on a divorcée, Monroe, and her burgeoning romance with an old cowboy, Gable. Monroe, who didn't like the script, was late for shoots and ultimately hospitalized. Huston spent much of the time inebriated in casinos. Gable died of a heart attack shortly after the film was belatedly finished. A year after the movie's release in 1961, Monroe died from a drug overdose.

On November 2, 1960, a British jury agreed that D. H. Lawrence's *Lady Chatterley's Lover* was not obscene or detrimental to public morals. The next day, publisher Penguin Books distributed 200,000 copies of the complete version. Here, a British tube passenger takes advantage of this new-found freedom. Similar cases in the United States in the late 1950s and early '60s helped usher in a new era of literary freedom and sexual liberation.

On November 4, 1960, six-year-old Ruby Bridges prepared for her first day at William Frantz Elementary School in New Orleans. Her mother told her: "Now, I want you to behave yourself today, Ruby, and don't be afraid. There might be a lot of people outside this new school, but I'll be with you." Due to a court-ordered integration law, the first-grader became the first (and only) black child enrolled in the school. For a while, in fact, Bridges was the only child in her class, as irate white parents and their children boycotted the school.

1960

October 21: Presidential candidates John Kennedy and Richard Nixon meet in New York for a fourth and final nationally broadcast debate. • Great Britain's first nuclear submarine, the *Dreadnought,* is launched by Elizabeth II at Barrow-in-Furness.

October 25: After his arrest during a sit-in demonstration, Martin Luther King, Jr., is given a four-month sentence in Atlanta for violating parole granted for an earlier traffic charge. • Baseball's American League approves the move of the Washington Senators to Minneapolis as well as the establishment of new teams in D.C. and Los Angeles.

November 8: In the U.S. presidential election, John Kennedy defeats Richard Nixon after garnering 49.7 percent of the vote compared to Nixon's 49.6 percent. • The Louisiana legislature passes 28 laws designed to block school integration. • In the first two-woman race for Senate in U.S. history, Margaret Chase Smith defeats Lucia Marie Cormier for Smith's U.S. Senate seat in Maine.

November 12: Disgruntled South Vietnamese army officers attempt, but fail at, a coup against President Ngo Dinh Diem. A crackdown in subsequent months will lead to more than 50,000 arrests and many executions.

November 14: A national TV audience watches six-year-old Ruby Nell Bridges become the first black child to attend William Frantz Elementary School after a federal court ordered the New Orleans school system to desegregate. *See* November 16, 1960.

November 15: The USS *George Washington,* the first U.S. submarine with nuclear missiles, is launched.

November 16: About 200 whites demonstrate against school desegregation on the steps of New Orleans City Hall. The protests are broken up with fire hoses. • Film star Clark Gable, 59, dies of a heart attack days after completing *The Misfits* with Marilyn Monroe. ➤

First-time author Harper Lee's *To Kill a Mockingbird* was published in 1960 to immediate acclaim. Her story of an innocent black man on trial for rape in the Deep South is told by a young, female narrator, whose sensitive and open-minded perspective raises the reader's awareness of injustice. The book touched the hearts of millions of Americans at a time when the nation was confronting true-life racial issues. Though *Mockingbird* earned Lee the Pulitzer Prize for fiction, she never wrote another novel. The book was made into a critically acclaimed film starring Gregory Peck in 1962.

John F. Kennedy celebrates his victory in the 1960 presidential election with his wife, Jackie, and his mother, Rose (*background*). The young Democratic senator garnered 303 electoral votes to 219 for his Republican opponent, Richard Nixon. However, JFK barely won the popular vote, amassing 34,226,731 to Nixon's 34,108,157. The shift of a few thousand votes in Illinois and Texas would have given Nixon the election. (Indeed, some Republicans alleged fraud in those two states, but no shenanigans were ever proved.) The closeness of the election reflected how deeply divided the nation was politically. The election was hardly an overwhelming mandate for change.

Ventriloquist Shari Lewis gives a kiss to Lamb Chop, her most famous hand puppet character. Lewis became a national phenomenon in fall 1960 after NBC replaced the legendary *Howdy Doody Show* with *The Shari Lewis Show*. She manipulated her fingers to move the mouths of her puppets, creating an intimacy not present in standard string puppeteering. The cute but sassy sweetness of her characters was immensely appealing, especially to children. Lewis, whose career spanned the last four decades of the 20th century, garnered numerous awards, including 12 Emmys.

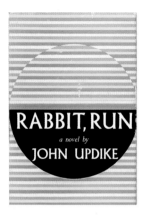

Rabbit, Run, a novel by prolific American author John Updike, was published in 1960. This story of a high school basketball star and unsuccessful young adult, Rabbit Angstrom, was the first in a series of four novels that delineate the course of Angstrom's life. *Rabbit, Run* focuses on Rabbit's failure to cope with the complexities of being a husband and father, as he figuratively and literally runs away from his responsibilities. The book is a marvel of carefully honed prose, and enjoyed popular and critical success. Updike was widely praised for the novel's poignancy, and obvious empathy for Rabbit.

South Vietnamese paratroopers take cover in Saigon as they participate in an unsuccessful coup against South Vietnamese President Ngo Dinh Diem in November 1960. Diem had become increasingly unpopular in 1960 after he centralized power in the hands of his family. This internal turmoil deeply concerned the Eisenhower Administration, which had wholeheartedly supported Diem (who, like the U.S., was determined to prevent the spread of communism from North Vietnam to his republic). By 1960 the administration was split over how to deal with Diem. Some wanted to push democratic reforms while others felt Diem needed time. Eisenhower, more worried about the threat of communism in Laos than Vietnam, essentially temporized and put little pressure on Diem. He left his successor, John F. Kennedy, with a very confused and troubled situation in South Vietnam.

Harvest of Shame, a powerful CBS documentary by famed reporter Edward R. Murrow, exposed the horrible conditions suffered by America's migrant workers. Broadcast on November 25, 1960, it featured scenes of impoverished workers who earned less-than-subsistence wages, had no sick or disability pay, and often lived in squalor. The show caused howls of outrage, especially from Florida Senator Spessard Holland, who argued that the documentary exaggerated conditions. Ironically, a few months later, Murrow—who had been appointed director of the U.S. Information Agency—tried to pressure the British Broadcasting Corporation not to show the film because of its negative image of the United States.

1960

This 1960 Soviet magazine cover reflects the USSR's view of itself as a dominant superpower. Premier Nikita Khrushchev bragged that the Soviet Union had "a broad range of rockets and in such quantity that we can virtually shatter the world." While such bellicose rhetoric no doubt frightened the average American, the Soviets in 1960 actually had only four intercontinental ballistic missiles. The United States was well ahead of its chief adversary in the nuclear arms race.

A family of four samples a den/fallout shelter in November 1960. After the Soviet Union successfully tested a nuclear weapon in late 1949, fallout shelters became increasingly popular items. They turned into a virtual fad from 1957 to '60 because of Sputnik (the Soviet orbital satellite) and John F. Kennedy's charge of a Soviet lead in missile development. Ranging from luxurious multiroomed structures to Sears prefab specials, shelters were dubious protection at best, as many Americans were duped by government promises of safety underground. As Columbia industrial engineering professor Seymour Melman noted, it was "futile, desperately futile, to construct fallout shelters."

In December 1960 a group of schoolchildren in Topeka, Kansas, practices survival techniques in case of a nuclear attack. This "duck and cover" maneuver was made popular in a short civil defense film of the same name, produced in 1950 and shown widely in schools during the 1950s and early '60s. Such drills became routine in American schools in this period, even though the government was misleading its people about the effectiveness of such tactics. Ducking and covering would be useless in the face of a nuclear bomb.

This 1960 album is the comedy recording of Mike Nichols's and Elaine May's revolutionary Broadway play. The "evening" in question consisted of a series of low-key yet biting satirical sketches that poked fun at social and cultural mores of the times. One famous sketch, "Bach to Bach," punctured the pretensions of two phony intellectuals who talked culture during a one-night stand. Nichols and May broke up in 1961 to pursue individual projects. Nichols would go on to win an Oscar as best director for *The Graduate* (1967).

The Pill

IN 1953 MARGARET SANGER, a pioneer in promoting contraception, approached reproduction specialist Dr. Gregory Pincus to fulfill a lifelong dream. Though the diaphragm had proven effective through decades of use, most women spurned it as uncomfortable and unwieldy. Sanger believed that if a more user-friendly means of contraception were available, unwanted pregnancies (as well as abortions) would be greatly reduced.

Dr. Pincus set to work on the project, supported by grants from International Harvester heiress Katharine McCormick. Soon Pincus joined forces with infertility specialist Dr. John Rock, and in 1954 the pair successfully tested a progesterone pill that prevented ovulation. In 1956 G. D. Searle & Co. submitted the first birth control pill, Enovid, to the Food and Drug Administration for approval, which was granted in May 1960. Commercial success was immediate; a half-million prescriptions were filled in 1960 alone.

Though lauded in some circles for providing married couples with an effective means of family planning, the arrival of the "miraculous tablet" did not come without controversy. Dr. Rock, a conservative Catholic, lobbied hard to win the Vatican's approval and became embittered by the

refusal. Meanwhile, African-American women who otherwise would have embraced the new technology were inhibited by prevalent rumors that the pill was an insidious form of mass sterilization that targeted the black community.

Concerns over side effects would plague the drug throughout the 1960s, but its popularity remained strong. By decade's end, millions of American women were on the pill. It also helped slow the postwar baby boom, which most historians say ended in 1964.

Rod Serling created and narrated the popular fantasy drama *The Twilight Zone*. Serling also wrote or adapted 99 of the 156 episodes that appeared on CBS from 1959 to 1964. Each episode began with Serling's understated but ominous exposition of the basic plot. (Serling had wanted Orson Welles to do the opening narration, but Welles wasn't interested.) In most episodes, ordinary people found themselves on the borderline between reality and fantasy—in that "Twilight Zone." Serling often tackled thorny social issues such as capital punishment, racism, and censorship. The show won two Emmy Awards and succeeded in syndication for decades after its initial run.

The Pill Relieves the "Burden"

THE PILL FOR ME didn't immediately fix anything in terms of my relationship with my husband, or improve it in that sense. What it gave to me was the sense of ownership of myself, which at that point in my life was very, very important. I could foresee at the age of twenty-three having another baby and another baby and another baby. And I was very disturbed, myself, about the loss of who I was. The loss of the investment that I'd made in my education, any future for me. Now that was considered a selfish motive at that time but that's how I felt. And so the idea that I could do something that would give part of me back to me was very important. And my husband was quite happy for me to use the pill, it wasn't a secret at all, and I think he was probably relieved because it took that burden away. So all in all, I think it was very, very positive.

—SYLVIA CLARK, ON THE INTRODUCTION OF THE BIRTH CONTROL PILL IN 1960

1960

November 25: CBS broadcasts *Harvest of Shame*. Hosted by Edward R. Murrow, the news special exposes the degradation and exploitation of millions of U.S. migratory workers. • John F. Kennedy, Jr., is born in Washington, D.C.

November 28: Novelist Richard Wright dies at 52.

December 5: A manifesto published in Moscow declares that Communist world victory will be achieved peacefully or, if necessary, through war. • In *Boynton v. Virginia*, the U.S. Supreme Court rules that segregation in interstate bus terminal restaurants is unconstitutional.

December 6: For the first time, the U.S. government publishes photos of the types of A-bombs dropped on Japan in 1945.

December 13: President-elect Kennedy announces the selection of Robert McNamara as secretary of defense.

December 16: A United Airlines jetliner collides with another plane above New York City and crashes to earth in a Brooklyn neighborhood; 134 people on the plane are killed. • President-elect Kennedy designates his brother, Robert F. Kennedy, as U.S. attorney general.

December 19: Forty-nine people die when the USS *Constellation*, a U.S. aircraft carrier under construction in Brooklyn, New York, catches fire.

December 20: Dedicated to the unification of a Communist Vietnam, North Vietnamese leader Ho Chi Minh organizes the National Liberation Front (NLF), which will aim to defeat the U.S.-backed government of South Vietnam.

December 30: Laos asks the UN for help with a reported invasion by North Vietnamese and possibly Red Chinese troops.

Columbia University Professor Charles Van Doren (*center*) answers questions after pleading not guilty to a perjury charge on December 1, 1960. Van Doren became embroiled in a well-publicized scandal after he appeared on the popular NBC quiz show *Twenty-One* in early 1957. He won $129,000 and became a pop culture hero. However, a defeated contestant claimed that the show's producers had fixed the contests. Van Doren initially denied the charges, but he later admitted that he had been fed answers and coached ahead of time. The scandal, some people have opined, contributed to America's "loss of innocence."

White housewives in New Orleans protest against public school desegregation. One woman carries a sign claiming that integration of African-American children into white schools is a "mortal sin." Opponents of desegregation did more than stage demonstrations and invoke the Bible. The state of Mississippi attempted to interpose its own authority in order to "protect" its citizens from "unjust" actions of the federal government. In Virginia, the Prince Edward County School Board simply shut down its schools from 1956 to 1960 when faced with court-ordered desegregation.

Martin Milner (*left*) and George Maharis welcome a hitch-hiker on board in this publicity still from *Route 66*. The popular television series, which ran on CBS from 1960 to '64, featured location shooting all along this legendary American highway. It was essentially an anthology show, featuring the varied adventures of these two unlikely friends—a Yale graduate (Milner) and a New York City tough guy (Maharis)—as they traveled what novelist John Steinbeck referred to as America's "mother road." Route 66, which ran from Chicago to Los Angeles, ultimately succumbed to the growing popularity of interstate highways.

Demonstrators in Algeria shout and wave flags on December 12, 1960, as fighting continued between French troops and Algerian rebels seeking independence. Algerian guerrillas had been fighting to expel France since 1954. In 1959 French President Charles de Gaulle suggested self-determination for Algeria at some point in the future. But French people living in Algeria as well as French paratroopers were so incensed that they launched an antigovernment revolt in January 1960. After the uprising was put down, Algerian independence fighters renewed their violence because of the slow pace of decolonization. The turmoil was not settled until 1962, when France granted its colony independence.

President-elect John F. Kennedy shakes hands with Robert S. McNamara, president of Ford Motor Company and Kennedy's choice for secretary of defense. McNamara had earned an MA in business administration and served as an Army Air Corps statistician during World War II. His rapid rise at Ford was a result of a fierce work ethic and a commitment to rational statistical analysis as the basis for decision-making. He brought this emotionally distanced style to his new job. McNamara became a leading advocate of the rational and flexible application of American power to assure that the Communists were not victorious in South Vietnam.

New & Notable

Books

Born Free by Joy Adamson
Growing Up Absurd by Paul Goodman
The Magic Christian by Terry Southern
The Making of the President
    by Theodore White
The Plague by Albert Camus
Rabbit, Run by John Updike
The Rise and Fall of the Third Reich
    by William L. Shirer
To Kill a Mockingbird by Harper Lee
The Waste Makers by Vance Packard

Movies

The Apartment
Butterfield 8
L'Avventura
La Dolce Vita
Elmer Gantry
The Little Shop of Horrors
The Magnificent Seven
Ocean's 11
Psycho
Saturday Night and Sunday Morning
Spartacus
Two Women
Where the Boys Are

Songs

"Are You Lonesome Tonight"
    by Elvis Presley
"Chain Gang" by Sam Cooke
"El Paso" by Marty Robbins
"It's Now or Never" by Elvis Presley
"Save the Last Dance for Me"
    by the Drifters
"Theme from 'A Summer Place'"
    by Percy Faith
"The Twist" by Chubby Checker

Television

The Andy Griffith Show
Candid Camera
My Three Sons
Route 66
Thriller

Theater

Becket
Bye Bye Birdie
Camelot
The Fantasticks
A Taste of Honey
The Unsinkable Molly Brown

The tail section of a United Airlines DC-8 lies smoldering in Brooklyn after a collision with a TWA Lockheed Super Constellation on December 16, 1960. The final death toll exceeded 130, including several people on the ground. An 11-year-old boy, traveling alone to visit his mother, initially survived the crash but died a few days later. An investigation showed that an instrument failure caused the TWA plane to stray off course.

Demonstrators in Great Britain protest against nuclear weapons on December 30, 1960. The "ban the bomb movement," spearheaded by the Campaign for Nuclear Disarmament (CND), achieved considerable notoriety in Britain in the late 1950s and early 1960s. Participants were concerned about the threat of nuclear war, the dangers of radioactive fallout from nuclear tests, and the amount of money being spent on bombs in hard economic times. CND and other protest groups had enough influence to concern British Prime Minister Harold Macmillan, who worried in a letter to President Eisenhower about "the difficult cross currents of opinions on the nuclear problem." The American equivalent of CND was the National Committee for a Sane Nuclear Policy (SANE), also founded in the 1950s and very active in the early '60s.

Fidel Castro

IN THE EARLY 1960S, John F. Kennedy had but one rival among foreign leaders who matched him in youth and charisma: Fidel Castro. A Cuban lawyer turned revolutionary, Castro enjoyed widespread popularity throughout Latin America while simultaneously being held in contempt by successive American administrations.

Born on a sugar plantation in 1926, Castro grew up resenting American political and military influence in Cuba. As a law student at the University of Havana, he became involved in student politics. In 1952, as Fulgencio Batista established a dictatorship in Cuba, Castro began to plot a revolution.

On July 26, 1953, Castro led about 150 rebels in an attack on more than 1,000 of Batista's soldiers. The rebellion was quashed, and Castro was tried for conspiracy, convicted, and sentenced to 15 years in prison. Pardoned after two years, Castro went to Mexico to train rebels. He returned in 1956 to Cuba, where he plotted the July 26th Movement in Sierra Maestra. Combining guerrilla warfare with promises of land reform, educational reform, and universal healthcare, he ran Batista out of the country on January 1, 1959. That year, Castro became prime minister of a new revolutionary government that soon began nationalizing American business interests.

Although Presidents Eisenhower and Kennedy were well aware of the abuses of the Batista regime, and that even some Americans idealized Castro as a revolutionary liberator, they waged an unwavering campaign to remove him from power. Both presidents approved the CIA plan to topple Castro by landing a force of Cuban exiles on the island to foment an uprising. When that ended in the Bay of Pigs disaster, Kennedy approved Operation Mongoose, a covert program that also failed to overthrow Castro.

In late 1961 Castro identified his government as Marxist–Leninist and established closer relations with the USSR. The next year, the Soviets installed nuclear missiles in Cuba. Following a tense two-week crisis, Kennedy succeeded in forcing the missiles' removal, but Castro remained. He ruled as Communist dictator of Cuba well into the 21st century.

Cuban soldiers stand next to an anti-aircraft battery near Havana in 1960. Relations between the U.S. and Cuba had deteriorated during late 1959 and 1960, as the Eisenhower Administration became increasingly convinced that Fidel Castro was tilting toward communism. By January 1960, Eisenhower was referring to him as "a madman," and on March 17, 1960, Ike authorized a program to overthrow the Cuban leader. As the year wore on, Castro—sensing a possible U.S. takeover—looked even more to the USSR for help. He also began preparing for a possible attack.

Fast Food Nation

IN THE 1950S CALIFORNIA restaurateurs Mac and Dick McDonald perfected the hamburger-making system. By using assembly line regimentation, they found they could maximize both efficiency and profits, serving fast food fast. The concept made them rich, and it attracted the attention of an aspiring entrepreneur named Ray Kroc.

While visiting the business that had bought so many of his milkshake machines, Kroc had a vision for the future. He felt that if he could apply his knowledge of franchising to the McDonald brothers' meticulously uniform and compartmentalized food handling, he could reshape the nation's eating habits.

Ray Kroc

Postwar America had seen the rise of convenience foods. This, coupled with a growing automobile culture, laid the groundwork for the success of fast food restaurants. The 100th McDonald's restaurant opened in 1959, and the 200th opened in 1960. A year later, arch rival Burger King went national. Throughout the 1960s, McDonald's competed with numerous new and long-established fast food restaurants, including Kentucky Fried Chicken, Dairy Queen, Burger Chef, Jack in the Box, White Castle, Red Barn, Taco Bell, and many more.

Kroc marketed his product to children via television. In the Washington, D.C., area, in 1963, viewers were introduced to Ronald McDonald for the first time, played by the clownish Willard Scott. The same year, Kroc served McDonald's 1 billionth hamburger on the *Art Linkletter Show*. By decade's end, the country reached the point of golden-arched homogeneity. At the time, few questioned the long-term implications of a generation raised on hamburgers and fries.

An employee of Radio Free Europe (RFE) broadcasts pro-American and anti-Communist messages to Soviet-controlled nations in 1960. RFE, the radio arm of the National Committee for a Free Europe, sent its first transmissions to Czechoslovakia on July 4, 1950. Funded in part by the CIA, it was a component of that agency's psychological warfare campaign. The Soviets, fearing RFE's impact, tried to jam its messages. On one occasion in 1959, a Czech diplomat went so far as to put poison in the station's cafeteria saltshakers. These attempts did not succeed in silencing RFE.

A group of young people act as they think "beatniks" would at a "beat" get-together. Bongo drums, sunglasses, and berets were part of the popular stereotype of this loosely connected group of artists and writers in the late 1940s, '50s, and early '60s. Most prominent among them were Jack Kerouac (who reportedly coined the term "beat," meaning beatific) and Allen Ginsberg. Their writing focused on disaffection with what they saw as American conformity and middle-class self-satisfaction. Ginsberg's poem "Howl" and Kerouac's novel *On the Road* best exemplified the Beat Generation's desire to

Kirk Douglas, as Spartacus, rides gallantly in the 1960 film of the same name. Directed by Stanley Kubrick and based on a Howard Fast novel, the film featured Oscar-winning set direction, spectacular battle scenes, and a stellar cast: Douglas, Peter Ustinov, Jean Simmons, Tony Curtis, and Laurence Olivier. As a slave rebelling against Roman authority, Spartacus certainly resonated with proponents of the modern civil rights movement. Kubrick sparked controversy by filming a nude bathing scene involving Olivier and Curtis, filled with homoerotic overtones. The scene was cut from the original release but restored for the DVD.

escape from traditional America, as an exchange between two of Kerouac's characters suggests: "Where we going, man?" "I don't know but we gotta go." Although the movement dissipated in the early 1960s, the beatniks' writings influenced many coming-of-age Baby Boomers.

Former Congo Prime Minister Patrice Lumumba sits dejectedly after being arrested by the forces of his political rival, Congolese President Joseph Mobutu, in December 1960. In the complex cauldron of Congo politics in the early 1960s, Lumumba was seen by his enemies, especially Mobutu, as a dangerous neutralist who might even seek the support of the Soviet Union. Although he was killed by supporters of Mobutu on January 17, 1961, the worldwide outcry actually prompted the Congolese president to proclaim his late rival a national hero.

1961

The Cold War Heats Up

ON APRIL 17, 1961, 1,400 CIA-trained Cuban émigrés, with the strong and enthusiastic backing of the Kennedy White House, disembarked from American Navy ships and hit the beaches of the Bay of Pigs on the southern tip of Cuba. Their mission: roll back the Communist, Soviet-allied government of Fidel Castro. The plan was simple. The small, armed contingent would ignite a popular revolution against the Castro regime. The groundwork had been laid by the CIA with a barrage of radio propaganda informing the Cuban people that their liberation from the dictator Castro was at hand.

There was only one problem: The people of Cuba were not ready to be liberated. The Cuban revolution was just two years old, and Castro—far from being perceived as a ruthless dictator by the majority of Cubans—instead seemed a liberator. That he was a Communist, allied with America's enemy, the Soviet Union, also seemed a good thing.

For nearly two-thirds of a century, since the Spanish–American War, Cubans had lived under the thumb of the United States and American-sponsored dictators. More than 60 years of American influence had left the majority of Cubans poor, ill-educated, and with few opportunities for dignified work. Thus, most Cubans supported the revolution of 1959 and cheered Fidel Castro when he thumbed his nose at the United States. "The revolution begins now," he had told the Cuban people. "It will not be like 1898, when North Americans came and made themselves masters of our country." Castro was seen by his people and, indeed, by many people throughout Latin America and in

"What right does a rich country have to impose its yoke on our people? Only because they have might and no scruples; they do not respect international rules. They should have been ashamed to be engaged in this battle of Goliath against David—and to lose it besides."

—FIDEL CASTRO, APRIL 23, 1961

In an ill-fated attempt to topple the Castro regime, 1,400 U.S.-backed Cuban exiles storm the beach on the southern coast of Cuba during the Bay of Pigs invasion on April 17, 1961. The failure of the poorly planned operation seriously embarrassed the young Kennedy Administration.

1961

Fidel Castro reacted defiantly to U.S. aggression toward Cuba, which included economic sanctions, assassination plots, and an attempted overthrow of his government. Here, he coolly partakes in "America's Game" just one month before the Bay of Pigs invasion.

Soviet Premier Nikita Khrushchev and President John F. Kennedy each saw how the other man measured up during their first and only meeting in Vienna, Austria, in June 1961. The Cold War enemies butted heads on several issues, including control over East and West Berlin. In two months, the Soviets would begin construction of the Berlin Wall.

the poor nations of the world, as a revolutionary hero who pointed the way to a more just and equitable future.

So, when the 1,400 men of Brigade 2506 landed at the Bay of Pigs, they were not greeted as returning heroes who came to save the Cuban people from communism. Instead, they were met by Cuban troops loyal to the revolution. The CIA radio broadcasts had not set off a populist revolution; they had served only to warn Castro of the imminent threat. The brigade was torn apart by gunfire. Those who survived the onslaught were captured and thrown into prison.

To ensure that the United States did not attempt to rush in and save the brigade, Soviet Premier Nikita Khrushchev immediately and pointedly told the world, "Cuba is not alone." Just three months earlier, on January 6, the Communist leader had drawn a line in the sand, declaring in a Moscow speech that the Soviet Union would champion third-world liberation struggles anywhere and everywhere they arose. John Kennedy, two weeks away from being sworn in as president, had been haunted by Khrushchev's declaration. He understood that if Khrushchev succeeded in defining the Soviet Union as the champion of the world's downtrodden masses who sought freedom and self-determination, Khrushchev also would succeed in defining the United States as the enemy of those freedom struggles.

Kennedy's first battle in the Cold War had turned into a humiliating disaster. Khrushchev, in the first meeting between the two heads of state in June 1961, let Kennedy know that he saw him as weak and ineffectual.

Kennedy had promised leadership in the Cold War during his successful campaign for the presidency. He had specifically chastised President Eisenhower and Vice President Nixon (his opponent in the 1960 race) for dropping the ball on Cuba and losing the small island nation to the forces of international communism. Cuba, he had exclaimed, just 90 miles off the coast of Florida, was a "dagger" pointed at the heart of America. When he was inaugurated on January 20, 1961, he proudly told the American people: "Let every nation know, whether it wishes us well or ill, that we shall pay any price, bear any burden, meet any hardship, support any friend, oppose any foe to assure the survival and the success of liberty. This much we pledge and more."

But in the midst of the Bay of Pigs operation, when it became clear that the brigade was outgunned, Kennedy decided not to "pay any price" to "support" the anti-Fidelistas. He refused to send in American air support, figuring that direct American involvement in the overthrow of Castro would alienate much of Latin America, and perhaps the world, against the United States. Kennedy and his handpicked team would have to find other venues and alternative means for proving their mettle in the Cold War.

The Kennedy Administration came to power confident that it could improve upon the Cold War record of President Eisenhower. They meant to move faster and more boldly on multiple fronts. Whereas Eisenhower had carefully vetted every major move with expert decision-makers, the Kennedy people meant to operate on the fly, without bureaucratic encumbrances. Journalist Henry Fairlie wrote that "the Kennedy team lived on the move, calling signals to each other in the thick of the action . . . like basketball players developing plans while the game moved on."

Kennedy's key advisers were all bold men who had risen fast through the "Establishment" ranks to become leaders in their respective fields. They included Secretary of Defense Robert McNamara, one of the "whiz kids" who had figured out how to quantify and systemize the Allied bombing campaigns during World War II. McNamara then jumped right to the top, taking over the helm of the Ford Motor Company before accepting his Kennedy Cabinet post. National Security Adviser McGeorge Bundy went to the White House straight from Harvard University, where he had been widely regarded as an "action-intellectual" of the highest order. He was a man who knew how to take ideas and turn them into workable plans that made things happen fast. Confident beyond their years, Kennedy and his talented team had failed at the Bay of Pigs but were ready for new challenges.

In 1961 Cold War policies poured out of the White House. Rather than concede to the romantic pull of Fidel Castro's revolutionary rhetoric, Kennedy promised Latin America a bigger and better idea (supported with American money): an Alliance of Progress. "Let us once again transform the American Continent into a vast crucible of revolutionary ideas and efforts," he proclaimed, "a tribute to the power of the creative energies of free men and women, an example to all the world that liberty and progress walk hand in hand."

Conceding that the Soviets had been dominating the space race (in 1961 Soviet cosmonaut Yuri Gagarin became the first man to reach outer space),

Kokomo, Jr., thinks it stinks that the Soviets put a man into space (Yuri Gagarin on April 12, 1961) before the United States could. The USSR had been dominating space exploration since its launch of Sputnik 1, the first man-made satellite, in 1957.

Kennedy appeared before a joint session of Congress on May 27 and declared it was "time for this nation to take a clearly leading role in space achievement." America, he promised, would put a man on the moon before the decade ended.

Fulfilling a campaign promise, Kennedy created the Peace Corps to show the world's poor that young Americans would live cheerfully among them and commit themselves to helping people help themselves. (By the end of 1961, hundreds of volunteers would be working in nine of the world's poorest nations.)

And in August, when the Soviet-backed East German government erected a wall to stop people fleeing from the totalitarian Communist state into free West Berlin, Kennedy sent American troop reinforcements to Germany to show the Communists that the United States stood by its allies. Despite the Bay of Pigs fiasco, Kennedy understood that the Cold War was evolving and intended to provide the means to fight the new battles.

In particular, the Kennedy White House understood that the battle between Communist dictatorship and Democratic capitalism was moving from the core nations of Europe to the periphery—to the decolonizing nations of Latin America, Africa, and Asia. To fight in these new arenas, Kennedy threw his energies behind a new military strategy, counterinsurgency, which was first championed by the CIA's Edward Lansdale in anti-Communist campaigns in the Philippines. This new strategy called for small numbers of American special-forces troops to train and assist allied soldiers to fight guerrilla-style wars against unconventional rebel forces. In 1961 Kennedy saw one nation tailor-made for a successful counterinsurgency campaign: Vietnam.

In the early hours of August 13, 1961, construction began on what was to become an ominous symbol of the Cold War, the Berlin Wall. As the city was physically split into two, so were many families, who remained separated for years to come.

The United States had become directly involved in Vietnam in 1954, after forces led by Ho Chi Minh, a longtime Communist-nationalist leader, had defeated the French imperialists that had controlled the country for nearly a century. The Eisenhower Administration hoped to create an independent, pro-Western government in South Vietnam by providing billions of dollars in military and economic aid and by training and supplying a modern army and air force. Despite these efforts, a coalition led by Minh—who had successfully consolidated his power in North Vietnam—was close to toppling the U.S.-supported government in the south and unifying Vietnam.

In spring 1961, to stave off defeat, Kennedy sent in an additional 400 Green Berets (Kennedy himself had approved the jaunty headgear from which these special-forces troops took their name). "Vietnam is the place," Kennedy said, where the United States would make "our power credible" to Communists everywhere. By late 1961 Kennedy had placed 3,200 American fighting men in Vietnam. Their sole job was to train the South Vietnamese in counterinsurgency and conventional military tactics. The die was not yet cast in Vietnam, but the mold was being struck.

Kennedy spent his first year in office focused on the Cold War. He worried little about the momentous changes going on at home. While he struggled to maintain American interests and to spread American ideals abroad, a very different battle of beliefs was occurring throughout the American South.

Beginning in May 1961, James Farmer of the Congress of Racial Equality (CORE) sent integrated teams of "Freedom Riders" on Greyhound bus rides through the Deep South. They were determined to show the nation—and the White House—the ugly face of "Jim Crow" racial segregation. In the Alabama cities of Birmingham and Montgomery, white mobs violently attacked the Freedom Riders for daring to challenge white supremacy. Ku Klux Klan members, with the open support of local police, clubbed Freedom Riders unconscious and knocked out their teeth. While President Kennedy tried to convince people of color around the world that the United States was on their side, newspapers in Africa, Asia, and Latin America flashed front-page photos of the racist mayhem.

The battle to spread American ideals of liberty and equality was going to demand more than just the Green Berets and Peace Corps. It was going to demand major reforms within the United States itself.

In fall 1961, 100,000 women staged a series of demonstrations criticizing the United States and Soviet Union for their continued atmospheric testing of nuclear arms. In New York (*pictured*), protesters marched outside the Russian Mission to the United Nations reminding people of the hazards that radiation could pose to children, particularly through the milk supply.

Freedom Riders were met with horrific violence when they ventured into Alabama in May 1961. Riders were beaten bloody in Birmingham and Montgomery, and their bus was bombed in Anniston.

1961: The U.S. Office of Civil Defense kicks off an approximately $200 million plan to provide fallout protection for a maximum number of Americans in minimum time. • Engineers and laborers in the Rocky Mountains near Colorado Springs, Colorado, carve more than 330,000 cubic yards of rock from the center of Cheyenne Mountain in order to create a $66 million headquarters for the North American Air Defense Command. • A model nuclear submarine produced by the U.S. toymaker Renwal is criticized by Vice Admiral Hyman Rickover for being excessively detailed, and likely to give the Soviets millions of dollars' worth of information about American nuclear subs.

1961: At Olduvai Gorge, Tanganyika, anthropologists Louis and Mary Leakey unearth human remains approximately 1.75 million years old. • The average weekly earnings for American workers in all manufacturing sectors is $94. • The beehive hairdo takes hold in the United States and elsewhere in the West. • Popular new toys include Rockem Sockem Robots and Johnny Reb Cannon. • A nationwide college-basketball betting scandal is exposed involving 37 players from 22 colleges, including St. John's, New York University, Columbia, Connecticut, and North Carolina State.

Early 1961: In a book-length tract called "The Politician," Robert Welch and his right-wing John Birch Society accuse presidents Dwight Eisenhower and Franklin Roosevelt of aiding the "international Communist conspiracy."

January: Congolese statesman Patrice Lumumba is murdered on orders from Moise Tshombe, the president of Katanga, which seceded from the Congo in 1960. *See* February 15, 1961.

January 2: Cuban Prime Minister Fidel Castro orders that the U.S. Embassy staff in Havana be reduced to 11 members within 48 hours.

In January 1961, a federal judge ordered the segregated University of Georgia to admit black applicants Charlayne Hunter (*back seat, left*) and Hamilton Holmes (*next to Hunter*). Judge W. A. Bootle found that the university had denied them admission because of their race and not—as the school claimed—because of overcrowding. Students welcomed the two African-Americans by sporting a large sign that read "Nigger Go Home!!!" and hurling bricks and pop bottles through Hunter's dormitory window. The school reacted by suspending Holmes and Hunter for, according to university officials, their own safety. Both students eventually would graduate from the university. Holmes would become a physician, and Hunter would work as a journalist for CNN and PBS.

President-elect John F. Kennedy contrasted sharply with the outgoing commander in chief, Dwight D. Eisenhower. The two were separated by age, religion, personality, geographical upbringing, and conceptions of presidential power. The youngest elected president in American history (age 43), Kennedy used his inauguration speech (*pictured*) on January 20, 1961, to display vitality, chart a fresh course of American international leadership, and swiftly mold the administration's image. He excited millions when he said: "Let the word go forth from this time and place . . . that the torch has been passed to a new generation of Americans."

On January 24, 1961, an Air Force B-52 crashed near Goldsboro, North Carolina. The bomber, which suffered in-flight structural failure leading to airborne disintegration, carried two MK39 thermonuclear devices—H-bombs. Each bomb packed about 250 times the firepower of the Hiroshima blast. One parachuted to the ground intact; the other free-fell and broke apart upon impact. Nuclear physicist Dr. Ralph E. Lapp said that five of the six interlocks on the latter bomb were set off by the fall, and that "only a single switch" prevented the bomb from detonating. Nuclear physicist Dr. Dietrich Schroeer stated that a detonation would have leveled homes within a five-mile radius and inflicted third-degree burns on people up to nine miles away.

The Soviet Union's 1957 launch of Sputnik with an intercontinental ballistic missile (ICBM) spurred the United States to further develop its own ICBM program. One tangible sign of success came on February 1, 1961, with the test launch of Minuteman (*pictured*)—a three-stage, solid-fuel ICBM with a range of 5,500 nautical miles. The successful launch was a political boon to President Kennedy, who had campaigned the previous year on the notion of a disadvantageous U.S.–Soviet "missile gap."

On February 1, 1961, the organization Women Strike for Peace protested outside both the U.S. Atomic Energy Commission's New York office (*pictured*) and the USSR's United Nations delegation building. At each location, they demanded a halt to nuclear testing and the arms race. Members would picket the White House, the Pentagon, and the UN headquarters in New York in protest of nuclear weapons and the Vietnam War.

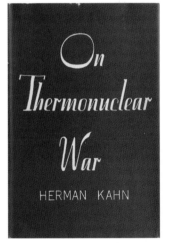

Herman Kahn, a military strategist employed by the Rand Corporation, sparked controversy with his book *On Thermonuclear War*. Kahn devised a number of strategies for fighting a nuclear war, and concluded that such a war—even with millions of casualties—could be won. Many critics were appalled by his calm objectivity in describing horrifying scenarios. Kahn was satirized in two 1964 films about nuclear war—*Fail-Safe* (by actor Walter Matthau) and *Dr. Strangelove* (by Peter Sellers).

1961

January 3: The United States terminates diplomatic relations with Cuba. • U.S. Representative Adam Clayton Powell, an African-American, becomes chairman of the House Education and Labor Committee. • Control rods mistakenly are removed from the core of a military experimental reactor in Idaho Falls, Idaho, causing a steam explosion that kills three technicians (one of whom is impaled by a control rod).

January 6: Soviet Premier Nikita Khrushchev gives a speech avowing Soviet support for wars of national liberation throughout the world. Some say the speech suggests that Moscow has every intention to undermine western influence by fanning war and subversion.

January 9: Charlayne Hunter and Hamilton Holmes integrate the University of Georgia. Two days later, hundreds of whites will gather outside Hunter's dorm building, some throwing rocks and bottles at her window.

January 10: *The New York Times* reports that guerrilla forces are training in Guatemala for U.S. action against Cuba. *See April 12, 1961.*

January 12: At a Washington, D.C., restaurant, Nigerian diplomat C. C. Uchuno is given his food in a bag and told to eat it outside.

January 17: In his farewell address, President Dwight Eisenhower warns against "the military-industrial complex."

January 18: Tom Dooley, American medical missionary in Southeast Asia, dies in New York City.

January 20: John F. Kennedy is inaugurated as the 35th president of the United States; Lyndon Johnson takes the oath of office as vice president. Kennedy declares: "Ask not what your country can do for you; ask what you can do for your country."

Elijah Muhammad (*right*) introduces Malcolm X in Chicago on February 26, 1961. Born in 1925 into a troubled environment, Malcolm Little began calling himself Malcolm X after his release from prison in 1952, signifying his break with "the white man's name." A convert to Muhammad's Nation of Islam (NOI), Malcolm earned a position of authority in the NOI due to his keen insights and dynamic speeches. Malcolm X was an ardent opponent of racial integration and nonviolent action. He argued that African-Americans should foster their own social institutions and defend against white racism by any means necessary. Malcolm X broke with the NOI in 1964 and recanted his claim that all whites were "devils."

The Kennedy Administration worried in March 1961 about the potential of an imminent Communist takeover of Laos. Officials discussed American military intervention to prevent such a takeover—in larger part to prevent a "domino effect" in Southeast Asia (with one country after another theoretically falling into Communist hands). The following month came the disastrous Bay of Pigs, however, which made Kennedy much more hesitant to use military force, and more inclined to choose a negotiated settlement instead. Later that year, he confided to an aide: "Thank God the Bay of Pigs happened when it did. Otherwise, we'd be in Laos by now—and that would be a hundred times worse."

On April 12, 1961, Soviet Air Force pilot and cosmonaut Yuri Gagarin (celebrated later on this Czechoslovakian stamp) became the first human being to circle Earth in space. Gagarin piloted Vostok I at a speed of 17,000 mph, then sat back as a computer guided his reentry. Once safely inside Earth's atmosphere, he ejected and parachuted to land. This Soviet aeronautical space success contributed to President Kennedy's announcement the following month—largely as a much-needed public relations response—to land a man safely on the moon by 1969.

In this 1961 political cartoon about the space race, Clifford "Baldy" Baldowski of the *Atlanta Constitution* paints the Soviets as far ahead of the United States. Slugger Nikita Khrushchev gets ready to belt a moon shot, while a puny John F. Kennedy strolls to the plate with only a space monkey and magazine stories about astronauts. In reality, the Soviets in 1961 were only slightly ahead of the Americans in the big race. Though Yuri Gagarin became the first person in space on April 12, Alan Shepard achieved the feat just 23 days later.

A Catch-22 Situation

A *CATCH-22* IS DEFINED AS "a condition or consequence that precludes success, a dilemma where the victim cannot win," according to the *Oxford English Dictionary*. That the phrase entered the popular lexicon is a profound tribute to writer Joseph Heller, a World War II Air Force bombardier who returned stateside to pen his landmark novel about the follies of war.

Catch-22's protagonist—Captain John Yossarian, a bombardier—spends most of his time scouring for loopholes in "Catch-22" of the Air Force code, "which specified that a concern for one's safety in the face of dangers...was the process of the rational mind." By declaring himself insane, Yossarian hopes to avoid bombing duty. But, as one fellow "inmate" explains, "Anyone who wants to get out of combat isn't really crazy." It's truly a Catch-22 situation.

The book (whose original title, *Catch-18,* was altered to avoid confusion with the concurrent Leon Uris novel *Mila 18*) was panned by *The New York Times* as "not even a good novel by conventional standards." But its savage indictment of militarism and bureaucracy made it a must-read for Vietnam War protesters. In fact, "Yossarian Lives" became a popular antiwar slogan. *Catch-22* went on to sell more than 10 million copies.

The 1961 Jaguar E-Type (called XKE in the States, where it sold for $5,595) produced a hyper-efficient 265 horsepower from a 231-cubic-inch inline six. The lithe two-seater easily posted quarter-mile times under 15 seconds, and a top speed of 140 to 150 mph. The flexible engine was happy at 10 mph or full-out, and a sophisticated suspension provided world-class handling. The E-Type's performance and stunning body (designed by engineer Malcolm Sayer and Jag founder William Lyons) made it an enduring classic.

January 23: A B-52 carrying two nuclear weapons crashes near Goldsboro, North Carolina. The bombs do not detonate. • Bob Dylan makes his debut in Greenwich Village in New York City, performing on open-mike "hootenanny" night at the Café Wha?.

January 25: In his first presidential news conference, President Kennedy announces that the Soviet Union has freed the two surviving crewmen of a USAF RB-47H reconnaissance plane shot down by Soviet fliers.

January 31: A male chimpanzee named Ham is recovered alive in the Caribbean after being carried to a height of 157 miles in a space capsule launched from Cape Canaveral, Florida.

January–April: North Vietnamese troops make repeated incursions into Laos. The U.S. responds with increased financial aid and advisers.

February 1: The U.S. Strategic Air Command launches the first solid-fuel rocket, the Minuteman, an intercontinental ballistic missile.

February 6: Civil rights demonstrators in Rock Hill, South Carolina, begin a "jail, no bail" policy. The strategy will be picked up in other cities, leading to the flooding of jails throughout the South.

February 15: A riot breaks out in the gallery of the United Nations among those impassioned by events in the Congo.

February 23: The National Council of Churches endorses birth control to limit family size.

February 25: In Memphis, Elvis Presley performs at a luncheon in his honor, his first performance since his discharge from the Army in 1960.

March: In a race with other high-tech companies, Bell Labs announces the first continuous-wave laser. • NBA rookie Wilt Chamberlain of the Philadelphia Warriors finishes the 1960–61 season with averages of 38.4 points and 27.2 rebounds per game.

Following the 1959 Cuban revolution, the U.S. Central Intelligence Agency (CIA) trained roughly 2,000 anti-Castro exiles in Guatemala for an invasion of their homeland. Ardent anti-Communists, the exiles—ideologically encouraged by both the Eisenhower and Kennedy administrations—believed their paramilitary invasion force would inspire widespread popular resistance to Castro's government. Their moment of truth would come during the CIA-supported Bay of Pigs invasion.

On April 17, 1961, approximately 1,400 CIA-sponsored Cuban exiles landed on the shores of *Bahía de Cochinos* (Bay of Pigs). Quickly combated by hostile locals and then the Cuban army (*pictured*), the expatriate troops expended an ample supply of ammunition in haste and panic. Two freighters, which carried the exiles' communications equipment and additional ammunition, were sunk by Castro's rocket-launching T-33 airplanes, causing two other supply ships to flee the area. Depleted of ammunition, the invasion force surrendered within 72 hours. It suffered 114 deaths.

"Anti-Castro forces struck their long-awaited invasion blow for liberation of Cuba Monday and claimed immediate successes. The counter revolutionary blows went in by air and sea with help from uncounted Castro foes rising inside Cuba.... Bearded Prime Minister Fidel Castro, his red-tinged government at stake, kept silent on how the battle was going.... [A]nti-Castro spokesmen claimed thousands of Castro's militiamen had deserted him at the first shot...."

—Erroneous wire story from April 18, 1961

Two of more than 1,100 captured exiles are pictured in April 1961. Poor U.S. intelligence and unrealistic expectations for the exiled expeditionary force doomed the invasion and further deepened hostilities between Cuba and the United States. After the Bay of Pigs fiasco, the U.S. government persisted in anti-Castro efforts, such as economic sanctions and assassination plots. However, the attempted overthrow of the Cuban leader only pushed him closer to the Soviet Union. One direct consequence, for example, was the Cuban–Soviet military agreement, which spawned the 1962 missile crisis.

The CIA's Ambitious Plans

JUST THREE MONTHS into his presidency, John F. Kennedy suffered his most humiliating foreign policy defeat at the Bay of Pigs in Cuba. The invasion of Cuba by a force of 1,400 Cuban exiles had first been conceived by the Central Intelligence Agency (CIA) under the Eisenhower Administration. Its failure led, for a time, to a reassessment of the agency's function.

The CIA was established in 1947 as part of an expansion of presidential authority over national security issues. Initially, the agency's function was clear: to gather and analyze foreign intelligence, particularly targeting the Soviet Union and its Communist allies. But under President Dwight Eisenhower, CIA Director Allen Dulles expanded the agency's role to include more ambitious covert operations that sometimes aimed to topple governments hostile to American political or economic interests.

In 1953, for example, after Iranian Prime Minister Mohammed Mossadegh nationalized the Anglo–Iranian Oil Company, the CIA backed a military coup that deposed him and established western control of the oil company. The following year, the agency orchestrated a coup that removed Guatemalan leader Jacobo Arbenz from power after he had confiscated property from the United Fruit Company as part of a land reform program.

In 1960, with these successful coups as models, the CIA turned its attention to Cuba. There, Fidel Castro's nationalization of American businesses seemed a direct challenge to American power. The success of the CIA plan depended on successfully training the Cuban exiles at camps in Guatemala, inserting them without detection at the Bay of Pigs, and, most critically, prompting a spontaneous general uprising of anti-Castro forces. However, none of these things happened. Some critics blamed the mission's failure on Kennedy for withholding air support, but the real problems were the CIA's poor planning and mistaken intelligence. In the aftermath, Allen Dulles resigned as CIA director.

March 1: In a message to Congress, President Kennedy recommends the establishment of "a permanent Peace Corps." *See* September 1961.

March 7: A boycott of stores in Atlanta ends as city officials agree to integrate lunch counters.

March 8: President Kennedy establishes the President's Committee on Equal Employment Opportunity.

March 10: Pro-Communist forces launch a major offensive in Laos.

March 13: Mattel's Ken doll, Barbie's "escort," becomes available in toy stores.

March 23: Football coach Bud Wilkinson is named to lead President Kennedy's youth fitness program.

March 28: President Kennedy sends Congress a revised defense budget shaped to hasten long-range missile capability.

March 29: The 23rd amendment to the United States Constitution is ratified, allowing Washington, D.C., residents to vote in presidential elections.

April: The White House reveals that President Kennedy likes to relax in a rocking chair. Sales of rockers jump nationwide.

April 9: The first elections are held in the Republic of Vietnam (South Vietnam) since the country's establishment in 1955. Reigning leader Ngo Dinh Diem, who the U.S. supports, is elected president with 88 percent of the vote.

April 11: The war-crimes trial of former Nazi SS functionary Adolf Eichmann opens in Jerusalem, Israel. *See* December 15, 1961.

April 12: Soviet cosmonaut Yuri Gagarin becomes the first human to successfully orbit Earth. • President Kennedy pledges that under no circumstances will the U.S. attempt an armed overthrow of the Castro government in Cuba. *See* April 17, 1961.

Italian director Federico Fellini's *La Dolce Vita* (*The Sweet Life*) created a popular and scandalous sensation in America in 1961. The film depicts a gossip columnist (played by Marcello Mastroianni) forever in search of juicy news items, leading him into a world of decadence quite unfamiliar to American movie audiences at the time. *La Dolce Vita*, which also stars Swedish beauty Anita Ekberg (*pictured*), features prostitutes, orgies, a suicidal girlfriend, and a nymphomaniac. Critically acclaimed as a work of art revealing modern society's amorality and deterioration, the film was as likely to be seen for its titillation value.

Through such films as *The Wizard of Oz* and *A Star Is Born,* and such songs as "Over the Rainbow" and "The Man That Got Away," Judy Garland became one of the entertainment industry's best-loved performers. The only obstacle in her career was herself: a lifelong, self-destructive love affair with drugs and alcohol, which nearly killed her in the late 1950s. However, Garland's dynamic performance at Carnegie Hall on April 23, 1961 (*pictured*), marked a resounding, if brief, comeback. She sang for two and a half hours, received several standing ovations, and left the audience wanting more. Garland won five Grammy Awards for the recording of this special performance.

In his 1961 exposé *A Nation of Sheep,* journalist William Lederer excoriated American foreign relations activities, especially in Asia. He condemned American decision-makers' ignorance about Laos, gullibility in Thailand, and willingness to support the "rascal and opportunist" Chiang Kai-shek in Taiwan. Moreover, he blasted Americans for not complaining about such errors—hence the title.

Urbanologist Jane Jacobs wrote *The Death and Life of Great American Cities,* a highly influential book that hit the stores in 1961. Jacobs challenged the whole idea of large-scale urban projects consisting of big, homogeneous developments, which she considered nothing more than little boxes stacked on top of each other. She opted for mixed-use neighborhoods, with a variety of structures serving different functions. According to reviewer Philip Landon, the work has had "phenomenal staying power" and has made Jacobs "the patron saint of . . . New Urbanists."

Cartoonist Clifford "Baldy" Baldowski illustrates President John F. Kennedy's trials and tribulations during his first 100 days in office. Baldy knew that Kennedy had promised to take the country to new heights. Unfortunately, JFK found himself stymied by a Congress that seemed far less willing to climb as high as he wanted to. Indeed, Kennedy spent much of his first three months in office mired in a divisive fight to expand the membership of the House Rules Committee so as to dilute the power of recalcitrant southern Democrats. He won that important battle, although it was not a high-profile victory. The media's tendency to measure Kennedy's performance against Franklin Roosevelt's first 100 days didn't help JFK's reputation as a leader.

A "space age" house emerges from the hills of Hollywood above Sunset Boulevard. Built in 1961 by experimental architect John Lautner, the octagonal house became one of the architectural wonders of Southern California. Its owner, Marco Wolff, Jr., was the well-connected son of a choreographer and film producer. The house perhaps symbolized the self-conscious futurism of the L.A. mind-set.

April 17: Anti-Castro rebels under the direction of the U.S.-based Cuban Revolutionary Council—with full knowledge and approval of the White House—land near Cuba's *Bahía de Cochinos* (Bay of Pigs). Cuban government troops mount a strong resistance, and casualties are heavy on both sides. *See* April 18, 1961.

April 18: President Kennedy warns the Soviet Union not to follow up on its offer to send military aid to Cuba. *See* April 20, 1961.

April 19: Laos announces that uniformed U.S. troops will enter the country as advisers to the Laotian army.

April 20: The last of the anti-Castro Cuban invaders are killed or captured at *Playa Girón*, near the rebels' original landing point at the *Bahía de Cochinos*. *See* April 24, 1961. ● Bell Aerosystems engineer Harold Graham makes a successful solo flight powered by a "rocket belt," a personal-propulsion device designed to allow infantry soldiers to fly above dangerous battlefields. Graham lifts about 15 feet above the ground and travels 112 feet at seven to 10 mph over 13 seconds.

April 23: Singer Judy Garland electrifies Carnegie Hall in New York. Her recorded performance, *Judy Garland at Carnegie Hall*, will win five Grammy Awards.

April 24: A White House statement says that President Kennedy assumes "sole responsibility" for the United States' role in the unsuccessful rebel invasion of Cuba. *See* June 14, 1961.

April 25: West Germany pays the U.S. $587 million in partial World War II reparations.

May: President Kennedy sends Vice President Johnson on a seemingly unimportant tour of Southeast Asia. LBJ praises South Vietnamese President Ngo Dinh Diem, calling him the "Winston Churchill of today." ● Alan Watts, an interpreter of Zen Buddhism, begins speaking on college campuses in the United States.

In response to the Soviets' successful launching of Sputnik in 1957, the National Aeronautics and Space Administration (NASA) was established in the United States the following year. NASA leaders formulated plans to put a manned aircraft into space, and in 1959 they selected their Mercury astronauts—one of whom was Alan Bartlett Shepard (*pictured*). On May 5, 1961, Shepard distinguished himself as the first American to enter space. During a 15-minute suborbital flight, he reached an altitude of 115 miles. President Kennedy proclaimed the successful flight as part of "the [Cold War] battle that is now going on around the world between freedom and tyranny."

The leading rocket engineer for the Nazis, Wernher von Braun surrendered to the United States after World War II. From that point on, he provided technical leadership to the U.S. in the fields of guided ballistic missiles and space-launch vehicles (for example, the Apollo program's Saturn rockets). More famously, he was a leading voice in the popularization of space flight. Braun likened American efforts in space to early world explorations, such as Columbus's. He argued that it was impossible—in olden times and the present—to cure all domestic social problems before exploring new frontiers. Braun delivered public addresses promoting space travel, collaborated on space films with Walt Disney, and wrote popular books on the subject.

When NASA selected its seven "right stuff" men for the Mercury project in 1959, it unofficially sponsored the "Mercury 13"—a largely forgotten group of women who prequalified for space training and travel. Chief among them was Jerrie Cobb (*pictured*), an award-winning pilot who had logged 10,000 flight hours in all manner of aircraft (about twice the number of hours logged by John Glenn). Cobb was the only woman of the Mercury 13 who passed all phases of physical and psychological testing. NASA originally believed women would be excellent candidates for space travel—especially during liftoff, because of their lighter weight. In 1961, however, the agency ruled that only military jet pilots (all of whom, at the time, were men) could qualify for the space program. The women's program was discontinued in July 1962.

The New Frontier

When Soviet cosmonaut Yuri Gagarin became the first human to orbit the Earth on April 12, 1961, the space race reached a heightened pitch. That year, *Life* magazine had exclusive access to the seven U.S. astronauts whom NASA busily prepared for its Mercury Program as part of this competition. "Spending hundreds of hours with the men and their families, following their training program, and getting to know them intimately," the magazine would make all-American heroes out of these "brave and patriotic" test pilots, the "prime candidates" for the "violent, historic event" of manned space travel.

Life provided candid photographs and in-depth profiles of the Mercury team, which included Alan B. Shepard, Jr.; Virgil "Gus" Grissom; John H. Glenn, Jr.; Donald K. Slayton; L. Gordon Cooper, Jr.; M. Scott Carpenter; and Walter M. Shirra, Jr. Eventually, the astronauts' deeds would capture the nation's attention like nothing else.

On May 5, 1961, Shepard became the first American in space when he blasted off in a Redstone MR 7 rocket that he named Freedom 7. He spent 15 minutes and 28 seconds in suborbital flight before his spacecraft splashed down in the Atlantic Ocean. Nine months later, John Glenn became the first American to orbit the Earth, doing so three times. Glenn spent four hours, 55 minutes, and 23 seconds in the cramped quarters of Friendship 7. NASA launched six of the seven astronauts into space as part of the Mercury Program, but Shepard and Glenn were the memorable heroes.

From 1961 to 1963, the Mercury Program achieved NASA's stated goals of orbiting humans in space, testing the human ability to function in space, and successfully recovering spacecraft and pilots. The program and its popular astronauts sparked American interest in the "New Frontier" of space and set the stage for the Apollo Program, which would take the first men to the moon by decade's end.

1961

May 1: Castro announces that Cuba is now a socialist nation and will no longer hold elections.

May 5: Alan Shepard becomes the first U.S. astronaut to achieve sub-orbital flight. Launched at Cape Canaveral, Florida, Shepard reaches a speed of 5,134 mph and travels 115 miles into space. He is recovered safely after splashing down 303 miles out at sea. • Black and white Congress of Racial Equality (CORE) volunteers board two buses bound for Louisiana and then Alabama. These "Freedom Riders" are out to test the federal law that outlaws segregation in interstate travel facilities. *See* May 14, 1961.

May 7: Incumbent President Ho Chi Minh, a Communist, easily wins reelection in the Democratic Republic of Vietnam (North Vietnam).

May 9: FCC Chairman Newton Minow, in a speech before the National Association of Broadcasters, excoriates the television industry for the vapidity of its programming, which Minow terms "a vast wasteland."

May 13: Legendary Hollywood star Gary Cooper dies at 60.

May 14: A white mob of about 200 attacks one of the two Freedom Ride buses in Anniston, Alabama, then firebombs it. Riders in the other bus are clubbed and bloodied by Ku Klux Klan members in Birmingham, Alabama. *See* May 20, 1961.

May 20: A new group of Freedom Riders arrives in Montgomery, Alabama. Police flee the scene just before the riders depart the bus, leaving them to the mercies of a large mob, which beats the riders as well as U.S. Justice Department representative John Seigenthaler. *See* May 24, 1961. • While Martin Luther King speaks at the First Baptist Church in Montgomery, several thousand white citizens surround the building and smash windows. Federal marshals disperse the crowd with tear gas.

A black woman is escorted from a "white" waiting room in a bus station in Dallas in May 1961. Even though the U.S. Supreme Court had ruled that segregation in public schools and on public transportation was illegal, many public facilities in the South remained segregated in 1961. Moreover, the White Citizens' Councils and Ku Klux Klan—by intimidating and threatening southern blacks and "nigger lovers"—were determined to keep it that way. Especially galling to many supporters of desegregation were separate waiting rooms in bus and train terminals, a situation that led to the Freedom Rides of 1961.

On May 14, 1961, while en route from Washington, D.C., to New Orleans, one of CORE's two buses of Freedom Riders was attacked by angry whites just outside Anniston, Alabama. The mob threw an incendiary bomb into the bus and beat its passengers as they fled. The following day, photos of the burning bus and severely injured riders appeared in newspapers throughout the world, staining the United States' image as the champion of the free world.

The other Freedom Ride bus that ventured through Alabama on May 14 stopped at the Birmingham bus station. When the riders departed the bus, an armed mob beat them bloody. Here, whites unload on white rider James Peck, who would need 50 stitches to close his gashes. Another rider, William Barbee, was seriously injured. Birmingham Public Safety Commissioner Bull Connor had known that the Freedom Riders were coming and that hostile whites would greet them. However, he posted no officers at the station because, he said, it was Mother's Day. Whites in Montgomery, Alabama, would beat another group of Freedom Riders on May 20.

Former Marine Robert F. Williams returned to his hometown of Monroe, North Carolina, in 1955. Elected president of the local NAACP, he was determined to shatter the KKK's influence in the region, meeting force with force if necessary. Williams laid out his beliefs in the widely read *Negroes with Guns* (1962), arguing that the time for passive  resistance was over. Williams spent much of the 1960s in self-imposed exile in Cuba, where he hosted the thunderclap of a program called "Radio Free Dixie." The militant broadcasts were widely heard in the U.S., and influenced many in the civil rights movement.

Freedom Riders

ON MAY 20, 1961, Freedom Rider Jim Zwerg of Wisconsin stepped off the bus in Montgomery, Alabama. White people armed with sticks and bricks descended on the bus station as if all reason had left them. That Zwerg, a white man, would have allied himself with Freedom Riders infuriated the waiting racists. His beating was just one of many bloody encounters between white mobs and integrated groups of Freedom Riders during 1961.

After the success of the sit-ins in 1960, the Congress of Racial Equality (CORE) decided to keep the pressure on southern establishments and federal authorities. With the Freedom Rides, they would test a recent Supreme Court decision that prohibited racial segregation in interstate travel.

In Washington, D.C., on May 4, 1961, CORE launched an integrated group in two buses on a dangerous journey through the Deep South to New Orleans. They would defy segregated restrooms, restaurants, and bus station waiting areas along the way. Outside Anniston, Alabama, on May 14, 200 angry whites forced one of the buses off the road, then slashed the tires, broke windows, and firebombed it. Then they attacked the riders. The Freedom Riders in the other bus faced their own horrors. When they got off the bus to use the facilities in Birmingham, the police gave the waiting mob 15 unrestrained minutes to beat the nonviolent passengers with lead pipes and clubs.

News photos of the injustice, and stories of the riders' bravery, inspired Americans and fueled the civil rights movement. Students from the Nashville area led a second round of Freedom Rides. After they were met with white mob violence in Montgomery on May 20, U.S. Attorney General Robert Kennedy finally sent federal marshals to keep calm in the city and protect the civil rights workers. The following night, an angry mob surrounded a black Montgomery church in which Martin Luther King, Jr., was speaking. The rioting whites kept people in the church much of the night. Three days later, the Nashville Freedom Riders continued their voyage to Jackson, Mississippi, where they were arrested. A judge sentenced them to 60 days in the state penitentiary.

The Freedom Riders forced the Kennedy Administration to become actively supportive of civil rights causes. The riders also helped to desegregate public accommodations in the South and rally the nation to the struggle for civil rights.

May 24: Twenty-seven Freedom Riders, accompanied by the Alabama National Guard, leave Montgomery for Jackson, Mississippi. They will be arrested in Jackson and sentenced to prison.

May 25: Reports state that President Kennedy is sending hundreds of "advisers" to train South Vietnamese soldiers in their fight against the National Liberation Front. • President Kennedy announces that the U.S. should commit to landing a man on the moon "and returning him safely to Earth" before the end of the decade.

May 29: During their visit to Paris, President Kennedy is overshadowed in popularity by his wife, Jackie.

May 30: General Rafael Trujillo, leader of the Dominican Republic, is assassinated.

May 31: The Union of South Africa becomes an independent republic no longer affiliated with the British Commonwealth.

June 3–4: President Kennedy and Soviet Premier Nikita Khrushchev meet in Vienna, Austria, to discuss the tense situation in Germany and, specifically, the physically divided city of Berlin.

June 6: Swiss psychiatrist and theorist Carl Jung dies at 80.

June 14: Cuban leader Castro agrees to accept 500 tractors, instead of the 500 bulldozers he had demanded, as ransom for 1,217 captured Cuban rebels. *See* April 8, 1962.

Mid-1961: Soviet propaganda blames Mickey Mouse for the flow of East Germans to West Germany, claiming that western "headhunters" blackmail the parents of East German members of a Mickey Mouse club.

June 17: Popular film actor Jeff Chandler, 42, dies following botched surgery.

June 24: Soviet Premier Khrushchev announces a new economic plan that he says will make the USSR the world's wealthiest nation.

Paying the Price for Freedom

JOHN LEWIS STARTED into a white waiting room in some town in South Carolina ... and there were several young white hoodlums, leather jackets, ducktail haircuts, standing there smoking, and they blocked the door and said, "Nigger, you can't come in here." He said, "I have every right to enter this waiting room according to the Supreme Court of the United States in the Boynton case."

They said, "Shit on that." He tried to walk past, and they clubbed him, beat him, and knocked him down. One of the white Freedom Riders ... Albert Bigelow, who had been a Navy captain during World War II, big, tall, strapping fellow, very impressive, from Connecticut—then stepped right between the hoodlums and John Lewis. Lewis had been absorbing more of the punishment. They then clubbed Bigelow and finally knocked him down ... and he didn't hit back at all. [They] knocked him down, and at this point police arrived and intervened. They didn't make any arrests.

—JAMES FARMER, NATIONAL DIRECTOR OF THE CONGRESS OF RACIAL EQUALITY (CORE),
RECALLING A 1961 FREEDOM RIDE

On May 22, 1961, Martin Luther King, Jr., flew to Montgomery, Alabama, to show his support for the Freedom Riders. While speaking at the First Baptist Church that evening, several thousand white citizens surrounded the church even though it was heavily guarded by federal marshals. The hostile whites threatened blacks inside, injured some of the marshals, and set fire to automobiles. To control the mob, the marshals employed tear gas—which wafted into the church. Those inside feared for their lives, including King, who did his best to calm the gathering. King then called Attorney General Robert Kennedy from a church phone. RFK called Governor John Patterson, who ordered the police and National Guard to disperse the crowd.

In mid-June 1961, Cuban leader Fidel Castro said he would be willing to ransom more than 1,200 prisoners from the Bay of Pigs invasion for 500 American tractors. President John F. Kennedy responded by initiating the Tractors for Freedom Committee, a private enterprise chaired by Eleanor Roosevelt that tried to raise enough money to meet demands. Partly because of a hostile conservative press, the committee soon disbanded. Ultimately, the prisoners were freed in 1962 in exchange for millions of dollars' worth of food and medicine, paid for by the U.S. government. No tractors were involved.

With wealthy Cubans having already fled to the United States during Fidel Castro's "socialist" revolution of 1958–59, the Cuban leader was left with the middle class as his major opposition. But rather than purge the bourgeoisie, he merely allowed it to emigrate to the United States, principally Miami. By 1961 the U.S. government was spending millions per month in assisting these new Cuban refugees. Before the federal government stepped in, however, the Catholic Church was the main source of assistance. It placed refugee children in its schools, necessitating an influx of Spanish-speaking nuns as teachers. The Church also found foster homes for Cuban children and provided free health care to Cuban families.

Demonstrators in the Dominican Republic hold up a Satanized portrait of dictator Rafael Trujillo, who was assassinated on May 30, 1961. Trujillo, although a firm anti-Communist, had become an embarrassment to the American government because of the brutality of his regime. Although it was not directly involved in his death, the Kennedy Administration was glad to see him gone. Unfortunately, political conditions in the island nation remained chaotic over the next few years, prompting U.S. military involvement in 1965.

Walter Lee Younger (played by Sidney Poitier) pleads with his mother, Lena (Claudia McNeil), in the 1961 film *A Raisin in the Sun*. Adapted from Lorraine Hansberry's award-winning play, the film centers around a poor black family that struggles with how to use a $10,000 insurance benefit after Lena's husband dies. Although the film emphasizes the power of faith more strongly than the play, it succeeds because it depicts a complex, nonstereotyped black family dealing with intensely human problems.

1961

July: IBM introduces the Selectric electric typewriter, which includes a "character sphere" instead of a type bar, keys, and carriage.

July 2: American author Ernest Hemingway, 61, commits suicide.

July 21: U.S. astronaut Virgil Grissom completes a suborbital flight, America's second. Grissom is safely recovered, but his capsule sinks into the ocean before it can be salvaged.

July 23: The Soviet Union claims that USA's launches of the Tiros III weather satellite and Midas III rocket-detection satellite are acts of espionage.

August: Civil rights leader Bob Moses begins a voter registration campaign in McComb, Mississippi.

August 7: USSR cosmonaut Gherman Titov is safely recovered after orbiting Earth 17 times in 25 hours, 18 minutes.

August 13: The Soviets order that the East–West Berlin border be closed. *See* October 27, 1961.

August 14: After seven years of imprisonment, Kenya leader Jomo Kenyatta is freed by the British government. He eventually will become prime minister of a free Kenya.

August 25: U.S. Secretary of Defense Robert McNamara announces that 76,500 reservists have been ordered to active duty.

September: As the frequency of attacks by the Vietcong increases, South Vietnamese President Ngo Dinh Diem requests more military aid from the United States. • Congress approves $30 million to finance the Peace Corps' first year of operation. • Hurricane Carla inundates the Texas coast.

September 1: The USSR resumes nuclear testing with a detonation over Soviet Central Asia. *See* October 12, 1961. • Finnish-born U.S. architect Eero Saarinen dies at 51.

President John F. Kennedy and the First Lady leave for dinner at the lustrous and fabled Palace of Versailles in France on June 1, 1961. Jacqueline Kennedy would create America's own fabled legacy—that of her husband's administration as Camelot—the symbolic, literary, and musical representation of daring and valor. In a *Life* magazine interview with Theodore White dated December 6, 1963, Mrs. Kennedy portrayed the former administration as "a magic moment in American history" in which "gallant men" did "great deeds" and held "barbarians beyond the walls."

The Kennedy–Khrushchev meeting in Vienna, Austria, on June 3–4, 1961, was largely inconsequential. The leaders' discussions about U.S.–Soviet relations and international tensions were cordial, and they talked about Cuba, mainland China, the space race, the Laotian situation, Berlin, and the possibility of a nuclear test ban. However, neither produced anything on paper or created even loose agreements to reduce Cold War hostilities. Khrushchev expressed to Kennedy his belief that the U.S. was intent on destroying Russia as a Communist power, while Kennedy rebutted that the USSR seemed intent on imposing its political will on others. The leaders left Vienna even more determined to stand firm, which would have serious implications the following year.

As a stylistically pioneering novelist, big-game hunter, deep-sea fisherman, and war reporter, Ernest Hemingway succeeded in personifying the image of a "man's man." Wounded in action during World War I, Hemingway first distinguished himself as a member of America's disenchanted "Lost Generation," writing *The Sun Also Rises* (1926) and *A Farewell to Arms* (1929). His 1952 novel, *The Old Man and the Sea,* earned him the Nobel Prize. Hemingway best described his laconic writing style in a 1933 private letter, stating that he continuously strove to make a picture of the world, boiled down. After suffering years of alcoholism and depression, he ended his own life with a shotgun on July 2, 1961.

Sophia Loren's acclaimed 1961 Italian film *La Ciociara* (*Two Women*) revealed to American audiences not only her already familiar beauty, but her dramatic abilities as well. Loren played the mother of a teenage girl in WWII-torn Italy. She tries to protect her daughter (Eleanora Brown) from the horrors of war, but fails—depicted in a devastating rape scene. A *New York Times* review described Loren's Oscar-winning performance as "lusty" as well as "grave and profound."

Chasing the Babe

THE STORY OF THE 1961 Yankees demonstrates the power of the press to cultivate public opinion. That year saw Babe Ruth's record of 60 home runs in one season under threat from sluggers Mickey Mantle and Roger Maris.

Though many people, Ruth's widow included, were loath to see the record shattered, sportswriters quickly made it known who the Babe's worthy successor was. Maris, an intense, taciturn man, was playing his second season in Yankee pinstripes. Though a magnificent power hitter with superb defensive skills, his tendency to take the fans' insults to heart did not endear him to the press. Mantle, conversely, was a sportswriter's dream: a hitting prodigy with the grit to play through injuries and a colorful character to boot.

Though the "M&M boys" had been good friends and roommates on the road, reporters portrayed them as rivals to heighten the drama. With pressure building as summer wore on, the mercurial Maris found it increasingly difficult to maintain calm in the face of the daily inanities the press subjected him to. "What's a .260 hitter like you doing hitting so many home runs?" they queried. "You've got to be a damned idiot," he once snapped back. In another era, Maris's perceived animosity toward reporters might have endeared him to the fans. But in 1961 it only made a capricious public all the more hostile. Playing baseball was one thing, but playing "the game" was something else.

After an injury forced Mantle out of the competition, disappointment that somehow "the wrong man" was in the running fueled more resentment. On October 1, just 23,154 fans at Yankee Stadium saw Maris belt No. 61. But there was little joy in the achievement. "All it brought me was headaches," he said.

Roger Maris (*left*) and Mickey Mantle with Claire Ruth, Babe Ruth's widow.

1961

September 5: French President Charles de Gaulle warns that the West should be prepared to defend its interests in Berlin and Germany, with force if necessary.

September 9: The U.S. Department of Defense announces that approximately 40,000 troops will be sent to Western Europe to bring the U.S. military presence there to "full combat" strength.

September 10: A crash at the Italian Grand Prix at Monza kills driver Count Wolfgang von Tripps and more than a dozen spectators. Ferrari, Tripps's sponsor, suspends all racing.

September 11: The World Wildlife Fund is founded. It will become the world's largest private international conservation organization.

September 12: Philosopher Bertrand Russell, 89, is sentenced to seven days' imprisonment by a London court for refusing to keep the peace during nuclear-disarmament demonstrations.

September 18: United Nations Secretary General Dag Hammarskjöld and 12 others are killed in a plane crash near Ndola, North Rhodesia.

September 19: The Department of Defense orders 73,000 National Guard and reservist troops to report by October 15 for active duty.

September 22: The Interstate Commerce Commission bans segregation at interstate travel facilities. The order will go into effect on November 1, 1961.

October: Kennedy aides General Maxwell Taylor and Walt Rostow recommend a stronger commitment to the problem in Vietnam. "If Vietnam goes, it will be exceedingly difficult to hold Southeast Asia," Taylor says. • The 22nd Congress of the Communist Party of the Soviet Union officially condemns former Soviet leader Joseph Stalin. *See* October 30, 1961.

As a lieutenant colonel in Heinrich Himmler's SS/SD, Adolf Eichmann acted as Nazi Germany's chief implementer of the "Final Solution"—the planned total annihilation of European Jews. Toward the end of World War II, he reported having slaughtered approximately six million Jews. In 1946 Eichmann escaped from Germany and fled to Argentina, where, in 1960, Israeli agents found and abducted him. In August 1961 Eichmann was convicted by an Israeli court for genocidal war crimes against the Jewish people. His public trial awakened millions to the horrendous atrocities committed during the Nazi Holocaust. He was hanged on May 31, 1962.

Jean Nidetch, a self-described FFH (Formerly Fat Housewife) from Queens, New York, held the first meeting of what would become Weight Watchers in September 1961. Discouraged when her motivation for losing weight seemed to be waning, she contacted some of her overweight acquaintances, and they shared stories about their food obsessions. Nidetch discovered that this organized empathy seemed to help, and in 1963 she incorporated that discovery. By 2004 the organization, owned by Heinz Company since 1978, boasted more than a million members.

Huldah Clark (*center*) chats with her new classmates at a secondary school in Moscow in September 1961. Clark's father said that because educational facilities in their home city, Newark, New Jersey, were inferior, he sent her to Russia to be schooled. The Soviets claimed the problem stemmed from racial discrimination. The USSR used race issues, especially continued segregation in the South, as a hammer to pound the U.S. for alleged hypocrisy. Such propaganda was especially embarrassing to an America trying to woo African countries just emerging from a colonialist past.

The now-defunct manufacturer of Renwal Blueprint Models sold the best and most accurate submarine model kits of the early 1960s. This nuclear-sub model, for example, shows the location and dimensions of the atomic reactor and gyro rooms. In fact, the model was *too* detailed for some U.S. Navy officials. Vice Admiral Hyman Rickover claimed that the model gave the Soviets millions of dollars' worth of information about American nuclear subs.

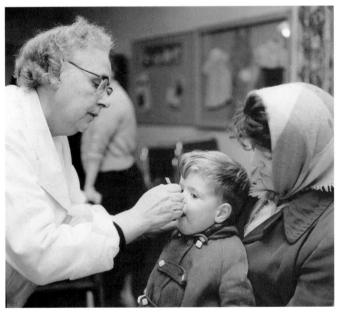

Polio, the dreaded infectious disease that paralyzed and killed children, struck more than 50,000 American children per year in the early 1950s. In 1954 Jonas Salk developed and introduced an effective killed-virus polio vaccine. In 1961 Albert Sabin's oral, live-virus vaccine was licensed and given to children on lumps of sugar. Throughout the early 1960s, millions of American children lined up for the sweet-tasting medicine. Within a few years, polio was all but eradicated in the United States.

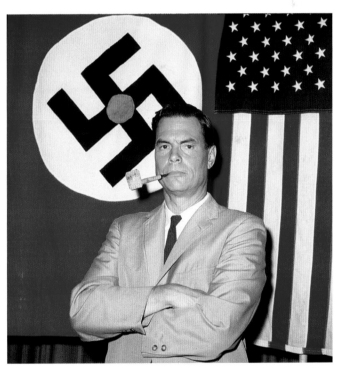

George Lincoln Rockwell—former Navy fighter pilot, traveling salesman, and Virginia gubernatorial candidate—was the founder and *"führer"* of the American Nazi Party. According to the party's current Web site, Rockwell was driven to national leadership because of "the nigger riots, economic chaos, cultural rot and Vietnam era treason of the 60's." His party even had its own "hate bus." Although Rockwell's followers numbered only a few hundred, he generated national media coverage that made him a minor celebrity. Rockwell was killed by a disgruntled former party member in 1967.

October 1: On the last day of the regular season, New York Yankees slugger Roger Maris belts his 61st home run, breaking Babe Ruth's single-season major-league record.

October 4: President Kennedy authorizes the training of French military personnel in the use of, and defense against, atomic weapons.

October 11: President Kennedy assures the government of South Vietnam that the U.S. will assist that nation in its defense against Communist guerrillas. • An X-15 rocket plane piloted by USAF Major Robert M. White reaches 217,000 feet—about 41 miles—a record for a winged, human-controlled aircraft. • Stage and film comic Chico (Leonard) Marx dies at 74.

October 12: The U.S. Public Health Service reports increased levels of radioactive iodine-131 in milk and fresh food in certain regions of the United States due to fallout from Soviet nuclear tests.

October 15: A complex U.S. defense test called "Sky Shield II" grounds all civil aircraft over the U.S. and Canada for 12 hours.

October 23: The Soviet Union test-detonates a 30-megaton A-bomb. It also announces a capability to destroy missiles in flight.

October 27: During the ongoing U.S./USSR dispute over free entry to Communist East Berlin by American citizens, U.S. and Soviet tanks line up and face each other at the *Friedrichstrasse* crossing between East and West Berlin. *See* November 23, 1961. • In its first test, a Saturn rocket is successfully fired from Cape Canaveral.

October 30: The Soviet Union test-detonates a 58-megaton A-bomb. • USSR's Communist Party Congress orders the body of Joseph Stalin removed from its place of honor near the body of Lenin in Moscow's Red Square. *See* November 11, 1961.

On June 15, 1961, East Germany's Communist Party leader, Walter Ulbricht, declared that "no one has the intention of constructing a wall" to separate East and West Berliners. On August 13, East German workers began to erect barbed-wire fencing to bisect the city. Four days later, Soviets began to secure the barrier with a 107-kilometer "anti-fascist protection wall" (in the words of East German propaganda). Here, on September 12, workers unload concrete slabs, which were intended to reinforce the wall so that heavy vehicles couldn't crash through it.

The Berlin Wall was about four meters high and often abutted East German apartment buildings and other structures. Hence, one could jump from an upper floor in East Berlin into West Berlin territory. This possible means of escape ended after border police bricked up windows that faced west. In 1962 workers constructed a second wall adjacent to the first. The well-lit corridor between the walls was guarded by watchdogs and armed soldiers in watchtowers. By 1989 hundreds of East Germans had lost their lives while attempting to escape.

The Berlin Crisis

On August 13, 1961, East German officials closed dozens of border crossings between East and West Berlin. They began building a wall to permanently block free passage between the two parts of the city. Over the next three months, tensions mounted in Washington and Moscow as people wondered if the wall might prompt another world war.

Following the defeat of the Nazis in 1945, the Allies divided Germany and its capital, Berlin, into four sectors, each individually administered by the United States, the Soviet Union, Great Britain, and France. Following the Soviets' 1948 attempt to blockade all of Berlin from West Germany, East Berlin became the capital of East Germany (in 1949) and the three western sectors unified to become West Berlin. Still, all of Berlin fell inside East Germany, a Soviet satellite.

At that time, people were free to move from one sector of Berlin to another. This meant that disillusioned citizens of East Germany could simply walk into West Berlin and escape communism. As a result, the population of East Germany dropped by two million after 1949. Soviet Premier Nikita Khrushchev did not like this scenario. He wanted either the western powers out of Berlin altogether or an agreement that would legitimate East Germany as autonomous and distinct from West Germany.

A U.S. Army tank in West Berlin

The construction of the Berlin Wall caught President John F. Kennedy by surprise. Tensions had been growing over free access to East Berlin by Americans, and the wall immediately made the situation worse. On one occasion, as American civilians continued to press for access to East Berlin, American and Soviet tanks faced each other at Checkpoint Charlie, the border crossing between East and West Berlin. The crisis eventually simmered down to a stalemate as the Americans and Soviets turned their attention to Cuba. The wall remained in place until 1989.

From the Other Side of the Wall

We learn in school that the Wall was built to protect us from capitalists who want to invade our socialist land. I used to believe that completely. When I was in the third grade, we visited a monument to a border guard who was killed by someone from the West. He was supposed to be like a hero for us, and I remember I thought he was. A lot of the kids did. But after a while I thought differently. Have you ever seen the Wall? If it was meant to keep them out, the land mines, soldiers, and self-shooting machines would be on the other side.

—Gritt, a 12-year-old resident of East Berlin

After a 35-month moratorium, the United States resumed nuclear weapons testing at the Nevada Test Site in Jackass Flats on September 15, 1961. In response to a Soviet test earlier that month, the U.S. set off a low-power nuclear device underground. Although there was little fallout from that explosion, the U.S. tested 123 additional weapons over the next two years, either in Nevada or in the Pacific Ocean, that *did* lead to radioactive fallout. The tests also heated up the arms race between the United States and the Soviet Union.

1961

October 31: SLATE organizes a vigil on the University of California–Berkeley campus after Premier Khrushchev's decision to resume atmospheric nuclear testing. Thousands around the country demonstrate as well.

November 1961–August 1962: Martin Luther King, Jr., leads a mass protest movement against segregation in Albany, Georgia. Hundreds of protesters are arrested. However, the demonstrations do not rouse the public's consciousness because the police refrain from abusing the demonstrators.

November 1: In San Francisco, drag entertainer Jose Sarria runs for a seat on the city council, making him the first openly gay candidate to run for elective office. He garners more than 5,000 votes.

November 2: Author, humorist, and cartoonist James Thurber dies at 66.

November 3: Burma's U Thant begins serving as the acting secretary-general of the United Nations.

November 6: More than 450 homes in the exclusive Bel Air enclave of Los Angeles are destroyed by aggressive wildfires.

November 9: At the Cavern Club in Liverpool, England, record store owner Brian Epstein sees the Beatles perform for the first time. He will become the band's manager in mid-December.

November 11: The Soviet city of Stalingrad is renamed Volgograd.

November 23: The Soviet military detains a U.S. Army train for 15 hours on the East German/West German border.

November 25: The nuclear-powered USS *Enterprise* aircraft carrier is commissioned at Newport News, Virginia. It is the largest, fastest, and most powerful warship the world has yet seen.

An emotionally drained Roger Maris sits in the New York Yankees clubhouse on September 30, 1961. At the time, he had belted 60 home runs and had one game left to break Babe Ruth's single-season longball record. The Yankees slugger was under enormous pressure, including from the many fans who simply did not want him to top the fabled Bambino. After Maris did crack No. 61 the next day, his achievement was tarnished when Major League Baseball Commissioner Ford Frick ordered that an asterisk be placed next to his record. Ford reasoned that Maris's record-setting season included more games (162) than Ruth's (154).

Though *Rocky and His Friends,* a black-and-white cartoon, premiered on ABC in 1959, NBC purchased the series shortly thereafter. The series was renamed *The Bullwinkle Show* and premiered as a color cartoon in September 1961. Main characters included (*left to right*) Bullwinkle J. Moose, Rocket "Rocky" J. Squirrel, and Russian spies Boris Badenov and Natasha Fatale. Although ostensibly a children's series, adults loved its irreverent satire of such institutions as international politics, fairy tales, movies, business, and even the Canadian Royal Mounted Police. The show ran on NBC until 1973.

By the early 1960s, jazz was finding its biggest audience among the young, urban, and college educated. A favorite among them was Dave Brubeck, a West Coast pianist who fronted a quartet beginning in the 1950s. The year 1960 saw his most acclaimed album, *Time Out,* become the first million-selling jazz record. Brubeck's experimentation with unusual time signatures matched Neil Fujita's abstract cover art. The catchy "Take Five," penned by saxophonist Paul Desmond, became a huge hit, contributing to *Time Out*'s massive success.

At an office equipment exhibition in Frankfurt, Germany, in October 1961, the IBM Corporation introduced the Selectric, an electronic typewriter with a rotating typing head smaller than a golf ball. The revolutionary typewriter also contained a memory-storage unit capable of reproducing data at a startling 960 letters per minute. The new machine also came with interchangeable type-style heads.

Building Up in Vietnam

IN MAY 1961, 400 GREEN BERETS—members of the U.S. Special Forces who were trained in counterinsurgency—arrived in South Vietnam. This addition of soldiers, along with an increase in other military advisers, represented President John F. Kennedy's first step toward a substantial expansion of the American commitment in Vietnam. Although the United States, under presidents Harry Truman and Dwight Eisenhower, had been involved in Southeast Asia since the 1940s, Kennedy's policies set the stage for American combat in Vietnam.

Kennedy wanted to make a stand in Vietnam after losing face with the Soviet Union three times in 1961. He was humiliated by the Bay of Pigs disaster and seemingly intimidated by Soviet Premier Nikita Khrushchev at a summit in Vienna. In addition, Kennedy supported a negotiated settlement in Laos (which borders Vietnam) in spring 1961 that led to Communist participation in the Laotian government. Fearing that more such settlements would make the United States appear weak, Kennedy ruled out a similar course in Vietnam.

When South Vietnamese leader Ngo Dinh Diem requested a dramatic increase in American economic support in 1961, Kennedy sent two trusted advisers, General Maxwell Taylor and National Security Council adviser Walt Rostow, to Saigon in October to survey the situation. Based on their grim report, including their assessment that the enemy, the Vietcong, already controlled much of the South Vietnamese countryside, some in the administration called for Kennedy to introduce combat troops to support South Vietnam. Kennedy rejected the idea, but he agreed to significant increases in both military advisers and economic aid.

By the time he was assassinated in November 1963, Kennedy had increased the number of American advisers in Vietnam to more than 16,000. He also approved their participation in combat operations. In 1962 and '63, those advisers instituted the Strategic Hamlet Program, which was designed to segregate peaceful peasants from the enemy guerrillas. In practice, the program further alienated rural people and fueled their support of the enemy.

Sergeant Stanley Harold, a U.S. military adviser, training South Vietnamese soldiers

November 29: Enos, a chimpanzee, becomes the first "American" primate to orbit the Earth. He orbits for three hours and 45 minutes in his Mercury 5 space capsule.

December 9: Tanganyika becomes an independent state within the British Commonwealth.

December 10: Motown Records scores its first No. 1 hit: "Please Mr. Postman" by the Marvelettes.

December 11: U.S. support for South Vietnam arrives with the aircraft carrier USS *Core* and her task group. Fighting power includes 400 pilots as well as airplanes, helicopters, and transportation crews. • The U.S. Supreme Court unanimously reverses the breach-of-peace convictions of 16 African-Americans who participated in a sit-in campaign in Baton Rouge, Louisiana.

December 12: In Montgomery, Alabama, police arrest 737 civil rights demonstrators.

December 13: Folk painter Grandma (Anna) Moses dies at 101.

December 14: President Kennedy sends a dispatch to President Diem pledging to help Vietnam "preserve its independence." Kennedy commits more advisers and equipment to the cause. • President Kennedy establishes the President's Commission on the Status of Women.

December 15: In Israel, former Nazi SS functionary Adolf Eichmann is sentenced to death for war crimes and crimes against humanity. *See* May 31, 1962.

December 21: The U.S. Army announces that a Nike-Zeus anti-missile missile has for the first time successfully intercepted a missile in flight.

December 22: James Davis of Livingston, Tennessee, becomes the first American soldier to die in Vietnam.

Born in Belgium in 1929 as Andrey Kathleen van Heemstra Ruston, Audrey Hepburn was the daughter of aristocratic parents. She went on to captivate moviegoers for more than 30 years with her on-screen charm and wit. Her best-known and career-defining role was that of Holly Golightly in Blake Edwards's 1961 *Breakfast at Tiffany's.* In partial contrast to the more outspoken feminism of the late 1960s, Hepburn personified in the film a fierce, womanly independence—but of a chic, cosmopolitan, and socially connected kind. Her other popular films included *Roman Holiday, The Unforgiven,* and *My Fair Lady.* Hepburn died of cancer in 1993.

Wilbur Post, played by Alan Young, stands by his good friend, the talking Mister Ed. A successor to the popular films starring Francis, the Talking Mule, *Mister Ed* ran on CBS from October 1961 to September 1966. Actor Allan "Rocky" Lane provided the deep voice of Ed, whom TV Land describes as "a sleek, intelligent, well read, up-on-current-events, glasses wearing, wise-cracking Palomino!" Mister Ed talked on the phone, surfed, played baseball, and routinely helped his buddy Wilbur out of jams (which Ed often initiated!).

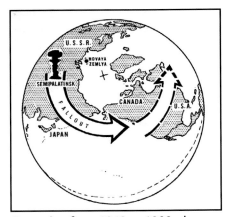

Operating from 1949 to 1989, the Soviet Union's Semipalatinsk nuclear test range spanned 18,000 square kilometers. The Soviets set off some 470 explosions, about 100 of which were atmospheric (until such testing was banned in 1963). The Degelen Mountain facility—which began operations on October 11, 1961—was the world's largest underground nuclear test site. A 2000 study found that Semipalatinsk "downwinders" had suffered abnormally high rates of lung, gastric, and esophageal cancers.

Organized in1957 by Quaker pacifists, the Committee for Nonviolent Action (CNVA) sought to protest and launch "direct action against the evil of nuclear tests." The pictured group—composed of pacifists, antinuclear activists, and students—walked from California to New York. They then sailed to Europe and proceeded walking to Moscow (*pictured*) in opposition to further nuclear tests. Later in the 1960s, the CNVA became involved in the civil rights and anti-Vietnam War movements.

The Peace Corps

TAPPING INTO THE COUNTRY'S reserve of earnest idealism, President John F. Kennedy launched the Peace Corps six weeks into his presidency. With a stroke of the pen, he pledged volunteers to work in largely Third World countries friendly to the United States. There, they would share their particular area of expertise while living among the locals.

Though both the concept and the program's name originated with Senator Hubert Humphrey (D–MN), the President was quick to recognize the political value of sending platoons of goodwill ambassadors around the globe. Moreover, striving toward such worthy goals as ending hunger and educating the poor benefited both sides. After all, as Indian Prime Minister Jawaharlal Nehru told Kennedy, "Young Americans could learn a lot from Indian villagers."

Never one to let charges of nepotism stand in the way of talent, the President appointed brother-in-law Sargent

A volunteer in the Philippines

Shriver as the Peace Corps' first director. As energetic as he was idealistic, Shriver adhered to the noble purpose, ensuring that the organization would not engage in intelligence gathering or propagandizing. Despite the original intent to recruit recent graduates, administrators were astounded to find adventure-loving volunteers of all ages and walks of life flocking to the program.

Mutual culture shock typified experiences in the Peace Corps. Idealistic volunteers from well-to-do families weren't prepared for the hardships of Third World living. Conversely, many inhabitants had never seen a white person before. Despite a rocky start, the Peace Corps' early successes convinced a once-skeptical Congress to approve funding to ensure a long-term commitment. Alongside the space program, the Peace Corps would become the most enduring legacy of Kennedy's New Frontier.

1961

New & Notable

Books

Black Like Me by John Howard Griffin
The Carpetbaggers by Harold Robbins
Catch-22 by Joseph Heller
Franny and Zooey by J. D. Salinger
The Moviegoer by Walker Percy
A Nation of Sheep by William J. Lederer
Stranger in a Strange Land
    by Robert Heinlein
Tropic of Cancer by Henry Miller
    (first legal U.S. publication)

Movies

Breakfast at Tiffany's
The Guns of Navarone
The Hustler
The Misfits
101 Dalmatians
The Parent Trap
Splendor in the Grass
West Side Story
Yojimbo

Songs

"Blue Moon" by the Marcels
"Crazy" by Patsy Cline
"Hit the Road, Jack" by Ray Charles
"Moon River" by Henry Mancini
"Runaround Sue" by Dion
    & the Belmonts
"Runaway" by Del Shannon
"Travelin' Man" by Ricky Nelson
"Where the Boys Are"
    by Connie Francis
"Will You Love Me Tomorrow"
    by the Shirelles

Television

Ben Casey
The Bullwinkle Show
Car 54, Where Are You?
The Defenders
Dr. Kildare
Hazel
Password
Top Cat

Theater

Come Blow Your Horn
How to Succeed in Business
    Without Really Trying
A Man for All Seasons
Night of the Iguana
Take Her, She's Mine

This six-year-old boy in San Francisco flies the only plane in the sky on October 14, 1961. That day, an air defense drill named Operation Sky Shield II—conducted by the North American Aerospace Defense Command (NORAD) in Colorado Springs, Colorado—grounded civilian aircraft across the United States. The purpose was to clear NORAD's Iconorama screen of all domestic interference so the Strategic Air Command could simulate and display a mock Soviet air attack.

The film adaptation of the award-winning musical play *West Side Story* played to huge audiences in 1961. This modern-day retelling of the Romeo and Juliet story features rival ethnic gangs: the Jets, a white gang from Manhattan, and the Sharks, a Puerto Rican immigrant gang. A Jet man (played by Richard Beymer) and a Shark woman (Natalie Wood) fall in love, with predictable results. Although the performances of Beymer and Wood were not critically acclaimed, the Leonard Bernstein–Stephen Sondheim score was a triumph. The movie won 10 Oscars, including best picture. Rita Moreno (*center*) was named best supporting actress.

The South Vietnamese Army attempts to root out the enemy in 1961. That year, the National Liberation Front—aka the Vietcong, slang for South Vietnamese Communists—stepped up its military operations in South Vietnam. Approximately 26,000 Vietcong launched multiple, successful attacks on South Vietnamese troops. South Vietnamese leader Ngo Dinh Diem responded by asking the Kennedy Administration for a dramatic increase in military aid.

As the Vietcong intensified their infiltration of South Vietnam in 1961, President Kennedy dispatched General Maxwell Taylor (*in ditch*) and National Security Council adviser Walt Rostow (*far right*) to the area in October for assessment and recommendations. Both recommended more U.S. advisers, more equipment, and even the introduction of combat troops. However, Kennedy, in the words of Secretary of Defense Robert McNamara, "flatly refused to endorse the introduction of U.S. combat forces."

Ho Chi Minh founded the Vietnam Republic in 1945 and became president of the Democratic Republic of Vietnam (North Vietnam) after the country's 1954 partition. In his youth, Ho had spent several years in France, becoming a founding member of the French Communist Party. Though a devout Communist, Ho maintained even stronger anti-imperialist and nationalist sentiments, which led to his

declaring Vietnam independent from France in 1945 and the defeat of France as a colonial power in 1954. Because he maintained strong ties with Communist powers China and the USSR, the United States believed it needed to prevent the reunification of Vietnam under a popular Ho Chi Minh. However, the U.S. seriously miscalculated the depth of Ho Chi Minh's nationalism. He was prepared to fight until the bitter end to unify his country.

John Paul Vann is best remembered as the subject of journalist Neil Sheehan's *A Bright Shining Lie,* a riveting account of American involvement in Vietnam. Vann was a U.S. military adviser to South Vietnamese government forces in the early 1960s. Vann supported American efforts against Vietcong insurgency, but he abhorred U.S. military strategy. He saw the futility of widespread

bombing, the lethargy of South Vietnamese troops, and local corruption. After his superiors turned a deaf ear to his concerns, Vann began leaking information about America's failing military strategy to journalists. Under Pentagon pressure, he resigned his commission in 1963. Vann later returned to South Vietnam as a civilian adviser with the Agency for International Development. He died in a helicopter crash in Vietnam's central highlands in 1972.

"Jackie would be sitting with some old guy who'd almost nodded off and suddenly ask a question so filled with implied indiscretion that this old guy's eyes would almost pop out of his head. And for the remainder of the conversation he'd practically be married to her in intimacy."

—LEM BILLINGS, FRIEND OF THE KENNEDYS

Washington Post journalist Alan Barth created a stir with his 1961 book, *The Price of Liberty*. He argued that America's anxiety about crime was leading to a police-state mentality that threatened American liberty, perhaps even more than internal subversion or external threats. The book focuses on unlawful arrests and other examples of over-zealousness on the part of law enforcement officers. Barth's thesis foreshadowed later court decisions limiting police powers.

Jackie Kennedy

As THE NEW FRONTIER GOT UNDERWAY, Jacqueline Kennedy proved a natural focal point for a nation fascinated with celebrity. Not only was she beautiful and charming, but she was only 31 years old—the youngest first lady since Frances Cleveland.

Jackie's exquisite fashion sense and innate elegance kept women around the country enthralled. Her penchant for Capri pants was widely imitated, as was her bouffant hairstyle. Jackie's tastes dictated the trends, making such designers as Cassini and Givenchy household names. Famously, her trademark pillbox hats remained a constant throughout her husband's tenure as president.

Jackie's aura of sophistication (her pursuits included sailing, horses, and the arts) also piqued Americans' interest. The President came to recognize this, viewing his wife as his secret weapon. During a state visit to France in June 1961, it was Jackie who the crowds turned out to see. Kennedy good-naturedly referred to himself as "the man who accompanied Mrs. Kennedy to Paris." Possessing a command of several languages, Jackie was naturally suited to the role of goodwill ambassador at a time of heightened tensions throughout the world.

Like JFK, Jackie raised people's expectations by setting an ideal. Appalled at the condition of her new home, she set about not so much to redecorate the White House but to restore it. Under her direction, the country was scoured for period-appropriate furnishings and art, turning the President's home into less of a transient hotel than a national treasure. State dinners became cultural events, with the world's leading artists and performers invited. The Kennedy years were a time of grace, style, and romance, and Jackie was the queen of Camelot.

American and Soviet troops and their tanks face off in Berlin on October 27, 1961. The incident reflected the tensions over that divided city that had risen since November 1958, when Soviet Premier Nikita Khrushchev had threatened to sign a separate peace treaty with Communist East Germany, thus compromising the independence of Berlin. President Kennedy affirmed the American commitment to defend the city. Although the Berlin Wall, built by the Communists in August 1961 to stem the brain drain from East to West Berlin, took some of the steam out of the crisis, anxieties still ran high.

On November 6, 1961, a small brushfire ignited in the Santa Monica Mountains in California. Winds soon fueled the small conflagration, driving it across Mulholland Drive and into the affluent Los Angeles community of Bel Air (*pictured*). More than 450 elegant homes burned to the ground. Though property damage was estimated at $25 million, no lives were lost. Actors Burt Lancaster and Zsa Zsa Gabor, singer Tex Williams, and comedian Joe E. Brown were among those who lost their homes. According to the *Los Angeles Examiner,* bandleader Lawrence Welk waited out the fire from his rooftop with a garden hose in hand.

The parents of James Davis—the first American killed in action in Vietnam—pose with a portrait of their deceased son. Davis had been one of 3,205 "advisers" sent to aid the South Vietnamese Army in its counterinsurgency efforts by the end of 1961. His job was to monitor and locate rebel Vietcong radio transmissions in the field. On December 22, the truck that Davis and 10 South Vietnamese soldiers were riding in hit a remote-controlled landmine. They survived the explosion but were gunned down immediately by the Vietcong. Within the next 12 months, the Kennedy Administration sent 8,000 additional advisers to South Vietnam.

An X-15 rocket plane is dropped by a B-52 bomber, then leaves a thick exhaust trail over Edwards Air Force Base in California. The X-15, a transitional vehicle between jet planes and space shuttles, was first tested in 1959. Its hypersonic speeds (up to six times the speed of sound, or Mach 6) and high altitudes (well above 100,000 feet) captured the public's imagination in the early 1960s. Pilot Bob White smashed speed records several times in 1961. When he broke Mach 6 on November 9, 1961, he also broke his right windshield.

1962

The Cuban Missile Crisis

ON MONDAY NIGHT, October 22, 1962, 100 million Americans—almost half the nation—gathered around their televisions. President John F. Kennedy had told the networks that he needed time to speak to the country about a matter of the gravest importance. The public knew that Kennedy had only bad news to share with them.

Hands clenched, grim-faced, Kennedy spoke from the Oval Office. He was haggard and drawn from lack of sleep. His speech lasted just 17 minutes. The Soviet Union had begun building a "nuclear strike capability" in Cuba, he said. They had lied about their actions. Their deadly weapons could reach tens of millions of Americans. This unprovoked aggression, he stated, "cannot be accepted by this country, if our courage and our commitments are ever to be trusted again either by friend or foe."

Speaking not just to the American people but to people everywhere in the world, President Kennedy laid down the gauntlet: "We will not prematurely or unnecessarily risk the costs of worldwide nuclear war in which even the fruits of victory would be ashes in our mouth—but neither will we shrink from that risk at any time it must be faced." The United States, Kennedy announced, would immediately begin a naval blockade of Cuba. If the weapons in Cuba were used against the American people, the Soviet Union would be destroyed by a massive retaliatory nuclear attack. The Soviets needed to stop their buildup in Cuba and withdraw all nuclear weapons or face further American actions.

"It shall be the policy of this nation to regard any nuclear missile launched from Cuba against any nation in the Western Hemisphere as an attack by the Soviet Union on the United States, requiring a full retaliatory response upon the Soviet Union. . . . I call upon Chairman Khrushchev to halt and eliminate this clandestine, reckless, and provocative threat to world peace. . . . He has an opportunity now to move the world back from the abyss of destruction."

—PRESIDENT JOHN F. KENNEDY, OCTOBER 22, 1962

In October 1962 the United States and USSR stood at the brink of nuclear war. The world breathed a sigh of relief on October 27 when Soviet Premier Nikita Khrushchev offered to remove missile bases in Cuba if the U.S. took down its bases in Turkey. By early November (*pictured*), Soviet missiles were on their way back to Russia.

President Kennedy would not accept the location of a Soviet nuclear arsenal just 90 miles off the coast of Florida. That night, he told the world that the United States would, if necessary, go to war with the Soviet Union to stop the Soviet buildup, even if that war led to nuclear apocalypse. Since the Soviet Union had first detonated an atomic device in 1949, matching the United States, the two superpowers had been marching in lockstep to this terrifying moment.

MEDIUM RANGE BALLISTIC MISSILE BASE IN CUBA
SAN CRISTOBAL

Aerial reconnaissance photos taken by U.S. spy planes showed concrete evidence of missile assembly in Cuba. Once operational, these missile sites would be capable of delivering nuclear strikes against numerous American cities.

Kennedy had known about the Soviet missile buildup in Cuba since early Tuesday morning, October 16. A U.S. Air Force spy plane had taken routine surveillance photos of Cuba on the 14th. Analysis of the photos revealed a shocking discovery: evidence of Soviet SS-4 intermediate-range ballistic missiles (IRBMs) on Cuban soil. Such missiles could reach Americans up and down the Southeast, taking out Miami, Atlanta, and dozens of other cities. No doubt existed about the situation; the photos were clear and conclusive.

The Soviets had put the weapons in Cuba for three reasons. First, they wanted to protect Cuba from the United States government, which had, since the Bay of Pigs invasion in 1961, continued to harass, subvert, and plan to take down the Castro regime. Second, the Soviets had discovered American nuclear weapons in Turkey, near the Soviet border, and wanted to retaliate. And third, the Soviets wanted to compensate for America's huge nuclear weapons advantage. The United States could launch a rapid attack on the USSR with about 2,000 nuclear weapons, while the Soviets had only about 340 weapons with which they could immediately strike the U.S.

Kennedy called an urgent meeting of his top administrative officials—the Executive Committee, known as EX-COMM—to plan the American response. The decision was made to keep the missile situation secret and for the President and his aides to maintain, as much as possible, their regular schedules. Without public scrutiny and political pressures, the Kennedy Administration believed they could better think through their response to the unfolding crisis. For seven days, the President and EX-COMM met in secret and debated the options.

First, they had to decide how seriously to take the Soviet action. The military Joint Chiefs had told Secretary of Defense Robert McNamara that the

During the first hours of the Cuban Missile Crisis, U.S. Air Force Chief of Staff Curtis LeMay forcefully argued for direct military intervention, including air strikes and an all-out invasion of Cuba.

Cuban missiles "substantially" changed the "strategic balance." McNamara disagreed, stating that the missiles changed things "not at all." President Kennedy had the last word on the matter: "This is a political strategy as much as military." The United States, he believed, could not allow the Soviets to bully the U.S., gain any sort of military advantage, or lie about their offensive actions. So, that bridge crossed, options were discussed.

The Joint Chiefs wanted to attack Cuba. Air Force General Curtis LeMay led the "hawks." He told the President: "If we don't do anything in Cuba, then they're going to push on Berlin, and push real hard because they've got us on the run. . . . I don't see any other solution except direct military action right now." Marine Corps General David Shoup, in an aside, told LeMay he was in full support of an attack: "Somebody's got to keep them from doing the goddamn thing piecemeal. . . . Do the son of a bitch, and do it right. . . ."

The civilian leadership was less sure. Early in the discussions, Undersecretary of State George Ball spoke out against a preemptive attack on the Cuban missile site: "We strike without warning, that's like Pearl Harbor. It's the kind of conduct that we might expect of the Soviet Union." The President's younger brother, Attorney General Robert Kennedy, who generally listened more than he spoke, chimed in: "I think George Ball has a hell of a point. . . . I think it's the whole question of, you know, assuming that you do survive all this . . . what kind of a country we are."

After a great deal of back and forth, the President and his civilian team opted for a compromise position. The President would order a naval blockade of Cuba, using force if necessary to turn back any Soviet ship that attempted to reach Cuba. Further, the United States would demand that the Soviets stop their buildup and withdraw missiles already sited on the island. And so Kennedy appeared on television on October 22 and told the American people what he felt must be done to ensure the security of the United States.

Americans overwhelmingly supported their young president, but they listened to him with dread. Many had feared this moment for more than a

With tensions running at an all-time high in the White House during the Cuban Missile Crisis, President Kennedy never had a more sober sense of his responsibility. Meetings and intelligence briefings were continuous as the President patiently made decisions intended to avoid global catastrophe.

1962

In Moscow's Red Square on May Day (May 1), 1962, senior Soviet leaders wave to parade-goers from atop the Lenin mausoleum. Soviet Premier Nikita Khrushchev (*second from left*) felt that President Kennedy was "weak" and "ineffectual," but it was Khrushchev himself who backed down during the missile crisis.

decade. Throughout much of the 1950s and right up through the President's announcement, Americans had been preparing for nuclear attack.

In schools, children as young as five had been drilled in "duck and cover" exercises, during which they curled up under their little desks to avoid dying from a nuclear explosion. Some families in America's burgeoning suburbs had built fallout shelters in their backyards or basements. They hoped they could somehow protect themselves from a nuclear blast, firestorms, and radiation that would be produced by a Soviet nuclear attack.

Some Americans, on hearing the President's words, tried to make specific plans to escape an attack. Earl Bailey, an aerospace engineer at Lockheed near Atlanta, hoped he would procure an advance warning of a Soviet missile launch. He and his wife worked out a complicated code that he would use to warn her, and they plotted an escape route that would take the family to the hills of western North Carolina.

The threat of nuclear annihilation seemed even more likely during the missile crisis, especially in states that were in immediate striking range of Cuban missile bases. In preparation for the worst, these schoolchildren in St. Petersburg, Florida, practice the "duck and cover" method during a disaster drill on October 25.

For a few years, a small minority of Americans had been speaking out against the nuclear "brinkmanship" policies practiced by America's Cold War presidents. The Committee for a Sane Nuclear Policy (SANE) had organized in 1957. In 1962 Students for a Democratic Society (SDS), a fledgling New Left group, had issued a manifesto, "The Port Huron Statement." The manifesto protested American nuclear policy, warning that "...we ourselves, and our friends, and millions of 'abstract' others we know more directly because of our common peril, might die at any time....Our work is guided by the sense that we may be the last generation in the experiment with living."

But in late October 1962, American citizens could do nothing but wait and see what would happen next. The whole world waited.

Soviet Premier Khrushchev, as the saying went, "blinked" first. He ordered Soviet ships not to advance on the American naval blockade. Frantically, Kennedy and Khrushchev traded telegrams, negotiating how to end the most dangerous crisis in Cold War history. Kennedy promised not to invade Cuba and secretly agreed to remove nuclear weapons from Turkey, just 150 miles from the Soviet border. In return, Khrushchev met the American demands: The missile sites in Cuba would be dismantled, and no more nuclear weapons would ever be sent to Cuba.

For Kennedy, acting tough had worked. Not only had the Soviets backed down completely, but Kennedy's apparent victory made him immensely popular with the American people. He and the men who followed him as commander in chief took that lesson to heart. It was a good lesson, it turned out, when dealing with the Soviet Union but a very bad lesson, it soon became obvious, when dealing with Ho Chi Minh and the anti-American forces in Vietnam.

In 1962 the American people still lived with a Cold War mentality. In so many ways, the early 1960s still felt like the "Ike Age" of the 1950s. "Big Girls Don't Cry" by the Four Seasons topped the record charts, and Tony Bennett's "I Left My Heart in San Francisco" won the Grammy for record of the year. Nobody was yet talking about moving to San Francisco and wearing flowers in their hair, as Scott MacKenzie would later sing. Still, as John Kennedy and most Americans celebrated the Cold War victory over the Soviets, massive changes were on the horizon and already beginning.

In Oxford, Mississippi, 29-year-old African-American Air Force veteran James Meredith forced the nation to confront the intransigence of racism and segregation. When Meredith tried to register at the University of Mississippi, he was met by violent mobs supported by the governor of the state. The nation watched transfixed as the 500 federal marshals President Kennedy had sent to protect Meredith were attacked by thousands of rioting whites.

And in a less dramatic but equally portentous event, author Ken Kesey's *One Flew Over the Cuckoo's Nest* was released. This award-winning novel, enormously popular with young people, attacked the conformity and rigid authoritarianism Kesey believed characterized American Cold War society.

The Cold War consensus that had ruled much of American life was beginning to fray—and soon would implode.

In spite of massive, violent opposition, James Meredith became the first African-American to attend the University of Mississippi on October 1, 1962. During his second day of classes, this effigy was hung in view of his dorm room window, then set ablaze.

1962: The Kennedy Administration defines a new U.S. defense policy, which shifts from "massive retaliation" to improved systems and failsafes for command and control. It announces the enlargement of conventional U.S. and NATO forces, the development of a second-strike force that could survive a sneak attack, and an increased commitment to undermine Communist activity designed to take over governments in developing nations. • The U.S. government prints and distributes 31 million copies of a Defense Department handbook entitled *Fallout Protection: What to Know and Do About Nuclear Attack.*

1962: Francis Crick and James Watson win a Nobel Prize for their work describing the structure of DNA. • The American Dental Association urges the dental profession to persevere against factions opposed to fluoridation of the U.S. water supply. • The FDA prohibits the sale of the sedative drug thalidomide after discovering it causes severe birth defects when taken by pregnant women. *See* March 2, 1962. • Sherry Finkbine, host of a children's television show in Phoenix, opts for an abortion after learning about the effects of thalidomide, which she has been taking. Amid death threats, she is denied the abortion by her hospital and goes to Sweden for the procedure.

1962: The U.S. Air Force begins spraying Agent Orange, a defoliant, to expose roads and trails used by Vietcong forces. The toxic chemical will cause perhaps hundreds of thousands of Vietnamese children to be born with deformities. • The Vatican excommunicates Cuban Communist dictator Fidel Castro from the Roman Catholic Church. • Illinois becomes the first state to repeal its sodomy laws. • *Ramparts,* a leftist publication, debuts.

Comedian Ernie Kovacs, here in a classic pose with a slightly bemused smirk and an ever-present cigar, died in an automobile accident on January 13, 1962. In the 1950s, he had been a pioneering television comic. His *Ernie Kovacs Show* featured novel skits that included talking books, living paintings, and a group of mechanical monkeys that played classical music. By 1960 Kovacs had become a movie star. His television shows clearly foreshadowed immensely popular later productions, such as *Laugh-In* and *Late Night with David Letterman.*

Eros, a handsomely packaged erotic quarterly, was introduced in 1962 to critical acclaim and intense controversy. Cerebral and artistic but obscene to some, the subscription-only magazine broke with traditional periodicals of the day with titillating pictures, a hard cover, and intelligent, often satiric editorial content. A collaboration between publisher Ralph Ginzburg and famed graphic designer Herb Lubalin, *Eros* lasted four issues until a campaign led by the National Office for Decent Literature landed Ginzburg in jail on obscenity charges.

The early 1960s witnessed the emergence of the giant retailers, Wal-Mart and Kmart. Both opened their doors in 1962, offering consumers virtually every household item imaginable under one roof. Kmart, in fact, opened 18 stores in '62 and sold more than $483 million worth of goods that year. America's growing suburbanization contributed to the stores' inception. It also prompted established downtown retailers, such as Sears and Montgomery Ward, to open stores in outlying shopping centers.

Bob Dylan, playing guitar and harmonica, records an album for Columbia Records. Born Robert Zimmerman in Duluth, Minnesota, in 1941, he discovered folk music in coffeehouses while attending the University of Minnesota in 1959. He began singing in some of them under the stage name Bob Dylan (after poet Dylan Thomas). Befriended by Woody Guthrie, Dylan became enamored with the work of the great folk singer and moved to New York City in 1961, partly so he could visit the hospitalized Guthrie in New Jersey. Dylan attracted a following while playing the folk club scene in New York's Greenwich Village. His 1962 debut album, *Bob Dylan,* featured traditional folk music as well as a Dylan original, "Song to Woody."

Dylan's Destiny

OUR LITTLE GROUP was helping plan the 1962 University of Michigan Folk Festival.... I said, "Why don't we just get Bob Dylan in the concert?" His album hadn't come out yet, so only those of us who'd gone to New York knew who he was. But we convinced them to put him on the show. Somebody drove Dylan from New York City and back, and we paid him a grand total of something like $100 for the weekend, including the car and driver. He did a few songs on Saturday and performed an entire concert by himself on Sunday....

Dylan didn't seem to want to hang with us; he really wasn't the friendliest type of fellow in those situations. But I think about it now and realize he was thinking about a very different world than we were. It was way advanced. He was already an artist; we were just thinking we'd become artists, because it was more fun than being a worker. Dylan had a much more purposeful musical existence; he had something to do.

—MARC SILBER

Demonstrators protesting nuclear weapons testing by both the United States and the USSR warm themselves with hot coffee on February 16, 1962. Organized by the Committee for a Sane Nuclear Policy (SANE) and Students for a Democratic Society (SDS), the demonstration drew at least 4,000 students to Washington, D.C. The coffee was delivered by a White House butler on behalf of President Kennedy. According to organizer Todd Gitlin, most of the protesters were "earnest short-haired young men wearing jackets and ties."

A Titan II missile waits in a silo launchpad 150 feet underground. The Strategic Air Command deployed the first squadron of Titan II missiles in 1962, giving the United States a two-stage, liquid-fueled, rocket-powered Intercontinental Ballistic Missile with significantly more power than Titan I. With a larger warhead and improved navigation, the missile gave the U.S. considerable political advantage in the Cold War.

1962

1962: The American auto industry finds success with midsize models positioned between compacts and full-size cars: Ford Fairlane, Mercury Meteor, and Chevy II. • AT&T introduces the T1 wideband phone line. It also experiments with digital transmission between switching offices in certain locations. • Women Strike for Peace, an anti-nuclear organization, holds its first national conference, in Michigan. • Amelia Newell opens a commune in Big Sur, California, offering her acreage to anyone who wants to settle there.

1962: The bossa nova, a rhythmic musical style from Brazil, achieves tremendous U.S. popularity—in record sales as well as on dance floors. • The comic album *The First Family*, featuring Vaughn Meader as President John F. Kennedy, becomes hugely popular. • Sweatshirts featuring faces of Beethoven, Brahms, or Bach become a clothing fad. They are embraced equally by lovers of classical music and by rock 'n' rollers (as a joke). • The British edition of *Vogue* magazine endorses the thigh-high miniskirt.

January: Bishop Burke of Buffalo, New York, says he forbids Catholic school students from dancing to Chubby Checker's "The Twist" or any other rock 'n' roll song. He calls the music lewd and un-Christian.

January 1: The Beatles get their first audition with a recording company, Decca Records, but are turned down.

January 9: The USSR and Cuba strike a $700 million trade agreement.

January 13: American comic actor, writer, and television star Ernie Kovacs, 42, dies in a freak, one-car accident.

January 15: During his first press conference of the year, President Kennedy is asked if any Americans in Vietnam are engaged in fighting. The President says "no" and moves on to the next question.

Astronaut John H. Glenn, Jr., suits up for a preflight training exercise in February 1962. Glenn was chosen to pilot the NASA spacecraft that would make the first manned orbital mission by the United States on February 20, 1962. Glenn had made his mark as a highly decorated Marine pilot in World War II and the Korean War. He later became a Navy test pilot, and in 1957 he set the transcontinental speed record from Los Angeles to New York. Glenn was chosen out of more than 500 talented pilots to be one of the seven original astronauts. His vast experience and coolness under fire, in addition to his degree in engineering, made him an ideal choice. Moreover, his clean-cut good looks, pleasant demeanor, and reputation for courage bolstered NASA's image.

These Soviet space toys, which include a model of Yuri Gagarin's spaceship Vostok, are testament to the space craze that hit the USSR in 1962. With John Glenn's successful flight that year, the fad spread across the United States, as well. Toy manufacturers produced such gems as Chief Robot Man and the Cragstan Mystery Action Satellite.

An American Atlas rocket carrying astronaut John Glenn's space capsule (Friendship 7) is launched from Cape Canaveral, Florida, on February 20, 1962. Glenn orbited Earth three times before splashing down in the Atlantic Ocean after four hours and 55 minutes. During the flight, he made numerous observations about his reactions and the universe he witnessed outside his craft, including the fact that he could eat and drink comfortably in zero gravity. In spite of several problems during reentry, Glenn landed safely. When asked in his debriefing if any unusual activity occurred during his flight, he stated, "No, just a normal day in space." On March 1, Glenn was honored with a tickertape parade in New York City.

A group of Special Forces troops (aka Green Berets) trains in a Virginia forest in March 1962. Special Forces were first organized in 1952 as the military's primary counterinsurgency unit. They achieved wide notoriety in the early 1960s when President Kennedy enthusiastically endorsed the concept of counter-guerrilla operations in Vietnam. He authorized the use of the jaunty green berets as head coverings, and increased the number of Special Forces troops from 2,500 to 10,000. Although these units served with great honor and courage in Vietnam, their training of South Vietnamese troops was insufficient to stem the Communist onslaught. After President Lyndon Johnson ordered U.S. combat troops to Vietnam in 1965, the Green Berets's role there focused on secret operations.

Jackie Kennedy stands for a group photo in front of the Taj Mahal during her March 1962 goodwill trip to India. In addition to accompanying her husband on official trips to Paris, Vienna, and Greece, Mrs. Kennedy traveled by herself to India, Italy, and Pakistan. Most observers—impressed by her youth, cultural interests, and sense of style—considered Jackie to be a splendid ambassador. She utterly charmed the Indians during her visit, especially when she revisited the Taj Mahal at night because she wanted to experience its beauty in the dark.

Judith Campbell Exner, pictured in 1960, the year she said she first met John F. Kennedy, was probably the most famous of the President's mistresses. Exner claimed to have served as an intermediary between Kennedy and mobster Sam Giancana. She also said she aborted the President's unborn child. Neither of these claims have been proven. What is clear, however, is that Kennedy had numerous sexual liaisons while president—including one with Exner—in what historian Robert Dallek calls his "reckless womanizing."

1962

January 17: Columbia University professor Charles Van Doren and other former contestants plead guilty to charges that they cheated on the TV quiz show *Twenty-One* in 1957.

January 19: Ballet star Rudolf Nureyev, a Soviet defector, makes his U.S. debut on network television.

January 30: Two members of the Flying Wallendas high-wire troupe die in an accident at the Shrine Circus in Detroit.

February 3: President Kennedy orders a ban on virtually all U.S. trade with Cuba.

February 7: American military strength reaches 4,000 in South Vietnam with the arrival of two Army aviation units.

February 10: U-2 spy plane pilot Francis Gary Powers is released in Berlin by the Soviets in exchange for convicted Soviet espionage agent Rudolf Abel.

February 14: First Lady Jacqueline Kennedy conducts a tour of the White House that's televised nationally on CBS and NBC.

February 16: Thousands of protesters participate in the first anti-nuclear march in Washington, D.C. The rally is organized by the Committee for a Sane Nuclear Policy (SANE) of Boston and the fledgling Students for a Democratic Society (SDS).

February 20: U.S. astronaut John Glenn orbits Earth three times, becoming the first American in orbit.

March: To combat the infiltration of Vietcong guerrillas in civilian villages in South Vietnam, Saigon and Washington begin the Strategic Hamlet program. Villagers will be relocated to the hamlets, which will be guarded by military personnel. • Barbra Streisand, 19, stars as Miss Marmelstein in the Broadway play *I Can Get It for You Wholesale*.

Rock Hudson prepares to plant a kiss on Doris Day in the 1962 film *Lover Come Back*. This was the second in a series of three popular Hudson–Day comedies, which included *Pillow Talk* (1959) and *Send Me No Flowers* (1964). *Lover* is both a screwball romantic comedy and a satirical look at advertising. With their good looks, charm, and genuine chemistry together, the Day–Hudson duo enjoyed huge box office appeal during the "innocent" early '60s.

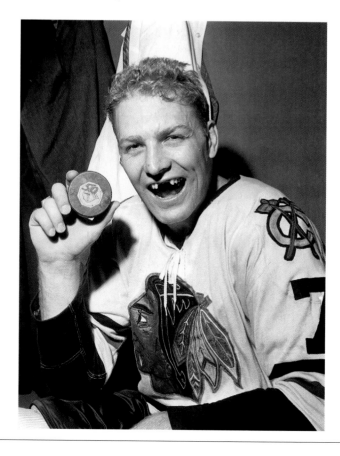

Chicago Black Hawk Bobby Hull flashes a toothless grin as he displays the puck with which he scored his 50th goal during the 1961–62 season. This goal, netted in the last game of the campaign, tied the NHL record reached by Maurice "Rocket" Richard and Bernie "Boom Boom" Geoffrion. Hull went on to repeat the feat four times. Known as the "Golden Jet," a speed demon with a ferocious shot, he was the most exciting NHL player of his era.

Wilt the Stilt

ON MARCH 2, 1962, while manning the middle for the NBA's Philadelphia Warriors, Wilt Chamberlain blew the minds of sports fans everywhere. Facing the New York Knicks, the 7′1″ center poured in 100 points, smashing his own NBA record of 78. During the 1961–62 season, Wilt "The Stilt" averaged 50.4 points and 25.7 rebounds per game.

Born August 21, 1936, in Philadelphia, Chamberlain became a national shot put champion and world-class decathlete at the University of Kansas. On the basketball court, he scored 52 points in his first collegiate game. Chamberlain left Kansas before graduating and toiled with the Harlem Globetrotters for a year. The Philadelphia Warriors signed him in 1959 at an unprecedented $65,000 per season.

Everything about the "Big Dipper" was unprecedented. He set a new standard for the game with his aggressive power moves, fall-away jump shots, and legendary endurance. Playing in a decade that saw basketball's attendance figures more than double, Chamberlain helped redefine the game. As *Sports Illustrated* summarized, he made the "white stars look like nothing."

During his 14-year NBA career, Chamberlain starred with the Philadelphia Warriors (1959–1962), San Francisco Warriors (1962–1965), Philadelphia 76ers (1965–1968), and Los Angeles Lakers (1968–1973). He often clashed with coaches and was accused by critics as being selfish and ego-driven. Yet for many people across the nation, most notably African-Americans, Wilt the Stilt was a heroic figure of power and independence.

South Vietnamese troops build a fortress for the people of Kham Duc in April 1962—part of the Strategic Hamlet Program developed by the governments of South Vietnam and the United States. The purpose of the program was to relocate villagers from their scattered homes to the new, guarded fortresses, thus protecting them from Vietcong guerrillas. Unfortunately, Vietcong penetration into the hamlets, along with reluctance on the part of peasants to leave homes where their ancestors were buried, made the program impracticable. Many villagers so resented their forced relocation that they joined forces with the Vietcong.

March 2: The sedative drug thalidomide is removed from Canadian shelves, as it has been shown to cause serious birth defects when taken by pregnant women. • Wilt Chamberlain of the Philadelphia Warriors scores an NBA-record 100 points versus the New York Knicks. He'll average a staggering 50.4 points per game for the season.

March 4: The first nuclear power plant in Antarctica begins operating at McMurdo Station.

March 5: After an almost 30-year tradition of aircraft excellence, the last Bendix race is held. Captain Bob Sowers pilots an Air Force B-58 Hustler from Los Angeles to New York in 2:00:56 to win the race.

March 9: The U.S. State Department affirms that U.S. pilots are flying training missions with South Vietnamese fliers.

March 15: Secretary of Defense Robert McNamara admits that U.S. military advisers in South Vietnam have returned fire against Communist guerrillas.

Spring: In a Greenwich Village café, Bob Dylan writes "Blowin' in the Wind" in a matter of minutes. The song catches on quickly around Village folk circles. • At a London fashion show, designer Mary Quant introduces the first in a line of vinyl dresses and coats.

March 26: The U.S. Supreme Court rules that no state can require racial segregation of interstate or intrastate transportation facilities.

April: After steel manufacturers, including U.S. Steel and Bethlehem Steel, announce major price increases, a furious President Kennedy compels them to rescind the increases.

April 3: The U.S. Department of Defense orders the complete racial integration of all military reserves, except the National Guard.

Communist troops at the Berlin Wall claim another victim. In April 1962 Klaus Brueske, a young East German, tried to drive his truck through a hole in the wall, but was gunned down by border guards. East Germans took desperate measures to escape in 1962. In September, 29 people tunneled under the wall. In November, eight escaped by crashing through gates in an armor-plated bus.

The Space Needle soars 605 feet above the grounds of the 1962 Seattle Century 21 Exhibition. The "World's Fair," as it was popularly known, covered 74 acres and had a 21st-century theme. Displays ran the gamut, from the high-tech World of Science to an adults-only, "topless" puppet show. More than 10 million people visited the extravaganza, including astronaut John Glenn and Rat Packer Sammy Davis, Jr. The Space Needle became an internationally known symbol for the Northwest's largest city.

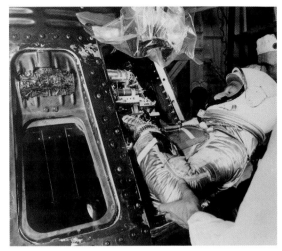

U.S. Secretary of Defense Robert McNamara strides purposefully along a village road during his May 1962 visit to South Vietnam. McNamara probably was the most influential of President Kennedy's advisers on the problem of Vietnam. Like most Americans, McNamara bought into the "domino theory," believing that if South Vietnam fell into Communist hands, other Southeast Asian nations also would fall to the Communists. McNamara recommended a graduated response to Communist advances, using money, materiel, and American military advisers to support South Vietnam. However, he did state as early as 1961 that "we should be prepared to introduce . . . combat forces if . . . necessary."

American astronaut Scott Carpenter is helped into his spacecraft by colleague John Glenn prior to blastoff on May 24, 1962. NASA launched this Aurora 7 mission to corroborate the success of the earlier manned orbital flight by Glenn. Carpenter successfully spent more than four hours in a state of weightlessness as he orbited Earth three times. NASA considered the mission a success, even though a technical problem caused the returning module to overshoot its intended target area by 250 miles. Carpenter was picked up unharmed by a backup ship.

The Trans World Airlines Terminal at New York's Idlewild Airport opened in 1962. Designed by noted Finnish architect Eero Saarinen, it featured curving contours, a soaring exterior, and a spacious interior—all suggesting a bird in flight. Saarinen was famous for his furniture as well, including the womb chair. He also designed the St. Louis Gateway Arch. To architecture critic Dennis Sharp, the TWA terminal was "self-assured, self-confident—even self-conscious." Sadly, Saarinen, who died in 1961, never saw his masterpiece completed.

April 8: Cuba announces that 1,179 prisoners taken in the 1961 Bay of Pigs invasion have been sentenced to 30 years in prison. All will be freed if a ransom of $62 million is paid. *See* April 14, 1962.

April 10: Stuart Sutcliffe, who played with the Beatles in 1960, dies of a brain hemorrhage at 21.

April 13: Welterweight boxer Benny "Kid" Paret, 25, dies from injuries suffered during his March 24 bout with welterweight champ Emile Griffith.

April 14: Sixty ill Bay of Pigs prisoners are released by Cuba after the U.S. promises to pay a $2.5 million ransom. *See* December 24, 1962.

April 21: The Seattle World's Fair opens. *See* October 21, 1962.

April 25: For the first time in three years, the U.S. resumes atmospheric nuclear testing, at Christmas Island in the Indian Ocean.

April 26: The U.S. spacecraft Ranger IV crashes on the moon, as intended, 64 hours after launch.

May: Tens of thousands of refugees from Red China stream into Hong Kong after the Chinese government unexpectedly relaxes border controls. The British government detains some 50,000 and forcibly repatriates them to China, but thousands more evade authorities and establish residency in Hong Kong. • During a visit to South Vietnam, Secretary of Defense Robert McNamara reports that "we are winning the war."

May 15: President Kennedy orders 4,000 Marines and other naval, air, and ground forces to Thailand to defend against a possible Communist incursion from Laos.

May 18: Teamsters President Jimmy Hoffa is indicted on charges of collecting money from an employer in violation of the Taft–Hartley Law.

In May 1961 President Kennedy issued Executive Order 10940 to establish a presidential committee on juvenile delinquency and youth crime. The committee was to recommend improvements to education and vocational training, as well as methods of crime prevention. A year later, on May 31, 1962, JFK noted that "30 or 35 or 40 percent of all our younger people across the country drop out of school before they've finished it." Central to the President's remarks was his feeling that "juvenile delinquency" was an unhelpful term. "It's really a question," he said, "of young people and their opportunity. . . ." In the meantime, many American teenagers spent idle hours unsupervised and ill-prepared to function in the America of Kennedy's New Frontier.

The career of singer Mary Wells took off in 1962. The first of the major stars for Berry Gordy's Motown Records, Wells recorded a string of hits that year, including "The One Who Really Loves You," "You Beat Me to the Punch," and "Two Lovers." In May 1964, during the height of Beatlemania, Wells soared to No. 1 on *Billboard*'s pop chart with "My Guy."

Engel v. Vitale

IN 1959 SCHOOL DISTRICT officials in Hyde Park, New York, required that children recite the following prayer in class: "Almighty God, we acknowledge our dependence upon thee and we beg thy blessings upon us, our parents, our teachers, and our country." A group of parents, believing in separation of church and state, sued the school district. The case was decided in the U.S. Supreme Court on June 25, 1962.

With one dissenting vote and two abstentions, the court decided that the school district's policy of prayer in school conflicted with the First Amendment guarantee of separation of church and state. The decision set off a firestorm of debate.

National Review, a conservative news magazine, called the decision "the fanatic logic of secularism." It accused the court of using its definition of the First Amendment as a "weapon to prevent the American people from the natural and normal experience of their faith." Indeed, 79 percent of Americans, according to a 1962 nationwide Gallup poll, favored the continuation of prayer in schools. The Catholic Church also criticized the ruling, and the Oklahoma City School District declared it would continue Bible readings in school.

Though many felt the court threatened religious liberty with its decision, others—including mainstream Protestant organizations, Jewish groups, and Christian publications such as *Christian Century*—backed the ruling. They argued that faith should be a private issue.

In 1963, in *School District of Abington Township v. Schempp,* the Supreme Court again ruled against prayer (and Bible reading) in schools. Debates about school prayer would rage throughout the decade and into the 21st century.

A church bulletin board illustrates the negative reaction many Americans had to *Engel v. Vitale,* the Supreme Court decision that prohibited mandated prayer in public schools. Here the decision is seen as a victory for Soviet Premier Khrushchev and communism. Other opponents, such as Reverend Billy Graham and Francis Cardinal Spellman, condemned the decision, and billboards demanding the impeachment of Chief Justice Earl Warren dotted America's highways. Supporters of the decision, including the American Civil Liberties Union, noted that students shouldn't be forced to participate in, or even listen to, state-supported prayer.

Rock 'n' roll idol Frankie Avalon allows himself to be tape-recorded by adoring fans. This photogenic Philadelphia native first hit the charts in 1958 with "De De Dinah," then recorded million-selling records— including his biggest hit, "Venus." Avalon's singing career was on the decline in 1962, although in '63 he would begin to star in a string of beach-party movies opposite Annette Funicello.

June 25: By a vote of 6–1, the U.S. Supreme Court holds in *Engel v. Vitale* that a daily reading in New York public schools of a prayer crafted by the state board of regents is unconstitutional.

June 27: President Kennedy warns Red China of American military intervention if that nation attacks the Formosan islands of Matsu and Quemoy.

June 28: In a landmark settlement of a libel case, jurors award radio personality John Henry Faulk $3.5 million in compensatory and punitive damages against a "watchdog" who branded Faulk a Communist sympathizer. Despite his vindication, CBS refuses to reinstate Faulk to his highly rated radio program.

July 3: After years of bloody warfare, France declares the independence of Algeria. The declaration follows an overwhelming affirmative vote for independence by the Algerian people.

July 6: For the first time, the U.S. explodes a hydrogen bomb on its own soil, underground at the Nevada proving grounds. • American author William Faulkner dies at 64.

July 9: Auroral displays are visible for thousands of miles following a U.S. test detonation of a 1.4-megaton thermonuclear device nearly 250 miles above Johnston Island in the Central Pacific.

July 9–August 4: Pop artist Andy Warhol makes a splash with his first art exhibit—32 paintings of Campbell's soup cans—at Ferus Gallery in West Hollywood, California.

July 10: An experimental U.S. satellite called Telstar, designed by AT&T's Bell Telephone Labs, is launched from Cape Canaveral. The satellite relays television images from Andover, Maine, to Britain and France.

July 20: President Kennedy names General Maxwell D. Taylor as chairman of the Joint Chiefs of Staff and appoints General Lyman Lemnitzer as U.S. commander in Europe.

Algerian soldiers weep with joy after their country gained independence from France. Algerians voted in favor of independence on July 1, 1962, and French President Charles de Gaulle declared the country an independent nation two days later. A French colony since 1830, Algeria began its rebellion against French rule beginning on November 1, 1954. The National Liberation Front (FLN) utilized guerrilla assaults to attack French positions for years. The liberation of Algeria marked another step in post-World War II European decolonization.

With a Thai boy by his side, an American soldier trains in Thailand in summer 1962. Although technically at peace, Thais were deeply concerned about the growing strength of Pathet Lao (Communist) forces in Laos, and feared that those forces would attack them. The Thai government allowed President Kennedy to station 5,000 American troops in Thailand to train for guerrilla warfare and intimidate the Communists. Later, when the Vietnam War heated up, the Thais provided about 12,000 troops to help America fight Communist forces. They also allowed U.S. planes to launch raids from bases in Thailand.

These two photographs show Honolulu's Diamond Head moments before and a split second after a U.S. nuclear weapon was exploded at Johnston Atoll, some 850 miles southwest of Hawaii. Night was momentarily turned into day. This was one of a series of 36 detonations in the spring and summer of 1962 at the Pacific testing grounds. Decades later, plutonium contamination from several aborted attempts remained in the atoll. These were the last U.S. atmospheric nuclear tests, which were banned by a 1963 treaty signed by the United States, Great Britain, and Soviet Union.

Pop artist Andy Warhol finished his *Campbell Soup Can, 19¢* in 1962. The son of a Pennsylvania coal miner, Warhol studied commercial art at Carnegie Mellon University and moved to New York City in 1949, where he worked as an illustrator. He emerged from relative obscurity in 1962 with his paintings of soup cans, which represented his view that commercial products could become subjects for artists. (Also, Campbell's soup was one of his favorite meals as a youth.) While many critics attacked Warhol for the banality of his subject matter, others saw his work as a telling comment on the impact of popular culture. Warhol would become the most famous Pop artist of the Sixties.

"The insects are winning: We're on a pesticide treadmill. The insects adapt to the particular insecticide used . . . forcing us to find ever deadlier new ones. . . . Thus the chemical war is never won, and all life is caught in its violent crossfire . . ."

—AUTHOR RACHEL CARSON, SILENT SPRING

Silent Spring

"THE FEW BIRDS seen anywhere were moribund; they trembled violently and could not fly. It was a spring without voices." With such foreboding lines, a mild-mannered former U.S. Fish and Wildlife biologist named Rachel Carson opened her wildly popular and controversial 1962 book, *Silent Spring.*

Carson's dire warnings about the destructive effects of the chemical pesticide DDT and other "elixirs of death" appeared first as a series of articles in *The New Yorker* in June 1962. When published as a book, her cautionary tale occupied *The New York Times* bestseller list for 31 weeks. A gifted writer, Carson sent chills into her readers with descriptions of an American landscape denuded by chlorinated hydrocarbons and an ecological system out of balance.

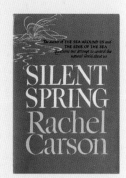

With *Silent Spring,* Carson redirected the discussion of nature and preservation in the early 1960s and helped to hatch the modern environmental movement with its emphasis on ecology. No longer was nature something "out there" to be preserved, but rather it was everywhere. "Man, however much he may like to pretend the contrary, is part of nature," Carson wrote. If water, soil, and birds—even the suburban front lawn— were at risk of contamination, so were people.

Silent Spring also pioneered a new tone for political activism. Carson presented an early feminist challenge to male experts and critics, who predictably referred to the book as an "emotional" outburst. Her critique of the booming chemical industry and the nascent war economy, and her emphasis on the personal responsibility of consumers, anticipated much of the country's grassroots activism of the 1960s. Carson died in 1964, eight years before Congress finally outlawed the use of DDT.

July 23: Jackie Robinson becomes the first African-American inducted into the Baseball Hall of Fame. • The Declaration on the Neutrality of Laos is signed in Geneva, Switzerland, by the U.S. and other nations.

August: In South Africa, Nelson Mandela is sentenced to five years in prison for leaving the country illegally. *See* June 12, 1964. • Billy Sol Estes, Texas millionaire and contributor to the Democratic Party, is indicted on charges of antitrust violations.

August 4: Film actress Marilyn Monroe, 36, dies in her California home from an overdose of prescription drugs.

August 6: Jamaica celebrates its independence from Britain's Commonwealth of Nations.

August 16: Beatles drummer Pete Best is fired by manager Brian Epstein and replaced by Ringo Starr.

August 17: An East German youth named Peter Fechter is slain by Communist border guards at the Berlin Wall.

August 29: Mal Goode becomes the first black news commentator for a television network, ABC.

September: Alone among America's states, Alabama, Mississippi, and South Carolina begin their school years with completely segregated school systems. Of the 3,047 southern and border-state school districts affected by the 1954 Supreme Court desegregation order, 960 have complied. • Harvard Professor Timothy Leary founds the International Foundation for Internal Freedom to promote LSD research. • Australian Rod Laver wins the U.S. Open to capture tennis's Grand Slam.

September 1: An earthquake in northwestern Iran kills 12,000 people. Another 10,000 are injured, and 100,000 are left homeless.

September 3: American poet and writer E. E. Cummings dies at 67. ➤

A young black activist goes limp as she is removed by local police from the Albany, Georgia, library in July 1962. The youth had staged a "read-in" at the segregated city library. Influenced by restaurant sit-ins, civil rights activists participated in various "ins" during the early 1960s, including swim-ins at segregated public pools and kneel-ins in churches. While their bold demonstrations often landed them in jail, these activists contributed mightily to the desegregation of the South.

On July 21, 1962, black citizens of Albany, Georgia, participate in a "pray-in" demonstration. Here, Chief of Police Laurie Pritchett orders the demonstrators to disperse. The Albany movement had begun in late 1961 when black improvement organizations targeted segregated facilities there. Martin Luther King, Jr., was arrested for demonstrating in Albany in December 1961, and the Albany movement continued throughout much of 1962. However, movement leaders failed to achieve their goals in Albany, largely because Chief Pritchett reacted nonviolently to their nonviolent protests. Hundreds of quiet arrests took the steam out of the movement. As historian Lee Formwalt noted, "King ran out of willing marchers before Pritchett ran out of jail space."

Helen Gurley Brown shocked conservative America with her 1962 book *Sex and the Single Girl*. Brown urged single women to find fulfilling careers and not feel guilty about premarital sex. As a pop culture figure, Brown became the Hugh Hefner of young single women. The success of her book led to a movie of the same name (whose plot had little to do with the book, but enhanced its popularity). In 1965 Brown became editor-in-chief of *Cosmopolitan*. She turned the rather stodgy magazine into a slick bible for young (and young-at-heart) women, quickly increasing its circulation to three million.

On the night of August 4–5, 1962, actress and Hollywood sex symbol Marilyn Monroe died from a barbiturate overdose. The police ruled that she had committed suicide. Monroe had been under psychiatric care (and prescribed numerous drugs by multiple doctors) and deeply depressed about her personal relationships with men. She was recently divorced from playwright Arthur Miller and was rumored to have had relationships with both John and Robert Kennedy. Her previous husband, baseball legend Joe DiMaggio, even blamed the Kennedys for her death. Monroe's apparent suicide became fodder for these British tabloids. The headline in the *Daily Sketch*, "GOODNIGHT HONEY...," is a dialogue quotation from the 1959 Monroe film *Some Like It Hot*.

British-born Alan Watts sorts through submissions for a haiku contest. After emigrating to the United States in 1938, Watts became widely known in the late 1950s and early '60s as an interpreter of Eastern religions. He began lecturing on college campuses, taking advantage of the popularity of his influential books, including *The Way of Zen*. Thousands of intelligent young people searching for alternatives saw in Watts a comprehensible guru, one who combined Eastern mysticism with fascinations for archery, calligraphy, cooking, and hiking in the wilderness.

1962

An apprehensive boy celebrates Jamaican independence on August 6, 1962. Presumably, he did not quite comprehend the joyousness of the occasion, as Jamaica ended more than 300 years of British rule. In 1961 the island's citizens had voted for complete independence from the British-dominated Federation of the West Indies. The United Kingdom fully accepted the decision. Princess Margaret and the Earl of Snowden joined 20,000 Jamaicans in the festivities at the national sports stadium.

On August 17, 1962, Sandra Wiseman, a nine-year-old British girl, became the first member of the public to receive a Telstar telephone call. Telstar, the first commercial communications space satellite, was developed by Bell Laboratories for American Telephone and Telegraph and launched under the auspices of NASA. Telstar transmitted television and telephone signals from the United States to Europe and became an overnight success. Indeed, polls showed that Telstar was better known in Britain than Sputnik, and it even became the subject of a popular rock instrumental by the Tornadoes. According to President Kennedy, the satellite proved to be "an outstanding example of the ways in which government and business can cooperate."

East German teenager Peter Fechter lies bleeding to death on the Communist side of the Berlin Wall on August 17, 1962. Fechter was shot by East German guards as he tried to scale the wall that had separated East and West Berlin since August 1961. As the guards ignored his cries for help, West Berliners nearly rioted, throwing stones across the wall and accusing the East German soldiers of murder. Fechter, the 50th East German known to be killed in 1961–62 while trying to escape, became a powerful symbol of the victims of Communist oppression.

On August 27, 1962, NASA's Mariner II spacecraft began its 109-day journey to the planet Venus. It reached its destination on December 14, becoming the first successful interplanetary probe. Before it lost contact, Mariner transmitted important scientific information back to NASA, including data about cosmic dust and solar winds. The launch was a major boost for the U.S. space program as well as a propaganda boon: America had beaten its Soviet rivals in at least this aspect of the space race.

Casey Stengel, manager of the New York Mets, contemplates his limited options during the team's debut season in 1962. The 71-year-old Stengel, who had managed the New York Yankees to seven world championships, watched in disbelief as his Mets lost a major-league record 120 games. Stengel quipped that the team showed "ways to lose I never knew existed." First baseman "Marvelous" Marv Throneberry typified the bumbling Mets. In one game, he slugged an apparent triple but was called out for not stepping on first *or* second base.

A salesperson pitches color television, the great status symbol of the early 1960s. Although RCA's David Sarnoff predicted that most American homes would have color TV sets by 1963, only about 3 percent of homes did that year. NBC's successful *Walt Disney's Wonderful World of Color,* introduced in 1961, sparked considerable interest but it was not until 1972 that more than half of American homes were equipped with color televisions. Not only were color TVs pricey in the 1960s, but conversion to color was also expensive for production companies and networks.

In 1962 pop singer Tony Bennett recorded his signature mega-hit "I Left My Heart in San Francisco." Bennett first performed this classic song at the Fairmont Hotel on Nob Hill in San Francisco, as he sang a hymn of praise to one of America's great cities. Bennett maintained his popularity in the midst of the rock revolution in spite of his mellow, crooner's style, which was more reminiscent of Frank Sinatra's than Elvis Presley's. In fact, Bennett would remain popular with young people well into the 21st century.

The Jetsons, a spin-off of the wildly popular Hanna–Barbera cartoon *The Flintstones,* premiered on ABC in September 1962. Although the show was pulled after 24 episodes, it became a cartoon classic. The traditionally nuclear Jetsons—and such characters as Astro the robot dog and the mean Mr. Spacely—lived in a futuristic society with a dazzlingly silly array of automated gadgets. The original episodes did so well in syndication that new episodes appeared from 1984 to 1987.

September 7: President Kennedy asks Congress for authority to call up 150,000 reservists if the Cuba situation worsens.

September 9: Red China shoots down a U.S.-built U-2 spy plane flown by Nationalist China.

September 11: Wernher von Braun, director of the Huntsville, Alabama, space center, tells President Kennedy that JFK's promise to land men on the moon before the end of the decade will be realized.

September 14: Twenty-nine people from East Germany escape by way of a tunnel (413 feet long, 20 feet deep) under the Berlin Wall.

September 18: Edward Kennedy, youngest brother of President John Kennedy, is elected to serve the state of Massachusetts in the U.S. Senate.

Autumn: Some 10,000 American military personnel are advising, training, and otherwise assisting South Vietnamese forces in the fight against the Communist North.

September 23: The recently completed Lincoln Center in New York City welcomes the New York Philharmonic for the first time.

September 25: With a first-round knockout, boxer Sonny Liston takes the heavyweight crown from Floyd Patterson.

September 26: Mississippi state police prevent African-American James Meredith, escorted by federal marshals, from registering at the segregated University of Mississippi. *See* September 30, 1962.

September 28: U.S. Secretary of Defense Robert McNamara says the U.S. is prepared to use nuclear weapons to protect American interests in Berlin. • Los Angeles Dodgers speedster Maury Wills logs his final stolen base of the season, No. 104, a major-league record.

In the early 1960s, many southern white women shared the same views as their men: that white liberals in the North were trying to destroy their way of life. They considered the forces for integration—the NAACP, the U.S. Supreme Court, the Kennedys, and Martin Luther King, Jr.—as the South's greatest enemies. According to these women, President John F. Kennedy was a tyrant and a treasonist who was worthy of impeachment.

Comedian Vaughn Meader's album *The First Family* flew off the shelves in 1962 and '63. With an uncanny ability to mimic the voices of the Kennedys, Meader amused millions with his sometimes gentle, sometimes acerbic satire. Especially pointed were jokes about the omnipresence of the Kennedys. In one sketch, a bedded down Jackie and Jack say goodnight to each other—then to Bobby, Ethel, Ted, Peter Lawford, and others. Another hilarious bit includes world summit leaders ordering sandwiches during a lunch break. Essentially a one-voice wonder, Meader saw his career as a comedian collapse after JFK was assassinated in 1963.

The television sitcom *The Beverly Hillbillies* ran on CBS from 1962 to 1971. After discovering oil on his backwoods property, the suddenly wealthy Jed Clampett (played by Buddy Ebsen, *far right*) moved his family to Beverly Hills, California. His kin included (*from left to right*) Jethro Bodine (Max Baer, Jr.), Elly May Clampett (Donna Douglas), and Granny (Irene Ryan). In each episode, culture clash was the premise of seemingly every joke. The popular series was enhanced by a catchy bluegrass theme song, performed by Flatt and Scruggs.

White segregationists throw bricks, rocks, and soda bottles at federal marshals in downtown Oxford, Mississippi. The protesters opposed the use of force to enroll James Meredith as the first African-American at the University of Mississippi. Governor Ross Barnett fanned the flames, saying on statewide television on September 30 that Mississippi was under siege by federal forces (referring to the many federal marshals who had escorted Meredith). During rioting in Oxford on September 30 and October 1, two people were killed and scores were injured.

James Meredith and Ole Miss

WHEN A 29-YEAR-OLD black transfer student named James Meredith tried to register at the all-white University of Mississippi in fall 1962, it took an army to get him through the door. Protected only by a court order requiring that he be allowed to enroll, the Air Force veteran decided to challenge the state's Jim Crow policies of segregation. He was met with fierce resistance.

Mississippi Governor Ross Barnett blocked Meredith's entrance to Ole Miss and adamantly defended the state's white supremacist policy. U.S. Attorney General Robert Kennedy ordered 500 U.S. marshals to defend Meredith and help him proceed with enrollment. As Meredith attempted to register on September 30, students

"fought hand to hand" with federal marshals, according to *The New York Times,* and several marshals were injured when the crowd pummeled them with bricks, bottles, pipes, and gas bombs.

As several thousand rioting whites from throughout the state gathered to threaten Meredith's safety and civil rights, not to mention the safety of the city, it became clear that more federal help was required. The President called in 23,000 U.S. troops to restore order. By the time rioting ended on October 1, 160 marshals had been injured and two white students had been killed. The ugly episode awakened the nation to white brutality in the South. As for Meredith, he enrolled at 8:30 A.M. on October 1. He graduated a year later.

September 30: Five hundred U.S. marshals escort James Meredith to the University of Mississippi. Meanwhile, a mob begins to riot on campus. President Kennedy federalizes the Mississippi National Guard and addresses the nation on television. *See October 1, 1962.* • Cesar Chavez starts the National Farm Workers Association (NFWA) in Fresno, California. The association will become a voice for the thousands of migratory farmworkers in the area. • The New York Mets set a major-league record with 120 losses.

October: The U.S. federal government begins to stock approximately 36,000 public buildings selected for use as civil defense shelters with food, water, and other provisions.

October 1: About 23,000 federal troops are needed to end the rioting at Ole Miss. Two men have been killed and hundreds injured. James Meredith enrolls at 8:30 A.M. *See August 18, 1963.* • After a series of guest hosts since Jack Paar's departure, Johnny Carson takes over as host of NBC-TV's *The Tonight Show.*

October 3: U.S. astronaut Wally Schirra orbits Earth six times.

October 5: The Beatles release "Love Me Do," which will climb to No. 17 on the British charts, making it their first hit.

October 9: Uganda becomes independent from Britain.

October 11: The Second Ecumenical Council of the Vatican (also known as Vatican Council II) convenes in Rome. It is just the 21st world gathering of Catholic Church leaders in the institution's 2,000-year history. Their agenda includes accessible language during Mass, avoidance of conflict with non-Catholics, and meaningful ritual.

October 15: U.S. spy plane photos reveal that Soviet-made, surface-to-surface, medium-range ballistic missiles are on Cuban soil. The White House keeps this information private for one week. *See October 22, 1962.*

Political cartoonist "Herblock" (Herbert L. Block) aims a bomb at the House Un-American Activities Committee in this 1962 drawing. The committee was in the midst of investigating a small pacifist group, Women Strike for Peace (WSP), which had been founded in November 1961. The doltish committee member who arrives late is sure that some aspect of what is being investigated must be un-American. According to the WSP's account, the women who testified "made a laughing-stock of HUAC."

"I Came In Late. Which Was It That Was Un-American—Women Or Peace?"

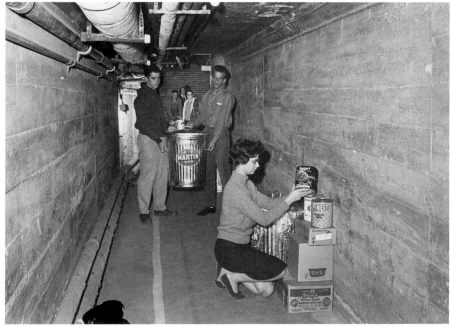

Students at National College in Kansas City stock a campus tunnel with supplies in October 1962 in case they have to take cover during a Soviet nuclear attack. Despite some misgivings, President Kennedy in May 1961 called for a tripling of federal spending on civil defense. He argued that the program was a kind of insurance policy that "we could never forgive ourselves for forgoing in the event of catastrophe." JFK may have been responding as much to Republican criticism as to a real hope of saving many lives. Nevertheless, in October 1962 the federal government began stocking with necessary provisions approximately 36,000 public buildings selected as civil defense shelters. Coincidentally, the Cuban Missile Crisis developed late that month.

Eleanor Roosevelt hosts *Prospects of Mankind,* a television series aimed at educating viewers about the prospects and perils of the future. Her efforts on the show indicated Roosevelt's commitment to public life long after the 1945 death of her husband, President Franklin Roosevelt. In 1961 President Kennedy reappointed Eleanor Roosevelt as a delegate to the United Nations. She encouraged the young president to negotiate with the Soviets—but with caution. In her last years, Roosevelt worked on her final book, *Tomorrow Is Now.* She died on November 7, 1962.

The cartoon character Mr. Zip helped the U.S. government convince Americans to accept a new mail coding system to speed up delivery. The ZIP code (for Zone Improvement Plan) was introduced by Postmaster General J. Edward Day in fall 1962. At a time when Americans feared being reduced to impersonal numbers, the perky Mr. Zip was an important "salesperson." He pitched his favorite code until his retirement in 1986.

The first James Bond film, *Dr. No,* premiered in Great Britain in October 1962. The plot of the movie, adapted from an Ian Fleming novel, places Bond in Jamaica looking for the whereabouts of a missing fellow agent. He experiences harrowing adventures, hair-breadth escapes, and glamorous sexual encounters. He emerges in the end by defeating villain Dr. No and getting the girl, played by the voluptuous Ursula Andress. Fans loved the movie, the concept, and especially Sean Connery as the suave, sexy, ingenious Agent 007. The Bond character was a natural for a generation in the throes of the Cold War and the sexual revolution. Stories about President Kennedy's penchant for Bond novels undoubtedly fueled the public's interest in *Dr. No* and its many sequels.

Led by Frankie Valli (*top*), the Four Seasons cranked out a string of hits, beginning with "Sherry" and "Big Girls Don't Cry" in 1962. The group's signature feature was lead singer Valli's piercing falsetto voice. The Four Seasons probably are the world's most successful white doo-wop group. By the 2000s, they had sold more than 100 million records.

October 16: The New York Yankees defeat the San Francisco Giants 1–0 in Game 7 of the World Series. With runners on second and third in the ninth inning, Yankees second baseman Bobby Richardson snares Willie McCovey's line drive to end the game.

October 20: Indian and Chinese forces exchange fire at Ladakh, India. Border disputes throughout the year contribute to a marked deterioration of India–China relations.

October 21: The Seattle World's Fair closes, ending a successful six-month run that attracted nearly 10 million visitors.

October 22: In a nationally televised address, President Kennedy announces a sea and air "quarantine" of offensive military supplies sent to Cuba. *See* October 23, 1962. • The first 10 Minuteman I ICBMs are placed on operational alert at Malmstrom AFB in Montana.

October 23: The USSR states that the U.S. embargo of Cuba forces the possibility of thermonuclear war. *See* October 25, 1962.

October 25: President Kennedy asserts that the U.S. blockade of Cuba will continue. He also agrees to have talks with United Nations Secretary General U Thant about possible U.S.–Soviet negotiations. *See* October 26, 1962. • Novelist John Steinbeck is awarded the 1962 Nobel Prize for Literature.

October 26: In a letter to President Kennedy, Soviet Premier Khrushchev offers to remove missiles from Cuba under United Nations supervision. The following day, in a public address, Khrushchev will demand that the U.S. do the same with the missiles it keeps in Turkey. *See* November 1, 1962. • Indian Prime Minister Jawaharlal Nehru requests U.S. military supplies to help with its territorial fight with Red China. The U.S. agrees.

October 30: The UN General Assembly votes 56–42 to deny the admission of Red China.

This declassified photograph, taken during the Cuban Missile Crisis in October 1962, shows a Medium Range Ballistic Missile (MRBM) launch site in San Cristobal, Cuba. Visible are a missile erector, fuel tank trailers, and oxidizer tank trailers. Photographs such as this convinced President Kennedy that the Soviet Union was attempting to accelerate its missile program and directly threaten the United States. This evidence also was used by Adlai Stevenson, the U.S. ambassador to the United Nations, to convince the world body of Soviet perfidy.

The Joint Chiefs of Staff pose for an official photograph. Pictured left to right are Earle Wheeler, Curtis LeMay, Maxwell Taylor, George W. Anderson, Jr., and David Shoup. The Joint Chiefs had advised President Kennedy to launch air strikes against the Soviet missile bases in Cuba and invade the small country. LeMay, former commander of the Strategic Air Command, was especially vociferous. He claimed that substituting a blockade for more direct military action was "almost as bad as the appeasement at Munich," in which Adolf Hitler bluffed and bullied the British in 1938. The President's brother, Attorney General Robert Kennedy, tried to steer the committee away from recommending an aggressive military response.

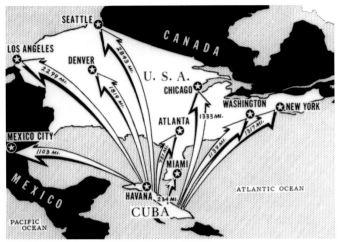

This map, drawn in October 1962, suggests the closeness of major U.S. cities to various points in Cuba that might harbor missiles. The medium-range Soviet missiles in Cuba could hit Miami and Atlanta with alarming ease, while the intermediate missiles had a range of about 2,100 miles, covering most of the United States. Young children across America picked up on the unease of adults and became terrified; many suffered sleeplessness, and prayed that they and their families would not be annihilated.

On October 22, 1962, passers-by in Los Angeles watch President Kennedy's televised address through a storefront window. Kennedy told upwards of 100 million viewers (the largest audience to watch a presidential address to that point) that the United States would not allow the Soviet Union's missiles to remain in Cuba. He announced a naval quarantine of the island to block further delivery of Soviet weapons. He also asserted that any nuclear missile attack on the United States from Cuba would be considered an act of war by the USSR and would warrant a full retaliatory attack on the Soviet Union. In general, Americans were calm but worried after the announcement.

With cameras clicking on October 23, President Kennedy officially approves the arms embargo against Cuba. The President wanted to avoid a rash provocation of the Soviets and thought that a "quarantine" (as Kennedy called it) gave him room to maneuver. The Soviets ultimately turned their ships around. However, scary moments arose when U.S. Admiral George Anderson claimed that he, not Kennedy, had the authority to order attacks on Russian ships. Secretary of Defense Robert McNamara disabused the admiral of that notion and proclaimed to an aide, "That's the end of Anderson."

Khrushchev Responds to JFK's "Threat"

YOU, MR. PRESIDENT, are not declaring a quarantine, but rather issuing an ultimatum, and you are threatening that if we do not obey your orders, you will then use force. Think about what you are saying! And you want to persuade me to agree to this! What does it mean to agree to these demands? It would mean for us to conduct our relations with other countries not by reason, but by yielding to tyranny. You are not appealing to reason; you want to intimidate us.

No, Mr. President, I cannot agree to this, and I think that deep inside, you will admit that I am right. I am convinced that if you were in my place you would do the same....

Unfortunately, people of all nations, and not least the American people themselves, could suffer heavily from madness such as this, since with the appearance of modern types of weapons, the USA has completely lost its former inaccessibility.

—LETTER FROM SOVIET PREMIER NIKITA KHRUSHCHEV
TO PRESIDENT KENNEDY, OCTOBER 24, 1962

November: The U.S. Post Office introduces Mr. Zip, a cartoon character created to prepare Americans for the upcoming Zone Improvement Plan (ZIP), which will add a five-digit code to all domestic addresses. All U.S. addresses are scheduled to have the code by July 1, 1963. • In Renton, Washington, Boeing unveils its new 727 airliner, which is designed to take off from and land on relatively short runways.

November 1: Fidel Castro publicly rejects any form of international inspection of Cuba. *See* November 2, 1962.

November 2: President Kennedy announces that Soviet missiles in Cuba are being dismantled and crated for shipment back to Russia. *See* November 12, 1962.

November 6 The UN General Assembly votes 67–16 to approve a request for UN sanctions against South Africa until it ends apartheid (institutionalized racial segregation).

November 7: Former First Lady Eleanor Roosevelt, a humanitarian political activist to the end, dies at 78. • As he concedes defeat in the 1962 California gubernatorial race, Richard Nixon informs reporters that they "won't have Nixon to kick around anymore." It is widely assumed that Nixon's political life has ended.

November 12: In a letter to President Kennedy, Soviet Premier Nikita Khrushchev confirms that all Soviet missiles have been removed from Cuba. *See* November 20, 1962.

November 16: Atomic spy David Greenglass is released from New York's Federal House of Detention after serving 9½ years of a 15-year sentence for espionage. His testimony was instrumental in sending his sister, Ethel Rosenberg, to the electric chair, for espionage.

November 18: Danish nuclear physicist Niels Bohr, known as "the father of atomic energy," dies at 77. ➤

On October 23, Cuban Prime Minister Fidel Castro delivers a fiery address to the Cuban people in response to President Kennedy's announcement of a naval quarantine of Cuba. Castro condemned U.S. actions, denied the presence of offensive missiles in Cuba, and concluded that he would "acquire the arms we feel like acquiring, and we don't have to give an account to the imperialists." Actually, Castro had allowed Soviets to station missiles on Cuban soil, but he had done so reluctantly. He feared that the missiles might provoke the United States and damage his image in other Latin American nations.

Checkout boys at a supermarket in Los Angeles wonder where to put all the cartfuls of groceries as Angelenos do some serious panic buying during the 1962 Cuban Missile Crisis. City Civil Defense Director Joseph Quinn had advised residents to buy two weeks' worth of supplies, but then added that they should remain calm! Although most Americans were gravely concerned about the crisis (it inspired Bob Dylan to write "A Hard Rain's A-Gonna Fall"), citizens did in fact remain calm. As scholar Tom W. Smith concludes, "There is little evidence of widespread stress, anxiety, or psychological harm" caused by the events of October 1962.

> "Do you, Ambassador Zorin, deny that the USSR has placed and is placing medium- and intermediate-range missiles and sites in Cuba? Don't wait for the translation! Yes or no?... I am prepared to wait for my answer until hell freezes over, if that's your decision. And I am also prepared to present the evidence in this room."
>
> —U.S. AMBASSADOR ADLAI STEVENSON TO SOVIET AMBASSADOR VALERIAN ZORIN AT A UN SECURITY COUNCIL MEETING, OCTOBER 25, 1962

U.S. Ambassador Adlai Stevenson (*center*) discusses the Cuban Missile Crisis during a UN Security Council meeting in New York on October 25. Although Stevenson initially doubted that Soviet missiles in Cuba posed a great threat to U.S. security, he forcefully attacked the Soviets in this meeting for lying about the existence of the missiles. He also defended President Kennedy's decision to quarantine the island. When Valerian Zorin, the Soviet ambassador to the UN, refused to say whether his country had stationed missiles in Cuba, Stevenson said he would wait "until hell freezes over" for the response. Ultimately, bilateral negotiations—not the UN—defused the crisis.

The fate of the world may have been saved by a secret conversation held between U.S. Attorney General Robert Kennedy and Soviet Ambassador Anatoly Dobrynin (*pictured*). Meeting on the night of October 26 at the Soviet Embassy, Dobrynin told Kennedy that the Soviets would consider removing their missiles from Cuba if the U.S. would remove its Jupiter missiles from Turkey. Robert Kennedy called the President, who responded favorably to the proposal. From there, the White House and Kremlin hammered out an agreement. Each would pack up their respective missiles, thus ending the crisis.

A Soviet freighter carrying missile parts sails away from Cuba on November 9, 1962. The press reported that the Soviets had agreed to remove the weapons after Kennedy had pledged that the United States would not invade Cuba. Aerial reconnaissance photos satisfied Washington that the missiles had been removed. On November 21, JFK proclaimed the quarantine terminated. In retrospect, analysts and historians determined that the crisis was precipitated, in large part, by Khrushchev's alarm at Kennedy's October 1961 proclamation of vast U.S. superiority in nuclear missiles.

1962

In October 1962, Johnny Carson first hosted *The Tonight Show* on NBC. The Nebraska-raised Carson, who had hosted ABC's popular quiz show *Who Do You Trust?*, turned *The Tonight Show* into a runaway hit and became an American cultural icon in the 1960s and beyond. Carson combined his sharp wit, Midwestern innocence, and East Coast sophistication in ways that appealed to millions of Americans. Such features as the opening monologue, Carnac the Magnificent, and the on-screen marriage of Tiny Tim and Miss Vicki in 1969 helped propel the show to late-night ratings dominance for three decades. His popularity undoubtedly altered the sleep and sexual habits of millions of Americans.

The Beatles weathered a turbulent year in 1962. The band from Liverpool, England, was rejected by Decca Records after their audition on January 1. Moreover, former member Stuart Sutcliffe died on April 10, and Ringo Starr replaced Pete Best as the group's drummer. Nevertheless, the Beatles—Starr, George Harrison, John Lennon, and Paul McCartney (*left to right*)—persevered. Throughout the year, they played more than 300 gigs in Great Britain and Germany. In October they released "Love Me Do," their first single for EMI Records and producer George Martin.

In *The Manchurian Candidate,* captured American soldier Raymond Shaw (played by Laurence Harvey, *standing*) undergoes brainwashing by Communist forces in Korea and is turned into a programmed assassin. This 1962 political thriller, directed by John Frankenheimer and starring Frank Sinatra, was a parable of Cold War intrigue. The film's complicated plot sees Shaw, managing to fight through his brainwashing, bring a twist to his mission to murder a presidential candidate.

Actresses Joan Crawford (*left*) and Bette Davis strike grim poses as sisters Blanche and Jane, respectively, in the scary 1962 film *Whatever Happened to Baby Jane?*. In a case of art imitating reality, the two aging actresses played two aging actresses. Jane hates Blanche, whose career is about to make a comeback via television, so she binds and gags her in the back bedroom of their spooky home. Reportedly, Davis and Crawford despised each other. In one scene, Davis kicks Crawford down some stairs, but allegedly the kick was for real. This film was the first of several horror thrillers about nasty older women, including *Hush . . . Hush, Sweet Charlotte,* starring Davis and Olivia de Havilland.

Richard Nixon addresses the press on November 7, 1962, after losing the California gubernatorial race. Nixon had run successfully for Congress in 1946 and the Senate in 1950, and he had served as vice president under Dwight Eisenhower from 1953 to 1961. He also nearly won the presidential election in 1960. In the race for governor, California Democrat Pat Brown defeated Nixon by almost 300,000 votes. Nixon, exhausted and defensive in this press conference, attacked the media for being unfair to him. He concluded with his famous promise: "You won't have Nixon to kick around anymore."

The Brill Building

BEFORE THE NEXUS of Sixties rock shifted to Liverpool and London, it was headquartered at 1619 Broadway in Manhattan at a music-publishing mecca known as the Brill Building—where Tin Pan Alley met teen pop.

More than 160 music publishers had offices in the building in the early 1960s. The "Brill Building sound" was the brainchild of record producer Don Kirshner (who would go on to form the Monkees) and his partner, Al Nevins. Kirshner attracted teams of young songwriters, among them Carole King, Neil Diamond, Neil Sedaka, Burt Bacharach, and a young kid from Queens, New York, named Paul Simon. Ensconced in tiny cubicles, these tunesmiths labored for about $150 a week, cranking out the hits that dominated America's pop music charts from 1958 to 1964.

Burt Bacharach

"[Kirshner] created this family of competitive siblings who all wanted to please him," recalled Brill songwriter Cynthia Weil. "And the way we pleased him was to write hit songs." The Brill era soundtrack boasted such standards as "The Loco-Motion," recorded by Little Eva, "Will You Love Me Tomorrow?" by the Shirelles, and "Breaking Up Is Hard to Do" by Neil Sedaka.

November 20: President Kennedy lifts the U.S. naval blockade of Cuba. Premier Khrushchev promises that all Soviet jet bombers will be removed from Cuba in 30 days. • President Kennedy signs an executive order that bans discrimination in government-sponsored housing. • Red China orders a cease-fire in its border war with India.

December: Ferocious snows and cold across the eastern and middle U.S. leave 112 people dead. Florida's citrus crop is badly damaged. • The Esalen Institute is founded near Monterey, California. Blending East and West philosophies, Esalen will attract philosophers, scientists, psychologists, artists, and religious thinkers to lead experimental workshops.

Early December: London suffocates beneath the worst smog in 10 years. It subsequently must deal with a particularly severe winter.

December 2: After visiting South Vietnam, Senate Majority Leader Mike Mansfield unnerves President Kennedy by saying that President Ngo Dinh Diem has wasted the $2 billion in aid that the U.S. has given to his country.

December 6: Thirty-seven miners die in Carmichaels, Pennsylvania, after being trapped in an underground explosion.

December 7: Internationally acclaimed Norwegian opera star Kirsten Flagstad, a preeminent Wagnerian soprano for 20 years, dies at 67.

December 15: British-born film star and director Charles Laughton dies at 63.

December 17: A federal jury in Washington, D.C., fines the U.S. Communist Party $10,000 on each of 12 counts of failing to register as an agent of the USSR.

December 24: The last of the more than 1,100 Bay of Pigs prisoners released by Cuba arrive in Miami.

One Day in the Life of Ivan Denisovich, a novel by Soviet dissident Alexander Solzhenitsyn, was published in 1962. The author had served with distinction in the Red Army during World War II, but he was arrested and sentenced to a Soviet labor camp in 1945 for writing a letter critical of Joseph Stalin. The novel, allowed to be published by Soviet Premier Nikita Khrushchev after it had been banned earlier, dealt with the excruciatingly painful attempts of one man to survive another day in a labor camp. Clearly autobiographical, it served as a telling criticism of the horrors of life under Stalin. In 1974 Solzhenitsyn was deported after writing his devastating memoir, *The Gulag Archipelago.* He settled in the United States.

A dog in Amsterdam models a flip hairdo wig created by a Dutch hairdresser in November 1962. The flip style competed with Jackie Kennedy's bouffant hairdo that year. Mattel Corporation's Barbie Doll may have worn the most famous flip in 1962, as Barbie's "do" influenced millions of young girls all over the world. Patty Duke would further popularize the flip on *The Patty Duke Show,* which debuted in 1963.

In 1962 William Burroughs's controversial novel, *Naked Lunch,* was published in the United States. A pastiche of allegory, science fiction, and nonlinear space and time, the work became the object of cult fascination. As critic Gary Kamiya put it, Burroughs was the "20th-century's drug culture's Poe," and the novel foreshadowed "the literature of pure experience." *Naked Lunch* also was important because it became the object of a celebrated obscenity trial in Boston in 1965. The court's ruling that the book was not obscene was a landmark that helped to end literary censorship in the United States.

A British bobby tries to protect himself from a suffocating smog that enveloped much of southern England on December 5, 1962. In spite of the 1956 Clean Air Act (passed after the great smog of 1952), some areas of Great Britain suffered from an excess of coal burning, which led to horrific incidents such as this one, in which 750 people died. This was, however, the last major smog incident, as the use of coal diminished.

The Ken Kesey novel *One Flew Over the Cuckoo's Nest* became a cult classic for many young people in the 1960s. Published in 1962, the novel focuses on a battle between McMurphy, a con man who pretends to be insane to escape work on a prison farm, and Nurse Ratched, the head nurse at the institution to which he is committed. McMurphy attempts to help fellow inmates gain a degree of autonomy, which leads ultimately to his own death after a lobotomy. As a symbol of individual rebellion against corporate authority, the story resonated deeply among cultural rebels.

Vatican II

IN 1962 POPE JOHN XXIII called the Second Vatican Council of Bishops in Rome to assess the state of the Catholic Church in the modern world. Through Vatican II reforms, the Church made its theology worldly, one that members could experience more personally.

The results of Vatican II, which did not close until 1965, were far-reaching. The Church replaced the Latin Mass with the vernacular, allowed meat on Fridays, and gave the laity increased power. Lay Catholics would replace many priests and nuns as teachers and as trustees for Catholic colleges and organizations. The Church also liberalized its relations with non-Catholics on such issues as heresy and marriage.

More profoundly, the Church encouraged its flock to directly engage the political struggles of the time. Catholic priests were allowed to take active roles in political struggle, be it practicing liberation theology in Central America or opposing the war in Vietnam. Priests Daniel and Philip Berrigan, activists in civil rights and anti-war movements, epitomized this new engagement. The brothers even became heroes of the New Left when they went "underground" to avoid charges of destroying draft records. Progressive organizations were formed as a result of Vatican II, including the Catholic Social Justice Lobby, the National Black Sisters Conference, and the National Office for Black Catholics.

Not everyone was happy with the liberalized Catholic Church. Wrote essayist Richard Rodriguez: "One Sunday I would watch dancers in leotards perform some kind of ballet in front of the altar; one Sunday there would be a rock mass. . . . I longed for the Latin mass. Incense. Music of Bach. Ceremonies of candles and acolytes." Rodriguez, though, was in the minority.

Pope John XXIII

1962

New & Notable

Books

All My Pretty Ones by Anne Sexton
Fail-Safe by Eugene Burdick and
    Harvey Wheeler
Pale Fire by Vladimir Nabokov
The Reivers by William Faulkner
Sex and the Single Girl
    by Helen Gurley Brown
Ship of Fools by Katherine Anne Porter
The Thin Red Line by James Jones

Movies

Days of Wine and Roses
Dr. No
How the West Was Won
Jules et Jim
Lawrence of Arabia
The Longest Day
The Manchurian Candidate
The Miracle Worker
The Music Man
To Kill a Mockingbird
Whatever Happened to Baby Jane?

Songs

"Can't Help Falling in Love"
    by Elvis Presley
"Don't Make Me Over"
    by Dionne Warwick
"Duke of Earl" by Gene Chandler
"He's a Rebel" by the Crystals
"I Left My Heart in San Francisco"
    by Tony Bennett
"The Loco-Motion" by Little Eva
"Monster Mash"
    by Bobby "Boris" Pickett
"Sherry" by the Four Seasons
"Soldier Boy" by the Shirelles
"Wipe Out" by the Surfaris

Television

The Beverly Hillbillies
Combat!
The Jetsons
The Lucy Show
McHale's Navy
The Match Game

Theater

*A Funny Thing Happened on the Way to
    the Forum*
Stop the World—I Want to Get Off!
A Thousand Clowns
Who's Afraid of Virginia Woolf?

Teamsters Union President Jimmy Hoffa appears at a news conference on December 23, 1962, after a judge declared a mistrial due to a hung jury in his conspiracy trial. A controversial labor leader, Hoffa was elected president of the Teamsters Union in 1957 after previous leader Dave Beck had been sentenced to prison. Hoffa was reelected in 1960. Convinced that Hoffa was involved in organized crime and racketeering, Robert Kennedy doggedly tracked Hoffa down. Kennedy did so first as chief counsel of the Senate committee investigating union corruption in the late 1950s, then as attorney general in his brother's administration, when he charged the Teamsters leader with misappropriating pension funds. Hoffa temporarily was able to escape the Kennedy net with the 1962 hung jury.

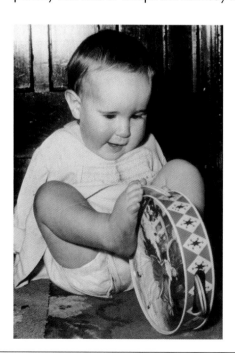

Richard Satherley (*pictured*) was born without arms because his mother took the antinausea drug thalidomide while she was pregnant. Marketed by a German company beginning in the mid-1950s, thalidomide became the drug of choice for combating morning sickness. However, the drug never was tested on pregnant animals, and mothers who took it bore children with severe birth defects. Because of the dedication of Frances Kelsey, a U.S. Food and Drug Administration evaluator, the drug never was approved for sale in the United States. However, some pregnant American women did take the drug while in Europe or Canada. A tightly controlled version of the drug is currently used, but only to treat leprosy.

民主和自由」传统……

肯尼迪：請允許我介绍一下是国「伟大的

江有生

In this 1962 cartoon from the Chinese Communist *People's Daily,* President Kennedy announces: "Allow me to show you some of the great democratic and free traditions of the USA." The saw is labeled "Smith Act" and the hammer "McCarran Act," pieces of congressional legislation designed to stamp out communism in the United States. Anti-Americanism in China and other Communist nations was especially virulent in 1962. Communist governments were upset by increased U.S. military aid to South Vietnam, U-2 spy plane surveillance flights over mainland China, and what the Chinese saw as an embarrassment for world communism during the Cuban Missile Crisis.

Peter O'Toole (as T. E. Lawrence, *right*) and Omar Sharif (as Sherif Ali) starred in *Lawrence of Arabia,* a 1962 epic directed by David Lean. The film follows the larger-than-life Lawrence as he attempts to create an Arab state during the chaos of World War I. Though the movie ran 216 minutes and featured no female characters, audiences were gripped by the story and mesmerized by the magnificent sights and sounds. The sprawling spectacle garnered seven Academy Awards, including best picture and best director.

SDS and the Port Huron Statement

O N JUNE 15, 1962, about 60 leaders of the newly formed Students for a Democratic Society (SDS)—most from elite universities—issued the Port Huron Statement in Port Huron, Michigan. It was the defining document of the New Left.

Authored primarily by Tom Hayden, a 22-year-old former editor of the University of Michigan's student newspaper and a civil rights activist, the Port Huron Statement set forth an "agenda for a generation." It began, "We are people of this generation, bred in at least modest comfort, housed now in universities, looking uncomfortably to the world we inherit." The statement itemized pervasive racism, the prospect of nuclear war, and the alienation of modern life as crises demanding "encounter and resolution."

The document argued that the goal of society should be more authentic human relationships: "We would replace power and personal uniqueness rooted in possession, privilege, and circumstance by power and uniqueness rooted in love, reflectiveness, reason, and creativity." Most important, the students called for a new "participatory democracy" in which matters "of basic social consequences"—in the workplace, in communities, in neighborhoods, on campuses—be discussed and decided by the people. The critique of modern society, coupled with the statement's optimistic view of human nature, inspired countless student activists for the rest of the decade and beyond.

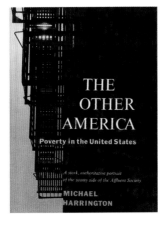

Michael Harrington's *The Other America,* published in 1962, was a scathing indictment of an affluent nation's inability to handle chronic poverty. Harrington believed that dealing with "the culture of poverty," which he claimed afflicted 50 million Americans in the early 1960s, required the government to embrace social planning and a substantial and lasting financial commitment. Political grandstanding and Band-Aid solutions were not sufficient. Harrington's book so impressed the Johnson Administration that the author was invited to serve as an adviser to Sargent Shriver in waging LBJ's War on Poverty.

1963

The Fight for Freedom

FANNIE LOU HAMER, a voting rights activist in Mississippi, expressed how a lot of African-Americans felt in the mid-1960s: "We're tired of all this beatin', we're tired of takin' this. It's been a hundred years and we're still being beaten and shot at, crosses are being burned, because we want to vote."

Beginning with the sit-ins of 1960, civil rights activists waged a nonstop, nonviolent, grassroots campaign for equal rights in the United States for three hard years. While protesters won some minor concessions from southern segregationists in towns and cities throughout the old Confederacy, they had not yet gained a significant national victory. President John F. Kennedy demonstrated concern about the inequities that plagued black Americans, but he had not yet committed the power of his presidency to the struggle for racial justice in the United States.

In 1963 civil rights movement leaders greatly escalated their campaign for equal rights. Kennedy, in the last months of his life, responded by pledging his full support to their cause. He vowed he would pass a monumental civil rights bill that would ensure that the American people lived up to their professed ideals of equality and liberty for all.

In early April 1963, Martin Luther King, Jr., and thousands of civil rights protesters took to the streets in Birmingham, Alabama, to focus the attention of the nation on the evils of racism in the Deep South. King and his allies had targeted Birmingham for one reason. As King told Kennedy, it was "by far the worst big city in race relations in the United States." King went to protest

"We are just getting started. We are going to continue demonstrations every day until the white people of Birmingham realize that we are going to get what we want.... We are going to fill all the jails in Birmingham. We are going to turn Birmingham upside down and right side up."

—MARTIN LUTHER KING, JR.

On August 28, 1963, 250,000 people gathered in what at the time was the largest civil rights demonstration ever held, the March on Washington for Jobs and Freedom. Enduring the hot summer sun, participants crowded the Lincoln Memorial to listen to speeches from leaders of various civil rights organizations. In his "I Have a Dream" speech, Martin Luther King, Jr., (*pictured*) inspired millions.

in Birmingham not because he thought reform there would be easy but because he expected it to be nearly impossible. He wanted northern whites in general and the Kennedy Administration in particular to see that only national intervention could end the racist practices of the Jim Crow South.

Project C—for confrontation—began uneasily in Birmingham. The openly racist police chief, Bull Connor, arrested the protesters as they marched through the streets or staged sit-ins at stores and restaurants that refused to serve African-Americans. King himself, leading by example, was arrested on Good Friday.

While in jail, King wrote his most famous statement on the necessity of nonviolent struggle against racist injustice. In the margins of a smuggled-in newspaper, in a sentence that ran some 300 words, he responded to white Americans who kept urging African-Americans to be patient: "[W]hen you have seen vicious mobs lynch your mothers and fathers at will and drown your sisters and brothers at whim; when you have seen hate-filled policemen curse, kick, brutalize, and even kill your black brothers and sisters with impunity... when you have to concoct an answer for a five-year-old son asking in agonizing pathos: 'Daddy, why do white people treat colored people so mean?'... when you are humiliated day in and day out by nagging signs reading 'white' and 'colored'... when you are forever fighting a degenerating sense of 'nobodiness'; then you will understand why we find it difficult to wait."

What white Americans saw on their television screens two weeks later moved many of them further into sympathy for the civil rights cause. On May 2, with the Birmingham protest a month old, the organizers upped the stakes by launching a massive march of children and young people. Six hundred were arrested. The next day, another thousand marched. With his jails already full, Bull Connor decided simply to attack the children. First, firefighters blasted youngsters with the full force of their hoses. They were knocked to the ground, rolled mercilessly along the concrete, and even smashed into brick walls. In addition, police brought out their German shepherds, who snapped at the protesters and bit several teenagers.

Network television cameras recorded the action. CBS news analyst Eric Sevareid summarized the result: "A newspaper or television picture of a snarling police dog set upon a human being is recorded in the permanent photoelectric file of every human brain." Throughout the United States—

The whole world watched as police and firefighters in Birmingham, Alabama, attacked anti-segregation protesters in spring 1963. Birmingham police released dogs and stung protesters with electric cattle prods. Meanwhile, local firefighters assaulted demonstrators with blasts of water strong enough to snap human bones.

Myrlie Evers consoles her son, Darrell, while attending the funeral of her late husband, slain civil rights activist Medgar Evers. During a funeral procession following the memorial service, at least 27 people were arrested when enraged African-Americans clashed with police in Jackson, Mississippi.

indeed, throughout the world—people saw the barbarous face of American racism, just as King and the movement activists had expected.

The events in Birmingham convinced President Kennedy that the time to act had arrived. Meanwhile, more controversy brewed in another part of Alabama. In June, Governor George Wallace refused to follow court orders permitting two black students to integrate the University of Alabama. After using federalized National Guard troops to force Wallace to back down, President Kennedy went on national television and threw himself, without equivocation, into the struggle for racial justice.

Kennedy gave one of the best speeches of his presidency, even though it was unscripted. "We are confronted primarily with a moral issue," he stated. "It is as old as the scriptures and as clear as the American Constitution. The heart of the question is whether all Americans are to be afforded equal rights and equal opportunities....A great change is at hand, and our task, our obligation, is to make that revolution, that change, peaceful and constructive." Echoing Martin Luther King, Kennedy asked white Americans, "Who among us would be content to have the color of his skin changed?...Who among us would then be content with counsels of patience and delay?" Kennedy promised to ask Congress to pass a comprehensive civil rights act that would guarantee that "race has no place in American life or law."

Horrifically, a few short hours after the nation heard their president, prominent civil rights activist Medgar Evers was shot in the back outside his Mississippi home by a white supremacist. His wife and young children ran outside, only to find Evers face down in blood. He died an hour later.

Civil rights leaders plot a route for the enormous number of people expected to attend the March on Washington for Jobs and Freedom. Shown (*left to right*) are A. Philip Randolph, president of the Brotherhood of Sleeping Car Porters; Roy Wilkins, executive secretary of the NAACP; and Anna Arnold Hedgeman, a leading proponent of women's rights and civil rights.

1963

An angry mother removes her child from Graymont School in Birmingham, Alabama, on September 4, 1963, after two black students were allowed admission. Earlier that year, a federal court mandated the desegregation of several Alabama school systems, including Birmingham's.

To pressure Congress into acting on the President's admonition, King and other mainstream leaders of the civil rights movement—most notably A. Philip Randolph and Bayard Rustin—organized the massive March on Washington for Jobs and Freedom. On August 28, 1963, an estimated 250,000 people gathered at the Mall in front of the Lincoln Memorial to rally support for civil rights legislation. White and black together, with movie stars mixing freely with poor sharecroppers, it was one of the most memorable events of the era. Despite warnings by FBI Director J. Edgar Hoover that the rally would become a violent riot, the entire day's event went off without a hitch—not counting some behind-the-scenes debates about the purpose of the event.

The more radical element of the civil rights movement coalition, the young activists associated with the Student Nonviolent Coordinating Committee (SNCC), wanted to indicate to the nation that they had little patience for compromised reform measures and little faith in the system of privilege. While Randolph succeeded in toning down the remarks of SNCC speaker John Lewis, the younger man's speech was still a powerful critique of politics-as-usual in the United States. He expressed deep disappointment with the Democratic and Republican party establishments alike, and blasted politicians who had made lucrative careers on compromise, abandoning their principles as they buckled to and even assisted the forces of exploitation. While few noted it at the time, the seeds of a far more militant black radicalism were being sown that day in Washington.

Far more noticeable was the climactic speech of Martin Luther King. By mid-1963 King was already a well-known public figure, but his nationally

On September 15, 1963, a bomb detonated under the steps of the Sixteenth Street Baptist Church in Birmingham, killing four girls, injuring 20 people, and destroying nearby cars, including this one. This was the eighth racially motivated bombing to occur in Birmingham in just six months.

televised speech that day made him a figure of extraordinary renown, even as many whites still believed him to be a dangerous radical. In his deliberate cadence and resonant baritone, King told Americans about his "dream." Someday, he believed, his "four little children will live in a nation where they will not be judged by the color of their skin but by the content of their character." Then, in an ecstatic tone, he prophesied a day "when all God's children, black men and white men, Jews and Gentiles, Protestants and Catholics, will be able to join hands and sing in the words of that old Negro spiritual, 'Free at last! Free at last! Thank God Almighty, we are free at last.'"

Passing the civil rights legislation that Kennedy had promised was no simple task. In fact, before the bill would reach the President's desk to be signed, the nation passed through a bloody veil of tragedy and despair. On September 15, 1963, a dynamite explosion tore apart the Sixteenth Street Baptist Church in Birmingham. It was Youth Day, and four black girls—all dressed in white—were killed in the blast. Some 20 other children were rushed to the hospital.

As word spread through Birmingham, a white preacher called short a pro-segregationist rally. Two teenage white boys, both Eagle Scouts, left the rally and on their way home shot and killed a 13-year-old black boy. When questioned by police, they could give no reason for their murderous deed. A prominent white Birmingham attorney, Charles Morgan, in a moment of overwhelming grief for the deaths, told reporters that all the city's whites were responsible: "We all did it." As historian Taylor Branch records, Morgan was made a "pariah" by Birmingham's white community for his remarks.

A sorrowful Jackie Kennedy holds the American flag that covered the coffin of her late husband, President John F. Kennedy, who was assassinated on November 22, 1963. JFK's successor, Lyndon Johnson—in a speech just five days after the murder—vowed to make the civil rights bill Kennedy's greatest legacy.

Then, on November 22, the nation was stunned by the assassination of President Kennedy, shot dead while riding in a motorcade in Dallas. America's handsome young president, who had, after a year of protests and racial violence, made passage of a monumental civil rights bill his highest priority, was gone.

While the nation mourned, Vice President Lyndon Baines Johnson was sworn in as president. Johnson promised the American people that he would carry out Kennedy's legislative agenda. Above all, the Texan stated without reservation, he would make the civil rights bill John Kennedy's greatest legacy. As the bloody year ended, one of the greatest legislative minds the American political system has ever produced went to work on passing the single most important federal act of the Sixties era—an omnibus civil rights act that would outlaw discrimination based on race in almost every area of American life.

1963

1963: Congress passes the Clean Air Act, allocating $95 million for research and cleanup efforts. • Fifty-two million Americans, one-third of the U.S. population, now drink fluoridated water. • The carbon dioxide laser is invented. It will be used as a cutting tool in surgery and industry. • In Iran, women are granted the right to vote, a program of the U.S.-backed Shah that causes violent, antisuffrage street demonstrations.

1963: Nancy Lotsey, age eight, joins the New Jersey Small-Fry League, becoming the first girl to participate in an organized all-boy baseball league. • McDonald's sells its billionth hamburger and introduces clown Ronald McDonald. • Borrowing from RCA's closed-cartridge, reel-to-reel tape system, Phillips introduces a smaller version that it calls the compact cassette tape. • The FBI begins collecting data on folk singer Phil Ochs.

Early January: An American plane carrying rice to South Vietnamese refugees is shot down over Laos by Communist Pathet Lao forces.

January 1: Undefeated Southern California defeats No. 2-ranked Wisconsin 42–37 in the Rose Bowl to win the national championship.

January 3: The Vietcong defeat a large force of American-equipped South Vietnamese soldiers in the Battle of Ap Bac. Three American helicopter crew members are killed.

January 11: The Whiskey-a-Go-Go opens on the Sunset Strip in Hollywood, California. It is billed as the first discotheque in the U.S., complete with caged female dancers.

January 29: American poet Robert Frost dies at 88.

January 31: U.S. Secretary of Defense Robert McNamara says "the war in Vietnam is going well and will succeed."

Belgian miner Albert Verbrugghe screams in anguish at a checkpoint in Jadotville, Katanga, on January 3, 1963. As he approached the checkpoint, Verbrugghe didn't stop his automobile. United Nations troops responded by firing machine guns at his car, killing his wife and friend and wounding Verbrugghe in the face. Katanga had witnessed enormous bloodshed since seceding from the Congo in 1960, necessitating the involvement of UN troops. Katanga President Moise Tshombe agreed to reunite his province with the republic in January 1963, but political turmoil continued in Katanga and the Congo for several more years.

Cast members of the British satirical television show *That Was the Week That Was* hold up their nameplates, led by David Frost. Immensely popular in Britain in 1962 and '63 because of its irreverence, the show reviewed the week's events while poking fun at the political and cultural establishment. An American version of the show ran on NBC from January 1964 to May 1965. From funny songs about prospective running mates for LBJ to Henry Cabot Lodge taking a polygraph test, little was sacred. Similar but more biting shows would emerge during the next 10 years, most notably *Laugh-In* and *Saturday Night Live.*

Robert Frost, shown in a characteristically thoughtful pose, died on January 29, 1963. Hailed by critics and readers alike as one of America's greatest poets, Frost won the Pulitzer Prize four times. His poems generally reflected his rural New England background, but they transcended his region as well. The poem "The Road Not Taken," for example, is set on a local country road but delves into such large human issues as loss and regret. In 1961 John F. Kennedy had asked his fellow Bostonian to read a poem at his presidential inauguration.

Patrons of the hip Los Angeles nightclub Whiskey-A-Go-Go dance the night away. The club opened in 1963 and became nationally prominent, in part because of its miniskirted "go-go" dancers, who did bumps and grinds in cages suspended above the floor. The club would attract such major groups as the Doors and spawn a number of clones in major American cities.

A terrified Melanie Daniels, played by actress Tippi Hedren, fends off a fowl attack in this poster for Alfred Hitchcock's *The Birds.* Hitchcock sought to make the horror in this movie glaringly realistic. During the filming of the climactic scene, birds were bound to Hedren's arms and legs while others were thrown at her. The ambiguous ending of the film cast a sense of impending doom over audiences, portraying human helplessness in the face of forces beyond our control.

The Cartwright clan made *Bonanza,* which ran on NBC from 1959 to '73, the most successful western television show of the 1960s. Dan Blocker, Michael Landon, Lorne Greene, and Pernell Roberts (*from top left, clockwise*) starred as Hoss, Little Joe, Ben, and Adam Cartwright. *Bonanza* centered around a thrice-widowed patriarch (Ben) and his three loyal sons as they carved out a place for themselves on their Ponderosa Ranch in Nevada in the 1860s. The show seemed to resonate with those in the 1960s who were seeking their own individual places in a complex society. *Bonanza* received its highest Nielsen rating, a 36.9 share, in the 1963–64 television season.

February 8–9: Iraqi Prime Minister Abdul Karim Kassem, suspected of Communist leanings, is killed by right-wing military officers who lead an armed revolution.

February 11: WGBH-TV in Boston begins airing *The French Chef* with Julia Child. The program will become a favorite on educational stations around the country.

February 21: The U.S. shrimp boat *Ala,* disabled in international waters about 60 nautical miles north of Cuba, is fired upon by Cuba-based, Soviet-built MiG fighter jets.

February 23: Quebec separatists bomb an English-speaking radio station.

February 25: The U.S. Supreme Court reverses the convictions of 187 African-Americans arrested in March 1961 in Columbia, South Carolina, during an antisegregation rally.

March: Polaroid introduces color film for its instant cameras.

March 4: William Carlos Williams, a physician and major U.S. poet, dies at 79.

March 5: Country-pop singer Patsy Cline, 30, is killed in a plane crash near Camden, Tennessee. Dying with her are performers Cowboy Copas and Hawkshaw Hawkins.

March 8: In the third revolution in Syria in 18 months, a Baathist faction overthrows the existing government in a bloodless coup.

March 17: Mother Seton, founder of the American Sisters of Charity, becomes the first American to be beatified by the Catholic Church. • A volcano in Bali, Indonesia, causes an estimated 11,000 deaths.

March 18: In *Gideon v. Wainwright,* the U.S. Supreme Court guarantees the right to counsel for every defendant.

March 21: The aging Alcatraz Federal Penitentiary in San Francisco Bay is permanently closed.

On February 11, 1963, American-born poet Sylvia Plath committed suicide in her London flat. She turned on the gas in her kitchen after leaving food and an opened window in the room that her two children occupied. Plath, who had a history of depression, also was troubled by marital problems with husband Ted Hughes (a British poet) and criticism of her first novel, *The Bell Jar.* The complete collection of Plath's tortured, emotionally powerful poetry would be published in 1981 and win a rare posthumous Pulitzer Prize.

Madalyn Murray and her sons, William (*left*) and Garth, stand outside the U.S. Supreme Court building on February 27, 1963. Through court action, Murray sought to ban the use of the Lord's Prayer and Bible reading in Baltimore's public schools. America's most famous atheist, Murray devoted her life to fighting for her vision of the separation of church and state. When the Supreme Court ruled 8–1 in her favor in this case, it triggered a massive public outcry that would continue into the 21st century. In 1964 *Life* magazine would refer to Murray as "the most hated woman in America."

Country music star Patsy Cline is shown backstage during a benefit concert on March 4, 1963, the day before she was killed in a plane crash. Born into poverty in West Virginia, Cline as a child sang along with the recordings of Grand Ole Opry stars. After some initial success in the mid-1950s, her career stalled until 1961, when she released "I Fall to Pieces," which rose to the Top 10 on both the country music and pop charts. In fact, Cline was one of the first country music singers to bridge the gap between country and pop, thus helping to pave the way for the likes of Garth Brooks and Shania Twain.

In the early 1960s, Roy Lichtenstein moved away from the reigning Abstract Expressionist style of the period and toward Pop Art, becoming one of the most important practitioners of the style. Lichtenstein became interested in comic book images after his son pointed to a Mickey Mouse comic book and said, "I bet you can't paint as good as that." He could, and thereafter Lichtenstein perfected a technique using oil and magna paint and Ben-Day dots that mimicked photographic reproduction. Lichtenstein became most famous for painting comic book panels that featured a beautiful female protagonist. For each, he employed bold colors, thick outlines, and speech balloons with comically melodramatic dialogue.

U.S. President John F. Kennedy joins Central American presidents in a group handshake in San Jose, Costa Rica, on March 18, 1963. From left to right are Miguel Ydigoras, Guatemala; Julio Rivera, El Salvador; Roberto Chiari, Panama; Ramon Villeda, Honduras; Kennedy; Francisco Orlich, Costa Rica; and Luis Somoza, Nicaragua. President Kennedy committed the United States to large-scale development aid to their countries. The precedent of the Cuban Revolution had fueled guerrilla uprisings in Central America, as the seeds of rebellion—hunger, poverty, and despair—festered in the cities and rural areas of those countries. Through financial support, JFK hoped to prevent another of USA's neighbors from falling into the hands of leftist rebels.

April 3: Martin Luther King, Jr., and the Southern Christian Leadership Conference (SCLC) launch a well-planned protest movement in Birmingham, Alabama. King's "Birmingham Manifesto" calls for desegregation of all businesses and public facilities in the city. The movement begins on this day with sit-ins in downtown stores. *See* April 12, 1963.

April 7: Yugoslavia's rubber-stamp parliament approves a new constitution making the country's current leader, Marshal Tito, president for life.

April 9: At a White House ceremony, President John F. Kennedy proclaims 88-year-old Sir Winston Churchill an honorary citizen of the United States—an accolade never before bestowed by the U.S. Congress upon a citizen of another nation.

April 10: The U.S. nuclear submarine *Thresher* breaks up and sinks in the Atlantic Ocean near Massachusetts while conducting deep-dive tests. All hands (more than 120) are lost.

April 11: The Vatican releases the encyclical letter *"Pacem in Terris,"* by Pope John XXIII, which calls for an end to the nuclear arms race.

April 12: Despite a state-court injunction against further demonstrations, Martin Luther King, Jr., Ralph Abernathy, and Fred Shuttlesworth lead a march to Birmingham City Hall on Good Friday. They are arrested, and King is placed in solitary confinement. *See* April 16, 1963.

April 15: A "Ban the Bomb" rally in Hyde Park, London, attracts some 70,000 people.

April 16: In his "Letter From Birmingham Jail," Martin Luther King, Jr., explains why black citizens cannot wait patiently for justice to be served. *See* May 2, 1963.

April 17: NFL Commissioner Pete Rozelle suspends Detroit Lions tackle Alex Karras and Green Bay Packers halfback Paul Hornung for betting on NFL games.

A publicity poster for the 1962 film *Mondo Cane* (*Dog World*) highlights its director, Gualtiero Jacopetti. Released in the United States in 1963, the film became the first in a cinematic genre known as "shockumentary." *Mondo Cane* features a series of bizarre scenes, including a woman in New Guinea suckling a pig, Thai restaurants serving dog (as a meal, not as a customer), Japanese farmers feeding their cows beer, and the results of radioactive fallout. Although much less gory than later such genre films, *Mondo Cane* was shocking at the time and made for great conversation at cocktail parties.

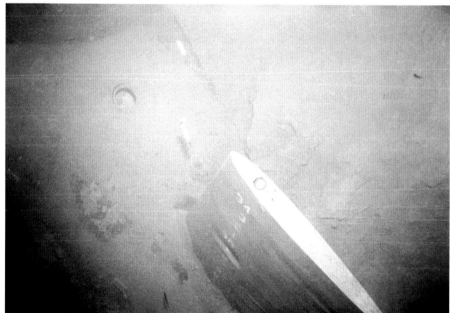

The remains of the rudder of the American nuclear submarine USS *Thresher* are photographed on the floor of the Atlantic Ocean. The sub went down on April 10, 1963, with all hands on board—112 military personnel and 17 civilian technicians. Considered the best new ship of its class, the *Thresher* was able to dive deeper and run quieter than any other submarine of its time. An investigation determined that a leak had developed in the engine room, which may have caused electrical problems that prevented the vessel from resurfacing. The Navy implemented new quality-control procedures after the tragedy.

The Profumo Affair

ON MARCH 22, 1963, British Secretary of State for War John Profumo told Parliament that "there was no impropriety whatsoever in my acquaintanceship with Miss Keeler." For weeks before his official statement, rumors of a sex scandal had swirled around the member of Conservative Harold Macmillan's Cabinet. In the following days, the lurid stories about spying and showgirls would be revealed as truth. The ensuing scandal rocked the conservative government and set off a round of national soul-searching in Great Britain concerning issues of sex, security, and the private lives of public servants.

On the surface, Profumo was a rich, upstanding member of the Tory government, with a brilliant career and a happy marriage to actress Valerie Hobson. But soon his private life became a matter of public concern when a "party girl" named Christine Keeler and a pimp for London Society, Dr. Stephen Ward, revealed Profumo's involvements with the lurid underbelly of London. The dogged London press revealed that Profumo had indeed carried on an affair with Keeler for many months while she simultaneously consorted with Yevgeny Ivanov, an assistant naval attaché to the Soviet Embassy in London. Ivanov was undoubtedly a spy, and the triangle exposed a Cold War Era security weakness in the British government in the wake of other scandals in Britain involving sex and government officials.

Profumo resigned in June 1963, though he claimed he had never breached security. Prime Minister Macmillan, who had stood by Profumo when the latter lied to Parlia-

John Profumo

ment, resigned in October, allegedly due to health problems. The Labour Party then ascended to power.

During the following months, the editor of *Punch* magazine said he believed that many Britons saw the scandal as the "embodiment of a hideous decline in national moral fiber." The years of Tory rule, according to *Punch*, "coincided with a remarkable new trend in the public discussion of sex. Suddenly, after decades of ignorance or reticence, the ordinary Briton began to talk openly of prostitution, abortion, contraception, [and] homosexuality...." The tragic and titillating details of the scandal, including Stephen Ward's suicide and revelations about British society, were published as the *Report Presented to Parliament by the Prime Minister by Command of Her Majesty September 1963*. It became a runaway bestseller on both sides of the Atlantic.

In 1963 model Mandy Rice-Davies (*left*) and showgirl Christine Keeler (*right*) were central figures in the sex scandal that rocked Great Britain and led to the resignation of Prime Minister Harold Macmillan. Keeler had an affair with John Profumo, Britain's minister of war, while simultaneously sleeping with Yevgeny Ivanov, a naval attaché at the Soviet Embassy in London. The Profumo–Keeler–Ivanov triangle raised legitimate security concerns. Profumo cut off his involvement with Keeler in a letter, which Keeler eventually made public. Keeler subsequently was jailed for perjury, then wound up living in squalid public housing in London. Rice-Davies, who also was intimate with powerful people, exploited her notoriety. She appeared in movies and ran a successful nightclub in Israel.

April 24: The Boston Celtics defeat the Los Angeles Lakers to clinch their fifth straight NBA title.

April 30: New Hampshire becomes the first state to offer a legalized lottery.

May: Buddhists begin to riot in South Vietnam after being denied the right to display flags during Buddha birthday celebrations. *See* June 11, 1963.

May 2: More than a thousand black schoolchildren march in Birmingham; 959 are arrested and sent by school buses to various jails. *See* May 3, 1963.

May 3: Black youths in Birmingham are blasted by firefighters with high-pressure hoses, clubbed by police officers, and attacked by police dogs deliberately let loose. The assault triggers outrage around the country and the world. *See* May 10, 1963.

May 6: Republic Aviation introduces the F-105F, a USAF two-seat super-sonic tactical fighter jet that carries combinations of nuclear and conventional weapons. The jet reaches a top speed of approximately 1,400 mph.

May 7: The communications satellite Telstar II is successfully launched from Cape Canaveral, Florida.

May 10: Birmingham city officials reach an agreement with the SCLC. The city promises to desegregate downtown stores and release all prisoners; the SCLC agrees to end its boycotts and demonstrations. In the evening, the Ku Klux Klan denounces the plan while bombs explode at the home of A. D. King (Martin Luther King's brother) and at the Gaston Motel (where MLK had been staying). Rioting ensues throughout the city.

May 12: Bob Dylan withdraws from *The Ed Sullivan Show* because he is asked to avoid performing his satirical song "Talkin' John Birch Paranoid Blues."

May 15: Hundreds of antisegregation demonstrators are arrested in Greensboro, North Carolina.

Members of the Birmingham Fire Department turn their fire hoses on a group of young protesters in early May 1963 during a demonstration against segregation in the Alabama city. During the same demonstrations, police used German shepherds against the marchers. Birmingham Public Safety Commissioner Eugene "Bull" Connor had ordered the attacks. Images of the violence, disseminated around the world, sparked outrage against racist practices in Birmingham, which Martin Luther King, Jr., had called "the most segregated city in America." Historians generally agree that the public outcry over Connor's odious tactics helped assure the passage of the Civil Rights Act of 1964.

Letter from Birmingham Jail

WE HAVE WAITED for more than 340 years for our constitutional and God-given rights. The nations of Asia and Africa are moving with jet-like speed toward gaining political independence, but we still creep at horse-and-buggy pace toward gaining a cup of coffee at a lunch counter. Perhaps it is easy for those who have never felt the stinging darts of segregation to say, "Wait." But when you have seen vicious mobs lynch your mothers and fathers at will . . . when you see the vast majority of your twenty million Negro brothers smothering in an airtight cage of poverty in the midst of an affluent society; when you suddenly find your tongue twisted and your speech stammering as you seek to explain to your six-year-old daughter why she can't go to the public amusement park that has just been advertised on television . . . and see depressing clouds of inferiority beginning to form in her little mental sky, and see her beginning to distort her personality by developing an unconscious bitterness toward white people . . . then you will understand why we find it difficult to wait.

—MARTIN LUTHER KING, JR., LETTER FROM BIRMINGHAM JAIL

After the massive arrest of children in Birmingham on May 2, Movement leaders assembled another 1,000 children to march the next day. Public Safety Commissioner Bull Connor decided to deter the demonstrators with fire hoses and police dogs. "I want 'em to see the dogs work," Connor said. While watching the attack dogs snap at black children, Connor added, "Look at those niggers run!" African-American Walter Gadsden (*pictured*), who did not take part in the demonstration, was at the wrong place at the right time for one of the most famous photographs of the civil rights movement.

At a May 10 press conference, Martin Luther King, Jr., and other SCLC leaders spelled out an agreement they had reached with Birmingham's Senior Citizens Committee, which represented the majority of the city's businesses. The terms: The city's lunch counters, fitting rooms, restrooms, and drinking fountains would be desegregated within 90 days; a process would begin that would ensure black employment in downtown stores; and all jailed demonstrators would be released. Bull Connor and Alabama Governor George Wallace soon denounced the settlement.

Benny Oliver, a former Jackson, Mississippi, police officer, kicks a black sit-in demonstrator in a segregated restaurant in Jackson in late May 1963. The Council of Federated Organizations (COFO), an umbrella organization of civil rights groups, coordinated protests against segregation in Mississippi in 1963. Especially influential was Medgar Evers, field secretary for the NAACP in Mississippi, who spoke out increasingly against racism in Jackson. Whites in Jackson responded by threatening and physically abusing black protesters.

May 25: The Organization of African Unity is founded to promote self-government, respect for territorial boundaries, and social progress throughout the continent.

May 27: The U.S. Supreme Court rules that the court will not tolerate foot-dragging in school desegregation.

June: President Kennedy tours Ireland.

June 3: Pope John XXIII (Angelo Giuseppe Roncalli) dies at 81. *See* June 21, 1963.

June 5: British War Secretary John Profumo resigns after admitting to having lied about his relationship with "party girl" Christine Keeler, who had carried on a simultaneous sexual relationship with a Soviet intelligence agent.

June 10: The Equal Pay Act is signed by President Kennedy. The measure is intended to halt payroll discrimination based on gender.

June 11: Escorted by federal troops, Vivian Malone and James Hood try to become the first African-American students to register at the University of Alabama in Tuscaloosa. Alabama Governor George Wallace stands defiantly in front of the schoolhouse door before eventually stepping aside. In the evening, President Kennedy informs the nation that he will push Congress to enact strong civil rights legislation. *See* June 19, 1963. • Thich Qaung Duc, a Buddhist monk, immolates himself in South Vietnam. The act is precipitated by longstanding upset among Vietnamese Buddhists with privileged, French-influenced Vietnamese Catholics. *See* July 30, 1963. • Dr. James D. Hardy performs the first human lung transplant, at the University of Mississippi at Jackson.

June 12: In Jackson, Mississippi, NAACP Field Secretary Medgar Evers is shot and killed in his front yard by Byron de la Beckwith, a white segregationist. ➤

> *"Do you realize that fluoridation is the most monstrously conceived and dangerous Communist plot we have ever had to face? I can no longer sit back and allow Communist infiltration, Communist indoctrination, Communist subversion, and the international Communist conspiracy to sap and impurify all of our precious bodily fluids."*
>
> —Satirical dialogue from the film Dr. Strangelove

New York Water Supply Commissioner Armand D'Angelo celebrates the fluoridation of the city's water supply in 1963. Years earlier, researchers had discovered that controlled amounts of the chemical fluoride could help prevent dental cavities. Over time, public health scientists recommended an optimum amount of fluoride concentration in water supplies. Although a number of cities fluoridated their water, some conservative groups—most notably the John Birch Society—claimed that fluoridation was part of a Communist plot to weaken America as a precursor to a Soviet invasion. The notion of a Communist plot was nonsense, and fluoride gradually became part of most Americans' water supply.

In this scene from the 1963 film comedy *The Nutty Professor,* Jerry Lewis (as Julius Kelp) eyes Stella Stevens (as Stella Purdy) as he inadvertently ignites a piece of paper in his lab. The famed comic actor appeared in 20 films during the 1960s, with *Nutty Professor* his signature performance. This zany portrait of Lewis as Dr. Jekyll and Mr. Hyde allowed him to be both goofy and sinister. Although dismissed by American critics, it was acclaimed in European film circles. *The Bellboy* (1960), which Lewis starred in and directed, was perhaps more appealing to Americans because of its brilliant sight gags, especially the infinite number of ways in which he took pratfalls.

Thich Quang Duc, a Buddhist monk, immolates himself on a Saigon street on June 11, 1963. Many South Vietnamese Buddhists chafed under what they saw as the anti-Buddhist and dictatorial regime of Catholic South Vietnamese President Ngo Dinh Diem and his brother, Nhu. The two American-supported leaders had banned parades on Buddha's birthday and arrested thousands of Buddhists in raids on pagodas, killing and maiming several monks. Nhu's wife hardly endeared her brother-in-law's government to the world when she quipped that she would be "willing to provide gasoline for the next barbecue." This event, and subsequent self-immolations, shocked millions of Americans and helped solidify growing opposition to Diem in the Kennedy Administration.

The first Chevrolet Corvette was produced in 1953. Only 315 were sold. But in 1963 Chevrolet introduced a totally revamped Corvette—the 1963 "Split Window" Sting Ray, designed by Bill Mitchell. The public fell in love with the car, leading to sales of 10,594 Sting Ray coupes in 1963, plus another 10,919 convertibles. The Corvette symbolized life in the fast lane, helping Americans push the boundaries of speed, freedom, and possibility.

Pop singer Dinah Shore flogs the purchasing power of S&H Green Stamps on the cover of this 1963 catalog. The stamps, originally introduced in 1896, became immensely popular in the 1950s and '60s. They were given out by retailers in amounts based on purchases, then redeemed through the Sperry and Hutchinson catalog for various goodies. In 1964 the S&H catalog had the highest circulation of any publication in the United States, and the company produced more stamps than the U.S. Post Office. The green stamps serve as a telling indicator of American consumerism and the power of advertising in post-World War II America.

The Motown Sound

IN THE MID-1950s, Berry Gordy, Jr., worked on the Ford assembly line, but he had much greater ambitions. The cowriter of "Money (That's What I Want)" was a natural entrepreneur. In 1959 he parlayed an $800 loan into an enterprise he dubbed Motown Records.

Along with singer/songwriter Smokey Robinson, Gordy discovered and cultivated talent, wrote hit material, pressed and distributed records, and put his acts on the road, keeping every aspect in house. Key to Motown's early successes was the familial atmosphere: No star was too big to assist in the process. Singers answered phones while musicians slid vinyl into sleeves. Even crooner Marvin Gaye played drums behind other acts.

In addition to Marvin and Smokey, Motown was responsible for making stars of Mary Wells, Martha Reeves, Stevie Wonder, the Temptations, the Four Tops, and, biggest of all, the Supremes. Correctly reading white America's taste for pop, Gordy assembled a stable of soulful, but nonthreatening, black singers. Peerless songwriting backed by superb instrumental work set the table for the biggest independent label success of the Sixties. Later years would see relations soured by jealousies, royalty disputes, and artistic acrimony, but for the bulk of the decade, Motown's golden era reigned "supreme."

George Wallace, the pro-segregation governor of Alabama, makes his "stand in the schoolhouse door" on June 11, 1963, as two black students attempt to register at the University of Alabama. Wallace, who had been elected governor in 1962 while promising "segregation now, segregation tomorrow, segregation forever," seemed to be defying a federal court order to proceed with desegregation. However, after making a speech in which he defended the Alabama constitution and attacked the federal government, he quietly stepped aside and allowed the students—Vivian Malone and James Hood—to register. Thus, the governor could claim that he had done his best for his constituency while staying within the framework of the law.

Berry Gordy, Jr. (*lower left*), and Motown musical artists, including Smokey Robinson (*rear*) and Stevie Wonder (*far right*)

Medgar Evers, Mississippi field secretary for the NAACP, was an articulate activist in the struggle for black rights in his home state. In the early 1960s, he investigated violent crimes against African-Americans and organized a boycott in Jackson against businesses that discriminated against black citizens. On May 20, 1963, Evers delivered a speech on local television denouncing segregation in Mississippi. In retaliation, Evers was shot and killed in front of his home on June 12. The alleged murderer, white supremacist Byron de la Beckwith, escaped conviction for the crime twice in the 1960s because of hung juries. He finally was convicted in 1994 and sentenced to life in prison.

Actress Elizabeth Taylor played the title role in the 1963 film *Cleopatra*. The hoopla that surrounded the making of the historical epic overshadowed the film itself. Originally projected to cost $2 million, its budget ballooned to a staggering $44 million. Taylor almost died during the filming, saved only by a tracheotomy. Off the set, Taylor and costar Richard Burton indulged in a torrid affair that destroyed their marriages. In spite of tremendous hype, the film lost money. Taylor actually vomited when she saw the finished product.

This photograph of an alleged flying saucer was taken in New Mexico on June 13, 1963, by a member of the Amalgamated Flying Saucer Clubs of America (headquartered in Los Angeles). It was a busy year for UFO aficionados, with several dozen sightings reported worldwide—from a luminous object in Argentina to a big fireball in Switzerland. Perhaps Cold War paranoia, combined with increasing testing of experimental aircraft and weather balloons, can help explain the UFO craze that continued throughout the 1960s. The U.S. government has never confirmed a single UFO as being from outer space.

ABC's *Combat!* was the longest-running (1962–67) and most critically acclaimed of television's World War II dramas of the 1960s. Veteran "method" actor Vic Morrow (*pictured*) starred as Sergeant Chip Saunders, the competent and toughly unsentimental K Company topkick who shepherds his men from D-Day to the liberation of Europe. Rick Jason costarred at Lieutenant Gil Hanley. Directors included Robert Altman and Richard Donner; among the guest stars were Robert Duvall, Dennis Hopper, Lee Marvin, James Caan, and Charles Bronson.

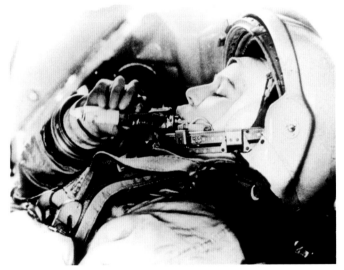

Valentina Tereshkova, a Soviet cosmonaut, practices eating in a flight simulator prior to her voyage into space. Tereshkova became the first woman to orbit the Earth on June 16, 1963, when she was launched aboard Vostok 6 for a 70.8-hour, 48-orbit flight. While Tereshkova never flew another mission, she became a public spokesperson for the USSR and received the United Nations Gold Medal of Peace. Although the United States had started a secret program to test women as potential astronauts in 1961, the first American woman in space, Sally Ride, did not make her flight until 1983, two decades after her Soviet counterpart.

June 16: Soviet cosmonaut Valentina Tereshkova becomes the first woman in space when she is successfully launched into orbit aboard Vostok 6.

June 17: The U.S. Supreme Court rules that no state or locality may require recitation of the Lord's Prayer or Bible verses in public schools.

June 19: President Kennedy submits a civil rights bill to Congress.

June 20: President Kennedy meets with civil rights leaders and agrees to their proposed March on Washington, which is intended to drum up support for the civil rights bill, school integration, and legislation for fair employment practices. *See* August 28, 1963.

June 21: Giovanni Battista Cardinal Montini is elected supreme pontiff of the Roman Catholic Church and will reign as Pope Paul VI. • In St. Louis, American Bob Hayes runs the 100-yard dash in 9.1 seconds to set a world record.

June 25: In a speech in Frankfurt, Germany, President Kennedy promises that the U.S. "will risk its cities to defend yours."

June 27: The U.S. Defense Department announces that the Armed Forces Reserves have been racially integrated.

July: Every address in the U.S. is assigned a five-digit zip code.

July 1: The British government reveals that Foreign Office worker Harold "Kim" Philby (now living in the Soviet Union) has admitted working for the Soviets since before 1946, and had warned British spies Donald MacLean and Guy Burgess of their imminent arrests in 1951. • The United Brotherhood of Carpenters, America's largest trade union, orders its locals to end racial discrimination.

July 11: Red China admits it will need 10 to 20 years to overtake the West in science, industry, and armaments.

As a 28-year-old freelance reporter, Gloria Steinem went undercover as a Playboy Bunny and kept a diary of her experiences, which appeared as a two-part feature in *Show* magazine in May and June 1963. The report was an understated yet blistering attack of the whole Playboy Club ethos. The Bunnies clearly were exploited, essentially serving as touts for the club's bottom line. For example, the club manual instructed Bunnies that "there are many pleasing means they can employ to stimulate the club's liquor volume." Steinem went on to become a leading voice in the American feminist movement.

Giovanni Battista Enrico Antonio Maria Montini became Pope Paul VI on June 21, 1963. He had the misfortune of following the jovial, photogenic, and ecumenical Pope John XXIII, who had promised the possibility of significant reform in the Catholic Church. Many non-Catholics and liberal Catholics perceived Paul VI as a comparatively conservative pope, especially because of his encyclicals confirming both the celibacy of priests and official Church opposition to all artificial means of birth control. These stances tended to overshadow his more progressive social letter, *Populorum progressio* (1967).

Frederico Fellini's film *8½* was released in the United States in summer 1963. Fellini fathered a whole new direction in cinema, shedding traditional narrative and using powerful imagery and fantasy to tell his stories. Most critics hail *8½* as a landmark in moviemaking history. The film stars Marcello Mastroianni as Anselmi, a successful Italian director who retreats to a spa outside Rome for rest and inspiration. But Anselmi is suffering a peculiar breakdown, and his memories, dreams, visions, and fantasies blur the line between what is real and what he imagines. Prior to this movie, Fellini had made seven feature films and one short ("half") film; hence the title *8½*.

The Boston Strangler

"ALBERT [DESALVO] so badly wanted to be the Strangler," testified Dr. Ames Robey, who had worked with police to solve the series of 13 brutal strangulation/sexual assaults that had rocked the Boston area from 1962 to 1964. DeSalvo actually confessed to the crimes, but evidence suggests he wasn't the killer. The real Boston Stranger—or, more likely, Stranglers—got away with the crimes.

The Boston Strangler rampage began on June 14, 1962, with the strangulation death of Anna Slesers, a 55-year-old seamstress living in Boston's Back Bay neighborhood. The woman had been sexually assaulted. Her apartment was ransacked but not burglarized, and her dead, naked body was posed in a provocative position. Five other women, all over 65, were murdered in similar fashion over the next two months. After a three-month respite, the criminal dubbed the Boston Strangler resumed, but with a different victimology. On December 5, 1962, 20-year-old Sophie Clark, an African-American student, was found strangled to death in her apartment. Over the course of the next 13 months, another six women in various areas of Boston were murdered, all but two of them under the age of 25.

DeSalvo emerged as a suspect, only to give detectives headaches. From 1961 to April 1962, he had served time for being the "measuring man"; he had taken measurements of women and stolen from them. The Boston Strangler murders occurred while he was a free man, from June 1962 to January 1964. In November 1964, DeSalvo was charged with the "green man" rapes—a series of rapes in Connecticut in which the perpetrator wore green work pants. In March 1965, while awaiting trial for the the Connecticut rapes, DeSalvo confessed to being the Boston Strangler.

Boston Police Commissioner Edmund McNamara described DeSalvo as a "blowhard" and braggart obsessed with fame. DeSalvo apparently had concocted a plan for collecting the Strangler reward money by confessing via a third party (a fellow inmate). Although DeSalvo impressed investigators with an immaculate recollection of crime-scene details, he may have gleaned much of the information from the in-depth press coverage of the murders.

Due to lack of evidence, DeSalvo never was tried for any of the Boston Strangler murders. However, he was sentenced to life imprisonment at Walpole State Prison for the series of rapes. DeSalvo was murdered in prison under suspicious circumstances in 1973—the night before he was scheduled to meet with a reporter to reveal the true identity of the Strangler.

Years would pass before DeSalvo would be exonerated from at least some of the Strangler charges. In 2001 DNA evidence from one of the Strangler's victims did not match that taken from the exhumed remains of DeSalvo. James Starrs, a professor of forensics science who was involved in the DNA testing, concluded: "If I was a juror [given the new evidence], I would acquit him [DeSalvo] with no questions asked."

U.S. President John F. Kennedy speaks to the approximately 60 percent of the West Berlin population who came to cheer him on June 26, 1963. This was part of a nine-day European trip designed to garner support for JFK's attempt to negotiate a nuclear test-ban treaty, and to assure Western Europeans of America's commitment to defend them against Communist threats. The visits to Ireland, Italy, and especially Berlin were great personal triumphs for the young president. West Berliners even forgave Kennedy for his famous verbal gaffe. When he said, "*Ich bin ein Berliner,*" he actually described himself as a jelly doughnut, not as a citizen of the divided city.

1963

July 15–25: The U.S. and USSR successfully negotiate a nuclear test-ban treaty, officially known as the Treaty Banning Nuclear Weapons Tests in Atmosphere, in Outer Space and Under Water. *See* August 20, 1963.

July 24: The Cuban government takes over the U.S. Embassy building and grounds in Havana.

July 26: The U.S. Defense Department authorizes military commanders to designate segregated businesses off-limits to military personnel.

July 26–28: The Newport Folk Festival in Rhode Island showcases such folk artists as Bob Dylan, Joan Baez, Pete Seeger, Phil Ochs, and Peter, Paul & Mary.

July 30: The USSR promises India missiles and MiG-21 fighter jets with air-to-air missiles if India is again attacked at its borders by Red China. • Approximately 60,000 Buddhist activists demonstrate against the Catholic-dominated South Vietnamese government of President Ngo Dinh Diem.

August: Lowell Skinner, a former U.S. serviceman, returns home to Akron, Ohio, after living for a decade in Red China. Skinner had been captured during the Korean War and had refused repatriation at war's end in 1953.

August 5: Craig Breedlove drives his J-47 jet-powered car, *The Spirit of America,* to a two-way average of 407 mph at Utah's Bonneville Salt Flats.

August 8: Near London, masked bandits rob a mail train of more than £2.6 million.

August 9: Patrick Kennedy, two-day-old son of the President and First Lady, dies after being born nearly six weeks premature.

August 18: James Meredith, the first African-American admitted to the University of Mississippi, becomes the first to graduate from that school.

Steve McQueen starred as Captain Virgil Hilts in the World War II film *The Great Escape,* which opened on the Fourth of July, 1963. Surrounded by a superb ensemble cast, including Donald Pleasence, James Garner, and Charles Bronson, the terminally cool McQueen organized a mass escape from Stalag Luft III, a German POW camp. Based on a true story, the film's fast-paced action, combined with dark humor, made it a popular hit.

Paul Stookey, Mary Travers, and Peter Yarrow (*left to right*) comprised the folk group Peter, Paul & Mary. Their 1963 hit "Puff the Magic Dragon" became the stuff of urban legend, as many listeners assumed that its lyrics told a subtle tale of marijuana toking. Not so, claimed Yarrow, who said that his college friend, Leonard Lipton, conceived the idea as a bittersweet comment on the loss of innocence entailed in growing up—just like the lyrics say. Peter, Paul & Mary also boasted *Billboard*'s No. 2 single of 1963, a cover version of Bob Dylan's civil rights anthem "Blowin' in the Wind," which they performed at the March on Washington in August.

The Folkies

THE TERM "FOLK MUSIC" covers much musical ground. Folk artists have sung everything from arcane traditional tunes to contemporary topical anthems. In the Sixties, voices for social change found folk music an ideal vehicle for expression.

Already tied to progressive causes going back at least as far as Woody Guthrie (1930s), folk music's direct approach and earnest simplicity soon found a receptive audience in the politically turbulent Sixties. New York's Greenwich Village became a proving ground for many folk artists, including Peter, Paul & Mary, Theo

Bob Dylan and Joan Baez

Bikel, and Phil Ochs. Perhaps the key figure spearheading the folk revival was Pete Seeger, the banjo-strumming activist whose "Where Have All the Flowers Gone?" became a folk staple. Under his tutelage and energetic promotion, a new generation of artists developed and flourished.

During the musical lull between early rock 'n' roll and the British Invasion, the popularity of ABC-TV's *Hootenanny* (1963–64) signaled mainstream acceptance of folk music. After the network banned Seeger for his controversial politics, the activist folkies stayed away. But Seeger didn't need the exposure, having by that time gotten the Newport Folk Festival up and running. Appreciative audiences gathered each year to hear the likes of Odetta and Joan Baez, among many others. But the biggest star was an enigmatic Minnesotan who called himself Bob Dylan.

Although he was initially viewed as a Guthrie wanna-be, Dylan's work soon transcended all labels, encompassing folk, blues, country, and rock. Compositions such as "A Hard Rain's A-Gonna Fall" and "Masters of War" demonstrated a lyrical sophistication and a gift for allegory. From his pen flowed the most enduring folk hits of the era, including "Blowin' in the Wind," "Mr. Tambourine Man," "It Ain't Me, Babe," and "The Times They Are A-Changin'."

In Japan, the 1954 film *Gojira* (*Godzilla*) was a gritty allegory about the horrors of nuclear war. But in America, the film was simply considered terrific drive-in fodder. Success of *Godzilla* led to a string of increasingly campy rubber-suit releases, which were dubbed in English for American audiences. The series reached its "pinnacle" in 1963, when an American legend met the Japanese icon in *King Kong vs. Godzilla*. An ambiguous ending left the winner of the battle in doubt.

Mary Tyler Moore and Dick Van Dyke entertained America as Laura and Rob Petrie on *The Dick Van Dyke Show*. The show, which ran on CBS from 1961 to 1966, ushered in the golden age of situation comedies. Aided by a brilliant ensemble cast—including Rose Marie, Morey Amsterdam, and the show's producer, Carl Reiner—it combined sweetness with a sharp comedic bite that echoed vaudeville. Moreover, the modern, feel-good nature of the show resonated with the Kennedy's Camelot. Moore, known for her Capri pants, was as much of a fashion trendsetter as First Lady Jackie Kennedy.

1963

August 20: Physicist Edward Teller, dubbed the "father of the H-bomb," concludes Senate testimony in which he publicly opposes the U.S.–USSR nuclear test-ban treaty. • While in South Vietnam, U.S. Ambassador Henry Cabot Lodge gets signals from Washington to support a military coup against President Ngo Dinh Diem. *See* November 1, 1963.

August 27: NAACP cofounder William Du Bois dies at 95.

August 28: In a civil rights event planned by A. Philip Randolph and Bayard Rustin, 250,000 people—many of whom are white—march to the Lincoln Memorial in Washington, D.C. Various civil rights leaders speak, including Martin Luther King, Jr., who delivers his "I Have a Dream" speech.

August 30: An emergency "hot line" teletype connection linking Washington, D.C., and Moscow becomes operational. It was established to help prevent breakdown of communication during political crises.

September 1: In Yokosuka, Japan, 100,000 people demonstrate against the proposed visit of U.S. nuclear-powered submarines to Japan.

September 9: All five of Alabama's district court judges issue a blanket restraining order prohibiting Governor George Wallace from blocking integration of schools in Tuskegee, Birmingham, and Mobile. *See* September 10, 1963.

September 10: President Kennedy federalizes the Alabama National Guard to prevent Governor George Wallace from using the troops to block desegregation.

September 15: A powerful bomb planted by Ku Klux Klansmen in a black church in Birmingham, Alabama, explodes, killing four girls who are inside the building.

September 19: A gay rights demonstration is held in New York City. Demonstrators protest against discrimination in the military. ➤

Future U.S. president Bill Clinton shakes hands with President John F. Kennedy on July 24, 1963. At the time, Clinton was a student leader of the American Legion Boys Nation. Kennedy's example of political courage in the face of great challenges made a strong impact on Clinton. In 1998 he addressed the same organization of young people and shared his memory of meeting Kennedy. Clinton said that JFK inspired young leaders to discuss "the kind of world we would inherit and about what we had to do about it."

British police investigate a London–Glasgow Royal Mail train stopped on a bridge shortly after it was robbed by at least 15 men on August 8, 1963. In what the British press dubbed "The Great Train Robbery," the bandits absconded with £2.6 million and didn't even use guns (although they did beat the train driver, Jack Mills, with iron bars). The gang members were captured, convicted, and sentenced to prison. In spite of the serious injuries to Mills, London tabloids tended to romanticize both the daring heist and the escapes.

American composer Samuel Barber, who attempted his first opera at age 10, composed his renowned *Adagio for Strings* in 1936. In 1963 he won a Pulitzer Prize for his *Piano Concerto No. 1*. Stated Schirmer.com: "Samuel Barber's music, masterfully crafted and built on romantic structures and sensibilities, is at once lyrical, rhythmically complex, and harmonically rich." Barber's opera *Antony and Cleopatra* premiered at the new Metropolitan Opera House in New York City on September 16, 1966. The audience showed its approval with 14 curtain calls.

The bubbly Annette Funicello (*on surfboard*) co-starred in the 1963 film *Beach Party* with frequent onscreen boyfriend Frankie Avalon (*upper right*). *Beach Party* launched Funicello, a former Mousketeer on *The Mickey Mouse Club,* as the queen of the popular beach movies. The lightweight films mesmerized teenagers (and unnerved adults) with a blend of fantasy, music, farce, and lust. Beach party movies coincided with the "dropping-out" lifestyle of the early 1960s.

Author Jessica Mitford, pictured in a burial crypt, wrote the 1963 exposé *The American Way of Death.* This classic piece of muckraking attacked the U.S. funeral industry for ripping off the public. For example, undertakers, who had recast themselves as "funeral directors," aggressively promoted overpriced coffins and expensive suits for the deceased, even when caskets were closed. Dying seemed to cost more than living. The No. 1 bestseller helped spur the Federal Trade Commission to establish standards for the industry for the first time.

Henry Cabot Lodge, U.S. ambassador to the Republic of Vietnam (popularly known as South Vietnam), presents his credentials to Republic of Vietnam President Ngo Dinh Diem in August 1963. At the time, many in the Kennedy Administration, including Lodge, were concerned that Diem, America's ally, was out of touch with his own people. The new ambassador suggested that Diem dismiss his brother, Nhu. Even President Kennedy publicly said that a change in personnel in the Republic of Vietnam was necessary. The South Vietnamese leader refused even to consider the possibility. Subsequently, Lodge encouraged South Vietnamese dissident military leaders by informing them, through a CIA contact, that the United States would not oppose a coup against Diem and his brother if one were to occur.

Scientist Edward Teller, known as the father of the H-bomb, testifies before the Senate Foreign Relations Committee on August 20, 1963. He spoke against the proposed treaty that would ban nuclear testing by the United States, Great Britain, and the Soviet Union. Along with the Joint Chiefs of Staff, he fretted that the crafty Soviets would figure out some way to cheat, thereby damaging U.S. security. Teller said the treaty was not a step toward peace but a step "away from safety and possibly a step toward war." Renowned Russian physicist Andrei Sakharov, on the other hand, opposed nuclear testing. He feared that radioactive fallout could kill hundreds of thousands of civilians.

"I Have a Dream"

FRUSTRATED BY THE U.S. government's inaction and weary of killings, clubs, and fire hoses, thousands of civil rights workers and their supporters converged on the nation's capital on August 28, 1963. They came from Birmingham and Montgomery and far-flung parts of the country. They came to march on Washington for "jobs and freedom," and they came to pressure Congress to pass proposed civil rights legislation. In all, about 250,000 people gathered around the reflecting pool in front of the Lincoln Memorial to hear various speakers, especially Martin Luther King, Jr., address the nation.

King delivered his "I Have a Dream" speech at the pinnacle of the civil rights movement, and he was aware of the moment's gravity. King's sermonic tones rose above the massive crowd: "I am happy to join with you today in what will go down in history as the greatest demonstration for freedom in the history of our nation." Millions of Americans watched the speech live on all three television networks. Toward the end of his speech, King began the famous refrain, "I have a dream that one day. . . ." He defined a "color-blind" society in which one day black and white children "will be able to join hands." He expressed his hope that his four children would not be "judged by the color of their skin but by the content of their character."

The famous lines offered Americans a dream of the future, but the speech was also a call to immediate action: "We have also come to this hallowed spot to remind America of the fierce urgency of now," King said. He offered Americans a foreboding choice between immediate freedom for African-Americans and "a rude awakening if the nation returns to business as usual." For the moment, King's speech was able to overshadow growing divisions between the non-violent SCLC and the younger, increasingly militant SNCC. Earlier in the day, for example, SNCC leader John Lewis had to be convinced to soften his more confrontational rhetoric before speaking to the crowd.

According to polls, Americans broadly supported the goals of the civil rights movement after the speech. Despite underlying fissures, the March on Washington was a high point in the movement and would provide the popular pressure to finally pass the momentous Civil Rights Act of 1964.

"Those who hope that the Negro needed to blow off steam and will now be content will have a rude awakening if the nation returns to business as usual. There will be neither rest nor tranquility in America until the Negro is granted his citizenship rights."

—MARTIN LUTHER KING, JR., FROM HIS "I HAVE A DREAM" SPEECH AT THE MARCH ON WASHINGTON, AUGUST 28, 1963

Demonstrators at the March on Washington cheer Martin Luther King, Jr., after his "I Have a Dream" speech. It was a glorious day not only for King but for all the civil rights activists who made the trip. "The heart of the American Negro was revealed today," said Senator Jacob Javits (R–NY). "This was an unforgettable demonstration. It was dignified, extraordinarily disciplined, and intensely patriotic." The March on Washington helped build the momentum that led to the Civil Rights Act of 1964 and King's Nobel Peace Prize that same year.

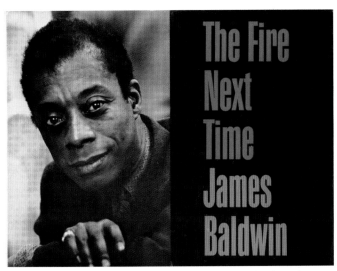

After Martin Luther King's speech about "brotherhood" at the 1963 March on Washington, many white Americans believed they were entering an era of improved race relations. James Baldwin was not so naive. His essay *The Fire Next Time* (1963) proved to be prophetic. He warned America: "Negroes of this country may never rise to power, but they are well placed indeed to precipitate chaos and ring down the curtain on the American dream." From 1965 to '68, major race riots would rage in numerous American cities.

U.S. Air Force Sergeant John Bretoski (*left*) and Army Lieutenant Colonel Charles Fitzgerald man the United States–Soviet Union "hot line" (actually a teletype machine) during a test run. On June 20, 1963, the White House and Kremlin had signed an agreement to set up the hot line, which became operational on August 30. The hot line enabled the two countries to send each other coded messages without delay on issues of international security. During the Cuban Missile Crisis, it had taken several hours for urgent communications to be transmitted, dramatically illustrating the need for improved means of détente.

Standing, Singing Together

AT THE DEMONSTRATION I saw Americans who were dedicated to the principles of individual liberty, political freedom, and the Constitution of the United States. I saw there an integrated audience. It has been said that one picture is worth a thousand words. Today, millions of the American people saw, by television, people of various races, creeds, and nationalities standing together, singing together, speaking together, walking together, playing together, and working together in the nations's capital. Let no one tell me it is ncessary to have segregation....

The participants were like actors in a mighty drama. Who was the audience, and where was the audience? Not here. The audience was back in every village, town, hamlet, city, and farm home in America—185 million people—because this great drama went out to the people this afternoon. I venture to say that there was more mass education on the issues of social justice and human rights in America than in all the history of our Republic.

—SENATOR HUBERT H. HUMPHREY (D–MN),
ADDRESSING THE SENATE ON AUGUST 28, 1963

The parents of Denise McNair hold a picture of their daughter, who died in a bombing in Birmingham, Alabama, on September 15, 1963. A blast at the Sixteenth Street Baptist Church killed Denise and three other African-American girls while injuring 20 other people. The bomb detonated under the church steps during Sunday school at 10:22 A.M. The explosion blew through the stone and brick wall. A stained glass window depicting Jesus on the cross remained intact, except the head was blown off. One of the sisters of the murdered girls survived with more than 20 pieces of glass in her face and eyes. The brutal act shocked the nation and emboldened civil rights activists.

The Avanti was created by Studebaker President Sherwood H. Egbert and famed industrial designer Raymond Loewy. A grand-touring automobile (based, ironically, on the frame of the humble Studebaker Lark), the Avanti had ample V-8 oomph. The Avanti R1 and the supercharged R2 boasted horsepowers of 240 and 290, respectively. A four-seat interior was inspired by aircraft ergonomics. More than 3,800 Avantis were produced for the 1963 model year ($4,445 base), but output dipped to 809 for '64, Avanti's final season. However, various niche manufacturers who cater to Avanti enthusiasts have kept the name and bodystyle alive.

Armed with a blazing fastball and knee-buckling curveball, Los Angeles Dodgers ace Sandy Koufax blew away National League hitters from 1963 to 1966, going 97–27. In 1963 he led the NL in wins (25–5), ERA (1.88), and strikeouts (306) en route to the Cy Young and Most Valuable Player awards—not to mention the World Series title. Classy and courageous, Koufax pitched for three years in almost constant pain from arthritis. He retired at the peak of his career, at age 30, in 1966.

the negroes
puerto ricans
jews beyond the melting pot
italians
and irish of
new york city

Beyond the Melting Pot, an influential and controversial book written by Daniel Patrick Moynihan and Nathan Glazer, was published in 1963. The two Harvard professors profiled the five major ethnic groups in New York City—Puerto Ricans, Jews, African-Americans, Italians, and Irish—and discussed how they clashed. The book exploded the "melting pot" myth in which, over time, people of all ethnicities would live harmoniously in America's cities.

Jazz pianist Thelonious Monk was one of the most important and innovative jazz performers and composers of the Bop Era, emerging in the late 1940s and impressing audiences for decades. Monk's piano style featured an active right hand with an equally active left one, as he combined stride and more angular rhythms using the whole keyboard. Many of his compositions, such as "Round Midnight" and "I Mean You," remain popular standards in the jazz repertoire. His 1963 album, *Monk's Dream,* was an artistic and critical triumph. In 1964 Monk became only the third jazz musician to appear on the cover of *Time* magazine.

Claes Oldenburg's *Two Cheeseburgers, With Everything* typified his singular approach to "Pop Art." The Pop Art movement began in reaction to the intellectualism of abstract expressionism, in vogue throughout the 1940s and '50s. Oldenburg used soft materials to depict hard objects. The unexpected sagging and contours that resulted challenged conventional perceptions. Oldenburg also experimented with scale, creating oversized versions of common items.

Comedian Woody Allen looks neurotically pensive in this 1963 publicity still. Allen, born Allen Stewart Konigsberg in 1935, changed his name for show business. As a teenager, he wrote jokes for such major television programs as *The Ed Sullivan Show* and *The Tonight Show*. In the early 1960s Allen attracted a loyal following as a stand-up comedian noted for his self-deprecating intellectual humor. He quipped that he cheated on a metaphysics exam by looking within the soul of the student sitting next to him. Allen launched his legendary filmmaking career by directing the 1966 comedy *What's Up, Tiger Lily?*.

Barbie and Ken were America's hottest couple in the 1960s—at least among kids. Barbie was introduced in 1959, with boyfriend Ken following in 1961. Although millions of little girls loved Barbie and took her as a role model, criticism of Barbie-as-sex-symbol did influence Mattel Corporation to introduce a less sexy friend, Midge, in 1964. Later incarnations of Barbie embarked on careers ranging from doctor to ballerina to astronaut. For most admirers in the 1960s, she was, in the words of one student of Barbiemania, "teaching [girls] what was expected of them by society."

Valachi Names Names

"**M**AFIA? WHAT'S THE MAFIA? There is not a Mafia," contended Joe Colombo, head of the Colombo crime family from 1964 to 1971. Many Americans—not to mention the FBI—wouldn't have challenged Colombo's denial of an organized national crime network. All that changed in 1963, when Joseph Valachi, a longtime "soldier" for the Genovese crime family, introduced America to the labyrinthine structure and practices of the Mafia.

Valachi, a dedicated "made man" since 1930, pled guilty to a narcotics charge in 1960. While in prison in 1962, he killed a man whom he thought was going to kill him. He offered to expose the inner workings of the mob in exchange for leniency.

In September 1963 Valachi appeared as the star witness before a Senate Subcommittee on Investigations known as the McClellan Committee. In nationally televised testimony, Valachi identified crime "families" in New York City and across the nation, fingering the bosses and senior officials in each group. He also provided a worm's-eye view of Mafia hierarchy and rituals: *capos, consiglieri,* blood oaths, and *omerta*—the Mafia code of silence that he had irrevocably ruptured.

"What Valachi did was beyond measure," said William Hundley of the U.S. Justice Department. "Before he came along, we had no concrete evidence that anything like this existed.... But Valachi named names.... In a word, he showed us the face of the enemy." Valachi lived until 1971, when he died in prison of natural causes.

September 27: In testimony before the Senate Permanent Investigations Subcommittee, Mafia "soldier" Joe Valachi identifies heads of organized crime in the U.S.

October: The U.S. works with West Germany to accomplish a military exercise called "Operation Big Lift," a massive, very quick airlift of an American armored division to West Germany, where GIs take control of prepositioned tanks. • *The Feminine Mystique,* by Betty Friedan, is published. The book reveals the unhappiness many American women feel with their traditional roles.

October 2: *CBS Evening News with Walter Cronkite* expands from 15 to 30 minutes. • Los Angeles Dodgers pitcher Sandy Koufax strikes out 15 New York Yankees to set a World Series single-game record.

October 10: Soviet troops block a U.S. military convoy in East Germany, preventing it from passing West checkpoint barriers.

October 11: President Kennedy endorses a report by the President's Commission on the Status of Women that documents widespread discrimination against American women. The report makes 24 specific recommendations. • Iconic French singer Edith Piaf dies at 47.

October 16: The New York City newspaper *New York Mirror* publishes its final edition.

October 22: About 225,000 Chicago public school students stay home in a one-day protest of *de facto* school segregation in the city.

October 31: Leaking propane gas causes an explosion at the Indiana State Fairgrounds in Indianapolis, killing some 70 ice-show spectators and injuring more than 350.

November: Touch-Tone telephone service is introduced, beginning a long phaseout of rotary phones. ➤

Running back Jim Brown, who led the National Football League in rushing in eight of his nine seasons, enjoyed his greatest campaign in 1963. The Cleveland Browns star set NFL records with 1,863 yards rushing and 6.4 yards per rush that season. Sports columnist Red Smith wrote, "For mercurial speed, airy nimbleness, and explosive violence...there is no other like Mr. Brown." Brown retired after the 1965 season and became a prolific movie actor.

An American military adviser instructs a member of the South Vietnamese army in the use of an automatic rifle in early October 1963. By the end of the year, 16,300 U.S. military personnel were in South Vietnam, up from about 900 at the end of 1960. According to the Kennedy and Johnson administrations, these were not officially combat troops; rather, their purpose was to teach the South Vietnamese military to fight the Communist insurgents on their own. In truth, these advisers often found themselves in combat, and several hundred were killed or wounded in the early 1960s.

President Kennedy signed the Limited Nuclear Test Ban Treaty on October 7, 1963. The treaty, agreed on among the United States, Great Britain, and the Soviet Union, prohibited nuclear testing in the atmosphere, outer space, and under water. A year earlier, Kennedy had ended the Cuban Missile Crisis that had brought the world to the brink of nuclear war. Leveraging his success, JFK accelerated negotiations with Moscow. But Kennedy's real goal, a comprehensive test-ban treaty, eluded him. In the ensuing decades, underground testing allowed for new and more advanced nuclear weapons.

Thomas Pynchon burst upon the literary scene in 1963 with his novel *V.* The story follows the life of Benny Profane, just released from the Navy. Profane is an irresponsible slacker until he gets involved with an ambitious man named Stencil, who is on a mission to find an elusive woman named V. The absurdist tale, steeped in contemporary jazz references, is widely considered to be the first postmodern fiction masterpiece.

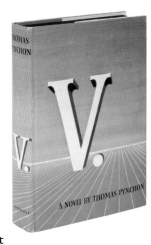

"There's no problem you can even put a name to. But I'm desperate. I begin to feel I have no personality. I'm a server of food and a putter-on of pants and a bedmaker, somebody who can be called on when you want something. But who am I?"

—MOTHER OF FOUR WHO LEFT COLLEGE AT AGE 19 TO GET MARRIED; QUOTED IN *THE FEMININE MYSTIQUE*, BY BETTY FRIEDAN

The Feminine Mystique

THE PUBLICATION OF Betty Friedan's *The Feminine Mystique* marked the start of a "second wave" in the history of American feminism. The book, which critiqued the suburban, middle-class homemaker role to which so many women felt limited, sold five million copies by 1970.

Friedan, who had attended Smith College and worked as a journalist in her 20s, gave up her professional aspirations for marriage and family. In 1957, at the 15-year reunion of her college class, Friedan administered surveys to women, asking them about their experiences since they left Smith. She combined their responses with an analysis of various cultural sources—women's magazines, for example.  Friedan concluded that millions of suburban, middle-class women were unhappy, lying awake each night wondering, *Is this all?*

Friedan indicted the "feminine mystique," an American cultural assumption, she charged, that women should be content to "glory in their own femininity." For middle-class women in America, the suburban home was not a haven of peace and calm in the postwar world but, rather, a "comfortable concentration camp." In order to find fulfillment, she argued, women needed to find their own identity—distinct from their husbands'—and their own vocations (here the book clearly targeted middle-class women; working-class and minority women had always worked).

The book touched a nerve, partly because some women in the 1950s had been moving into the workforce, trying to negotiate the dual roles of work and family when cultural expectations dictated that the home should be the primary obligation. Moreover, the civil rights movement had so successfully focused the nation's attention on discrimination that many women now saw the limits on their lives as a similar injustice. Describing women's unhappiness as "the problem that has no name," Friedan spoke for millions. In 1966 Friedan cofounded and became the first president of the National Organization for Women.

An artificially evolved coal miner (played by David McCallum, pictured with actress Jill Haworth) works his magic in *The Outer Limits,* an inventive science fiction show that ran from 1963 to '65 on ABC. Moody and highly literate, the show tackled large social issues such as racism, the dangers of nuclear power plants, and government violations of privacy. Each episode began with the chilling announcement, "There is nothing wrong with your television set." Such guest stars as Bruce Dern and Sally Kellerman made audiences tremble and consider bizarre possibilities.

Veronica "Ronnie" Bennett, her sister Estelle Bennett, and cousin Nedra Talley (*left to right*) comprised the stylish Ronettes. Signed by producer Phil Spector in 1963, the Ronettes were probably the most popular "girl group" of the early 1960s, peaking with "Be My Baby" in 1963. They also helped popularize the beehive hairdo, which was all the rage in the early '60s. "Everybody wanted the beehive, even women with real, real short hair," said Margaret Vinci Heldt, creator of the hairstyle. "They looked more like anthills than a beehive, then they got bigger and bigger and became hornet's nests."

This 1963 propaganda poster from the People's Republic of China (PRC) proclaims that "American imperialism must be driven out of South Vietnam." The Chinese Communists feared that anti-Communist forces, led by the United States, were trying to encircle the PRC. During the 1960s, more than 300,000 Chinese served in North Vietnam in support roles.

West Germans watch the deployment of American military forces in their country in October 1963. Operation Big Lift was a major U.S. military maneuver in which 14,500 combat-ready troops were flown from the United States to West Germany. The Kennedy Administration wanted to show the Soviets and East Germans that it could rapidly reinforce NATO units in Europe in case of a Communist military provocation.

On October 30, 1963, several dozen demonstrators protested U.S. involvement in Vietnam across the street from a hotel where President John F. Kennedy was attending a reception. Opposition to the Vietnam War, although still modest in 1963, was growing. Pundits such as journalist Walter Lippmann and political scientist Hans Morgenthau wrote critiques of American policy, while Senator Mike Mansfield and French President Charles de Gaulle warned JFK about deepening involvement. However, because so few U.S. soldiers had been killed or wounded, "the war in Vietnam was still not a major political issue for most Americans," according to historian Mel Small.

South Vietnamese General Duong Van Minh walks joyfully down the streets of Saigon in November 1963 after leading the coup that overthrew President Ngo Dinh Diem. Nicknamed "Big Minh" because of his large frame, he rose to importance during the mid-1950s when he helped Diem quell internal threats. He gradually grew disillusioned with Diem's rule, organized the coup, and ordered the deaths of Diem and Diem's brother, Nhu. Minh ruled for just two months before being ousted by General Nguyen Khanh. Eleven years later, it would be Minh, as acting president, who would surrender South Vietnam to invading North Vietnamese troops.

South Vietnamese President Ngo Dinh Diem (*right*) and his brother, Ngo Dinh Nhu, lay slain after a successful coup against the Diem government on November 1–2, 1963. Though U.S. officials did not actively participate in the coup, they knew beforehand that it was going to happen and did nothing to prevent it. In fact, adviser McGeorge Bundy, acting for President Kennedy, informed U.S. Ambassador Henry Cabot on October 30 that "it is in the interests of the U.S. Government that [the coup] should succeed." Diem and Nhu were captured while hiding in a church and then killed by agents of the coup leaders. When President Kennedy heard of the deaths, he reportedly "rushed from the room with a look of shock and dismay on his face." Later he said that the White House had to "bear a good deal of the blame" for the deaths.

In 1963 Chrysler Corporation loaned to VIPs 55 prototypes of its newly built, turbine-powered (as opposed to piston-driven) automobile, a project it had been working on since the 1930s. Although the company recommended diesel fuel for the innovative vehicle, it could run on any flammable liquid, including "jet fuel, home heating oil, peanut oil, tequila, and even Chanel No. 5," according to *Barracuda Magazine*. Ever-restrictive EPA regulations pushed Chrysler to dump the project.

November 1: The South Vietnamese army overthrows President Ngo Dinh Diem. *See* November 2, 1963.

November 2: South Vietnamese President Ngo Dinh Diem, 62, and his brother, Ngo Dinh Nhu, are murdered by the South Vietnamese military.

November 14: AFL–CIO President George Meany says in a convention speech in New York City that automation is "a curse to society" that could wreck the U.S. economy.

November 20: The United Nations Commission on Human Rights adopts a declaration to eliminate all forms of racial discrimination.

November 22: At 12:30 P.M., CST, President Kennedy is shot and mortally wounded while riding in a motorcade in Dallas. Texas Governor John Connally is seriously wounded. • Later, Dallas patrolman J. D. Tippit is shot and killed, probably by alleged presidential assassin Lee Harvey Oswald. • Aboard Air Force One at 2:39 P.M., CST, Vice President Lyndon Johnson is sworn in as president of the United States. His wife, Lady Bird, and JFK's widow, Jackie, are among the witnesses. *See* November 24, 1963. • Novelist and essayist Aldous Huxley dies at 69.

November 24: Suspected Kennedy assassin Lee Harvey Oswald is shot and killed by Dallas nightclub owner Jack Ruby. The murder is inadvertently broadcast live on NBC-TV as Oswald is being moved by Dallas and federal authorities. *See* November 25, 1963.

November 25: The remains of President Kennedy are buried at Arlington National Cemetery.

November 27: In an address to a joint session of Congress, President Johnson declares his full support of the Kennedy legislative agenda, and urges the earliest possible passage of a national civil rights bill.

On November 22, 1963, President John F. Kennedy, Jackie Kennedy, and Texas Governor John Connally (*in front of JFK*) get ready to ride to the Dallas Trade Mart, where Kennedy was to speak. The President went to Texas to raise campaign money and mend political fences. The conservative and liberal factions of the Democratic Party in Texas (led by Governor Connally and Senator Ralph Yarborough, respectively) had been feuding; Kennedy hoped he could use his charm to get the two sides to stop their fussing. The Kennedys had spent time in San Antonio and Houston, cheered by thousands. The trip to Dallas would be tragic.

This is the view Lee Harvey Oswald had from the sixth floor of the Texas School Book Depository in Dallas on November 22, 1963. Oswald reportedly fired three shots at the presidential limousine as it passed by the building, using a 6.5 millimeter rifle purchased from a Chicago mail-order house. One shot missed while the other two found their targets. The first, called "the magic bullet" by critics of the Warren Commission Report, allegedly hit Kennedy in the back, exited his throat, then managed to strike Governor John Connolly in the back and wrist. The third and fatal bullet struck the President in the head.

The Assassination of JFK

ELECTED BY THE SLIMMEST of majorities three years earlier, President John F. Kennedy planned to go all out for reelection in 1964. Though the campaign's official start was months away, in autumn he began laying the groundwork, visiting states crucial to his interests.

The South posed particular concerns, with conservative Democrats blocking many of his key initiatives. Making matters worse, a feud in Texas between Senator Ralph Yarborough and Governor John Connally threatened to fray JFK's carefully crafted party unity. By scheduling personal appearances in Texas's major cities, the President believed he could resolve intrastate tensions while boosting his own poll numbers.

Kennedy's planned visit to Dallas provoked special trepidation. A month earlier in Dallas, UN Ambassador Adlai Stevenson was besieged by right-wing extremists, spat upon, and struck by a demonstrator's placard. Though Texas suffered a black eye nationally, the mood in what the President would term "nut country" was hardly repentant. *The Dallas Morning News* ran a full-page ad sardonically headlined "Welcome Mr. Kennedy," detailing a list of perceived grievances. Meanwhile, instigators handed out leaflets accusing the President of treason.

When John and Jackie Kennedy arrived in Dallas on November 22, safety concerns seemed unfounded, as enthusiastic crowds offered a robust, Texas-styled greeting. To be sure, a large part of the warmth was directed at the First Lady, who was making a rare campaign appearance. At breakfast in Fort Worth, her carefully staged late arrival maximized attention, prompting the President to good-naturedly recall being similarly overshadowed in Paris.

The downtown motorcade was timed to coincide with the lunch hour, ensuring a full turnout. Texas First Lady Nellie Connally, while riding with the Kennedys in a limousine convertible, burst with delight. "Mr. President," she remarked, "you certainly can't say Dallas doesn't love you." Moments later, three rifle shots were fired into the limousine, blasting open the President's skull and severely wounding Governor Connally.

Word of the tragedy first reached the country six minutes later. Millions of midday programming viewers were jarred alert with the words, "Three shots were fired at Pres-

Jackie Kennedy cradling her husband moments after the fatal shot

ident Kennedy's motorcade today in downtown Dallas." Though he was clinically dead, doctors continued working on the President until the futility was fully recognized.

Meanwhile, in the aftermath of the shooting, dozens of bystanders and several police officers stormed the grassy area near the triple underpass, searching frantically for a gunman believed to be in the vicinity. Other officers encircled the Texas School Book Depository building, where some witnesses reported seeing a rifle sticking from an open window.

Official word that Americans had lost their president came at 1:48 P.M. Twenty minutes earlier, Dallas patrolman J. D. Tippit was shot dead in the street. Police swarmed to the suburb of Irving, tracking Tippit's killer. The search ended at a movie theater with the arrest of 24-year-old Lee Harvey Oswald, a onetime Marine who had lived in Russia. Though authorities had been keeping tabs on Oswald, no one had considered him a potential risk.

As circumstantial evidence tying Oswald to both killings accumulated, the prisoner vehemently maintained his innocence. "I'm just a patsy!" he declared to hordes of reporters besieging the Dallas City Jail. Any hopes for his day in court to resolve matters ended with his slaying two days later at the hands of Dallas nightclub owner Jack Ruby. The weekend of stunning events came to a somber close on November 25 at Arlington National Cemetery, where world leaders gathered to bid farewell to America's fallen president.

1963

November 29: President Johnson names U.S. Supreme Court Chief Justice Earl Warren to head an investigation into the assassination of President Kennedy.

December: The long-awaited measles vaccine becomes available. It eventually will reduce measles cases by more than 90 percent. • Running back Jim Brown of the Cleveland Browns sets NFL records for yards rushing (1,863) and yards per carry (6.4). • An X-15 rocket plane reaches an altitude of 100,000 feet at Mach 6.06.

December 6: Former First Lady Jackie Kennedy and her children, Caroline and John, Jr., move to the Georgetown district of Washington, D.C.

December 7: The District Court of Tokyo declares that the atomic bomb attacks on Hiroshima and Nagasaki were illegal acts of hostility.

December 8: Frank Sinatra, Jr., is kidnapped at gunpoint from his motel in Lake Tahoe, Nevada. He will be released three days later after a ransom is paid by his father.

December 9: The Studebaker Corporation announces it will end automobile production in the United States but will continue in Hamilton, Ontario, Canada.

December 12: Kenya gains independence from Great Britain. Jomo Kenyatta becomes the new nation's first prime minister.

December 20: West Berliners, under special dispensation from the East German government, begin to cross into East Berlin for Christmas visits with relatives.

December 22: American entertainer Paul Robeson, a proponent of communism, arrives in the U.S. from London following a five-year U.S. exile.

December 26: "I Want to Hold Your Hand" by the Beatles is released, sparking Beatlemania in the U.S.

President Kennedy slumps in the backseat of his limousine as Jackie ministers to him and Secret Service Agent Clinton Hill mounts the back of the vehicle. The shooting took place at approximately 12:30 P.M., and the limousine arrived at Dallas's Parkland Hospital within a few minutes. Doctors worked furiously to revive the young president but were unable to deal with the massive brain damage. His death was officially announced at 1:48 P.M. The Warren Commission Report later criticized the Secret Service for numerous lapses, including not having in place a policy to search all buildings along the route of the motorcade.

Inside the Trauma Rooms

A FEW MINUTES BEFORE they brought in the body of the president, a Secret Service agent burst into the trauma room, waving a submachine gun. Everyone in the room hit the floor.

A man in a dark business suit ran in after him. The agent knocked him out with one punch, and as the man slid down the wall, he reached into his coat pocket and pulled out an FBI badge.

A second later, a gurney bearing the president, surrounded by an emergency room team, rattled past and disappeared into Trauma Room One, right across from John's. That door, too, slammed shut. Like me, another woman in a pink suit, also splattered with her husband's blood, stood forlornly in the hall.

—NELLIE CONNALLY, *FROM LOVE FIELD*, BY CONNALLY AND MICKEY HERSKOWITZ

Vice President Lyndon Johnson, flanked by Jackie Kennedy (*right*) and his wife, Lady Bird Johnson (*left*), takes the presidential oath of office. Texas Federal District Judge Sara Hughes swore in LBJ on Air Force One a few hours after President Kennedy's death. Johnson, not realizing that he legally had become president at the moment JFK died, wanted to be sure he had full presidential power. Johnson insisted that Jackie stand next to him. According to historian Robert Dallek, he felt that "she owed it to the country to endorse the transition of power by her presence." Dallek also points out that Johnson, like the whole nation, was "in a state of shock" because of the tragic events of the day.

The front page of the Soviet periodical *Nedelya* features a photograph of slain American President John F. Kennedy. World reaction was deeply sympathetic to the United States and the Kennedy family. Willi Brandt, mayor of Berlin, lamented that "a flame went out."

From the Soviet Union came an outpouring of grief and sympathy. Premier Nikita Khrushchev praised JFK for both his toughness and his willingness to negotiate. Most poignantly, *The New York Times* reported that a 15-year-old Russian boy ran a mile in the dark and cold to tell an American high school classmate the tragic news.

Lee Harvey Oswald speaks to the press after being formally charged with the murder of President Kennedy. He denied any involvement in the assassination. Oswald's troubled life had included truancy from school, a stint in the Marines, time in the USSR, a return to the United States with his Russian wife, participation in pro-Castro activities in New Orleans, and employment in October 1963 by the Texas School Book Depository. After allegedly firing the fatal shot, Oswald left the scene of the crime. He went to his boarding house, allegedly shot and killed Dallas police officer J. D. Tippit, and tried to hide in a movie theater. He was arrested at the theater as a suspect in the Tippit shooting. Soon after, he was charged with JFK's murder.

Dallas nightclub owner Jack Ruby shoots alleged Kennedy assassin Lee Harvey Oswald as the accused is being escorted out of the Dallas Municipal Building. Oswald later died of his wounds. For much of his life, Ruby owned nightclubs and was in and out of trouble with the law. He also associated with known mobsters, a fact that has led some conspiracy theorists to place him in the middle of a mob plot in which Oswald was hired to kill the President and then silenced by Ruby. (This is one of many conspiracy theories that have never been proved, including ones that blame Fidel Castro and the CIA.) Ruby's 1964 conviction for murder was overturned on a technicality, but he died of cancer in jail in 1967 while awaiting a second trial.

New & Notable

Books

The American Way of Death
  by Jessica Mitford
By the North Gate by Joyce Carol Oates
City of Night by John Rechy
The Collector by John Fowles
The Feminine Mystique by Betty Friedan
The Fire Next Time by James Baldwin
The Learning Tree by Gordon Parks
V. by Thomas Pynchon

Movies

The Birds
Blood Feast
Cleopatra
8½
From Russia with Love
The Haunting
Hud
It's a Mad, Mad, Mad, Mad World
Lilies of the Field
Tom Jones

Songs

"Another Saturday Night"
  by Sam Cooke
"Be My Baby" by the Ronettes
"Da Doo Ron Ron" by the Crystals
"Heat Wave" by Martha
  and the Vandellas
"Hello Muddah, Hello Fadduh"
  by Allan Sherman
"I Saw Her Standing There,"
  by the Beatles
"It's My Party" by Lesley Gore
"Louie, Louie" by the Kingsmen
"She Loves You" by the Beatles
"Surf City" by Jan & Dean
"Surfin' USA" by the Beach Boys

Television

Burke's Law
The Fugitive
Let's Make a Deal
My Favorite Martian
The Outer Limits
The Patty Duke Show
Petticoat Junction

Theater

Barefoot in the Park
Enter Laughing
Luther
Oliver!

"Now I think that I should have guessed it could not last. I should have known that it was asking too much to dream that I might have grown old with him and see our children grow up together. So now he is a legend when he would have preferred to be a man."

—Jacqueline Kennedy, *Look* magazine, November 17, 1964

Members of the Kennedy family grieve for the fallen president during the funeral procession. John F. Kennedy left behind daughter Caroline, wife Jacqueline, brother Robert, and son John (*front, left to right*) as well as brother Ted (*back row, far left*). Drawn slowly in a caisson pulled by six white horses, the President's body was buried in Arlington National Cemetery, with an eternal flame marking his grave. Hundreds of dignitaries marched in the procession, including French President Charles de Gaulle and Britain's Prince Philip. The funeral's most poignant moment, as shown here, came when son John saluted as his father's casket passed by.

In spring 1963, the Beatles recorded their first long-playing album, *Please Please Me*. That LP, which boasted such hits as the title track, "I Saw Her Standing There," and "Twist and Shout," sparked "Beatlemania" in Europe. Then, on November 22 (just hours before President Kennedy was shot), the group released *With the Beatles* in the U.K. and Europe. That album would dislodge the earlier LP from a six-month reign at the top of the charts. In January 1964, as the Beatles single "I Want to Hold Your Hand" was skyrocketing to No. 1 on the U.S. charts, *Meet the Beatles!* (containing remixed material from their two British albums) hit stores in the States.

Lyndon Johnson

CRUDE, OVERBEARING, AND RUTHLESS, yet compassionate, thoughtful, and generous—Lyndon Baines Johnson was a complicated man, to say the least.

Johnson launched his political career in Texas when he was elected to the U.S. House of Representatives in 1937. A staunch supporter of Franklin Roosevelt's New Deal, LBJ worked his way up the political ladder, eventually claiming a seat in the U.S. Senate. By 1955 he was Senate Majority Leader and one of the most powerful Democrats on Capitol Hill.

In 1960 Johnson sought his party's nomination for the presidency, but lost to the more youthful and charismatic John F. Kennedy. Despite a clash in interests and personalities, the headstrong Texan accepted Kennedy's offer to run as vice president. Johnson's background gave the ticket vital southern support and ultimately helped swing the election in Kennedy's favor.

As vice president, Johnson was relegated to the sidelines, and many Cabinet members ridiculed him behind the scenes. Such mockery, along with the lack of inherent power in the office of the vice presidency, weighed heavily on Johnson's mind and was, to him, humiliating. But as fate would have it, an assassin's bullet propelled him into the position he had always coveted.

As the new president, Johnson affirmed his allegiance to Kennedy's agenda. "This nation will keep its commitments [in] South Vietnam," he declared in a speech just five days after the assassination of his predecessor. "We will carry on the fight against poverty and misery and disease and ignorance in other lands and in our own. We will serve all the nation, not one section or one sector or one group—but all Americans."

By and large, Johnson stuck to his promises, launching an array of "Great Society" social reforms, forcing through groundbreaking civil rights legislation, and escalating the war in Vietnam. He served as president during seven of the most turbulent years in American history.

Young Mau Mau fighters march in Kenya in December 1963. Since the late 1800s, Kenya had been a colony of Great Britain, which confiscated the farming land of natives and imposed other exploitive laws. The Mau Mau rebels emerged in the late 1940s, and for more than a decade they waged guerrilla warfare, focusing on British loyalists. Though tens of thousands of Mau Mau fighters were arrested, the rebels persevered until December 12, 1963, the day Kenya gained its independence. During a solemn ceremony, the last Mau Mau fighters handed over their weapons to Kenya's new prime minister, Jomo Kenyatta.

Frank Sinatra, Jr., talks to reporters for the first time after being released by kidnappers on December 11, 1963. His mother, Nancy, offers support. A singer himself, Frank Junior was taken from his hotel room at Lake Tahoe at gunpoint by three men, who let him go after Frank Senior paid a ransom of $240,000. Eventually, the perpetrators were caught and most of the money returned. However, the young Sinatra's career was dogged by false rumors that the snatch had been orchestrated by Junior as a publicity stunt designed to jump-start his career.

1964

Boomers Embrace the Beatles

On February 7, 1964, the Beatles arrived on Pan Am flight 101 from London at the newly renamed John F. Kennedy International Airport in New York City. Although it was the British band's first trip across the Atlantic, they already were insanely popular in the United States. On the tarmac, the Fab Four—John Lennon, Paul McCartney, George Harrison, and Ringo Starr—were greeted by several thousand teenagers, most of them screaming girls who strained their outstretched arms to get that much closer to the men of their dreams. It took about 100 police officers to keep the four lads with mop-top haircuts and mod black boots from being engulfed by their rapturous fans. About 200 reporters and disk jockeys were there to record the historical event.

Beatlemania was about to take America by storm. As the Associated Press declared, 1964 "was the year of the Beatles." At the same time, AP noted, it was the "Year of the Kids." Youth culture in the 1960s, comprised of 70 million post-World War II Baby Boomers, was a tidal wave that rolled right over an older generation's traditional mores and established lifestyles. The Beatles rode that wave better than anyone, giving their millions of fans a soundtrack to their first kiss, their first love, and—for many soon thereafter—their first toke of marijuana.

The Beatles began playing music together (initially with Pete Best instead of Starr on drums) in their native Liverpool, a tough, working-class port city. There, visiting Americans introduced records by the likes of Howlin' Wolf,

> *"My mother hates them, my father hates them, my teacher hates them. Can you think of three better reasons why I love them?"*
>
> —Young Beatles fan

On February 9, 1964, *The Ed Sullivan Show* introduced Americans to a soon-to-be cultural phenomenon known as Beatlemania. As the Fab Four were broadcast into tens of millions of living rooms across the nation, the character of a new generation was forever transformed.

Muddy Waters, Bo Diddly, Chuck Berry, and Buddy Holly to the local music scene. From this stew pot of styles, the Beatles developed their own sound. It included elements of London pop ballads, skiffle (a type of folk music characterized by improvised instruments), and the hard-charging, beat-driven American music. In fact, the name *Beatles* was a takeoff of Buddy Holly's backup band, the Crickets.

Like the Sixties-era youth culture to which they would be so important, the Beatles crossed national boundaries—even in their early years. In 1961 the band gained a popular following in the raucous music clubs of Hamburg, Germany. In 1963, under the professional guidance of manager Brian Epstein, the Beatles enjoyed their first big hit in England, "Please Please Me." By early 1964, "I Want to Hold Your Hand" was a transAtlantic monster hit, and they were ready to make their mark in the United States.

Two days after arriving in New York, the Beatles appeared on *The Ed Sullivan Show,* America's top-rated variety program. More than 72 million Americans tuned in, setting a record for an entertainment show. The live studio audience was ecstatic, squealing and screaming throughout the Beatles' performance, nearly drowning out the music. Nonetheless, Americans got the idea. Some observers recalled the hysteria over Elvis Presley a decade before. Others enjoyed the band's apparent joy and physical abandon, and suggested that the Beatles might just be what America needed to perk up its spirits.

Among more conservative Americans, the Beatles' antic style of performance, their mod style of dress, and the hard beat of their music was not nearly so welcome. Even before the band first stepped foot in the United States, anti-Beatles groups had formed across America. One of them, in Detroit, vowed to "stamp out the Beatles." When John Lennon was asked by a reporter about the Detroit group's campaign, he impishly replied: "First of all, we have a campaign of our own to stamp

Just prior to their first trip to the United States, the Beatles relax in a Paris hotel room with the manager who was pivotal to their success, Brian Epstein. After signing the boys in 1962, Epstein smartened up their appearance with matching suits and instructed them not to swear or smoke on stage. Pictured (*left to right*) are John Lennon, George Harrison, Epstein, Ringo Starr, and Paul McCartney.

It was all-out pandemonium at every venue the Beatles played during their first U.S. tour in August/September 1964. This ecstatic fan reaches out for drummer Ringo Starr in Indianapolis.

out Detroit." American teenagers loved the Beatles for that kind of flip witticism, even as it annoyed many adults. (Two years later, Lennon would incite large numbers of religious Americans to near hysteria by taking his ironic iconoclasm much further, informing them that "Christianity will go.... We're more popular than Jesus now.")

In 1964 the Beatles, under Epstein's firm hand, kept their rebellious spirit under control. In their early days playing in Liverpool and then Hamburg, they cultivated a working-class swagger and often performed in black leather. Epstein mainstreamed their look. He dressed the Fab Four in stylish suits and kept their long hair (long by the crew-cut standards of the early 1960s) neatly trimmed. Boyish and winning, the Beatles were far from confrontational during their first year in the United States. As Epstein understood, the Beatles needed to *appear* to play by the rules if they wanted to make it big in the music business. Because they did, Ed Sullivan and other mainstream entertainment industry types were happy to expose the group to a mass audience.

Beatlemania triumphed throughout the year. In addition to two more appearances on *Ed Sullivan,* they toured the U.S., Europe, and Australia. On April 4, their songs occupied the top five slots on the *Billboard* music chart: "Can't Buy Me Love," "Twist and Shout," "She Loves You," "I Want to Hold Your Hand," and "Please Please Me." The group's first movie, *A Hard Day's Night,* premiered in London on July 6. A cheapie that cost just $600,000 to produce, the film set the record for the highest grossing rock 'n' roll movie, eclipsing Elvis's *Viva Las Vegas.*

The film's title song, "A Hard Day's Night," demonstrated that the Beatles were more than just another cute boy band. It featured, as John Lennon biographer Jon Weiner writes, "more complicated chord changes than anything in rock music, eleven chords in all; the opening chord gained fame as the most complex and baffling one." The Beatles were extraordinary artists, and their influence on their fellow musicians and young people throughout the Sixties was simply unparalleled.

The Beatles' appeal to their young audience transcended their music and even their wit and charm. The band had an amazing feel for the youth culture zeitgeist. If it was hip and new, the Beatles were interested in it, explored it, and then usually exposed it—musically or otherwise—to their fans. So, in February 1964, the Beatles visited 22-year-old boxer Cassius Clay, a brash upstart whom the Fab Four recognized as one of their own.

On February 25, 1964, Cassius Clay upset the brutish Sonny Liston, scoring a seventh-round technical knockout to become the new heavyweight champion of the world. Young, brash, and vociferous, Clay appealed to the rebellious youth of America.

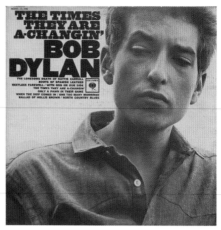

By the time his third album, *The Times They Are A-Changin'*, was released in 1964, Bob Dylan already had been embraced by the anti-establishment as a prophet. Capturing the spirit of the times, some of Dylan's songs, most notably "Blowin' in the Wind," became anthems for various protest movements.

Mario Savio (*left*), leader of the Free Speech Movement (FSM), meets folk singer and movement supporter Joan Baez. The FSM was born at University of California–Berkeley in fall 1964 after university leaders had attempted to restrict the involvement of students in political activities. Savio and other students had been trying to raise funds for the civil rights movement.

A few days later, Clay shocked the world by defeating the heavily favored heavyweight champion, Sonny Liston. "I'm the greatest!" shouted the new champion. The next day, the champ announced to a startled American public, accustomed to bland and accommodating black boxing champions such as Floyd Patterson, "I don't have to be who you want me to be. I'm free to be who I want." The champion was speaking specifically to his decision to become a member of the Nation of Islam. But, more generally, he was voicing a rebelliousness of spirit that many young people around the country respected and, in their own ways, sought to emulate. The Beatles and much of hip, young America cheered on the newly named Muhammad Ali.

Later that year, the Beatles met another of the Sixties' great rebels, Bob Dylan. Dylan was, among hipper young people, already a well-known performer. His 1963 album *The Freewheelin' Bob Dylan* featured the socially conscious song "Blowin' in the Wind," which would become the anthem of young activists in the mid-1960s. Dylan was not yet a star when the Beatles decided to hang out with him at their New York City hotel room, but they saw in him what tens of millions of other young people would eventually perceive: Dylan was a visionary musician who could put voice to a generation's dreams and nightmares as well as anyone.

The musicians talked all night and right up to daybreak, mainly about writing and performing music. Sometime during this legendary meeting, Dylan lit up a joint, and the Beatles—for the first time—got stoned. Soon thereafter, their music would reflect that intoxicating influence, and Beatles fans got the point. As Todd Gitlin writes in *The Sixties*, referring to the druggy turn in rock music, "The word got around that in order to 'get' the song…you had to smoke this apparently angelic drug. It wasn't just peer pressure; more and more, to get access to youth culture, you had to get high." The Beatles, always it seemed, pointed out their generation's path.

While the Beatles, Dylan, and other rock artists supplied the generational soundtrack and a hip style of nonconformity, thousands of other young people were making their own history in 1964. They rebelled against the status quo and demanded that their elders live up to their own self-proclaimed ideals. At the University of California at Berkeley, students fed up with administrators' hypocrisy formed the Free Speech Movement (FSM). They asked how university administrators could deny students the right to free speech on campus even as they proclaimed that they were teaching young people to become good citizens. In response to the university's suppression of students' rights, FSM leader Mario Savio declared: "There comes a time when the operation of the machine becomes so odious, makes you so sick at heart that you can't take part...and you've got to put your bodies upon the levers, upon all the apparatus and you've got to make it stop."

That same kind of moral fervor moved thousands of young whites and blacks to join together in the 1964 Mississippi Freedom Summer struggle against racial discrimination. And it led young people, according to their differing political predilections, to form and participate in such organizations as the Students for a Democratic Society (SDS), Young Americans for Freedom (YAF), and Student Nonviolent Coordinating Committee (SNCC).

By 1964 the seeds of massive generational rebellion had begun to bloom. Meanwhile, in a significant paradox, the seeds of a new conservatism also were germinating. In Garden Grove and other white, middle-class suburbs in Orange County, California, voters who had had their fill of Kennedy/Johnson liberalism organized with impressive focus. They agitated for a right-wing agenda at the local, state, and national levels. These "new conservatives" supported Republican nominee Barry Goldwater in the 1964 presidential election. Although Goldwater was trounced by President Johnson, his campaign reenergized the party, and the new conservatives persevered. Within just a very few years, conservatism would dominate mainstream politics.

Democratic and Republican supporters each rented half of this building in St. Louis during the 1964 presidential campaign. Losing in a landslide to incumbent Lyndon Johnson, ultraconservative Arizona Republican Barry Goldwater managed to carry only his own state and five in the Deep South, where he had widespread support for his opposition to the Civil Rights Act.

Ironically, perhaps, it was a president of liberal domestic politics, Lyndon Johnson, who was moving the nation toward a war against communism that soon would push many young people into confrontation with traditional authority. On August 4, 1964, after a purported North Vietnamese attack on two American naval ships in the Gulf of Tonkin, Johnson informed the American people that he had authorized retaliatory "air action" against enemy targets. At the President's request, Congress subsequently passed a resolution authorizing Johnson "to take all necessary measures to repel any armed attack against the forces of the United States." Though few yet noticed it, a "hard rain" had started to fall in America.

1964: Support for the Big Bang Theory, regarded as the best available theory about the origin and evolution of the universe, is adopted by additional scientists after American physicists Arno Penzias and Robert Wilson observe cosmic background radiation—the heat left over from the suspected explosion. • American physicists Murray Gell-Mann and George Zweig independently come to the same conclusion that quarks exist. Quarks are fundamental matter particles that are constituents of neutrons and protons.

1964: The Soviet Union attempts to end baptism, eliminate religious instruction in the home, and curtail church attendance by those under age 18. • Malcolm X makes a Muslim pilgrimage to Mecca, then tours the Middle East and Africa. • The mass-transit bullet train, which can travel at 120 mph, begins operation in Japan • Designer Rudi Gernreich introduces a topless bathing suit and topless evening dress.

1964: The oldest of the Baby Boomers turn 18. • The "mop-top" haircut, made popular by the Beatles, becomes all the rage on both sides of the Atlantic. Some schools ban the hairstyle. • The success of the Beatles sparks the British Invasion. British pop groups that hit it big in the U.S. include the Rolling Stones, the Dave Clark Five, the Animals, and Gerry & the Pacemakers.

January 7: U.S. students at U.S.-administered Balboa High School in the Canal Zone run up an American flag in defiance of a prohibitive directive from Panama's governor. Panamanian students hoist Panama's flag next to the U.S. banner, touching off a riot. Over several days, at least 25 people, including four U.S. soldiers, are killed and hundreds injured.

January 8: In President Johnson's first State of the Union address, he vows to end racial discrimination and poverty, and eliminate threats of war abroad.

Panamanian students struggle with police over a torn flag of Panama during riots in early 1964. On January 7, American high school students in the Canal Zone had raised Old Glory in front of their school without also hoisting a Panamanian flag, as required by an agreement between the two nations. When Panamanian students tried to rectify the error on January 9, a riot ensued. Fighting continued over the next three days, with a death toll of at least 25 and $2 million in property damage. The incident indicated a clash of nationalisms in the ambiguously situated Panama Canal Zone—an American enclave within a sovereign nation.

In this still from *Dr. Strangelove, Or: How I Learned to Stop Worrying and Love the Bomb*, General Jack D. Ripper (Sterling Hayden, *right*) tries to convince British Captain Lionel Mandrake (Peter Sellers) that the dirty "Russkie Commies" are trying to sap his "vital bodily fluids" through fluoridation. In this wickedly funny black comedy, directed by Stanley Kubrick, Ripper launches a nuclear attack on the USSR, which cannot be called back by a flustered U.S. president (also played by Sellers). When it looks like the world will end in a nuclear holocaust, U.S. defense analyst Dr. Strangelove (again played by Sellers) sees hope for the future if he and other top American leaders can hide in mine shafts with thousands of beautiful young women to repopulate the nation. *Dr. Strangelove* is considered one of the most intelligent and important satires in American film history.

South African black leader Nelson Mandela makes a point to South African teacher C. Andrews in a meeting in 1964. Mandela had been a major anti-apartheid activist since 1942, when he joined the African National Congress (ANC). He initially supported nonviolent protest as a tactic to end racial segregation, but in 1961 he became commander in chief of *Umkhonto we Sizwe* (Spear of the Nation), the military wing of the ANC. Mandela was convinced that only a more militant approach could dislodge the system of racial oppression. Reacting to threats of violence, the South African officials sentenced Mandela to life in prison in June 1964. He lived behind bars until 1990, when apartheid was crumbling.

A British soldier discovers two Turks, killed by Greeks, in Cyprus in 1964. This Mediterranean island was a British colony until 1960, when it was granted its independence in a treaty that provided power sharing between the island's Greek majority and Turkish minority. Hostility between the two groups continued. When Greek-speaking President Archbishop Makarios proposed amendments to the constitution, which Turks saw as a power grab, Turkish Cypriots rebelled. Turkish members of government refused to serve, and sporadic fighting continued through most of 1964.

The Surgeon General Speaks

LUNG CANCER. Mouth Cancer. Esophageal Cancer. Emphysema. On January 11, 1964, the Surgeon General of the United States took the fun out of smoking. The result of decades of accumulated data and the work of an assembled panel of 10 experts, Surgeon General Luther L. Terry's report, "Smoking and Health," sought to "reach some definitive conclusions on the relationship between smoking and health in general."

The 387-page report did just that. The U.S. Department of Health, Education, and Welfare concluded, "Cigarette smoking is a health hazard of sufficient importance in the United States to warrant appropriate remedial action." It warned that numerous health hazards were directly linked to the number of cigarettes smoked and the duration of a smoker's habit. Reaction to the news varied. Some people took up pipe and cigar smoking as alternatives, with some doctors even recommending the change. One Detroit tobacconist reported that customers came into the shop with doctors' prescriptions. In San Francisco, sales of "ladies pipes" increased.

Tobacco companies saw stock prices dip, but federal price supports and crop controls for tobacco continued. As a result of the report, Congress directed the Federal Trade Commission to draft and enforce regulations related to any unfair and deceptive advertising claims of the industry. These efforts eventually led to warning labels ("Smoking may be hazardous to your health"). From 1965 to 1997, smoking prevalence among U.S. adults decreased from 42.4 percent to 24.7 percent.

1964

January 13: The U.S. Supreme Court rules as unconstitutional a Louisiana statute requiring that the racial heritage of political candidates be listed on all electoral ballots.

January 18: The Federal Trade Commission proposes a selective ban on cigarette advertising.

January 20: *Meet the Beatles,* the first Beatles album available in the U.S., hits record stores.

January 21: Carl Rowan is appointed director of the U.S. Information Agency by President Johnson. Rowan becomes the highest-ranking African-American in the federal government, and the first African-American to sit on the National Security Council.

January 23: The 24th Amendment, which outlaws poll taxes, is ratified.

January 27: U.S. Senator Margaret Chase Smith (R–ME) announces her candidacy for the 1964 GOP presidential nomination, making her the first woman to seek the nomination of a major U.S. political party.

January 29: U.S. film star Alan Ladd dies at 50.

January 29–February 9: The Winter Olympics are held in Innsbruck, Austria.

January 30: South Vietnamese General Nguyen Khanh overthrows the country's ruling military junta in a bloodless coup, and is declared head of state. *See* August 21, 1964.

February: After an investigation triggered by Indiana Governor Matthew Welsh, it is announced that the lyrics of the hit song "Louie, Louie" by the Kingsmen are not obscene.

February 4: Red China accuses the USSR of seeking world domination in collusion with the U.S.

February 7: The Beatles, making their first trip to the U.S., are greeted by thousands of screaming fans at the John F. Kennedy International Airport in New York. *See* February 9, 1964.

On February 9, 1964, the Beatles made their first appearance on *The Ed Sullivan Show,* one of the most exciting events in television history. CBS had received more than 50,000 requests for tickets in a studio that held 703. More than 72 million Americans watched as the Fab Four sang five of their hits—"All My Loving," "Till There Was You," "She Loves You," "I Saw Her Standing There," and, finally, "I Want to Hold Your Hand." At 8 o'clock that evening, normal activities in the United States came to a standstill. Sullivan (*pictured*), the host of the longest-lasting variety show in American television history, would feature the Beatles eight more times.

Cassius Clay pounds Sonny Liston in a heavyweight championship bout on February 25, 1964. After winning by a technical knockout in the seventh round, Clay screamed "I shocked the world!" and "eat your words!" to reporters. Many in boxing's establishment despised Clay because of his cockiness and audacious behavior. But some Americans found him a breath of fresh air, laughing at such Clay-isms as "If you want to lose your money, then bet on Sonny." Immediately after the bout, Clay announced that he had converted to the Nation of Islam and changed his name to Muhammad Ali. At the time, most Americans viewed the separatist Nation of Islam as a threat to the country and its core beliefs.

A South Vietnamese peasant displays the lifeless body of his child to South Vietnamese troops. The child was killed on March 19, 1964, during a battle between South Vietnamese and Communist Vietcong troops. During the first half of 1964, President Johnson continued John Kennedy's basic strategy of providing advisers and materiel to the South Vietnamese military, which did the bulk of the fighting. As Vietcong successes mounted, however, the Joint Chiefs of Staff urged that the war be increasingly Americanized. While not totally ruling out the possibility, LBJ certainly wanted to delay any escalation because, in the words of historian Robert Schulzinger, the President "hoped to downplay the Vietnam story" in the run-up to the 1964 presidential election.

Irish author Brendan Behan engages in his favorite pastime—tossing back a cold one. Behan spent much of his youth in jail and reform school for crimes ranging from sabotage to attempted murder. His most famous works—the novel *Borstal Boy* and the play *The Hostage* (both of which premiered in 1958)—were based on his own incarcerations and pro-Irish activism. His fiercely anti-establishment views and evangelical hedonism made him something of a role model for some Sixties rebels in the United States. Behan died on March 20, 1964, of acute alcoholism at age 41.

A huge Soviet-style billboard in Cuba advertises 1964 as Cuba's "Year of the Economy." Whether the program succeeded or not is debatable. Marxist economist William Stodden stated that the Cuban people enjoyed a better life in 1964 than they did before Fidel Castro took power in 1959. However, Cuba's economic output stagnated during the early 1960s. In 1964 the Organization of American States slapped economic sanctions on the island nation, forcing it to continue to rely heavily on Soviet economic assistance.

February 9: More than 72 million viewers watch the Beatles on *The Ed Sullivan Show* on CBS. *See* February 11, 1964.

February 10: Columbia Records releases Bob Dylan's album *The Times They Are A-Changin'*. The title track becomes an anthem for the times.

February 11: The Beatles perform their first U.S. concert at the Washington (D.C.) Coliseum. • The first John F. Kennedy half dollar is struck.

February 13: Former Vice President Richard Nixon condemns the tactics of civil rights leaders as irresponsible. He says that civil disobedience, demonstrations, boycotts, and violations of property rights will hurt the cause in the long run.

February 21: The U.S. freighter *Exilona* docks at Odessa with the USA's first-ever peacetime shipment of grain to the USSR.

February 25: Brash boxer Cassius Clay, a 7-1 underdog, knocks out heavyweight champion Sonny Liston in the seventh round in Miami Beach, Florida. After the fight, Clay proclaims his devotion to the Nation of Islam and declares his name as Muhammad Ali.

March: Secret U.S.-backed bombing raids begin against the Ho Chi Minh trail inside Laos. The raids are conducted by Laotian mercenaries flying old American T-28 Trojan trainer fighters. • In Chicago, large numbers of students boycott the city public schools to protest *de facto* segregation. • The California State Department of Education reports that many textbooks of American history distort the history of African-Americans in order to appease southern school districts.

March 2: Protesting interference with treaty rights, local Native Americans conduct "fish-ins" on the Puyallup River, south of Tacoma, Washington.

Senator Allen Ellender (D–LA) displays a calendar illustrating the determination of most southern Democratic senators to filibuster the 1964 Civil Rights Act into oblivion. They almost succeeded, managing to tie up the legislation with a torrent of words from April through early June. Ultimately cloture was voted, largely because of the work of Republican Minority Leader Everett Dirksen (IL), whom President Johnson lobbied furiously. Once passed, the landmark bill provided the legal basis for the desegregation of public facilities (such as restaurants) and gave the federal government more power to enforce public school desegregation.

Murder of Kitty Genovese

A FRONT-PAGE STORY in *The New York Times* blared: "37 Who Saw Murder Didn't Call the Police." The article described the shocking death of 28-year-old Catherine "Kitty" Genovese on Friday, March 13, 1964. Genovese was stabbed 17 times by her assailant, raped, and left to die in a vestibule of her apartment building in the otherwise staid community of Kew Gardens, Queens.

The killer, a married Queens homeowner named Winston Mosley, was quickly apprehended and confessed to two other murders. What made the Genovese murder such a watershed case was less its brutality than the fact that at least 37 neighbors had seen Genovese's struggle and heard her anguished cries but didn't call the police. They enabled the perpetrator to return two more times over a 30-minute period to complete the crime.

Witnesses' justifications for their apathy ranged from "we thought it was a lover's quarrel" to "I was tired." The murder soon became a national cause célèbre. Social psychologists propounded such theories as the "Bystander Effect," in which individuals are paradoxically less likely to report a crime if many people are witnessing it.

The murder ultimately changed the way citizens reported crimes. Instead of calling local precincts, Americans, beginning in 1968, could call 911—an anonymous emergency number instituted by AT&T.

Rare is the comedy that gets better reviews for its opening credits than the rest of the film, but such was the case with Blake Edwards's *The Pink Panther* (1964). In the movie, a jewel thief (David Niven) pursues a rare gem called the "Pink Panther," while bumbling Inspector Clouseau (Peter Sellers) tries to catch him. To begin the film, Friz Freleng created an animation sequence featuring a cool, strutting, pink panther. Henry Mancini's pitch-perfect instrumental theme guaranteed lasting fame for the character, which was spun off into a television cartoon by decade's end.

Houses lie in shambles after a major earthquake struck Alaska on March 27, 1964. Measuring 9.2 on the Richter Scale, the quake hit on Good Friday with an epicenter about 75 miles east of Anchorage. The quake and tsunami that followed caused more than 120 deaths in the sparsely populated state. Damage occurred as far away as Oregon and California, where more people died because of tsunamis. This was the second largest earthquake ever recorded.

A relatively small crowd strolls through the New York World's Fair, located in Flushing Meadows, Queens. The fair, which ran from April to October in both 1964 and 1965, was held in conjunction with the 300th anniversary of British forces gaining control over New York from the Dutch. New York City Park Commissioner Robert Moses, who had taken charge of the fair's planning in 1960, hoped to develop a major park on the site. More than 50 million people visited the 140-plus pavilions and major entertainment venues. However, the fair lost money, and Moses's dream of a grand, permanent park never reached fruition.

New York City police arrest James Farmer, national director of the Congress of Racial Equality (CORE), after he led a sit-in at the 1964 New York World's Fair on April 22. As demonstrators protested alleged civil rights violations at the fair, police arrested about 350 of them for disorderly conduct. On the same day, other protesters engaged in a "stall-in" in Brooklyn, hoping to prevent fair-goers from reaching their destination. The bold demonstrations signified that the civil rights movement was moving from the South to the North, and using increasingly confrontational tactics.

March 4: A jury in Chattanooga, Tennessee, finds Teamsters President Jimmy Hoffa guilty of tampering with a federal jury in 1962. *See* July 1964.

March 11: Cambodians riot in protest against U.S. policy in Vietnam.

March 12: Approximately 15,000 white parents march across the Brooklyn Bridge to protest a plan to achieve racial balance with busing in New York City schools.

March 13: Catherine "Kitty" Genovese, 28, is stabbed to death near her home in Kew Gardens, Queens, New York, in full view of 37 neighbors, not one of whom summons police or tries to intervene.

March 14: A jury in Dallas finds Jack Ruby guilty of "murder with malice" in the death of Lee Harvey Oswald, and sentences him to death.

March 23–24: In Jacksonville, Florida, police use clubs to break up a peaceful anti-segregation demonstration. Rioting ensues. Almost all of the 400 people arrested are black.

March 25: Senator J. William Fulbright (D–AK) delivers a Senate speech, "Old Myths and New Realities," in which he challenges the assumption that Cuba is a threat to the Western Hemisphere. The Johnson Administration is outraged.

March 26: Secretary of Defense Robert McNamara announces that the U.S. will provide South Vietnam with an additional $50 million annually to expand its armed forces by 50,000 men.

March 27: At least 120 people die in southern Alaska following a powerful earthquake and tidal waves.

April 4: British anthropologist Louis Leakey, in association with *Nature* magazine, announces the discovery at Olduvai Gorge, northern Tanganyika, of evidence of *Homo habilis,* a heretofore unknown species of prehistoric man who lived about 1.75 million years ago.

Singer Dionne Warwick had intended to become a high school music teacher until she was discovered by composer Burt Bacharach in 1961. At the time, Warwick's group was singing backup for a Drifters song Bacharach had written. In 1962 Warwick recorded a song composed by Bacharach and partner Hal David, "Don't Make Me Over," which eventually reached No. 21 on the *Billboard* chart. In 1964 she recorded Bacharach and David's "Walk on By," which became a huge hit. By combining a clear soprano voice with a gutsy soul sound, Warwick became a pop music diva in the 1960s.

President Lyndon Johnson visits an Appalachian family on April 24, 1964, as he shows his commitment to fighting poverty in the United States. With the 1964 election only a few months away, it was also a dramatic photo opportunity. On May 22, in a rousing address at the University of Michigan, LBJ officially proclaimed his war on poverty as part of his plan for a Great Society. "For half a century we called upon unbounded invention and untiring industry to create an order of plenty for all of our people," Johnson declared in his speech. "The challenge of the next half century is whether we have the wisdom to use that wealth to enrich and elevate our national life, and to advance the quality of our American civilization."

Lenny Bruce

"I'VE BEEN ACCUSED of bad taste," said comedian Lenny Bruce, "and I'll go down to my grave accused of it and always by the same people—the ones who eat in restaurants that reserve the right to refuse service to anyone."

Bruce first gained notoriety in the 1950s thanks to a satirical, iconoclastic wit that engaged such taboo subjects as racial fears, sexual fantasies, and presidential foibles. Having previously been arrested on both obscenity and drug charges, Bruce's career collapsed in April 1964, when he was busted just prior to performing at the Cafe au Go Go in Greenwich Village. Police had audiotaped a previous performance, in which Bruce's routine ranged from married men who prefer sex with barnyard animals to a sketch insinuating that Jackie Kennedy was trying to

dodge the bullets that killed her husband, not shield him. Manhattan Criminal Court judges convicted Bruce of obscenity, though they freed him pending appeal.

The ordeal proved too much for the beleaguered comedian, who secluded himself in his Los Angeles home. After completing his autobiography, *How To Talk Dirty and Influence People,* Bruce succumbed to illegal drugs on August 3, 1966, when he was found dead at home—a syringe still in his arm.

Bruce proved a sacrificial lamb in the crusade for freedom of expression, which opened the doors for comedians, shock jocks, rappers, and other iconoclasts. Bruce was portrayed in the 1974 film *Lenny,* starring Dustin Hoffman.

A playbill for the Broadway musical *Funny Girl* promotes its stars, Barbra Streisand and Sydney Chaplin. The musical, based on the life of Fanny Brice, was a rags-to-riches story that appealed to the public and critics alike. Streisand, a popular cabaret singer in the early 1960s, had won a New York Drama Critics supporting actress award for her role in *I Can Get It for You Wholesale* in 1962. But it was her performance in *Funny Girl* that catapulted her into the national spotlight. She also received two Grammy Awards in 1964 for *The Barbra Streisand Album.* Her powerful voice and fine acting skills made her a megastar in the 1960s and beyond.

Jubilant fans celebrate the Boston Celtics' sixth consecutive National Basketball Association championship after the team defeated the Wilt Chamberlain-led San Francisco Warriors in the 1964 NBA Finals. They hoist on their shoulders Celtic standouts Tommy Heinsohn (*left*) and Bill Russell (*right*). Legendary coach Red Auerbach (*center*) sports a victory cigar. Boston was spearheaded by center Russell, who exemplified Auerbach's commitment to hard-nosed defense and rebounding. Boston would extend its title-winning streak to eight in 1966.

April 5: General Douglas MacArthur, commander of Allied Forces in the Pacific during World War II, supreme commander of U.S. Occupation Forces in Japan (1945–50), and commander of UN forces during the initial stage of the Korean War, dies at 84.

April 6: Beatles songs fill the first five positions on *Billboard*'s Hot 100 chart: "Can't Buy Me Love," "Twist and Shout," "She Loves You," "I Want to Hold Your Hand," and "Please Please Me."

April 17: Ford introduces the Mustang, a sporty car that quickly will become popular among young adults.

April 18: A National Aeronautic Association press release announces that Geraldine Mock of Columbus, Ohio, has become the first woman to complete a solo flight around the world.

April 22: President Johnson opens the New York World's Fair.

April 26: SNCC members form the Mississippi Freedom Democratic Party (MFDP) as an alternative Democratic party in Mississippi. *See* August 22–27, 1964. • The former Sultanate of Zanzibar merges with the former Republic of Tanganyika to create what will be known as Tanzania.

April 28: President Johnson sends Congress a $228 million plan to alleviate poverty in the 10-state Appalachian region.

May: The U.S. State Department states that the U.S. is flying reconnaissance flights over Laos to obtain intelligence information about Communist Pathet Lao forces.

May 2: Northern Dancer, a two-year-old colt, wins the Kentucky Derby in a record time of 2:00. He is the first Canadian horse to win the race.

May 8: President Johnson waives a legal requirement that would force FBI Director J. Edgar Hoover to retire at age 70, on January 1, 1965.

White House visitors seem amused as they watch President Lyndon Johnson lift his beagle, Her, by the ears. The President regularly lifted both Her and his other beagle, Him, by the ears until photos of him doing so hit the papers. A number of animal lovers protested, and Republican Senate Majority Leader Everett Dirksen gave LBJ a hard time. According to Kansas State Professor Ronnie Elmore, Johnson worried about "how negative the photos were and how they were going to affect [his] political career."

One of the signature automobiles of the 1960s, the Ford Mustang was unveiled in April 1964. Developed in a remarkably quick 18 months, the Mustang introduced the affordable sporty car tradition with a base price tag of only $2,372—half that of the Chevrolet Corvette. The Mustang was built on a humble Ford Falcon platform, but to young Americans it represented style, speed, and freedom. Exciting luxury options included center console and deluxe wheel covers. From April 1964 to August 1965, Ford sold 680,989 Mustangs.

Baby Boomers Come of Age

FROM 1946 TO 1964, the United States experienced an explosion in its birthrate, reversing years of steady decline. Whether the surge was due to postwar optimism, economic expansion, or a sense of civic duty, more Americans were having more babies than ever before. Indeed, in 1947 nearly a million more babies were born than in 1945. A greater number of people were getting married and a very high percentage of them were becoming parents. In the postwar years, couples were having an average of 3.2 kids.

By the mid-1960s, the first wave of Baby Boomers came of age. Their generation, however, was very different from their parents'. Never before had an entire population grown up with the threat of nuclear holocaust. Schoolchildren of the postwar era learned to "duck and cover" in case of an attack by the Soviet Union. This threat of utter annihilation was coupled with economic growth, suburbanization, and cultural homogenization, all of which conspired to shape postwar America.

Perhaps one of the most significant and far-reaching generational changes was the rise of television. In 1946 only 8,000 American households reported owning a TV set. Ten years later, the figure stood at a whopping 35 million. Television not only served as a source of family entertainment, but it also brought unprecedented commercialization into the home. Economic prosperity meant more purchasing power, and television was the perfect medium to advertise goods to a new generation of consumers.

Student at Mills College

These societal and cultural changes came to define the Boomers and determine their worldview. Even more significant was the effect they were beginning to have on the nation's culture and politics. By the mid-1960s, many Boomers embraced the new "counterculture" and were coalescing into a formidable political force that used direct-action tactics to protest the escalating war in Vietnam.

In awarding "Man of the Year" for 1966 to the "25 and Under" generation, *Time* magazine noted, "Never before have the young been so assertive or so articulate, so well educated or so worldly." The Baby Boomers, the magazine continued, were "not just a new generation, but a new kind of generation."

Peruvian soldiers try to control a riot at an Argentina–Peru soccer match on May 24, 1964. A referee had disallowed a Peruvian goal in the final two minutes of the Olympic qualifying contest, which led thousands of Peru supporters to charge the field. The stampede and rioting caused 318 deaths and approximately 500 injuries in one of the worst sports disasters in history.

May 19: The U.S. State Department reveals that microphones have been found hidden throughout the U.S. Embassy in Moscow.

May 22: In a speech at the University of Michigan, President Johnson uses the phrase "Great Society" for the first time to describe his vision for a nation of equality and equal opportunity.

May 23: The *Los Angeles Free Press*, an underground newspaper, is founded.

May 25: In a unanimous ruling, the U.S. Supreme Court holds that Prince Edward County, Virginia, must reopen public schools that, because of local resistance to racial integration, have been closed since 1959.

May 27: Indian nationalist Prime Minister Jawaharlal Nehru dies at 74.

May 30: Drivers Eddie Sachs and Dave MacDonald are killed in a crash at the Indianapolis 500. The winner is A. J. Foyt.

June: Comedian Lenny Bruce goes on trial in New York City after being arrested in Greenwich Village on obscenity charges during a performance. • Malcolm X leaves the Nation of Islam and founds the Organization of Afro-American Unity.

June 1: Cuban dictator Fidel Castro accuses the U.S. of waging bacteriological warfare against Cuba. • In a unanimous decision, the U.S. Supreme Court orders Alabama to permit the NAACP to resume activities in that state. • The Rolling Stones arrive in the United States to begin their first U.S. tour.

June 10: The U.S. Senate votes to end a 57-day filibuster spearheaded by southern segregationists, removing the final barrier to enactment of the Civil Rights Bill.

June 11: Martin Luther King, Jr., is among those arrested by local authorities in St. Augustine, Florida, during anti-segregation demonstrations. *See* June 18, 1964.

Ann-Margret and Elvis Presley cut a rug in the 1964 film *Viva Las Vegas*. The King of Rock 'n' Roll starred in 31 movies, 26 in the 1960s alone. Elvis's manager, Colonel Tom Parker, orchestrated the numerous movie deals, though after awhile Presley's heart wasn't in it. While many of Elvis's films were forgettable, *Viva Las Vegas* was a popular hit that featured a fun plot and exciting chemistry between the two stars.

Jawaharlal Nehru, India's first prime minister, died on May 27, 1964. In 1919 Nehru had joined the Indian National Congress, where he followed the lead of Mahatma Gandhi in the fight for India's independence from Great Britain. Nehru, who was jailed nine times for civil disobedience, became India's first prime minister in 1947, a post he held until his death. His firm policy of nonalignment and neutrality in the Cold War often irritated U.S. policymakers, as did his pursuit of India's claim to Kashmir. Nehru was succeeded by Lal Bahadur Shastri, another Gandhi protégé. When Shastri died in 1966, Nehru's daughter, Indira, became prime minister.

Singers Florence Ballard, Mary Wilson, and Diana Ross (*top to bottom*) comprised the Supremes, one of the most successful singing groups of the 1960s. Each of the Supremes hailed from the same housing project in Detroit. When they wanted to sign with the up-and-coming Motown label, owner Berry Gordy told them to finish high school first—advice they heeded. Beginning with "Where Did Our Love Go" in June 1964, the group enjoyed a string of hit songs that year. Buoyed by a thumping beat and joyous harmony, the Supremes remained successful throughout the 1960s. Ross and Wilson went on to solo careers, while Ballard died in poverty in 1976.

American fashion designer Halston helps Italian actress Virna Lisi choose from an array of his famous hats in 1964. Roy Halston Frowick had burst onto the scene in 1961 when Jackie Kennedy, for her husband's inauguration, wore Halston's pillbox hat—a simple design that became a nationwide craze. Indeed, simplicity was the signature feature of Halston's fashion philosophy. His creations helped make New York City the couture capital of the world in the 1960s.

Hollywood models relax poolside while wearing the original topless bathing suit, or monokini, in June 1964. This daring fashion innovation was designed by Rudi Gernreich. One of the leading fashion gurus of the "mod" Sixties, Gernreich specialized in unisex and futuristic looks. Ultimately, he hoped that both men and women would wear his monokini—as well as shave off all their head and body hair. The monokini may have symbolized the emerging sexual revolution, but very few women actually bought and wore the audacious suit.

Famed Sixties comedian Soupy Sales takes a pie in the face while consorting with a duck. After graduating from college, Sales honed his comedic skills on the road in West Virginia. By 1964 his *Soupy Sales Show* led local ratings in New York City, and two years later the show went nationwide. In addition to his pies, Sales was famous for attracting major celebrities, such as Frank Sinatra, and for slipping adult humor into a show aimed at children. For example, he once asked his kiddie viewers to take the "little green pieces of paper" from their parents' wallets and mail them to him.

The popular magazine *Famous Monsters of Filmland* was one reflection of the monster craze of the early and mid-1960s. First published in 1958 by James Warren and science-fiction enthusiast Forrest J. Ackerman, the magazine featured a combination of lurid photos, plot summaries, and interviews to whet the whistle of any horror fan. This July 1964 issue included an interview with actor Christopher Lee (who often played Dracula) and an article about the film *The Flesh Eaters,* in which a crazy scientist breeds minuscule flesh-eating creatures who ungratefully gobble up their daddy.

1964

June 12: In South Africa, black anti-apartheid activist Nelson Mandela is sentenced to life in prison following convictions on charges of sabotage.

June 18: The UN Security Council votes 8–0 to condemn South Africa's policy of apartheid. • An anti-segregation "swim-in" takes place in a pool at the Monson Motor Lodge in St. Augustine, Florida. Monson's manager James Brock retaliates by spilling hydrochloric acid into the pool while the protesters are still in the water.

June 19: After 83 days of debate, the U.S. Senate passes the Civil Rights Bill, 73–27. *See* July 2, 1964. • U.S. senators Ted Kennedy (D–MA) and Birch Bayh (D–IN) are injured in a private plane crash while en route to the Massachusetts Democratic Convention. The pilot and Kennedy aide Edward Moss are killed.

June 20: Golfer Ken Venturi wins the U.S. Open despite suffering from heat prostration during a 36-hole final day at Congressional Country Club, near Washington, D.C.

Summer: Bob Moses heads the Freedom Summer Project in Mississippi. Thousands of people, many of whom are white college students from the North, help black Mississippians register to vote. Whites in the state react to the threat with shootings, bombings, beatings, and other acts of violence. • The Provos, an early Sixties counterculture group, stage their first "happenings" in Spui Square in Amsterdam.

June 21: Civil rights workers James Chaney, Michael Schwerner, and Andrew Goodman are arrested in Philadelphia, Mississippi. Following release, the three disappear. *See* August 4, 1964.

June 22: The U.S. Supreme Court votes 6–3 that the denial of U.S. passports to Communists, as provided for by the Internal Security Act of 1950, is unconstitutional.

Keith Richards, Mick Jagger, Charlie Watts, Brian Jones, and Bill Wyman (*left to right*) formed the rock band the Rolling Stones. The most popular British Invasion band besides the Beatles, the Stones rocked (and partied) harder than the Fab Four and appealed to a more rebellious sect. The Stones toured the United States beginning in June 1964. That month, their single "It's All Over Now" became their first No. 1 hit in the United Kingdom. The Stones broke through in the U.S. in 1965 with the classic "(I Can't Get No) Satisfaction."

In St. Augustine, Florida, on June 18, 1964, black civil rights activists conduct a "swim-in" at the Monson Motor Lodge pool. James Brock, the motel manager, is so incensed that he dumps acid into the water. The next day, Brock added an alligator to the mix to discourage those seeking desegregation. Martin Luther King, Jr., and SCLC colleague Ralph Abernathy joined the demonstrators in St. Augustine. Not only were both eventually arrested, but someone shot a bullet through the window of the cottage in which King was staying. The events in St. Augustine illustrated the determination of the protesters and the continued resistance to integration by many white Southerners.

MISSING CALL FBI

THE FBI IS SEEKING INFORMATION CONCERNING THE DISAPPEARANCE AT PHILADELPHIA, MISSISSIPPI, OF THESE THREE INDIVIDUALS ON JUNE 21, 1964. EXTENSIVE INVESTIGATION IS BEING CONDUCTED TO LOCATE GOODMAN, CHANEY, AND SCHWERNER, WHO ARE DESCRIBED AS FOLLOWS:

ANDREW GOODMAN   **JAMES EARL CHANEY**   **MICHAEL HENRY SCHWERNER**

RACE:	White	Negro	White
SEX:	Male	Male	Male
DOB:	November 23, 1943	May 30, 1943	November 6, 1939
POB:	New York City	Meridian, Mississippi	New York City
AGE:	20 years	21 years	24 years
HEIGHT:	5'10"	5'7"	5'9" to 5'10"
WEIGHT:	150 pounds	135 to 140 pounds	170 to 180 pounds
HAIR:	Dark brown; wavy	Black	Brown
EYES:	Brown	Brown	Light blue
TEETH:		Good: none missing	
SCARS AND MARKS:		1 inch cut scar 2 inches above left ear.	Pock mark center of forehead, slight scar on bridge of nose, appendectomy scar, broken leg scar.

This FBI poster features three civil rights workers who disappeared in Mississippi on June 21, 1964, during Freedom Summer. Andrew Goodman (*left*) and Michael Schwerner (*right*) were white volunteers from New York, while James Chaney (*center*) was a local black advocate. After being arrested, briefly jailed, and released by Neshoba County Deputy Sheriff Cecil Price, the three civil rights workers disappeared. A massive search was organized while the story made headlines nationwide—in part, no doubt, because two of the men were white. After six weeks, their bodies were discovered buried in an earthen dam. All three had been shot and Chaney savagely beaten.

Burmese diplomat U Thant reigned as secretary general of the United Nations from November 1961 through 1971. In his first term (1961–66), Thant was deeply involved in several successes, including the establishment of a peacekeeping force in Cyprus in 1964. More intractable problems dogged much of his tenure, however, especially the Vietnam War. In spite of numerous efforts to bring the warring sides together, the UN played virtually no role in bringing peace to Vietnam. Nor was U Thant able to solve many of the organization's nagging financial problems.

"Maybe we're not going to get very many people registered this summer. Maybe, even, we're not going to get very many people into freedom schools. Maybe all we're going to do is live through this summer. In Mississippi, that will be so much."

—BOB MOSES, DIRECTOR OF THE MISSISSIPPI FREEDOM SUMMER PROJECT, JUNE 14, 1964

Freedom Summer

"A DOMESTIC FREEDOM CORPS will be working in Mississippi this summer. Its only weapons will be youth and courage. We need your help now." On the campuses of such elite universities as Yale, Michigan, and Stanford, students found flyers with these stirring words stapled to kiosks and reader boards in 1964. Robert Moses, the man behind Mississippi Freedom Summer, wanted African-Americans in Mississippi to take hold of their power and to lead themselves. But at the same time, he needed leverage to help register black voters. Moses and the Student Nonviolent Coordinating Committee (SNCC) invited northern, white student volunteers to act—in Moses's words—as "an opening wedge for further pressure."

Entering 1964, only 6.7 percent of eligible black voters were registered to vote in Mississippi. Through relentless intimidation and violence, whites had kept blacks off the voting rolls. SNCC activists believed that by sending a thousand white student volunteers house to house in rural Mississippi, and by setting up "Freedom Schools," they could register more voters for the 1964 election and bring national scrutiny to bear on voting rights in the South.

SNCC's experiment with an integrated Freedom Summer led to conflicts between white student upstarts and veteran black activists. But such internecine problems paled in comparison to the ferocity of racist resistance and terror tactics, which included shootings, bombings, and beatings.

Early in the summer, three young civil rights workers—James Chaney, Michael Schwerner, and Andrew Goodman—were abducted by the Neshoba County deputy sheriff and then handed over to a Ku Klux Klan mob. They shot the two white men and beat Chaney with a chain, crushing his bones before shooting him three times. Their bodies were found two months later buried in an earthen dam. Seven men eventually were convicted of conspiracy in the murders.

Freedom Summer workers succeeded in registering thousands of black voters. Meanwhile, the violence perpetrated by the white racists backfired on them. The injustices in Mississippi helped spur Congress to pass the Voting Rights Act of 1965, which allowed federal officials to step in and register voters, thus ensuring everyone's right to vote.

1964

June 23: Jack Kilby receives a patent for his 1958 invention, the integrated circuit, which will revolutionize the electronics industry.

June 24: The Federal Trade Commission announces that beginning in 1965 cigarette packages will carry a warning about the health hazards of smoking.

June 29: In an address televised from Mexico City, Juana Castro, sister of Cuban dictator Fidel Castro, condemns her brother's authoritarian government, calling Cuba "an enormous prison surrounded by water."

July: Lieutenant General William C. Westmoreland assumes command of the U.S. military in Vietnam. • More than 100 members of the SDS (Students for a Democratic Society) and ERAP (Economic Research and Action Project) organize the poor in nine U.S. cities. • Teamsters President Jimmy Hoffa is convicted of conspiracy to misuse the union's pension fund as well as mail and wire fraud. • Former Harvard professor Timothy Leary holds LSD sessions in Millbrook, New York. • With "Where Did Our Love Go," the Supremes score their first of five consecutive No. 1 hits.

July 1: General Maxwell Taylor, chairman of the Joint Chiefs of Staff, is appointed by President Johnson as the new U.S. ambassador to South Vietnam.

July 2: The U.S. House approves the Civil Rights Bill 289–126. In a televised ceremony later in the day, President Johnson signs the Civil Rights Act of 1964.

July 15: Senator Barry Goldwater (R–AZ) is nominated as the GOP candidate for president on the first ballot at the Republican National Convention.

July 18–21: One person is killed and more than a hundred are injured during rioting in Harlem and Brooklyn.

On July 3, 1964, Pickrick Restaurant owner Lester Maddox pulls a gun on African-Americans attempting to enter his segregated Atlanta eatery, even though the 1964 Civil Rights Act, passed earlier that year, had made such discrimination illegal. Maddox also used an axe handle to shoo away customers of the "wrong color." As a symbol of resistance to civil rights, Maddox closed shop in August 1964 rather than accede to the law. Incredibly, Maddox parlayed his popularity among white segregationists into a successful run for the Georgia governorship in 1966, using axe handles as his central campaign icon. Maddox was unable to stem the tide of desegregation, however, and eventually appointed several African-Americans to posts in state government.

Malcolm X (*second from left*) meets Muslim cleric and educator Sheik Abdel Rahman Tag (*right*) in Egypt in July 1964. As a Nation of Islam leader from the early 1950s until early 1964, Malcolm's charismatic speaking style electrified thousands of African-Americans. He had preached that whites were blue-eyed devils and that integration was nothing but tokenism. In 1964, after a rift with Nation of Islam leader Elijah Muhammad, Malcolm visited Africa and the Mideast, where his interaction with nonblack believers in Islam helped change his attitudes toward whites. In early 1965, Malcolm was working with more moderate civil rights organizations when he was assassinated.

> *"The surest path to nuclear war is for us to lull Russia into the misconception that we will never use the nuclear weapons. If and when so convinced, Russia will attack; and then, in defense of our freedom and our way of life, we will definitely strike back with all the power at our command. The bombs will fall."*
>
> —Barry Goldwater

Goldwater and the Right

IN THE PRESIDENTIAL election of 1964, Democratic incumbent Lyndon Johnson trounced Republican Barry Goldwater, who captured only 39 percent of the popular vote. Columnists wrote obituaries for the GOP, arguing that the nomination of a candidate from the far right wing of the Republican Party killed the party's future prospects. But while the 1960s are often remembered as the heyday of American liberalism, Barry Goldwater's campaign actually marked the start of a conservative ascendancy in America.

Goldwater (*right*) and running mate William Miller

Goldwater was born in Phoenix in 1909. His disdain for liberalism grew out of the Great Depression, when he came to regard the Roosevelt Administration's expansion of federal power as a threat to individualism and self-reliance. After serving as a pilot in Asia during World War II, Goldwater returned to Phoenix and began a political career. In 1952 Arizonans elected him to the United States Senate.

At the height of Cold War hysteria, Goldwater defended Senator Joseph McCarthy and became identified with militant anticommunism. In 1960 he published the best-selling *The Conscience of a Conservative*. Goldwater voted against both the 1963 Nuclear Test Ban Treaty (as needlessly weakening American defense) and the 1964 Civil Rights Act (as an abuse of federal power).

In 1964's bitter presidential primary campaign, Goldwater called for "carrying the war to North Vietnam" and for Social Security to be made voluntary. The campaign polarized the Republican Party, but Goldwater edged moderates Nelson Rockefeller, George Romney, and William Scranton for the nomination when he won the June California primary.

Campaigning against LBJ's characterizations of him as a warmonger and conservative extremist, Goldwater defiantly asserted that "extremism in the defense of liberty is no vice." Despite the outcome at the polls, Goldwater's grassroots campaign crystallized a New Right voting block that proved instrumental in electing Ronald Reagan president 16 years later.

Protesters take a shot against Republican presidential nominee Barry Goldwater during the 1964 GOP convention in San Francisco. The sign identifies Goldwater with cross burnings practiced by the Ku Klux Klan. When he voted against the Civil Rights Act of 1964, the Arizona senator seemed to align himself with white segregationists. An editorial in *The New York Times* proclaimed that Goldwater's nomination had reduced "a once great party to the status of an ugly, frustrated faction." California Governor Pat Brown, a Democrat, went further when he said, "The stench of facism is in the air."

1964

July 27: The U.S. sends 5,000 more troops to South Vietnam, bringing the total to 21,000.

July 30: The Medicare Act is signed by President Johnson. It's the first government-operated health insurance program for Americans age 65 and older.

July 31: The U.S. Ranger 7 spacecraft crashes on the moon, as planned, after relaying 4,316 high-quality, closeup photographic images of the moon's surface, taken off kinescope by six Vidicon video cameras.

August 2: Three North Vietnamese PT boats allegedly fire on the U.S. destroyer *Maddox* in the Gulf of Tonkin, about 30 miles off the coast of North Vietnam. *See* August 4, 1964.

August 2–4: Riots rage in black and Puerto Rican neighborhoods in Jersey City, New Jersey. Dozens of people are arrested.

August 3: American novelist and short-story writer Flannery O'Connor dies from lupus at 39.

August 4: President Johnson orders retaliatory attacks against North Vietnam for alleged attacks on the destroyer *Maddox*. The U.S. military reports a second attack by North Vietnamese torpedo boats on the *Maddox* and, for the first time, on the *Turner Joy*. *See* August 5, 1964. • The bodies of missing civil rights workers James Chaney, Michael Schwerner, and Andrew Goodman are found buried in an earthen dam outside Philadelphia, Mississippi. *See* December 4, 1964.

August 5: The U.S. bombs North Vietnamese naval craft, bases, and oil storage depots in a five-hour raid along 100 miles of North Vietnam's coast. *See* August 7, 1964.

August 7: The U.S. Senate votes 88–2, and the House votes 416–0, to pass the Gulf of Tonkin Resolution, which approves U.S. action in Vietnam and gives President Johnson whatever war powers he deems necessary.

Psychologist and LSD guru Timothy Leary (*front*) and Neal Cassady, the model for the hero of Jack Kerouac's *On the Road,* share a laugh aboard Ken Kesey's bus. Kesey, himself a noted novelist, along with assorted friends and relatives (dubbed the Merry Pranksters) boarded a 1939 vintage bus in July 1964 in California and headed across the country spreading joy and dope. Made famous in journalist Tom Wolfe's *The Electric Kool-Aid Acid Test,* the Pranksters were prototypes of the hippie phenomenon, which soon would become a major part of American popular culture.

A longtime congresswoman, Senator Margaret Chase Smith (R–ME) took a stab at the presidency in 1964. Back in 1940, Smith had succeeded her late husband in the House of Representatives, where she served until elected to the Senate in 1948. Smith earned acclaim for her public attack on Red-hunting Senator Joseph McCarthy in 1950. Although she did not receive the support of Maine's Republican Party machinery, she was overwhelmingly reelected in 1954, '60, and '66. In 1964 she became the first woman ever to have her name placed in nomination for the presidency by a major party. She received 27 votes at the convention.

Young black girls flee police during a race riot in New York City in July 1964. The disturbances began in Harlem on July 18 after a white police officer killed a black teenager. A protest against the alleged police brutality turned violent, as some demonstrators attacked law enforcement officers. The riot spread to the Bedford-Stuyvesant area of Brooklyn the next day. Ultimately, one person was killed, more than 100 were injured, and hundreds were arrested. This event prefigured larger race riots later in the decade, such as those in Los Angeles, Detroit, and Newark, New Jersey.

Two young African-Americans staff the Freedom Press office during Freedom Summer in Mississippi in 1964. More than a thousand volunteers—most of them white college students from the North—went to Mississippi that summer to help educate and register black voters. Freedom Summer volunteers faced extraordinary hostility from local white segregationists, and more than 60 black churches, businesses, and homes were attacked. A number of volunteers were beaten by mobs, and more than a thousand civil rights workers—both natives and out-of-staters—were arrested. Black organizers in such groups as SNCC often were ambivalent about white participation as well.

A young woman talks on Bell Telephone System's new "Picturephone." Bell unveiled this innovation at the World's Fair in New York City in spring 1964. Though thousands lined up in New York and at Disneyland (where a similar device was located) to make calls, users generally didn't like the Picturephone. The equipment was too bulky and the picture too small. Despite technological improvements over the years, the Picturephone still failed—largely because people didn't want callers staring at their faces.

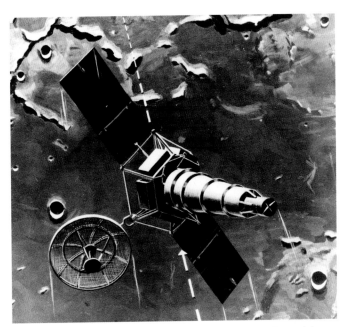

This artist's drawing shows how NASA's Ranger 7 would approach the moon. Launched on July 28, 1964, the unmanned craft was designed to crash on the lunar surface after taking a series of high-resolution photographs. NASA would then use the photos to help plan future missions to the moon. The mission was a resounding success. Ranger 7 reached its destination three days after launch and transmitted more than 4,000 photographs before impact.

1964

August 11–13: Race riots rage in Elizabeth and Paterson, New Jersey.

August 12: Ian Fleming, author of the James Bond novels, dies at 56.

August 19: The Beatles kick off a 24-city North American tour, their first on the continent, with an appearance at the Cow Palace in San Francisco.

August 21: In Saigon, students and Buddhist militants protest against General Khanh's military regime.

August 22–27: The Mississippi Freedom Democratic Party (MFDP) arrives at the Democratic National Convention in Atlantic City, New Jersey, and asks that its 68 delegates be seated. The Democratic Party rules that only two seats will be given, a compromise that the MFDP rejects.

August 26: President Johnson and Vice President Hubert Humphrey are nominated by acclaim at the Democratic National Convention in Atlantic City, New Jersey.

August 29: Racially motivated rioting in Philadelphia moves Mayor James Tate to quarantine 125 city blocks.

August 31: The Food Stamp Act is signed into law. The goals of the program are to help low-income individuals buy more food, to improve nutrition, and to expand the market for agricultural products.

September: After banning all politicking outside the school's main gate, University of California–Berkeley President Clark Kerr suspends eight students for political activities. *See* October 1, 1964.

September 1: The Census Bureau reports that California has surpassed New York as the most populous state.

September 3: The Wilderness Act, which calls for the creation of a National Wilderness Preservation System, is signed into law by President Johnson. ➤

North Vietnamese torpedo boats speed away after attacking the USS *Maddox,* an American destroyer, on August 2, 1964. The attack, in the Gulf of Tonkin off the coast of North Vietnam, allegedly was followed on August 4 by a second assault on the *Maddox* and its sister ship, the *Turner Joy.* The first attack did take place, but the American ship had been using electronic intelligence to spy on North Vietnam, thus provoking the Communist attack. Almost all experts now conclude that the second attack never took place. Nonetheless, it served as the official excuse for the passage of the Gulf of Tonkin Resolution, the congressional act that provided the legal basis for U.S. escalation of the war in Vietnam.

Political cartoonist Clifford "Baldy" Baldowski punctures Lyndon Johnson's efforts to portray himself as the "pacifist" candidate during the 1964 presidential election campaign. To Baldy, LBJ was as much a hawk on Vietnam as his Republican challenger, Barry Goldwater. In reality, Johnson was conflicted about Vietnam. To the press he tried to downplay the issue, and when pushed he said he would not send U.S. combat troops there. For Johnson, Vietnam was a catch-22 situation. In a May 26 telephone conversation, he told adviser McGeorge Bundy: "I don't think it's [Vietnam] worth fighting for, and I don't think we can get out."

Gulf of Tonkin Resolution

Facing criticism from Republican presidential candidate Barry Goldwater and others for not using more military force in Vietnam, President Johnson approved several covert operations in the summer of 1964. For Johnson, this constituted a reasonable middle path between overt war and maintaining the current course of providing economic aid and military advisers to South Vietnam. However, the covert operations soon led to a dramatic escalation of the American war in Vietnam.

In late July, two American destroyers, the *Maddox* and the *Turner Joy*, patrolled the Gulf of Tonkin off the coast of North Vietnam. They were participating in covert missions designed to gather intelligence on enemy coastal radar sites. On August 2, North Vietnamese torpedo boats unsuccessfully attacked the American destroyer *Maddox*. The next day, the two destroyers resumed their patrols even closer to the coast, and on

President Johnson, talking to the press after the attacks

August 4 both ships reported being under attack.

It later became clear, however, that no attacks took place at all on August 4. The *Turner Joy* fired on ships visible on its radar but not visible on the *Maddox*'s, and the *Maddox* detected ships with its sonar equipment not detected by the *Turner Joy*. Commanders on both ships later conceded that nervous sonar and radar men, combined with unusual weather patterns, prompted the false reports.

In Washington, however, President Lyndon Johnson described the events as unprovoked, "deliberate attacks" against American forces. He asked Congress for a joint resolution authorizing him to take "all necessary measures to repel any armed attacks...and to prevent further aggression." The administration did not tell Congress about the dubious nature of the attacks or the covert operations in which the American ships had been engaged.

The resolution passed overwhelmingly, allowing Johnson to call the shots in Vietnam without any legal or political complications. Within a year, more than 150,000 American combat troops were in Vietnam.

A truck driver shows his support for Teamsters Union President Jimmy Hoffa in August 1964. Representing the feelings of many Teamsters, the driver felt that Hoffa had been railroaded by U.S. Attorney General Robert Kennedy, who many claimed used tactics that violated basic civil liberties. After a hung jury in his 1962 trial for stealing from the union's pension fund, Hoffa was retried and found guilty in January 1964. He managed to stave off imprisonment until 1967, when he began serving an eight-year sentence. In 1971 his sentence was commuted by President Richard Nixon to time served.

1964

Members of the Dave Clark Five pose in this publicity still from their film *Having a Wild Weekend.* Part of the "British Invasion" of pop music groups in the mid-1960s, the Dave Clark Five hit No. 1 on the British pop charts in January 1964 with their catchy composition "Glad All Over," knocking the Beatles' "I Want to Hold Your Hand" from the top spot. Altogether, the DC5 recorded 17 *Billboard* Top 40 hits. By staying with the same upbeat formula, however, the group gradually lost fans to more inventive acts, including the Beatles themselves.

Fans scream their lungs out at one of the Beatles' concerts during their 1964 North American tour, which ran from August 19 through September 20. The band played a phenomenal 32 shows in 33 days, as they broke attendance records in major arenas in the United States and Canada. Hysteria spread from San Francisco, where 9,000 screaming teenagers awaited the Beatles in the airport reception room, to Convention Hall in Atlantic City, where the boys had to escape postconcert crazies by sneaking away in a laundry truck. The Beatles even drew 23,000 fans at the Gator Bowl in Jacksonville, Florida, only a day after Hurricane Dora had blown through the town.

The Beatles' first movie, *A Hard Day's Night,* premiered in America to rave reviews in August 1964. This mock documentary followed "the boys" during one day in their busy lives. Unlike previous rock movies, which featured cheesy love stories and stand-up singing performances, *Night* is a free-spirited romp, ingeniously directed in black and white by Richard Lester. The music is great, of course, but the underlying theme of the film is liberation. The characters (meaning the Beatles) constantly violate convention and establishment norms—for example, escaping from the recording studio and running like kids in an open field. As film critic Roger Ebert put it, "The Beatles were obviously not housebroken."

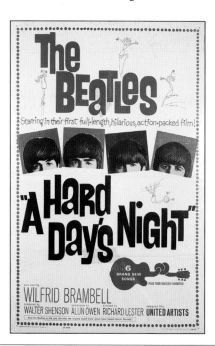

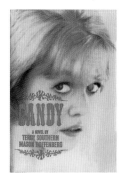

Candy was a salacious novel written by Terry Southern and Mason Hoffenberg. The novel traces the life of a naive, young sexpot, Candy Christian, who maintains her optimism in spite of unfortunate encounters with mystics, psychoanalysts, and various sexual predators. *Candy* originally was published in France by Maurice Girodias's Olympia Press in 1958, but was immediately banned because of its "obscene" content. American publisher Putnam issued the book in 1964, and it went on to become a bestseller.

Mississippi civil rights activist Fannie Lou Hamer testifies before the Credentials Committee of the Democratic National Convention in August 1962. Hamer was a leader of the Mississippi Freedom Democratic Party (MFDP), which challenged the all-white slate of delegates chosen by the regular Democratic Party in Mississippi. One of 20 children, Hamer was a sharecropper and plantation timekeeper from 1944 to 1962. When she tried to register to vote in '62, she lost her job, then became a field secretary for SNCC. Her heartfelt pleas on national television won the sympathetic understanding of many. When the MFDP was offered two nonvoting, at-large members to the '64 convention as a compromise, Hamer argued that they were "token rights, on the back row, same as we got in Mississippi." The MFDP's efforts contributed to public awareness of disenfranchisement in the South.

Clint Eastwood played "The Man With No Name" in A Fistful of Dollars. This 1964 film, by Italian director Sergio Leone, was the first in a long line of "spaghetti westerns," meaning westerns produced in Italy. Within its convoluted plot, stranger-in-town Eastwood manages to trick two gangs of outlaws into killing most of each other's members, save for a few whom he dispatches himself. Reviewer Dennis Schwartz wrote that "violence is glorified by [a] hero who is as amoral as the villains," setting the tone for many westerns to follow. Eastwood shot the film while on hiatus from his popular TV series, Rawhide.

Lyndon Johnson, who had governed the United States without a vice president since November 1963, chose Hubert Humphrey—a popular liberal senator from Minnesota—as his running mate at the 1964 Democratic National Convention (pictured). LBJ and HHH waged an immensely successful campaign, trouncing the Republican ticket in the general election. They succeeded partly because Republican Barry Goldwater kept shooting himself in the foot—attacking the War on Poverty in West Virginia, for example, and implying he might use nuclear weapons in Vietnam. All the while, Johnson and Humphrey successfully painted themselves as peace candidates. The two never were personally close, however. Johnson ultimately kept Humphrey at arm's length after the Vice President, in 1965, began to criticize LBJ's Vietnam policy.

September 7: Viewers see the first and only television airing of the so-called "daisy spot," on behalf of the Johnson presidential campaign. In the ad, a little girl plucks petals from a daisy and a male voice-over counts down from 10 to one; at the climax, the ad cuts to a nuclear blast. The message is that GOP candidate Barry Goldwater will lead the U.S. to nuclear holocaust.

September 9: William Willis, 70, completes a 200-day, 11,000-mile journey on a raft across the Pacific Ocean.

September 11: In Egypt, the Palestine Liberation Organization (PLO) is founded. The organization proclaims Israel an illegal state.

September 14: The Roman Catholic Church begins use of the vernacular (local language), rather than Latin, in the administration of the sacraments (except holy orders). Also, the Third Session of the Second Vatican Council in Rome is the first to admit women as observers. *See* November 29, 1964.

September 18: Martin Luther King, Jr., has an audience with Pope Paul VI despite efforts by the FBI to prevent the meeting.

Fall: The American Academy of Pediatrics blames "tired child syndrome" on television.

September 25: The United Auto Workers initiates a strike against General Motors that will last five weeks.

September 27: The Warren Commission, which investigated the assassination of President Kennedy, releases its findings: One man, Lee Harvey Oswald, is responsible.

October 1: University of California–Berkeley graduate student Jack Weinberg is arrested for setting up a civil rights information table on campus. In protest, students surround the police car he's in for 32 hours. *See* December 2–3, 1964. ➤

Powered by a rocket belt, Peter Kedzierski flies over the entrance of the California State Fair on September 2, 1964. Perfected in 1961 by Bell Aerospace engineer Harold Graham, this form of individual propulsion had been in the works ever since the fictional Buck Rogers used it in the 1920s. It was initially designed to allow soldiers to fly over battlefields, but Bell attempted to sell it commercially. Although it became something of a novelty hit at county fairs and the like, the rocket belt never sold well, mainly because of its short duration time. Thirteen seconds just wasn't worth the cost for most people.

Dick Van Dyke (*left*) and Julie Andrews (*right*) starred in the 1964 box office hit *Mary Poppins*. The story of the magical English nanny who brings joy to a stuffy London upper-class family garnered five Oscars, including best actress for Andrews and best musical score. Its combination of live action and animation made it especially appealing to children, who loved to repeat Poppins's favorite word: supercalifragilisticexpialidocious!

Marguerite Oswald, the mother of alleged Kennedy assassin Lee Harvey Oswald, casts a jaundiced eye on her copy of the *Warren Commission Report,* which was issued in September 1964. Although critical of security lapses by the Secret Service and the FBI, the commission concluded that Mr. Oswald had acted alone in killing the President. His mother did not buy this argument, in part because her son had never told her that he planned to do it. When she testified before the Warren Commission, she concluded, darkly, "Gentlemen, you are making a very big mistake."

The Warren Commission

THE SHOCK OF PRESIDENT John F. Kennedy's assassination was outdone only by the subsequent shooting of prime suspect Lee Harvey Oswald on live television. Mindful of the effect that wild speculation could have on public morale, President Lyndon Johnson moved quickly to calm the waters. One week after the assassination, he appointed a panel to investigate the events surrounding the murders of Kennedy and Oswald.

Chief Justice Earl Warren headed the committee, which also included former CIA Director Allen Dulles, who had been fired by Kennedy after the 1961 Bay of Pigs debacle. Capitol Hill legislators from both sides of the aisle rounded out the body, including Congressman Gerald Ford (R-MI). Johnson's executive order deliberately superseded all other investigations in progress, including those by the FBI, the Secret Service, and authorities in Dallas.

Under pressure to wrap things up before the fall presidential campaign, the Warren Commission released its findings in September 1964. (Observed Johnson upon receiving their work: "It's heavy.") With a thick summary and 26 volumes of testimony and evidence, the impression of a complete, thorough inquiry was conveyed. The findings contained no surprises, and merely reinforced what had been asserted all along: that Oswald and his slayer, Jack Ruby, both acted alone, and that there was no evidence of a conspiracy.

Despite support from *The New York Times* and laudatory praise from other media, including CBS, public confidence in the report was shaky. A number of books critiquing the investigation became best-sellers—some lurid and sensationalistic, others meticulous and scholarly. Evidence that U.S. intelligence agencies had been less than forthcoming with pertinent information would later justify the skepticism.

By 1966 polls showed that two-thirds of the public had doubts about the official findings. Even Johnson himself told an interviewer, "I never believed Oswald acted alone, although I can accept that he pulled the trigger."

A decade later, in 1976, a House Select Committee on Assassinations was formed to investigate both the Kennedy and the Martin Luther King, Jr., assassinations. Their findings differed from the Warren Commission, noting "probable conspiracy" without further details, but did not vindicate either Oswald or King's convicted assassin, James Earl Ray.

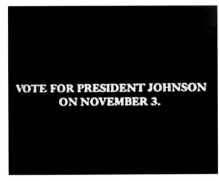

The "daisy spot" was one of the most famous political television advertisements in American history. The ad shows a little girl pulling petals off a daisy while counting up to 10. A male voice then counts down: "10, 9, 8. . . ." After the "1," we see a huge nuclear explosion while a voice-over by President Lyndon Johnson intones, "These are the stakes—to make a world in which all God's children can live or to go into the dark." Run on September 7, 1964, during the heat of the presidential campaign, the ad clearly suggested that Republican nominee Barry Goldwater was a trigger-happy cowboy who could not be trusted with his finger on the nuclear button. After Goldwater's people complained about the advertisement's first showing, the "daisy spot" never aired again.

1964

Robert Kennedy is mobbed by supporters as he campaigns for a U.S. Senate seat in New York in September 1964. Deeply depressed after his brother's assassination, Kennedy had stayed on as U.S. attorney general, but he and President Lyndon Johnson simply did not get along. LBJ did not want RFK as a running mate in 1964, referring to Bobby as "that little runt." When Kennedy resigned to run for a New York Senate seat, opponents claimed that he was a power-hungry carpetbagger from Massachusetts. Yet an energetic and upbeat campaign, combined with Johnson's landslide victory in the presidential race, propelled Kennedy to a 700,000-vote victory over Republican incumbent Kenneth Keating. The junior senator later became a thorn in LBJ's side by vocally opposing the Vietnam War.

Samantha Stephens (played by Elizabeth Montgomery) twitches her nose to make a bottle of bubbly pour itself in this publicity still from *Bewitched*. Her mother (played by Agnes Moorehead) and husband (actor Dick York) look on. This highly successful situation comedy, which ran on ABC from 1964 to '72, hooked its audiences with its skilled ensemble cast and unlikely but affecting plots. Typically, the nice witch, Samantha, tried—but mainly failed—not to use her craft at the behest of her "normal" husband. Numerous sight gags and some sharp social commentary helped garner the show more than 20 Emmy nominations during its run.

Gilligan's Island, which ran on CBS from 1964 to 1967, became a cult phenomenon in spite of (or perhaps because of) its silly premise. Seven people, supposedly representing a cross section of American life, are stranded on a deserted island. The title character, played broadly by Bob Denver (*third from right*), is the bumbling first mate of the cruise boat that sank. His fellow castaways include the captain, a fabulously rich husband and wife, a movie actress, a college professor, and an all-American girl. Many episodes deal with attempts to get off the island, which usually are thwarted by Gilligan's lovable ineptness.

A young boy happily plays with a GI Joe action figure (as opposed to a "doll"), whose face and physique are the composite of 28 Medal of Honor winners. GI Joe was introduced by toy manufacturer Hasbro in 1964 and has been in production ever since. In the mid- to late 1960s, Joe was a true military man, which undoubtedly reflected Middle America's support of the U.S. mission in Vietnam. By 1969, however, some Joes left the service and became adventurers who captured wild animals and recovered mummies.

High-speed bullet trains were introduced in Japan in 1964. Going as fast as 125 mph, they initially connected Tokyo to the major cities of Nagoya, Kyoto, and Osaka. As the system expanded with even faster trains, it helped fuel the Japanese "economic miracle." Several European countries developed their own bullet train systems, but the idea never took hold in the United States—largely because of cost issues, the great expanses of land to be covered, and America's love affairs with the automobile and air travel.

Members of the United Auto Workers walk out at the Cadillac Assembly Plant in Detroit on September 25, 1964. This was the first national strike against an automaker in 13 years. The chief issues separating the union and General Motors were health care and overtime. After a five-week impasse, the union won major concessions, including an attractive medical benefits package for retirees as well as company-funded life and disability insurance.

The soul-singing Righteous Brothers (*foreground*) appear on ABC's *Shindig* while backed by regular show members: the female Blossoms, the male Wellingtons, and the *Shindig* dancers, who also danced in cages. This rock 'n' roll variety show, created by British producer Jack Good, premiered in September 1964. Taking advantage of the resurgence of interest in rock engendered by the British Invasion, the show included fast-paced, nonstop music interrupted only by commercials. In its two-season run, *Shindig* featured such high-powered groups as the Beatles, the Supremes, the Rolling Stones, and the Who.

October 5: Fifty-seven East Berliners escape to West Berlin through a tunnel.

October 10: The Summer Olympics open in Tokyo. The city showcases the new monorail during the Games. *See* October 24, 1964.

October 14: Martin Luther King, Jr., age 35, becomes the youngest person to win the Nobel Peace Prize.

October 15: The Kremlin strips Nikita Khrushchev of all government and Communist Party offices, and ousts him from power. His successors are Aleksei Kosygin (premier) and Leonid Brezhnev (first party secretary). • The St. Louis Cardinals defeat the New York Yankees 7–5 in Game 7 of the World Series.

October 16: Red China announces the detonation of the first Chinese atomic bomb, in a test in western China.

October 20: Herbert Hoover, 31st president of the United States, dies at 90.

October 24: The Summer Olympic Games conclude. The U.S. wins the medal standings with 188 points, one more than the USSR's total. Swimmer Don Schollander leads the Americans with four gold medals. • Zambia, formerly Northern Rhodesia, gains independence.

October 27: Urging voters to support Republican presidential hopeful Barry Goldwater, actor Ronald Reagan delivers his "A Time for Choosing" speech on national television. It is considered one of the most successful political fund-raising speeches in history. • Art Arfons breaks a land speed record in Utah, pushing his *Green Monster* to 544.134 mph.

October 29: A collection of precious gems that includes the "Star of India," the world's largest sapphire, is stolen from New York's American Museum of Natural History.   ➤

Television's Addams family, including Gomez (John Astin, *standing behind chair*) and Morticia (Carolyn Jones, *sitting in chair*) poses for the camera. Based on the successful cartoon characters created by Charles Addams in *The New Yorker*, *The Addams Family* ran on ABC from 1964 to 1966. The family itself was peculiar in its good-humored ghoulishness, but especially appealing were the show's supporting characters. They included the diminutive Cousin Itt (Felix Silla), whose long hair covered his whole body; Lurch (Ted Cassidy), the 6'9" butler who mainly inquired, "You rang?"; Thing, a disembodied hand; and Fester (Jackie Coogan), the scheming, zombie-like uncle.

Lily Munster, played by Yvonne De Carlo, offers her Frankensteinish husband, Herman (Fred Gwynne), a large ladle of God-knows-what in a publicity still for *The Munsters*. This popular "monster" comedy debuted on CBS on September 24, 1964, and ran for two years. Like *The Addams Family,* its counterpart on ABC, *The Munsters'* humor derived from the juxtaposition of horror with the ordinary. Grandpa was a vampire, son Eddie was part vampire and part werewolf, and the whole family worried about niece Marilyn, who looked like a sorority girl—obviously too normal. The show was created by Joe Connelly and Bob Mosher, the duo who previously produced *Leave It to Beaver.*

Free Speech Movement

"LAST SUMMER I WENT to Mississippi to join the struggle there for civil rights," said student activist Mario Savio in 1964. "This fall I am engaged in another phase of the same struggle, this time in Berkeley."

University of California–Berkeley had been a haven for nascent student radicalism since the late 1950s, but collegians returning for the fall 1964 semester were confronted with a new set of rules: Students were henceforth prohibited from setting up tables on campus to promote "off-campus" causes such as civil rights. Fortified by their civil rights experience, however, student groups across the political spectrum defied the ban. The Free Speech Movement (FSM) was born, inaugurating a decade of protest on college campuses.

The first major flare-up took place on October 1. After FSM activist Jack Weinberg attempted to set up tables on campus, administrators called the police. The police car soon was surrounded by thousands of students singing civil rights songs, and was trapped there for 32 hours. In the ensuing months, the campus administration made a pretense of negotiating with activists, all the while blackballing them in the press as Communists. The breaking point came on December 2, when FSM protesters were confronted by about 600 police officers. The officers arrested 773 students—the largest mass arrest in California history.

The administration's heavy-handed tactics ultimately sealed its own doom. On December 8, the university faculty

Mario Savio at Berkeley

voted overwhelmingly in support of the Free Speech Movement and against the police. They also crafted a set of liberalized political school rules, which the administration ultimately accepted. On January 4, 1965, the FSM held its first legal rally.

The success of the Free Speech Movement was tarnished by lingering student mistrust of university officials—and of adults in general. Students throughout the country believed wholeheartedly in Jack Weinberg's credo: "Don't trust anyone over 30."

University of California–Berkeley graduate student Jack Weinberg was arrested on campus on October 1, 1964, for refusing to leave a table at which he was handing out civil rights literature. Though Weinberg had acted in violation of university regulations, he was supported by hundreds of his fellow students. After learning that Weinberg had been arrested, students swarmed around the police car, preventing it from moving for 32 hours. The events that day sparked the Free Speech Movement at Berkeley.

1964

"My husband was a business executive and we entertained a lot, and I complained once to my doctor about feeling anxious before social occasions. So he gave me the pills, and I'd have a quarter here and a quarter there—all my friends did—and we felt marvelous and just floated through our lives."

—Valium user Bev Mason

In 1964 Baltimore Colts quarterback Johnny Unitas was named the National Football League's Player of the Year. Six years earlier, Johnny U had led the Colts to an overtime win against the Giants for the NFL championship—a contest many consider the greatest game in NFL history. Unitas, one of the few quarterbacks who called his own signals at the time, went on to set NFL career passing records with 40,239 yards and 290 touchdowns. The crewcut-sporting field general was voted the Player of the Decade for the 1960s as well as the "Greatest Player in the First 50 Years of Pro Football."

Mother's Little Helper

IN APRIL 1964, Dr. Theodore H. Greiner of Baylor University's College of Medicine told *Newsweek* that "milder tranquilizers are used sort of like vitamins. If a doctor can't quite pin a person's problem down, he's apt to write a tranquilizer prescription." As disquieting as Greiner's words were, his assessment of Americans' use (or abuse) of psychoactive prescription drugs was more or less on the mark. Indeed, ingestion of sedatives was so widespread in the 1960s that *Consumer Reports* ran a feature on the drugs, announcing, "It pays to shop around for tranquilizers."

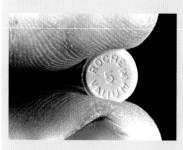

Diazepam, more commonly known by its marketed brand name Valium, became the most commonly and extensively prescribed of the minor tranquilizers, even though it would prove to be physically addictive. By the end of the decade, Valium use had quite literally reached epidemic proportions, as tens of millions of Americans were taking the drug. Perhaps even more startling was that women were more than twice as likely to take valium, leading to the drug's nickname, "Mother's little helper."

Many critics claimed that the pharmaceutical industry used slick, deceptive advertising in medical journals and trade magazines, erroneously touting Valium and other sedatives as perfectly safe, non-addictive cure-alls. They charged that the advertisements presented women as powerless, neurotic, and completely at the mercy of their male physicians, who, with minor tranquilizers, could redirect the confused and anxious female patient to her proper role as contented housewife and mother.

Others placed the blame directly on the medical establishment and argued that doctors were over-prescribing sedatives, leading to the "medicalization" of everyday problems. One such critic wondered, "[O]nce daily living is defined as a disease, how logical is it for us to attempt to treat that disease?" Valium use escalated throughout the 1960s and peaked in the mid-1970s, then declined in subsequent years.

A god-like urban planner oversees a scale model of Columbia, Maryland, a community completely planned by urbanologists in 1963–64. A major contractor, the Rouse Company, employed a range of educators and sociologists to help it plan this new town from the ground up. With permission to create higher residential densities than usual, along with flexibility in mixing land uses, Rouse broke ground in 1966 amid great fanfare. Columbia's planners sought to integrate a pleasing design with livability to create the opposite of urban sprawl and decay.

Soviet Premier Nikita Khrushchev was ousted as leader of the USSR and Soviet Communist Party on October 15, 1964. Officially, he was relieved of duty because of age and ill health. In reality, other Soviet political and military leaders were disturbed by the weak performance of the economy (especially in agriculture), the perceived blow to Soviet pride during the Cuban Missile Crisis, and the growing rift with China. Ultimately, Leonid Brezhnev succeeded Khrushchev as first secretary of the Party.

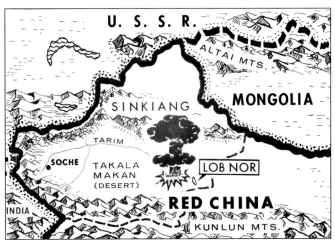

A UPI artist renders the first nuclear test by the People's Republic of China (PRC), which occurred on October 16, 1964. The inscription on a monument to the event states that the test made "a great contribution to breaking the nuclear monopoly and safeguarding world peace." This propaganda may have more than a grain of truth in it, since both the United States and Soviet Union saw the explosion as a threat. The existence of the Chinese bomb probably made President Lyndon Johnson more cautious with his military strategy in Vietnam, fearing a war with the PRC.

Bob Hayes (right) not only won the 100-meter dash at the 1964 Tokyo Olympics, but he anchored USA's 4 X 100-meter relay team (pictured) to gold. The United States won more gold medals (36) than any other nation, although they trailed the USSR in total medals, 96–90. Swimmer Don Schollander led the American effort by winning four gold medals, while American swimmers Sharon Stouder and Kathy Ellis earned four medals each. American Joe Frazier, a future rival of Muhammad Ali, won the gold in heavyweight boxing. Inevitably, politics played a part in the Games. South Africa was banned from the Olympics because of its racist policy of apartheid.

Herzog, a classic novel by noted American author Saul Bellow (shown), hit bookstores in 1964. The title character in this complex novel of ideas is a philosophy professor. He muses about growing up Jewish in the 20th century, the breakup of his second marriage, and the failure of his career. Though not an easy read, Herzog became influential as a work that combined complicated philosophical issues and fascinating characters in a contemporary setting.

November: Albert DeSalvo is arrested and charged with a series of rapes in Connecticut. Later, he will confess to multiple Boston-area murders and be dubbed the Boston Strangler.

November 3: President Johnson and Hubert Humphrey score a landslide victory over the Barry Goldwater–William Miller ticket. • Former U.S. Attorney General Robert Kennedy is elected U.S. senator from New York. • California voters pass by an overwhelming margin Proposition 14, which repeals the state's fair-housing laws.

November 18: During a lengthy interview with reporters, FBI Director J. Edgar Hoover objects to the Warren Commission report's criticism of his agency, and dismisses the report in general as Monday-morning quarterbacking. He also calls Martin Luther King, Jr., a "notorious liar," and labels American judges "bleeding hearts."

November 24–26: Belgian paratroopers occupy Stanleyville, Congo, and liberate about 2,000 white hostages from Congolese rebels.

November 29: Major changes in Roman Catholic liturgy, including English prayer and response, take effect in the U.S.

December: Thousands of North Vietnam Army soldiers arrive in the Central Highlands of South Vietnam. They provide organization and leadership to the Vietcong, and arm them with sophisticated weaponry (courtesy of Russia and China).

December 1: Aides of President Johnson, including Secretary of State Dean Rusk, National Security Adviser McGeorge Bundy, and Secretary of Defense Robert McNamara, recommend a policy of gradual military escalation in North Vietnam.

December 2–3: University of California–Berkeley students, protesting the suspensions of several fellow Free Speech Movement activists, stage a sit-in protest on campus. More than 700 demonstrators are arrested.

In November 1964 California citizens were asked to support a ballot initiative favoring Community Antenna Television (CATV), popularly known as pay TV. Voters, though, were not impressed by the display of all of the extra channels (11). They defeated the proposition by a 2–1 majority. Voters were undoubtedly influenced by a public relations campaign, launched by the three commercial networks, opposing the idea.

Grease spots are all that remain of several U.S. aircraft destroyed in a November 1, 1964, Communist mortar attack on the Bien Hoa air base in South Vietnam. Four Americans died and dozens of people were wounded. In spite of the provocation, President Johnson was reluctant to escalate American involvement in the war only a couple days before the 1964 presidential election. His political strategy throughout that year had been to keep the war on the back burner.

General Maxwell Taylor, U.S. ambassador to the Republic of Vietnam (South Vietnam), confers with Secretary of Defense Robert McNamara on November 27, 1964, prior to meeting with President Johnson. Taylor urged the President to increase American military operations in Vietnam and to avoid negotiations with the Communists. The National Security Council concurred, and in December 1964 LBJ approved a plan by which the administration would stress to the world the importance of the war and prepare for the possibility of more direct U.S. intervention, including bombing North Vietnam. This set the stage for the escalation that occurred in the spring of 1965. Johnson, incidentally, was increasingly pessimistic about the effectiveness of the South Vietnamese Army (ARVN). When the idea of turning the ARVN loose on the North emerged, he exploded that it would be like sending "a widow woman to slap Jack Dempsey."

The Failure of Strategic Hamlets

AT A PLACE CALLED Hoa Phu [in the province of Long An], for example, the strategic hamlet built during the previous summer now looked like it had been hit by a hurricane.... A local guard explained to me that a handful of Vietcong agents had entered the hamlet one night and told the peasants to tear it down and return to their native villages. The peasants complied without question. From the start, in Hoa Phu and elsewhere, they had hated the strategic hamlets, many of which they had been forced to construct by corrupt officials who had pocketed a percentage of the money allocated for the projects. Besides, there were virtually no government troops in the sector to keep them from leaving. If the war was a battle for "hearts and minds" ... the United States and its South Vietnamese clients had certainly lost Long An.

—AUTHOR STANLEY KARNOW, *VIETNAM: A HISTORY*

American pop singer Sam Cooke was shot to death on December 11, 1964. A motel manager killed Cooke after the singer had struggled with a woman he had allegedly picked up that night. Cooke's career had begun in the 1950s with a gospel group called the Soul Stirrers. After going solo, he combined the gospel tradition with soul and rock 'n' roll in such mega-hits as "You Send Me" (1957) and "Chain Gang" (1960). He became one of early rock's most important figures.

At a time when long, roomy, big-engine cars dominated the U.S. automobile market, a strange little vehicle called the Beetle began to wiggle its way into American consciousness in the mid-1960s. In a whimsical sales campaign, VW suggested that buyers heed the headline (*above*). Many did. The rounded, petite Volkswagen (German for "people's car") was originally built with the support of Adolf Hitler. Reintroduced after World War II, it appealed to a generation of young Americans in search of economy and the exotic. The little bug and the subsequent Volkswagen Microbus became enduring symbols of the counterculture.

December 4: The FBI arrests 21 white men in conjunction with the June 1964 murders of three civil rights workers in Mississippi. *See* October 20, 1967. • President Johnson issues an executive order that bars discrimination in federal-aid programs.

December 7: The U.S. Supreme Court unanimously rules that Florida laws prohibiting cohabitation of whites and blacks are unconstitutional.

December 11: As Cuban revolutionary Che Guevara addresses the United Nations, a bazooka shell is fired at the UN building from across New York's East River. It falls short of the Manhattan riverbank. • Rhythm and blues singing star Sam Cooke, 33, is shot to death in a motel office.

December 12: President Johnson welcomes the first group of VISTA (Volunteers in Service to America) workers to the White House. VISTA will sponsor a range of programs to help the nation's poor.

December 14: In *Heart of Atlanta Motel v. United States,* the U.S. Supreme Court upholds the power of Congress to prohibit discrimination in privately owned hotels.

December 15: The Canadian House of Commons votes, 163–78, to adopt a new national flag: a red maple leaf on a white field, with vertical red bars at both ends of the banner.

December 19: The East German government opens the Berlin Wall for about two weeks to allow holiday visits to the East by West Berliners.

December 20: General Khanh and officers Cao Ky and Van Thieu lead a successful military coup in South Vietnam, ousting General Minh.

December 24: A bomb blast in U.S. officers' quarters in Saigon, South Vietnam, kills two Americans.

After members of the Free Speech Movement had been suspended by the school, University of California–Berkeley students staged a sit-in protest on campus on December 2–3. More than a thousand people filled Sproul Hall, including folk singer Joan Baez, who inspired protesters with her rendition of "We Shall Overcome." Governor Pat Brown, fearing anarchy, called in a force of 600 law enforcement officials, who arrested 773 protesters. Here, arrestee No. 479 poses for an impromptu mug shot.

Savio: We Won't Compromise

MANY STUDENTS HERE at the university [California–Berkeley], many people in society, are wandering aimlessly about.... They are people who have not learned to compromise, who for example have come to the university to learn to question, to grow, to learn—all the standard things that sound like clichés because no one takes them seriously. And they find at one point or other that for them to become part of society, to become lawyers, ministers, businessmen, people in government, that very often they must compromise those principles which were most dear to them....

The "futures" and "careers" for which American students now prepare are for the most part intellectual and moral wastelands.... But an important minority of men and women coming to the front today have shown that they will die rather than be standardized, replaceable and irrelevant.

—MARIO SAVIO, *AN END TO HISTORY*

James Bond (played by Sean Connery) is held prisoner by Pussy Galore (Honor Blackman) in the 1964 film *Goldfinger*. Considered by many critics to be the best of the Bond movies, the film features the evil machinations of Auric Goldfinger (Gert Frobe) as he tries to corner the world gold market. Bond, secret agent extraordinaire, manages to foil the plot at the last minute with the help of the provocatively named Miss Galore, who has deserted her employer, Mr. Goldfinger, mainly because of Bond's enticing sex appeal. It was all great fun for James Bond buffs.

Characters Allison Mackenzie (Mia Farrow), Constance Mackenzie (Dorothy Malone), and Dr. Michael Rossi (Ed Nelson), pictured from left to right, stroll down a sidewalk in *Peyton Place*. This revolutionary television soap opera premiered on ABC in fall 1964. In a scheduling experiment, the show ran in prime time twice a week. *Peyton Place* was based on the 1956 novel by Grace Metalious. Its plot exposed the dark secrets of a small New England town that on the surface was filled with virtue and piety. The strong sexual content—although not graphic—and excellent acting helped make the experiment a rousing success. *Peyton Place* lasted until spring 1969.

Eliza Doolitle (played by Audrey Hepburn) demonstrates her class to Henry Higgins (Rex Harrison), her mentor, in the 1964 film version of *My Fair Lady*. Based on the Lerner and Lowe 1956 Broadway musical, this film was both popular and critically acclaimed. It won three of the four major Academy Awards for the year: best actor (Harrison), best director (George Cukor), and best picture. Its appeal owed much to its faithful adaptation of the play, with witty dialogue, sumptuous costumes, and brilliant tunes and lyrics. Moviegoers also enjoyed the film's rags-to-riches storyline as well as Hepburn's many charms.

New & Notable

Books

Candy by Terry Southern
    & Mason Hoffenberg
Herzog by Saul Bellow
In His Own Write by John Lennon
The Psychedelic Experience
    by Timothy Leary
Understanding Media
    by Marshal McLuhan
Why We Can't Wait
    by Martin Luther King, Jr.
With Shuddering Fall
    by Joyce Carol Oates
You Only Live Twice by Ian Fleming

Movies

The Carpetbaggers
Dr. Strangelove
Fail-Safe
A Fistful of Dollars
Goldfinger
A Hard Day's Night
Mary Poppins
My Fair Lady
Woman in the Dunes

Songs

"Everybody Loves Somebody"
    by Dean Martin
"Fun Fun Fun" by the Beach Boys
"I Want to Hold Your Hand"
    by the Beatles
"Leader of the Pack"
    by the Shangri-Las
"My Guy" by Mary Wells
"Wishin' and Hopin'"
    by Dusty Springfield

Television

The Addams Family
Bewitched
Gilligan's Island
Gomer Pyle, USMC
Jeopardy
The Man from U.N.C.L.E.
The Munsters
Peyton Place
Shindig!

Theater

After the Fall
Fiddler on the Roof
Funny Girl
Hello, Dolly!

Gunsmoke, the longest-running prime-time drama in American TV history, ran on CBS from 1955 to 1975. In 1964 the cast included (*left to right*) James Arness (Marshal Matt Dillon), Burt Reynolds (blacksmith Quint Asper), Ken Curtis (Festus Hagen), Amanda Blake (Miss Kitty), and Milburn Stone (Doc Adams). *Gunsmoke* boasted a strong set of characters who displayed both courage and vulnerability. Marshal Dillon was sometimes beset with doubts, Doc struggled with a drinking problem, and Miss Kitty had a somewhat shady reputation as a saloon owner.

Tevye (played by Zero Mostel) tries to bargain with God in the lilting song "If I Were a Rich Man" in the Broadway musical *Fiddler on the Roof*. When it opened on September 22, 1964, some criticized the play for having limited appeal. Yet it became a huge hit, winning nine Tony Awards and running for a record-breaking 3,242 performances on Broadway. Set in a small Jewish village in Russia, *Fiddler* clearly transcends its ethnicity. Tevye's major conflict comes when his daughter wants to marry a poor tailor rather than the middle-aged butcher he has chosen for her. The debate over retaining beloved traditions versus freedom of choice resonated with many Americans in the turbulent Sixties.

Media as the Message

THE EMINENTLY QUOTABLE Marshall McLuhan was a professor at the University of Toronto. Coining the phrase "the media is the message," he laid out his observations about technology and mass communications in a series of highly touted works.

In 1964's *Understanding Media: The Extensions of Man,* McLuhan asserted that the *content* of a received message is less important than the vessel, or *media,* that conveys it. McLuhan postulated that human perceptions had become conditioned to respond to the context of a message, rather than the message itself. The various media were characterized as either "hot" or "cool." Books were an example of the for-

mer, exemplifying an individual, nonparticipatory activity. Cool media included participatory, group pursuits, such as television (and eventually the Internet).

McLuhan saw the rise of technology, beginning with the invention of writing, as a force of alienation from our "true" social natures. Individual activities led to the "detribalization" of the social order. Conversely, McLuhan believed that electronics represented an extension of our selves, leading inexorably toward a "retribilization" that would restore mankind's "sensory imbalance." While wildly popular on campuses throughout the decade, McLuhan's work was just as often dismissed among academics as pseudointellectual claptrap.

Characters Napoleon Solo (Robert Vaughn, *left*) and Illya Kuryakin (David McCallum) stand at the ready with state-of-the-art automatic weapons in the cult television spy classic *The Man from U.N.C.L.E.* Running from 1964 to 1968, the show sprang from the spy craze of the mid-1960s. Solo, an American, and Kuryakin, a Russian, are good-guy agents who battle the evil villains of THRUSH. The 105 episodes were even campier than the James Bond films from which *U.N.C.L.E.* drew inspiration.

Martin Luther King, Jr., (*right*) and associate Andrew Young (*next to King*) arrive at FBI headquarters in early December 1964 to try to end the tension between King and FBI Director J. Edgar Hoover. King had asked for the meeting when he learned that Hoover had called him "the most notorious liar in the country" after King had criticized the FBI's investigations of attacks on civil rights workers. In the meeting, King and Hoover discussed issues for about an hour. Hoover, though, wasn't through with MLK. During the height of the controversy, the FBI sent him a threatening anonymous letter, urging King to commit suicide. If not, they would bare his "filthy, abnormal fraudulent self" to the nation. In December, King received the Nobel Peace Prize.

1965

The War Escalates

I N LATE 1965 American soldiers fought their first major battle in Vietnam. In the Ia Drang Valley of the Central Highlands, heavily outnumbered American troops struggled for 34 days against three regiments of well-armed, well-trained regular soldiers of the People's Army of Vietnam. During the worst four days of the bloody combat, 234 American soldiers were killed. Altogether, 305 American fighting men lost their lives in the forested valley. Most of the dead were just 19 or 20 years old.

At one point in the battle, the North Vietnamese troops appeared ready to break through the Americans' defensive perimeter. From the battalion's command post, a simple, desperate coded call went out over the radio: "Broken Arrow." It meant, "American unit in danger of being overrun." From all over South Vietnam, American planes streaked to the battle zone and, one after another, dropped bombs and napalm on the enemy.

The commander of the American forces, Harold G. Moore, later wrote: "Among my sergeants were three-war men—men who parachuted into Normandy on D Day and had survived the war in Korea—and these old veterans were shocked by the savagery and hellish noise of this battle.... We were dry-mouthed and our bowels churned with fear, and still the enemy came on in waves."

The American forces finally did defeat the enemy at Ia Drang, inflicting thousands of casualties. To those who subscribed to the "body count" method of scoring a war (a reasoning that the Pentagon would promote), the U.S.

"So, when we marched into the rice paddies on that damp March afternoon, we carried, along with our packs and rifles, the implicit convictions that the Viet Cong would be quickly beaten and that we were doing something altogether noble and good. We kept the packs and rifles; the convictions, we lost."

—MARINE LIEUTENANT PHILIP CAPUTO

Heeding a warning from U.S. troops that their village, Qui Nhon, was going to be bombed, this South Vietnamese mother and her children wade through a murky river to safety. Throughout the war, American soldiers besieged villages in search of male Vietcong. Women, children, and the elderly often had to flee to save their lives.

achieved a resounding victory at Ia Drang. However, this was not the kind of triumph that promised to end the war on terms the American people would find acceptable.

The Vietnam War was not supposed to have become an American killing ground. No president had planned for it, and the American people had not expected to see their young men fighting a protracted land and air war in Southeast Asia. By 1965 the war had progressed in increments. One seemingly logical decision had led to the next until massive American military intervention had become, at least to President Lyndon Johnson and most of his closest advisers, the only reasonable strategic move.

Direct American involvement in Vietnam had begun in 1954 at the direction of President Dwight Eisenhower. The French, who had colonized Indochina a century earlier, were defeated on the field of battle after nearly 10 years of war by Vietnamese fighting for their independence. The Vietnamese were led by Ho Chi Minh, a Communist revolutionary and an uncompromising nationalist. The United States had been providing its French allies with financial aid. With the French defeated, Eisenhower feared that the rise of a Communist nation in the heart of Southeast Asia could be a major setback in the Cold War. He feared a "domino effect," in which other nations in the region would turn, as well, to communism.

Avoiding sniper fire, this soldier moves carefully through the underbrush outside the perimeter of the Ia Drang Valley. A major turning point in the war, the bloody four-day battle at Ia Drang in November 1965 was the first large military engagement between U.S. and North Vietnamese forces.

Eisenhower decided to try to build an anti-Communist independent nation in South Vietnam, while conceding Communist control in North Vietnam. It would be the United States' first major experiment in nation-building in the developing world. If it was successful, Eisenhower believed, it could be a model for many decolonizing nations in Asia, Africa, and parts of Latin America.

By the time John F. Kennedy took office, the struggle to build a separate anti-Communist nation in South Vietnam was not going well. The American-supported government in the south was corrupt and largely indifferent to the needs of its people. Many Vietnamese in the south had turned against the government, and some had joined or were supporting the armed resistance group, the National Liberation Front (NLF), commonly called the Vietcong. The NLF worked closely with Ho's Communist government in the north, and by 1961 it was fighting a guerrilla-style war.

By late 1963, Kennedy had increased America's military advisers to more than 15,000 and had contributed tremendous military and financial aid to the South Vietnamese government. In addition, the Kennedy Administration supported a military coup in South Vietnam that resulted in the death of America's handpicked Vietnamese leader, Ngo Dinh Diem. Despite these efforts, Kennedy's aides told the President that the struggle against communism in Vietnam was failing. They advised that unless the United States stepped in militarily, the South Vietnamese government would collapse and Vietnam would be unified under the control of Ho Chi Minh.

Having as their only task the training and assistance of the South Vietnamese military, U.S. "advisers" were not supposed to engage the enemy unless under direct attack. That policy shifted on March 8, 1965, when 3,500 Marines splashed ashore at Da Nang, becoming the first U.S. combat troops to set foot in Asia since the Korean War. Here, Marines march captured Vietcong to detention centers.

No one will ever know what policy Kennedy would have pursued in Vietnam. When Lyndon Johnson took over the presidency and was informed about the failures in Vietnam, he mournfully stated that he felt like a catfish that had "grabbed a big juicy worm with a right sharp hook in the middle of it." Johnson wanted to focus all his energies on creating what he called the "Great Society," an America in which hunger, poverty, and ignorance were abolished and all Americans had the right to equal opportunity and the basic resources they needed to realize their own ambitions. But to maintain political support for his immense domestic spending programs, Johnson believed he had to stave off an embarrassing defeat in Vietnam.

Thus, Johnson increased American military personnel—still acting only as advisers to the Army of the Republic of Vietnam—to approximately 20,000 by summer 1964. And after a purported attack (the evidence remains murky) by North Vietnamese torpedo boats on two American destroyers off the coast of Vietnam in the Gulf of Tonkin on August 4, 1964, Johnson convinced Congress to pass a resolution giving him the power to escalate American military involvement in Vietnam. Campaigning against "hawkish" Republican Barry Goldwater in the 1964 presidential election, Johnson claimed that when it came to Vietnam he was the "peace candidate." Still, despite his more "dovish" campaign rhetoric, Johnson knew that he faced hard choices in Vietnam.

A contemplative President Johnson meets with General Earle Wheeler, chairman of the Joint Chiefs of Staff, on July 27, 1965. Wheeler had argued strongly for a rapid military buildup in South Vietnam and continued bombing raids in the north. The following day, the President revealed his commitment to Americanize the war in Vietnam by deploying an additional 50,000 troops.

In early 1965, Secretary of Defense Robert McNamara and National Security Adviser McGeorge Bundy both warned the President that the United States faced a "disastrous defeat" in Vietnam if a more aggressive military policy was not quickly implemented. Convinced by the arguments of most of his key advisers, Johnson decided he had to act more aggressively to stave off an imminent Communist victory in Vietnam. He hoped that by incrementally increasing the pressure against the combined force of the South

Vietnam-based National Liberation Front and the armed might of North Vietnam, he could convince Ho Chi Minh to negotiate a peaceful settlement to the conflict. Then, Johnson hoped, he could focus the nation on waging a "war on poverty" and creating his "Great Society."

So, after an attack by the NLF on the barracks of American Marine advisers in Pleiku on February 6, 1965, which killed eight Americans, Johnson took the fight to the North Vietnamese. He ordered a sustained bombing campaign of North Vietnam called Operation Rolling Thunder. Then, to protect the American air bases used in the operation, Johnson ordered 3,500 more Marines to Vietnam. A few weeks later, in early April, he sent additional Marines. This time, he gave orders permitting the Marines to begin limited offensive operations against enemy forces operating near the U.S. air bases. Thus, the United States had begun an air war and then a ground war against the Vietnamese enemy.

Anti-Vietnam War protesters hang on to a troop train in Berkeley, California, on August 12, 1965. The train eventually slowed to a stop, and police led the demonstrators away from the tracks. Though most Americans supported the war effort in 1965, many young "radicals" railed against it. An organized antiwar demonstration on April 17 in Washington, D.C., drew 20,000 people.

On April 7, in his first major address about Vietnam, Johnson defended his decision to escalate American military involvement. At Johns Hopkins University, the President declared: "We fight because we must fight if we are to live in a world where every country can shape its own destiny.... The first reality is that North Vietnam has attacked the independent nation of South Vietnam. Its object is total conquest." He went on to echo President Eisenhower's fears of a domino effect: "Let no one think for a moment that retreat from Vietnam would bring an end to conflict. The battle would be renewed in one country and then another.... [A]ggression is never satisfied." While the President never asked for a formal declaration of war, this speech marked Johnson's commitment to waging a battle in Vietnam with no clear route to victory.

In 1965 more than two-thirds of Americans surveyed supported U.S. military intervention in Vietnam. If the American people then had been aware of some of the secret documents circulating through the executive branch, they might have felt differently. Secretary of Defense McNamara, for example, had received a memo from his chief adviser on Vietnam in mid-1965 that contradicted much of what LBJ had told the public. It stated that 70 percent of the reason for the U.S. to continue fighting was "to avoid a humiliating U.S. defeat," and just 10 percent was to help the South Vietnamese "enjoy a...freer way of life."

Very few Americans in 1965 publicly challenged U.S. policy in Vietnam. Most opponents were from the "radical" fringe of American political life: Communists, socialists, pacifists, militant civil rights activists, and a new breed of young leftists. In March 1965, some of the young radicals joined professors at the University of Michigan to hold a "teach-in" on the war. Soon, dozens of other campuses staged similar events.

On April 17, the first national protest against the war was held in Washington, D.C., sponsored by a then relatively obscure New Left group called Students for a Democratic Society (SDS). Before a crowd of about 20,000, SDS President Paul Potter denounced U.S. conduct by identifying the stated motives for American involvement as shams, and insisting that neither democracy nor decency guided U.S. foreign policy. While the protest did receive some mass media attention, most Americans trusted that their government was pursuing a just and necessary policy in Vietnam.

By the end of 1965, more than 180,000 American fighting men were serving in Vietnam. Since college students, professionals, and skilled workers received draft deferments, most American servicemen in Vietnam came from those youth who

To demonstrate against voting injustice in Alabama, activists were determined to march from Selma to the state capital in Montgomery, 54 miles away. On the first attempt on March 7, 1965, state troopers routed marchers with clubs and tear gas on the Edmund Pettus Bridge. Led by Martin Luther King, Jr., demonstrators completed a successful march 18 days later.

were not bound for college. As a partial result, African-American Army troops and Marines made up nearly 20 percent of all war casualties in 1965—even though blacks comprised less than 12 percent of the U.S. population. This unfair burden did not go unnoticed by black activists, further radicalizing many of them. The injustice played as an ugly backdrop to the protests in Selma, Alabama, that led to the Voting Rights Act of 1965 and to the destructive race riot that exploded in the Watts neighborhood of Los Angeles in August.

In general, public support for the war and overall military morale remained strong in 1965. Even so, the only real victory American troops achieved that year was keeping the unpopular government in South Vietnam from falling to the combined force of the NLF and the North Vietnamese Army. Few Americans had any idea of the immediate and eventual costs of the war—reduction of spending on American domestic policies, increased taxes, international ignominy, loss of American lives, massive death and destruction in Vietnam (and neighboring Laos and Cambodia), and a polarized, angry society. The wounds opened by direct American military intervention in Vietnam in 1965 would take decades to heal.

1965

1965: Feeling pressure from North Vietnam, Russia begins providing surface-to-air missiles to Hanoi. • The M16 automatic rifle is introduced for use by U.S. military forces. • Disc jockey Adrian Cronauer entertains troops in Vietnam via Armed Forces Radio. • Two significant underground newspapers are launched: *The East Village Other* in Greenwich Village, New York, and the *Los Angeles Free Press* in California.

1965: Congress passes the Water Quality Act in an effort to limit water pollution. • As contraception and abortion issues come to the forefront of the public's consciousness, members of the Catholic Church begin to organize Right to Life groups. • Poet Allen Ginsberg coins the term "flower power."

Early 1965: Underground chemist Owsley Stanley's synthesized crystalline LSD becomes available on the streets.

January: African-American players who arrive in New Orleans for the American Football League All-Star Game are denied access to social clubs—even by gunpoint. When the black players say they will boycott the game, AFL Commissioner Joe Foss decides to move the contest to another city. • French designer André Courrèges startles the fashion world with his 1965 collection, which emphasizes ultrashort skirts; helmet-like headgear; flattened, geometric bodylines; white kid boots to midcalf; and enormous round goggles. • A new dance called "The Jerk," made popular on Top 40 radio stations by the Larks, is popular in discotheques across the U.S.

January 2: University of Alabama quarterback Joe Namath signs a rookie-record $400,000 contract with the New York Jets of the American Football League.

University of Alabama football coach Paul "Bear" Bryant comforts his quarterback, Joe Namath, after a 21–17 loss to Texas in the Orange Bowl on January 1, 1965. Namath perked up the next day when he signed a $400,000 pact with the New York Jets of the American Football League—the fattest rookie football contract to that time. Namath would become one of professional football's most successful and colorful quarterbacks as he helped make the AFL competitive with the National Football League. Bryant would become a larger-than-life icon in the South, winning five national championships in his 25 seasons at Alabama.

Sir Winston Churchill, the wartime prime minister of Britain and champion of democracy, suffered a stroke in January 1965. His family reported that in a moment of fleeting consciousness, Churchill uttered his last words: "I am so bored with it all." In his famous "Iron Curtain Speech" given in the United States in 1946, Churchill had helped define the Cold War standoff that would shape the foreign policy agenda of the West during the 1960s. An accomplished historian, painter, and soldier, Churchill retired from politics in 1955 at age 80 and died 10 years later on January 24, 1965.

Dallas County Sheriff Jim Clark scuffles with the SCLC's C. T. Vivian in Selma, Alabama, on February 5, 1965. After Vivian compared Clark to Hitler, one of Clark's deputies responded by punching Vivian in the face. Several times in January and February, Clark and his men turned back activists as they attempted to register to vote. These demonstrations launched the first phase of the Selma Project, a Martin Luther King-led campaign that included marches and civil disobedience in the city. In the first week of February, police arrested hundreds of marchers in Selma, many of whom were children, and sent them to jails and makeshift jail yards. The demonstrators' efforts weren't in vain, however. On February 4, a federal judge ordered Selma's registrar to process at least 100 voter applications per day.

A group of anti-Vietnam War protesters blocks the entrance to the headquarters of the United States Mission to the United Nations on February 19, 1965. Organized by the Committee for Nonviolent Action, some 30 demonstrators (14 of whom were arrested) called for the withdrawal of all U.S. troops from Vietnam a few days after President Johnson launched air strikes against North Vietnam. This protest was indicative of the small but slowly growing opposition to the war.

"Respect me, or put me to death."

—MALCOLM X

The Murder of Malcolm X

O N FEBRUARY 21, 1965, Malcolm X appeared at the Audubon Ballroom on Broadway and 165th Street in Harlem to give one of his firebrand orations. As he launched into his speech, a scuffle broke out on the ballroom floor. "Get your hand out of my pocket!" someone shouted. Distracted, Malcolm's security guards rushed to the scene to quell the disturbance. Moments later, three gunmen charged the stage and opened fire, killing one of the most powerful spokesmen of black liberation.

The three assassins were members of the Nation of Islam (NOI), an African-American religious sect that Malcolm had left in March 1964 after years of serving as one of its chief lieutenants. Headed by the self-proclaimed prophet Elijah Muhammad, NOI blended elements of Islam with a racial cosmology that cataloged blacks as God's chosen people and whites as "devils." Malcolm's breech with the organization came after he learned that Muhammad had engaged in extramarital affairs and had fathered several illegitimate children—a discovery that he began relating in his speeches.

Top NOI officials such as Louis X (Farrakhan) tried to discredit Malcolm, labeling him a hypocrite and a traitor. Such denunciations only led the estranged Muslim leader to broaden his criticism, as he charged Muhammad with financial corruption and with distorting the teachings of the Koran. Soon the death threats began, growing ever more frequent as 1964 drew to a close. Always the realist, Malcolm recognized that his days were numbered: "Every morning when I wake up, now, I regard it as having another borrowed day," he mused in his autobiography. Nevertheless, silence was not in Malcolm X's nature. He continued to speak out against NOI and white racism until his assassination.

1965

January 4: In his State of the Union message, President Lyndon Johnson outlines his plans for a "Great Society."

January 20: Lyndon Johnson and Hubert Humphrey are inaugurated as president and vice president, respectively. • Indonesian President Achmad Sukarno announces his nation's complete withdrawal from the United Nations.

January 24: Winston Churchill, British statesman and former prime minister, dies at 90.

January 27: Johnson aides McGeorge Bundy and Robert McNamara advise the President that limited military involvement in Vietnam is not succeeding and the U.S. must either escalate its commitment or withdraw its troops.

January–February: Senators Frank Church and George McGovern speak out against the Vietnam War.

February: Senator William Fulbright holds congressional hearings on the U.S. role in Vietnam. • American opinion polls find a 70 percent approval rating for President Johnson and 80 percent approval for U.S. involvement in Vietnam.

February 1–2: More than 700 protesters, including Martin Luther King, Jr., and many children, are arrested in Selma, Alabama. The national TV networks showcase the drama. *See* March 7, 1965.

February 7: The Battle of Pleiku erupts when Vietcong attack a U.S. base at Pleiku in Vietnam's central highlands. In just 15 minutes, eight U.S. soldiers are killed and 126 are wounded.

February 8: Vietcong guerrillas blow up U.S. barracks at Qui Nhon, killing 23 American soldiers.

February 15: Canada's new national "maple leaf" flag is raised officially for the first time. • Musician and singer Nat "King" Cole dies at 45. ➤

Time magazine made General William C. Westmoreland its Man of the Year for 1965. Here, the commander of U.S. forces in South Vietnam poses with three combat-ready Hawk antiaircraft missiles on February 21, 1965. Westmoreland, who had served with distinction in North Africa during World War II, designed the ground strategy in Vietnam and helped lay the foundation for the war's expansion, beginning with more than 100,000 troops in 1965. Westmoreland's critics faulted him for overusing helicopters, over-reliance on ground forces, and not paying good enough attention to insurgency.

Trans World Airlines flight attendants picket against the airline's policy requiring stewardesses to retire at age 35. In February 1965 their union struck against this rule as well as for higher wages and shorter hours. The same year also saw the emergence of Braniff Airline flight attendants as sex symbols. Braniff had hired an advertising agency to put some oomph in its business, and Mary Wells of Jack Tinker and Partners did just that when she had stewardesses' uniforms redesigned to be sexier. As she put it, "When a tired businessman gets on an airplane, we think he ought to be allowed to look at a pretty girl."

Selma to Montgomery Marches

ON MARCH 7, 1965, about 600 civil rights marchers tried to cross the Edmund Pettus Bridge in Selma, Alabama. They were greeted at the end of the bridge by a sea of Alabama state troopers—some on horseback, others slapping billy clubs against their palms. As the demonstrators stood quietly, troopers charged the crowd. They flailed their clubs, lobbed tear gas canisters, and aimed shotguns at the scattered and terrified marchers as they drove them back across the bridge. That violent day forever would be remembered as "Bloody Sunday."

The unsuccessful march from Selma to Montgomery was part of a coordinated effort to draw public attention to the plight of black voters in Alabama and the Deep South. In January 1965, Martin Luther King, Jr., and the SCLC had announced a voter registration project for Selma. SNCC decided to join the movement, too.

Each time Selma's black citizens attempted to register to vote that January, they were turned back by Sheriff Jim Clark and his deputies. Through a series of demonstrations, civil rights workers hoped to force confrontations and compel the federal government to intervene. On February 18, in the nearby town of Marion, local authorities showed no restraint, beating protesters bloody and killing a civil rights worker named Jimmie Jackson. The March 7 march was scheduled to commemorate Jackson's death.

Images of police brutality during Bloody Sunday drew hundreds of black and white protesters from throughout the country for a second procession on March 9. King was to lead more than 2,000 marchers across the bridge to Montgomery. However, when they reached another line of troopers at the end of the bridge, King, after a prayer, decided to turn the crowd around (to the dismay of militants in the movement). President Lyndon Johnson had quietly urged King to cool down the protests in exchange for assurances that voting rights legislation would go forward.

Soon after the aborted second march, local thugs attacked three white ministers from the North. One of the ministers, James Reeb, died from his injuries. This violent episode brought an even larger national outcry (largely because Reeb was white), including solidarity protests throughout the nation. Johnson brought Alabama Governor George Wallace to the White House for two hours of intimidation, and on March 15 Johnson addressed a joint session of Congress to push for passage of the Voting Rights Bill.

On March 21 protesters began a third march from Selma, this time protected by a federalized Alabama National Guard. They arrived in Montgomery four days later. A jubilant crowd of nearly 50,000 people, including celebrities such as Harry Belafonte and Ella Fitzgerald, gathered in triumph at the Capitol.

In August Johnson signed the Voting Rights Act, which abolished poll taxes and literacy tests, and allowed federal examiners to man polling stations in the South. After the bill passed, the number of registered black voters in Alabama increased dramatically. It was the high-water mark of the civil rights struggle.

On the morning of March 7, 1965, about 600 people departed from Selma's Brown Chapel on a protest march. Their goal was to draw national attention to their demands for voter rights in the United States. As the group, led by SNCC Chairman John Lewis and SCLC organizer Hosea Williams, traversed the Edmund Pettus Bridge, a small army of Alabama state troopers waited for them on the other side. The troopers ordered the marchers to turn back. After a moment of eerie silence, troopers in gas masks, including many on horseback, began attacking the unarmed protesters with billy clubs and tear gas, injuring at least 50 people. The mayhem would be remembered as "Bloody Sunday."

This 1965 political cartoon by Clifford "Baldy" Baldowski reflected the views of many whites at the time, including some white liberals. It insinuates that African-Americans somehow needed to *earn* acceptance—presumably, in part, by making less noise and mounting fewer demonstrations. Of course, no American citizen needs to "earn" civil rights, which are guaranteed on the basis of citizenship alone. This tendency to stereotype African-Americans as somehow undeserving was part of a growing white backlash against civil rights activism.

Martin Luther King, Jr., and his wife, Coretta Scott King, lead the third march toward Montgomery, Alabama. After two aborted attempts to march on the capital, and weeks of violent attacks by white mobs and law enforcement officials, SCLC and SNCC leaders finally completed their journey on March 25, 1965—just days after Johnson's historic speech announcing the Voting Rights Bill. Enduring rainy weather and occasional racist taunts— but protected by federal troops— thousands of demonstrators completed the five-day, 54-mile march. Marchers kept up their spirits by singing "freedom songs," such as "We Shall Overcome."

"It is wrong—deadly wrong—to deny any of your fellow Americans the right to vote in this country." President Lyndon Johnson aimed these words at lawmakers and the American public, who watched Johnson's address to a joint session of Congress on March 15, 1965. The President was promoting the Voting Rights Bill, which he promised would "strike down restrictions to voting in all elections—federal, state, and local—which have been used to deny Negroes the right to vote." Civil rights activists were buoyed when Johnson ended the speech with the movement's own slogan: "And we shall overcome."

Approximately 25,000 protesters gathered in front of the Montgomery, Alabama, capitol building on March 25 to celebrate the culmination of the Selma movement for voting rights. Martin Luther King, Jr., addressed the sea of weary marchers, assembled celebrities, and national media, proclaiming: "Selma, Alabama, became a shining moment in the conscience of man. . . . There never was a moment in American history more honorable and more inspiring than the pilgrimage of clergymen and laymen of every race and faith pouring into Selma to face danger at the side of its embattled Negroes." On August 6, just a few months after the movement to register African-Americans in Selma had begun, President Johnson signed the Voting Rights Act of 1965. The act prohibited discriminatory election practices.

Late on March 25, 1965, a civil rights activist from Detroit named Viola Liuzzo drove triumphant marchers from Montgomery back to Selma. She and a young African-American named Leroy Moton were traveling down a lonely road when a carload of three Ku Klux Klansmen and an FBI informant drove up beside them. One of them shot Liuzzo twice in the face, killing her. The FBI apprehended the three Klansmen, although evidence would suggest that the FBI informant may have been the one who fired the shot. Later, the FBI leaked false information to smear Liuzzo, stating that she had been a Communist who had abandoned her five children to have sexual relationships with black civil rights workers. A white jury acquitted the three KKK suspects of murder, although a subsequent jury convicted them of violating Liuzzo's civil rights.

Marchin' to Heaven

IT WAS SUCH A BEAUTIFUL, sunshiny day. And I walked along with Rachel for a while and we kept looking up at the sky. And there was a sign that somebody was carrying—a placard or banner, I mean—which said the whole thing that was on my mind.

It said that we weren't marching fifty miles; instead, we were marching to cover three hundred years.

My family and Rachel's family were all with us that day and we went about ten miles down the road. We were singing *Ain't Gonna Let Nobody Turn Me 'Round* as we came up to some buses pulled off alongside the road. We stopped there, and that's when Dr. King saw us.

"Are you marching all the way?" he asked, and the way he said it and the way he was smiling told me he was quite proud.

And I told him, "I don't know 'cause my momma said I had to come back home. She didn't give me permission."

"Aren't you tired?" he says.

And me and Rachel shrugged and grinned, and I said, "My feet and legs be tired, but my soul still feels like marchin'."

So he said that we had walked far enough for little girls and he wanted us to get on the bus and go back to Selma. So we said we'd do that and he touched us on the head and went on down the road. I remember standing there a long time and watching those people marching along. I would never forget that sight.

And I said to Rachel, "It seem like we marchin' to Heaven today."

And she says, "Ain't we?"

—SHEYANN WEBB, *SELMA, LORD, SELMA: GIRLHOOD MEMORIES OF THE CIVIL-RIGHTS DAYS*

February 21: Civil rights activist and leader Malcolm X, 39, is assassinated by a faction of the Nation of Islam.

February 23: Popular British-born film comedian Stan Laurel, longtime screen partner of Oliver Hardy, dies at 74.

March 2: In Operation Rolling Thunder, more than 160 U.S. and South Vietnamese warplanes launch reprisal raids against North Vietnamese military targets.

March 4: Two thousand Soviet students protesting USA's role in Vietnam attack the U.S. Embassy in Moscow, breaking 170 windows.

March 7: To protest the denial of voting rights and police brutality, about 600 marchers in Selma, Alabama, begin a 54-mile trek to Montgomery. As they try to cross the Edmund Pettus Bridge that leads out of Selma, they are attacked by state troopers and local police, who use tear gas, clubs, chains, and electric cattle prods. Dozens of marchers require medical treatment. Numerous congressmen are among the many who express their outrage. *See* March 9, 1965.

March 8: The U.S. Supreme Court rules that U.S. citizens do not need to believe in the existence of a supreme being in order to claim conscientious objector status on religious grounds.

March 9: Martin Luther King, Jr., leads a group of ministers and others across Selma's Edmund Pettus Bridge. Instead of challenging the line of police, the group says a prayer and then retreats. One marcher, white minister James Reeb from Boston, is attacked by whites later in the day and will die from his injuries. *See* March 13, 1965. • President Johnson authorizes the use of napalm, a jellied gasoline, as an antipersonnel weapon in Vietnam.

March 11: The U.S. commences Operation Market Time to disrupt North Vietnamese sea routes used to funnel enemy supplies.

Soviet cosmonaut Alexei Leonov, the first human spacewalker, is pictured in this still frame from the documentary *The Man Walking in Space*. During his orbit of the Earth on March 18, 1965, Leonov left the safety of his Voskhod II spacecraft to whirl through space for about 10 minutes at 18,000 mph. Tied to safety only by a tether, Leonov floated in space with "dreamlike gyrations," according to *Time* magazine. The achievement proved the Soviets' technical prowess in the Cold War space race. It also took the wind out of NASA's impending Gemini mission.

The Sound of Music, a Rodgers and Hammerstein stage musical, came to the silver screen in 1965. The film, which starred Julie Andrews and Christopher Plummer, told the true story of the von Trapp Family Singers, Austrians who had fled from the Nazis in the 1930s. Critics thought the musical was sentimental and saccharine. However, the public embraced this feel-good movie and its classic tunes—such as "Do Re Mi," "Climb Every Mountain," and "My Favorite Things"—making it one of the biggest blockbusters in cinema history. The film earned Oscars for best director, picture, and score.

The wreckage of a North Vietnamese PT boat burns in the Song Ging River as a U.S. Navy reconnaissance jet flies overhead. As part of Operation Market Time on March 11, 1965, American aircraft, in a joint operation with the South Vietnamese Navy, bombed North Vietnamese sea routes used to move supplies into the South. The operation succeeded in severing coastal supply lines, forcing the North to use overland supply routes, most notably the Ho Chi Minh Trail.

After eight weeks of U.S. bombing in North Vietnam, a car bomb exploded outside the U.S. Embassy in Saigon on March 30, 1965, killing 22 people. The blast ripped through the building, aiming a message of defiance at the United States' efforts to force negotiations. "Outrages like this," President Johnson responded, "will only reinforce the determination of the American people and government to continue and to strengthen their assistance and support for the people and government of Vietnam." In the following months, Johnson would increase the number of punitive raids on the north.

In February 1965 President Johnson deepened American involvement in the Vietnam War, approving General William Westmoreland's request for two battalions of Marines to protect the American air base at Da Nang. As South Vietnamese troops battled Vietcong amassed south of the beach, U.S. Marines moved ashore at Red Beach on April 10, 1965 (*pictured*). Three months later, Vietcong destroyed three aircraft in a mortar attack on the base. In August, seven Marines were killed while searching for Vietcong. As American soldiers destroyed Vietcong villages, CBS cameras recorded the drama. The footage generated controversy back home, as Americans wondered where this war was headed.

March 13: During a conference at the White House, President Johnson warns Alabama Governor George Wallace that segregationist violence must not be repeated. *See* March 15, 1965.

March 15: President Johnson, addressing a joint session of Congress, requests the passage of a strict voting rights bill. *See* March 21–25, 1965.

March 16: Quaker Alice Herz, 82, immolates herself in Detroit as a protest of the Vietnam War.

March 18: Soviet cosmonaut Alexei Leonov becomes the first human to "walk" in outer space when he leaves his Voskhod II spacecraft.

March 20: Against Wichita State, Princeton basketball star Bill Bradley scores 58 points, setting an NCAA Tournament record.

March 21–25: Martin Luther King, Jr., leads a five-day march in Alabama from Selma to Montgomery. Thousands of activists participate in the 54-mile journey, singing freedom songs and sleeping in tents. *See* March 25, 1965.

March 24: An all-night student-teacher discussion of the war in Vietnam and the nascent peace movement is held at the University of Michigan. The event is the first of what will be known as "teach-ins."

March 25: About 25,000 tired but proud marchers reach Montgomery, Alabama, where Martin Luther King, Jr., delivers a stirring speech on the steps of the state capitol building. Later in the day, Viola Liuzzo, a white woman from Detroit who participated in the march, is murdered by members of the Ku Klux Klan.

April: The U.S. Congress enacts the Elementary and Secondary Education Act of 1965, allocating $1.3 billion for public education.

"The eighth wonder of the world," boasted promoter and financier Roy Hofheinz of America's first domed stadium. The Astrodome, completed in 1965, stood as a testament to the increasing popularity of professional sports in the 1960s. The dome's Lucite roof eventually was darkened because the glare had prevented players from catching fly balls. But the lack of natural light killed the grass, necessitating the introduction of "Astroturf"—which baseball purists despised. As the Philadelphia Phillies' Richie Allen said, "If a horse won't eat it, I don't want to play on it."

On April 11, 1965, a series of spectacularly destructive twisters struck the Midwest—including Illinois (*pictured*)—injuring at least 5,000 people, killing more than 250, and causing $250 million in damage. Meteorologists had warned residents that low pressure was building in eastern Kansas, but nobody anticipated the 45 twisters that would rip through "Tornado Alley," leaving a shattered landscape of upended trailers, ripped-up sidewalks, and leveled buildings. On an expressway outside of Detroit, a twister flipped a bus onto its roof, killing four passengers. President Johnson flew to the Midwest with U.S. congresspersons to tour the damage.

As a secretary at Motown Records in the early 1960s, Martha Reeves (*right*) was asked to sing as a replacement in a session with Rosalind Ashford and Betty Kelly. The women went on to form Martha and the Vandellas in 1962. Known for their earthy vocals, the group enjoyed a series of hits, including "Heat Wave" (1963), "Dancing in the Streets" (1964), and "Nowhere to Run" (1965). The group's success coincided with that of the Supremes, Motown's other hugely popular female trio.

Rod Steiger starred in director Sydney Lumet's film *The Pawnbroker*, a bleak fictional drama that explored the inner turmoil and suppressed emotions of Holocaust survivor Sol Nazerman. Steiger's character, who runs a pawnshop in Spanish Harlem during the mid-1960s, is unable to reconcile the past and connect with his young, Hispanic employee. The Holocaust, a largely taboo topic up through the 1950s, was discussed more openly in the 1960s. Elie Wiesel's memoir *Night* was published in 1960, while the war-crimes trial of Nazi Adolf Eichmann was televised in '61. *The Pawnbroker* offered another cathartic release for Jewish-Americans.

A group of American soldiers demonstrates in New York City on April 17, 1965. The men supported the war in Vietnam and opposed the growing number of young men claiming conscientious objector status. According to a Lou Harris poll in 1965, more than 66 percent of Americans approved of President Johnson's course in Vietnam. And though antiwar sentiment was gathering steam, students on such college campuses as Yale and Michigan State University gathered sizeable petitions backing U.S. policy and expressing disapproval of civil disobedience. Veterans groups also orchestrated pro-American and pro-war rallies. But as the war raged on and more men were drafted, the pro-war contingent became less vocal and its numbers dwindled.

"This . . . is London." With these memorable words, Edward R. Murrow started each report from London during the Battle of Britain and established himself as the voice of a generation. As a CBS television reporter after the war, Murrow's Peabody-winning programs influenced public opinion. His broadcasts included critical reporting about McCarthyism and investigative specials, such as "Harvest of Shame" (about the plight of migrant farm workers). Murrow worked for two years as the head of the U.S. Information Agency for the Kennedy Administration, but he felt stifled in his diplomatic role. A three-pack-a-day smoker, Murrow suffered from lung cancer and died at age 57 in 1965.

1965

April 9: The brand new Astrodome, the country's first domed stadium, hosts its first baseball game—the Houston Astros versus the New York Yankees in a preseason contest.

April 11: Tornados in the Midwest cut across six states and kill more than 250 people, including some 140 in Indiana.

April 14: Richard Hickock and Perry Smith are hanged for the 1959 murder of a family in Kansas. The case was the basis for Truman Capote's bestselling 1965 book *In Cold Blood*.

April 17: Some 15,000 gather in Washington, D.C., to protest the Vietnam bombing campaign by the U.S. • The Mattachine Society, the leading gay organization in the U.S., pickets the White House for equal rights.

April 25: Secretary of State Dean Rusk condemns U.S. academics who are publicly critical of the American role in Vietnam.

April 27: U.S. radio and television broadcaster Edward R. Murrow dies at 57.

April 28: President Johnson announces the landing of U.S. Marines in the Dominican Republic, which is torn by civil war. The U.S. military's goal is to quell the uprising of Communist-oriented rebels and help bring order to the country.

May: Drop City, a commune and artist colony, is founded near the Colorado–New Mexico border. • Eastman Kodak introduces Super 8 home-movie film, which comes in cartridges that require no threading into the camera. *See* Summer 1965.

May 1: America's YF-12 Blackbird aircraft sets records for speed (2,070 mph) and altitude (80,257 feet).

May 3: The first U.S. Army combat troops, a total of 3,500 men, arrive in Vietnam.

An American soldier protects a food distribution center in Santo Domingo, Dominican Republic, on May 9, 1965. After Rafael Trujillo's 30 years of brutal, U.S.-supported rule ended with his assassination in 1961, the Dominican Republic entered an era of civil war. Juan Bosch, a social democrat whom President Kennedy thought might be a Communist sympathizer, reigned as president for seven months in 1963 before being ousted by Dominican military leaders. When Bosch's military supporters attempted a coup in 1965, the United States used the pretext of imminent Communist takeover to send more than 20,000 troops to the island nation in April and May. The American soldiers crushed the rebellion and assisted civilians. The Organization of American States eventually brokered a cease-fire, and the country attained relative stability after Joaquin Balaguer took office in 1966.

THE GREEN BERETS

ROBIN MOORE

Brilliant, inspiring tales of the little known but crucially important arm of U.S. defense, the crack teams of the Special Forces – true-life heroes who have made the Green Beret a badge of honor in the jungles of Vietnam and the world over.

Robin Moore's book, *The Green Berets*, glorified the Special Forces counter-insurgency unit of the U.S. Army, and was a bestseller in 1965. At age 36, Moore had been given permission to undergo Green Beret training and "guest-serve" with the unit in Vietnam. Though the book was fact-based, security concerns required that Moore write the book as fiction—and even at that, some D.C. politicians were outraged that Moore had related "secret" information. But because of intense, positive interest in the elite group, the general public was unfazed. According to a Gallup poll, two-thirds of Americans supported U.S. activity in Southeast Asia in 1965.

On May 15, 1965, radio broadcasters linked 122 campuses in a nationwide "teach-in" that presented views against and in favor of the war. Here, former Kennedy Administration adviser Arthur Schlesinger, Jr., speaks out in favor of U.S. strategy. Faculty at the University of Michigan had organized the first teach-in on March 24, 1965, and other teach-ins sprouted up on campuses throughout the country. During the teach-ins, which often lasted all night, students and their professors discussed the history of the Vietnam conflict as well as U.S. policy in Vietnam. The phenomenon helped ignite student antiwar organizing.

On May 25, 1965, Muhammad Ali and Sonny Liston dueled in a rematch of their 1964 heavyweight championship bout. Midway through the first round, Ali landed a short right that knocked Liston flat on his back. Referee Jersey Joe Walcott tried to maneuver Ali to a neutral corner. Ali did not obey for 17 seconds—time enough for Liston to recover. Walcott allowed the fight to resume but stopped it almost immediately, when *The Ring* magazine founder Nat Fleischer insisted from ringside that Liston should have been counted out. Ali was declared the winner by knockout. Meanwhile, fans wondered if the single punch had really been strong enough to floor Liston.

The Credibility Gap

AFTER THE AUGUST 1964 passage of the Gulf of Tonkin Resolution, which was in effect a declaration of war, few Americans questioned President Lyndon Johnson's policies in Vietnam. But when Johnson announced retaliatory air strikes on North Vietnam in early 1965, he inadvertently roused resistance among the American public. His subsequent deployment of combat troops triggered protests.

On March 24, faculty and students at the University of Michigan, the scene of Johnson's "Great Society" speech a year earlier, announced the country's first "teach-in." More than 3,000 students and faculty members attended an overnight gathering to discuss U.S. involvement in Vietnam. The first such on-campus demonstration sparked an outbreak of other teach-ins at universities across the country. The proliferation of teach-ins revealed that universities were fast becoming the center of the antiwar movement.

As these peaceful protests attracted notice, the Johnson Administration was put on the defensive. Attempting to defuse the situation, the President gave an address at Johns Hopkins University to explain his position. Surrogates likewise were dispatched throughout the country, but to little avail. Reporters, increasingly aware of the unmistakable divergence between events in Southeast Asia and what they were being told by the White House, found they were not alone. Some Capitol Hill lawmakers also were becoming upset with the dissembling, and went public with their criticism. Even war supporters felt that LBJ, by not leveling with Congress, put at risk the credibility of the administration.

A copy editor coined a damning phrase to describe the phenomenon: a "credibility gap." *Washington Post* reporter Murray Marder brought the term into general use, giving the press a handle for the pattern of deception regarding the war. For Johnson, official obfuscation was a political necessity in order to shepherd his bills through Congress. But once the media caught on, a turning point was reached for the administration's relations with both journalists and the public.

1965

May 13: Hoping North Vietnam will be open to negotiations, the White House announces the first bombing pause.

May 15: A national "teach-in," held in Washington, D.C., is broadcast to 122 campuses.

May 25: Muhammad Ali retains his world heavyweight boxing championship by knocking out Sonny Liston in the first round.

June: Folk singer Joan Baez and scholar Ira Sandperl open the Institute for the Study of Nonviolence in Carmel Valley, California. • Alton Kelly opens the Red Dog Saloon in Virginia City, Nevada. With its psychedelic atmosphere, it will become a popular watering hole for Bay Area bohemians.

June 3: U.S. astronaut Ed White takes a 21-minute space walk outside the Gemini 4 spacecraft, piloted by Jim McDivitt, becoming the first American astronaut to achieve the feat. • President Johnson asks Congress to approve elimination of silver from dimes and quarters.

June 5: The U.S. State Department admits for the first time that American ground troops in South Vietnam are engaging Vietcong in combat.

June 7: In *Griswold v. Connecticut,* the U.S. Supreme Court invalidates an 1879 Connecticut law prohibiting birth control. • Oscar-winning actress Judy Holliday dies of cancer at 43.

June 8: Nearly 17,000 protesters attend an anti-Vietnam War rally at Madison Square Garden in New York City.

June 11: About 7,000 people crowd into Royal Albert Hall in London to hear beat poets Allen Ginsberg, Laurence Ferlinghetti, and Gregory Corso. The event is billed as the first "happening." • It is announced that the Beatles will be awarded the Order of the British Empire.

A small group of gay rights activists pickets the White House on May 29, 1965, to protest federal government discrimination against "the nation's second largest minority"—15 million homosexuals. The group of nine men and three women represented the Mattachine Society of Washington. The activist group had begun in Los Angeles in the 1950s as a response to the increasing harassment and institutional discrimination that homosexuals faced during the Cold War. The Washington protest targeted the issue of less-than-honorable discharges given to gays in the Armed Forces. The Mattachines protested the government's refusal to hire homosexuals or even discuss the situation.

On June 3, 1965, Major Edward H. White, Jr., left the relative safety of his Gemini 4 capsule to walk in space. Tethered to the craft only by a cord (through which he communicated with the capsule), he floated 110 miles above Earth for 21 minutes. White not only became the first American spacewalker, but he bettered the previous 10-minute space walk of Soviet cosmonaut Alexei Leonov. Americans listened to radio broadcasts of White's voice as he floated through the void.

Ralph Nader

In 1965 General Motors, the largest corporation in the United States, hired a private detective to follow, harass, and dig up dirt on a gangly young lawyer from Winsted, Connecticut. That lawyer was Ralph Nader.

Born in 1934 and educated at Princeton, Nader by 1965 was still fresh from Harvard Law School and working in Washington, D.C., as a Senate staff consultant on highway safety. A muckraker in the progressive reform tradition, Nader made his exhaustive findings public in the bestseller *Unsafe at Any Speed*. The book exposed the roots of the unsafe vehicle problem in the United States. Nader singled out GM's rear-engine Corvair, showing how the profitable company had sacrificed safety for style in the car's construction. As a result of his exposé, sales of the car dropped by 93 percent. Nader argued that car safety could "be improved only by the forging of new instruments of citizen action."

GM's spying fiasco backfired, and when the president of General Motors apologized before a congressional committee, Nader's reputation as a crusader for consumer rights and safety was assured. In the wake of his book, the National Traffic and Motor Safety Act (1966) was passed, setting new safety standards for the automobile industry.

Nader went on to forge a career-long crusade to make the workings of government transparent and accessible to public citizens. A believer in institutions *and* their reform, Nader and his task force of young lawyers, known as "Nader's Raiders," gained hero status among the young reformers of the Sixties generation. They encouraged whistle-blowing and battled corporate power. They also exposed lapsed regulation on a wide range of issues, from auto safety to food and drugs to environmental concerns such as nuclear energy and air pollution.

Nader's efforts and example of research, advocacy, and reform led directly and indirectly to such enduring "Naderite" entities as the Center for the Study of Responsive Law (1968). He also pushed hard and successfully for class-action lawsuits against big corporations whose products were unsafe or harmful to the environment. By the late 1970s and early 1980s, some critics believed his style of activism had seen its day. But as a presidential candidate in two recent elections, Nader showed that his message of reform and persistence would live on.

Estelle Griswold (*left*), executive director of Planned Parenthood in New Haven, Connecticut, and Cornelia Jahncke, president of the Parenthood League of Connecticut, celebrate their U.S. Supreme Court victory in June 1965. After they had provided contraception information to a married couple, Griswold and Jahncke were convicted under an 1879 Connecticut law that criminalized assisting anyone seeking contraception in the state. In *Griswold v. Connecticut,* the Supreme Court ruled that the law infringed on citizens' right to privacy and was thus unconstitutional. American couples became more reliant on contraceptives in the mid-1960s, ending the postwar baby boom.

June 12: The South Vietnamese government of Phan Huy Quat, a physician, is overthrown by air force officer Nguyen Cao Ky, fewer than four months after Quat's takeover.

June 13: Major General Nguyen Van Thieu leads a military triumvirate that takes control of the South Vietnamese government.

Summer: The new, federally funded Head Start program runs for eight weeks. It is designed to help pre-school children of low-income families meet their emotional, social, health, nutritional, and psychological needs. • Wham-O Manufacturing Company's Super Ball, a small, extraordinarily bouncy sphere made of polybutadiene and sulfur, becomes a massive sales success and sweeps America. By November, Wham-O's factory in San Gabriel, California, will produce 170,000 a day. • Eastman Kodak introduces the Flashcube Kodak Instamatic camera, which permits four flash pictures to be taken without changing bulbs. • Paraphernalia, a new "mod" clothes store, opens on Madison Avenue in New York City.

July 3: Trigger, the horse of cowboy film star Roy Rogers, dies at 33.

July 14: UN ambassador and two-time Democratic presidential candidate Adlai Stevenson, 65, dies in London.

Mid-July: The Mariner 4 Mars probe flies to within 6,100 miles of Mars, sending back pictures of a cratered, waterless world.

July 17: Red China announces a technical- and economic-assistance agreement with North Vietnam.

July 20: Following a fact-finding trip to South Vietnam, U.S. Secretary of Defense Robert McNamara admits that the military situation there has deteriorated, despite U.S. involvement. See July 28, 1965.

Nguyen Cao Ky, the head of the Republic of Vietnam (South Vietnamese) air force, was named premier of the Republic of Vietnam in June 1965 after he participated in a coup that overthrew Phan Huy Quat. While in the air force, Ky dressed in a jaunty style, proudly showed off his Vietnamese wife whose eyes were "westernized" through surgery, and publicly praised Adolf Hitler. Ky served as vice president from 1967 to 1971. He fled the country in 1975 and settled in Los Angeles, where he ran a liquor store. His career illustrates the difficulty the U.S. experienced in fostering effective leadership in South Vietnam.

Adlai Stevenson, a two-time Democratic Party candidate (1952 and 1956), died on July 14, 1965. In his obituary, *The New York Times* described the intelligent, articulate, and witty politician as an "idol to the eggheads." In 1961 Stevenson had been named U.S. ambassador to the United Nations. In that role, he debated and helped negotiate the Cuban Missile Crisis and oversaw the signing of the 1963 treaty to ban underground testing of nuclear devices. Always a reluctant politician, Stevenson said the UN job "has been a terrible drill."

> *"[T]he draft was on their necks, school was a boring hassle, jobs all seemed dead end, family life was becoming unbearable, conflicts with authorities were turning serious and dangerous."*
>
> —HISTORIAN CHRIS APPEY, ON WHY ENLISTING IN THE MILITARY SEEMED TO BE THE BEST OPTION FOR MANY YOUNG MEN

During 1965 the monthly military draft increased from an average of 17,000 men to 35,000, increasing troops in Vietnam to 125,000. Across the country, 18-year-olds could look forward to the induction process. They would be inoculated, be fitted for uniforms, have their heads shaved, and be assigned temporary barracks before being shipped off to basic training. A *Life* magazine cover story in 1965 detailed this induction process for nervous mothers and their sons. Lieutenant General Lewis B. Hershey, the director of Selective Service, told young men, "If you know what you want to be, then go to college. If not, go in the service." A disproportionate number of draftees were working-class youths. They would comprise the bulk of infantry riflemen and more than half of the battlefield deaths.

In England after World War II, slot car racing became a popular leisure activity. American GIs brought the hobby home to the U.S., setting up race tracks in suburban basements around the country. Young males perfected designs for their miniature race cars and built elaborate tracks for their electric cars. Elvis Presley got caught up in the craze and relaxed with a 155-foot "King" track at Graceland. By 1965 Americans had transformed the popular fun into competitive sport, forming clubs throughout the country. Ed Sullivan even hosted a high-stakes race on his CBS variety show.

Wham-O!

"WHAM-O!" WAS THE SOUND heard when a generation of children let fly projectiles from their slingshots in the 1950s. It also inspired the name of the famous toy company that made a variety of colorful, plastic, novelty toys in the 1960s. Founded by Arthur "Spud" Melin and Richard Knerr in 1948, Wham-O encouraged Americans to swing their hips with the Hula Hoop, spin Pluto Platters, and even buy $119 do-it-yourself bomb shelter kits.

In the 1960s, Wham-O's greatest success, and children's greatest joy, derived from its sales of sidewalk skateboards, Super Balls, and Frisbees. In the second half of the decade, the company sold more than 20 million of the unpredictably bouncing, plum-colored Super Balls. The Frisbee, which originated during the UFO craze of the 1950s, became popular among the American youth culture during the 1960s. College students flicked the disk between classes, and high school students in New Jersey invented Ultimate Frisbee—an airborne derivation of soccer.

Creating wacky fads as well as lasting fixtures of American popular culture, the Wham-O Manufacturing Company helped to define fun in the 1960s and beyond.

1965

July 24: Bob Dylan decides spontaneously to perform several rock-laced songs at the Newport Folk Festival, angering folk purists.

July 28: President Johnson announces that U.S. troop strength in South Vietnam will be increased from 75,000 to 125,000, and that draft call-ups will be doubled.

July 30: President Johnson signs a landmark Medicare bill after spending many months twisting arms at the American Medical Association.

July–August: Berkeley students and protesters sit on railroad tracks and hang onto the train cars in an attempt to stop troop trains from leaving the Bay Area.

August: CBS televises the destruction of suspected Vietcong villages by U.S. troops, generating controversy. • Barry McGuire's hit protest song "Eve of Destruction" is banned by some radio stations. • *The Berkeley Barb,* a counterculture newspaper, begins publication. • Author Ken Kesey and his Merry Pranksters host an LSD party for the Hell's Angels at Kesey's six-acre spread south of San Francisco.

August 1: Unidentified flying objects are sighted over Kansas, Texas, Oklahoma, New Mexico, Colorado, South Dakota, Nebraska, and Wyoming.

August 6: President Johnson signs the Voting Rights Act of 1965. *See* August 10, 1965.

August 8: American writer Shirley Jackson dies at 45.

August 9: Singapore secedes from Malaysia and becomes an independent nation. • An explosion and fire at the U.S. Titan II missile silo in Searcy, Arkansas, kills 53 civilian employees.

August 10: Federal examiners begin registration of African-American voters in Alabama, Mississippi, and Louisiana.

A young couple strolls through the Chelsea section of London. This area was considered the home of the miniskirt, a modest example of which is worn by the woman seen here. Introduced by fashion designer Mary Quant in 1965, the miniskirt—which rose six inches above the knee—quickly became "the thing" among hip young women on both sides of the Atlantic. For many cultural conservatives, this "London look," which also included bobbed hair and tall vinyl boots, exposed too much thigh and no doubt prefigured the collapse of western civilization.

Mary Quant, an art school graduate turned fashion designer, helped define the look of swinging London in the 1960s. Her designs included miniskirts, skinny ribbed sweaters, and white, patent plastic, knee-high, lace-up boots. With her own design house and boutique, Quant contributed to the "mod" and "Chelsea girl" looks while making fashion both affordable and accessible to a growing youth market. Quant mass-produced her bold color combinations and patterns for the American market as well.

Noted American author Shirley Jackson died at age 45 of cardiac arrest on August 8, 1965. Her most famous story, "The Lottery," is the chilling tale of a small-town gambling ritual that leads to the socially accepted public execution of the "winner." Jackson's personal eccentricities caused some of her neighbors to claim that she wrote with a broomstick for a pen. However, her stories of seemingly ordinary, often bucolic characters caught in macabre circumstances made her a favorite, especially among college and high school students.

"Little Stevie Wonder" was only 12 years old when he signed with Motown Records in 1962. His 1963 album, *Recorded Live—The 12-Year-Old Genius,* was the first record to top both the pop and R&B charts. After dropping "Little" from his stage name, the blind singer and master of harmonica, piano, and drums toured in 1965. The following year, Wonder's soul hit "Uptight (Everything's Alright)" topped the pop and R&B charts again. A multiple Grammy winner, Wonder enjoyed continued success throughout the 1960s and '70s, championing various social and political causes along the way.

Annie Maude Williams of Selma, Alabama, holds up her new voting eligibility certificate on August 10, 1965. Within weeks of the August 6 passage of the Voting Rights Act, federal examiners fanned out across the South to help register voters. After enduring a century of intimidating violence, illegal poll taxes, literacy tests, and other means of disenfranchisement, more than 27,385 African-Americans in Alabama, Mississippi, and Louisiana were quickly registered. With the U.S. government finally enforcing federal law, the act dramatically changed voting in the South. In Williams's state of Alabama, black registration grew from 66,000 in 1960 to 241,000 six years later.

Pakistani soldiers patrol the Kashmir front during the war that raged between India and Pakistan over Kashmir in 1965, from early August to late September. The dispute had its origins in the 1947 British partition, which pitted Muslims and Hindus against each other in a struggle over contested territory. The 1965 war also was weakly linked to the Cold War, as Pakistan was a longtime ally of the United States while India had ties to the Soviet Union. With U.S.-supplied jets, tanks, and other arms, Pakistan fought India on multiple fronts in Kashmir as well as on the Indian–Pakistani border, and with air attacks on Indian cities. Tank battles between the two countries were the largest since World War II.

August 11–16: Massive rioting, triggered by the arrest of a black man for drunk driving, occurs in the Watts section of Los Angeles. Thirty-four people are killed and nearly 4,000 are arrested.

August 13: In Chicago, violence erupts following a rally protesting the death of an African-American woman, who had been hit by a fire truck. Seventy-five people, including 18 police officers, are injured.

August 15: The Beatles play 12 songs in 35 minutes before 56,000 fans at Shea Stadium in New York City.

August 17: Cleveland newspaperman Robert Manry arrives at Falmouth, England, after piloting his 13½-foot sailboat, *Tinkerbelle,* across the open Atlantic for 78 days, covering a distance of 3,200 miles. The boat becomes the smallest ever to make the eastward crossing.

August 18–24: In Vietnam, U.S. Marines engage in "Operation Starlite," the first major U.S. ground operation.

August 30: President Johnson signs into law legislation that prohibits the destruction of draft cards.

September: Only 110 of 5,135 public school districts in the 17 southern states have made moves to desegregate their classrooms, as mandated by Title VI of the Civil Rights Act of 1964. • The United Farm Workers Organizing Committee calls a strike against California grape growers, with the aim of establishing a trade union and the right to bargain collectively. • The U.S. Army successfully test-fires the tube-launched, optically tracked, wire-guided (TOW) portable antitank missile. • Miniskirts, a favorite in Europe last year, catch on in the U.S. • The phenomenal success of the British "Supermarionation" show, *Thunderbirds,* sparks a surge in toy production in the United Kingdom. ➤

An unlikely source provided significant insight into chimpanzee behavior. Jane Goodall grew up in England raised on Tarzan stories and *The Jungle Book.* At 23 and armed only with some secretarial training, she went to Kenya, landing a job with anthropologist Dr. Louis Leakey within months. Assigned to observe the daily life of chimpanzees, Goodall recorded numerous revelations, including proof of their tool-making abilities. Her work revealed chimps' behavioral kinship to humans, with evidence of community order, social hierarchy, and affection. Goodall became the world's preeminent primatologist.

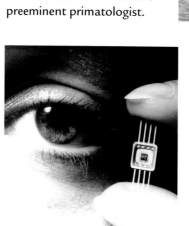

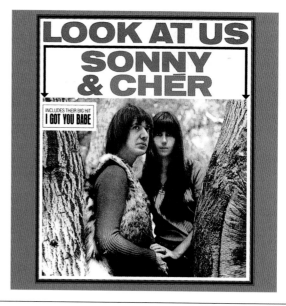

A woman holds a microchip smaller than her eye in 1965, a year in which the microelectronics industry boomed. Intel scientist Gordon Moore promulgated Moore's Law that year, four years after the first planar integrated circuit was developed. He postulated that a new generation of memory chips would appear every couple of years and that each would be smaller in size but with greater memory capacity—a prediction that has largely held true. This boom marked the beginning of the information revolution.

Under the tutelage of studio wunderkind Phil Spector, Sonny Bono mastered every facet of the music business. In 1964 he pushed his girlfriend, background singer Cherilyn Sarkisian, into the spotlight to sing his tune "Baby Don't Go." Her stage fright led to his joining her in the vocal booth, serendipitously creating Sonny and Cher. A year later, "I Got You Babe" became a huge hit, partly due to their image as a pair of offbeat but harmless lovebirds.

"I looked up and I just saw a fire; the air was just full of smoke, and I glanced over and I saw a large fire over toward where I live at; I just saw things burning, burning, burning. Everywhere I looked I saw a fire."

—WATTS RESIDENT RECALLING THE RIOT

The Watts Riot

IN THE MIDDLE of a heatwave on August 11, 1965, a crowd began to gather around a motorist named Marquette Frye and a police officer who had stopped him on suspicion of drunk driving. This scene, so familiar to the citizens of the Watts neighborhood of Los Angeles—where tensions between white police officers and African-Americans ran high—soon exploded into violence. Years of pent-up anger erupted in six days of rebellion, resulting in 34 deaths and nearly a thousand injuries.

The Watts riot was a reaction to the specific condition of segregation in California. In 1964 the California Real Estate Association successfully persuaded voters to pass Proposition 14. Prop 14 overturned the Rumford Fair Housing Act, which had prohibited racial discrimination. Squeezed into increasingly confined ghettos and with a 30-percent unemployment rate, black Angelenos reached the breaking point.

Whites, many of whom were surprised by the violence so soon after the passage of the Civil Rights Act, found that segregation and civil rights were not just southern issues. In

Police arresting a rioter in Los Angeles on August 12

the succeeding years in the Sixties, race riots would erupt in Chicago, Detroit, Cleveland, and numerous other northern cities.

Three stores burn to the ground on Avalon Boulevard during the 1965 Watts riot. Angered by discrimination and police brutality, thousands of black citizens of Los Angeles rebelled in mid-August 1965, yelling "Burn, baby, burn!" as they looted and committed arson in this primarily African-American area. While temperatures approached 100 degrees, more than 1,000 fires raged in the city. One firefighter was killed and 136 firefighters were injured.

Alone in his 13½-foot sailboat *Tinkerbelle*, Robert Manry of Cleveland, Ohio, successfully charted his way from Falmouth, Massachusetts, to Falmouth, England, in summer 1965 in the smallest boat ever known to have made the eastbound trip. After his 3,200-mile, 78-day adventure across the open Atlantic, a crowd of more than 20,000 greeted him as he steered his way into Falmouth Harbor in the late afternoon of August 17.

Dao Hong Lien, an 18-year-old factory worker, practices her marksmanship while training with the local self-defense unit in Vinh, North Vietnam. As U.S. bombers attacked the North Vietnamese countryside and cities in the spring of 1965, detachments of civilians were pressed into service. The high command's strategies required that every man, woman, and child be prepared to defend their homes against the enemy, to the death. In fighting a war of attrition against superior forces, maintaining hostilities as long as possible in a test of wills became key to survival.

Corporals James Williams (*left*) and Frank T. Guilford drag a wounded Marine to an evacuation helicopter after Vietcong guerrillas attacked a supply column on Vietnam's Van Tuong Peninsula. The attack came on the second day of Operation Starlite, the United States' first major ground operation in Vietnam, which raged from August 18 to 24, 1965. U.S. Marines waged a series of preemptive strikes against 1,500 Vietcong, who were planning to assault the American airfield at Chu Lai. Forty-five Marines and 614 Vietcong guerrillas were killed. The victory boosted U.S. troop morale.

Vietnam: Dead and Brown

IN ASIA VEGETATION is always lush, but now when you fly over parts of Vietnam you can see the dead, brown surface of the areas which have been sprayed with weed killers. You see the areas that were sprayed on purpose, and the places defoliated by accident. Ben Cat…was almost completely destroyed by accident; 3000 acres were transformed into the tropical equivalent of a winter forest….A Catholic refugee village, Honai, along Highway 1 in South Vietnam…was sprayed by mistake. All its fruit trees died. United States Air Force planes were defoliating the jungle along Highway 1, but the wind shifted and blew the killer spray towards the villages instead. In a supreme irony, the jungle now stands in the background, lush and thick, while the villages are barren.

—JOURNALIST BERNARD FALL

A member of the Vietnam Day Committee, a University of California–Berkeley antiwar group, tries to stop a troop train in August 1965. Some 60 members of the committee took part in this demonstration, one of many that occurred in the Bay Area in 1965. Taking a cue from civil rights protesters, these antiwar advocates practiced nonviolent civil disobedience to make their point. This demonstration was a precursor to a larger one in Oakland later that fall, when thousands marched against the war.

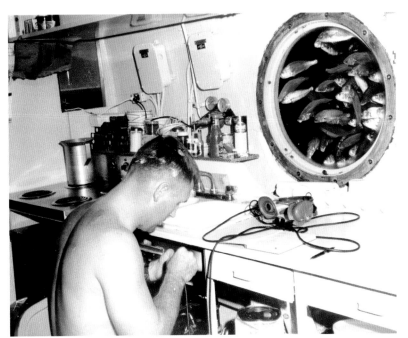

A school of fish keeps aquanaut Berry Cannon company on the ocean floor near San Diego in the small underwater habitat known as SeaLab II. From 1964 to 1969, the U.S. Navy built a series of underwater dwellings to experiment with saturation diving methods and the psychological aspects of human isolation over extended periods of time. Although considered to be a success, the program was scrapped in 1969 during the operations of SeaLab III, when Cannon died as he descended toward the dwelling without wearing the proper equipment.

Dorothy Dandridge battled racial discrimination in Hollywood and American culture throughout her career. The talented, sensitive, and troubled black actress and singer possessed star quality, but she was consigned to "black roles" throughout the 1940s and '50s. In her last major film role, she starred opposite Sidney Poitier in the musical *Porgy and Bess* (1959). But with few decent parts available to African-Americans at the time, she returned to performing as a nightclub singer. Her personal life, too, was difficult. She became deeply involved with powerful director Otto Preminger, who would not marry her because of her color. Dandridge's marriage to Jack Denison, a white restaurateur, led to the actress's bankruptcy. Dandridge, just 41, died in her West Hollywood apartment on September 8, 1965, a possible suicide by barbiturates.

1965

September 1: The Pakistani army crosses the international boundary separating Pakistan and the disputed Kashmir province, ostensibly part of India but unrecognized as such by Pakistan. *See* Early September 1965.

September 4: Albert Schweitzer, a French–German mission doctor, theologian, and philosopher, dies at 90.

Early September: India continues its armored incursion into West Pakistan and disputed Jammu territory. Troops engage in what is considered to be the fiercest tank battle since World War II.

September 8: Oscar-nominated film actress and singer Dorothy Dandridge dies at 41.

September 24: Executive Order 11246 requires federal agencies and federal contractors to take "affirmative action" in overcoming employment discrimination.

September 29: North Vietnam announces it will try downed U.S. pilots as war criminals.

October: The two-year New York World's Fair ends with attendance of 51,607,307, which is short of the projected 70 million.

October 3: President Johnson signs a bill abolishing U.S. immigration quotas.

October 4: Pope Paul VI arrives in New York, becoming the first pope to set foot in North America. On this day, he confers with President Johnson, addresses the UN, and delivers a sermon to 90,000 people at Yankee Stadium in the Bronx.

October 14: In Game 7 of a hard-fought World Series, L.A. Dodgers pitcher Sandy Koufax shuts out the Minnesota Twins for a 2–0 win and the championship.

October 15: The first public burning of a draft card is perpetrated by 22-year-old David Miller in New York City.

➤

Hogan's Heroes, which debuted in 1965, was an unlikely television comedy set in a German prisoner-of-war camp during World War II. Each episode featured the shenanigans of wily American Hogan (Bob Crane, *center*), who used the prison camp as a base of operations for anti-German sabotage. Under the clueless watch of bumbling German Sergeant Schultz (John Banner, *left*) and idiotic Colonel Klink (Werner Klemperer, *right*), the prisoners ran an elaborate system of escape tunnels and clandestine communications. Klemperer was Jewish, and his family had fled from the Nazis during World War II. He agreed to play Klink only if his character was presented as a fool.

Completing a 17-year project, workers finally placed the 10-ton keystone at the top of the 630-foot-high St. Louis Gateway Arch in October 1965. Eero Saarinen, the architect responsible for such other famous modernist landmarks as the TWA terminal at New York's JFK Airport, designed this centerpiece for the $29 million riverfront park complex on the Mississippi. The stainless steel Gateway Arch commemorated the city's role as a gateway for western explorers and pioneers.

LBJ's "Great Society"

PRESIDENT LYNDON JOHNSON was nothing if not ambitious. He had seen the effects of President Franklin D. Roosevelt's New Deal in curing society's ills, and it moved him. With a mastery of the legislative branch acquired during his tenure as Senate majority leader, Johnson was determined to craft a legacy that would outshine FDR's.

LBJ's chance came with his unexpected ascendancy to the presidency in November 1963. Recognizing the unique opportunity before him, he proceeded to push President John F. Kennedy's languishing civil rights legislation through Congress, which came to fruition in July 1964. This victory, he hoped, would set the stage for programs of his own design. Confident in his abilities to reshape America with the stroke of his pen, Johnson began planning what he called the "Great Society."

College student Janet Lewis, volunteering for a housing program

In May 1964 LBJ announced his intentions at the University of Michigan. "We have the power to shape the civilization that we want," he declared. In Johnson's view, an array of problems needed attention for society to achieve greatness: Poverty must be eradicated; full employment must be pursued; college education should be the rule rather than the exception; and the basic needs of all Americans from infancy to old age should be addressed. While maintaining that it wasn't enough merely to throw money at society's ills, Johnson was fully prepared to take advantage of the robust economy. Likewise, the public seemed willing to go along with his idealism, at least initially.

LBJ declared "war" on poverty. His Equal Opportunity Act was tailored to silence critics by offering the poor a "hand up," not a "handout." It called for job training, targeting the young before they could fall into the poverty cycle. Medicare and Medicaid were two planks of his reelection campaign that helped define him as the voice of compassion against Republican opponent Barry Goldwater. Emboldened by his landslide reelection win, Johnson sent these and a raft of other bills before the 89th Congress.

Predictably, conservatives felt his proposals went too far, while liberals declared that they fell short. Both sides could agree that the Voting Rights Act of 1965 was a major corrective for festering civil rights concerns. But the President's widening domestic scope included beautification and urban renewal provisions, transportation and job safety outlines, clean air and water mandates, and immigration reform. Head Start, an education program aimed at preschoolers, provided Johnson and the public with tangible evidence of the Great Society's success.

Unfortunately, setting such high expectations only provoked backlash when efforts fell short. Riots erupted in long-neglected urban areas, polarizing Johnson's support base among the middle-class, who resented being called upon to, in effect, subsidize looting. Conversely, the unmistakable paternalism of such heavy-handed "cures" became a sensitive issue, especially within minority communities. Johnson's own party questioned the creation of a huge, faceless bureaucracy, believing that it could only distance the federal government from the real concerns and needs of the disadvantaged it was intended to help. But the fatal weakness within Johnson's ambitions was underfunding necessitated by the escalating war. Attempting to have guns *and* butter effectively doomed his Great Society and, beyond that, put a heavy strain on the economy.

Johnson's attempt at a Great Society resulted in programs that became central aspects of American life, most notably Medicare, Medicaid, Head Start, and an expansive Food Stamp program. However, many of his antipoverty programs were dismantled because of lack of funding and lack of political support. LBJ's Great Society ultimately was overshadowed by his failed Vietnam policies, leaving a stained legacy.

An American soldier test-fires an M16 rifle in 1965. The weapon was developed to give troops a rifle with less recoil, more accuracy at short distances, and lighter ammunition than the previous M14. First introduced in Vietnam in 1965, the M16 got mixed reviews. For some, it was a powerful and efficient weapon. However, its tendency to jam when not properly cleaned caused some soldiers to complain bitterly about its effectiveness. (Only belatedly did the military realize that the weapon needed to be cleaned frequently.) The M16 nonetheless became standard issue.

A soldier guards a captured Indonesian man during a bloody purge of Communist Party members in the wake of an aborted coup on September 30, 1965. It remains unclear whether the coup was an internal Indonesian military dispute or a U.S.-orchestrated event meant to undermine the Communist-friendly and anti-neocolonial regime of President Sukarno, as some argued. The result was indisputable. Fiercely anti-Communist Major General Suharto soon displaced the teetering Sukarno and commenced killing more than 500,000 Communists and others throughout Indonesia.

A B-52 Stratofortress drops a load of 750-pound bombs over the coast of North Vietnam. The mission was part of the bombing campaign against the north that began in March 1965 and continued until October 31, 1968. The campaign, called Operation Rolling Thunder, effectively destroyed Communist supply lines and provided a justification for increased numbers of troops to defend U.S. airbases. President Johnson and his advisers chose targets from a short list every Tuesday during luncheons at the White House. Johnson and Secretary of Defense Robert McNamara hoped the bombing would force negotiations, but they underestimated the resolve of North Vietnamese leader Ho Chi Minh. The strategy was also criticized for targeting civilians and for putting U.S. pilots at risk. Of the 745 U.S. military prisoners-of-war eventually returned by North Vietnam, 457 were flyers downed during this operation.

Pope Paul VI blesses more than 90,000 people at Yankee Stadium in the Bronx on October 4, 1965, at the end of his 32-hour pilgrimage to the United States. His "Sermon on the Mound" was the climax of a visit during which he met with President Johnson and spoke at the United Nations. His address to the UN stressed the need for peace in the world at a time of escalating Cold War conflict and criticism of U.S. policy. The Pope's pilgrimage reflected the more worldly approach of the Catholic Church in the era after Vatican II.

During the grape harvest in October 1965, Filipino farm workers went on strike. Here, picketers in the fields near Delano, California, hold placards that read *"Huelga"* ("Strike"). Cesar Chavez's Farm Workers Association also joined the strike to obtain better working conditions, union recognition, and an increase in wages for mostly Mexican-American and Filipino farm workers. During the six-week strike, 44 people (including ministers) were arrested. Americans empathized with the plight of farm workers in the California industry, leading to a successful nationwide boycott of table grapes.

Cesar Chavez

DURING THE HARVEST of September 1965, farm workers from the San Joaquin Valley crowded into the meeting hall of Our Lady of Guadalupe Church in Delano, California. United Farm Workers banners hung down from a balcony that was "jam-packed" with "people coming out of the rafters," as Cesar Chavez remembered it. *La Causa* (The Cause) was in motion. That day, Mexican-American farm workers joined in a successful strike with Filipino grape harvesters and brought Chavez into the national spotlight.

Cesar Estrada Chavez was born on March 31, 1927, in Yuma, Arizona. When he was a child in the late 1930s and early 1940s, his family joined the swelling migrant labor force that made California's factory farm system possible. Chavez experienced firsthand the poverty and exploitation of the fields. After serving in World War II, Chavez returned to California, where a nascent Chicano movement had already begun to grow in the barrios of Los Angeles.

In the 1950s Chavez worked with the Community Service Organization (CSO), a group that organized Mexican-American voters. By the 1960s he used his organizing skills to help farm workers on a state level through the National Farm Workers Association. In fall 1965, the union, co-led by Dolores Huerta, launched a general strike of more than 2,000 workers over a 400-square-mile area. The strike and an effective national boycott paralyzed growers.

Holding signs that announced *"Huelga"* ("Strike"), Chavez and *La Causa* helped ignite a drive for labor rights and Mexican-American civil rights. Inspired by his Catholic faith and influenced by Gandhi, Chavez's nonviolent movement coincided with the civil rights movement. He even invited members of CORE and SNCC to join strikers.

La Causa was a huge success. By 1970 two-thirds of grapes in California were under union control. Chavez's cause became part of the broader movement in the 1960s to instill ethnic pride and protect equal rights for Mexican-Americans and all Hispanics in the West and through-

1965

A reviewer for *The New York Times* called Roman Polanski's *Repulsion* "the *Psycho* of '65." Polanski, a 32-year-old director and Jewish survivor of Nazi-occupied Poland, followed the international success of his first film, *Knife in the Water* (1962), with this psychological horror film. It starred Catherine Deneuve (*pictured*) as the sexually repressed, murderous heroine. The film conveyed Deneuve's building madness with creative uses of sound and arresting visual technique. *Repulsion* pushed new boundaries for English-language cinema, as it depicted rape and suggested incest.

Actors Jonathan Harris (as Doctor Smith, *left*) and Billy Mumy (Will Robinson) are stalked by yet another outer-space creature in the television series *Lost in Space,* a sci-fi takeoff on *Swiss Family Robinson* that premiered in 1965. Though originally centered around the adult parents in the cast, focus soon shifted to the scene-stealing Mumy as well as the prissy, cowardly Harris, raising the camp factor considerably. A robot named Robot, who had more personality than most of the characters, added to the tongue-in-cheek merriment.

A Love Supreme, the signature album of noted jazz saxophonist John Coltrane, was released in 1965. Coltrane first made a name for himself playing alto sax with the Miles Davis Quintet in the late 1950s. He left Davis in 1960 and soon became a leading proponent and practitioner of "free jazz"—an even more unstructured and improvisational style than the "be-bop" he played with Davis. Wrote Davis of Coltrane: "[N]ot only was he a great and beautiful musician, he was a kind and beautiful and spiritual person that I loved. . . . He was a genius. . . ." Coltrane died of liver failure in 1967 at the age of 40.

Ann Downey watches as searchers comb the Saddleworth Moors for her 10-year-old daughter, Lesley, one of six young people who were murdered by Myra Hindley and Ian Brady in 1965. The pair of office workers lured strangers from the streets of Manchester, England, and then raped and viciously killed them. Hindley and Brady, who photographed and even tape-recorded Lesley Downey as they tortured her, became the most hated serial killers in British history. The two were convicted of murder and sentenced to life in prison in 1966.

President Lyndon Johnson often shocked people with his forthright, even crude manner. After surgery to remove his gall bladder and a kidney stone, LBJ sat with reporters on the golf course at Bethesda Naval Hospital on October 20, 1965. To the reporters' surprise, he lifted his blue knit sport shirt and pointed to the 12-inch scar under his right rib cage. "We had two operations for the price of one," he explained to the startled press. Before leaving the hospital, the President visited Marines wounded in Vietnam, a war that would increasingly dominate his presidency after 1965.

Tom Wolfe and New Journalism

IN 1963, AFTER BEING pink-slipped by the *New York Herald Tribune* during a newspaper strike, journalist Tom Wolfe accepted a freelance assignment about California hot rod culture for *Esquire* magazine. The problem was that Wolfe couldn't write a finished piece about the topic—or so he thought.

Wolfe submitted to *Esquire* editor Byron Dobell a 49-page written apology mixed with random notes he took while documenting the youthful hot rod subculture. Instead of nixing Wolfe, Dobell expunged the preamble apology and ran Wolfe's notes as the finished article. They became one of 22 short essays in Wolfe's first book, *The Kandy-Kolored Tangerine-Flake Streamline Baby* (1965).

Wolfe's book gave birth to so-called New Journalism, a highly subjective and interpretive form of reportage that dispensed with "journalistic objectivity" in favor of a novelistic concentration on sound, sight, surface, and emotion. A hybrid that emerged from this form was the "nonfiction novel," epitomized by Truman Capote's searing *In Cold Blood* (1966) and Norman Mailer's Pulitzer Prize-winning *The Armies of the Night* (1968), which chronicled the antiwar movement.

Other practitioners of New Journalism included Joan Didion and Hunter S. Thompson. The latter turned New Journalism's often gruff and surreal subjectivity into an even headier brew known as "Gonzo Journalism." Thompson, who wrote while stoned, tried to rouse readers with provocative material.

Tom Wolfe

October 16: Scores of demonstrations in the U.S. and abroad, involving more than 100,000 people, protest American involvement in Vietnam.

October 28: The keystone is placed on top of the "Gateway to the West" arch in St. Louis, completing its construction.

October 30: U.S. warplanes mistakenly bomb the South Vietnamese village of De Duc, about 300 miles northeast of Saigon, killing 48 civilians. • Approximately 25,000 citizens march in Washington, D.C., supporting U.S. involvement in Vietnam.

November: The (Daniel Patrick) Moynihan Report is released. It warns that core problems of racial unrest—welfare dependency, joblessness, high divorce rate, and illegitimate births—are spiraling toward a social crisis. • Ralph Nader's *Unsafe at Any Speed* is published. The book condemns the American auto industry for producing unsafe vehicles. • Nationalist Party candidate Ferdinand Marcos defeats incumbent Philippines President Diosdado Macapagal by nearly 670,000 votes. • Author Ken Kesey and his Merry Pranksters hold a public "acid test" in Santa Cruz, California.

November 2: Republican–Liberal ticket candidate John V. Lindsay is elected the first GOP mayor of New York since Fiorello La Guardia (1934–45). • American Quaker Norman Morrison burns himself to death in front of the Pentagon to protest U.S. involvement in Vietnam.

November 6: The San Francisco Mime Troupe holds a party at Bill Graham's Calliope Ballroom. The Fugs and the Jefferson Airplane are among the bands that appear.

November 9: New York City and parts of eight northeastern states, Ontario, and Quebec are blacked out by an enormous power failure. Twenty-five to 30 million people are affected. ➤

Victor Moscoso poses with the psychedelic imagery that he made into an art form as part of the poster scene of the mid-1960s. Formally trained at the San Francisco Art Institute, Moscoso defined the look of the psychedelic era with his designs of posters, album covers, and comic strips in *Zap*. As the youth culture began "turning on" to LSD and other psychedelic drugs, and as they gathered for light shows and "acid tests" in San Francisco locations such as the Avalon Ballroom, Moscoso created a complementary aesthetic of organic lettering and trippy images that were used to spread the word.

Bill Graham was part of San Francisco's art scene in the early 1960s. He also was an expert event organizer and a skilled businessman. On November 6, 1965, he staged a legal defense fund benefit for a group he managed, the San Francisco Mime Troupe (city officials had declared the troupe's act obscene). For his venue, Graham selected the Fillmore Theater, which had opened as a dance hall in 1912. It was later a roller rink and finally a music venue. From 1965 until Graham's last concert on July 4, 1968, the Fillmore soared with acts as diverse as Moby Grape and Lenny Bruce; Jefferson Airplane and Miles Davis.

A disabled mother joins a group of University of California–Berkeley students in a protest against the war in Vietnam on November 1, 1965. This Vietnam Day demonstration was one of many staged by Berkeley students and their allies in 1965. Most of the demonstrators agreed with the woman that going to prison for draft evasion was preferable to death in an unjust war. Scenes such as this proved that the growing antiwar sentiment was not confined just to college students.

Quaker pacifist Norman Morrison burned himself to death in front of the Pentagon on November 2, 1965, to protest American involvement in Vietnam. Secretary of Defense Robert McNamara, who witnessed the event from his office window, recalled that he "reacted to the horror of this action by bottling up my emotions," even though he realized that it was "a tragedy." Morrison was survived by his wife and three young children. Alice Herz, an 82-year-old pacifist, immolated herself in Detroit in March 1965, and Roger LaPorte did the same in front of the UN building a week after Morrison's death. U.S. involvement in the Vietnam War continued for another eight years.

An American soldier sets fire to the roof of a South Vietnamese hut in November 1965. The dwelling was allegedly part of a Communist training camp. It was standard procedure for U.S. troops to destroy villages thought to be controlled by the Vietcong or its sympathizers. The most famous of such episodes was captured on film by reporter Morley Safer in August 1965 and broadcast on national television. Marine Corps Headquarters claimed that Safer had given a Marine the lighter and asked him to torch the hut, but the charges were never proved and Safer denied them.

Soldiers of the U.S. 1st Cavalry Division (Airmobile) carry the body of a comrade killed during a battle in the Ia Drang Valley. Ia Drang marked the first major engagement between U.S. soldiers and North Vietnamese Army (NVA) regulars inside South Vietnam. From November 14 to 16, 1965, hundreds of NVA were killed by U.S. troops, who used helicopters to deliver soldiers directly into fierce firefights. The battle also marked the first use of B-52 air support to assist combat troops. During the battle, 79 Americans were killed and 121 were wounded.

This *Rhodesia Herald* headline announces the colony's unilateral Declaration of Independence from Britain on November 11, 1965. Led by recently elected Prime Minister Ian Smith, Rhodesia sought independence from British rule while insisting that the 220,000-person white minority would maintain apartheid rule over four million black Rhodesians. Smith's political party said that Rhodesia's black population would become violent if it shared power. British Prime Minister Harold Wilson denied approval of independence unless Rhodesia's majority black population had meaningful rule. In the face of trade sanctions and almost unanimous UN condemnation, Smith said his party would rather go down fighting than crawling on their hands and knees.

In the middle of rush hour on November 9, 1965, the entire northeastern U.S. power grid collapsed. The cascading outage moved down from Buffalo, New York, spreading throughout the eastern grid and affecting a total of 80,000 square miles, including eight states and parts of Canada, and about 25 million people. New York City (*pictured*) was worst hit. In the dark for 13 hours, New Yorkers slept on the floor of Grand Central Terminal waiting for trains that never came. Moreover, 600,000 New Yorkers sat in immobile subways underground or in elevator shafts. No crime or looting accompanied the blackout. In fact, many New Yorkers proved heroic, carrying the elderly up stairs in apartment buildings and volunteering to direct traffic at intersections. Others enjoyed romantic dinners by candlelight. However, contrary to a popular myth, the number of births in New York did not skyrocket nine months later.

On November 27, 1965, six weeks after the nationwide "Vietnam Day" marches, about 20,000 citizens staged a March on Washington for Peace in Vietnam. *Newsweek* reported that during the protest, "a coalition of respectable peace groups," headed by the Committee for Sane Nuclear Policy (SANE), had problems with such younger "left-wing" groups as the Youth Against War and Fascism (*pictured*). Before the escalation of the war, the "old left" had dominated the movement. But increasingly during 1965, younger groups, such as the Students for a Democratic Society (SDS), helped shape the mounting opposition to war.

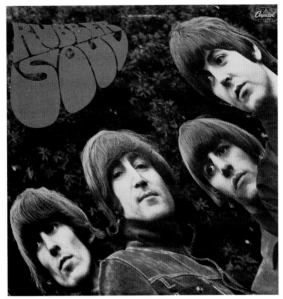

In late 1965 the Beatles released *Rubber Soul,* their sixth studio album. It marked a departure from their earlier work in that it reflected the influence of a variety of musical styles. "Drive My Car" is classic rock combined with blues, while "Nowhere Man" is much lighter rock. The signature piece, "Norwegian Wood," is a haunting, slow number in which the band used the sitar for the first time. In August 1965 the Beatles toured America. Two months later, they were awarded the prestigious MBE (Member, Order of the British Empire) honor by Queen Elizabeth.

In 1965 and '66, NASA launched 10 Gemini missions in preparation for an eventual voyage to the moon. Astronauts had to test their abilities for orbital maneuvering, rendezvous and docking, reentry, and long-duration flight if they ever hoped to land on the moon. On December 18, 1965, Gemini 6 (*pictured*) and Gemini 7 met above the Pacific Ocean, achieving the first-ever manned rendezvous in space. Gemini 7 came within a foot of Gemini 6, proving the feasibility of docking in space.

Julie Christie (*left*) and Omar Sharif (*right*) starred in *Dr. Zhivago,* director David Lean's sweeping epic based on Boris Pasternak's 1958 novel. Many reviewers criticized the sappy love story set against the serious backdrop of the Russian Revolution, but audiences enjoyed the film's lush, spellbinding visual style. The movie helped propel Christie to stardom, as she forever became associated with "Lara's Theme." The story follows Zhivago, a stoic poet who is torn between the love of two women and embroiled in the political upheaval of the time. The story reflects Pasternak's real-life experiences of repression in the Soviet Union.

November 11: Southern Rhodesia declares independence and assumes the name Rhodesia.

November 14–16: In the Battle of Ia Drang Valley in South Vietnam, U.S. Army troops wage their first major battle against North Vietnamese Army regulars (NVA). U.S. troops are supported by B-52 air strikes. About 2,000 NVA and 79 Americans are killed. *See* November 17, 1965.

November 16: Bill Ham produces the first psychedelic light show at the Red Dog Saloon in Virginia City, Nevada.

November 17: In the aftermath of the Ia Drang battle, 155 American troops are killed in an ambush. • After a vote of 47-47, the UN General Assembly refuses to seat Red China. A two-thirds affirmative vote is needed.

November 18: Henry Wallace, former U.S. vice president (1941–45) and Progressive Party candidate for president (1948), dies at 77.

December: The U.S. Selective Service inducts 40,200 men for military service, up from the 5,400 inducted in January 1965. • U.S. troop levels in Vietnam reach 184,300. • General William Westmoreland is named "Man of the Year" by *Time* magazine. • North Vietnamese officials meet with American antiwar activists Tom Hayden, Herbert Aptheker, and Staughton Lynd in Hanoi. • The Deacons of Defense and Justice, an armed, black self-defense group, is formed in Jonesboro and Bogalusa, Louisiana.

December 5: A manned A4E Skyhawk attack jet, carrying a B43 thermonuclear bomb, rolls off a USS *Ticonderoga* elevator and sinks off the coast of Japan.

December 8: The Vatican II Council closes.

December 20: Independent reports suggest that U.S. field commanders in Vietnam are authorized, under specific circumstances, to pursue Vietcong forces into Cambodia.

Chris Hillman, Dave Crosby, Mike Clark, Jim McGuinn, and Gene Clark (*left to right*) comprised the Byrds, an experimental pop band out of Los Angeles. In December 1965 the group released "Eight Miles High." The song, which was perceived as the first "psychedelic" rock hit because of its alleged aural rendition of an LSD high, was banned by many radio stations. Previously, the Byrds worked mainly in the folk rock idiom, releasing an especially successful cover of Bob Dylan's "Mr. Tambourine Man" in summer 1965. Led by guitarist and songwriter McGuinn, the group's record sales never rose to the level of its art.

Trumpeter Herb Alpert proved an unlikely pop star. Too grown up for kids but too lightweight for "serious" music fans, Alpert nonetheless found a niche satisfying millions with his mariachi-flavored single releases. Beginning with 1962's "The Lonely Bull," he recorded a steady stream of evocative originals (such as "Tijuana Taxi" and "Mexican Shuffle") and reworked standards, scoring big with 1965's "A Taste of Honey." Herb Alpert & the Tijuana Brass was ubiquitous throughout the decade, heard on television's *The Dating Game* as

well as a popular chewing gum commercial. *Whipped Cream & Other Delights* was a smash in 1965, partly because of its provocative (and widely imitated) cover art featuring model Dolores Erickson, three months pregnant at the time of the shoot.

Popular actress Audrey Hepburn wears an example of the Moon Girl Collection, a wildly popular style that designer André Courrèges introduced in 1964 and that other designers soon adopted. His thigh-high skirts, shiny white boots that rose to mid-shin, and trouser suits helped define hip youth fashion in the mid-1960s.

Charles Schulz's Peanuts became big business by the mid-1960s, as an array of toys and clothing attested. With only television left to conquer, *A Charlie Brown Christmas* premiered in December 1965. In the first of their prime-time holiday specials, the Peanuts cast turns Charlie Brown's sickly Christmas tree into a beautiful creation while Linus explains the true meaning of the holy holiday.

Ferdinand Marcos, the newly elected president of the Philippines, appears with his wife, Imelda, on inauguration day on December 30, 1965. Marcos had spent $8 million to inundate the impoverished country with pamphlets, placards, and tear-jerker biographical movies. The couple had charmed voters during the campaign with their good looks and the duets they performed. Forecast as a close election, pitting his Nationalist Party against the Liberal Party of Diosdado Macapagal, Marcos ran on an anticorruption, anticrime, pro-American platform to win in a landslide. In the 1970s Marcos would declare martial law and appoint himself president for life. By 1986 the Marcoses were exiled because of their corruption.

Bobby Tatroe (*right*) stands with *Wingfoot Express* designer Walt Arfons just prior to their assault on the world land speed record in September 1965. Powered by 15 solid-fuel rockets, *Wingfoot Express* was designed to crush the earlier land speed record of 536 mph set by Walt's brother, Art, in 1964. *Wingfoot* never managed the feat, but in November 1965 *Spirit of America* driver Craig Breedlove did by reaching the astonishing speed of 600.6 mph, a record that stood for almost five years. From 1963 through 1965, the world land speed record was shattered 11 times.

1965

New & Notable

Books
Ariel by Sylvia Plath
The Autobiography of Malcolm X
    by Alex Haley
The Green Berets by Robin Moore
The Making of the President, 1964
    by Theodore White
Manchild in the Promised Land
    by Claude Brown
The Painted Bird by Jerzy Kosinski
A Thousand Days by Arthur Schlesinger, Jr.

Movies
Alphaville
Beach Blanket Bingo
Darling
Doctor Zhivago
Repulsion
Sands of the Kalahari
The Sound of Music
Thunderball
Von Ryan's Express

Songs
"Downtown" by Petula Clark
"Eve of Destruction"
    by Barry McGuire
"(I Can't Get No) Satisfaction"
    by the Rolling Stones
"I Got You, Babe" by Sonny and Cher
"Mr. Tambourine Man" by the Byrds
"Stop! In the Name of Love"
    by the Supremes
"Yesterday" by the Beatles

Television
The Dating Game
The Dean Martin Show
The F.B.I.
Get Smart
Green Acres
Hogan's Heroes
I Dream of Jeannie
I Spy
Lost in Space
The Smothers Brothers Show
The Wild, Wild West

Theater
Cactus Flower
The Killing of Sister George
Man of La Mancha
Marat/Sade
The Odd Couple

West Coast Pop artist Mel Ramos borrowed from the "low-art" styles of popular culture and design, such as comics, pinups, and advertising imagery, to create a new art form. Ramos's photorealistic paintings combined artists' classical subject—the female nude—with icons of American culture, such as fast food, cola, and name-brand cigarettes. Many gallery owners were reluctant to show his paintings, which they felt walked the line between art and girlie magazine pictures. This painting, "Virnaburger," invokes the image of screen starlet Virna Lisi.

Bill Cosby (*standing*) and Robert Culp blast away in this promotional still from the television espionage show *I Spy*, which ran on NBC from 1965 to 1968. Producer Sheldon Leonard took a chance when he cast African-American standup comedian Cosby in one of the lead roles. Cosby was brilliant as Alexander Scott, winning three consecutive Emmys as best male actor in a dramatic series. The show combined classically exotic locations and spy drama with what critic John Cooper calls "the personal side of espionage and the toll it took on those who practiced it."

Warhol's "Silver Factory"

"**I** COULD NEVER finally figure out if more things happened in the Sixties because there was more awake time for them to happen in [since so many people were on amphetamine]," mused Pop artist Andy Warhol, "or if people started taking amphetamine because there were so many things to do.... It was probably both."

That question likely was discussed at Warhol's famous Factory, established in 1963 in New York. A cross between an artist's loft and an avant-garde commune, the "Silver Factory"—named after the silver foil that covered it entirely—was the gestation site for some of Warhol's finest Pop Art projects and intentionally obscure underground films. One of his films, *Empire* (1964), was an eight-hour, stationary shot of the Empire State Building at night.

Because of his long experience as a commercial artist, Warhol kept the Factory humming with star-struck acolytes he called "art workers." They churned out a steady and profitable flow of Warhol prints, posters, even shoes. The Factory also was the place where the artist's enormous silkscreens, arguably the most famous of his works, were produced. In these respects, the "Factory" name was literal, and not at all ironic. The Factory was, most publicly, the stomping ground for Warhol's celebrity-obsessed coterie of "superstars"—fashion plates such as "poor little rich girl" Edie Sedgwick (who died of a drug overdose in 1971), filmmaker Paul Morrissey, and Billy Name, the Factory's reclusive concierge who spent most of his time in a back closet. The Factory's propensity for sex, drugs, and sadomasochistic exhibitionism contributed to the burgeoning Sexual Revolution.

In the 1930s, Bob and Joe Switzer first combined the dyes and resins that created this glowing fluorescent paint later marketed as Day-Glo. During World War II, the substance allowed the United States military to make highly visible signs for signaling. The technology transferred easily to civilian use. Not only was it used to make the plastic coating for roadside cones, but advertisers used it to catch the consumer's eye on billboards and other advertising. In the 1960s, Day-Glo came alive under the black light and ultraviolet lights of the psychedelic counterculture.

"If you buy my lamp," promised Craven Walker, the British inventor of the lava lamp, "you won't have to buy drugs." Originally called the Astro Lamp in Europe, its gold base contained small light holes that shone like stars. Above, light-warmed goo undulated through a choice of yellow or blue liquid, mesmerizing everyone in the room. Sales of the lamps soared as psychedelia spread through Europe and America in the mid-1960s.

Andy Warhol with Ultra Violet (*left*) and Viva

1966

NOW Fights for Women's Rights

O N JUNE 20, 1966, Congresswoman Martha Griffiths, a Republican from Michigan, rose on the floor of the U.S. House of Representatives. Emphatically, Griffiths denounced the Equal Employment Opportunity Commission (EEOC), the federal agency charged with enforcing the 1964 Civil Rights Act, for failing to sustain the law in its entirety—"not just the part of it that they are interested in," she said.

The monumental, 28-page law clearly stated in Title VII that job discrimination—whether based on race, color, creed, national origin, or sex—was a federal crime. Yet the EEOC, Griffiths had learned, ignored one-third of all the complaints it had received because those complaints came from women alleging that they had suffered from job discrimination due to their gender. EEOC staffer Frances Cousens had already, unapologetically, admitted Griffiths's charge, arguing: "Complaints about sex discrimination . . . diverted attention and resources from the more serious allegations by members of racial, religious, and ethnic communities."

Griffiths was furious over the agency's "specious, negative, and arrogant" indifference to discrimination routinely practiced against working women. She also knew that until women organized to fight this inequity, little if anything would be done about it.

Just 10 days after Griffiths's angry speech, representatives from state commissions on the status of women met in Washington, D.C., for their third annual meeting to discuss women's issues in the United States. At the top of

"I charge that the officials of the Equal Employment Opportunity Commission have displayed a wholly negative attitude toward the sex provisions of Title VII. I would remind them that they took an oath to uphold the law. . . ."

—CONGRESSWOMAN MARTHA GRIFFITHS (R–MI), SPEAKING ON THE HOUSE FLOOR OF THE U.S. HOUSE OF REPRESENTATIVES, JUNE 20, 1966

Three young women face off with members of the U.S. Senate while propelling women's liberation issues into the national spotlight. In 1966 the Equal Employment Opportunity Commission's failure to enforce title VII of the Civil Rights Act prompted 28 women, including *Feminine Mystique* author Betty Friedan, to each contribute $5 toward the formation of the National Organization for Women (NOW).

1966

Three weeks after its inception, NOW members asked that President Johnson make comprehensive efforts to provide "true equality" for all, including women, within his Great Society. Founding members of NOW included (*left to right*) Dorothy Haener, Sister Mary Joel Read, Anna Hedgeman, Betty Friedan, Inez Cassiano, Richard Graham, and Aileen Hernandez.

the agenda for many of these women was the question of how to convince the EEOC to enforce the law that prohibited job discrimination on the basis of gender. They had invited a host of high-powered women's rights activists to help formulate a plan, including Betty Friedan, author of the 1963 bestseller *The Feminine Mystique.* The book had explored "the problem with no name," which eventually would be called sexism.

During a working lunch in Washington, Friedan got a brainstorm and scrawled across a napkin "NOW," the National Organization for Women. She later wrote that the group's mission would be "to take the actions needed to bring women into the mainstream of American society." Friedan championed "full equality for women, in full equal partnership with men."

NOW officially was launched on October 29, 1966, with Friedan as president. The group started with just 300 members and little grassroots support. Right from the start, NOW members believed that their cause was broader than just fighting against overt discrimination in the workplace. NOW's founding statement of purpose called for a better health care system, a national system of child care, pregnancy leave, and a host of other institutional changes that would enable women to participate equitably in the workplace and, indeed, in all aspects of public life.

Boldly, NOW's statement challenged views on appropriate gender roles that were widespread in American society. The organization turned its back on the assumption that the male should assume the role of sole breadwinner. Further, the group objected to the custom that home, housework, and children were the only things that might occupy a woman's mind and time. The often exhausting responsibilities of work and domestic life, NOW stated, must be shared by men and women. Male-female relationships should be partnerships. These feminist beliefs struck many Americans in 1966 as radical attacks on traditional verities. NOW, in the short-term, faced an uphill political struggle.

At their second national conference, two founders of NOW, Dr. Kathryn Clarenbach (*left*) and Betty Friedan, announce the adoption of a "Bill of Rights for Women" to be presented to candidates during the 1968 presidential campaign. The directive called for the adoption of an Equal Rights Amendment (ERA) to the U.S. Constitution.

It did not face that struggle alone. In April 1966 another statement about discrimination against women appeared in *Liberation,* a radical movement magazine. Written by Casey Hayden and Mary King, longtime activists in the southern civil rights struggle and the student New Left, "A Kind of Memo" was a three-page essay that targeted two problems: sexism within movement culture itself and the societal sexism that limited women's life opportunities. The authors asked their fellow activists to ponder questions that ranged from "who cleans the freedom house, to who accepts a leadership position, to who does secretarial work, and to who acts as spokesman for groups." Hayden and King also asked their colleagues to interrogate "those institutions which shape the perspectives about men and women: marriage, child-rearing patterns...."

As "A Kind of Memo" circulated among female activists, some, especially African-American activists, dismissed it (not unlike the EEOC staffers) as an irrelevant distraction from a more pressing concern. Racism, they argued, was a far more serious problem in the United States. But some women in the movement felt differently. "It was stunning in its effect on me," one woman recalled. "I read it and reread it, and shared it with all my friends. Eventually we started a group in Washington and met on a regular basis to discuss the issues...."

Gender discrimination was not the only issue demanding attention from female activists in 1966. Here, members of Women Strike for Peace wave paper doves in New York City on February 9, 1966. The women prepared to board a train for Washington, D.C., to protest the war in Vietnam.

The Students for a Democratic Society (SDS), the main organization of the New Left, followed up on the Hayden and King memo by taking up the "woman question" at a national meeting. The organization's newsletter, *New Left Notes,* described the workshop on "man-woman issues" as "fruitful," but very few men at the conference saw the need to pursue any new policies or behaviors. Many of the women in attendance, however, most of whom were long accustomed to taking a backseat to the men in the organization, were inspired by the discussions and realized that they were participating in a historic moment. One of them, Nanci Hollander, had a kind of epiphany: "We've just started a women's movement." Still, no one knew exactly what to do next.

The young female activists who were inspired by "A Kind of Memo" were more radical than most of the women first associated with NOW. The NOW activists, above all, intended to lobby the EEOC and Congress to push for legally protected equality for women. NOW primarily was interested in individual rights and equal treatment before the law. Movement women believed that more systemic changes were necessary. The Hayden and King memo urged that private human problems be viewed as public problems. The memo further noted that persons in positions of power must create people-friendly institutions, instead of bending people so that the institutions are the main benificiaries of the system.

In 1966 these more radical women were just beginning to formulate how they might "shape institutions" to create a society in which women had the freedom, responsibility, and opportunities to participate equitably with men in creating a more just world. These feminist social-justice activists not only struggled to move an anti-sexist agenda forward, but were hampered by a barrage of other problems and challenges that year.

Within the movement culture of 1966, far-reaching changes were occurring. First, the civil rights struggle was fast entering a new, fragmented phase. Martin Luther King, Jr., moved to Chicago to take on housing segregation in the North, but he was profoundly disheartened by what he found. In a protest march in nearby Cicero, while the police watched, whites hurled bottles, bricks, and vicious racist curses at the protesters. And on a hot summer day, when a small fracas developed between police and local black residents, King was unable to calm an angry mob. Right before King's eyes, a riot broke out in which three black people were killed by stray bullets and 533 African-Americans were arrested. King was shocked. "A lot of people have lost faith in the establishment," he said. "They've lost faith in the democratic process. They've lost faith in nonviolence."

Civil rights demonstrators march down a street in Cicero, Illinois, a suburb of Chicago, protesting unfair housing discrimination. Led by Martin Luther King, Jr., protesters were confronted by angry white residents who shouted racial epithets, made threats, and hurled rocks from every direction. Marchers were met with so much hatred that King said he expected to be shot at any moment.

In Mississippi, SNCC activist Stokely Carmichael was in full agreement with King's diagnosis. After being released from jail (he had been arrested on spurious charges while leading a "March Against Fear" in Mississippi), Carmichael roared to a large crowd: "The only way we're gonna stop them white men from whuppin' us is to take over. We've been saying 'freedom' for six years and we ain't got nothin'. What we're gonna start saying now is Black Power!"

Soon after, SNCC's leaders decided to expel all white members from the organization and commit themselves to the uncertain but fierce course of "Black Power." While King tried to find a path that could unite all progressive Americans in a struggle for racial and economic justice, many of the movement's younger and most committed black activists turned away from the goal of integration. Instead, they sought to control the political and cultural life of their own black communities.

Black Power militants wanted to stop white policemen from enforcing brutal "street justice" in their ghetto communities. They wanted to elect black leaders to represent their political needs. And they wanted to oversee the education their children received in their community schools. Black Power supporters wanted African-Americans to reject white standards of beauty and a Eurocentric view of the world and instead to celebrate their own history and their own culture.

While this radical—even separatist—turn developed within the African-American community, more and more white activists focused on the antiwar cause. In late 1966, 385,300 Americans were serving in Vietnam. Even though "The Ballad of the Green Berets" topped the music charts and most Americans supported the war effort, a vocal minority was beginning a nationwide effort to stop the war and bring the troops home. White activists began organizing draft-resistance centers and university-based antiwar protests.

One of these activists, Staughton Lynd, saw the antiwar campaign as a natural next step in the "movement." He felt that the antiwar activism of white radicals would echo and perpetuate the spirit of challenge and commitment that characterized Freedom Summer of 1964 and the drive to register black voters. Throughout 1966, as the Vietnam War heated up and the likelihood of either victory or peaceful settlement grew increasingly remote, more and more Americans, not just radicals, began to speak out against the deadly "quagmire."

Thus, almost all radical female activists in 1966 continued to expend their energies fighting for causes other than their own liberation. Not until mid-1967 would the militant women's liberation movement begin to take clear form. But even before the provocative actions of the women's lib radicals made headlines, NOW activists began digging in for the long haul. As historian Ruth Rosen explains, Betty Friedan's living room in New York City became a policy think tank; local chapters began opening up around the country; and the United Auto Workers, key supporters of many progressive causes in the Sixties, supplied a long-distance phone line and copy machines.

What little media coverage NOW received in its earliest days was almost all negative, and usually overripe with sexist mockery. For example, *The New York Times'* account of NOW's first convention was headlined "They Meet in Victorian Parlor to Demand 'True Equality'" and ran just below an article about turkey recipes. However, the feminist activists of NOW pushed on. Gradually, they would create the political infrastructure to take on "the problem with no name" and put an end to discrimination against women in the United States.

During the March Against Fear in Mississippi in June 1966, a civil rights activist showcased an image that would soon become the national symbol for the Black Panther Party. The civil rights movement was indeed becoming more militant. In a speech during the march, SNCC leader Stokely Carmichael roused the crowd with his cries of "Black Power."

1966

1966: The National Welfare Rights Organization is founded. Its aim is to federalize Aid to Families with Dependent Children by building local welfare rolls. • The first gay community center opens, in San Francisco. • Between 400 and 1,000 American youths flee to Canada during the year to avoid the draft. • The first direct-dial international telephone calls are made, with no operator assistance required. • Milton Bradley's new Twister game becomes a nationwide craze.

Early 1966: The U.S. Department of Defense estimates that the war in Vietnam costs the U.S. $1 billion a day. • RCA introduces integrated circuits in its television sets, marking the first use of the technology in mass-consumer products.

January 1: U.S. law now requires a warning to appear on all packages of cigarettes: "Caution: cigarette smoking may be harmful to your health."

January 1–13: New York City's subway and bus systems are shut down by a Transport Workers Union strike. At the outset, union president Mike Quill publicly tears up a court order intended to force his people back to their jobs.

January 8: The largest "acid test" yet takes place at the Fillmore Auditorium in San Francisco.

January 10: India and Pakistan sign a peace accord. The two countries will withdraw forces to the positions they occupied before the onset of the 1965 hostilities over Kashmir.

January 11: A U.S. military spokesperson announces the infiltration of North Vietnamese anti-aircraft battalions into South Vietnam.

January 12: In his State of the Union address, President Lyndon Johnson vows that the U.S. will remain in Vietnam until Communist aggression is stopped. • *Batman*, starring Adam West, debuts in prime time on ABC-TV. The first guest villain is Frank Gorshin as The Riddler.

South Vietnamese, accompanied by U.S. soldiers, take cover from Vietcong fire near Saigon in January 1966. From 1965 through 1972, more than a million civilians died in South Vietnam. Civilians often were caught in the crossfire in free-fire zones controlled by the Vietcong. In an effort to destroy popular support for the Vietcong in the South and drive civilians into areas controlled by the South Vietnamese government, U.S. forces destroyed a third of the cropland and half the villages in the South. Such actions created many refugees and deep resentment toward the U.S. from people with cultural practices connected to villages, homes, and ancestral graves.

Soldiers of the U.S. First Cavalry Division drag a Vietcong soldier from a bunker during Operation Masher in an area north of Bong Son. President Johnson later softened the name of the operation to White Wing. From January to March 1966, those conducting the mission attempted to eliminate the Vietcong and North Vietnamese Army presence from four valleys in the Binh Dinh Province. The effort exemplified the Americans' "search and destroy" strategy, in which they employed overwhelming technology and firepower to inflict casualties and weed out the enemy. The North Vietnamese left the region by March, although the U.S. strategy of attrition generally failed during the war.

The U.S. Defense Department used this template (*right*) to notify American citizens that their loved ones had been killed in the Vietnam War. Mary Brophy of Ewing, New Jersey, was among the thousands of mothers who received a dreaded telegram. During a blizzard on the night of January 29, 1966, a cab driver delivered the news that 21-year-old Dennis Brophy, a former altar boy, had been killed in action. "I started hollering," the mother said. "I remember saying, 'My son! My beautiful boy!' They had to bring a priest and doctor over for me. They gave me a shot to put me out."

"THEY WON'T GET US TO THE CONFERENCE TABLE . . . WILL THEY?"

This 1966 political cartoon by *Denver Post* cartoonist Pat Oliphant illustrates Ho Chi Minh's determination to outlast his U.S. adversaries in Vietnam no matter what the cost in lives. In the 1950s, Ho had demonstrated to the French that his forces were willing to absorb 10 deaths for every French one, and he seemed determined to follow the same strategy in the American war. In spite of such historical evidence, the Johnson Administration still believed that U.S. military might would wear the Communists down.

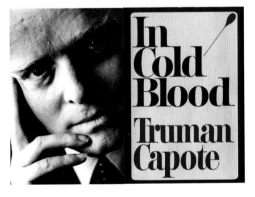

In 1966 Truman Capote published *In Cold Blood,* his pioneering study of a senseless 1959 mass murder in rural Kansas. Perry Smith and Dick Hickock, in a botched robbery attempt, killed four members of the Clutter family—an event that traumatized the small town of Holcomb. Capote interviewed the principals, including the two perpetrators, but he also invented dialogue and explored the minds of characters in ways that a fiction writer would. In essence, Capote created a new genre: the "nonfiction novel." This approach would be employed by Tom Wolfe and Hunter S. Thompson, among others, in what would become a literary and journalistic revolution.

Indira Gandhi, the daughter of India's famous postindependence leader, Jawaharlal Nehru, was first elected to Parliament in 1964. When Prime Minister Lal Bahadur Shastri died suddenly of a heart attack in 1966, members of Parliament jockeyed for power. They eventually placed Gandhi in power as a compromise candidate who they believed could be easily manipulated. Instead, she turned out to be a tough leader with consummate political skills. Gandhi held power during a tumultuous period of Indian history, 1966 to 1977. She was reelected in 1980 but was assassinated in 1984 by her Sikh bodyguards.

January 17: An American B-52 carrying four nuclear devices collides with a U.S. jet refueler and splashes into the Mediterranean Sea off the coast of Spain. *See* January 20, 1966.

January 19: Following the death of Prime Minister Lal Bahadur Shastri, Indira Gandhi (daughter of the late Prime Minister Jawaharlal Nehru) is elected prime minister of India by Parliament.

January 20: Washington announces that three of four nuclear devices that splashed into the Mediterranean Sea following a B-52 bomber's collision with a refueling jet have been recovered, and that the search for the fourth continues. *See* April 7, 1966.
• President Johnson appeals to North Vietnam for peace negotiations.

January 21: Bill Ham produces the first Grateful Dead light show, in San Francisco's Longshoremen's Hall.

January 28: Large-scale U.S. "search and destroy" operations begin against the Vietcong. • The U.S. Senate Foreign Relations Committee questions the legality of the United States' involvement in Vietnam. *See* February 1966.

January 31: Following a 37-day moratorium, the U.S. bombing campaign against North Vietnam resumes. Senator Robert F. Kennedy (D–NY) criticizes President Johnson's decision to resume the bombing, stating that the U.S. may be headed in a direction "that leads to catastrophe for all mankind."

February: Senator J. William Fulbright (D–AR), chairman of the U.S. Senate Foreign Relations Committee, conducts televised hearings about the status and purpose of the Vietnam War.

February 3: The first "soft" landing on the moon is achieved by the USSR, with its Luna 9 spacecraft.

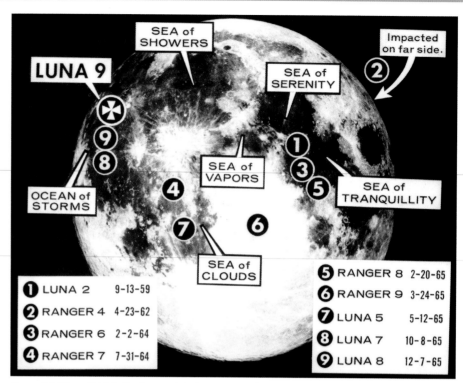

From 1959 to 1966, Soviet and U.S. spacecraft made planned crash landings on the moon, as indicated by numbers 1 through 9. But it was not until 1966 that the Soviets made the first successful soft landing of an unmanned spacecraft on the moon, landing their number 9 in the Ocean of Storms on February 3. Once on the lunar surface, Luna 9 sent back images to Earth. The U.S. soon followed with a successful soft landing of Surveyor 1 on June 2. The increasingly successful U.S. landings set the stage for the first manned trip to the moon.

Nico (*left*) and Lou Reed of the Velvet Underground practice together in 1966. Hailed by music historian Piero Scaruffi as "the most influential band in the entire history of rock music," the Underground began playing in 1964 and soon was represented by Andy Warhol. Their first album, *The Velvet Underground and Nico* (1967), included such cult hits as "Femme Fatale" and "Black Angel's Death Song." Featuring dissonance and atonality, as well as macabre lyrics, the Underground was a precursor to the punk rock that shook pop music in the 1970s.

The Generation Gap

A protester smokes a prodigious reefer at a demonstration to legalize marijuana in 1966. Called by many names—pot, dope, weed, ganja—marijuana became the drug of choice for many young people in the mid- and late 1960s. "Pot heads" developed their own rituals, which included roach clips, rolling papers, passing the joint, and "getting stoned." Marijuana's illegality (it was outlawed in the United States during the 1930s) underlined the hypocrisy of an older generation that accepted highly addictive alcohol and yet outlawed the relatively mild weed.

IN THE MID-1960s, millions of young Americans believed they could defeat an encrusted Establishment of elders by the sheer force of numbers. Behind the polemics, however, lay an unresolved problem with "generation gap" rhetoric.

The chasm between the generations was a function of demographics. *Esquire* magazine determined that by the end of 1965, half of the American population would consist of under-25 Baby Boomers. But the "generation gap" was also the product of a predominantly white cultural zeitgeist that exalted novelty and shunned convention in spheres ranging from music to fashion—as well as youth's perception that adults were hopelessly "out of touch" with new ideas. Millions of youngsters accepted Free Speech Movement hero Jack Weinberg's quote—"Don't trust anyone over 30"—as the credo for their generation. But many young people did not rebel; in fact more youngsters supported the Vietnam War than did people over 65.

What Sixties youth never resolved was whether the "generation gap" was literal—numerical age determined one's social politics—or if "youth" was a more inclusive metaphor that like-minded adults could access. After all, most of the counterculture's chief luminaries, such as Allen Ginsberg and Timothy Leary, had long since passed the age of 30. The confusion about whether the "generation gap" was literal or a metaphor is pronounced in Yippie activist Jerry Rubin's 1970 "manifesto" *Do It!*, in which he alternately enjoins kids to kill their parents while asserting that "age exists in your head."

While "generation gap" polemics fomented an us-versus-them cosmology and would become a major political issue in the 1968 presidential election, many graying adults enthusiastically adopted the Sixties' youth-centered mores, particularly the sexual ones.

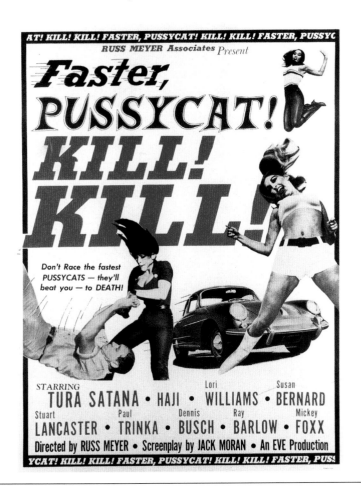

Director Russ Meyer helped define the skin flick genre in the late 1950s. But by 1966 he had taken the sexploitation genre to new heights with such films as *Mud Honey, Europe in the Raw,* and—most notably—*Faster, Pussycat! Kill! Kill!*. The movie's Pop Art fantasy style and high-energy, quick-cut filmmaking excited audiences. *Pussycat* stars three large-breasted action heroines who dominate men with karate chops, fast cars, and their own desires—an inversion of the typical male-centered action film. Critics continue to debate whether the film is an empowering portrayal of women or merely exploitation.

1966

February 23: Following a January 1966 shoot with London fashion photographer Barry Lategan, 16-year-old Leslie Hornsby, also known as Twiggy, is declared the "Face of 1966" by the *Daily Express.*

February 28: Gemini astronauts Charles Bassett and Elliott See are killed when their T-38 jet trainer strikes a building at Lambert–St. Louis Municipal Airport.

March: The National Farm Workers Association organizes Mexican-American migrant grape pickers for a protest march to Sacramento, California. They demand better wages and working conditions. • Astrophysicist J. Allen Hynek, scientific consultant on UFOs to the U.S. Air Force, informs a news conference that a high-profile UFO sighting in south Michigan was nothing more than "swamp gas."

March 1: The Soviet spacecraft Venus 3 becomes the first man-made object to touch another planet when it crashes onto the surface of Venus.

March 9–10: Communist troops attack and overrun the U.S. Special Forces base at A Shua, which is located about five miles from the Laotian border and sits astride the NVA invasion route to Hué and Da Nang. Some 200 U.S. Special Forces and South Vietnamese irregulars are killed or captured. Two years later, the base will become a Communist staging point for the Tet Offensive.

March 16: The U.S. spacecraft Gemini 8 lands prematurely but safely after an alarming pitch and yaw of the capsule and docking vehicle in space leads to a loss of maneuverability. • The Soviet satellite Cosmos 110 returns to Earth with two dogs after 22 days in orbit.

March 21: The U.S. Supreme Court votes 5–4 to uphold the obscenity conviction of Ralph Ginzburg, publisher of *Eros,* a quarterly hardcover.

In February 1966 U.S. Cabinet officials and President Johnson met with the South Vietnamese leadership in Honolulu. Here, Secretary of Defense Robert McNamara (*left*), who privately had begun to question the war, discusses strategy with South Vietnamese President Nguyen Van Thieu (*right*), while Johnson and Premier Nguyen Cao Ky talk in the background. Allies of convenience, the men maintained an outward appearance of confidence. Nevertheless, while the death toll escalated, a coherent policy for the war remained elusive.

In 1964 General Motors' Pontiac division, under John DeLorean, introduced the Tempest, a midsized car with a big 389-cubic-inch engine. Though GM did not officially create cars for racing in the early 1960s, the company selected Pontiac to produce the first "muscle" car, called the GTO, based on the Tempest platform. By 1966 (*pictured*), with a V-8 engine and a 333-horsepower base (360 horsepower optional), the GTO—nicknamed "The Goat"—was a favorite of young, male drivers who coveted power and speed.

A virulent attack on the justifications for the Vietnam War, *The Arrogance of Power* (1966) helped to legitimize the growing antiwar sentiment in the United States. Written by Senator J. William Fulbright (D–AR), the book heavily criticized the delusional and imperialistic attitudes of a Congress that failed to set limits upon itself as military intervention in Indochina continued to escalate.

THE ARROGANCE OF POWER

SENATOR J. WILLIAM FULBRIGHT

Starring Adam West as Batman and Burt Ward as his sidekick Robin, *Batman* debuted as an ABC midseason replacement in 1966 and ran for two years. This campy takeoff of the comic book superhero subtly mocked the Sixties establishment with over-the-top square heroes and delightful villains who had all the fun. Making full use of color television, the series mimicked the bright colors of comics. It also recreated the comic book look with tilted frames and such words as "Pow" and "Zap" appearing in bursts during fight scenes. Famous stars lined up to play the villains, including Cesar Romero as the Joker, Burgess Meredith as the Penguin, and Eartha Kitt as Catwoman.

In a pop music era still dominated by the sweet and conservative teen sounds of such singers as Annette Funicello and Connie Francis, Nancy Sinatra burst onto the public stage in the mid-1960s. The daughter of Frank Sinatra, Nancy sported big hair and a tough, no-nonsense style. After scoring her first hits overseas, Sinatra brought the swinging London look—miniskirts and go-go boots—to the United States. With such hits as "Sugar Town" and "These Boots Are Made for Walking" (which hit No. 1 in late February 1966), Sinatra adopted a commercial rebel persona that appealed to teenage girls.

The Mamas and the Papas strike appropriately puckish poses for the cover of their 1966 hit album, *If You Can Believe Your Eyes and Ears.* Formed in 1964 by (*left to right*) John Phillips, "Mama" Cass Elliot, Denny Doherty, and Michelle Phillips,

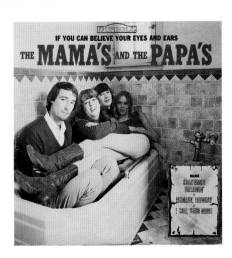

the group took advantage of John's immense writing and arranging skills. This album featured such hit singles as "Monday, Monday" and "California Dreamin'"; the latter became an anthem of the West Coast good life. The band combined beautiful, universally appealing harmonies with a lifestyle that was clearly countercultural. They broke up in 1968 due to artistic and personal conflicts.

1966

March 22: General Motors President James Roche apologizes before the Senate Subcommittee on Traffic Safety for GM's investigation into the private life of consumer advocate Ralph Nader.

March 25: Anti-Vietnam War protests are staged in eight U.S. cities and seven foreign cities, including a demonstration in New York that draws 25,000. The New York rally is staged by veterans of World War I, World War II, and the Korean War. Veterans burn or destroy their discharge papers. • The U.S. Supreme Court declares, 6–3, that poll taxes are unconstitutional.

March 31: The French government announces that it will complete its withdrawal from NATO by July 1966, and that all foreign personnel and installations on French soil must be removed by April 1, 1967.

April: Activists bombard the New York Stock Exchange with antiwar leaflets.

April 3: Black Mississippi cotton workers pitch tents near the White House to dramatize their need for decent housing.

April 7: A U.S. H-bomb lost in the crash of a B-52 off the coast of Spain is recovered after an 80-day search.

April 8: Leonid Brezhnev is elected secretary general of the Soviet Communist Party—the top leadership position in the Soviet Union.

April 12: B-52 bombers, capable of carrying 100 bombs each, are used to destroy targets in North Vietnam for the first time.

April 14: Sandoz Pharmaceuticals, the only authorized distributor of LSD, discontinues distribution and recalls its supply just one month after *Life* published a negative cover story about LSD. ➤

On March 8, 1966, Biddle Duke (*shirtless, left*), the American ambassador to Spain, along with Manuel Fraga (*speaking*), Spain's information and tourism minister, went for a swim in the 58-degree sea off the coast of Palomares, Spain. They hoped to allay public fears after a midair collision had dropped one undetonated U.S. hydrogen bomb into the Mediterranean and three onto the Spanish mainland. During the 1960s, the United States kept nuclear-loaded B-52s in the air constantly, ready at a moment's notice to drop their payloads. On one of these routine flights over Spain on January 17, a B-52 collided with an air tanker. The bombs that were dropped on land spread some plutonium but did not detonate. The fourth bomb eventually was recovered from the sea.

Nelson's Pillar in Dublin, Ireland, which commemorated the victory of British Admiral Horatio Nelson at the Battle of Trafalgar, lies in ruins after being bombed in March 1966. Although no one was ever charged with the crime, police blamed the Irish Republican Army (IRA) since many Irish nationalists saw the monument as an affront—and because 1966 was the 50th anniversary of Dublin's failed Easter Rising against British rule. Considerable violence raged in Northern Ireland during 1966 as well, especially by militant Protestant groups such as the Ulster Volunteer Force, which promised to execute members of the IRA "mercilessly and without hesitation."

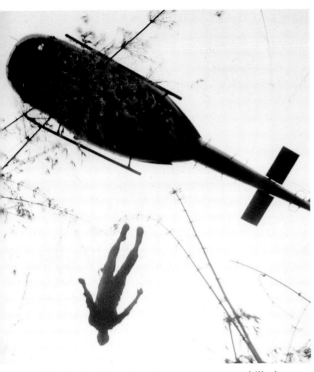

The body of an American paratrooper killed near the Cambodian border in 1966 is raised to an evacuation helicopter. By March of that year, the Pentagon reported that more than 2,000 fighting men had been killed in combat in Vietnam since the previous summer, when President Johnson ordered ground forces into the country. The report brought the overall death toll of Americans to more than 2,500 since 1961.

In 1960 North Vietnamese leader Ho Chi Minh organized the National Liberation Front (NLF) to infiltrate politically unstable South Vietnam. The NLF, Minh hoped, would spark an uprising in the south that eventually would result in the reunification of the country. South Vietnamese President Ngo Dinh Diem gave the NLF its derisive nickname of "Vietcong," which was short for Vietnamese Communists. The NLF used guerrilla tactics, including terror and assassination, to destabilize South Vietnam, and by 1963 it had control over or the support of most villages in the South. However, approximately 850,000 Vietcong lost their lives in the war, far more than the 58,000 U.S. soldiers who died in combat.

In South Vietnam in 1966, U.S. troops unleash napalm, a highly incendiary jellied gasoline. While the ostensible purpose of napalm was to clear vegetation and enhance air power, it often killed and maimed civilians. Napalm's manufacturer, Dow Chemical, became the target of antiwar demonstrations, and napalm itself came to symbolize the inhumanity of the war. Napalm would later be responsible for health problems among U.S. soldiers.

1966

The Peace Movement

DURING THE WEEKEND of March 25–27, 1966, more than 100,000 people turned out in 80 cities and towns across America to join in the Second International Days of Protest against the Vietnam War. More than 20,000 rallied in New York City alone. Such protests demonstrated that various constituencies, though they had little central coordination, could come together in large numbers to oppose President Lyndon Johnson's escalation of the war. As Johnson increased the number of American ground troops to more than 380,000 by the end of 1966, dissenters laid the foundation for what became the most significant antiwar movement in the nation's history.

The earliest protests against the war came primarily from historically pacifist and religious groups. In 1964 and 1965, the Fellowship of Reconciliation, the War Resisters League, and the American Friends Service Committee, for example, organized many of the earliest demonstrations against American intervention in Vietnam. Following the nonviolent teachings of Henry David Thoreau, Mohandas Gandhi, and Martin Luther King, Jr., this growing core of dissidents signed antiwar petitions and supported draft resistance. Some even refused to pay federal taxes.

In California, one group of homemakers briefly blocked trucks carrying napalm, the jellied gasoline explosive dropped from American planes on Vietnamese combatants and civilians alike. In June 1966 *The New York Times* ran an ad signed by 6,400 academics that called for an end to the war. And on college campuses across the country, students and faculty continued a string of "teach-ins" that had begun the previous year.

Equally significant, many former military men and politicians began to question the administration's handling of the war. David Shoup and James Gavin (retired generals) and George Kennan (the Truman Administration's architect of Communist containment) testified before Congress that the war should be ended as quickly as possible. Moreover, some of President Johnson's key allies in the Senate, including Majority Leader Mike Mansfield and Foreign Relations Committee Chairman J. William Fulbright, broke with the President over the war. Others, such as Robert Kennedy, George McGovern, and Eugene McCarthy, soon followed.

People's rationale for opposing the war varied. Some protesters characterized the conflict as illegal because the

Protesters outside the U.S. Embassy in London in 1966

President's authority to wage war did not come from a Congressional declaration of war. Others described it as immoral because of the high level of civilian casualties in North and South Vietnam. Meanwhile, even among those who generally supported the strategy of containing communism, some challenged the premise that American national security was at risk. Of course, most who protested the war did so because hundreds of American soldiers were dying each month in a war with no clear purpose.

As combat escalated in 1966 and 1967, antiwar protests became more confrontational. In particular, the Resistance—a loosely linked national coalition—called for draft-age men to openly defy the draft by turning in their selective-service cards in public ceremonies. Rather than flee the country or feign illness, draft resisters followed the example of civil rights leaders by confronting the government nonviolently.

In October 1967, Stop the Draft Week, which coincided with a massive march on the Pentagon, rattled Johnson so much that he mounted his own publicity campaign in which the commander of American forces, William Westmoreland, predicted a quick victory. When North Vietnam's Tet Offensive shattered that notion early in 1968, Johnson stopped the escalation. Similarly, President Richard Nixon took notice on October 15, 1969, when a nationwide moratorium was staged. That day, literally millions of Americans skipped work and school to participate in antiwar events.

These anxious young men prepare to take the draft-deferment test that was instated in March 1966. The test helped local draft boards decide which students deserved in-school deferment status. Similar to the SAT, the test consisted of 150 multiple-choice questions to be answered within three hours. One young man wore a sign on his back while taking the test. It read, "Score High or Die."

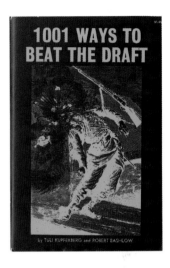

1001 Ways to Beat the Draft, by Tuli Kupferberg and Robert Bashlow, became an underground cult favorite when it was published as a booklet in 1966. Kupferberg, a founding member of the radical rock group the Fugs, advised young men to marry their sister or grope J. Edgar Hoover to evade military service. Actually, to avoid the draft, many men took the perfectly legal routes of occupational or educational deferment. Others avoided the draft thanks to letters from friendly doctors. One young man drank two pounds of honey before his physical exam, hoping the sugar spike would fool the Army doctors. It didn't.

Approximately 3,000 people in San Francisco demonstrated against the Vietnam War on March 26, 1966. They were part of the nationwide Second International Days of Protest, organized by the National Coordinating Committee to End the War in Vietnam. On the 26th, some 100,000 people protested in 80 American cities, a number not much larger than the First Days of Protest held the previous October. By 1967, however, the number and size of such demonstrations would increase significantly.

1966

April 22: An Electra prop-jet, which was chartered to transport U.S. Army recruits from Fort Ord, California, to Fort Benning, Georgia, misses the runway and crashes, killing more than 80 servicemen and crew members.

April 23: For the first time, Communist aircraft attack U.S. planes in force over North Vietnam.

April 27: The "Moors Murder" trial of stock boy Ian Brady, 28, and typist Myra Hindley, 23, opens in Chester, England. The lovers are accused of torturing, sexually molesting, and killing three children. Both defendants will be sentenced to life in prison.

April 28: Center Bill Russell leads the Boston Celtics to their eighth consecutive NBA championship.

April 30: Two Suffolk County, New York, police officers who attempt to arrest a black motorist for speeding are assaulted by black men and women who take the gun from one officer and shoot him three times in the legs.

May 3: The U.S. government admits that U.S. forces fired into Cambodia following a Communist attack mounted from the Cambodian side of the Cambodia–South Vietnam border.

May 7: A power surge inside a BWR prototype nuclear reactor in Kelekess, USSR, irradiates two workers. The chain reaction is stopped when two sacks of boric acid are thrown onto the reactor.

May 11: The U.S. State Department acknowledges that the U.S. government has declined to agree with Red China that neither would be the first to use nuclear weapons against the other.

May 12–13: Students attempt to seize the administration buildings at City College of New York and the University of Chicago.

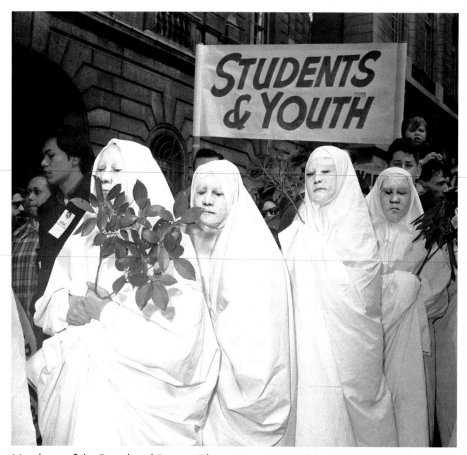

Members of the Bread and Puppet Theater troupe participate in an anti-Vietnam War protest in New York City on March 26, 1966. Founded in 1962 by Peter Schumann—a German-born dancer, musician, and sculptor—the group was in the vanguard of experimental theater with its use of human-scale puppets. In 1966 Schumann took his theater to the streets with a group of masked performers whose dreamlike dances honored Americans who had immolated themselves in protest of the war.

A Frustrated Generation

WELL, THIS GENERATION has been taught, you know, that there shouldn't be any phonies or anything, and then suddenly you find that the whole, everything is phony, I mean adults are phony. They say one thing and they mean another and they say that America's the greatest country, you know, and here we have all these problems between races and they, they don't listen to you and, and I guess that's why, you know, you just get frustrated, and I guess it's come out more in this generation 'cause there's been a sort of loss of interest in, in money, you know, and before this, in the fifties, they were always interested in money and getting ahead, and now we're ahead and we're supposed to be at the peak, you know, affluence and everything, but you know, really we're just as bad as we were when we started, it seems, because everything is phony and the world's all a mess. I, I guess that's why we're revolting so.

—FEMALE HIGH SCHOOL STUDENT, AGE 16, WASHINGTON, D.C., AS QUOTED IN *SCHOOLING FOR WHAT?*

Leonid Brezhnev, general secretary of the Soviet Communist Party, addresses the 23rd Party Congress in March 1966. After Soviet Premier Nikita Khrushchev was ousted from power in 1964, Brezhnev emerged as the most powerful Soviet leader. He rose to power primarily by appealing to the conservative state bureaucracy, which yearned for stability. As head of the party, Brezhnev halted de-Stalinization and employed repressive tactics against dissidents. While continuing the policy of limited détente with the West, he aggressively built up Soviet nuclear capacity. American policy-makers generally saw him as less flexible than Khrushchev, and were disturbed by his continued support of the Communist insurgency in Vietnam.

Alfie propelled actor Michael Caine to stardom in the role of a selfish, womanizing Cockney in swinging London during the 1960s. Due to his own East London background, Caine lent authenticity to the character that exemplified the "angry young man" period that had prevailed in British theater during the late 1950s and early '60s. Like the plays of Joe Orton and John Osborne, *Alfie* explored the class conflicts of postwar Britain and the explosive anger of working-class men. The film also features an interesting technique: Caine's character often speaks directly to the camera without other characters noticing.

Newsweek called it a "White House Camp-in" when a group of 90 displaced black farm workers from Mississippi pitched tents in front of the White House on April 3, 1966. The protesters, mostly cotton-industry workers from the Delta, hoped to draw attention to the plight of poor southern farm workers, many of whom had been dispossessed of land or jobs due to their fight for civil rights. They pressured the President to create literacy programs and job training, and to assist them with grants to build homes.

May 13: Federal funds are withheld from 12 school districts in Louisiana, Alabama, and Mississippi because the districts are in violation of school desegregation guidelines.

May 14: Approximately 15,000 demonstrators gather in Washington, D.C., to protest U.S. policy in Vietnam; 8,000 war protestors circle the White House.

May 15: South Vietnamese troops loyal to Premier Ky take control of Da Nang, South Vietnam, from rebel, anti-American South Vietnamese army units allied with anti-government Buddhists.

Mid-May: Chinese dictator Mao Tsetung reappears following a public absence of nearly six months. *See* July 25, 1966.

May 20: The U.S. sells tactical aircraft to Israel for the first time.

May 26: Buddhist students in Hué, South Vietnam, burn the U.S. Cultural Center and library. *See* June 19, 1966.

May 30: After months of civil war in Nigeria, Odumegwu Ojukwu, the governor of the Nigerian Eastern Region, declares his region independent. It is renamed the Republic of Biafra. • Japanese students in Yokosuka, Japan, demonstrate against the visit of the U.S. nuclear submarine *Snook.*

June: U.S. Selective Service chief Lewis Blaine Hershey tells the House Armed Services Committee that he favors special emphasis on drafting high school dropouts and other underprivileged young males to give them "educational, physical, and moral training." Critics see the plan as a way to utilize still more poor whites and blacks as "cannon fodder." *See* October 1, 1966. • Anti-American students riot in Colón and Panama City, Panama. Two students are killed by police.

By the mid-1960s, urban areas had grown into sprawling metropolitan messes in need of solutions, as illustrated by *Washington Post* cartoonist Herbert Block. Chief among the concerns were crowded and poor neighborhoods, transportation shortfalls, and racial discrimination. The solution, championed by private-sector developers and the government, was "slum clearance." Because of Vietnam War spending, however, only a small portion of urban-focused anti-poverty and slum-clearance programs saw federal support. "If the war in Vietnam should end," said a White House source in 1966, "the war on poverty and the rebuilding of our cities would become top priorities for government spending."

"Help"

VISTA volunteer Sally Leipzig helps an impoverished girl make a paper caterpillar in Newark, New Jersey, in April 1966. After the Peace Corps' success in the early 1960s, President Kennedy suggested the formation of VISTA, short for Volunteers in Service to America. The program finally came to fruition as part of President Johnson's War on Poverty in 1965. By '66 more than 3,600 VISTA volunteers had fanned out across the United States to help battle "poverty in the midst of plenty." VISTA sponsored a range of projects, including credit unions, block-watch clubs, and the first Job Corps and Head Start programs.

By 1966, the Beach Boys had come a long way from surf music. Group *auteur* Brian Wilson was relentless in his ambition, pushing the band's recordings into uncharted waters. The Beach Boys worked with some of L.A.'s best session players, who helped turn Wilson's introspective musings into profound pop symphonies. The result was a groundbreaking song cycle he called *Pet Sounds,* which featured such innovative classics as "Wouldn't It Be Nice," "God Only Knows," and "Sloop John B." The Beach Boys' ongoing creative competition with the Beatles would spur the latter band into creating its 1967 masterwork, *Sgt. Pepper.*

Nguyen Cao Ky, who became premier of South Vietnam in June 1965 following a military coup, was supported by President Lyndon Johnson but despised by many of his countrymen. In early 1966, anti-government and anti-U.S. protests swept South Vietnam. Dissent reached a fevered pitch during the "week of anger" in April 1966, especially in Da Nang (*pictured*). That city was the headquarters of Ky's key rival to power, Thich Tri Quang, who had broad support among students, the left, Buddhist monks, and even military officers. Demonstrators paraded through the streets carrying signs that read "Down with U.S. Obstruction." Ky dispatched troops to Hué and Da Nang to restore order and arrest anti-government demonstrators.

Leslie Hornby, better known as Twiggy, defined London's "Mod" style in the mid-1960s. After being named the "Face of 1966" by the London *Daily Express*, Twiggy graced myriad fashion magazines with her doe eyes, long eyelashes, pixie haircut, and shockingly thin figure (31–22–32). The 5′6″, 90-pound model wore the miniskirts and space-age androgynous clothes of such designers as Mary Quant. Her Twiggy Enterprises sold everything from clothing and false eyelashes to a Twiggy doll. Some claim Twiggy's popularity triggered America's obsession with slim figures—and the health problems that accompanied it.

In 1966 the John Birch Society boasted 100,000 members and a network of regional offices. Founded by businessman Robert Welch in 1958 to combat communism, the radical right-wing group was named for an Army Air Force captain who was murdered by Chinese Communists shortly after the end of World War II. Birchers believed that the United States was dominated at its highest levels by Communists. They considered everyone from Dwight Eisenhower to CIA chief Allen Dulles to be part of a vast Communist conspiracy. Despite their radical beliefs, the Birch Society gained the support of many politicians and wealthy conservatives during the 1960s. With their radio programming and widely distributed publications, the Birchers helped fuel the nascent conservative movement.

1966

June: Some 750,000 copies of the Beatles' *Yesterday and Today* album are recalled in the U.S. because of the album's "butcher" cover, which pictures the Beatles with decapitated dolls, blood, and raw meat. • The American Football League merges with the National Football League. The AFL and NFL champions will face each other in a game called the Super Bowl beginning in January 1967.

June 3–6: Gemini 9, carrying Tom Stafford and Eugene Cernan, splashes down safely after 44 Earth orbits as well as a record two-hour, nine-minute space walk by Cernan.

June 4: A three-page antiwar advertisement signed by 6,400 teachers and professors is published in *The New York Times.*

June 5–6: Wearing a pith helmet, James Meredith begins a one-man "March Against Fear" from Memphis, Tennessee, to Jackson, Mississippi. On the second day, he is shot and wounded by a sniper. *See* June 7–26, 1966.

June 7–26: James Meredith, Martin Luther King, Jr., and others complete the "March Against Fear." On June 23, marchers are clubbed and tear-gassed by police in Canton, Mississippi.

June 10: Big Brother and the Holding Company, a new band featuring singer Janis Joplin, plays at the Avalon Ballroom in San Francisco for the first time.

June 13: In *Miranda v. Arizona,* the U.S. Supreme Court rules 5–4 that constitutional guarantees against self-incrimination include restrictions on police interrogation of an arrested suspect. • A major battle of the Vietnam War is fought in Kontum, in Vietnam's Central Highlands; 565 North Vietnamese soldiers are reported killed.

June 19: South Vietnamese troops and police crush anti-government resistance in the city of Hué.

On June 6, 1966, civil rights activist James Meredith was a day into his March Against Fear when he spotted a man pointing a gun at him in Hernando, Mississippi. Meredith dove to the ground, but the sniper shot him in his back and legs. In terrible pain, Meredith dragged himself to the edge of Highway 51 before being taken to Memphis for treatment. Upon his recovery, he completed the march.

After a sniper incapacitated James Meredith during his March Against Fear, representatives of the major civil rights groups made a rare appearance together in Memphis for a news conference on June 7. Included were Stokely Carmichael (*third from right*) of SNCC, Martin Luther King (*second from right*) of the SCLC, and Floyd McKissick (*far right*) of CORE. The leaders announced they would complete Meredith's march. During the March Against Fear, the rhetoric of SNCC and CORE became more militant. Led by Carmichael, activists began trumpeting "Black Power."

Stokely Carmichael and Black Power

"WHAT DO YOU WANT?" shouted Stokely Carmichael. "Black Power!" answered the crowd gathered in Greenwood, Mississippi. On that hot June evening in 1966, with clenched fist thrust skyward, the young radical SNCC leader signaled a significant move away from the integrationist and nonviolent moral agenda of the civil rights movement and toward the language of power.

Carmichael began his activist career as a Howard University student in the early 1960s. He endured the brutal experience of the Freedom Rides, registered voters during Mississippi Freedom Summer in 1964, and helped launch the black-based Mississippi Freedom Democratic Party. After his experience registering black voters in Mississippi (amid the constant fear of racist violence) and as the elected chair of SNCC in 1966, Carmichael increasingly felt he was betrayed by white liberals. He gave voice to the growing impatience among younger civil rights activists who no longer endorsed Martin Luther King's nonviolent resistance strategies.

Carmichael's leadership helped to launch the Black Power movement for self-determination that dominated the second half of the 1960s and shifted the civil rights movement's orientation toward a more urban, northern audience. Inspired in part by the separatist ideas of Malcolm X, Carmichael served as the prime minister of the Black Panther Party for a brief period before breaking with the organization. He changed his name to Kwame Touré and embraced pan-Africanism before emigrating to Guinea in 1969.

On June 10, 1966, Billie Jean King won her first of three consecutive Wimbledon titles. A fierce battler on the court, King was also a determined activist. She took strong stands against the elitist and corrupt system of the United States Lawn Tennis Association, and she spoke out against the unequal treatment that women faced as professional athletes. By the 1970s, King had become a hero to feminists as well as to advocates of gay and lesbian rights.

June 29: U.S. warplanes bomb Communist fuel depots near Haiphong and Hanoi, the closest raids yet to those major North Vietnamese cities. • The National Organization for Women (NOW) is founded in Washington, D.C., with 28 members.

July: Tennis star Billie Jean King wins her first of three straight women's singles titles at Wimbledon. • Boeing announces it will undertake significant production of the new 747 jumbo jet, which will carry 400 to 500 passengers. The first delivery to the airlines is scheduled for 1969.

July 5: In Belfast, Northern Ireland, a 30-pound concrete block is dropped on a car in which Queen Elizabeth and Prince Philip are riding. Neither is injured.

July 6: North Vietnamese radio reports that captured American pilots have been paraded through the streets of Hanoi.

July 8–August 19: A strike by the International Association of Machinists cripples operations of five major U.S. airlines: United, Trans World, Northwest, National, and Eastern.

July 10: Martin Luther King, Jr., leads 30,000 protesters from a rally at Soldier Field to Chicago's City Hall. *See* July 12–15, 1966.

July 12–15: Racially motivated riots that shake Chicago's west side are quelled by National Guardsmen. *See* August 26, 1966.

July 14: Drifter Richard Speck invades a Chicago apartment inhabited by female student nurses and murders eight of them. One woman, who hides beneath a bed, survives. *See* April 15, 1967.

July 15: Operation Hastings is launched by U.S. Marines and South Vietnamese troops against the enemy in Quang Tri Province. It is the largest combined military operation by U.S. and South Vietnamese forces to date.

This June 1966 Herblock cartoon refers to Republican Senate Minority Leader Everett Dirksen's criticism of President Johnson's failure to keep congressional leadership adequately informed about administration policy in Vietnam. Johnson was stung by the rebuke, especially since he had a close alliance with Dirksen on such issues as civil rights. The President needed the support of moderates such as Dirksen to counter doves, who wanted the U.S. to withdraw, and hawks, who wanted to expand the war. Johnson did call a meeting of congressional leaders shortly after this cartoon appeared.

"Ev Tu?"

Miranda v. Arizona

IT'S HARD TO IMAGINE a TV crime drama without hearing, "You have the right to remain silent." In 1966 a 5–4 U.S. Supreme Court decision made "Miranda rights" the law of the land. The *Miranda v. Arizona* decision was one in a series of rulings that signaled the high court's continued commitment to equal-protection rights in the decades following World War II.

Under Chief Justice Earl Warren, the court overturned the conviction of Ernesto Miranda for kidnapping and rape. After a review of Miranda's case and other instances of improper interrogation and forced confession, the court decided that evidence obtained illegally in this way was therefore inadmissible. The majority opinion argued that in order to protect a defendant's Fifth Amendment right protecting against self-incrimination, and to guarantee the 14th Amendment right to due process, police would be required to inform suspects of their rights before questioning. The Miranda warning read as follows:

You have the right to remain silent. Anything you say can and will be used against you in a court of law. You have the right to speak to an attorney, and to have an attorney present during any questioning. If you cannot afford a lawyer, one will be provided for you at government expense.

Like the *Brown v. Board of Education* decision of 1954 (which prohibited segregation in public schools) and the Civil Rights Act of 1964, the *Miranda* decision established a national standard of justice—one that was based on the Bill of Rights and that superseded local custom.

Robert Indiana, an important Pop artist, created "LOVE" in 1966. Describing himself as a "people's painter," Indiana contemplated the conflicted personal identities and national meanings encompassed by the American Dream. He also explored dichotomies such as high and low culture. This particular image reached iconic status, appearing on 320 million postage stamps in the 1970s and in other commercial incarnations.

Workers put the finishing touches on the Whitney Museum of American Art in June 1966. A cube-shaped structure sheathed with granite on the outside—with suspended concrete, open-grid ceilings inside—the bizarre design generated considerable controversy. Its Hungarian-born architect, Marcel Breuer, wanted it to have substance in a small space and "not look like a business or office building [or] like a place of light entertainment." The Whitney Museum maintained a policiy of no permanent exhibits.

Edward Albee's first full-length play, *Who's Afraid of Virginia Woolf?*, was made into the Mike Nichols-directed film starring Elizabeth Taylor (*right*), Richard Burton (*background*), and George Segal (*left*) in 1966. The story of a couple's disintegrating marriage—full of bitterness, recriminations, and destructive revelations—reflected the roiling conflicts just below the surface of middle-class marriages during the 1960s. The film's foul language and frank themes broke with censorship codes at the time, but the star power of Taylor helped give Nichols the clout to get the film made. Taylor won an Oscar for her performance.

On June 27, 1966, ABC introduced a daytime soap opera that starred vampires, werewolves, and witches. Using such devices as time travel and parallel universes, *Dark Shadows* followed the drama and history of the Collins family of Collinsport, Maine. The soap, which appealed to both children and adults, centered around a gothic hero named Barnabas Collins (*pictured*), a 172-year-old vampire played by Jonathan Frid. The program ran for five years and became a cult favorite, inspiring feature-length movies, games, and trading cards.

July 21: Gemini 10 splashes down safely after more than 70 hours in space. The mission accomplished rocket propulsion of the spacecraft through 475 miles of space, a rendezvous with two Agena rockets, a docking maneuver, and two space walks.

July 23: National Guardsmen in the Hough area of Cleveland impose order after a week of racially motivated violence and looting. • Stage and film actor Montgomery Clift dies at 45.

July 25: Chinese photos of a "healthy" Mao Tse-tung, swimming "nine miles" in the Yangtze River, appear throughout China two months after Mao's reappearance following a half-year absence from public view.

July 26: The U.S. State Department responds to South Vietnamese Premier Ky's stated willingness to invade North Vietnam, noting that the U.S. has no interest in prosecuting a wider war.

July 29: *Datebook,* an American teen magazine, publishes an out-of-context quote in which John Lennon says the Beatles are more popular than Jesus. Radio stations in the South will respond by banning Beatles music.

July 30: For the first time, U.S. warplanes bomb the demilitarized zone (DMZ) separating North and South Vietnam.

Late July–Early August: African-Americans and Puerto Rican-Americans battle police for several days in Perth Amboy, New Jersey.

August: U.S. General William Westmoreland declares that a Communist takeover of South Vietnam is "impossible."

August 1: Architectural student Charles Whitman kills 15 and wounds 31 from a sniper's perch atop a clock tower at the University of Texas at Austin. He is shot and killed by police.

August 3: Comedian Lenny Bruce, 40, dies from a drug overdose.

Psychologist Virginia E. Johnson (*left*) and gynecologist William H. Masters (*right*) authored the best-selling 1966 book *Human Sexual Response,* a groundbreaking and frank discussion of sex in the United States. Their work built on Alfred C. Kinsey's famous survey of sexual behavior in the 1940s and '50s. However, Masters and Johnson took it a step further by examining sexual activity in the laboratory, measuring the physical responses of 700 men and women. Critics called their work immoral, an intrusion into a sacred realm. Negative reaction aside, Masters and Johnson portrayed sex as healthy and natural, demystifying a taboo subject for the generation that would forge the sexual revolution.

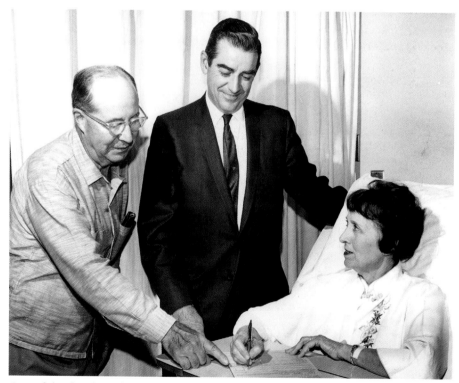

One of the first beneficiaries of the Medicare Program, Lillian Grace Avery, signs her Medicare forms at Edward Hospital in Naperville, Illinois, on July 1, 1966. The Medicare bill had passed in 1965, and the program went into effect in 1966, providing national health insurance for people over the age of 65 as well as the seriously disabled. While Medicare's quality of care varied, the costs of the program ballooned as the population aged and the system expanded.

A grinning group of Baby Boomers enjoys a round of Twister. Introduced in 1966 by Milton Bradley Company, the game involved placing hands and feet on colored circles depending on where the spinner landed. Because Twister led to a precarious and often risqué comingling of limbs, the game became especially popular at college parties—with drinking and stripping sometimes part of the fun.

Jacqueline Susann struggled for years as an actress, but her magnetic personality brought her into contact with many of Hollywood's biggest stars. When she turned to writing, her real-life experiences embellished by her considerable imagination engendered compelling, if lurid, prose. Her first novel, *Valley of the Dolls,* prompted readers to guess which real-life show-biz figures were being depicted. Though critically lambasted as "trash," powerful hype fueled sales, giving Susann the notoriety she craved. A 1967 film version starred Patty Duke and Sharon Tate.

Richard Speck, an unemployed ore boat worker passing through Chicago, went on a killing spree on the city's South Side on July 14, 1966. Speck, who had a history of crime and drug use, broke into a townhouse where student nurses lived. Speck killed, and in some cases raped, eight of the students, all in their twenties. One nurse survived by hiding under a bed. The brutal nature of the murders, which included stabbings and strangulation, shocked the nation. Speck originally was given the death penalty, but the sentence was changed to life imprisonment after the U.S. Supreme Court ruled the death penalty unconstitutional in 1972. Speck died in prison in 1991.

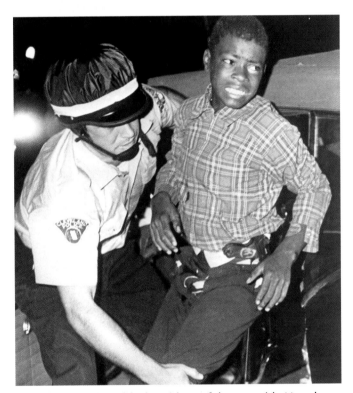

On July 18, 1966, a black resident of the east-side Hough neighborhood of Cleveland entered the 79ers Café to ask for a glass of ice water. The white bartender refused him the courtesy, providing just enough spark for a violent riot in a city that was on the edge. Rioters chanted "Black Power" as they moved through the streets of Hough, looting stores, setting buildings afire, and committing random acts of violence. Four people were killed and many were injured, including 12-year-old Ernest Williams (*pictured*). Most of Cleveland's 60,000 African-Americans lived in the cramped, two-square-mile Hough neighborhood, where crime rates were high and police empathy was almost nonexistent.

1966

August 4: *The New York Times* publishes a "Black Power" manifesto elucidated by the Student Nonviolent Coordinating Committee (SNCC).
• Ground breaking begins for the construction of the World Trade Center in New York City.

August 8: U.S. surgeon Michael E. DeBakey successfully implants the first completely artificial heart into a 37-year-old patient.

August 9: U.S. warplanes mistakenly attack two South Vietnamese villages, killing 63 civilians.

August 10: The U.S. Treasury Department suspends production of the $2 bill.

August 13: China's Communist Party Central Committee announces its endorsement of the nation's "great proletarian cultural revolution," a shift to harshly ideological communism.

August 15: Israeli and Syrian ships and warplanes battle for three hours in and near the Sea of Galilee.

August 16: A Soviet MiG-21 fighter jet falls into western hands when an Iraqi pilot defects to Israel.

August 22: The U.S. Department of Labor notes that the July 1966 Consumer Price Index rose to a record high, confirming that 1966 is the most inflationary year in the U.S. since 1957.

August 23: An enormous demonstration of the Communist Chinese Red Guard in Peking calls for the eradication of every trace of western influence.

August 26: Chicago politicians, real estate agents, and civil rights activists agree on a 10-point program to end discrimination in housing, ending a monthlong series of civil rights demonstrations in the city. ➤

Captured American airmen, clothed in prison uniforms and looking dejected, are paraded through the streets of Hanoi in July 1966. The Democratic Republic of Vietnam released a total of 565 American military POWs by the end of the war. Most POWs were aviators and many of them were officers, shot down during the Rolling Thunder bombing campaign that spanned from 1965 to 1968. During that period, POWs were held in 11 different prisons in the north. They were isolated, malnourished, kept in stocks, and in many cases brutally tortured in an effort to break their morale.

Two U.S. Marines protect a soldier who was wounded during Operation Hastings in northern South Vietnam on July 30, 1966. General William Westmoreland, who wanted Marines to engage in large-unit combat, sent them against a strong North Vietnamese contingent in Hastings. The operation achieved an 8–1 kill ratio, but it hardly destroyed Communist capabilities in the area. Indeed, some critics say that by pulling the Marines away from successful civilian-pacification efforts, Hastings actually harmed American prospects in the area.

Charles J. Whitman, a former scoutmaster and Marine who everyone remembered as an All-American boy, climbed to the top of the clock tower at the University of Texas in Austin on August 1, 1966. From his perch, he aimed at the people below and began shooting. Earlier that summer, Whitman had told a psychiatrist that he didn't feel right, complaining of headaches and murderous rage toward his father,  whom he hated for beating his mother. Whitman turned that rage outward, killing his mother and his wife before fatally shooting 15 and wounding 31. Police eventually climbed the tower and gunned him down. The shootings brought fresh discussion of legislation to regulate the sale of firearms.

The Endless Summer

On any day of the year it's summer somewhere in the world. Bruce Brown's latest color film highlights the adventures of two young American surfers, Robert August and Mike Hynson who follow this everlasting summer around the world. Their unique expedition takes them to Senegal, Ghana, Nigeria, South Africa, Australia, New Zealand, Tahiti, Hawaii and California. Share their experiences as they search the world for that perfect wave which may be forming just over the next Horizon. **BRUCE BROWN FILMS**

With a hip surf guitar soundtrack and beautiful photography, filmmaker Bruce Brown's *The Endless Summer* (1966) captured the free and easy lifestyle of two surfers (Robert August and Mike Hynson) as they searched the world for the perfect wave. Accompanied by Brown's humorous narration, this lifestyle portrait follows the surfers from the waves of Hawaii to the beaches of South Africa. Considered the ultimate surfer film, *The Endless Summer* portrayed the beach subculture more authentically than the many Elvis and Annette Funicello vehicles.

"We're more popular than Jesus now." When John Lennon uttered those words to a (London) *Evening Standard* reporter, he was supporting his belief that Christianity was a declining religion. After the teen magazine *Datebook* published just the one quote, out of context, many Americans were outraged. Evangelical Christian groups staged "Beatles burnings," during which young people (including those pictured in Waycross, Georgia, on August 12, 1966) were encouraged to toss their Beatles albums into the fire. Lennon later apologized, saying, "I suppose if I had said television was more popular than Jesus, I would have gotten away with it. I'm sorry I opened my mouth."

The Cultural Revolution

WHEN THE RED GUARDS came to Bai Di's home in early autumn 1966, Di knew what their intentions were. His father, a university professor in the town of Harbin in northeastern China, was suspected of being a capitalist sympathizer. The Red Guards, most of whom were teenagers, proceeded to rummage through and confiscate the family's belongings.

"They took things like family photo albums and some of [my mother's] clothes," recalled Di. "[T]he Red Guards took away my favorite books. Among them were *A Thousand and One Nights, Grimm's Fairy Tales,* and *A Hundred Thousand Whys,* a children's encyclopedia on science."

Chairman Mao Tse-tung launched his Great Proletarian Cultural Revolution in the mid-1960s in hopes of "reeducating" the Chinese masses.

Red Guards in Peking, China, honoring Chairman Mao Tse-tung

The aging Mao feared that Russia's retreat from hardline Stalinism would be replicated in China after his death. In order to avoid such a fate, Mao turned to the nation's suggestible youth, whom he organized into the Red Guard. Their mission was to do away with all western influence, cleanse the Communist Party of "revisionism," and restore ideological purity. Intellectuals, professors, teachers, Westerners, Buddhists, and suspected "rightists" were targeted. The Guards carried out the most extensive purge in Communist China's history, destroying houses of worship, sacking foreign schools, raiding homes, and looting museums.

Although the dogma of the Cultural Revolution led to institutionalized terror, Mao and his radical reforms were seemingly supported by most Chinese people. Cowed citizens hung pictures of the chairman in their homes, cars, and offices. Foreign correspondents who elected to ignore the brutality and fear that ruled China naively claimed that Mao's government enjoyed enormous popular support.

In truth, the Red Guard youth set loose by Mao hounded and tormented numberless citizens, many of whom ended up in horrific "reeducation" camps where they were brutalized, worked to death, or killed outright. Years of Chinese economic progress and intellectual achievement were blasted to bits, and the nation was set on a backwards course that it would not begin to reverse for 20 years.

Nevertheless, the "cult of Mao" flourished because of coercion and because Mao and his lieutenants insisted they were creating a more efficient Chinese government characterized by social justice and gender equality.

The legacy of the Cultural Revolution remains a point of debate among scholars. One of the most enduring questions is the extent to which the Chinese people were forced to embrace the chairman and his reforms. Although the youthful and naive Red Guard happily implemented the sanctioned anarchy, their invasive and barbarous tactics frightened many of the wary into going along with the Maoist torrent. Protest was virtually invisible, and many foreign visitors took note only of the cleanliness of public streets and the apparent physical fitness of the populace.

The reality of the Revolution was seen clearly by an Austrian journalist who commented on how people were compelled to do gymnastics daily. The reporter knew the regimen was disliked by many, but it was healthy and, as with much else in China, the participants had no choice.

By 1966, 73-year-old Mao Tse-tung was pondering his ideological legacy. On May 16, the Chinese Communist Central Committee announced, with Mao's blessing, the start of the Great Proletarian Cultural Revolution, which exhorted students to come together in revolutionary fervor as the Red Guard. They were instructed to violently purge China of intellectuals and "imperialists," and destroy the "four olds": old culture, old thought, old customs, and old practices. In Peking on September 28 (*pictured*), Mao greeted enthusiastic Guard members.

Soon after Martin Luther King, Jr., joined marchers in Chicago's Marquette Park on August 5, 1966, a white counterprotester hit him in the head with a rock. "It hurts," King said at the time, "but it's not an injury." King's Freedom Movement in Chicago addressed the issue of segregated housing, which plagued northern cities and had contributed to recent riots. King and his supporters sent out white and black "testing" teams to Chicago-area neighborhoods that were closed to blacks. Where they found segregated housing practices, King initiated marches through the neighborhoods. Civil rights workers faced brutal and virulent backlash from large white crowds, often without adequate police protection.

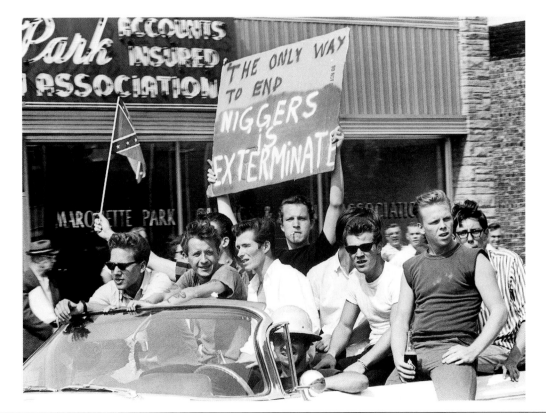

In response to the Martin Luther King-led demonstrations in Chicago, white residents of the city's Marquette Park neighborhood staged their own demonstration on August 5, 1966 (*pictured*). While much of the South Side of Chicago was largely African-American, some neighborhoods were all-white—and residents were determined to keep them that way. King told reporters that he had never seen such racial hatred, even in such Ku Klux Klan strongholds as Mississippi and Alabama.

1966

August 31: Congress makes the burning of Selective Service (draft) cards a federal offense punishable by up to five years' imprisonment.

September: Timothy Leary launches the League for Spiritual Discovery and coins the phrase "Turn on, tune in, drop out." • George Harrison of the Beatles visits India to study the sitar with Ravi Shankar. Harrison will bring the instrument's "psychedelic sound" to Beatles music. • Slugger Frank Robinson of the Baltimore Orioles wins the American League Triple Crown, leading the circuit in batting average (.316), home runs (49), and runs batted in (122).

September 2: A bill signed by Alabama Governor George Wallace declares the school desegregation guidelines of the U.S. Office of Education "null and void" in his state.

September 6: South African Prime Minister Hendrik Frensch Verwoerd, 64, is stabbed to death in Parliament by a parliamentary messenger who says Verwoerd has sponsored too much legislation benefiting non-whites. Verwoerd will be succeeded by Balthazar Vorster, minister of justice, police, and prisons.

September 8: The science-fiction television show *Star Trek* premieres on NBC.

September 9: The National Traffic and Motor Vehicle Safety Act, a program to reduce motor vehicle crashes, is signed into law.

September 16: The New Metropolitan Opera House in the Lincoln Center for the Performing Arts in New York City opens with the world premiere of Samuel Barber's *Antony and Cleopatra*.

September 17: Leading German operatic tenor Fritz Wunderlich, 35, dies in an accidental fall.

A Phantom F4B fires rockets at a Vietcong position in September 1966. This all-weather, twin-engine, tactical fighter-bomber was the mainstay of U.S. air power in Southeast Asia beginning in 1964. The Phantom, which reached speeds of 1,600 mph at high altitudes, also was used on reconnaissance missions and to destroy North Vietnamese MiG-17 fighters. From 1965 through 1973 the U.S. lost more than 500 Phantoms, 430 of them in combat.

Workers poured the first concrete for the World Trade Center in New York City in September 1966. The soaring towers, the tallest in the world for a brief time (1972 to 1974), exemplified the modernist style of their Seattle-born architect, Minoru Yamasaki. The 1,368- and 1,362-foot-tall skyscrapers were part of a complex of seven buildings that made up the 16-acre site. In reshaping whole blocks of lower Manhattan, the developers hoped the structures would revitalize the area. The idea of the project, and the buildings themselves, would be much maligned in the 1960s and '70s as arrogant examples of power and bad modernist taste. But when terrorists killed thousands working in the buildings on September 11, 2001, and obliterated them from New York's skyline, the twin phantoms transcended time and space as tragedy.

Star Trek

TELEVISION'S TRADITIONAL USE of outer-space themes in entertainment changed forever with the premiere of *Star Trek* on NBC on September 8, 1966. Gene Roddenberry, a successful producer and scriptwriter, conceived a futuristic storyline set aboard an exploratory Starfleet spaceship, the *Enterprise*. Unlike typical science-fiction fare, his creation would be plot- and character-driven—in a word, *cerebral*. Roddenberry intended for the series to be a commentary on the tumult of his own times, exploring such weighty themes as war and race relations.

True to his vision, the *Enterprise* was manned by a racially diverse crew (including a Russian) under the command of Captain James T. Kirk (William Shatner). The show's success left an imprint on popular culture, with such phrases as "He's dead, Jim," "Live long and prosper," and "Beam me up, Scotty" entering public consciousness (although the last was never actually uttered on the show). Roddenberry's relations with NBC were always uneasy. The "satanic" look of Vulcan Mr. Spock (Leonard Nimoy) raised network concerns, and an interracial kiss between Captain Kirk and black crew member Uhura (Nichelle Nichols) pushed the envelope as a television first.

William Shatner, DeForest Kelly, and Leonard Nimoy

Star Trek appealed mostly to children and teenagers—not adults—which turned off advertisers and led to its cancellation after three seasons. Nevertheless, the *Star Trek* phenomenon lasted for decades due to syndication, television spinoffs, and related movies. Revenue from *Star Trek* merchandise alone has generated more than $4 billion.

On the morning of October 21, 1966, children assembled in the courtyard of Pant-glas Junior School in the village of Aberfan in South Wales. Just then, a mountain of mine tailings suddenly gave way, sending two million tons of slag down upon the children. The slide engulfed the school and 20 homes in the village, killing 116 children and 28 adults. People from the village dug through the rubble for nearly a week before recovering all the bodies. The disaster has been called the worst tragedy in the history of Wales.

1966

September 18: In a report to the United Nations General Assembly, Secretary General U Thant criticizes U.S. policy in Vietnam. • Valerie Percy, 21, daughter of Republican Senate candidate Charles Percy, is beaten and stabbed to death by an intruder in the family home in Kenilworth, Illinois.

September 20: The underground newspaper *The San Francisco Oracle* begins publication.

September 21: A proposed constitutional amendment that would allow voluntary prayer in public schools fails to muster the two-thirds majority required for Senate passage.

September 23: U.S. officials report that American forces are defoliating jungles near the demilitarized zone (DMZ) with sprayed chemicals.

September 28–October 1: The Hunter's Point area of San Francisco is hit by a violent racial riot after a police officer shoots and kills a black youth who ran from a stolen car. The National Guard is called in, 359 people are arrested, and 51 people are injured.

October: The U.S. Selective Service calls up 46,200 men, the highest one-month total since the Korean War. • In Oakland, California, Bobby Seale and Huey Newton form the Black Panther Party. The militant black organization advocates violent self-defense, political awareness, economic empowerment, and community involvement and activism in pursuit of collective self-determination.

October 1: Secretary of Defense Robert McNamara launches "Project 100,000" to increase America's military manpower by lowering the mental and physical requirements of draftees. • Albert Speer and Baldur von Schirach, two top-ranking Nazis sentenced to 20 years' imprisonment at Nuremberg in 1946, are released from Germany's Spandau Prison.

"My advice to people today is as follows: If you take the game of life seriously, if you take your nervous system seriously, if you take your sense organs seriously, if you take the energy process seriously, you must turn on, tune in, and drop out."

—Timothy Leary

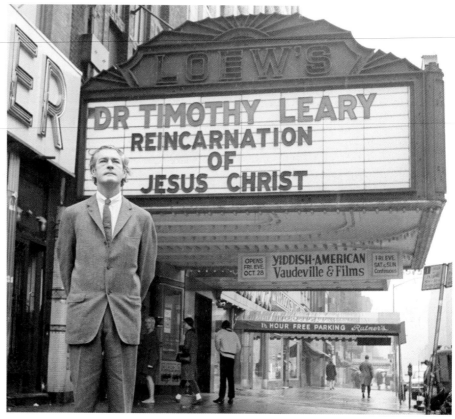

Psychologist Timothy Leary promotes his religious sect, League of Spiritual Discovery (LSD), an amalgam of eastern religions and mystical psychedelic revelation. Leary was the preeminent psychedelic evangelist of the 1960s. He encouraged Americans to "turn on" to the mystical experiences of LSD, "tune in" to the "message," and "drop out" of mainstream society. Fired from Harvard in 1963 for his unorthodox methods—including dispensing LSD to his students as part of his research—Leary set up his own privately funded institute on a donor's estate in upstate New York. In 1967 Leary took his show on the road, visiting college campuses.

British folk rocker Donovan Leitch, professionally known by his first name, released the album *Sunshine Superman* in 1966. Born in Glasgow, he began performing in folk clubs in the U.K. in 1964. According to *Rolling Stone,* Donovan by 1965 was considered the British answer to Bob Dylan because of "his topical acoustic ballads and introspective demeanor." Influenced by the Beatles, *Sunshine Superman* took on a psychedelic tone, with its references to beatniks and LSD, and became Donovan's signature album. The cut "Season of the Witch" is a classic.

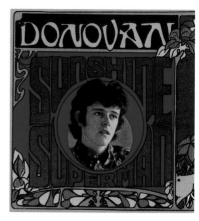

Dropping Acid

"**W**E MUST ALWAYS REMEMBER to thank the CIA and the army for LSD," noted John Lennon shortly before his death in 1980. "They invented LSD to control people, and what they did was give us freedom."

Indeed, the tale of LSD starts out like a Cold War spy novel. The drug that eventually would become the signature sacrament of the Sixties counterculture, LSD (lysergic acid diethylamide) was first synthesized in 1938 by Dr. Albert Hoffman for Sandoz Laboratories in Switzerland. The hallucinatory drug was taken up by the CIA in the 1950s, when the agency experimented with it as a potential truth serum as part of MK-ULTRA, the CIA's major drug and mind-control program during the Cold War. Meanwhile, the U.S. Army tried briefly to use the drug as an interrogation device.

By the early 1960s, LSD was prescibed by psychiatrists to treat a range of neuroses. Some of the drug's new acolytes, however, decided to redirect the flow of LSD to broader recreational usage. Ken Kesey, whose bestseller *One Flew Over the Cuckoo's Nest* was written under the influence, decided to "turn on" the California populace through a series of "acid tests." These essentially were LSD parties where people took the drug while grooving to the music of the Warlocks, later known as the Grateful Dead.

On the East Coast, Dr. Timothy Leary became infatuated with LSD while a scientist at Harvard University, then became the country's foremost proponent of LSD during

Acid test participant

the '60s. Leary formed the League for Spiritual Discovery and coined the mantra "Turn On, Tune In, Drop Out."

Despite incidences of "bad trips," and perhaps because of the drug's ability to inspire curiosity and controversy, LSD became the lifeblood of the psychedelic culture. "Acid rock" became a new music genre. The drug inspired the music of numerous artists, from the Byrds ("Eight Miles High") to the Beatles. By 1966 *Life* magazine estimated that more than one million doses of LSD had been consumed. That same year, the drug was made illegal by the U.S. government.

In fall 1965, writer and psychedelic evangelist Ken Kesey and his band of Merry Pranksters began spreading the news about LSD, a hallucinogenic drug that at the time was legal. Psychedelic posters began to appear asking young people if they had what it took to pass the "acid test." By 1966 many had, and that year around the Bay Area the Trips Festival attracted more than 2,400 curious people. The acid tests were held in large halls, where participants sipped LSD-laced Kool-Aid, donned outrageous costumes, and enjoyed the light shows that accompanied the usual house band—the Grateful Dead. On Halloween 1965, the Pranksters staged the Acid Test Graduation (*pictured*). In October 1966 lawmakers made LSD illegal in California.

1966

October 3: The Soviet Union announces a far-reaching military and economic aid package for North Vietnam.

October 5: The Enrico Fermi "Fast Breeder" nuclear reactor near Detroit suffers a partial core meltdown after broken sheet metal is swept up the coolant flow, blocking the system. The reactor is permanently disabled.

October 6: LSD becomes illegal in California.

October 7: The USSR orders the expulsion of all Chinese students from Soviet soil.

October 15: President Johnson signs a bill providing for the creation of a federal Department of Transportation, to be represented by a new Cabinet post.

October 21: A rain-saturated slag heap in the mining town of Aberfan, Wales, slides down a hillside and buries houses and a school, killing 116 children and 28 others.

October 26: President Johnson travels from Manila to Cam Ranh Bay, South Vietnam, where he spends more than two hours with U.S. troops.

October 29: Pope Paul VI declines to adjust the Vatican's position on birth control, reaffirming traditional Catholic teaching on the issue.

November: The Red China government openly launches brutal campaigns against Chinese novelists, playwrights, philosophers, historians, and other intellectuals perceived to have links to "bourgeois revisionism."

November 5: A ravaging flood in Florence, Italy, damages crucial Renaissance art, including "A Crucifixion" by Giovanni Cimabue.

November 7: During a visit to Harvard University, Secretary of Defense Robert McNamara is booed, and his limousine surrounded, by angry antiwar students.

President Lyndon Johnson's visit to South Vietnam on October 26, 1966, was kept secret until the last moment, when Air Force One dropped sharply to a landing at Cam Ranh Bay, avoiding potential anti-aircraft fire. The President addressed a cheering crowd of 7,000 soldiers. "Make no mistake about it," Johnson said. "The American people whom you serve are proud of you. There are some who may disagree with what you are doing here, but that is not the way most of us feel...." Johnson spent a few hours on the ground, shaking hands and eating a pork chop dinner with the troops. He then boarded Air Force One and headed to the Philippines.

Heart surgeon Michael E. DeBakey holds one of the artificial heart pumps that he invented and successfully implanted in patients in 1966. DeBakey designed the device as a left ventricle bypass, which allowed a damaged ventricle to rest and heal during heart surgery. DeBakey pioneered multiple heart-technology inventions and surgical techniques. He also is credited with developing the Mobile Army Surgical Hospitals (MASH) used during the Korean War.

Ronald Reagan was a reluctant candidate for governor of California in 1966. Holmes Tuttle (a Los Angeles automobile dealer) and other Republican fund-raisers had to talk the actor into running against the popular incumbent governor, Democrat Pat Brown. During the campaign, Reagan accused Brown of excessive government spending, welfare giveaways, and high property taxes. Reagan also argued that the most important issue of the campaign was "the morality gap" between liberals and conservatives. Despite Democrats' attempts to paint Reagan as a right-wing extremist, he won the 1966 campaign on a platform that would later carry him to the nation's highest political office.

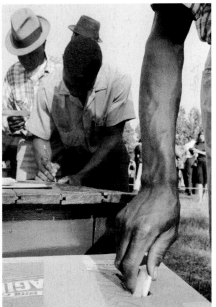

After President Lyndon Johnson signed the Voting Rights Act in August 1965, southern blacks—for the first time since Reconstruction—could vote in elections without racist barriers and the threat of violent retaliation. Within three weeks after the law's enactment, federal registrars signed up 27,385 African-Americans in Alabama, Mississippi, and Louisiana. By 1966, voters in Alabama (*pictured*) and other states cast their ballots in major elections. In 1969 Charles Evers, brother of Medgar Evers, would become the first elected black mayor in Mississippi since Reconstruction.

In 1966 the defiant, pro-segregation governor of Alabama, George Wallace (*left*), was prevented from running for governor again because of the state's term-limit law. His wife, Lurleen Wallace, ran in his place and won, becoming the first female governor in the Deep South. Seen here after voting, Lurleen promised Alabamians that George would essentially continue to make administrative and policy decisions, which he did. During her tenure, Lurleen opposed antipoverty grants for African-Americans. She also attempted to place state schools under police power to fight court-ordered desegregation. Lurleen Wallace died of cancer in 1968 at age 41.

1966

November 8: Republican candidate Ronald Reagan is elected governor of California, defeating incumbent Edmund "Pat" Brown by nearly a million votes. • Edward Brooke, the Republican attorney general of Massachusetts, becomes the first African-American elected to the U.S. Senate since Reconstruction. • Lurleen Wallace is elected governor of Alabama, with 67 percent of the vote. Her husband, Governor George Wallace, is prohibited by law from serving consecutive terms.

November 13: Astronaut Buzz Aldrin takes a two-hour, nine-minute space walk.

November 16: Sam Sheppard of suburban Cleveland, once a prominent doctor who was convicted of killing his wife in 1954, is acquitted after spending nine years in prison.

November 19: Notre Dame and Michigan State play to a 10-10 tie in football. They each will finish the year at 9-0-1 and be declared co-national champions.

November 24: Operation Attleboro, a large-scale "search and destroy" mission north of Saigon, is completed. The death toll includes 155 Americans and 1,106 North Vietnamese.

December: *Time* magazine names the "Twenty-five and Under" generation as its "Man of the Year."

December 14: U.S. bombers level the village of Caudate near Hanoi, creating an outpouring of criticism from around the word.

December 15: Entertainment mogul Walt Disney dies at 65.

December 26: Black nationalist Maulana Karenga, creator of the holiday Kwanzaa—an alternative to Christmas—celebrates the holiday for the first time, with friends and family.

December 31: By year's end, the U.S. troop level in Vietnam reaches 385,000. More than 5,000 U.S. soldiers have been killed.

Robert McNamara faces a hostile student crowd at Harvard University on November 7, 1966. The secretary of defense was despised at many college campuses. That spring, students at New York University and Amherst had walked out when he received honorary degrees. He was even hooted when he spoke at his daughter's graduation at Chatham College. Harvard, where he went to talk to Henry Kissinger's class, almost exploded. McNamara tried to defuse potential violence by telling the students that he "was tougher" than them as well as "more courteous." Those comments, however, only inflamed antiwar passions. At Harvard, McNamara had to escape through a tunnel.

A replica of Michelangelo's David stands over the flood-damaged streets of Florence, Italy, the birthplace of the European Renaissance. In November 1966, the Arno River burst its banks and ravaged the city with water up to 10 feet deep. The flooding forced Florentines to their rooftops, punched holes through the Ponte Vecchio (a medieval bridge), and killed at least 87 people. The muddy waters submerged priceless sculptures, paintings, and manuscripts in the city's museums and libraries. Mayor Piero Bargellini said that the "damage is incalculable."

McNamara Goes to Harvard

AFTER SEVERAL FALSE ALARMS and one attempted decoy maneuver, [Secretary of Defense] Robert McNamara emerged in a police car on a narrow back street. While a dozen SDSers sat down around the car, others passed the signal over the walkie talkies around the block, and the thousand began running towards McNamara. Within moments, he was surrounded by what must have looked to him like a mob of howling beatniks...delighted to have trapped the Secretary. McNamara told the crowd: "I spent four of the happiest years on the Berkeley campus doing some of the same things you're doing here. But there was one important difference: I was both tougher and more courteous." After laughter and shouts, he shouted vehemently, "I was tougher then and I'm tougher now!" The audience loved it. Mac was blowing his cool—

unable to handle himself, quite possibly scared. A few PL-types [Progressive Labor Party Movement] in front were jumping up and down screaming "Murderer! Fascist!" Mac tried to regain his composure and said "Look fellas, we had an agreement..." A girl shrieked "What about your agreement to hold elections in 1956?" Things seemed to be breaking up. The police moved in and whisked McNamara into Leverett House; an SDS leader, fearing violence in the streets, took the microphone and ordered all SDS people to clear the area. The disciplined shock troops of the revolution turned and dispersed quickly, McNamara was hustled out through steam tunnels, and everyone went home to watch themselves on TV.

—*NEW LEFT NOTES,* THE NATIONAL NEWSPAPER OF THE
STUDENTS FOR A DEMOCRATIC SOCIETY (SDS)

During an antiwar demonstration in New York City in November 1966, Lieutenant Travis Tuck burns his military discharge papers in protest of U.S. involvement in Vietnam. Though veterans were never a large presence at protests, their opposition to the war gave weight to the antiwar effort. In 1967 six former soldiers started Vietnam Veterans Against the War, an organization that rapidly grew to 30,000 members.

British-born Jean Shrimpton, according to some cultural historians, was the world's first "supermodel." After appearing on the cover of *Vogue* for the first time in 1962, she was named Model of the Year by *Glamour* magazine in 1963. "The Shrimp" wrote her autobiography in 1965, and starred in the film *Privilege* in 1967. Shrimpton's sister, Chrissie, also lived in the limelight, even dating Mick Jagger for a spell.

1966

"Hey, hey, we're the Monkees." Davy Jones (*standing*), Michael Nesmith, Peter Tork, and Micky Dolenz (*left to right*) comprised this band, which was invented for television in 1966. NBC-TV producers hoped their teen-oriented program, *The Monkees,* which they styled after the Beatles film *A Hard Day's Night,* could compete with the popular *Batman* show on ABC. The band members had little musical experience and did not play instruments on their first album. But with the help of Don Kirshner, president of Colgems records, the group became phenomenally successful. Their first album, *The Monkees,* sold more than a million copies, while the single "Last Train to Clarksville" hit No. 1 on the U.S. pop charts.

The Avalon Ballroom, which sat on the border of the Haight-Ashbury district of San Francisco, became an epicenter for the "freak" explosion of the mid-1960s. The building's old swing dance hall—with its ornate interior and bouncy, spacious wooden dance floor—served as the ideal venue for promoter Chet Helms's concerts. From 1966 to 1968 (when he lost his permit), Helms drew crowds from the burgeoning psychedelic community. His concerts combined trippy light shows with the music of such bands as the Grateful Dead and Big Brother and the Holding Company. Bill Graham, who ran the competing Fillmore, said that hippies of the day considered Avalon "the *real* church."

Writer Susan Sontag, a college graduate by age 18, was something of a Renaissance woman: social activist, lecturer, playwright, novelist, and filmmaker. She first entered public consciousness in 1963 with her novel *The Benefactor.* But it was her collection of essays, *Against Interpretation* (1966), that established her reputation as an intellectual force. Her essays cover a variety of aesthetics, most notably in "Notes on Camp." In that essay, she defines camp and offers examples, such as Tiffany lamps, Swan Lake, and "stag movies seen without lust."

Paul Simon and Art Garfunkel first appeared as Tom and Jerry in the late 1950s, even playing Dick Clark's *American Bandstand.* After college, however, they reinvented themselves as folk singers. Simon's intelligent social commentary and poetic lyrics along with Garfunkel's pretty harmonies led to a breakthrough for the duo in 1966. Their *Sounds of Silence* LP included such classics as "Homeward Bound," "I Am a Rock," and the chart-topping "The Sound of Silence." Simon and Garfunkel's biggest success came with their soundtrack for the 1967 film *The Graduate.* "Mrs. Robinson" and other songs from the film contributed to the restless feel of the late 1960s.

New York City discotheques such as Arthur and Cheetah became increasingly popular in the mid-1960s. They especially appealed to the city's gay community, which, according to music historian Piero Scaruffi, was reacting against "rock music's domination of the airwaves" and the counterculture's tendency to "demonize dance music." Discotheques featured up-tempo music that you could dance to. Disco music would enter the mainstream in 1975 (thanks in part to Van McCoy's megahit "The Hustle") and dominate the latter half of that decade.

Richard Kiley (*pictured*) starred as Don Quixote and Irving Jacobson played Sancho Panza in the Broadway production of *Man of La Mancha*. The play parallels the life of Cervantes, the writer, and the exploits of his character, Don Quixote. The musical's classic song, "The Impossible Dream," summed up a testament to idealism that resonated with audiences at the time. *Man of La Mancha*, the third-longest running musical of the 1960s, later was adapted into a film starring Peter O'Toole as Quixote and James Coco as Sancho Panza.

Ravi Shankar helped inject the classical sitar sounds of India into the music of the Sixties. Shankar had begun to spread Indian ragas, the melodic elements of his music, to the West back in the late 1950s. But it was when he met Beatles guitarist George Harrison and taught him to play the difficult-to-master, 700-year-old instrument that the sitar really hit the scene. Harrison played the sitar for the Beatles' 1965 hit "Norwegian Wood," and after that seemingly every rock band—for better or worse—had to have the exotic and psychedelic-friendly sounds in their music. Shankar set up a sitar school in Los Angeles and gave concerts throughout the 1960s.

1966

New & Notable

Books

The Arrogance of Power
    by J. William Fulbright
The Crying of Lot 49
    by Thomas Pynchon
Human Sexual Response by William
    Masters and Virginia Johnson
In Cold Blood by Truman Capote
Rush to Judgment by Mark Lane
Three Years in Mississippi
    by James Meredith
Valley of the Dolls by Jacqueline Susann

Movies

Alfie
Blowup
Fantastic Voyage
Faster, Pussycat! Kill! Kill!
The Fortune Cookie
Lord Love a Duck
Persona
Seconds
Who's Afraid of Virginia Woolf?

Songs

"The Ballad of the Green Berets"
    by S/Sgt. Barry Sadler
"California Dreamin'"
    by the Mamas and the Papas
"Good Vibrations" by the Beach Boys
"Last Train to Clarksville"
    by the Monkees
"Nowhere Man" by the Beatles
"Paint It Black" by the Rolling Stones
"These Boots Are Made for Walkin'"
    by Nancy Sinatra
"Wild Thing" by the Troggs

Television

Family Affair
Mission: Impossible
The Monkees
The Newlywed Game
Star Trek
That Girl
The Time Tunnel

Theater

Cabaret
I Do! I Do!
The Killing of Sister George
The Lion in Winter
Mame
Man of La Mancha

American infantrymen fan across a field in South Vietnam during Operation Attleboro. This "search and destroy" mission involved 22,000 soldiers from American and South Vietnamese (ARVN) units operating 50 miles north of Saigon during November 1966. Communist forces suffered more than 3,000 casualties, while U.S./ARVN dead, wounded, and missing were fewer than 700. Although it was a U.S. "victory," critics said that, for Attleboro and similar operations, U.S. leaders were putting too much emphasis on military aspects of the war and were failing at the political war—the need to win the "hearts and minds" of South Vietnamese peasants.

Betty Friedan, the first president of the National Organization for Women (NOW), addresses an audience in New York City on November 21, 1966. Stung by the Equal Employment Opportunity Commission's indifference to women's issues, many advocates were stirred to action. The newly formed organization raised awareness of gender discrimination while simultaneously pushing for change. NOW's first vice president was a man, symbolizing the fairness that would come by enforcing existing policy. In 1967 NOW would generate considerable controversy by demanding repeal of all laws regulating abortion.

The Spy Craze

Long before Austin Powers, the Sixties made the spy a veritable pop icon. The spy vogue is synonymous with the career of James Bond, Agent 007, based on the novels by Ian Fleming and first incarnated on screen by Sean Connery. The box office success of the first James Bond film, *Dr. No* (1962), generated six Bond sequels in the Sixties.

Less-enduring American versions of the Bond formula included the Matt Helm movies, starring Rat Pack swinger Dean Martin. The trend soon filtered down to television with such hit spy shows as *Get Smart* (1965–1970), *The Man from U.N.C.L.E.* (1964–1968), and *I Spy* (1965–1968), the only genre show to headline a black actor, Bill Cosby. *The Avengers* (airing on ABC from 1966 to 1969) was a British import that featured Diana Rigg as Emma Peel, whose martial arts prowess was matched by a keen intellect and a kinky fashion sense.

Espionage pop culture bore a paradoxical relationship to the actual Cold War. While reinscribing the polarities of communism versus free world, the satirical gamesmanship of these shows also parodied Cold War espionage—a stance inconceivable in the 1950s. In doing so, they marked the transition from Fifties "brinkmanship" to the mutual coexistence ethic of Seventies détente.

Get Smart's Don Adams and Barbara Feldon

Already a hit television show in Britain, *The Avengers* debuted on ABC in the United States on March 28, 1966. This secret-agent series followed the highly skilled team of proper Englishman John Steed (played by Patrick Macnee, *pictured*) and the beautiful and brilliant Mrs. Emma Peel (Diana Rigg, *pictured*). The duo solved mysteries and discovered espionage plots and other odd goings-on throughout the British countryside. The show, often filmed in a style that verged on avant-garde, was acclaimed for its sexiness and wit.

Walt Disney, a tidy, restrained man who turned an animated mouse into an empire, died at age 65 on December 15, 1966. Disney pioneered a cartoon film company in the 1920s and broke through in 1928 with *Steamboat Willie,* an animated film that featured Mickey Mouse. The Walt Disney Company went on to produce 18 animated feature films before Walt's death, including such classics as *Snow White and the Seven Dwarfs, Bambi, Pinocchio,* and *Fantasia*. Despite his pleasant demeanor, Disney was an aggressive businessman who also worked with HUAC during the 1950s to finger leftists in his own studio.

1967

Summer of Love

ON JANUARY 14, 1967, 20,000 people gathered for the Human Be-In—
"a Gathering of the Tribes"—in Golden Gate Park. Some celebrants
dressed as Plains Indians or Afghan nomads. Others wore monk
robes or Indian saris, paisley blouses or tie-dyed shirts, cowboy hats or turbans.
People wore whatever made them feel good or what they believed manifested
their "inner selves." Poet and scene-maker Allen Ginsberg had opened the day
by ritually circling the field while chanting a Hindu blessing. On low risers, the
Grateful Dead, Big Brother and the Holding Company, Jefferson Airplane,
and other bands rocked out. Between sets, Jerry Rubin—then a Berkeley antiwar organizer—called for an alliance between the San Francisco hipster scene
(comprised of hippies) and the East Bay antiwar radicals. LSD apostle Timothy Leary, seemingly under the influence of his favorite sacrament, gave a
bleary benediction.

Most people paid only occasional attention to the stage events. They were
not there to be somebody's audience. They *were* the event. They wandered,
played their own musical instruments, and sat in circles passing around marijuana joints. No one got hurt, nobody started a fight, and almost everybody
really did seem to have a splendid time. The Human Be-In was the preamble
for what would become in a few months a mass media extravaganza: the Summer of Love.

This counterculture had been taking root in the San Francisco Bay Area
for years. In the mid-1950s, a Beat scene was firmly established in the North

> *"I was suddenly aware
> of this whole scene.
> Something was going
> on. . . . I went to the
> Haight-Ashbury for
> about two months. The
> Summer of Love. . . . I felt
> I had fallen into some
> Utopia whose millen-
> nium had arrived. I was
> heedless of the future,
> and my past as well."*
>
> —MARC BARASCH, A TEENAGER
> FROM LOS ANGELES

The mass media dubbed the warm months of 1967 the "Summer of Love," and paid particular attention to San
Francisco's Haight-Ashbury district. In truth, the Haight's mellow vibe had peaked a couple years earlier. By 1967
the lovin' continued, but the district also was flooded with vulnerable teenage runaways, hardcore drug pushers,
and other predators—even busloads of curious, middle-class tourists who came to gawk at "the hippies."

Beach district. Jack Kerouac, Allen Ginsberg, Gary Snyder, and other talented artists gave shape to the Beat aesthetic. They blended a faith in Eastern forms of spirituality with a disregard for conventional social mores to create new forms of prose and poetry. Poet Lawrence Ferlinghetti had opened City Lights Bookstore as a source for the new literature and as a creative vortex for the evolving scene. These elder statesmen, most of whom were in their mid-40s in 1967, inspired and often supported the new generation of seekers and artists who coalesced around the intersection of Haight and Ashbury in San Francisco.

By 1967 the neighborhood had become a mecca for young people looking to create an affordable alternative community. In January of the prior year, Ron and Jay Thelin had opened the Psychedelic Shop at 1535 Haight Street. Inspired by LSD (the drug was legal in the United States until October 1966), the store offered books about drug experiences and mystical states by writers such as Timothy Leary, Aldous Huxley, and Joseph Campbell. The store also sold finely wrought, locally made crafts meant to dazzle and surprise the mind's eye. It was the first "head" shop. Everything in the store fit an emerging ethos that scorned the mass-produced commodities of an automated society.

A group of artists/activists, several of whom had been members of the avant-garde theater group known as the Mime Troupe, regrouped as the Diggers. They named themselves after a 17th-century utopian movement that had fought unsuccessfully to create an egalitarian, collective society in preindustrial England. Preaching a doctrine of "free," the San Francisco Diggers cooked up scavenged food and handed it out to anyone who showed up at their Golden Gate Park site. The Diggers also set up the Free Store, which turned "profit motive" on its backside by simply giving away clothes, toys, furniture, and anything else that came their way.

The Diggers, as well as many other creative men and women dedicated to rethinking everyday life, staged imaginative parades, public theatrical events, and whimsical makeovers of the neighborhood's public spaces. Calling themselves "life actors," they aimed to show people that the future did not have to be an incremental extension of the present but was open to the power of their collective imagination. The Human Be-In, at the beginning of 1967, was the most extravagant of these free festivals.

Throughout 1967 other similar alternative communities burgeoned. In New York City's Lower East Side, Abbie Hoffman took direct inspiration from

The explosive Beat poet Allen Ginsberg was about 20 years older than the typical San Francisco hippie, but his orientation was definitely youthful. As a young man, Ginsberg had struggled with his homosexuality and middle-class aspirations until liberating himself through his writing. In the 1960s he was a high-profile antiwar activist and a vocal advocate of LSD. Here, he exhorts the crowd at San Francisco's 1967 Human Be-In festival.

the Diggers. He, too, established a free store and began organizing community events. In Old Town in Chicago, the 14th Street neighborhood in Atlanta, Dinkytown in Minneapolis, Venice Beach in Los Angeles, and numerous college towns, young people worked to create their own alternative culture. Each was unified by illegal drug use and a collection of head shops, record stores, and clothes boutiques.

The emerging national hippie culture featured an increasingly recognizable look: long, flowing hair for both young men and women; brightly colored clothes that often borrowed stylistically from India, Africa, and Latin America; and a penchant for bare feet, no undergarments, and a casual attitude toward personal hygiene. Alternative newspapers, attuned to this sensibility, sprung up everywhere: *The Great Speckled Bird, The East Village Other, Vortex, The Seed, Kudzu,* and eventually hundreds of others with a combined circulation of several million. Here and there, new FM radio stations emerged, such as KMPX in San Francisco and listener-sponsored WBAI in New York. These stations played psychedelic (LSD-inspired) music that both influenced and reflected this national, and even international, alternative culture.

Most of this psychedelic music first emerged in the Bay Area from such bands as the Grateful Dead, Jefferson Airplane, Quicksilver Messenger Service, and Big Brother and the Holding Company. The music was a cultural glue that bonded together the "paisley ghettos." Songs included long guitar riffs, fierce amplification and electronic distortion, druggy lyrics, and running times that far surpassed AM radio's commercially acceptable three minutes. Yet by 1967, this new music expanded far beyond the Bay Area scene. That year, the once cute and cuddly Beatles released a spectacular psychedelic pop album titled *Sgt. Pepper's Lonely Hearts Club Band.*

Sgt. Pepper featured the sounds of an Indian sitar, farm animals, and numerous stereophonic effects best appreciated, their fans understood, while stoned. One of the Beatles' hit singles, "All You Need Is Love," was a paean to the new hippie credo: "love can turn the world around." In just three years, the Beatles and a substantial part of their audience had traveled quite a distance from the sweet silliness of "I Want to Hold Your Hand."

In June 1967 the pop music industry, primarily based in Los Angeles, and the countercultural music of the Bay Area joined forces at the Monterey International Pop Festival. Such commercially successful bands as the Mamas and

The Diggers were a self-described "anarchist guerrilla street theater group" in California determined to exist outside the fishbowl of mass-produced culture. They urged people to develop "personal authenticity" by living in accord with their impulses and dreams. Digger Free Food, seen here, was not charity but an expression of community, and regard for the value of the individual.

Marijuana was the recreational drug of choice for many youngsters. If not always of the highest quality, it certainly was readily available. This young woman tokes up on the tour plane of America's pre-fab, "squeaky-clean" rock group, the Monkees.

the Papas, which featured beautiful vocal harmonies, met up with Big Brother and the Holding Company. Big Brother was fronted by the howling, blues-singing Janis Joplin, a white woman who, many at the time said, sang like a black woman. Also at the festival, India sitar player Ravi Shankar transfixed the crowd for hours, and Jimi Hendrix shocked even his fellow musicians with his outrageous, feedback-driven guitarmanship.

As tens of thousands milled through the Monterey Fairgrounds, the record industry realized the commercial possibilities of a far more eclectic, adventurous, and free-form style of pop music. In 1967 the boundaries that had loosely separated commercial pop music and alternative, counterculture rock completely disintegrated. By mid-1967 not just the music but the entire hippie style was, suddenly, everywhere in the United States.

The mass media proclaimed 1967 the "Summer of Love." *Time, Life, Newsweek,* and other mainstream magazines sent reporters to the Haight-Ashbury to cover America's newest "fad." Tour companies arranged for sightseers to view the hippies from the comforts of air-conditioned buses. Caught up in the mass media hoopla, tens of thousands of teenage runaways, not really sure how they would fit in, made their way to San Francisco and other hippie enclaves.

Writer Joan Didion spent several weeks during the "Summer of Love" observing the Haight-Ashbury scene for *The Saturday Evening Post.* She was appalled: "We are seeing the desperate attempt of a handful of pathetically unequipped children to create a community in a social vacuum.... They are less in rebellion against the society than ignorant of it, able only to feed back certain of its most publicized self-doubts, Vietnam, Saran-Wrap, diet-pills, the Bomb."

By the fall, the Diggers were at least in partial agreement with Didion's analysis. They believed the countercultural experiment was becoming overrun

Thousands of youngsters who drove, thumbed, and took buses to San Francisco, such as this inexperienced panhandler in the Haight-Ashbury district, discovered that food and shelter almost always cost money, just like anywhere else. Too many kids spent their days hungry and cold, and many were robbed and otherwise exploited.

by clueless kids who could not take care of themselves, let alone create a viable new culture. On October 6, 1967, the Diggers held a mock funeral for the "Death of Hippy" in the Haight-Ashbury.

Still, by the end of the 1960s, business executives would start sporting long hair, suburban parents would experiment with marijuana, and college students would form food co-ops. Moreover, health practitioners would ponder alternative medicines, and mainstream Americans would accept Eastern spiritual practices (such as meditation and yoga) as antidotes for their daily stresses.

Such lifestyle changes would come later. In 1967 the Vietnam War was raging and race riots were tearing apart many of America's big cities. Millions of Americans, not just hippies, aggressively challenged mainstream American values and political beliefs. Many of them rejected the hippies' "peace and love" ethos, believing that more aggressive protest was required. A few even decided that armed resistance was the only response to American injustices.

In May, the newly formed Black Panther Party staged a protest rally at the state capitol building in California. Panthers co-leader Bobby Seale declared, "[As] the aggression of the racist American government escalates in Vietnam, the police agencies of America escalate the repression of black people throughout the ghettos.... The time has come for black people to arm themselves against this terror before it is too late." Black Power advocate H. Rap Brown was even more explicit: "We will no longer sit back and let black people be killed.... We are calling on full retaliation."

Antiwar protesters, too, had grown frustrated over their government's escalating violence in Vietnam and the public's general indifference to the deaths of hundreds of thousands of Vietnamese. At a massive, nonviolent, antiwar protest at the Pentagon in October, about 700 demonstrators were arrested for trespassing on the Pentagon grounds. Afterward, antiwar protest leader Dave Dellinger noted that he and others wanted to create negative consequences at home because of America's conduct in Vietnam. It had become necessary to throw sand into the gears of the war machine, and to disrupt normal life for as long as the government perpetuated the the war. Pro-war Americans were infuriated by the increasingly aggressive antiwar movement. After a protest at the University of Wisconsin ended with a brutal police attack on the student demonstrators, a Wisconsin state assemblyman commended the police and added, "Shoot them if necessary. I would...it's insurrection." By the end of 1967, Americans were beginning to draw lines in the sand, daring each other to cross the ugly divide. The Summer of Love was over.

Twenty-year-old Marine Corporal Michael Wynn of Columbus, Ohio, was photographed in Da Nang, South Vietnam, sporting a helmet with his own variation of the hippie slogan "Make Love, Not War." Combat was frightening, and whether or not individual soldiers agreed with at-home protesters, they knew what sort of mind-set they needed to cultivate in order to survive.

1967

1967: Throughout the year, 952 American men are convicted of violations of United States draft laws. • The Mobilization to End the War in Vietnam is formed. • Congress enacts the Age Discrimination Act of 1967, prohibiting employment discrimination against Americans 40 and older. • The Environmental Defense Fund (EDF) is founded.

January 1: The Hell's Angels Motorcycle Club hosts a free rock concert at the Panhandle of Golden Gate Park, not far from the Haight-Ashbury.

January 3: Jack Ruby, 56, a Dallas nightclub owner who shot and killed alleged John F. Kennedy assassin Lee Harvey Oswald in 1963, dies in prison while awaiting retrial.

January 5: The U.S. Department of Defense announces that 5,008 U.S. soldiers died in Vietnam in 1966.

January 6: U.S. and South Vietnamese troops launch a major offensive against the Vietcong in the Mekong Delta region of South Vietnam.

January 8–26: Operation Cedar Falls becomes the largest U.S./South Vietnam offensive to date, with 16,000 American and 14,000 South Vietnamese troops.

January 9: The U.S. House Democratic Caucus votes to remove Representative Adam Clayton Powell, Jr., (D–NY) as chairman of the House Education and Labor Committee. Powell is under investigation for alleged misconduct. *See* April 11, 1967.

January 10: President Lyndon Johnson asks the 90th Congress to levy a 6 percent surcharge on corporate and personal incomes to fund the American effort in Vietnam. • Staunch segregationist Lester Maddox is elected governor of Georgia by the state legislature, 182–66.

January 14: The Human Be-In is held at San Francisco's Golden Gate Park, attracting hippies, antiwar militants, and Hell's Angels.

A civil rights pioneer who organized rent strikes and fed Harlem's poor during the Great Depression, Adam Clayton Powell, Jr., became a popular and flamboyant lawmaker after being elected to Congress in 1944. Powell attained power and privilege as chairman of the House Education and Labor Committee, and by the 1960s he was a supporter of black militants. In 1967 his enemies accused him of using taxpayers' money to bankroll his personal spending. In January, the House Democrats stripped him of his Committee position, an action that Powell described as a northern-style lynching. Later, the Supreme Court ruled that Congress had violated the law. Powell was reelected but deprived of seniority.

American soldiers fire from an armored personnel carrier during Operation Cedar Falls in early 1967. The largest combined U.S.–South Vietnam operation to that point in the war, it was designed to clear Vietcong from an area about 20 miles north of Saigon. In addition to engaging the enemy, U.S. forces relocated thousands of peasants from their native villages, such as Ben Suc, to newly built, more secure ones—then leveled the old ones. According to reporter Jonathan Schell, the Americans seemed "bent on annihilating every possible indication that Ben Suc had ever existed." Nevertheless, Vietcong forces were again operating in the area six months later.

The "Limited War"

In early 1967, after pressure from Congress, the United States military announced substantial improvement in its treatment of Vietcong and North Vietnamese prisoners of war. In 1967 an estimated 2,500 POWs were held. But Vietcong suspects, who often were difficult to discern from civilians, continued to endure harsh treatment. Here, a U.S. soldier holds an M16 rifle to the head of this woman as she is questioned by a South Vietnamese police officer. Atrocities were frequent on both sides during the war, including rape, torture, and mutilation of the dead.

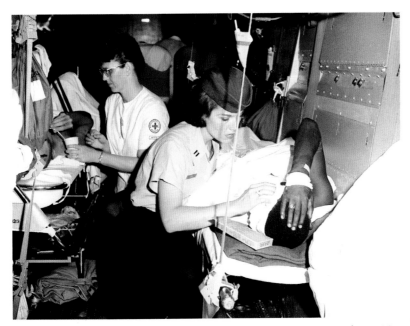

Of the approximately 7,500 women who served in Vietnam, at least 80 percent of them worked in the nurse corps of the various branches of the service. Most were volunteers and generally inexperienced militarily, but they faced many of the same emotional and physical rigors of war that the soldiers on the front did. After the war, hundreds of nurse veterans suffered from post-traumatic stress disorder. Only in recent years has the role of women and nurses in Vietnam been properly recognized. On Veterans Day in 1993, a statue commemorating women's roles in the military was unveiled on the Mall in Washington, D.C.

BY 1967 AMERICAN FORCES under the command of General William Westmoreland engaged in what many critics called a "limited war." Despite the dramatic increase in American troops and sustained daily bombing of North Vietnamese targets, the Johnson Administration and Westmoreland limited the ground war to "search and destroy" missions in South Vietnam. They deliberately ruled out a ground invasion of North Vietnam (and the use of tactical nuclear weapons), largely out of concerns that such actions might provoke Chinese military intervention in support of their Communist neighbor. The administration also feared a breakdown in American–Soviet relations, then in a period of relative calm.

As a result, a war of attrition developed in the south, making "body counts" of enemy dead the primary measure of military success. The American public, accustomed to the World War II example of military victory achieved through coordinated ground invasions of enemy territory, grew frustrated with sporadic engagements with enemy guerrillas—sometimes over the same hill captured and abandoned the previous week. Over time, critics seized on the idea of "limited war" as the main culprit in America's defeat in Vietnam.

At the same time, others argued that American power in Vietnam had not been materially limited at all. At its peak, American troop levels exceeded 550,000 men and women, with a total of 2.6 million serving in Vietnam over the course of the war. American planes dropped more than seven million tons of ordnance on North and South Vietnam, and they dumped more than 19 million gallons of chemical weapons (mostly herbicides) on South Vietnam. This immense firepower secured "victory" for American and South Vietnamese forces in every major engagement with the enemy. Over nearly 10 years of combat, 3.2 million Vietnamese died. The war cost the United States nearly 58,000 lives and $170 billion.

1967

January 15: The Green Bay Packers defeat the Kansas City Chiefs 35–10 in Super Bowl I. • U.S. bombers make their first strikes against the Hanoi area in North Vietnam since December 1966. • The Rolling Stones perform "Let's Spend the Night Together" on *The Ed Sullivan Show.* They honor Sullivan's request by changing the words "the night" to "some time." *See* September 17, 1967.

January 16: In Macon County, Alabama, Lucius D. Amerson becomes the first black sheriff in the South since Reconstruction.

January 18: Albert DeSalvo, the alleged "Boston Strangler," is sentenced to life imprisonment for 10 counts of sex offenses, robbery, and assault.

January 21–22: Managua, Nicaragua, is struck by violent street demonstrations protesting the pro-U.S. politics of presidential candidate Anastasio Somoza Debayle.

January 22: China's *People's Daily* newspaper exhorts radical Red Guards to seize power across the nation.

January 23: President Johnson asks Congress for Social Security hikes ranging from 15 percent to 59 percent. They would be funded by a payroll-tax increase in 1968.

January 27: Three U.S. astronauts—Gus Grissom, Edward White, and Roger Chaffee—die in a Cape Kennedy launch-pad fire during tests after a spark ignites pure oxygen in the capsule. • Sixty nations, including the U.S. and USSR, sign a United Nations treaty calling for peaceful uses of outer space.

February: *Ramparts* magazine reveals that the CIA has been subsidizing and thus infiltrating university student organizations for 15 years, notably the left-of-center National Student Association (NSA). • Chicano movement activist Jose Angel Gutierrez forms *La Raza Unida* (The United Race) as an organizing tool and the first Chicano political party.

Green Bay Packers halfback Elijah Pitts gains six yards against the Kansas City Chiefs in the first Super Bowl game, won by the Packers 35–10 in Los Angeles on January 15, 1967. Green Bay quarterback Bart Starr, who threw for 250 yards and two touchdowns, was named the game's MVP. The newly created contest pitted the champions of the National Football League and the upstart American Football League. After the game, Packers coach Vince Lombardi fueled a rivalry between the two leagues when he said, "Kansas City is a good football team," but "their team doesn't compare with the top NFL teams."

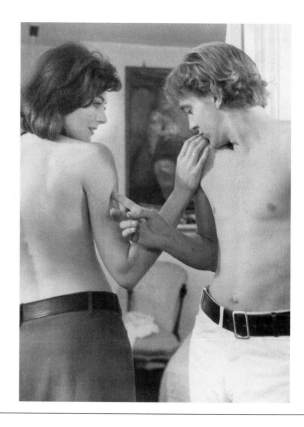

By the late 1960s, the youth audience for movies was harder for Hollywood to pin down. Films with a hip sensibility (such as *Bonnie and Clyde*) as well as art films and foreign films drew audiences of young people in search of the authentic or challenging. The highest-grossing art film in 1967 was Michelangelo Antonioni's *Blowup.* The story follows the experiences of a trendy and alienated London photographer (played by David Hemmings, *pictured*) who may have witnessed a murder through the lens of his camera. The film also stars Vanessa Redgrave (*pictured*) as a mysterious woman implicated in a possible scandal.

In January 1967 the Jefferson Airplane touched down for a concert at the Human Be-In in San Francisco and began gathering a counterculture audience for their brand of psychedelic rock. Singer Grace Slick joined the Airplane from another Bay Area band called

the Great Society, and brought with her two songs that soon became hits on her new band's 1967 release, *Surrealistic Pillow*. The song "Somebody to Love" took the album to the top 10, but those "in the know" were blown away by the hit "White Rabbit." The song criticizes hypocrisies of mainstream society and advocates drug use through metaphorical *Alice in Wonderland* references.

Tragedy struck the U.S. space program on January 27, 1967. An electrical fire engulfed the Apollo 1 command module during a launch-pad test in preparation for the first Apollo/Saturn manned flight. The accident killed all three astronauts aboard the craft: Virgil "Gus" Grissom, Edward White II, and Roger Chaffee (*left to right*). Grissom was a veteran of the Mercury and Gemini missions, and White had distinguished himself as part of the Gemini program. Americans had grown close to these space heroes and their families after years of *Life* magazine profiles and interviews. The accident led NASA to reassess its safety measures. It published a report in April that recommended major design and engineering modifications that would improve safety significantly.

Grace and Janis

MANY MUSIC HISTORIANS CLAIM that rock 'n' roll music reached its peak in 1967. The Beatles released their landmark *Sgt. Pepper* album, and the first large-scale outdoor rock festival, Monterey Pop, took place that June. Two of the acts appearing were fronted by female singers, Grace Slick and Janis Joplin. In the parlance of the times, each was the *yin* to the other's *yang*.

Jefferson Airplane was a San Francisco band founded by singer Marty Balin. Though its first album was an unremarkable folkie effort, the Airplane soared to greater heights after Slick joined the band. Slick, a former model who had sung with the Great Society, brought two powerhouse songs to the Airplane: "Somebody to Love" and "White Rabbit." The latter, which melded Lewis Carroll imagery with Ravel's *Bolero*, was largely viewed as a paean to the drug culture. Slick's cerebral, ironic persona would support the band's increasingly political direction.

With Janis Joplin, however, all politics was personal. The embodiment of blues writ large, Joplin fronted Big Brother and the Holding Company, a Bay-area band noted mostly for its uncanny ability to elude proper tuning. Joplin, a transplanted Texan, was as "hot" as Slick was "cool." With her, what you saw was what you got: riveting, soul-baring performances that left both singer and audience emotionally drained.

A rebel against conformity, Joplin drew attention with her outlandish stylings and outrageous behavior. She eventually partied herself to death, falling victim to a drug overdose at age 27 in 1970. In subsequent decades Joplin, like Slick, would be hailed as one of the greatest voices in rock history.

Grace Slick

Janis Joplin

February 4: The racially integrated crew of U.S. aircraft carrier *Franklin D. Roosevelt* is confined to the ship after the carrier docks at Cape Town, South Africa, because of that nation's policy of apartheid.

February 10: The 25th amendment to the U.S. Constitution is adopted. It deals with issues of succession of the vice president to the presidency.

February 12: Mick Jagger and Keith Richards are arrested in England for drug possession.

February 13: After peace efforts fail, President Johnson announces that the U.S. will resume full-scale bombing of North Vietnam.

February 16: Thirteen U.S. helicopters are lost in South Vietnam, a single-day record.

February 18: The President's Commission on Law Enforcement and Administration of Justice reports that one-third of Americans keep firearms, and that one-third feel that to walk outside at night is unsafe. • New Orleans District Attorney Jim Garrison announces he has evidence of a conspiracy in the assassination of President John F. Kennedy, and will launch an investigation. *See* March 22, 1967. • American physicist J. Robert Oppenheimer, a key figure in the U.S. development of the atomic bomb, dies at 62. • A medical-supply ship funded by the Philadelphia Quakers leaves Tokyo for North Vietnam.

February 22: About 70 miles north of Saigon, more than 25,000 U.S. and South Vietnamese troops launch Operation Junction City, the most aggressive U.S./South Vietnam offensive of the war.

February 27: The U.S. military command in Saigon acknowledges that the U.S. has been placing mines in North Vietnam's rivers.

February 28: Publisher Henry Luce (*Time, Life, Fortune, Sports Illustrated*) dies at 68.

A sufferer of depression for most of her life, Anne Sexton was encouraged by her doctor to write poetry as a way to deal with her black moods. Her work was "confessional" in that it dealt with the continuing cycle of breakdown and recovery in her own life. *Live or Die* (1966) won the Pulitzer Prize for poetry in 1967. Sexton answered the question posed in the title of that work when she committed suicide in 1974. Her last book, published posthumously, was entitled *The Awful Rowing Toward God.*

Artist Peter Max strikes a pose with many of his works in the background. Born in Berlin, Max moved to the United States in 1953 and studied at the Art Students' League in New York. He began experimenting with photo collages in the early 1960s, then turned to what he called his "cosmic '60s style." These works featured unusually bold juxtapositions of color, which were psychedelic in nature. His posters and album covers became popular icons in the late 1960s.

"[S]everal teachers . . . would be taken out there and shot in public. The family members were not allowed to cry, instead they had to praise the Red Guards that they were doing the right thing. Some teachers were buried alive. On the roof of the building over there, four teachers were forced to sit on a pack of explosives, and they were ordered to light the explosives themselves."

—A TEACHER IN CHINA DESCRIBING THE WRATH OF STUDENTS AT HIS SCHOOL DURING THE CULTURAL REVOLUTION

By 1967 the nationalist zeal of the Red Guard reached its peak. All over the world, television viewers witnessed China's young people waving the "Little Red Book" of Chairman Mao Tse-tung's quotations. During demonstrations throughout the country, young people shouted slogans and sang songs of the revolution. As revolutionary fervor surged, the army, the Red Guard, and workers began to battle each other in the countryside. High government officials were purged, and anti-Mao uprisings threatened the stability of the government.

In 1966 Mao Tse-tung closed the nation's schools and unleashed the revolutionary zeal of millions of young people on his country. Despite the efforts by the Chinese establishment to rein in the Red Guard, their youthful energies rolled over the country, rooting out the "Four Olds": old customs, old habits, old culture, and old ideas. By 1967 the Red Guard began to divide into factions and purge its own members. Here, at the height of the near-anarchic period, Red Guards humiliate members of their own ranks.

The Humiliation

O N THE ATHLETIC FIELD and farther inside, before a new four-story classroom building, I saw rows of teachers, about forty or fifty in all, with black ink poured over their heads and faces so that they were now in reality a "black gang." Hanging on their necks were placards with such words as "reactionary academic authority So-and-So," "class enemy So-and-So," "capitalist roader So-and-So," "corrupt ringleader So-and-So," all epithets taken from the newspapers. On each placard was a red cross, making the teachers look like condemned prisoners awaiting execution. They all wore dunce caps painted with similar epithets and carried dirty brooms, shoes and dusters on their backs. Hanging from their necks were pails filled with rocks. I saw the principal; the pail around his neck was so heavy that the wire had cut deep into his neck and he was staggering. All were barefoot, hitting broken gongs or pots as they walked around the field, crying out, "I am black gangster So-and-So." Finally they all knelt down, burned incense and begged Mao Tse-tung to "pardon their crimes."

—RED GUARD KEN LING, FROM HIS BOOK
THE REVENGE OF HEAVEN

March 4: The Presidential Selective Service Commission recommends an end to graduate-student deferments and calls for a lottery system of selection by which 19-year-olds would be called up first.

March 6: Svetlana Alliluyeva, daughter of late Soviet dictator Joseph Stalin, seeks asylum in the U.S.

March 7: Teamsters leader Jimmy Hoffa begins an eight-year federal sentence for jury tampering.

March 9: Thai Prime Minister Thanom Kittikachorn announces that U.S. warplanes have used Thai bases for bomb runs against North Vietnam.

March 12: Indonesia's Provisional People's Consultative Congress strips President Sukarno of the executive and ceremonial powers he has held since 1945, and passes power to General Suharto.

March 13: Senator Eugene McCarthy (D–MN) introduces the Equal Rights Amendment, intended to eliminate gender discrimination.

March 18–19: Liberian tanker ship *Torrey Canyon* runs up on a reef off the southwest coast of England and spills 117,000 tons of crude oil into the ocean. Severe damage to seabirds and seabird colonies results.

March 19: A rain-loosened hillside slides into a resort at Rio de Janeiro, Brazil, killing more than 400 people.

Spring: Chinese dictator Mao Tse-tung reopens schools across China because Red Guard activity is close to anarchy. In response, the Guard storms institutions in Peking.

Spring–December: Riots and violent fighting occur across China between workers, Red Guards, and the army.

March 22: A grand jury in New Orleans, encouraged by New Orleans District Attorney Jim Garrison, indicts local businessman Clay Shaw for conspiracy in the assassination of President John F. Kennedy.

Beginning on February 22, 1967, the operation code-named Junction City combined 22 battalions from the U.S. Army with South Vietnamese forces in attacks on Vietcong strongholds in the Tay Ninh province. By the end of this "search and destroy" mission, the largest U.S. military offensive of the war, the operation had led to the deaths of nearly 3,000 Vietcong and 282 U.S. soldiers. The mission was successful in terms of the U.S. "body count" strategy at the time, which equated the high numbers of dead Vietcong with victory and progress in the war. However, the result of Junction City, rather than to undermine the Vietcong's secure areas, simply drove the guerrillas over the border into the Cambodian sanctuary area. There they continued to resupply and fight on.

From the beginning of U.S. involvement in Vietnam, women's groups were among the many peace organizations that pressured Congress and the President to negotiate a settlement with the North Vietnamese. On February 13, 1967, 2,500 members of Women's Strike for Peace, including many mothers and family members of soldiers, marched on the Pentagon, demanding to meet with Secretary of Defense Robert McNamara.

The Baby Boom hit Southern California with special force, given the many Americans who had moved there during and after World War II. Thus, a large number of relatively affluent teenagers emerged on the scene in the mid-1960s, and many of them flocked to the club-rich area of L.A. known as the Sunset Strip. A riot broke out on the strip on November 12, 1966, when a thousand demonstrators protested the tight enforcement of curfew regulations. Some youths hurled rocks, while others tried to set fire to a bus. Producers of the film *Riot on Sunset Strip*, which was rushed to theaters by March 1, 1967, tried to profit from the notoriety of the young rebels.

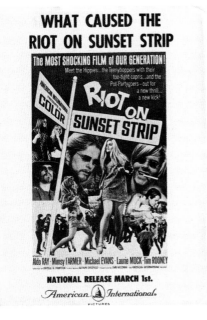

This 1967 Cuban poster depicts a Chinese dragon coiled around a rifle. Created as part of a "Week of Solidarity with the Peoples of Asia" celebration, it illustrates Communist Cuba's determination to present a united front with the People's Republic of China and, especially, Communist North Vietnam in its war against the United States and South Vietnam. The Cuban government viewed as positive anything that troubled its neighbor to the north.

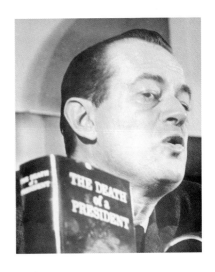

After the assassination of John F. Kennedy, the Kennedy family commissioned William Manchester (*pictured*) to write *Death of a President*. Manchester put together a detailed, exhaustive reconstruction of the days before and after Kennedy's assassination. He concluded that Lee Harvey Oswald, unequivocally, was the lone gunman. Despite Manchester's findings, millions of Americans still believed in various conspiracy theories.

In its short career as a band, Buffalo Springfield combined folk rock, country sounds, protest, and poetry to create a wide-ranging and highly influential style. As a result, the band shaped the sound of rock music beyond the decade and propelled talented musicians to fame. Stephen Stills (*left*) and Neil Young (*right*) were two original members of the band, which produced the hit song "For What It's Worth" in 1967. The song focused on the growing generation gap between younger, sign-carrying antiwar protesters and the older middle class.

1967

April: West German authorities arrest British extremists who planned to assassinate U.S. Vice President Hubert Humphrey during an official visit.

April 1: UN Secretary General U Thant urges the U.S. to declare a unilateral truce in Vietnam.

April 4: Martin Luther King, Jr., condemns the U.S. government's Vietnam policy in a speech at Riverside Church in New York.

April 5: Grayline begins bus tours of the Haight-Ashbury.

April 7: Top-40 DJ Tom Donahue begins a "progressive" rock format at KMPX-FM in San Francisco. It is the nation's second FM rock station, following WOR-FM in New York.

April 11: In a special election, Adam Clayton Powell, Jr., is reelected to the U.S. House of Representatives from the 18th Congressional District (Harlem) in New York.

April 14: Visiting Saigon, former Vice President Richard Nixon declares that antiwar protests back in the U.S. are "prolonging the war."

April 15: More than 100,000 antiwar demonstrators, including Martin Luther King, Jr., march through New York to the UN. The march is part of the antiwar movement's Spring Mobilization, which also sponsors a march on this day in San Francisco.
• Following 49 minutes of deliberation, a Chicago jury finds Richard Speck guilty of the 1966 mass murder of eight student nurses.

April 19: Officials try to physically remove K. (Kathrine) Switzer from the Boston Marathon after she is identified as a female entrant. She finishes the race anyway.

April 20: U.S. bombers strike the North Vietnamese port city of Haiphong for the first time.

On March 18, 1967, the giant oil tanker *Torrey Canyon* ran aground on rocks in the English Channel. The disaster released more than 117,000 tons of crude oil into the sea. British authorities bombed the ship so it would sink and stop spreading pollution. The *Torrey Canyon* wreck, followed by a series of oil spills and other environmental disasters during the late 1960s, would draw widespread public outrage and attention, and galvanize a growing environmental movement.

"Aden Is a 'Little Vietnam' for Britain," read a *New York Times* headline in July 1967. The British had ruled Aden, the port city of Yemen (an Arabic nation), since 1839. However, rebellion in Aden broke out in 1963. British troops did their best to quell demonstrators, especially this soldier, pictured on April 4, 1967. Eventually, however, Aden's Arabic population achieved its dream of liberation. Helicopters lifted the last British troops from the city on November 30, 1967.

Martin Luther King, Jr., had long opposed the war in Vietnam. However, he had avoided the topic in public speeches in order to avoid the interference with civil rights goals that criticism of the President's policies might create. By 1967, though, as more and more mainstream Americans began to actively oppose the war, King put his weight behind antiwar efforts. On April 15, 1967, King participated in a large antiwar protest march in New York City, linking arms with Dr. Benjamin Spock (*left*) and Monsignor Charles O. Rice. Earlier in the month, King said, "This war is a blasphemy against all that America stands for."

In 1967 the U.S. Supreme Court reviewed the first test case challenging the constitutionality of a 1965 law prohibiting the burning of draft cards. During the Vietnam era, the government assigned every draft-age man a number and card that he was required to carry at

all times. The 1965 law was made in response to a rash of card burnings that year. The draft card law would be upheld by the Supreme Court in 1968. However, the symbolic and political act of burning draft cards would continue at rallies as a public rejection of the war and the government's efforts to turn individuals into numbers.

Ali's Biggest Fight

On February 25, 1964, 22-year-old Cassius Clay defeated heavily favored Sonny Liston for the world heavyweight boxing championship. This should have put him on top of the world, but a news conference the next day marked the beginning of an ugly battle between the new champ and the press, the public, boxing, and ultimately the United States government.

What had been an open secret for several years was confirmed: The fighter was a member of the Nation of Islam (NOI), a follower of Elijah Muhammad. To most Americans, NOI was an extremist group out to destroy the "white devils." Clay, still evolving in his beliefs, was never that excessive, merely embracing the Nation's outlook on justice, morality, and black pride. Dispensing with his "slave" name, he became Muhammad Ali ("worthy of praise"). Many sportswriters refused to refer to him by anything but his birth name.

In February 1967 Ali, who was 28–0 at the time, was ordered to report for induction into the Army in Houston on April 28. Ali showed up and took his physical, but he refused to be sworn in to the military, claiming he was "exempt as a minister of religion for Islam." To the press, he said, "I ain't got nothing against them Vietcong." Invoking conscientious objector status, Ali further elaborated that "the real enemy of my people is right here." The World Boxing Association responded by stripping Ali of his title, claiming he was "a very poor example" for the world's youth.

In June 1967 an all-white jury in Houston found Ali guilty of draft evasion. The judge gave him the maximum sentence, five years and a $10,000 fine, although his conviction eventually was overturned by the U.S. Supreme Court. Nevertheless, the entire episode kept Ali away from the ring from March 1967 to October 1970—the prime years of his career. Said his trainer, Angelo Dundee, "The best Muhammad Ali is the one we never saw."

April 21: A military coup in Greece ousts Prime Minister Panayotis Kanellopoulos, appoints Konstantinos Kollias in his place, and hands real power to the military and King Constantine. Greek Communists and other leftists are rounded up for deportation, and civil rights are suspended nationally. • Tornadoes near Chicago kill 56 people, injure 1,500, and cause $20 million in property damage.

April 24: Soviet cosmonaut Vladimir M. Komarov dies during the reentry of spacecraft Soyuz I. He is the first person known to have died in space. • Colorado becomes the first state to liberalize abortion laws, okaying legal abortion if a pregnancy results from rape, incest, or other specific conditions. • General William Westmoreland says that antiwar demonstrators give the typical North Vietnamese soldier encouragement because he hopes "that he can win politically that which he cannot accomplish militarily."

April 24–May 11: More than 150 American troops are killed in battles in the hills of Khe Sanh.

April 27: The Expo '67 World's Fair opens in Montreal.

April 28: U.S. General William Westmoreland assures a joint session of Congress that the U.S. "will prevail in Vietnam over the Communist aggressor."

May 1: CBS, NBC, and ABC are joined by a new television network, the United Network, which begins operations with a 90-minute, nightly variety show originating from Las Vegas. The network has 100 affiliate stations. Weak revenue will force it to shut down after a month. • Elvis Presley marries Priscilla Ann Beaulieu in Las Vegas.

May 2: Thirty armed Black Panthers march past California Governor Ronald Reagan and into the state house to voice their views about oppression of blacks. ▶

In 1967 the Boston Marathon was still an all-male race. This changed when a woman who registered with a gender-neutral name, K. Switzer, left the starting line with everyone else. When a race official, John "Jock" Semple, realized a woman was in the race, he attempted to rip the number from her back. However, he was blocked by Kathrine Switzer's burly boyfriend, Thomas Miller. Switzer completed the race. According to *The New York Times,* "her presence in the men's race drew cheers from the crowd." Switzer's run represented another effort by women in the Sixties who broke down gender barriers in sports and other aspects of public life.

Svetlana Alliluyeva, daughter of late Soviet leader Joseph Stalin, defected from the USSR in 1967. Having found God and her voice as a writer, the famous daughter talked to the American press at the Plaza Hotel in New York on April 26. Alliluyeva's press conference interrupted midday soap operas on television, and her story and image dominated U.S. tabloids for weeks. The defection not only scored political points for the United States during the Cold War, but Alliluyeva won over the press and American public. Wrote a *New York Times* reporter, "Moscow has reason to be apprehensive over the impact of Stalin's daughter on the mass mind; she is charmingly videogenic."

The U.S. and Soviet pavilions face each other at the 1967 Montreal World's Fair, called Expo '67. Commemorating the 100th anniversary of the Canadian Confederation, the yearlong fair featured exhibitions from more than 90 countries and welcomed more than 50 million visitors. The American exhibit was housed in a futuristic, 20-story geodesic dome of glass and plastic, designed by visionary architect Buckminster Fuller. The fair inspired the name of baseball's Montreal Expos, who began play in the National League in 1969.

This 1967 "shock" advertisement sponsored by the Sierra Club illustrates the environmental group's attempts to preserve California's redwood forests. A number of competing bills went before Congress that year concerning the establishment of a national park involving the great trees. In a compromise that provided less than what the Sierra Club wanted—but more than the minor additions proposed by timber interests—Congress established Redwood National Park, which comprised 58,000 acres.

Elvis Presley and Priscilla Beaulieu cut their wedding cake after marrying in Las Vegas at the Aladdin Hotel-Casino on May 1, 1967. The pair would later don the same wedding garb and recreate the scene at Graceland for friends and family who could not attend the small ceremony in Sin City. Despite the happy scene, Presley's career was at an all-time low, characterized by a seemingly endless string of uninspired singles and films. *Clambake,* which opened the same year, was Elvis's 25th picture.

Black Panther Party

ON MAY 2, 1967, Bobby Seale, Huey Newton, and a group of armed revolutionaries arrived at the California State Capitol in Sacramento. The group of young African-American activists donned leather jackets, boots, and berets. They carried an arsenal of M-1 rifles, 12-gauge shotguns, and .45 caliber pistols. As they moved through the halls of the Capitol building, intimidated reporters and photographers backed away. That day, the Black Panther Party for Self-Defense burst into the American consciousness.

Seale and Newton had organized the Black Panthers a year earlier in Oakland. They traveled to Sacramento to lobby against gun-control legislation before the State Assembly, which sought to restrict their public display of firepower. The Panthers were inspired by the self-defense orientation of Malcolm X and the self-reliance ethic of black nationalism. Calling themselves the "people's party," the BPP mixed basic community improvement—such as food programs, legal assistance, and medical clinics—with calls for violent revolution

Bobby Seale and Huey Newton

against what they saw as the colonizing white power structure.

At its height, the Black Panthers boasted only 1,000 core members and operated in 35 cities and 19 states. But their larger-than-life reputation and the slogan "Off the pigs!" obsessed law enforcement, especially FBI Director J. Edgar Hoover. The Panthers saw themselves as the vanguard in the movement for revolutionary socialism. They not only talked about offing the pigs, they engaged in gun battles with police officers. At least 20 Black Panther members were killed in battles with police.

The FBI used its COINTELPRO program to infiltrate and undermine the BPP, causing Newton to complain that the Panthers were being "harassed, persecuted, and killed across the country" for "trying to pass the truth on to the people." On December 4, 1969, police sprayed 90 bullets into the Chicago Panther headquarters, executing Fred Hampton and Mark Clark. The BPP lost much of its influence by the early 1970s and disbanded in 1982.

Black Panther Party Chairman Bobby Seale and 30 heavily armed Panthers marched on the California State Capitol Building on May 2, 1967. That spring, the Oakland police had been pushing the California State Assembly to pass legislation that would ban such displays of firepower in public places, targeting the Panthers in particular. The Panthers, masters of flamboyant and confrontational style, took their opposition straight to the source. The demonstration, much to the Panthers' delight, made national headlines. It also infuriated California Governor Ronald Reagan, who would become one of the party's fiercest enemies.

Uncle Sam wants YOU nigger

Become a member of the world's highest paid black mercenary army!

Support White Power — travel to Viet Nam you might get a medal

Fight for Freedom . . . (in Viet Nam)

Receive valuable training in the skills of killing of other oppressed people

(Die Nigger Die — you can't die fast enough in the ghettos.)

So run to your nearest recruiting chamber

SNCC leader Stokely Carmichael distributes antiwar leaflets at a Georgia induction center in 1967. "Receive valuable training in the skills of killing off other oppressed people!" reads the satirical recruitment advertisement. SNCC led the vanguard of black activists opposed to the Vietnam War. They felt that African-Americans had more than enough battles to fight in their own country. As the leaflet states, "you can't die fast enough in the ghettos."

In spring 1967 British philosopher Bertrand Russell organized the unofficial "International Tribunal on War Crimes," held in Stockholm, Sweden. The trial sought to assign blame for war crimes and condemn officials found responsible. In particular, the tribunal criticized the U.S. bombing of civilians in North Vietnam. Among the many notable antiwar activists presented as witnesses was French philosopher Jean-Paul Sartre (*pictured, wearing glasses*). He explained that the tribunal "had no mandate from anyone," but that the "tribunal's legitimacy derives simultaneously from its powerlessness and universality." President Lyndon Johnson said the tribunal was "highly regrettable."

A Houston police officer stands over some of the nearly 500 students arrested during a riot at Texas Southern University on May 16, 1967. During a rally on the all-black campus, someone fired shots that killed a police officer. The shooting led to a crackdown on the campus as Houston police moved through student dormitories, damaging student property in their search for firearms and other weapons. The uprising came close on the heels of a riot just days earlier at Jackson State College. The incidents revealed both black anger and white fear—as well as whites' willingness to use firepower and force to stop unrest.

May 2–10: Philosopher Bertrand Russell organizes (but is unable to attend) a War Crimes Tribunal at Stockholm, Sweden. Russell, moderator Jean-Paul Sartre, and investigators claim evidence of U.S. violations of international law in Vietnam.

May 9: With nearly 60 percent of South Vietnamese villages now under Vietcong control, President Johnson appoints Robert W. Komer to form the Civil Operations and Revolutionary Center (CORDS). The organization will provide $850 million in food and supplies, as well as military training, to villagers to win their "hearts and minds." • U.S. pianist and reporter Philippa Schuyler, 35, a onetime child musical prodigy, dies in a helicopter crash in South Vietnam during an evacuation of schoolchildren.

May 12: Black activist H. Rap Brown becomes chairman of SNCC following the resignation of Stokely Carmichael.

May 13: Chinese Premier Chou En-Lai warns that China will intervene if North Vietnam is threatened with invasion. • About 70,000 marchers surge along New York City's Fifth Avenue in a demonstration of support for U.S. troops in Vietnam.

May 14: The Provos, a radical political organization in Amsterdam that inspired San Francisco's Diggers, disband. • New York Yankees slugger Mickey Mantle belts his 500th career home run.

May 15: American naturalistic painter Edward Hopper dies at 84.

May 16: Tennessee's Butler Law, the "Monkey statute" that prohibits the teaching of evolution in public schools, is repealed.

May 19: U.S. bombers raid Hanoi in North Vietnam for the first time. • U.S. Marines and South Vietnamese troops attack in the DMZ (demilitarized zone) for the first time.

One survivor is carried to safety while another shimmies down a rope to escape the L'Innovation department store fire in Brussels, Belgium, on May 22, 1967. Three hundred and twenty-two people perished in one of the most devastating conflagrations in history. Although some suspected that the fire was started by a Communist-sponsored group protesting the sale of U.S. goods in the store, no sabotage was ever proved. The L'Innovation blaze was Europe's worst peacetime fire since 1881, and led to stricter Belgian fire-safety standards and regulations.

In 1959 Mildred Jeter and Richard Loving (*both pictured*) received suspended one-year jail sentences for violating Virginia's ban on interracial marriages. Their judge stated: "Almighty God created the races white, black, yellow, malay, and red, and he placed them on separate continents. . . . The fact that he separated the races shows that he did not intend for the races to mix." At the time that the U.S. Supreme Court ruled on their case, in *Loving v. Virginia* in June 1967, 16 states had outlawed such marriages. Those laws were nullified when the Supreme Court ruled that a ban on interracial marriage constituted an abridgement of the equal-protection and due-process clauses of the 14th Amendment.

The Six-Day War

For six days in early June 1967, all-out war raged between Israel and its Arab neighbors. Despite the short duration of the conflict, the death toll was astonishingly high, as well as lopsided. Nearly 15,000 Egyptians, Syrians, and Jordanians lay dead with tens of thousands more wounded. Israel, on the other hand, lost about 700 soldiers.

While the outcome of the Six-Day War was perfectly clear, its origins were, and remain today, an issue of debate. In 1948, in the wake of the Holocaust, the region of Palestine was divided into the state of Israel (for Jews) and the Kingdom of Jordan (for Arabs). Many Palestinian Arabs never accepted the plan, and in 1966–67 Palestinian guerrillas launched heavy attacks against Israel. Israel responded with air strikes against Syria and Jordan, nations Israel blamed for harboring terrorists. Angered by what they believed to be unjust aggression, the two Arab countries, along with Egypt, began to amass troops along the Israeli border in hopes of deterring future attacks.

World leaders called for a peaceful solution, and Egyptian President Gamal Nasser hinted that the UN should assume control over the escalating crisis. Such attempts at diplomacy were in vain. On June 5, Israel launched a massive air attack against its neighbors, striking targets deep within Egypt and Syria. The air raids were followed by a

Israeli soldier examining a target in Port Suez, Egypt

lightning ground assault that resulted in a decisive Israeli victory. Israel occupied the Sinai Peninsula, the Golan Heights, the Gaza Strip, the West Bank, and all of Jerusalem.

Though Egypt, Syria, and Jordan suffered a serious defeat, Palestinian Arabs in the newly occupied areas were the biggest losers. Some 200,000 refugees left the territory seized by Israel, fleeing to Jordan. Some Palestinians, however, remained, including one youth who prophetically declared, "We will stay here until we can fight again and take back our land."

"We shall not complain anymore to the UN about Israel. The sole method we shall apply against Israel is total war, which will result in the extermination of Zionist existence."

—Voice of the Arabs, an Egyptian radio station; May 18, 1967

Refugees from the West Bank make their way across the River Jordan on the damaged Allenby Bridge in the aftermath of the Six-Day War. Carrying children in their arms and possessions packed in sacks, the refugees walked to Jordan as the Israeli army secured control in the West Bank. Whether forced out or leaving by choice, an estimated 200,000 refugees amassed on the east side of the river. In the days after the occupation, *The New York Times* reported that the Israeli government promised "humanitarian treatment of refugees and Jordanian citizens from the territory."

1967

May 22: A fire of unknown origin sweeps through L'Innovation, a major Brussels department store, and several blocks of nearby buildings, killing 322 people. • African-American poet and writer Langston Hughes dies at 65.

May 24: United Arab Republic (UAR) President Gamal Abdul Nasser threatens Israel with "annihilation" if it attempts to run the UAR blockade of the Gulf of Aqaba. The brewing crisis prompts an emergency meeting of the UN Security Council. *See* June 1, 1967.

May 26: The FDA reports that banana peels do not contain psychedelics, defusing the popular rumor.

May 30: Biafra declares its independence from Nigeria. • Hippies and Puerto Rican–Americans clash at New York's Tompkins Square Park on the lower east side of Manhattan.

June: The Mobile Riverine Force, comprised of elements of the U.S. Army and Navy, begins operations. It will successfully deny Vietcong usage of inland waterways in the Mekong Delta. • The New Buffalo commune is founded in Arroyo Hondo, near Taos, New Mexico. It will become a mecca for hippies.

June 1: Major General Moshe Dayan is named defense minister of Israel. *See* June 5, 1967.

June 2: A visit to West Berlin by the U.S.-supported Shah of Iran provokes clashes between students and police. • The FCC requires that all U.S. radio and television stations that air ads for cigarettes also air warnings of smoking's dangers.

June 5: In a preemptive move, the Israeli air force and army strike deeply into Syria and the UAR. *See* June 6, 1967. • France conducts its first nuclear test away from the Sahara Desert—at the Moruroa Atoll in the Pacific Ocean.

Moshe Dayan, the heroic commander of Israeli forces during the war with Egypt in 1956, was named minister of defense by Prime Minister Levi Eshkol on the eve of the Six-Day War in 1967. Dayan led a full-scale battle against the United Arab Republic that helped assure victory for Israel. He later brokered the cease-fire. Dayan was part of the new guard of Israeli leaders who hoped to modernize Israeli political, social, and economic institutions. He went on to become an important peace negotiator in the 1970s.

Following a fierce battle with Jordanian troops on June 7, 1967, Israeli soldiers gained control of the Old City of Jerusalem and the Western Wall, the remnant of Solomon's Second Temple. Since Israel's 1948 wars with Arab states, the site of deep significance for Jewish people had been off-limits. After reclaiming the Wailing Wall on June 7, soldiers wept and prayed while Israeli civilians waited outside the city gates for a chance to touch the structure. Israeli workers immediately demolished the Arab Moghrabi Quarter, which was sited at the Wall and dated to about 1320. Later, buildings south of the old Quarter were razed, and the cleared area was paved.

Big Brother and the Holding Company bash away behind the star-making performance of Janis Joplin at the Monterey Pop Festival, held in Monterey, California, in June 1967. Though outdoor concerts featuring rock bands weren't new, never had such an array of international talent been assembled on such a large scale. Among the featured acts at the top of their game were Buffalo Springfield, Simon & Garfunkel, the Byrds, and Moby Grape. Performances by Joplin, the Who, Otis Redding, and Jimi Hendrix became the stuff of legend, prompting many to declare in 1967 that rock music had reached its zenith.

The Dirty Dozen, a 1967 film by director Robert Aldrich, created a new prototype for the over-the-top war movie. Lee Marvin plays the officer who commands a pack of criminals, rejects, and killers who are promised pardons when recruited for a suicide mission behind German lines. The testosterone-driven thrill ride includes Charles Bronson, Donald Sutherland, Trini Lopez, John Cassavetes, George Kennedy, and Ernest Borgnine, with Cassavetes earning an Oscar nomination. The next year, ABC-TV capitalized on the popular movie with a knock-off series called *Garrison's Gorillas.*

After Jayne Mansfield modeled for a 1954 photo shoot for General Electric, GE officials wouldn't allow her photos to be shown because they considered her "too sexy." Mansfield went on to become an immensely popular model, Broadway leading lady, and B movie star—a rival to Marilyn Monroe. From 1955 to 1967, she appeared in at least one film each year, including *The Girl Can't Help It, Will Success Spoil Rock Hunter?,* and *Too Hot to Handle.* On the foggy Louisiana night of June 29, 1967, with her star fading, the car in which Mansfield was traveling smashed into the back of a slowed truck. She and two companions died upon impact.

1967

June 6: Israeli forces roar across the Sinai Desert and into Jordan. UAR President Nasser closes the Suez Canal and severs diplomatic relations with the U.S. The UN Security Council adopts a Soviet proposal for a Middle East cease-fire. Israel agrees with the proposal on the condition that the Arab states do likewise. *See* June 7, 1967.

June 7: The air forces of Jordan, Syria, and Iraq are destroyed by Israel. Jordan agrees to the UN cease-fire proposal. *See* June 8, 1967.

June 8: The UAR agrees to the UN cease-fire proposal. • Israeli aircraft and torpedo boats mistakenly attack a U.S. communications ship about 15 miles off the Sinai coast, resulting in the deaths of 34 Americans. *See* June 9, 1967.

June 9: Israel has complete control of the Sinai Peninsula approaches to the Suez Canal. When Syrian artillery violates a cease-fire, Israeli armor and infantry drive deep into that country, breaching the West Wall. *See* mid-June 1967.

June 10: American film star Spencer Tracy dies at 67. His final film is the mildly controversial race drama *Guess Who's Coming to Dinner*.

June 12: In *Loving v. Virginia*, the U.S. Supreme Court strikes down laws in 16 states that prohibit interracial marriage.

Mid-June: Thousands of UAR soldiers stranded in the Sinai Desert following hostilities with Israel die of thirst.

June 16: The Monterey Pop Festival begins. The bill includes Jimi Hendrix, Laura Nyro, the Byrds, Jefferson Airplane, the Grateful Dead, Simon & Garfunkel, the Who, and Otis Redding.

June 17: Red China announces a successful test-detonation of a hydrogen bomb, that nation's first.

June 20: Heavyweight boxing champion Muhammad Ali is sentenced to five years in prison and fined $10,000 for draft evasion.

Along with sex and drugs, rock 'n' roll was integral to the psychedelic scene in San Francisco's Haight-Ashbury district. From the beginning, or soon after they began dropping acid, Jerry Garcia (*pictured*) and the Grateful Dead invented the new sound that perfectly matched the improvisational and anti-authoritarian ethos of the time. They played free concerts in the Haight and Golden Gate Park, and were the house band for Ken Kesey's legendary acid tests. They also played numerous concerts at the Avalon Ballroom. Garcia lived at 710 Ashbury, not far from where this photo was taken. Rock queen Janis Joplin also lived nearby, at 112 Lyon.

A Bad Trip

I WAS SITTING in a room with four or five friends, and someone else came into the room. It was a guy about sixteen or seventeen, wearing an alligator shirt and chinos and sneakers, a crewcut. He said hello to everybody in the room, and they said hello back. I said hello to him, and he said hello to me. And then I looked at him and he was me.

I was so scared that the top of my head felt like it had a hinge in the back and a beam of white light shot out, blew the top of the head off. My persona was on the beam of white light and we went all the way up into the sky, out of house, out of body, up into the stratosphere with the stars and everything. "Blow your mind." I got utterly petrified. I said, Get yourself together, man, you are going crazy. And I tried to talk, and I couldn't. So I started to crawl around the room.

My buddies were all zonked out. "What are you doing?" I said, "I have to go down to Haight Street." "Why?" "I have to tell everybody that there is a God. And that there is an objective reality. I have to spread the message." I'm crawling around on all fours. These guys popped up and grabbed me by my feet and pulled me back. "You go out to Haight Street like that and we're going to have to come get you out of the ward tomorrow."

—STAN KAPLAN, RECALLING AN LSD EXPERIENCE

The year 1967 marked the beginning of one of rock's longest running phenomenons. Following their inception as the Warlocks two years earlier, the Grateful Dead became the virtual house band for San Francisco's Haight-Ashbury, ground zero of the acid-drenched counterculture. Touring virtually nonstop thereafter, the band built a following with their idiosyncratic blend of folk, blues, and psychedelia. Jerry Garcia and his tie-dyed cohorts possessed adroit improvisational chops, rarely playing the same tune the same way twice.

The Cheshire Cat from *Alice in Wonderland* stares enigmatically in this widely popular 1967 poster by Joe McHugh. A prolific poster artist, McHugh and his wife, Irene, founded East Totem West, a small production company in San Francisco. McHugh wasn't afraid to admit that his artwork "had something to do with LSD." "It was that acid change of mind," he added. "And I felt proud of it, blessed to be part of that whole movement, privileged to have the opportunity."

Underground radio pioneer Tom Donahue rejected the overly commercial and formulaic Top 40 radio style of the 1950s and introduced a thought-provoking and often controversial medium. By 1967, AM radio—referred to by Donahue as a rotting corpse—had alienated many listeners by dictating instead of reflecting their musical tastes. The increased sophistication of rock music and its following was the impetus for a more experimental style that Donahue brought to the FM airwaves at KPMX in San Francisco. Providing the sound for a new generation, stations such as KPMX dared to play album-oriented rock songs longer than three minutes in length while featuring laid-back DJs who spoke *to* audiences instead of at them.

Young people paint flowers on each other's faces in San Francisco. Such scenes were common in the mid-1960s, as youth flooded into the district to "fly their freak flags." The Haight's funky, ornate Victorian houses and compact business district provided the perfect atmosphere for hippie culture to thrive. In the head shops, vegetarian cafés, and free clinic, hippies socialized and developed their collective endeavors. Off the street and behind the batik window curtains, in the rooms of recycled furniture and homemade artwork, they experimented with LSD and new sexual freedoms.

1967

Summer: The Haight-Ashbury district of San Francisco swells with up to 100,000 young people.

June 23–25: President Johnson and Soviet Premier Alexei Kosygin meet in Glassboro, New Jersey, to discuss a wide range of issues. Red China accuses the U.S. and USSR of colluding to harm China.

June 27: Israel's Knesset (parliament) passes legislation making Jerusalem a united city under Israeli control. *See* July 10, 1967.

June 29: American stage and screen star Jayne Mansfield, 34, is killed in a car crash in Louisiana.

July: The Stockholm Conference on Vietnam attracts more than 400 unofficial delegates from scores of nations. Moscow-based groups and nonaligned peace organizations are among those who participate.

July 2: Congress passes the Selective Service Act reform, which ends deferments for graduate students and puts them in a pool to be drafted.

July 7: U.S. and South Vietnamese troops take heavy losses in fighting near the U.S. Marine base at Con Thien, south of the DMZ. • Secretary of Defense Robert McNamara arrives in South Vietnam, where General Westmoreland presses him for additional troops.

July 10: Israel rejects a UN decree that its reconfiguration of Jerusalem is invalid.

July 12–17: The rumor of a white police officer killing a black taxi driver sparks a race riot in Newark, New Jersey. The National Guard is called to restore order. Rioting results in 26 fatalities, 1,200 injuries, and 1,400 arrests.

July 17: Revolutionary jazz saxophonist John Coltrane dies at 40.

July 18: A new law passed by the U.S. House of Representatives makes crossing state lines in order to incite a riot a federal offense. ➤

This young hippie woman epitomized the fashion values and basic attitudes of many young people in the late 1960s. The orange reflects an appreciation of natural health, while the long hair and subdued makeup suggest an embrace of natural, open spirituality and gender roles. The paisley clothing shows an appreciation of wild patterns and bright colors. And the sweet but enigmatic smile puts a human face on the "Summer of Love." These were the outward manifestations of an idealized philosophy that many young people, to their credit, successfully pursued, not as a lifestyle but as a way of life.

In her famous 1967 essay "Slouching Toward Bethlehem," Joan Didion wrote that in San Francisco "missing children were gathering and calling themselves 'hippies.'" Such songs as "San Francisco" by Scott McKenzie and increased media attention drew young people "with flowers in their hair" to the utopia by the bay. But many young people left home simply to escape the insufferable generational conflicts within their families. Their parents' suburban values clashed with the youth movement's rejection of the war, the draft, and what young people saw as the prevailing death culture of "Amerika." In San Francisco, many runaways found their freedom but also fell victim to drugs, disease, and/or hunger. The Haight-Ashbury police station's bulletin board displayed photographs of the area's many runaways.

Volunteers at the Haight-Ashbury free medical clinic unload donated supplies. Created in 1967 by San Francisco physician Dr. David Smith, the clinic was designed to tend to the health needs of the thousands of young people who flocked to the city. Smith, who firmly believed that "health care is a right, not a privilege," relied on a small grant from the city and the good graces of scores of donors. Licensed physicians and medical students worked at the clinic, treating a number of drug-related problems and other illnesses of the young and hip.

Members of the British rock band the Who hoped they would die before they got old—at least that's what they declared in their 1965 single "My Generation." For the Who (Keith Moon, Pete Townshend, John Entwistle, and Roger Daltrey, *left to right*), this was a reasonable assertion, given their onstage pyrotechnics and habit of destroying their instruments. But there was method behind the anarchy. Guitarist Pete Townshend's anthemic songwriting belied the band's image as a group of dissonant rowdies. His artistic ambitions would reach full flower with the "rock opera" *Tommy* in 1969, securing the band's place among rock's immortals. In 1978 drummer Keith Moon would fulfill the credo they had aspired to years earlier, dying of a drug overdose.

David Hockney helped launch the Pop Art movement in England during the 1960s with his technically sophisticated and humorous images. Yet he also spent much of the decade in the United States, where his art took on a more naturalistic look. Hockney's favorite subject matter included California scenes of young men, sun-soaked landscapes, and blue skies. With "Bigger Splash," Hockney created a play between the sterility of Southern California and the disruptive and exciting splash of an unseen diver.

1967

In 1966 the U.S. began bombing Hanoi, the capital city of North Vietnam, to demoralize the population and damage the north's industrial infrastructure. On May 4, *Nhan Dan,* the North Vietnamese Communist Party newspaper, explained that the people of North Vietnam were prepared to "sacrifice all." Facing 250 to 300 bombing flights a day, North Vietnam's citizens devised inventive strategies for survival, including this one-person bunker snapped on July 5. In villages near Hanoi, residents used dirt and bamboo ribbing to create durable bomb shelters.

Vietnamese farmer Vo Hieu stands next to a memorial marker in Vietnam's central province of Quang Ngai. The memorial says, "On July 5, 1967, American invaders in one operation savagely killed 23 civilians." The "invaders" were an elite U.S. Army unit known as Tiger Force. The platoon, composed of 45 highly trained paratroopers, was tasked to spy on and terminate suspected Communist units. According to a Pulitzer Prize-winning exposé by *The* (Toledo) *Blade* in 2003, the force actually was responsible for the murder and maiming of scores of innocent civilians from May to November 1967. In the 1970s the Pentagon investigated allegations of illegal behavior, but no charges were brought, and many of the pertinent records are missing from the National Archives.

Tiger Force: Army's Top Killers

I HEARD A RADIO transmission from battalion. They had been asked what to do with the prisoner we had. The reply that came back was something like, take care of them like you would a horse with a broken leg, or words to that effect. Green was told to take care of the prisoner. Green made a big deal about it, letting the prisoner know that he was going to be killed. The prisoner was tied down and gagged. Green actually tortured him with a knife, jabbing him in the throat, cutting it a little at a time, finally cutting his throat and killing him. I cannot say specifically who witnessed this besides myself, but there were quite a few people around....

We, Tiger Force, were told by the officers that when we went into an area anything moving, man, woman, or child, was to be killed, as they were not supposed to be there. We were constantly being told how good we were, how our body count was always the highest and what a good job we were doing.

—TIGER FORCE SOLDIER MICHAEL J. ALLUMS

The Riots of '67

A man lies dead on a Newark, New Jersey, sidewalk during rioting that lasted from July 12 to 17, 1967. In the city with the nation's highest black unemployment rate, high residential segregation, and a notoriously corrupt white city administration, it took only the rumor that a white policeman had beaten a black taxi driver to touch off the explosion. Governor Richard J. Hughes called in the National Guard, which fired more than 13,000 rounds during the riot. Approximately 1,200 people were injured and 25 were killed.

Just days after the Newark riot, the city of Detroit erupted in flames. A police raid on an illegal saloon on July 23 triggered six days of firebombing, violence, and looting. African-Americans expressed their rage over police brutality, housing discrimination, and the city's black unemployment, which was double the national average. The violence grew beyond the control of Michigan Governor George Romney, requiring President Johnson to call in the National Guard. With tanks and machine guns, troops occupied the city and quelled the uprising, firing up to 150,000 rounds. Ultimately, 4,000 people were arrested and 43 people died.

AT AROUND 3 A.M. ON JULY 23, 1967, Detroit police raided an illegal after-hours club, arresting all of the 80-plus African-American patrons. As the suspects were rounded up and stuffed into patrol cars, residents of the area began to gather at the scene. By 8 A.M. more than 3,000 people filled the streets, and soon bottles and rocks were flying and buildings burning.

For five days during that hot July, Detroiters—most of whom were black—burned and looted. After the smoke cleared, 43 people lay dead, more than 1,000 were injured, and about 4,000 had been arrested.

Detroit was only one of numerous American cities that witnessed uprisings. Newark, Cleveland, Louisville, Washington, New York, Atlanta, Birmingham, Minneapolis, Cincinnati, Buffalo, San Francisco, Boston, Wichita, and Nashville all suffered varying degrees of riot-related anger and damage during the summer of 1967.

Tensions in black communities had been brewing for years. Due to discriminatory housing practices and deindustrialization (which led to unemployment), inner-city African-Americans were packed into decaying ghettos and had few, if any, opportunities. Nevertheless, most whites blamed the riots on African-Americans. Detroit Mayor Jerome Cavanagh claimed that "a carnival spirit" drove the rioters and that there was "a sense of euphoria in the air." Black Power proponent Ron Karenga voiced a different viewpoint: "[W]e have to distinguish between riots and revolts," he said. "Riots are illegal. A revolt is legitimate because it is what a people must do in order to express self-defense, self-determination, and self-direction."

By the end of the summer, President Lyndon Johnson had formed the National Advisory Commission on Civil Disorders. Headed by Illinois Governor Otto Kerner, the commission issued an exhaustive report on the causes of the urban crisis. The report stated: "White racism is essentially responsible for the explosive mixture which has been accumulating in our cities since the end of World War II." The report further noted that black ghettoization and white exodus only compounded the situation.

Initially, the Kerner commission's findings fell largely on deaf ears. It was not until the assassination of Martin Luther King, Jr., and another round of devastating riots in 1968 that Congress finally took action. The result was the Fair Housing Act of 1968, which officially made discrimination illegal when selling or renting property.

1967

July 19: A U.S. Boeing 727 airliner collides in midair with an off-course Cessna 310 above Hendersonville, North Carolina. All 82 people aboard the planes, including three in the Cessna, are killed. • A racially motivated riot hits Minneapolis.

July 20: The first National Black Power Conference is held in Newark, New Jersey.

July 22: Important U.S. poet and biographer Carl Sandburg dies at 89.

July 23–28: In Detroit, police raid an illegal African-American drinking establishment, angering blacks in the area. A riot ensues, resulting in 43 deaths, 1,200 injuries, and 4,000 arrests.

July 24: Racial violence hits Cambridge, Maryland, after SNCC Chairman H. Rap Brown urges an audience of 400 to "burn this town down." In the ensuing fracas, Brown in nicked in the head by shotgun pellets. *See* August 14, 1967.

July 27: President Johnson appoints Illinois Governor Otto Kerner to head an investigative committee charged with explaining the rash of racially motivated riots.

July 29: The USS *Forrestal* is badly damaged by fire while off the Vietnamese coast; 134 sailors are killed, and 60 planes and helicopters are destroyed or damaged.

August: The first issue of *The Los Angeles Advocate* (which will become *The Advocate*), the first national gay and lesbian news magazine, hits newsstands. • The British Embassy in Peking is sacked by Red Guards. • The Dior fashion house introduces the maxi-coat.

August 1: FBI Director J. Edgar Hoover tells President Johnson that "outside agitators" played key roles in the summer's race riots. • Washington, D.C., is struck by race riots.

"People are bitter. White people gyp you all the time. I went to a gas station at Wyandotte and Michigan to get a tire changed. It was raining and the man wouldn't change it. Then he wanted to charge me $12 to change it because I'm a Negro. That kind of stuff is wrong. I've been looking for this riot to happen for years."

—Detroit auto worker

President Johnson (*center*) ponders his options on July 24 while his advisers communicate with federal troops, who are trying to quell the riot in Detroit. Johnson struggled with the constitutional aspects of sending troops into Detroit. Republicans, especially Michigan Governor George Romney, later accused the President of playing politics with his hesitation to assert federal power. Soon after the riots, Johnson appointed Governor Otto Kerner of Illinois to chair the National Advisory Commission on Civil Disorders. The commission eventually would determine that white racism was the root cause of the insurrections.

"If America don't come around, we're going to burn America down!" An hour after SNCC Chairman H. Rap Brown spoke those words to a crowd in Cambridge, Maryland, on July 24, 1967, local residents exchanged gunfire with police. Several hours later, a fire destroyed a black school and most of the city's black businesses. The next day, the FBI arrested Brown, charging him with flight to escape prosecution for inciting arson in the city. Maryland Governor Spiro Agnew blamed Brown for the riot and vowed, "It shall now be the policy of this state to immediately arrest any person inciting to riot, and to not allow that person to finish his vicious speech."

Political cartoonist Herblock (Herbert Block) offers his take on congressional reaction to the widespread urban disturbances in 1967. He compares modern America to Rome under Nero, who fiddled while the fire he purportedly started burned down the city. According to Herblock, the 90th Congress had failed to address underlying social and economic problems that were the root causes of racial conflagrations in many American cities. He implies that at least some action on urban-assistance programs and gun control would help prevent future problems.

Fiddler

On July 29, 1967, during her first combat deployment off the coast of Vietnam in the Gulf of Tonkin, the aircraft carrier USS *Forrestal* became the site of a tragic fire. At 10:52 A.M., a Zuni rocket accidentally fired from a parked F-4 Phantom, streaked across the flight deck and ruptured the 400-gallon fuel tank of an A-4D Skyhawk. Fuel from the tank ignited and spread over the deck of the carrier, engulfing planes and men in flames and setting off multiple explosions. The accident killed 134 crew members.

Vietnam Summer

ON APRIL 23, 1967, television camera crews followed Martin Luther King, Jr., and Dr. Benjamin Spock as they went house to house in Cambridge, Massachusetts, talking to families about the Vietnam War. This canvassing of homes kicked off a program they called Vietnam Summer, in which college-age students across the country reached out to American families on the war issue, hoping to mobilize more and more people against it. But, as King and Spock walked the streets between homes, a group of young men heckled them. One carried a sign that said, "King Get the Hell Out of Harvard." Divisions over the war could not have been more apparent.

Despite more than two years of growing protest against the American war in Vietnam, peace activists grew increasingly frustrated in 1967 as the war's escalation continued. U.S. troop levels had risen to more than 500,000. Organizers designed Vietnam Summer to turn politically inactive middle-class Americans into a powerful antiwar lobby by sending thousands of volunteers into hundreds of communities across the country to talk about the war. The idea had first been conceived by Gar Alperovitz, a fellow at the Kennedy School of Government's Institute of Politics at Harvard University. He modeled it after Freedom Summer, the 1964 civil rights project that injected more than a thousand college students into Mississippi to run Freedom Schools and register voters.

Organizers chose Cambridge as the national headquarters for Vietnam Summer and staffed it with 11 people and 100 recruiters. Eventually, more than 4,000 volunteers took to the streets of 770 of their own communities as part of the nationwide project. The effect of Vietnam Summer on the American people is virtually impossible to gauge, though most scholars have concluded that it did not succeed as well as its movement forebear.

August 3: President Johnson announces that another 45,000 to 50,000 American troops will be sent to Vietnam by July 1968. ● Johnson requests from Congress a 10 percent income-tax surcharge, to help limit inflation.

August 9: The U.S. Senate Armed Services Committee begins hearings concerning the influence of civilian advisers on military planning.

August 14: SNCC Chairman H. Rap Brown is indicted by a Maryland grand jury on charges of inciting to riot in Cambridge, Maryland, the previous month.

August 15: Martin Luther King, Jr., calls for a massive campaign of nonviolent civil disobedience so that African-American demands will be met. ● A large Picasso sculpture is unveiled at Chicago's Civic Center. It will be variously described as a baboon, a dog, and a human being.

August 16: The Senate Foreign Relations Committee undertakes an investigation of the 1964 Gulf of Tonkin resolution to determine whether it provides sufficient basis for U.S. policy in Vietnam. *See* November 16, 1967.

August 17: Broadcasting from Havana, Cuba, black American civil rights activist Stokely Carmichael exhorts U.S. blacks to arm for "total revolution."

August 18: California Governor Ronald Reagan says the U.S. should get out of Vietnam because "too many qualified targets have been put off limits to bombing."

August 19–23: A race riot strikes New Haven, Connecticut.

August 21: The U.S. State Department admits that two American jets have been shot down over China after veering off course.

August 24: The Beatles meet Maharishi Mahesh Yogi at a lecture on transcendental meditation in London. They will study and train with him.

Bonnie and Clyde, starring Warren Beatty and Faye Dunaway, was a youth allegory that appealed to the Sixties generation. The 1967 film used "mod" nostalgia, shockingly graphic violence, and the portrayal of sexual confusion to tell the story of the infamous bank-robbing couple. At first panned by many critics and undercut by Warner Bros., director Arthur Penn's film struck a chord with its tragicomic tale of youthful rebellion on the road. Critic Bosley Crowther wrote that the film conveyed "a sense of the pathos of youngsters who . . . recklessly play with fire without care or a thought of what they're doing until they are fatally burned."

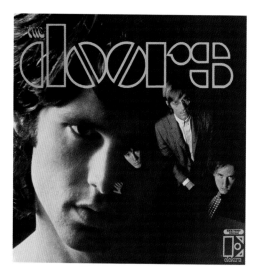

In 1967 the Doors' self-titled album and their song "Light My Fire" were both top-10 hits. The band's simple, tight combination of drum, guitar, and organ put to music the mystical and often dark themes of death and insanity that characterized the lyrics of singer Jim Morrison (*dominant image*). Starting out as the house band at the Whiskey-A-Go-Go in Los Angeles, the Doors soon developed a cult following among counterculture youth, who were attracted to the band's psychedelic themes and Morrison's outrageous behavior on stage. On December 9, 1967, Morrison was arrested in New Haven, Connecticut, for public obscenity during a concert. Other arrests followed. The Doors were a major force in rock music until Morrison died in Paris of heart failure on July 3, 1971.

Throughout 1967 New Orleans District Attorney Jim Garrison grabbed headlines with his flamboyant style and numerous accusations of conspiracy surrounding the assassination of President John F. Kennedy. In 1967 Garrison prosecuted a businessman named Clay Shaw, linking him to Kennedy assassin Lee Harvey Oswald and to a wide-ranging conspiracy involving Cubans, former CIA operatives, and right-wing Americans in a coordinated plot to kill the president in Dallas. (Shaw was quickly acquitted.) In a *Playboy* magazine interview, Garrison claimed that a "precision guerrilla team of at least seven men" was directly involved in Kennedy's murder. His challenge to the official story of the Warren Report deepened suspicions and bred conspiracy theories at a time when many Americans had begun to question their government's motives in Vietnam and at home.

In his formative years, Jimi Hendrix was deeply influenced by blues singer Muddy Waters and rocker Little Richard, in whose band he played. A revolutionary guitar player, Hendrix formed his own group, the Jimi Hendrix Experience, in 1967. Their debut album, *Are You Experienced,* became a major influence on the counterculture, especially after an appearance at the Monterey Pop Festival that year. Cuts from the album, including "Purple Haze" and "Foxey Lady," became cult classics. Hendrix rocked the nation with his electric performance of "The Star-Spangled Banner" at the 1969 Woodstock Festival, in which his guitar wailed, soared, and echoed the sound of bombs bursting in air. Hendrix died of a drug overdose in 1970 at age 27.

Actor David Janssen starred in television's longest-running chase, *The Fugitive.* Loosely based on the sensational Dr. Sam Sheppard murder case of the 1950s, Janssen played Dr. Richard Kimble, a man wrongly accused of murdering his wife. Escaping incarceration, he doggedly pursued the real culprit—an elusive "one-armed man"—across the country. Superbly scripted and acted, *The Fugitive* kept viewers riveted. The series finale in 1967, in which the pursuer finally confronts his quarry, was watched by a record 72 percent of the viewing audience.

August 25: Leftists Abbie Hoffman and Jerry Rubin enter the New York Stock Exchange and shower the trade floor with dollar bills. Traders scramble for the money. • American Nazi Party leader George Lincoln Rockwell is shot to death as he leaves a laundromat in Arlington, Virginia. The shooter is a disgruntled aide.

August 27: Brian Epstein, 32, discoverer and manager of the Beatles, commits suicide.

August 30: The New York chapter of the National Organization for Women pickets *The New York Times*, protesting the paper's sex-segregated job listings.

August 31: The National Conference for a New Politics opens a five-day convention in Chicago. Some 3,000 delegates from leftist, community, and civil rights groups fail in their attempt to create a joint presidential election strategy for 1968.

Late August: FBI Director J. Edgar Hoover instructs his counter-intelligence program to "expose, disrupt, misdirect, [and] discredit" the Black Panthers.

September: Chinese dictator Mao Tse-tung tells the Chinese people that nothing will be gained if China is allowed to fall into two, warring philosophical camps. • The Thai government sends 2,500 men of the Queen's Cobra Division to South Vietnam to fight against Vietcong and North Vietnamese regulars.

September 3: The military-backed ticket of Nguyen Van Thieu (president) and Nguyen Cao Ky (vice president) easily wins reelection in South Vietnamese general elections. The U.S. State Department vigorously defends the election's integrity.

September 11–October 31: Two miles south of the DMZ, U.S. Marines are besieged by the North Vietnamese Army at Con Thien. The U.S. responds with 281,000 rounds and B-52 air strikes, killing more than 2,000 NVA.

At 5:00 A.M. on September 3, 1967, Swedish drivers officially switched from the left to the right side of the road. As this scene from Stockholm attests, the adjustment wasn't easy. Sweden was the last of the western nations—except Ireland and Great Britain—to switch to the right side. H-hour (for the Swedish word *Höger*, which means *right*), the name given to a mammoth $120 million undertaking, included switching signs and signals nationwide in an instant. But Swedes had been prepared. The Walt Disney Company had even created short films starring Donald Duck to educate schoolchildren about the hazards they might face.

A 1966 raid on a Los Angeles gay bar stirred gay pride activist Dick Michaels to action. Working with partner Bill Rand, Michaels published the first issue of *The Los Angeles Advocate* in summer 1967. The publication tackled a range of issues targeting what was then a largely underground community, with few daring to go public. By 1969 *The Advocate* went national. That same year, the Stonewall Riots in Greenwich Village galvanized the burgeoning gay rights movement, with *The Advocate* on the front lines to rally the troops.

U.S. officials estimated that at least 180 Americans had been taken prisoner by February 1967, either by North Vietnamese or by the Vietcong. That year, the Pentagon also listed 139 servicemen captured by the enemy and 335 missing. Many of the missing were pilots shot down over North Vietnam. Here, a young North Vietnamese woman or girl marches an airman out of the jungle at gunpoint in September. This photo is evidence of a nation totally mobilized for war against the Americans, who had been bombing the country relentlessly.

In September 1967, Black Power advocate Stokely Carmichael outraged many Americans when he traveled to North Vietnam to meet with officials in Hanoi. Here he confers with Truong Chinh, chairman of the Committee of the National Assembly. Carmichael also met with Hoang Bac, assistant secretary general of the Vietnamese Committee of Solidarity with Afro-Asian People. "In a sense, our struggle is a common struggle," Carmichael told his hosts, "and in this sense we are comrades." He went on to assert that like the Vietnamese government, he wanted to "stop cold the greatest destroyers of humanity, the American leadership."

Agent Orange

WHILE COVERING THE VIETNAM WAR, journalist John Pilger noticed genetically deformed children in villages in the Mekong Delta. "[W]henever I asked about them," he recalled, "people pointed to the sky; one man scratched in the dust a good likeness of a bulbous C-130 aircraft, spraying."

In an effort to demoralize and uncover the enemy, U.S. forces laid waste to huge areas of South Vietnam with chemical defoliants such as Agent Orange. One of 15 defoliants used in the war (chemical giant Monsanto was the largest supplier), Agent Orange killed broadleaf tropical foliage. U.S. aircraft rained herbicide liquid down on people and jungles below. Four planes could cover a 1,000-foot-wide swath of jungle in a single pass.

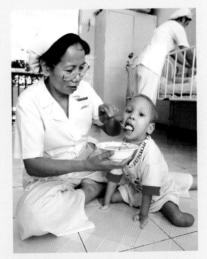

The child of parents exposed to Agent Orange

From 1962 to 1971, American forces sprayed more than 20 million gallons of Agent Orange alone, defoliating more than 5,182,000 acres of land. After the war, the U.S. officially recognized that the dioxin in Agent Orange caused Hodgkin's disease, soft tissue carcinoma, and other diseases. By century's end, about a million Vietnamese had been affected by defoliants. About 50,000 of them were children born with serious deformities as a result of their parents' exposure to the chemicals. Numerous fetuses never reached full term.

"Perhaps the most gruesome legacy of Agent Orange is to be found in a locked room in Tu Du Obstetrical and Gynecological Hospital in Saigon," wrote journalist Hugh Warwick. "Here the walls are lined with jars containing aborted and full term foetuses."

September 17: The Doors perform "Light My Fire" on *The Ed Sullivan Show.* Singer Jim Morrison ignores Sullivan's request to omit the supposedly drug-related lyric "higher," and instead *emphasizes* the word during the performance. *See* December 9, 1967.

September 20: Britain's 58,000-ton *Queen Elizabeth II* is launched. *See* September 22, 1967.

September 22: The British ocean liner *Queen Mary* sails for Britain from New York for the final time. The ship subsequently will be purchased by Long Beach, California, for use as a hotel and museum.

September 25: The Dali Lama arrives in Tokyo, his first trip abroad since leaving Chinese-occupied Tibet for India in 1959.

September 29: American novelist Carson McCullers dies at 50.

October: Dr. Benjamin Spock, Reverend William Sloane Coffin, Jr., and others return draft cards to the U.S. Justice Department.

October 1: *Wall of Respect,* a large mural on Chicago's South Side, is dedicated. The dramatic wall depicts images of accomplished African-Americans.

October 2: Thurgood Marshall is sworn in as the U.S. Supreme Court's first African-American justice. • Narcotics agents raid the Grateful Dead's house in the Haight-Ashbury and arrest band members Bob Weir and Pigpen. • Carl Yastrzemski of the Boston Red Sox captures the last Triple Crown of the century with a .326 batting average, 44 home runs, and 121 runs batted in.

October 3: American folk singer Woody Guthrie dies at 55.

October 8: Cuban revolutionary Ernesto "Che" Guevara, 39, is mortally wounded in Bolivia during a battle between guerrillas and the Bolivian army. He will die the following day.

From 1967 to 1970, Sally Field (*above*) played a former surfer girl turned nun in the popular ABC situation comedy *The Flying Nun.* Like other 1960s fantasy sitcoms, such as *Bewitched* and *I Dream of Jeanie, The Flying Nun* evinced the psychedelic tendencies of television writers and producers at the time. In a decade full of popular nun pictures—such as *The Sound of Music* and *The Singing Nun*—Field played Sister Bertrille, a nun who, when the wind was right, could put on her cornette and lift off into the sky.

Sidney Poitier (*left*) and Rod Steiger (*right*) starred in the 1967 movie *In the Heat of the Night,* a film so thick with racial tension that it wasn't screened in the Deep South. Steiger, a bigoted small-town sheriff, spars with Poitier, an educated, northern police detective who is drawn into a murder investigation while visiting his mother in Sparta, Mississippi. The film portrays American racism and injustice as well as the possibility of reconciliation, as the two strong characters work together to solve the murder mystery. In one famous moment, a wealthy southern racist slaps Poitier in the face. Poitier's response, against the backdrop of riots and racial unrest, electrified audiences when he immediately returned the blow. Both the film and Steiger won Academy Awards.

Marines move a wounded comrade during a siege of their hilltop outpost near Con Thien in South Vietnam, two miles south of the demilitarized zone (DMZ). During their long-range artillery duel with North Vietnamese soldiers in September and October, Marines were pounded with 42,000 rounds of ammunition. The U.S. responded with 281,000 rounds along with B-52 air strikes, finally driving the enemy back into North Vietnam on October 4. The Communists ultimately saw losses of more than 2,000 soldiers.

Thurgood Marshall (*top right*), the famous NAACP lawyer who argued the *Brown v. Board of Education* case in 1954, was named U.S. solicitor general in 1965 and sworn in as a U.S. Supreme Court justice in October 1967. Marshall became the first African-American to serve on the nation's highest court. As a justice, he brought to the court an ongoing commitment to equal protection under the law and a frequent voice of dissent in a court dominated by conservatives. Until his retirement in 1991, Marshall significantly advanced civil liberties and pushed for racial and gender affirmative action.

Haitian dictator François Duvalier was nicknamed "Papa Doc" because of his medical background and his self-image as the father of his country. Duvalier was elected president in 1957, with the support of the military, and named himself president for life in 1964. His regime was enormously corrupt and oppressive, killing as many as 30,000 people. Political opponents were routinely executed while his brutal personal militia, the Tonton Macoutes (meaning *bogeymen* in Haitian Creole), terrorized the public. After bombs were detonated near Duvalier's palace in 1967, 20 *Garde Présidentielle* officers were executed. Duvalier died in 1971 and was succeeded by his son, "Baby Doc."

October 11: A major exhibition of works by Pablo Picasso opens at New York's Museum of Modern Art.

October 12: The St. Louis Cardinals defeat the Boston Red Sox 7–2 in Game 7 of the World Series.

October 16: The antiwar movement kicks off "Stop the Draft" week at Selective Service offices across the country. Forty demonstrators, including folk singer Joan Baez, are arrested.

October 18: Job recruiters from Dow Chemical, a manufacturer of the war weapon napalm, are driven away from the University of Wisconsin-Madison by student protesters.

October 20: An all-white jury in Philadelphia, Mississippi, convicts seven men of conspiracy in the 1964 murders of three civil rights workers.

October 21: More than 50,000 antiwar activists, led by David Dellinger, demonstrate at the Lincoln Memorial and the Pentagon; 400 are arrested. Poet Ed Sanders, the San Francisco Diggers, and others park a flatbed truck outside the Pentagon and perform an "exorcism," chanting, "Demons, out!"

October 23: The American Basketball Association (ABA), a rival to the NBA, tips off its first season with its trademark red, white, and blue basketball.

October 26: The federal government eliminates draft deferments for anybody who violates draft laws or interferes with recruitment.

October 27: Four people, including Father Philip Berrigan, enter the Baltimore Customs House and pour duck blood on draft records.

October 28: Black Panther Party Defense Minister Huey Newton is charged with murder, intent to commit murder, and kidnapping following a traffic stop in West Oakland, California, during which one police officer was killed by gunfire and another wounded. ➤

Las Vegas odds-makers tagged the Boston Red Sox as a 100–1 longshot to win the 1967 world championship. However, they underestimated the power of Yaz. By smashing .326 with 44 homers and 121 runs batted in, outfielder Carl Yastrzemski won the American League Triple Crown—the last in the majors in the 20th century. Moreover, his theatrics in the final 12 games of the season (.523 with five homers) propelled Boston to the World Series. The Red Sox lost to St. Louis in seven games, ending what New Englanders had dubbed the "Impossible Dream" season.

By October 6, 1967, the "Summer of Love" was well over, as was the scene in the overly hyped hippie enclave of Haight-Ashbury in San Francisco. The happy times had given way to a season of intense media scrutiny, frequent police busts, gawking tourists in Gray Line tour buses, and a steady influx of the nation's lost teenagers in search of escape and stimulation. The unique hip utopia that had been blooming since mid-decade was dying on the vine, and many hippies had already headed out to rural communes. To celebrate the "death of the hippie," some members of the community decided to hold a mock funeral. They carried a faux dead hippie through the streets before staging a mournful "burial."

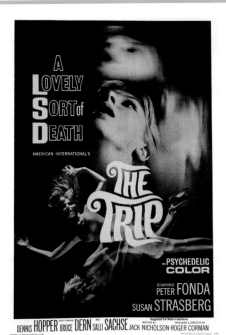

As Hollywood's big-studio system began to lose its grip on the 1960s youth audience, a new breed of film-makers, writers, and actors stepped into the vacuum. Roger Corman, working with a Jack Nicholson screenplay, directed the 1967 film *The Trip,* starring Peter Fonda and Dennis Hopper. As part of the Fonda character's "freak out," the film attempts to convey an acid trip with kaleidoscopic color patterns, images of painted women wandering on the beach, and a cloaked figure on horseback—all accompanied by an acid rock score. *The Trip* was successful enough to give Hopper, Fonda, and Nicholson the green light for their next project together, *Easy Rider.*

Scenes such as this one from *I Am Curious (Yellow)* explain why the film piqued people's interest in the late 1960s. Released in Sweden in 1967, (but not in the U.S. until 1969), the film combined documentary footage with a fictional story as it explored contemporary Swedish mores, especially sexual ones. Because it included brief glimpses of full frontal nudity, it offended many Americans but nonetheless played to full houses.

Sgt. Pepper

I F YOU LOOK REALLY CLOSELY at the album cover, you'll see it, confided Beatle John Lennon: "Two of us are flying, and two aren't." Evidently, he and George Harrison had "dropped acid" for the photo shoot.

Behind the cover of the Beatles' *Sgt. Pepper's Lonely Hearts Club Band,* released on June 1, 1967, lay an even bolder message: The Fab Four had clearly embraced the counterculture. The hallucinatory images in "Lucy in the Sky with Diamonds" more than hinted at the LSD experience, as did its presumed acronym, "LSD." The song "A Day in the Life," which Lennon described as "the only one in the album written as a deliberate provocation to people," was banned by the BBC for implied drug references.

Sgt. Pepper is notable for launching the "art rock" trend of concept albums. Yet its enduring appeal owes more to its lush orchestration and the nostalgia-tinged sensibility of such ballads as "When I'm 64" and "She's Leaving Home"—the theme song of every female runaway who made the exodus to the Haight-Ashbury that summer.

From the depth of our hearts we sing

1967

In October 1967 Che Guevara was killed in Bolivia at the hands of troops trained by the CIA and the U.S. Green Berets. Guevara, the charismatic hero and skilled guerrilla tactician of the Cuban Revolution in the 1950s, eventually tired of his role in Cuba's new government. He renounced his citizenship and vanished from the Cuban scene in spring 1965. Rumors had it that he had gone to Vietnam or the Congo, keeping the flame of revolution and anti-imperialism burning. Che's departure from Cuba and the mystery of his fate appealed to New Left radicals who sought out uncompromising rebel heroes on the run. Che's famous bearded visage appeared on T-shirts and posters throughout the decade.

During the nationwide "Stop the Draft Week" in mid-October 1967, the SDS and other groups launched efforts to disrupt the government's ability to wage war. Students from the Bay Area went to the source, the induction center in downtown Oakland where young men were daily unloaded from buses and processed through the system. From October 16 to 20, different protest groups gathered at the entrance of the center and put their bodies before the wheels of the war machine. Some women held signs that read, "Women say yes to men who say no," and the crowd chanted, "Don't go! Don't go!" During the first day of protest (*pictured*), 124 pacifists were quietly arrested. The next day, more than 2,000 militants around the center clashed with police in riot gear.

Corporations such as Dow Chemical, Honeywell, Lockheed, and General Dynamics directly profited from the war in Vietnam. Increasingly, protesters made the connection between homegrown companies and the carnage abroad. Dow Chemical in particular became the object of protesters' rage for its manufacture of napalm—the jellied gasoline that the military used to incinerate people and foliage in Vietnam. On October 18, students protested at the University of Wisconsin–Madison against the on-campus recruiting activities of Dow Chemical. Riot police tried to control unruly protesters, who chanted, "Dow burns babies!"

During "Stop the Draft Week," young men across the country burned their draft cards and activists clashed with police. The week climaxed with the March on the Pentagon on October 21. More than 50,000 people, including a mixture of radical student activists and the previously apolitical counterculture, joined together to bring the war home to the war-makers. The crowd assembled at the Lincoln Memorial to hear folk singer Phil Ochs and listen to speeches before moving across the Arlington Bridge to their destination: the Pentagon.

On October 21, Military Police were called out to guard the Pentagon from the onslaught of activists. The soldiers faced a diverse mix of angry protesters—Black Power advocates, the Diggers (a counterculture group), Vietnam Veterans Against the War, and middle-class liberals. During struggles with police that day, more than 600 people were arrested for trespassing. Another 47 were hospitalized after being beaten and tear-gassed by police.

Father Philip Berrigan (*pictured*) and his brother, Father Daniel Berrigan, both engaged in radical protest against the war in Vietnam. Philip, who also worked in the civil rights movement, became a leading voice of nonviolent revolution in the United States. On October 27, 1967, he and three other protesters entered

a Baltimore Selective Service office and poured animal blood onto hundreds of files. On another occasion, he and others raided a different Selective Service office and burned agency files. Berrigan was sentenced to nine years in prison for both acts and remained a controversial figure after his release.

October 31: A feminist group that later will be called the New York Radical Women begins in New York.

November: The United Kingdom abandons plans to build an airfield on Aldabia Island, in the Indian Ocean, when it becomes clear that construction would destroy the world's only natural habitat of giant tortoises.

November 4–22: A costly battle for Hill 875 in Vietnam's Central Highlands at Dak To, near the Cambodian border, ends with the U.S. Army's capture of the hill.

November 7: Black mayors are elected in Cleveland (Carl Stokes) and Gary, Indiana (Richard Hatcher).

November 9: U.S. Surveyor 6 makes a soft landing on the moon. • The first issue of *Rolling Stone,* a music and counterculture magazine published and edited by 21-year-old Jann Wenner, hits newsstands.

November 11: The Vietcong release three captured African-American GIs in Cambodia. A VC radio broadcast describes the gesture as showing "solidarity and support" for the freedom struggle of American blacks.

November 15: USAF Major Michael Adams becomes the first fatality of the X-15 rocket-plane program when he is unable to pull out of a descent begun at 260,000 feet.

November 16: The U.S. Senate Foreign Relations Committee approves a resolution that U.S. engagement in Vietnam be restricted, and that President Johnson bring the conflict before the UN Security Council for possible resolution. President Johnson rails against critics of his Vietnam policy, labeling them "extremely dangerous" and "irresponsible."

November 23: Attendees at a national Black Youth Conference, including UCLA basketball superstar Lew Alcindor, vote to boycott the Olympic Games.

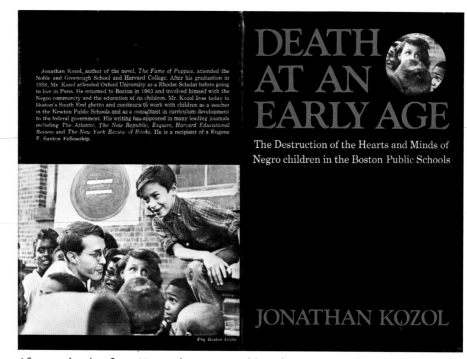

Jonathan Kozol, author of the novel, *The Fume of Poppies,* attended the Noble and Greenough School and Harvard College. After his graduation in 1958, Mr. Kozol attended Oxford University as a Rhodes Scholar before going to live in Paris. He returned to Boston in 1963 and involved himself with the Negro community and the education of its children. Mr. Kozol lives today in Boston's South End ghetto and continues to work with children as a teacher in the Newton Public Schools and as a consultant in curriculum development to the federal government. His writing has appeared in many leading journals including *The Atlantic, The New Republic, Esquire, Harvard Educational Review* and *The New York Review of Books.* He is a recipient of a Eugene F. Saxton Fellowship.

DEATH AT AN EARLY AGE

The Destruction of the Hearts and Minds of Negro children in the Boston Public Schools

JONATHAN KOZOL

After graduating from Harvard, a young, white educator named Jonathan Kozol began teaching at elementary schools in Boston's mainly black Roxbury district. Kozol was shocked by inadequate and rotting buildings, overcrowded classrooms, corporal punishment of students, and the outdated racist books and readers that stunted and scarred students and their potential for success. In his classroom, Kozol challenged the prevailing belief within the school system that black students were unteachable or stupid. He was fired for his ideas and methods, but in 1967 he published *Death at an Early Age,* which describes these conditions for a public audience. An immediate sensation, the book made Kozol a leader in educational and social reform.

Novelist Richard Brautigan became a major cult figure in the 1960s, largely due to his 1967 book *Trout Fishing in America.* A series of loosely joined short sketches, the book is unified only by continuing references to trout fishing, especially in the author's native Northwest. (The references include a character, a hotel, and a book all named "Trout Fishing in America.") One critic said Brautigan was like Ernest Hemingway but with "the disillusioned eyes of a flower child." The book certainly appealed to the puckish, self-referential, and modernistic side of the counterculture.

Introduced in late 1967, *Rolling Stone* soon would become the first widely distributed American publication to give serious coverage to rock music and the counterculture. Conceived by Jann Wenner and music critic Ralph Gleason, *Rolling Stone* intentionally broke away from traditional music trade papers and fan magazines with cutting-edge interviews and intelligent commentary. Wenner also had a knack for hiring extraordinary talent. Early contributors included photographer Annie Liebowitz and writers Hunter S. Thompson, Abe Peck, and Tom Hayden. Now an American institution, *Rolling Stone* succeeded in the late 1960s as the voice for a new generation.

George Segal was one of the Pop artists of the 1960s, along with Andy Warhol, Roy Lichtenstein, and others. However, his work drew from more personal and humanistic sources. Early in the decade, he began to communicate images of the American vernacular by creating humanlike figures out of bandages and white plaster. The plaster and mixed-media piece seen here, "Cinema," was completed in 1963. Like much of Segal's work, it communicates a peculiar sort of loneliness. In Chicago in 1968, Segal would hold his first one-man show of his fascinating and impassive sculptures.

Rock's first "super group" came into being in 1966 when alumni of the Graham Bond Organisation and John Mayall's Blue-breakers joined up to form Cream. Former Yardbird Eric Clapton was a renowned blues prodigy in England before he, Jack Bruce, and Ginger Baker decided to form a "power trio." Their heavy sound, exemplified by extended soloing, laid the groundwork for other rock bands. *Disraeli Gears,* featuring the hits "Strange Brew" and "Sunshine of Your Love," typified their psychedelic blues approach.

November 27: Craig Rodwell opens Oscar Wilde's in lower Manhattan. It is believed to be the first gay bookstore in the U.S. • The Chicago Women's Liberation Group conducts its first meeting.

November 29: President Johnson announces the resignation of Secretary of Defense Robert McNamara, who has accepted an offer to serve as president of the World Bank (International Bank for Reconstruction and Development). • U.S. Treasury Secretary Henry Fowler tells the House Ways and Means Committee of "substantial" recent losses of U.S. gold reserves.

November 30: Senator Eugene McCarthy (D–MN) announces his candidacy for the 1968 Democratic presidential nomination.

December: The National Organization for Women (NOW) holds demonstrations at Equal Employment Opportunity Commission locations across the country, including New York City, San Francisco, and Chicago. • The Navajo Indian reservation at Fort Sumner, New Mexico, is snowed in, necessitating a government airdrop of food, hay, and medical supplies.

December 3: A South African surgical team headed by Dr. Christiaan Barnard successfully transplants the heart of a 24-year-old female accident victim, Denise Darvall, into the chest of 55-year-old Louis Washkansky. *See* December 21, 1967.

December 4: Martin Luther King, Jr., announces he will kick off a national Poor People's Campaign in spring 1968. • Stage and film actor Bert Lahr, best known as the cowardly lion in *The Wizard of Oz,* dies at 72.

December 6: President Johnson asks American businesspeople to hold down prices, and for workers to modify wage demands.

As African-Americans mobilized politically and voted in higher numbers in the late 1960s, they targeted mayoral elections in northern cities. On November 7, 1967, Carl B. Stokes (*pictured*) and Richard Hatcher became the first black mayors elected in major American cities—Cleveland and Gary, Indiana, respectively. Hatcher faced what became an ominous trend: emerging "white backlash" among lower- and middle-class white voters and a divided and unsupportive Democratic Party. Many African-Americans did rise to power in northern cities in the late 1960s and 1970s, but all the while white people fled to the suburbs—taking their tax money with them and leaving the cities economically depressed.

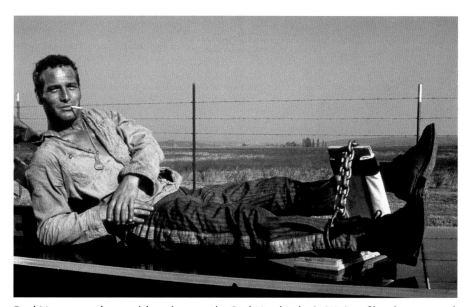

Paul Newman relaxes with a cigarette in *Cool Hand Luke* (1967), a film that assured the actor's image as a tough, handsome rebel. Newman portrays a cool loner who stands up to the repressive system, symbolized by a brutal chain-gang boss played by George Kennedy (who won an Oscar for his performance). Newman's character appealed to those with long-held American ideals of stand-alone independence. It also resonated with young Americans engaged in their own acts of rebellion.

Biafra Starves

IN THE LATE 1960S, people turned on their TV sets to see African children with stomachs distended and skin stretched taut against their ribs. These images of starving refugees awakened the world to the plight of Biafrans.

On May 30, 1967, the eastern region of Nigeria, dominated by the Igbo tribe, seceded, calling itself the Republic of Biafra. The Igbo declared independence after years of nationwide conflicts along cultural, economic, and religious lines with the Hausa tribe in the West. In fighting in 1966, approximately 30,000 Igbo had been massacred.

The Organization of African Unity greeted Biafra's effort to readjust colonial boundaries with little enthusiasm. Nige-

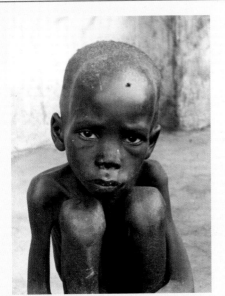

ria met the secession with a brutal war and merciless blockade. Nigeria blockaded Biafra's harbors and roads, and restricted the flow of food and medicine to many starving refugees.

As the world looked on, an estimated two to three million people died from war and starvation from July 1967 to January 1970. At its worst, the crisis killed an estimated 8,000 to 10,000 people each day.

At first, the Cold War superpowers did little to assist Biafra. But the horrific news finally spurred a worldwide relief effort when citizens of the U.S. and Western Europe pressured their governments to send food and aid. Biafra capitulated to Nigeria and—as a Republic—ceased to exist in January 1970. The terrible scenes placed African politics and conflicts before the eyes of the world.

During a televised press conference on November 17, 1967, President Lyndon Johnson made a bold, impassioned speech, attempting to connect with viewers and defend his policies in Vietnam. One headline read, "Johnson Comes Out Swinging." As he moved toward the election season, Johnson argued that the war was progressing well despite the drumbeat of criticism he faced from antiwar protesters. At the time, Johnson had an all-time low approval rating of 23 percent, according to a Harris Poll released that week.

An American soldier, lugging his M60 machine gun, waits to be evacuated during a monthlong series of battles known collectively as the Battle of Dak To. In late 1967, U.S. troops held off North Vietnamese attacks on American positions near the Laotian and Cambodian borders. Assisted by massive air strikes and South Vietnamese ground assaults, U.S. forces managed to maul four Communist regiments, thus preventing their participation in the upcoming Tet Offensive. Almost 300 Americans and some 1,600 North Vietnamese died in the battles.

December 9: In a White House ceremony, Lynda Bird Johnson, daughter of the President, marries Charles Robb, who later will become governor of Virginia. • Jim Morrison of the Doors becomes the first rock star to be arrested during a performance. Police arrest him when he exposes himself on stage during a concert in New Haven, Connecticut.

December 10: A twin-engine plane carrying Memphis recording star Otis Redding and members of the Bar-Kays crashes in fog-shrouded Lake Monona, near Madison, Wisconsin, killing Redding and all but one of the others.

December 14: Biochemists at Stanford University announce successful synthesis of DNA.

December 15: The Silver Bridge, a suspension-type bridge spanning the Ohio River at Point Pleasant, West Virginia, and Kanauga, Ohio, collapses at evening rush hour, dumping at least 75 cars and trucks into the river; 60 people are killed or missing.

December 21: South African Louis Washkansky dies 18 days after becoming the world's first heart-transplant patient. Cause of death is double pneumonia; the heart beat strongly to the end. • U.S. and South Vietnamese troops mount a major offensive in and around the DMZ. • A massive antiwar demonstration in Washington, D.C., includes civil disobedience at the Pentagon, which results in 400 arrests.

December 31: At a New Year's Eve get-together, Abbie Hoffman, Jerry Rubin, Paul Krassner, Dick Gregory, and others pronounce themselves "Yippies" and make plans to attend the Democratic National Convention in Chicago in July 1968. • In -14 degree weather in Wisconsin, the Green Bay Packers defeat the Dallas Cowboys 21–17, clinching their third straight NFL title. • Approximately 486,000 American troops have served in Vietnam in 1967.

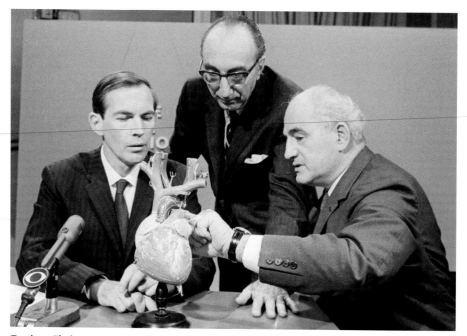

During Christmas season in 1967, the "Miracle in Cape Town" captured the world's attention. On December 3, South African doctor Christiaan Barnard (*left*) replaced the diseased heart of 55-year-old Louis Washkansky with the heart of a young woman killed in a traffic accident. The procedure, which required a 30-member surgical team, was the world's first successful heart transplant operation. Washkansky, who joked that he was "a new Frankenstein," died 18 days after the surgery—not of heart failure but of double pneumonia. Here, Barnard discusses the procedure with fellow heart specialists Dr. Michael DeBakey (*center*) and Adirn Kantrowitz.

Otis Redding started out in Georgia inspired by the sounds of Little Richard. Throughout the early 1960s, he recorded a series of soulful ballads. On June 16, 1967, while dressed in a blue silk and mohair suit, Redding took the stage at the Monterey Pop Festival. He blew away the audience of hippies and white middle-class young people, many of whom had never heard soul music—and certainly no one like Redding. On December 10, 1967, Redding's life was cut short when his plane crashed into Lake Monona near Madison, Wisconsin. Just three days before his death, Redding recorded "(Sittin' on) The Dock of the Bay," an uncharacteristically serene song about sitting next to San Francisco Bay. The posthumous release soared to No. 1 on the pop charts.

A model displays false eye-lashes made of real hair and fake flower petals. Poet Allen Ginsberg had coined the term "Flower Power" as the counterculture's alternative to military aggression. First painted on faces and micro-buses, the symbol of hippie values was soon incorporated into mainstream fashions. In the late 1960s, American women wore flowers in their hair and bought flower-patterned dresses.

"Dirty fascist!" screams this student at a police officer at the University of Wisconsin in Madison. The antiwar rally occurred during another nationwide "Stop the Draft Week" in December 1967. Dozens of officers and students were injured during the Madison melee, as police used tear gas and billy clubs to disperse the crowd. Also that week, antiwar protesters hoping to block induction centers and slow the war machine held large protests in midtown Manhattan, near the Rockefeller Center Christmas tree and holiday shoppers. The New York protest also targeted weapon-making Dow Chemical Company. In New Haven, Connecticut, three women and 27 men out of a crowd of 300 were arrested as they shouted, "Hell no! We won't go!" in front of an Armed Forces induction center.

The Graduate

"I JUST WANT TO SAY one word to you," a business mentor tells homecoming college graduate Ben Braddock. "Plastics." Seemingly capturing the youthful angst of the day, *The Graduate*—which launched the career of actor Dustin Hoffman—hit movie screens in December 1967. It eventually grossed more than $100 million.

The secret of its success was that audiences could interpret *The Graduate* either as a treatise on generation-gap alienation or as a perversely romantic tale of an aimless youngster. Braddock lounges in his pool, has an affair with the matronly vixen next door (Anne Bancroft), then absconds with her daughter after she marries a preppy jock. Director Mike Nichols won an Oscar for his work, while Simon & Garfunkel provided a blissful soundtrack (which included "Mrs. Robinson").

Because the film played it safe by eschewing the generational warfare of so-called "movement movies" such as *Bonnie and Clyde* (1967) and *Easy Rider* (1969), some film scholars have taken it to task. David James notes that "the fact that a protest as timid and trivial [as Ben Braddock's] should have been received as the sign of a generational revolt testifies to the paucity of Hollywood's responsiveness to the crises of the times." Most critics, however, consider *The Graduate* a classic. An American Film Institute panel rated it as the seventh best American film of the 20th century.

1967

New & Notable

Books

The Chosen by Chaim Potok
The Crisis of the Negro Intellectual
 by Harold Cruse
Death of a President by William
 Manchester
Division Street: America by Studs Terkel
Rosemary's Baby by Ira Levin
Trout Fishing in America
 by Richard Brautigan

Movies

Bonnie and Clyde
Cool Hand Luke
The Dirty Dozen
Don't Look Back
The Graduate
Guess Who's Coming to Dinner
Point Blank
Thoroughly Modern Millie
To Sir with Love
Weekend
Who's Minding the Mint?
You Only Live Twice

Songs

"Alice's Restaurant" by Arlo Guthrie
"All You Need Is Love" by the Beatles
"Georgy Girl" by the Seekers
"Happy Together" by the Turtles
"Light My Fire" by the Doors
"Ode to Billie Joe" by Bobby Gentry
"Piece of My Heart" by Big Brother
 and the Holding Company with
 Janis Joplin
"Purple Haze" by Jimi Hendrix
"Respect" by Aretha Franklin
"Ruby Tuesday" by the Rolling Stones
"To Sir With Love" by Lulu
"White Rabbit" by Jefferson Airplane

Television

The Carol Burnett Show
Dragnet
The Flying Nun
Gentle Ben
Ironside
Mannix
Mr. Rogers' Neighborhood

Theater

The Birthday Party
Hallelujah, Baby!
The Homecoming
Rosencrantz and Guildenstern Are Dead

The successful film *Guess Who's Coming to Dinner* starred Sydney Poitier (*left*), Katharine Houghton (*center*), and Spencer Tracy (*right*), as well as Katharine Hepburn. The movie dramatizes the conflicts surrounding the impending marriage of a brilliant black doctor and a white suburbanite. Outside of the mainstream, the film and Poitier were criticized for espousing easy liberal sentiments without honestly portraying race or class divisions in the United States. For years, Poitier had struggled to create smart and realistic African-American characters that defied persistent Hollywood stereotypes. After this film, black audiences questioned Poitier's depictions of unthreatening and polite role models of blackness.

Michigan Governor George Romney greets troops in Cu Chi, South Vietnam, on Christmas 1967. Romney was considered a promising Republican candidate for president until two incidents in 1967 tarnished his reputation. The first was the Detroit riot in June, which reflected badly on his leadership. Later in the year, Romney stated that when he had visited Vietnam in 1965 to assess the military and political situation in the country, the U.S. military had given him "the greatest brainwashing that anyone can get." The statement made the electorate uneasy and ended Romney's chances to win the 1968 presidential nomination.

The first *Zap Comix*, puckishly numbered 0, features a hairy, naked man being, well, zapped. Created by San Francisco cartoonist and former greeting card designer Robert Crumb, *Zap* broke comic book conventions by featuring sex, drugs, profanity, and panels that poked fun at Jesus. It became an instant cult classic in the late 1960s, and was published sporadically into the 1990s. Crumb went on to become America's most famous alternative comic artist.

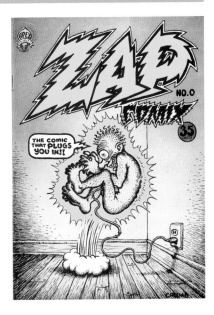

Aretha Franklin showcased her soulful, powerful voice while singing gospel in her father's church in Detroit, but success in the secular world came hard. In the early 1960s, Columbia Records tried to launch her into the mainstream with pop and jazz standards, but that went nowhere. Only at Atlantic Records, under the auspices of producer Jerry Wexler, did the right mix coalesce, as Wexler combined Aretha's piano and vocal stylings with soulful material and the Muscle Shoals Rhythm Section. Immediately, Franklin enjoyed commercial success, beginning with "I Never Loved a Man" in 1967. A torrent of classics followed, including "Chain of Fools," "A Natural Woman," and, most famously, her reworking of Otis Redding's "Respect" in 1967. She eventually would be dubbed the "Queen of Soul."

The Soviet government newspaper *Izvestia* described Bob Hope as "a promoter of aggression" for taking his USO tour to the troops in Vietnam during the early weeks of 1967. The newspaper exclaimed, "Nearly naked girls were singing. More naked girls were dancing. In the intervals Bob clowned." Hope and his troupe entertained standing-room-only crowds at Air Force bases around Southeast Asia. He told running jokes about General Westmoreland, and he showed off sex symbol Raquel Welch (*pictured*) to boost morale. While troops appreciated the entertainment, the American counterculture criticized Hope's decision to take his show to an unpopular war.

1968

Revolts and Crackdowns

O N A COLD MORNING in Chicago on April 26, 1968, several students at the Francis Parker School trooped through the front doors wearing black armbands. Word buzzed through the school: The armband was a protest against the war in Vietnam. Soon, dozens of the high schoolers wore the black band. Later in the day, students held a teach-in. Young men and women, some still in their early teens, explained why the war was wrong and must be stopped.

Parker was not the only school caught up in antiwar activism that day. The grassroots Student Mobilization Committee had put out the call for a day of protest by students against the Vietnam War. More than a million young people—as well as sympathetic teachers, staff, and administrators—responded with locally organized rallies, marches, teach-ins, and school walkouts.

Just three years earlier, antiwar protesters had been considered part of a fringe movement, easily dismissed by the Johnson Administration and the nation's mass media. By spring 1968 the antiwar forces in the United States numbered in the millions, and protests rang out in thousands of communities. The Vietnam War had polarized the nation, and President Lyndon Johnson's failed military policy had torn apart his own Democratic Party.

The Vietnam War was far from the only discordant element in the United States in 1968. Race riots, assassinations, and the increasingly radical turn of both the student and civil rights movements made many Americans afraid

> *"[W]hile the police were beating up the demonstrators in Chicago, you could see the Russian soldiers chasing Czech civilians in Prague. . . . But, for the record, the Chicago police are much more brutal."*
>
> —THE BERKELEY BARB

In August 1968 Chicago police cracked down hard on antiwar protesters attracted to the city by the Democratic National Convention. The overtly pugnacious attitude of Mayor Richard J. Daley was perceived by many activists as a direct challenge, and was interpreted by many police as permission to freely Mace, beat, and kick defenseless demonstrators. This moment from August 28, with on-duty officers chewing cigars as they manhandle a protester, suggests the breakdown of proper police procedure.

that the nation was coming apart at the seams. A small minority decided by 1968 that revolution was the only cure for American society's ills.

At the beginning of 1968, President Johnson feared that the Vietnam War was going to cost him reelection. He was right. In late 1967, Johnson had been forced to sign an unpopular tax increase to help pay for the war. To help his political situation, Johnson had asked his commander of U.S. forces in Vietnam, General William Westmoreland, to return to the United States and reassure the American people about the course of the war. Westmoreland complied, telling the national press corps: "I am very, very encouraged.... We are making real progress.... We have reached an important point where the end begins to come into view." This so-called "light at the end of the tunnel" speech catastrophically blew up in the faces of Westmoreland and Johnson on January 31, 1968, when the Vietcong launched a major offensive throughout South Vietnam during Tet, the Vietnamese New Year.

Movement icons Abbie Hoffman, Timothy Leary, and Jerry Rubin (*left to right*) held a New York press conference on February 21, 1968. They announced plans to utilize "a million" leftist demonstrators and "flower guerrilla" tactics to embarrass President Johnson at that summer's Democratic National Convention in Chicago.

While the Vietcong were, in fact, soundly defeated on the battlefield, the Tet Offensive demonstrated to the American people that the Vietnam War was far from over and would lead to many more American casualties. Other kinds of costs—moral and ethical—also became clearer to the American people during the U.S. military response to the offensive. For instance, in order to root the Vietcong out of Ben Tre, a city of 140,000 people, American bombers unleashed their full fury on the community. An American officer tried to explain the decision to level Ben Tre: "It became necessary to destroy the town to save it."

To better understand the course of the war, trusted CBS television news anchor Walter Cronkite traveled to Vietnam. He reported back to the American people that what he had witnessed could be described only as a frustrating stalemate that would be extremely difficult to resolve. Amid the bad news, American public opinion turned against Johnson's war. As historian Terry Anderson notes: "Polls from January to March [1968] recorded one of the most profound opinion shifts in history. Earlier, hawks had outnumbered doves 60 to 24 percent; a month later doves led hawks 42 to 41 percent." Johnson had lost the support of the American people.

Evidence of that loss of support became clear on March 12 at the New Hampshire Democratic presidential primary. The relatively obscure Eugene McCarthy, a U.S. senator from Minnesota campaigning against Johnson's

Vietnam War policy, pulled off an extraordinary upset, winning 42 percent of the vote against the incumbent president of the United States. His campaign had been waged not with big-money supporters or a mass-media blitz but instead by thousands of young volunteers. College students, "McCarthy's Kids," had gone "clean for Gene." Young men sheared their long hair and young women traded in blue jeans for skirts and sweater sets before setting out to convince voters to support the antiwar senator.

Totem or warning? A human skull, probably of a Vietcong soldier or Vietnamese civilian, decorates an American encampment somewhere in Vietnam in October 1968. The coarsened emotions of soldiers are a byproduct of any war, but they had not been as pointed since the American military's Pacific experience during World War II.

After McCarthy's shocker, Robert Kennedy, New York senator and younger brother of the assassinated president, announced that he, too, would challenge Johnson's renomination. Just a couple of weeks later, on March 31, Johnson dropped his own bombshell. Appearing on television, LBJ told the American people that he was withdrawing from the presidential campaign in order to focus all his attention on ending the Vietnam War.

Even before Americans could make sense of this dramatic turn, another event shocked the country. Martin Luther King, Jr., the nation's apostle of nonviolent social protest, was struck down by an assassin's bullet on April 4. He was killed in Memphis, Tennessee, where he had gone to lend his moral authority to a strike by the city's garbage collectors—his first effort in a campaign to create a multiracial coalition of poor people in the United States.

As news of King's death rocketed around the nation, some African-Americans, most of them young, exploded in fury over the murder. In Washington, D.C., just blocks from the nation's Capitol Building, mobs looted stores and then put them to the torch. Fires burned out of control less than a mile from the Senate office buildings where the 1964 Civil Rights Act had been crafted. In Chicago, hundreds of fires burned against the night sky. Mayor Richard Daley demanded that the police "shoot to kill any arsonists...[and] shoot to maim or cripple anyone looting any stores in our city."

While some Americans were appalled by Daley's order, many more enthusiastically supported his fierce call for order at any price. Riots had torn apart some 130 cities. By the time rioting subsided a week later, approximately 21,000 people had been arrested, 3,000 injured, and 46 killed. In order to maintain order, approximately 130,000 soldiers and National Guardsmen patrolled America's city streets.

Flags across America were lowered to half-staff following the April 4, 1968, assassination of Martin Luther King, Jr. However, the gesture was small solace to 12-year-old Howard Jeffery, who kept somber vigil at the U.S. Capitol. Other mourners expressed their rage in the streets of America's cities.

Responses to the violence varied dramatically across the nation's political spectrum. Stokely Carmichael, who had coined the phrase "Black Power" two years earlier, spoke for the most militant of the black activists. "When white America killed Dr. King," he said, "she declared war on us." Ominously,

President Johnson's decision not to seek the 1968 Democratic nomination flung the doors wide for New York Senator Robert F. Kennedy. RFK had great appeal across a broad spectrum of Democratic voters, and was perceived by many as America's best hope to disentangle itself from Vietnam. The dream ended on June 5 with an assassin's bullet.

Former Vice President Richard Nixon, whose political obituary had been written in 1962, resurrected himself in 1968 with an effective appeal to America's apprehensive "silent majority." He became the GOP presidential nominee, and narrowly won the White House.

he concluded, "Now that they've taken Dr. King off, it's time to end this nonviolent bullshit." A *Chicago Tribune* editorial spoke for the many whites who felt that the time had come to get tough with all the troublemakers who were creating disorder in the United States. The piece painted demonstrators as opportunists who had taken advantage of a permissive climate to lay war guilt at the country's doorstep. The writer predicted that if permissiveness were to continue, so would the "rioting."

Robert Kennedy, who was on a campaign stop in Indianapolis when King was killed, struggled to find meaning in the horror. Rather than retreat from Indianapolis's tense streets, Kennedy went to the community's black ghetto to share his feelings of anguish over the assassination. Like few other public figures during that hard time, Kennedy sought not scapegoats but a path by which all Americans could move forward together.

No one will know if RFK might have succeeded in helping the American people move down that path of wisdom. On June 5, after narrowly winning the California Democratic Party presidential primary, he, too, was struck down by an assassin's bullet. It was almost more than the nation could bear.

When the Democratic Party met in August to nominate its candidate for president, the antiwar faction of the party, though vocal, was not as powerful within party ranks as outsiders might have assumed. Johnson's announcement that he would not seek reelection came too late for Vice President Hubert H. Humphrey to join the primary fray. Regardless, Humphrey came to the convention with strong support from the party establishment because of his insider credentials, name recognition, and veteran liberal leadership record. McCarthy's support was fervent but not broad, and party delegates distrusted his insurgency campaign. HHH easily won the nomination.

Even as Humphrey was celebrating his victory, some 10,000 antiwar demonstrators massed in protest in downtown Chicago. While almost all of the protesters were peaceful, a few demonstrators, including members of the increasingly militant New Left group Students for a Democratic Society, threw rocks at police officers who were refusing to allow the protesters to hold an antiwar march.

On previous nights, the police had battled protesters in nearby Lincoln Park, some of whom had gathered there for a "Festival of Life" planned by the Yippies, a theatrical group of agitators led by Abbie Hoffman and Jerry Rubin. On the night of Humphrey's convention victory, the police moved in on the protesters and anyone else caught in their path in full view of network television cameras. While protesters chanted "the whole world is watching," police began cracking heads and spraying Mace. South Dakota Senator George McGovern, who had tried to rally the antiwar delegates at the convention, watched in horror from his hotel room just above the melee. "Do you see what those sons of bitches are doing to those kids down there?" he said.

Most American citizens disagreed with McGovern's analysis. According to surveys, Americans overwhelmingly supported the police action. After so many months of riots and mayhem, a majority of Americans seemed to want, above all, assurance of law and order.

Republican Richard Nixon provided that assurance. He told the electorate that if he were their president, he would answer not to the protesters but to the "forgotten majority—the nonshouters and the nondemonstrators, the millions who ask principally to go their own way in decency and dignity...." While he actually received fewer votes than he had in his losing bid for the presidency in 1960, Nixon managed to win the prize he had long sought.

By the end of 1968, the United States was a polarized nation, torn apart by a failed policy in Vietnam and rife with racial tensions and violence. But the U.S. wasn't the only country in turmoil. Throughout 1968, young people revolted all around the world. In May, university students in Paris fought police in the streets. They ignited a national strike that briefly united workers and students in a massive movement for a more open and humane society.

In Mexico City, shortly before the Summer Olympics began there, soldiers and police opened fire on students marching for political and economic reform, murdering hundreds of young men and women. In the spring, Czechoslovakian political reformers fought to break free of the heavy hand of the Soviet Union and create "socialism with a human face." But in August, the Soviets arrived with tanks and crushed the peaceful Czech revolt.

In Tokyo, Rio de Janeiro, Rome, Seoul, and many other cities, young people—tired of the Cold War global order that had been created a generation earlier—rejected the political status quo and clashed in the streets with government forces. In 1968, even as the forces of reaction regained the upper hand, a nearly worldwide protest movement—often naive and even misguided—struggled to imagine and create a more democratic, free, and peaceful world.

The attempt of Czech Party Secretary Alexander Dubcek, a Communist reformer, to cultivate "socialism with a human face" in his country was at odds with the philosophy of conservative Communists in the Soviet Union and other Warsaw Pact nations. Czechoslovakia's liberal movement was bloodily crushed in August, when Soviet and other Warsaw Pact troops and armor ripped through Prague.

1968

1968: A Gallup poll reports that 78 percent of Americans feel that morals are in decline; 67 percent believe that religious influence on daily life is on the wane. • The Mexican American Legal Defense and Education Fund, the first national Chicano civil rights legal organization, is founded. • The National Abortion Rights Action League (NARAL) is founded by Bernard Nathanson and Lawrence Lader. • California furniture designer Charles Prior Hall invents the waterbed. • The Children of God, a counterculture religious cult, takes root. • Mattel unveils its new "Christie" doll, Barbie's African-American counterpart.

January: Alexander Dubcek, first secretary of the Czechoslovak Communist Party, initiates reforms in his country to bring about "socialism with a human face." *See July 27, 1968.* • Tokyo's landmark Imperial Hotel, designed by Frank Lloyd Wright and built in 1916, is razed because of structural problems following earthquakes and modest guest capacity.

January 1–June 15: More than 220 major antiwar demonstrations, involving some 39,000 students, take place on approximately 100 U.S. campuses.

January 4: Cambodia accepts delivery of aircraft and anti-aircraft guns from Red China.

January 12: AT&T announces its designation of 911 as an emergency number throughout the United States.

January 14: The Green Bay Packers rout the Oakland Raiders 33–14 in Super Bowl II.

January 15: In Washington, D.C., the Jeanette Rankin Brigade—a coalition of women's peace groups—demonstrates against the Vietnam War.

Singer Eartha Kitt (*right*) chats with Lady Bird Johnson (*center*) after a luncheon at the White House on January 18, 1968. Kitt sparked controversy when she told the First Lady that the Vietnam War was groundless and was the main reason why the country was having trouble with its youth. Her comments brought Mrs. Johnson to tears. Kitt subsequently was investigated and smeared by the CIA, whose files described her as "a sadistic, sex nymphomaniac . . . rude, crude, shrewd, difficult." Blacklisted in the United States, Kitt was forced to continue her career in Europe.

Eskimo dogs help American officials investigate the crash of a U.S. B-52 bomber. The plane, carrying four unarmed hydrogen bombs, went down on January 21, 1968, about eight miles from the Thule Air Base in Greenland. The crash caused serious diplomatic problems with Denmark, which controlled Greenland. The Danes were upset that the U.S. planes had carried nuclear weapons into Danish air space. Some evidence suggests that although all the bombs were officially "accounted for," one might not have been recovered. Like the crash of a B-52 over Spain in 1966, this incident incited European objections to such flights.

In January 1968 anti-American demonstrators in Japan protest the visit of the nuclear-powered aircraft carrier USS *Enterprise.* An even larger demonstration against the war in Vietnam and the Japanese–American alliance took place in June 1968, when 141 police and 70 students were injured in Osaka. Many Japanese students, like pockets of students all over the world, adopted an aggressive stance against what they viewed as American imperialism. Memories of Hiroshima and Nagasaki made the Japanese especially sensitive about nuclear issues.

This poster, advertising a nonexistent movie, satirizes American involvement in the Vietnam War. The type style used for the movie's title is reminiscent of posters for the epic *Ben-Hur,* while the copy utilizes black humor to attack the war and its political dimensions. Historian Michael Doyle, who ran a "head shop" during the Vietnam era, recalls that this poster was a big seller.

"What You Need Is Something New, Like This"

Political cartoonist Herblock takes issue with Richard Nixon's attempt to create a new image of himself. Throughout 1967 and early '68, the former Vice President attempted to soften his persona. As he said to reporter James J. Kilpatrick, the "Tricky Dick" albatross was "a brutal thing to fight." Nixon sought to emphasize his support for civil rights, for example, in an attempt to overcome his image as mean and devious through "absolute candor." To Herblock, it was all a façade.

1968

January 16: After their initial New Year's meeting, the Youth International party (Yippies) is founded. Members include Country Joe and Fish, the Fugs, Allen Ginsberg, Arlo Guthrie, Abbie Hoffman, Paul Krassner, Phil Ochs, and Jerry Rubin. • Terrorists in Guatemala shoot and kill two U.S. military attachés.

January 18: Invited to a White House luncheon, black entertainer Eartha Kitt embarrasses the First Lady, Lady Bird Johnson, by commenting on serious issues, such as the Vietnam War and black youth crime. Kitt subsequently will become the subject of a CIA investigation. • The British House of Commons votes 304–9 to reduce Britain's role as a world power, and to reduce domestic welfare payments.

January 19–21: Riot police battle Japanese students who wish to storm the U.S. naval base at Cape Iorizaki, following the anchoring there of the nuclear-powered U.S. aircraft carrier *Enterprise. See* June 7, 1968.

January 21: Communist forces lay siege to the U.S. Marine base at Khe Sanh, South Vietnam. *See* April 5, 1968. • North Korean infiltrators are foiled in their attempt to assassinate South Korean President Park Chung Hee. Thirty-one infiltrators are killed by South Korean police. • An American B-52 bomber carrying four unarmed H-bombs crashes into the ocean near Thule, Greenland.

January 23: The U.S. intelligence-gathering ship *Pueblo* is captured by North Korean patrol boats off the Korean coast. Commander Lloyd Bucher and his crew are interned. *See* December 22, 1968.

January 30: On this Vietnamese lunar new year (Tet), North Vietnamese and Vietcong troops launch bold attacks against Saigon. *See* January 31, 1968.

On January 31, 1968, two American soldiers lie dead within the walls of the U.S. Embassy in Saigon following a predawn attack by 17 Vietcong troops. The January 31 insurgency violated the cease-fire usually observed during the *Tet Nguyen Dan* (Lunar New Year), demonstrating considerable audacity. Though the invaders were dispatched with little difficulty, images of the fight being brought to U.S. turf damaged morale in the United States.

Smoke billows over Saigon following a series of coordinated attacks staged by the North Vietnamese during the Tet Offensive. By launching an assault on major cities during the country's biggest holiday, Communists took advantage of the celebrations to move troops and transport weapons undetected. Though the Vietcong hoped to spark popular uprisings throughout the south, they instead incurred tremendous civilian casualties. Nonetheless, by boldly striking symbolic targets, they scored a huge psychological victory. Americans accustomed to fighting in rural areas now faced the prospect of urban guerrilla warfare. After the Tet Offensive began, the majority of the American public wanted the U.S. out of Vietnam.

The Tet Offensive

On January 30, 1968, at 2:45 in the morning, an explosion rocked the U.S. Embassy in Saigon. Vietcong guerrillas began their assault by blowing a hole into the wall of the embassy compound. American forces eradicated the threat after a six-hour firefight, but the assault signaled the start of the Tet Offensive, a carefully coordinated attack timed to hit numerous targets throughout South Vietnam during *Tet Nguyen Dan*, the Lunar New Year.

The planning for this "General Offensive, General Uprising," conceived by North Vietnamese General Vo Nguyen Giap, began months earlier and unfolded in two phases. First, in a series of "border battles," the North Vietnamese and Vietcong engaged in conventional combat intended to draw American and South Vietnamese forces to the interior of the country and away from the heavily populated areas. Battles at Con Thien, Dak To, and especially Khe Sanh succeeded in distracting American military leaders from a growing guerrilla presence in cities and larger towns.

Capitalizing on the traditional cease-fire during Tet, the second phase began when a combined force of 84,000 North Vietnamese regulars and Vietcong guerrillas took part in an enormous offensive. They targeted 36 of 44 provincial capitals, five of six autonomous cities, 64 of 245 district capitals, and more than 50 hamlets. Most of the fighting in these places ended within two weeks, with the Americans and South Vietnamese inflicting devastating casualties on the attackers. However, a month was needed to reclaim the imperial capital, Hué, and parts of Saigon.

General Giap had hoped that the offensive would spark an uprising among the South Vietnamese people, and the toppling of the Saigon government, but no uprising occurred. Instead, as many as 40,000 North Vietnamese and Vietcong were killed, and they failed to hold any territory.

But Giap achieved an enormous political victory by shocking not only the American military command, but the American people as well. In fall 1967, as antiwar sentiment in the United States reached new heights, and as public opinion polls showed support for the war dropping steadily, President Lyndon Johnson had brought General Westmoreland home for a publicity tour. In a widely covered speech, the general assessed the prospects of American victory, saying, "I have never been more encouraged in my four years in Vietnam." He predicted that the North Vietnamese and Vietcong would soon fold.

A Marine helps a wounded friend in Hué, South Vietnam

However, the Tet Offensive made Westmoreland and, by extension, Johnson look foolish. Americans wanted to know how the war could be winding down if the enemy was staging a massive offensive—and so brazenly penetrating the U.S. Embassy, no less.

This proved to be the turning point in the war. With public opinion polls showing Americans doubting the wisdom of the present course, and with many of his advisers now questioning the utility in fighting on, Johnson rejected Westmoreland's request for 206,000 additional troops and replaced the general as commander of American forces in Vietnam.

On March 31, 1968, in a nationally televised address, Johnson announced that he would suspend the bombing of North Vietnam and would seek peace negotiations. At the end of the speech, he stunned the country by stating that he would neither seek nor accept the Democratic nomination for reelection as president. Richard Nixon would soon inherit the war.

1968

January 31: Martial law is declared in Saigon as Communist attacks spread to include the presidential palace and the U.S. Embassy. *See* February 13, 1968.

January 31–March 2: In the Battle for Hué during the Tet Offensive, North Vietnamese Army (NVA) and Vietcong troops systematically execute more than 3,000 "enemies of the people," including South Vietnamese government officials, captured South Vietnamese officers, and Catholic priests. The battle for the city results in the deaths of more than 5,000 NVA and more than 200 Americans.

January 31–March 7: In the Battle of Saigon during the Tet Offensive, 35 NVA and Vietcong battalions are defeated by 50 battalions of American and Allied troops that had been positioned to protect Saigon. *See* February 1, 1968.

February 1: In Saigon, Brigadier General Nguyen Ngoc Loan, South Vietnam's police chief, shoots a suspected Vietcong guerrilla in the head. The execution is captured on film by an Associated Press photographer. • Richard Nixon enters the race for the 1968 Republican presidential nomination. • Priscilla Presley, wife of Elvis Presley, gives birth to a daughter, Lisa Marie.

February 2–10: Garbage collectors strike in New York City, with refuse piling up at a rate of 10,000 tons each day.

February 6–18: The Winter Olympic Games are held in Grenoble, France. Celebrated French skier Jean-Claude Killy wins the downhill event, while American Peggy Fleming earns a gold medal in figure skating.

February 7: Referring to Ben Tre, South Vietnam, a U.S. major tells Peter Arnett of the Associated Press, "It became necessary to destroy the town to save it."

In one of the most famous of all journalistic photographs, South Vietnamese police chief Nguyen Ngoc Loan executes a Vietcong suspect in Saigon on February 1, 1968. AP photographer Eddie Adams caught the exact moment of impact, and an NBC cameraman filmed the whole sequence. The photograph appeared on the front pages of many U.S. newspapers the next day, fueling public opposition to the war. Americans also saw the execution on NBC, including the final seconds in which a fountain of blood streamed from the head of the corpse. It was later reported that this suspect had been part of a team that had killed the family of Loan's best friend.

In the South Vietnamese city of Hué, a young girl gathers spilled rice during a rare moment of calm. The former imperial capital, heretofore untouched by war, became the scene of some of the bloodiest fighting during the Tet Offensive. On January 31, Communists swept into Hué from three directions, occupying the sprawling Imperial Citadel. Marines stationed nearby found themselves hamstrung by orders to minimize damage to historic structures, necessitating brutal house-to-house combat. Eventually, heavy fire from both sides reduced half the city to rubble. The Communists were expelled within three weeks, but graves discovered later revealed the horrific toll exacted upon thousands of citizens during the occupation.

Police officers in Orangeburg, South Carolina, stand over the bodies of two wounded youths on February 8, 1968. After college students had demonstrated against a whites-only policy at a local bowling alley on February 6, demonstrators confronted police on the 8th. Police responded by firing at the protesters, claiming that students had fired first. Three demonstrators were killed and 27 were wounded. A week of violence followed, which necessitated the arrival of National Guard units. Nine patrolmen were indicted in federal court, but each was acquitted of all charges.

Figure skater Peggy Fleming was the darling of the 1968 Winter Olympics in Grenoble, France. Fleming had finished sixth in 1964, but in '68 she easily won the gold medal, with all nine judges ranking her first. Her beauty and grace made her immensely popular among Americans, who were in desperate need of a feel-good story. Not surprisingly, Fleming helped create a surge of interest in figure skating. As her coach, Carlo Fassi, said, "She made [skating] appear so easy and lovable, a lot of little girls fell in love with it."

Actor Charlton Heston is collared by two of his simian adversaries in the 1968 film *Planet of the Apes.* In this sci-fi classic, Heston plays an American astronaut stranded on an Earthlike planet where primitive humans swing from vines while nonhuman primates rule the roost. Humans are used for target practice and kept in zoos. In the famed final scene, Heston escapes from his captors only to discover the Statue of Liberty half-buried on a beach; he's on a future Earth that had been devastated by nuclear war. This popular film generated four sequels, a television series, and an animated show.

February 8: In Orangeburg, South Carolina, state and local police fire on a crowd of about 100 unarmed black students protesting a segregated bowling alley. Three students are killed and 27 are wounded. • Alabama Governor George Wallace enters the presidential race as an Independent candidate.

February 10: A special commission reports that the National Guard and state and local police used excessive and unjustified force against black citizens during 1967 racial disturbances in Newark, New Jersey.

February 13: The U.S. rushes 10,500 emergency combat troops to South Vietnam in response to Communist attacks in Saigon and elsewhere.

February 16: The U.S. National Security Council abolishes occupational and graduate student draft deferments. • John Lennon and George Harrison of the Beatles arrive with their wives in Rishikesh, India, for an extended study of transcendental meditation with the Maharishi Yogi. Band members Paul McCartney and Ringo Starr will join them.

February 18: Coordinated Vietcong rocket and mortar attacks are mounted against U.S. and South Vietnamese military garrisons from the Central Highlands to the Mekong Delta. • The U.S. State Department announces the highest weekly casualty count of the Vietnam War so far, with 543 Americans killed in action.

February 21: A Delta Air Lines jet carrying 109 people is hijacked over Florida, and the pilot is forced to land the plane in Cuba. It's the first of 12 planes hijacked to Cuba in 1968.

February 25: Pete Seeger performs "Waist Deep in the Big Muddy," a song that mocks America's involvement in the Vietnam War, on *The Smothers Brothers Comedy Hour.* CBS had refused to allow Seeger to perform the song in its entirety back in September 1967.

Walter Cronkite, anchorman for the *CBS Evening News* and one of television's most respected journalists, traveled to Vietnam in February 1968 as the Tet Offensive was winding down. After his return, on a February 27 CBS special, he opined that "the bloody experience of Vietnam" would "end in a stalemate." He concluded that because military victory was impossible, the U.S. should enter into serious negotiations. President Johnson, who watched the broadcast, reportedly said, "If I have lost Walter Cronkite, I have lost Mr. Average Citizen."

Landing Under Fire

ALL AIRCRAFT ATTEMPTING TO LAND at Khe Sanh received heavy ground fire, including .50-caliber machine gun, mortar, and artillery rounds. The crew chief had us lay our gear bags on the floor beneath us to shield our bodies from ground fire that might penetrate the underside of the chopper. Needless to say, we were all very nervous and "puckered" at the thought of .50-caliber rounds ripping through the thin underbelly of the chopper beneath us! We would circle down through a heavy cloud cover and have only a few seconds with the tailgate on the ground to disembark with all of our gear. As we began our descent, we saw tracer rounds streaking past the windows through the thick clouds. The crew chief shouted that we would have less than ten seconds on the deck, and we had better be off the ramp or know how to fly!

Incoming mortars and artillery rounds exploded all around the landing area. The pilot didn't even land the chopper. The crew chief lowered the tailgate to the ground as the chopper hovered and we were dumped out like a heap of garbage from the rear of a sanitation truck. We scattered like rats for the nearest trenchline or bunker and waited in sheer terror for what seemed like an endless barrage to be over. The chopper disappeared into the clouds without retrieving any of the casualties it had come for, and the incoming rounds finally ceased. We huddled for at least another twenty minutes before mustering the courage to crawl out from the relative safety of the trenches, and we made our way across the airfield. We found our gun positions along the northern perimeter of the runway and settled in with our beleaguered comrades to rest and be briefed about the situation at hand.

—U.S. ARMY LIEUTENANT BRUCE M. GEIGER, DESCRIBING THE SIEGE AT KHE SANH

The Siege at Khe Sanh

ON JANUARY 21, 1968, nine days before the start of the Tet Offensive, North Vietnamese forces attacked a Marine position in Khe Sanh, killing 14, wounding 43, and destroying 1,500 tons of explosives. This spectacular assault signaled the start of a 77-day siege of Khe Sanh.

Located just 14 miles south of the demilitarized zone (DMZ), and near the main highway extending from Laos to the South Vietnamese coast, Khe Sanh attracted American attention as early as 1962. At first, it served as a Special Forces outpost for gathering intelligence. However, in response to increased North Vietnamese activity near the DMZ in early 1967, American commanders sent a Marine regiment to hold a number of hills in the region. By late 1967, in coordination with attacks on Con Thien (near the DMZ), the North Vietnamese cut off Route 9, the primary supply route for the American garrison at Khe Sanh.

American GI in Khe Sanh

In January 1968, forces from three separate North Vietnamese divisions gathered near Khe Sanh. American commander William Westmoreland marshaled a defense force of more than 6,000 ground troops (mostly Marines) to hold the base. He also launched Operation Niagara, a sustained air attack on North Vietnamese positions. Westmoreland believed that the North Vietnamese were launching a preemptive strike against the Marines. In fact, the enemy implemented the siege at Khe Sanh primarily as a diversionary tactic, to draw American forces to remote areas and away from the cities, where it hoped to spark a general uprising with the Tet Offensive.

Fierce fighting at Khe Sanh lasted from January to April, while American planes dropped food, drink, and supplies to hungry, thirsty, frightened Marines. Eventually, the dropping of more than 100,000 tons of bombs devastated the North Vietnamese and prevented an American defeat.

Supplies are parachuted to U.S. Marines under siege in Khe Sanh, South Vietnam, on February 29, 1968. North Vietnamese Army (NVA) troops had begun surrounding the isolated base in late 1967. President Johnson feared a repeat of the French defeat at Dien Bien Phu in 1954, but General William Westmoreland assured him that the base would be held. U.S. forces beat back a number of NVA assaults over the next two months, aided by massive B-52 attacks, although the NVA was successful at destroying an outlying post at Lang Vei in early February. The Communist attacks were diversions to draw American attention from urban areas assaulted during the Tet Offensive.

February 27: After his trip to Vietnam, *CBS Evening News* anchor Walter Cronkite tells viewers that he is certain "the bloody experience of Vietnam is to end in a stalemate."

February 28: Honoring a request by General William Westmoreland, General Earle Wheeler—chairman of the Joint Chiefs of Staff—asks President Johnson for an additional 206,000 soldiers and mobilization of reserve units in the U.S. *See* March 10, 1968.

February 29: The National Advisory Commission on Civil Disorders issues its report on the race riots that have plagued the country. The committee focuses the blame on poverty, discrimination, unequal enforcement of the law, substandard education, and inferior housing and public services.

March–May: The Cuban government expropriates ("nationalizes") some 60,000 small businesses in an attempt to rid the island nation of "bourgeois values."

March 1: Washington attorney Clark Clifford is named the new U.S. secretary of defense by President Johnson.

March 6: Despite a commutation to life in prison from Queen Elizabeth II, three black Africans convicted of murder are hanged at a maximum-security prison in Salisbury, Rhodesia, in clear Rhodesian defiance of Britain.

March 10: *The New York Times* reports that the White House has denied General Westmoreland's request for an additional 206,000 troops in Vietnam. • It is reported that a Soviet submarine with three nuclear-armed missiles has sunk 750 miles off the coast of Oahu, a Hawaiian island.

March 11: American and South Vietnamese forces launch a massive offensive against the Vietcong in the Saigon area.

March 12: Minnesota Senator Eugene McCarthy wins 42 percent of the vote in New Hampshire's Democratic presidential primary, dealing a major blow to President Johnson. ➤

A North Vietnamese youth stands in rubble caused by a U.S. bombing attack on Haiphong in early March 1968. As part of Operation Rolling Thunder, U.S. planes had been bombing North Vietnam since March 1965. The bombing was gradually expanded to include major industrial and port targets, such as Haiphong. This was one of the last Rolling Thunder missions. President Johnson stopped the bombing of most of North Vietnam on March 31, 1968, in an attempt to speed up the peace process. In fact, the aerial campaign did little to destroy the will of the Communists, even though the U.S. was running out of useful targets in the North.

Mary Beth Tinker and her brother, John, display the two black armbands that they wore to their Des Moines, Iowa, high school to protest the Vietnam War. When they were suspended from classes, their father sued. Although lower courts dismissed the suit, the U.S. Supreme Court on March 4, 1968, agreed to hear the case. In 1969 it ruled 7–2 that the students did have a right to protest, arguing that they did not "shed their constitutional rights to freedom of speech or expression at the schoolhouse gate."

Secretary of State Dean Rusk (*right*) appears before the Senate Foreign Relations Committee on March 11, 1968. Rusk was grilled on live television for 11 hours over two days. Many senators were outraged when they read a *New York Times* report that General William Westmoreland had requested that an additional 206,000 troops be sent to Vietnam. They wanted answers from the secretary. Rusk explained that Johnson had made no decision about the size of the American forces and that a number of options were being considered. In fact, Johnson wrote in his memoir that he had "firmly decided against sending anything approaching 206,000 additional men to Vietnam." The controversy caused by the report led to increasingly fatalistic views of the war, and of the Johnson Administration.

Counter-demonstrators march in opposition to student protesters in Poland in March 1968. A number of Polish students had hit the streets in previous days, primarily because of strict censorship imposed by the government. When six prominent professors were dismissed for supporting the students, almost 2,000 young people defied an order not to demonstrate and gathered to demand the reinstatement of their mentors. More than 1,600 students were expelled and forced to reapply for admission. This was a highly visible indication of the worldwide nature of youth discontent in the 1960s.

Sheepherders try to rescue surviving members of their flock after a U.S. Army nerve gas test got out of hand in Utah's Skull Valley. On March 13, 1968, at the Dugway Proving Ground, an orientation test of a deadly nerve gas had taken place. The Army later admitted that a shift in wind might have caused the gas to spread into sheep-ranching areas. Some 5,000 of the animals died, and the Army suspended the tests and ultimately compensated ranchers. No evidence exists that any humans were affected, although one Utah veterinarian said that many of the sheep could have been saved had the military been more forthcoming.

> *"We huddled 'em up. We made them squat down.... I poured four clips into the dinks.... [T]he mothers kept hugging their children.... [W]e kept on firing."*
>
> —U.S. Army Private Paul Meadlo, describing his part in the My Lai Massacre

The My Lai Massacre

AT EIGHT IN THE MORNING on March 16, 1968, soldiers from Charlie Company, 1st Battalion 20th Infantry of the Americal Division, entered My Lai 4, a hamlet in the village of Song My near the northern coast of South Vietnam. Encountering no enemy guerrillas, members of Charlie Company—particularly those in a platoon led by 24-year-old Lieutenant William Calley—systematically massacred more than 300 unarmed civilians, many of whom were marched into a ditch on Calley's orders and mowed down with machine gun fire. Helicopter pilot Hugh Thompson saved the lives of a few civilians when he landed his craft in front of an advancing group of soldiers and threatened them with his own machine guns.

Several factors had caused the soldiers to act in an unacceptably aggressive manner. Two days earlier, a popular sergeant was killed and several others were injured by a Vietcong booby trap. Soldiers sought revenge. On a higher level, military leaders encouraged and rewarded kills because the higher the body count, the more it seemed the U.S. was winning the war. For angry and bloodthirsty Charlie Company soldiers, the line between enemy and ally blurred. Every Vietnamese became the enemy.

Calley's Army superiors succeeded in keeping news of the massacre from breaking for 18 months. But after journalist Seymour Hersh published the first full account of the event, the subsequent investigation and trial preparations divided a country already polarized by the war. Although military courts indicted 25 men, including Calley, for war crimes, only Calley received a prison sentence. Charges were dropped against Calley's divisional commander, General Samuel Koster.

Consequently, many Americans saw Calley as a scapegoat. Soon after his conviction, a sympathetic record, "The Battle Hymn of Lieutenant Calley," sold 200,000 copies.

Civilians rounded up to be killed by Charlie Company soldiers

Responding to this public sympathy, President Richard Nixon intervened. He first moved Calley to house arrest, and then, through the Pentagon, reduced his sentence from life imprisonment to just three years.

As Calley's trial unfolded, Vietnam Veterans Against the War held the Winter Soldier hearings, in which dozens of veterans testified that they had seen similar war crimes in Vietnam. Such revelations, coupled with the Calley controversy, demoralized even supporters of the war.

A gruesome photo taken by Army photographer Ron Haeberle in March 1968 shows some of the more than 300 South Vietnamese civilians slaughtered by American soldiers during the My Lai Massacre. Among the photographs Haeberle took was one showing American soldiers taking a lunch break during the killings. The only U.S. casualty was Private Herbert Carter, who shot himself in the foot in the late afternoon after taking heroin. Chillingly, one American participant, Varnado Simpson, admitted that "from shooting them, to . . . scalping them, to . . . cutting out their tongue. I did it."

Enjoying the Massacre

WITHOUT A DIRECT ORDER, the first platoon also began rounding up the villagers. . . . Sledge remembered thinking that "if there were VC around, they had plenty of time to leave before we came in. We didn't tiptoe in there."

The killings began without warning. . . . Stanley saw "some old women and some little children—fifteen or twenty of them—in a group around a temple where some incense was burning. They were kneeling and crying and praying, and various soldiers . . . walked by and executed these women and children by shooting them in the head with their rifles."

There were few physical protests from the people; about eighty of them were taken quietly from their homes and herded together in the plaza area. A few hollered out, "No VC, no VC. . . ." Women were huddled against children, vainly trying to save them. Some continued to chant, "No VC." Others simply said, "No. No. No."

Carter recalled that some GIs were shouting and yelling during the massacre: "The boys enjoyed it. When someone laughs and jokes about what they're doing, they have to be enjoying it." A GI said, "Hey, I got me another one." Another said, "Chalk up one for me." Even Captain Medina was having a good time. Carter thought: "You can tell when someone enjoys their work." Few members of Charlie Company protested that day. For the most part, those who didn't like what was going on kept their thoughts to themselves.

By nightfall the Viet Cong were back in My Lai, helping the survivors bury the dead. It took five days. Most of the funeral speeches were made by the Communist guerrillas. Nguyen Bat was not a Communist at the time of the massacre, but the incident changed his mind. "After the shooting," he said, "all the villagers became Communists."

—JOURNALIST SEYMOUR HERSH,
MY LAI 4: A REPORT ON THE MASSACRE AND ITS AFTERMATH

March 13: Antigovernment student demonstrations spread across Poland.

March 13–14: Approximately 5,000 sheep are found dead in Skull Valley, Utah, downwind from the U.S. government's Dugway Proving Ground, where tests of airborne biological weapons are undertaken. Dugway is located 85 miles southwest of Salt Lake City.

March 14: Senator Robert F. Kennedy tells President Johnson that he will agree to stay out of the presidential race if he can lead a committee that would chart a new course in Vietnam. Johnson turns down the offer. *See* March 16, 1968.

March 16: U.S. ground troops from Charlie Company rampage through the village of My Lai, South Vietnam, killing more than 300 civilians, including babies. The three-hour killing spree ends when three American fliers intervene. The massacre won't be made public for more than a year. *See* August 4, 1969. • New York Senator Robert F. Kennedy announces his candidacy for the Democratic presidential nomination. • Right- and left-wing students battle at Rome University in Italy.

March 22–23: During a conference at Lake Villa, Illinois, activists from the National Mobilization to End the War in Vietnam (MOBE), the SDS, and the Yippies outline protest plans for the Democratic National Convention in August. *See* August 23, 1968.

March 26: The "Wise Men"—Dean Acheson and other elder-statesmen policymakers—gather at the White House for lunch with the President. Although they were advocates of an interventionist foreign policy immediately after World War II, the majority of the six advises U.S. withdrawal from Vietnam.

Right- and left-wing students battle on the steps of Rome University's Literature School in March 1968. During the 1967–68 academic year, 19 of Italy's 33 state universities experienced student disruptions. Part of the problem was overcrowding, with the University of Rome employing only 300 professors to teach 60,000 students. By March 1968, about a half million Italian students were on strike. Many protested the Vietnam War; most called for the hiring of more professors and demanded more say-so in governing the very hierarchical university system. The unrest managed to close the University of Rome for much of March.

Howard University students tape a sign reading "Black University" to the window of the school's administration building. Students occupied the building in March 1968 to publicize their demands for more courses dealing with African-American issues at the predominantly black university. This was one of several such demonstrations at U.S. institutions of higher education in 1968. Many called for the establishment of black studies courses and programs.

On March 31, 1968, Lyndon Johnson announced in a nationally televised speech that he would neither seek nor accept the Democratic nomination for president in 1968. LBJ also stated that he had ordered an end to the bombing of most of North Vietnam and had begun the process of negotiations to end the war. He said he elected not to run because he needed to devote his full attention to Vietnam, unhindered by any partisan activities. Although he did not mention it in his speech, Johnson also was deeply concerned about his health. His decision to resign was almost universally praised as a great act of patriotism, even by such critics as William Fulbright. As biographer Robert Dallek points out, "The response to Johnson's announcement was the most positive expression of national support since his landslide election in 1964."

"Clean for Gene"

IN 1967 YOUNG DEMOCRATS began to search for a presidential candidate who would run on a peace platform. Allard Lowenstein, the "Dump Johnson" leader, first approached a skeptical Senator Robert Kennedy, who immediately declined. Antiwar Senator Eugene McCarthy had no such qualms. Though Lowenstein's overtures barely registered with him, the popular liberal could not ignore the mass revulsion millions of Americans felt toward President Lyndon Johnson's foreign policy. The antipathy of college students moved him the most, and his message would resonate strongest among them.

Few pundits who observed McCarthy in action gave him much of a chance. Dry and erudite, the poetry-spewing candidate came on like a latter-day Adlai Stevenson. Among a populace that barely tolerated intellectuals even in the best of times, McCarthy's egghead persona might have doomed him. However, he correctly sensed a constituency eager for someone to express their dismay with the country's direction.

McCarthy's secret weapon was the army of young idealists he tapped into. He encouraged legions of antiwar protesters of every stripe to become, with proper grooming, part of the campaign. Soon, campuses across the country became recruiting centers for those eager to get "Clean for Gene."

Once news of the Tet Offensive was fully digested, McCarthy's stock improved with a war-weary public. In the New Hampshire primary on March 12, 1968, he finished a strong second to his own party's incumbent. Johnson announced his stunning withdrawal before the month was up, although another obstacle lay ahead. The reconfigured tableau drew Robert Kennedy into the race, stirring bitterness within McCarthy's ranks that even RFK's June assassination could not mitigate.

Though McCarthy would soldier on, his momentum was lost. Resistance from the party's power brokers effectively doomed any real chance he had of wresting the nomination away from Vice President Hubert Humphrey.

1968

March 28: Martin Luther King, Jr., marches with sanitation workers on strike in Memphis, Tennessee. The protest turns violent, resulting in the death of a 16-year-old boy and the arrests of 280 people. *See* April 3, 1968.

March 31: In a nationally broadcast address, President Johnson tells the American people he will neither seek nor accept the Democratic presidential nomination. He also announces that he has ordered a bombing halt over North Vietnam.

April: Twelve TWA flight attendants file a complaint with the EEOC against the airline for sex discrimination. The suit states that female flight attendants make less than their male counterparts. • Federally Employed Women (FEW) is founded to end gender-based discrimination in civil service jobs.

April 2: Minnesota Senator Eugene McCarthy wins 57.6 percent of Wisconsin's Democratic primary vote, compared to 35.4 percent for President Johnson.

April 3: The U.S. and North Vietnam agree to start the peace process by initiating direct contact of their respective diplomatic representatives. *See* May 10, 1968. • At Mason Temple Church in Memphis, Martin Luther King, Jr., delivers his "I've been to the mountaintop" speech, in which he says he is not worried about dying. *See* April 4, 1968.

April 4: A sniper assassinates civil rights leader Martin Luther King, Jr., 39, in Memphis, Tennessee, as King stands on a motel balcony. *See* April 4–mid-April.

April 4–mid-April: News of Martin Luther King's murder triggers rioting in more than 120 American cities over several days. An estimated 46 people (41 of them African-American) are killed, more than 3,000 are injured, and more than 20,000 are arrested.

Black sanitation workers and civil rights activists march in Memphis, Tennessee, in late March 1968 under the watchful eyes of National Guardsmen. Martin Luther King, Jr., went to Memphis to assist the black workers, who were striking because of poor working conditions and a wage scale that was lower than that of comparable white workers. When some young black protesters resorted to violence during a March 28 demonstration, King called for a peaceful follow-up march. On April 3, King made his famous "I've been to the mountaintop" speech in a Memphis church. He would live only one more day.

Martin Luther King, Jr., (*second from right*) and three aides—Hosea Williams, Jesse Jackson, and Ralph Abernathy (*left to right*)—stand on a balcony at the Lorraine Hotel in Memphis. The civil rights leaders were on their way to dinner on April 4 after learning that a federal court had approved a new march permit for civil rights activists and striking sanitation workers. A few seconds after this photo was taken, gunfire crackled and King fell, mortally wounded by a shot to the throat. He was pronounced dead at 7:05 P.M.

Assassination of Martin Luther King, Jr.

BY 1968 MARTIN LUTHER KING, JR., had received more than 50 death threats. He told a crowd at a Memphis church on April 3, 1968, "I may not get there with you, but...we as a people will get to the promised land."

King was 39 years old, in his 12th year as a nationally recognized civil rights leader. Though his philosophy of nonviolent protest was on the wane (militant activists trumpeted "Black Power"), King's activism had broadened in recent years. After the passages of the Civil Rights Act of 1964 and Voting Rights Act of 1965, he turned his attention to the problems of the northern ghettos, the plight of America's poor, and ending the war in Vietnam.

On April 4, as King left for dinner with associates Ralph Abernathy, Hosea Williams, and a young SCLC worker named Jesse Jackson, a sniper shot King in the neck. He died an hour later. James Earl Ray, a smalltime criminal, was later arrested for the shooting. Many people, however, including King's children, do not believe Ray was the assassin.

In its tribute to the fallen leader, *Ebony* magazine noted that King, a man who had "consorted with kings and queens and who had been consulted by his nation's presidents," selflessly spent his last days helping striking sanitation workers in Memphis. King led marches in Memphis in support of labor and to draw public attention to economic inequality in the United States. Simultaneously, King was planning a "Poor People's Campaign," which was set to culminate with a march on Washington for economic justice later that spring.

The country's black ghettos reacted violently to King's death. About 700 fires burned in Washington, D.C. Chicago residents looted and burned businesses despite Mayor Richard Daley's order to police to "shoot to kill" arsonists and "shoot to maim" looters. In all, violence and destruction tore apart more than 130 communities. King's death effectively ended the nonviolent phase of the movement for civil rights.

President Lyndon Johnson (*seated with back to camera*) appears deep in thought as aides watch television coverage of the assassination of Dr. Martin Luther King, Jr. In the wake of the tragedy, LBJ canceled a planned trip to Hawaii, phoned King's widow, Coretta Scott King, to express his sadness, and urged all Americans to avoid violence and pray for "peace and understanding throughout this land." The President also arranged to meet with civil rights leaders and pushed the FBI to spare no effort in finding the assassin.

1968

April 5: The Vietcong siege of the U.S. Marine base at Khe Sanh, South Vietnam, is lifted.

April 6: In Oakland, police ambush prominent members of the Black Panthers, killing Bobby Hutton and wounding Eldridge Cleaver and Warren Wells.

April 8: The Federal Bureau of Narcotics (FBN) merges with the Bureau of Drug Abuse Control (BDAC) to form the Bureau of Narcotics and Dangerous Drugs (BNDD).

April 10: President Johnson names General Creighton Abrams as the new U.S. commander in Vietnam.

April 11: President Johnson signs the 1968 Civil Rights Act, which bans discrimination in the sale or rental of housing. The bill also gives federal protection to civil rights workers and makes it a federal crime to cross state lines for the purpose of inciting a riot.

April 23–24: New York's Columbia University is rocked by violent student demonstrations, which cause the campus to be closed on the 24th. *See* April 30, 1968.

April 26: The U.S. Department of Defense establishes a riot-control center based at the Pentagon. • The largest-ever U.S. H-bomb is exploded in a test 3,800 feet below ground in the Nevada desert, 100 miles northwest of Las Vegas.

April 27: Vice President Hubert Humphrey announces his candidacy for the Democratic presidential nomination.

April 30: New York Governor Nelson Rockefeller announces his candidacy for the Republican presidential nomination. • New York City police remove Columbia University students and other protesters who have occupied university buildings for five days.

"The dream of Dr. Martin Luther King, Jr., has not died with him. Men who are white—men who are black—must and will now join together as never in the past to let all the forces of divisiveness know that America shall not be ruled by the bullet, but only by the ballot of free and of just men."

—President Lyndon Johnson

Photographs capture National Guardsmen on the smoldering streets of Washington, D.C., (*right*) and the ruins of burned-out buildings in Chicago (*below*) in April 1968. After the assassination of Martin Luther King, Jr., major racial disturbances broke out in more than 120 American cities. An estimated 46 people, most of them African-American, died in the riots, while some 3,000 were injured and more than 20,000 were arrested. In Washington, barbed wire and machine guns were placed around government buildings. In Chicago, nine people were killed and more than 2,500 were arrested.

Yolanda King (*center*), daughter of Martin Luther King, Jr., stares out the window of an automobile as the family leaves for Dr. King's funeral on April 9, 1968. The major candidates for president—Nixon, Kennedy, Humphrey, and McCarthy—attended the services, and some 50,000 people marched in the funeral procession. King was survived by his wife, Coretta, and four children: Yolanda, Martin Luther III, Dexter, and Bernice.

Radical German students protest after an attempt on the life of Rudi Dutschke, one of their leaders. Nicknamed "Red Rudi," Dutschke had been severely wounded when shot in the head by Josef Bachmann, a young neo-Nazi, on April 11, 1968. As a leader of the German Socialist Students League, Dutschke had coordinated a number of violent demonstrations in 1967 and early 1968. The league opposed the Vietnam War, demanded that West Germany officially recognize East Germany, and called for democratization of higher education in Germany. Interestingly, West Berliners, grateful for U.S. support, strenuously opposed the anti-American demonstrations.

Wounded U.S. Army troops are carried to safety during Operation Pegasus, a successful attempt to lift the Communist siege of Khe Sanh in South Vietnam in April 1968. The operation succeeded that month, and American commander Creighton Abrams ordered the base officially closed on July 5. During the siege, from late November 1967 to April 1968, at least 15,000 North Vietnamese troops died. Two hundred Americans were killed as well, with another 400 killed in action in the Khe Sanh sector from April through June. To some critics, the decision to abandon the base represented the height of futility—to suffer so many casualties for a piece of land that was not even kept.

April 30–May 3: In the Battle of Dai Do, a battalion of U.S. Marines nicknamed the "Magnificent Bastards" squelches North Vietnam's effort to open an invasion corridor into South Vietnam along the demilitarized zone.

May: Turkish students at Istanbul University declare Anti-NATO Campaign Week.

May 2–3: Militant left-wing students of the University of Paris (France) take over a lecture hall and a suburban campus. Students riot and clash with police in Paris. *See* May 13, 1968.

May 3: A U.S. Electra turboprop airliner flying through a rainstorm near Dawson, Texas, explodes, killing all 85 people on board.

May 5: The Vietcong launch "Mini Tet," a series of rocket and mortar attacks against Saigon and 119 cities and military installations throughout South Vietnam.

May 6: Topping-out ceremonies are held at the John Hancock Center in Chicago, the world's tallest residential/office building.

May 7: Robert Kennedy wins Indiana's Democratic presidential primary.

May 10: Peace talks open in Paris. The U.S. delegation is led by W. Averell Harriman, while North Vietnam's representative is Xuan Thuy.

May 13: France is hit by a general strike of hundreds of thousands of workers and students. *See* May 20, 1968.

May 14: FBI Director J. Edgar Hoover instructs units of the COINTELPRO (counter-intelligence program) to disrupt New Left activities across the country.

May 16: The Midwest and Mississippi Valley are raked by tornadoes that greatly damage Illinois, Indiana, Arkansas, and Iowa; 70 people are killed.

Cast members of *Hair* ham it up. This famed rock musical opened on Broadway in April 1968. Its plot focused on the attempts of its main character to avoid induction into the military, although specifics of the play often changed according to where it played on the road. *Hair* was the first Broadway show to be based on rock music and to include male and female full-frontal nudity. Its energetic songs (especially "Age of Aquarius"), youthful and enthusiastic actors, and anti-establishment message made it a critical and commercial success. It ran for 1,750 performances on Broadway and spawned 14 national touring companies.

Dr. David Bowman, played by Keir Dullea, is bathed in the eerie light of HAL the computer in the 1968 film *2001: A Space Odyssey*. This parable of the origin and destiny of humankind represents director Stanley Kubrick at his most adventurous and complex. Running more than two hours and containing hardly any dialogue, the film features a calmly evil computer and stunning visual effects while telling a puzzling, metaphysical tale. The movie's ambiguity, especially its strange ending (which features a giant fetus in space as the astronaut/hero dies and is reborn), sparked numerous debates at cocktail parties.

Anti-Vietnam War protesters march down Fifth Avenue in New York City on April 27, 1968. The demonstration attracted 87,000 people and led to 60 arrests. Also on the 27th, some 200,000 New York City students boycotted classes. A similar demonstration in Chicago that day resulted in 15 injuries during confrontations with police. And on the same day in New York, 16-year-old high school student Ronald Brazee died of burns; he had set himself on fire to protest the war.

Czech Prime Minister Alexander Dubcek addresses Communist Party leaders in Prague on May 1, 1968. Dubcek was the son of Slovakians who had lived for a time in the United States. He rose to power in the Czech Communist Party by following the Soviet line, but by 1967—as second-ranking leader—he became convinced that economic and social reforms were necessary in his country. When he became prime minister in early 1968, Dubcek called for the abolition of censorship, regularized relations between church and state, and liberalization of the economy. The Soviets, who strenuously opposed these doctrinal deviations, would take action in August.

A befuddled professor peers around a door to see that his classroom has been occupied by Columbia University students in late April 1968. The Columbia branch of the SDS, led by Mark Rudd, organized a demonstration against the university to protest the school's ties with the Institute for Defense Analysis (seen as being complicit in the Vietnam War) and the building of a gymnasium that would require the leveling of black and Hispanic homes. In the course of the protests, four campus buildings were occupied, including Hamilton Hall, which was taken over by militant black students. Police arrested hundreds of students and injured dozens. Ultimately, Columbia President Grayson Kirk resigned. The sit-ins inspired other such actions at American universities.

1968

May 17: Brothers Phil and Daniel Berrigan, both Catholic priests, and seven others invade the Selective Service office in Cantonsville, Maryland, steal hundreds of draft files, and then burn them outside. They're promptly arrested.

May 20: France is crippled as millions of workers take control of factories, mines, and offices.

May 21: The U.S. nuclear submarine *Scorpion* is lost somewhere in the Atlantic while on its way to base at Norfolk, Virginia; 99 men are lost.

May 28: Eugene McCarthy bests Robert Kennedy in Oregon's Democratic presidential primary.

June 1: Helen Keller, author and advocate for the handicapped, dies at 87.

June 3: Aspiring writer Valerie Solanas shoots Pop artist Andy Warhol at his "Factory" workplace, wounding him severely.

June 5: An assassin standing at close range shoots and mortally wounds New York Senator Robert Kennedy at the Los Angeles Ambassador Hotel shortly after Kennedy claims victory in the California Democratic presidential primary. A Palestinian man named Sirhan Sirhan is wrestled to the floor by bystanders. *See* June 6, 1968.

June 6: Senator Robert Kennedy, 42, dies of gunshot wounds suffered the day before. • President Johnson orders Secret Service protection for all major presidential candidates.

June 7: The June 2 crash of the USAF F-4C Phantom jet at Kyushu (Japan) University motivates 15,000 student protesters across Japan. *See* June 15, 1968.

June 8: James Earl Ray, alleged assassin of Martin Luther King, Jr., is arrested at London's Heathrow Airport. *See* March 10, 1969.

A boy mourns his 12-year-old sister, who was slain in Saigon during the "Mini Tet" offensive of May 1968. As they had in January, Communists launched a second ambitious assault, this time targeting 119 cities and military positions throughout South Vietnam. The challenge was met with retaliatory air strikes by U.S. bombers, who strafed the enemy with napalm and heavy explosives. Though the U.S. was successful from a military standpoint, inflicting thousands of enemy fatalities, scenes like this record the heavy price civilians paid throughout the war.

Xuan Thuy, North Vietnam's chief negotiator at the Paris Peace Talks, arrives at the French Foreign Office on May 10, 1968. Called for by President Johnson in his March 31 resignation speech, the talks began on May 13 and moved at a glacial pace. Negotiations stumbled on the issue of what kind of table would be used. South Vietnamese chief delegate Nguyen Cao Ky refused to sit at the same table with the National Liberation Front delegate, fearing that it would symbolize equality of status. As the table debate raged on, thousands died in the war, with neither side seriously willing to consider compromise.

Eruption in Paris

URING A RIOT in Paris's Latin Quarter on May 24, 1968, students used hatchets and saws to cut down dozens of trees to use as barricades against the police. More than a thousand people were injured that day and night, the bloodiest encounter in three-plus weeks of student and worker protest in France.

Charles de Gaulle, France's hard-line, anti-Communist president, characterized the protests, university occupations, and general strike as the work of a few groups in revolt against consumer and technological society. The protests, however, were much more than that. They were part of the broad international youth movement that rocked the United States, China, Czechoslovakia, and other countries in 1968. The New Left student movement in France expressed a variety of anarchist, socialist, and Third World solidarity stances. And like their counterparts in the United States, they protested the war in Vietnam and de Gaulle's support of it.

Student demonstrators also reacted to specific domestic grievances. Frustrated by crowded, impersonal universities and dwindling prospects for employment, young protesters sought increased control over their destinies. On May 2, students occupied a lecture hall at a suburban campus of the University of Paris. The next day, in response to disciplinary actions against its leaders, several hundred students demonstrated at the Sorbonne in Paris. This set the stage for a series of intense battles with police, which resulted in mass arrests and injuries.

On May 10, more than 30,000 students drove the police out of the Latin Quarter. Over the next month, at least nine

Students in Paris during a riot on May 13

million workers, including the National Union of University Teachers and aircraft manufacturers, went on strike in solidarity with the students. Leftist leader Francois Mitterrand pushed for a transitional government, as the uprising almost brought down the Gaullist government.

The revolts achieved university reform for students and substantial wage concessions for unions, but the solidarity soon diminished. Ultimately, the eruptions in May helped the status quo when de Gaulle's party—fortified by conservative French voters who sought law and order—reached an absolute majority in the National Assembly in late June. Nonetheless, Paris '68 remained a triumphant moment for the Left.

A mule-driven wagon, symbolizing poverty among black Americans, slowly wends its way down a street in Washington, D.C., in May 1968. This was part of the Poor People's Campaign, a demonstration organized by Martin Luther King, Jr., and carried out by aides Ralph Abernathy and Jesse Jackson after King's assassination. The protest attracted between 50,000 and 100,000 demonstrators to the nation's capital from May 13 to June 24, 1968. Some of them erected an encampment of tents—called Resurrection City—on the Mall. The demonstrators called for a guaranteed annual income and an economic bill of rights. But with its most charismatic leader dead and the Vietnam War at center stage, the protest fizzled. After six weeks, police ultimately moved into Resurrection City with tear gas and drove the protesters out.

1968

June 14: Pediatrician Benjamin Spock and three others are convicted in a federal district court in Boston of conspiring to commit violations of the Selective Service Act.

June 15: About 25,000 university students across Japan demonstrate against American involvement in Vietnam and Japan's alliance with the U.S. In Osaka, 141 police and 70 students are injured when 2,000 riot police attempt to turn back 3,000 demonstrators. *See* June 26, 1968.

June 19: The Poor People's Campaign in Washington, D.C., concludes with a Solidarity Day March of 50,000 people. *See* June 24, 1968.

June 20: Brazilian police battle antigovernment student demonstrators in Rio de Janeiro. *See* June 26, 1968.

June 23: The war in Vietnam becomes the longest in U.S. history.

June 24: D.C. police use tear gas to close Resurrection City, the primary encampment for participants in the Poor People's Campaign.

June 25: The U.S. House of Representatives passes a bill making it a crime to burn or otherwise desecrate the American flag.

June 26: Earl Warren resigns as chief justice of the U.S. Supreme Court, citing his age, 77. President Johnson nominates Justice Abe Fortas to succeed Warren. *See* October 2, 1968. • Thousands of Brazilian students, priests, nuns, teachers, writers, and workers march in Rio de Janeiro to protest police brutality and other antidemocratic practices. • The Japanese flag flies over Okinawa and other Bonin Islands for the first time since the U.S. gained control in 1945. The U.S. has agreed to the reversion of the island's control to Japan.

June 27: President Johnson asks Congress to approve a constitutional amendment lowering the voting age to 18. ▶

Senator Robert F. Kennedy campaigns for the Democratic presidential nomination in Detroit on May 15, 1968. Kennedy had announced his candidacy in March in the same room, the Senate Caucus Room, where his brother had proclaimed his candidacy in 1959. In a sense, RFK entered the race on the coattails of Senator Eugene McCarthy's strong showing in the New Hampshire primary. But Kennedy had far more appeal than McCarthy, as he reached out to minorities while attacking America's policy in Vietnam. Calling for serious negotiations to end the war and government programs to help the poor, he seemed to be on the road to the nomination and victory in November.

This image of a smiling girl with a workman's pickax replica and a toy machine gun was Albania's dubious contribution to marking International Children's Day on June 1, 1968. One of the poorest and most rigidly Communist countries in the world, Albania had been ruled with an iron fist by Marxist dictator Enver Hoxha since the mid-1940s. He employed brutal tactics to enforce his rule, exiling, imprisoning, and murdering countless thousands of his opponents. In 1967 Hoxha outlawed all religion in his country, making Albania the world's only official atheist state. He died in 1985.

Sirhan Bishara Sirhan, the accused assassin of Robert Kennedy, was a young Palestinian, originally from Jordan, who lived with his mother and two brothers in Los Angeles. He harbored a deep hatred of Israel and was angry with Kennedy for what he considered pro-Israel remarks. In a notebook that police found in his home, Sirhan had written, "RFK must be disposed of." The notebooks also threatened UN Ambassador Arthur Goldberg, who was Jewish. In spite of his lawyers' pleas that Sirhan suffered from diminished capacity, he was convicted of murder and sentenced to be executed. He escaped that fate when the U.S. Supreme Court voided the death penalty in 1972. In 2003 Sirhan was denied parole for the 12th time.

What Was Lost with RFK

"THE SIXTIES CAME TO AN END in a Los Angeles hospital on June 6, 1968," wrote speechwriter Richard Goodwin. That evening, Senator Robert F. Kennedy (D–NY) succumbed to gunshot wounds inflicted by deranged Jordanian terrorist Sirhan Sirhan.

Hours earlier, Kennedy had been celebrating his narrow victory over Democratic rival Eugene McCarthy in the vital California primary. His victory increased the possibility that RFK would win the Democratic nomination in the 1968 presidential race. As Kennedy confided to an adviser, "I'm the only candidate against the war who can beat [Vice President Hubert] Humphrey."

After President Lyndon Johnson's surprising announcement on March 31, 1968, that he would not seek reelection, the Democratic race for the presidency came down to three men. Humphrey had strong support among Democratic Party bosses. But the American people at large—and youth in particular—looked alternately to Kennedy and Senator McCarthy to heal a nation fractured by war, race riots, student protest, and generational conflict.

McCarthy held a stronger antiwar position than Kennedy, who professed vaguer claims for a negotiated settlement. But, as historian Terry Anderson observed, RFK "*seemed* more radical," due to his longer hair, Kennedy mystique, and profound empathy for the have-nots. His voter support was particularly strong among minorities, the poor,

Robert Kennedy moments before he was shot

blue-collar workers, and young women, who chased after him as if he were the fifth Beatle. To these groups, RFK represented the last gasp of an increasingly weathered Sixties idealism, a stance the candidate wore on his sleeve. "Some people see things as they are and say, 'Why?'" he intoned during the campaign. "I see things that never were and ask, 'Why not?'"

After Kennedy's assassination, many student activists definitively repudiated reform politics. Some espoused an increasingly violent and alienated politics of confrontation, which synchronized perfectly with presidential candidate Richard Nixon's pledge to crack down on student radicalism.

John Wayne, playing Colonel Mike Kirby, calls for assistance in the 1968 film *The Green Berets*. Based on Robin Moore's popular novel about U.S. Special Forces in the Vietnam War, this simplistic movie, which Wayne also co-directed, appalled critics with its false depiction of the war. Colonel Kirby convinces an antiwar journalist, played by David Janssen, that the Berets are stout fellows fighting for a noble cause, and that they'll go out of their way to give a Vietnamese kid a chocolate bar. The film also includes embarrassing visual gaffes. The most famous occurs in the final shot when the sun sets over the South China Sea in the east! According to film critic Penelope Gilliat, *The Green Berets* is "best handled from a distance and with a pair of tongs."

Actress Mia Farrow has a knife ready for followers of Satan, the father of her child, in the 1968 film *Rosemary's Baby,* based on the best-selling book of the same title by Ira Levin (1967). Directed by Roman Polanski in his American debut, the movie told the story of a nice young couple whose seemingly innocuous elderly neighbors are minions of Satan. The oldsters must provide a woman for their master to impregnate in order to bring a new little devil into the world. The film's success rests in Polanski's ability to overlay the ordinary with utter horror. The film features superb supporting acting, especially by Ruth Gordon as the devil's ditsy chief matchmaker.

General Creighton Abrams took over as U.S. commander from William Westmoreland in July 1968. Abrams had been considered one of the best combat officers during World War II, serving under George Patton. His primary mission as commander in Vietnam was to implement President Nixon's "Vietnamization" strategy by turning the bulk of the fighting over to the South Vietnamese. Although Abrams had private doubts about the efficacy of the strategy, he nonetheless oversaw the ultimate departure of U.S. troops in January 1973.

The year 1968 witnessed the growth of feminism, led by such figures as freelance journalist Gloria Steinem (*far right*), New York City NOW President Ti-Grace Atkinson (*bottom left*), and writers Germaine Greer (*bottom right*) and Kate Millett (*near right*). Millett's *Sexual Politics,* published in *New American Review* that year, was an especially influential attack on male domination. Also in 1968, activists such as Bernadine Dohrn attacked male chauvinism in Students for a Democratic Society (SDS), while the Women's International Conspiracy from Hell (WITCH) was founded in New York. Most American feminists took a moderate approach to issues, supporting such proposals as legalization of abortion and federally financed day care centers.

June 28: Due to the high cost of the war in Vietnam, President Johnson signs a bill that calls for a 10 percent surcharge to income taxes.

July: The American Indian Movement (AIM) is founded in Minneapolis in reaction to discriminatory practices by police in the arrest of Native Americans in the area. The movement will spread nationally.

July 1: The Phoenix program is established to crush the secret Vietcong infrastructure (VCI) in South Vietnam, believed to be 70,000 strong. • The Treaty on the Non-Proliferation of Nuclear Weapons (NPT) is signed by the United States, Great Britain, and Soviet Union.

July 15: Aeroflot and Pan American World Airways initiate the first direct air service between the U.S. and Soviet Union.

July 22–26: Members of NOW picket *The New York Times,* urging the end of sex-segregated job advertising.

July 23: Five men whom authorities describe as black nationalists open fire on a police cruiser in Cleveland. Shootings lead to the deaths of seven African-Americans and three police officers. National Guard troops are called in to maintain order in the city.

July 26: The New York offices of Grove Press, the publisher of left-wing books as well as the *Evergreen Review,* are bombed, allegedly by Cuban exiles unhappy with *Evergreen*'s publication of diaries of deceased Cuban revolutionary Che Guevera.

July 27: Czechoslovak Communist Party leader Alexander Dubcek announces in a radio and TV address that Czechoslovakia has chosen its own political path, independent of the USSR, and will not deviate from it. *See* August 20, 1968.

July 29: The Roman Catholic Church publishes *Humanae Vitae* (*Of Human Life*), a reiteration of the Church's 1930 ban on artificial contraception.

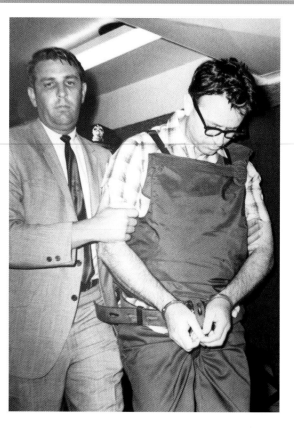

James Earl Ray is led to his cell in Memphis on July 19, 1968. The FBI had identified Ray as the probable assassin of Martin Luther King, Jr., after his prints were found on the alleged murder weapon and a witness placed him running from a rooming house from which the shots were fired. Ray had fled abroad after King's death and was apprehended at London's Heathrow Airport on June 8, 1968. Although Ray pleaded guilty to the crime and was sentenced to 99 years in prison, he later recanted. Ray died in prison in 1998. Interestingly, the King family believes that he was not the assassin, and a number of conspiracy theories have emerged.

On July 23, 1968, a shootout occurred between police and black nationalists in Cleveland, leaving three police officers and seven nationalists dead. Cleveland's mayor, African-American Carl Stokes, sent in the National Guard (*pictured*), then agreed to pull them and police out after turning over responsibility to a group of 109 community members who agreed to keep order. The violence shook a city that had witnessed riots in 1966 as well as earlier in '68.

New York City police investigate the bombing of the offices of *Evergreen Review* on July 26, 1968. Founded by Barney Rosset in 1957, *Evergreen* published radical left-wing material. In 1968, for example, it published John Schultz's "Pigs in the Park," a biting indictment of the Chicago police force's behavior during the Democratic National Convention. Anti-Castro Cubans, opposed to *Evergreen*'s celebratory cover image of Marxist hero Che Guevera, may have committed the bombing.

President Lyndon Johnson listens to a tape from his son-in-law, Chuck Robb, on July 31, 1968. Robb, Lynda Bird Johnson's husband, had left for Vietnam in late March to command a Marine Corps infantry company. This personal connection to the war—Johnson said that Robb's departure left his daughter "lonely and bewildered"—only heightened the President's unhappiness. In July 1968 the Paris Peace Talks were stalled, and Secretary of Defense Clark Clifford was pessimistic about the war. Johnson's hopes that a negotiated settlement might have a meaningful start on his watch became increasingly unrealistic.

Paul Krassner was perhaps most noted for editing the *Realist* (1958–74), a radical magazine considered pornographic by many. He also was a stand-up comedian and cofounder of the Yippie Party. In the mold of Lenny Bruce, Krassner became a cult figure on college campuses, where he often gave one-man shows in the 1960s. Krassner received the ultimate compliment from fellow satirist George Carlin, who stated, "This man is dangerous—and funny; and necessary."

July 30: Mexican college students battle police and federal troops during antigovernment demonstrations in Mexico City. *See* September 24, 1968.

August 1: President Johnson signs a $5.3 billion bill providing for 1.7 million low-cost housing units. • Some 4,500 American troops arrive in South Vietnam, bringing the U.S. total to 541,000.

August 8: Former Vice President Richard Nixon wins the Republican presidential nomination on the first ballot at the GOP National Convention. Nixon surprisingly selects Maryland Governor Spiro Agnew as his running mate. • U.S. troops on patrol in Mekong Delta inadvertently kill 72 civilians during a firefight with Vietcong.

August 9: Detroit's newspapers resume publication after a 267-day strike, the longest in U.S. history.

August 10: South Dakota Senator George McGovern announces his candidacy for the Democratic presidential nomination.

August 20: The USSR engineers a late-night military invasion of Czechoslovakia, with troops from the USSR, Poland, East Germany, Hungary, and Bulgaria. Czech Communist Party Secretary Alexander Dubcek and other Czech leaders are arrested. *See* August 21, 1968.

August 21: In a secret meeting, the Czech Communist Party reelects Alexander Dubcek and pledges to resist the Soviet-instigated invasion. The USSR claims it entered Czechoslovakia because the Czech government requested assistance. *See* September 13, 1968.

August 23: Members of the Youth International Party (Yippies) and their presidential candidate, Pigasus (a pig), are arrested at the Chicago Civic Center, the location slated for the Democratic National Convention. *See* August 26, 1968.

Czechoslovakians wave their nation's flag atop an overturned truck as other Prague residents surround Soviet tanks on August 21, 1968. The country, especially its capital, had experienced a burst of cultural, intellectual, and artistic freedom because of liberalization under Premier Alexander Dubcek, especially his ending of iron-handed censorship. The hopes for increased and continuing liberalization were dashed when Soviet leader Leonid Brezhnev, fearing infection of other Communist bloc nations, ordered the invasion, thus ending what was known as "Prague Spring."

"She Might Have Invaded Russia"

Washington Post editorial cartoonist Herblock wasn't the only one who felt that Soviet leader Leonid Brezhnev had overreacted in Czechoslovakia. World opinion was harshly critical of the Soviets' heavy-handed suppression of reforms instituted by students, artists, and writers during the "Prague Spring." When the push toward an open society started gaining momentum, Soviet tanks rolled in to shut down the "counter-revolution." Still, acts of civilian-led resistance delayed the installation of a government more to the Kremlin's liking for nine months.

Crushed Hope in Czechoslovakia

AT AROUND 11:00 P.M. ON AUGUST 20, 1968, Soviet tanks accompanied by hundreds of thousands of troops from Poland, Hungary, and East Germany roared across Czechoslovakia's border. When dawn broke the following day, the country was firmly under Soviet control.

The impetus for this dramatic military invasion was Czech leader Alexander Dubcek and the political and economic reforms that he and the Czechoslovak government were attempting to carry out. Hardly a capitalist, Dubcek merely hoped to give his country's lagging economy a boost. "We are not changing the general line of internal and foreign policy," he noted in a speech preceding the invasion, "but we must give serious thought to ways of contributing to faster socialist development in our country." For the USSR, such sentiments were a threat to the entire Communist bloc.

The roots of what came to be known as "Prague Spring" can be traced back to early 1968, when Dubcek replaced the more conservative Antonín Novotný as the first secretary of the Czechoslovak Communist Party. Shortly after assuming leadership, Dubcek loosened restrictions on free speech and tolerated a more assertive and often critical press. He also opened economic negotiations with the West without Soviet approval.

But probably the biggest threat to the USSR's hegemony was talk of multiple political parties. Initially, Soviet Secretary Leonid Brezhnev hesitated, hoping that the growing

Prague residents responding to the Soviet invasion

"crisis" would resolve itself. However, under pressure from hawks in the Politburo who asserted that "defense of socialism is the highest internationalist duty," Brezhnev ordered military action.

Neither Dubcek nor the Czechoslovak military put up a fight, and Soviet officials immediately arrested and detained the popular leader. However, the spirit of liberal reform persisted in Czechoslovakia, as students and workers united in vocal opposition to the USSR's military occupation. They were joined by the United States and its NATO allies, who claimed that Soviet actions only heightened tensions between the East and West.

A man tries to minister to some of the people wounded and killed in downtown Prague on August 21, the first day of the Soviet-led invasion. The focus of the assault was the capital city, where civilians—often armed only with fruit and vegetables—tried to fight off hundreds off Soviet and other Communist-bloc tanks. Buoyed by the promise of increased political and artistic freedom, protestors had taken to the streets eagerly, but Moscow reacted with ferocious brutality. Ultimately, more than 100 resisters were killed. Popular support for Alexander Dubcek ran high—scrawled on one exterior shop wall were the words "Viva Dubcek"—but the leader was arrested, taken to Moscow, and expelled from the Communist Party.

August 26: The Democratic National Convention opens in Chicago. Antiwar and other demonstrators clash with Chicago police following an 11:00 P.M. curfew. *See* August 27, 1968.

August 27: Following an "Unbirthday Party for President Johnson," about 2,200 antiwar demonstrators still on the streets past the 11:00 P.M. curfew tussle with Chicago police in Lincoln Park. *See* August 28, 1968.

August 28: Presidential candidate Hubert Humphrey and running mate Edmund Muskie win nomination on the first ballot at the Democratic National Convention. Outside the convention hall, violence between Chicago police and antiwar demonstrators escalates, bringing many injuries and charges of police brutality. One 18-minute battle is captured by TV cameras and will be broadcast around the world. *See* Late August 1968.

Late August: Chicago Mayor Richard Daley orders local radio stations to avoid playing "Street Fighting Man" by the Rolling Stones during the Democratic National Convention for fear it would spark rioting. *See* December 1, 1968.

August 31–September 4: Earthquakes in northeast Iran kill 30,000 people, injure 17,000, and leave 100,000 homeless.

September: Berkeley, California, becomes the first U.S. city of more than 100,000 people to entirely desegregate its public schools. • McDonald's adds the hearty Big Mac burger to its menu.

September 7: Several women's liberation organizations, including the National Organization of Women (NOW), target the Miss America Beauty Pageant in Atlantic City, New Jersey. As part of the protest, women toss brassieres into a "freedom trashcan." ➤

Members of the Yippie Party, including Jerry Rubin (*second from right*), honor the party's 1968 presidential candidate, Pigasus, on August 23 in Chicago. The Yippies were founded in early 1968 as a satirical comment on the failure of mainstream parties. Nominating a pig both echoed a favorite radical insult aimed at the police ("pigs") and suggested the bankruptcy of the usual types of candidates. Rubin was famous for such guerrilla theater in the 1960s. He appeared before the House Committee on Un-American Activities dressed as a Revolutionary War soldier, and threw dollar bills onto the floor of the New York Stock Exchange.

While the Democratic National Convention didn't commence until later in the day, protesters and police clashed in the early morning of August 26. Hundreds of marchers, who had been at odds with police throughout the night, converged at Grant Park. When they swarmed around the statue of Civil War General John Logan, police wielded nightsticks to clear the area. Police and protesters skirmished in Lincoln Park later in the day and the following evening, with police employing tear gas each time. Officers even clubbed reporters and nonprotesting area residents.

The Chicago Convention

IN AUGUST 1968, Democratic Party delegates converged in downtown Chicago for their national presidential convention. So, too, did angry Vietnam War protesters, media-savvy provocateurs, and law enforcement officials intent on ensuring the peace by any means necessary. What resulted would be termed a "police riot" by government investigators.

Chicago police on the eve of the convention

With his standing as "kingmaker" at risk, Chicago Mayor Richard J. Daley had lobbied hard to host his party's convention. Though he expected demonstrations, Daley had solidified his reputation as a no-nonsense magistrate four months earlier with his infamous "shoot to kill" directive against looters in the aftermath of the Martin Luther King assassination. Both he and party officials felt secure in his ability to handle any trouble.

Protest groups with differing agendas headed to Chicago. The National Mobilization Committee to End the War in Vietnam (MOBE) wished to make its points peaceably. Others wanted to push the establishment's buttons. Asserting that *their* brand of revolution was "fun," Abbie Hoffman and Jerry Rubin brought a nominee of their own to town, the cloven-hoofed "Pigasus." As leaders of the Youth International Party (Yippies), they sought to simultaneously challenge reactionary authorities while scoring maximum media exposure. This they achieved with such stunts as the disclosure of "plans" to lace the city's water supply with LSD. Local officials took the bait. In addition to 12,000 police officers, Daley called upon thousands of National Guardsmen and Army regulars to secure the city.

Meanwhile, a divided Democratic Party arrived to nominate President Lyndon Johnson's successor. Hubert Humphrey's nomination seemed secure; however, with followers of dove candidates George McGovern and Eugene McCarthy in attendance, a contentious floor battle was certain.

Supporters of McCarthy joined the thousands of protesters who had assembled in the city's Lincoln Park. Officially denied permission to camp out in the park overnight, the crowd defied the order to vacate, thereby precipitating violent encounters with police from August 25 to 28. While police swung nightsticks and unleashed tear gas, students retaliated with rocks and fisticuffs. The unexpectedly brutal nature of the clashes escalated, with both sides drawing the worst from each other. Part of the savagery was fueled by mutual resentment. Blue-collar cops couldn't understand the antics of what they perceived to be spoiled, upper-class college kids, while protesters saw confirmation of their own rhetoric: The cops were as bad as Nazi storm troopers.

Events climaxed outside the party headquarters at the Conrad Hilton Hotel on August 28. Banned from proximity to the convention center, some 7,000 demonstrators gathered for their last chance at getting their voices heard. Cannily placing the spectacle before the glare of television lights, they chanted, "The whole world's watching!" Viewers saw the police unleash a furious assault on protesters and bystanders alike. Police singled out newsmen for abuse; indeed, to flash press credentials seemed to invite further harm.

Tempers also ran high inside the International Amphitheater. At the podium, Senator Abe Ribicoff denounced the "Gestapo tactics" being employed outside. This brought Mayor Daley to his feet, shouting an epithet at Ribicoff that his apologists later clarified as "faker."

Humphrey and running mate Edmund Muskie won the nomination, but the disastrous week fatally wounded their chances for victory in November. In fact, the events in Chicago weighed heavily on all participants. Said one police officer: "After all this is over, I'm quitting the force."

1968

Mayor Richard J. Daley (*center*) brought the 1968 Democratic National Convention to Chicago thanks to his close ties to President Johnson and his insistence that his police force could maintain law and order. Daley denied permits to antiwar protesters, allowing them to gather only in the Grant Park bandshell—far away from the International Amphitheater, where the convention was held. When protesters grew hostile or tried to march, the police—with Daley's support—often turned aggressive. In the convention hall, Senator Abraham Ribicoff infuriated Daley by denouncing the "Gestapo tactics on the streets of Chicago."

Feeling the Heat in Chicago

AT THE SOUTHWEST ENTRANCE a skinny, longhaired kid skidded down the sidewalk, and four overweight cops leaped on him, chopping strokes on his head. His hair flew from the force of the blows. A dozen small rivulets of blood began to cascade down the kid's temple and onto the sidewalk. He was not crying or screaming, but crawling in a stupor toward the gutter. When he saw a photographer take a picture, he made a V sign with his fingers.

A doctor in a white uniform and Red Cross armband began to run toward the kid, but two other cops caught him from behind and knocked him down. One of them jammed his knee into the doctor's throat and begun clubbing his rib cage. The doctor squirmed away, but the cops followed him, swinging hard, sometimes missing.

A few feet away a phalanx of police charged into a group of women, reporters, and young McCarthy activists standing idly against the window of the Hilton Hotel's Haymarket Inn. The terrified people tumbled backward through the glass. The police then climbed through the open window and began to beat people, some of whom had been drinking quietly in the hotel bar.

—REPORTER JACK NEWFIELD, *THE VILLAGE VOICE*

"The world hears those demonstrators making their noise. The world doesn't hear me and it doesn't hear a single person I know. . . . Fancy, fast-talking students, gabby they are, gab, gab."

—WIFE OF AN AMERICAN FIREMAN

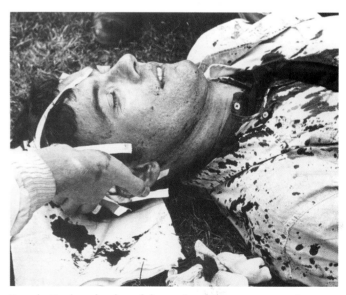

Rennie Davis, a leader of the antiwar movement, was beaten unconscious during a confrontation between antiwar demonstrators and police at the 1968 Democratic National Convention in Chicago. This disturbance took place on Wednesday, August 28, after 10,000-plus protesters gathered in Grant Park. When a demonstrator began to lower an American flag and replace it with a red shirt, police charged the crowd. Davis would be arrested as one of the "Chicago Seven."

Vice President Hubert Humphrey (*left*) and Maine Senator Edmund Muskie celebrate their nominations to the Democratic ticket amid chaos both inside and outside the convention center. Humphrey had entered the presidential race after President Johnson's stunning March 31 declaration of his retirement. Following the assassination of candidate Robert Kennedy, Humphrey became the top Democratic candidate thanks to support from party power brokers. However, he faced an uphill battle up to election day. Many antiwar Democrats refused to support someone so closely identified with Johnson's policies, and the public viewed the convention's divisive spectacle with great distaste. At the close of the convention, Humphrey was well behind Republican presidential candidate Richard Nixon in the polls.

The *Berkeley Barb* takes aim at the Chicago police force in this cover story on the Democratic National Convention in August 1968. Founded in 1965 in conjunction with an antiwar protest, the *Barb* was one of America's first underground newspapers. It consistently took radical, anti-establishment stands, including support for the Yippie Party. This cover equates Chicago's official response to antiwar demonstrators at the convention with the Soviet invasion of Czechoslovakia, another August 1968 event. The cover is the work of underground comics artist Spain Rodriguez, and features his anarchist character "Trashman."

A women's rights activist protests at the Miss America Pageant in Atlantic City on September 7, 1968. Organized by the New York Radical Women, some 400 demonstrators attacked the beauty pageant for reducing women to sex objects. Some of the women tossed their brassieres into the "freedom trashcan," while others hanged contest emcee Bert Parks in effigy. In spite of substantial criticism of the protest, it marked a watershed moment in feminist activism. The year 1968 also saw the birth of important women's liberation publications, such as *Lilith*.

September 8: Black Panther leader Huey Newton is found guilty of voluntary manslaughter in the October 28, 1967, shooting death of Oakland police officer John Frey. Newton is sentenced to two to 15 years in prison.

September 9: Chicago Mayor Richard J. Daley, stung by harsh criticism regarding the conduct of his city's police force during the Democratic National Convention, states: "The policeman isn't there to create disorder; the policeman is there to preserve disorder." • Arthur Ashe becomes the first black male tennis player to win the U.S. Open championship.

September 13: The Czech National Assembly, now firmly under the thumb of the Soviet Union, approves direct censorship of the press. *See* October 4, 1968.

September 14: Detroit Tigers hurler Denny McLain becomes the first major-league pitcher since 1934 to win 30 games in a single season. He'll finish 31–6.

September 16: Presidential candidate Richard Nixon appears on NBC-TV's top-rated *Laugh-In*. He exclaims, "Sock it to *me?*"

September 24: Mexico City police and students battle for 24 hours, resulting in 15 deaths. *See* October 2, 1968.

September 25: Police in Lima, Peru, use tear gas and water cannons to disperse political demonstrators.

September 30: The U.S. posts its 900th aircraft loss over Vietnam.

October: Operation Sealord, the largest combined naval operation of the entire Vietnam War, begins. More than 1,200 U.S. Navy and South Vietnam gunboats and warships will target NVA supply lines from Cambodia to the Mekong Delta.

October 1: A Communist Party rally in China conspicuously relegates the formerly exalted Red Guard activists to subordinate roles. ➤

Lloyd Bucher, commander of the USS *Pueblo,* answers questions at a North Korean press conference in September 1968, eight months after the Communist nation captured his vessel near that country's coast. Bucher's ship was an intelligence-gathering vessel disguised as a freighter. After it was stopped by North Korea on January 23, 1968, Bucher refused to allow boarding, precipitating an attack by North Korean vessels. Bucher and 81 crew members were imprisoned and tortured. President Johnson, already tied down in Vietnam, chose the path of negotiation. The U.S. admitted to spying (but later repudiated the admission), and the captain and crew were released in December. To some, the incident represented American weakness in the face of a clear attack.

A bystander examines bullet holes in the window of a Black Panthers headquarters in Oakland, California, on September 12, 1968. Two dozen Oakland police officers had fired the shots. The Panthers were targeted by law enforcement agencies throughout the 1960s, especially the FBI and its secret COINTELPRO (counterintelligence program). The program's purpose, in the words of J. Edgar Hoover, was "to expose, disrupt, misdirect, discredit and otherwise neutralize" domestic radical organizations. The Black Panthers headed that list in the late 1960s. The steps taken against the Panthers included propaganda, such as fabricated letters, to cause internal dissent. The FBI also framed a California Black Panther leader, Geronimo ji Jaga, for the 1968 murder of schoolteacher Caroline Olsen.

Police scour the wreckage of the Naval ROTC Building at the University of California–Berkeley on September 13, 1968. The wood-framed building suffered significant damage from a dynamite explosion—one of several destructive incidents at Berkeley in 1968. In June, police and demonstrators clashed when protesters tried to shut down Telegraph Avenue in support of French student rebels. In October, protesters occupied and trashed Moses Hall in response to the university regent's refusal to allow black radical Eldridge Cleaver to teach an accredited course. Nationwide, students participated in more than 200 major demonstrations on college campuses in 1968. Many were directed at ROTC installations because of the program's perceived complicity in preparing students to fight in the Vietnam War.

Law and Order

"**I** DON'T THINK a looter should ever be shot unless he tries to escape arrest," stated Spiro Agnew, Richard Nixon's vice-presidential candidate, in August 1968. As Nixon, Hubert Humphrey, and George Wallace squared off in what would prove to be a highly contested election, the issue of law and order became a key issue. From 1960 to late in the decade, crime skyrocketed, with the murder rate up more than 30 percent and assaults up nearly 70 percent. Moreover, televised images of black urban rioters and angry antiwar protesters put many Americans on edge.

The debate, however, was not over whether the nation had a problem with law and order, but rather how to deal with it. While noting that effective law enforcement was imperative, Democrats such as Humphrey generally believed that unemployment and poverty were the root causes of crime, and therefore the solution was to create jobs and clean up ghettos. Conservatives, on the other hand, scoffed at social explanations, and instead stressed the need for harsher punishments and a more forceful, unfettered police presence. Both Nixon and Wallace accused liberal judges and politicians of coddling criminals and hindering police by placing too much emphasis on civil liberties.

Ultimately, conservatives proved to be more in touch with what Nixon termed the "silent majority." A solid 80

A crackdown in Memphis in March 1968

percent of Americans felt that law enforcement had broken down, and more than 60 percent believed that the police should "shoot to kill" looters. When the ballots were counted, Humphrey garnered less than 43 percent of the popular vote, while Nixon and Wallace racked up a combined 56 percent.

Republican presidential candidate Richard Nixon parades down a Philadelphia street in September 1968. Nixon had stayed active politically since his loss in the 1962 California governor's race, especially by courting state political leaders. He had convinced many that there was a "new" Richard Nixon—gentler and less combative. In fact, one of his major campaign slogans—"Bring Us Together"—suggested a more compassionate candidate. Nixon promised to find a way to end the Vietnam War with honor. Yet he also relied heavily on the promotion of law and order as well as an appeal to southern racial conservatives, such as South Carolina Senator Strom Thurmond.

The term "silent majority," coined by conservative journalist Otto Scott in 1968, referred to nonprotesting, middle-of-the-road Americans who worried about economic and social stability and wanted an honorable peace settlement in Vietnam. During a televised speech on November 3, 1969, President Nixon called upon the silent majority to support his stance in Vietnam. The silent majority apparently *was* a majority; a Gallup poll taken just after Nixon's speech showed that the President had an approval rating of 68 percent.

St. Louis Cardinal Bob Gibson (*left*) and Detroit Tiger Denny McLain (*right*) blew away hitters in baseball's Year of the Pitcher in 1968. The intimidating Gibson went 20–9 with 13 shutouts and a stunning 1.12 earned-run average. McLain won 31 games, becoming the majors' first 30 game-winner since Dizzy Dean in 1934. The Cardinals and Tigers faced each other in the 1968 World Series. Although Gibson won two games to McLain's one, the Tigers took the series 4–3, coming back from a 3–1 deficit. Ironically, it was another pitcher, Detroit's Mickey Lolich, who emerged as the series hero. He logged three victories, including a 4–1 win in the final game against Gibson.

Clarence Williams (*left*), Michael Cole (*center*), and Peggy Lipton (*right*) starred in the hip television show *The Mod Squad.* First aired on ABC in September 1968, the show became an immediate sensation, especially among younger viewers. The three stars were young and savvy and seemed to enjoy their work as members of an undercover police unit. Speaking the cool slang of the day—including "solid," "groovy," and "keep the faith"—they worked such colorful venues as go-go clubs and motorcycle rallies. The show had a solid five-year run, losing steam as the stars grew older and the Sixties mood evaporated.

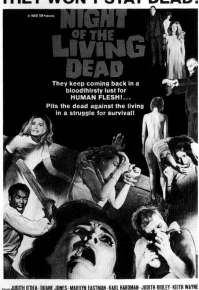

When *Night of the Living Dead* hit theaters in October 1968, it was a shocking departure from horror movie conventions. The film was shot almost like a home movie and at a frighteningly leisurely pace. The source of the horror is never really explained, and its themes of cannibalism (the dead come back to eat the living) and matricide broke taboos. So, too, did the casting of an African-American, Duane Jones, as the hero. Director George Romero would go on to make two sequels, and produce a remake of *Night* on the strength of the original cult classic.

Big Brother and the Holding Company grew from the fertile Bay Area counterculture and music scene of the mid-1960s. When Janis Joplin joined the band in 1966, Big Brother moved away from its famous 15-minute jam sessions to more structured songs that complemented Joplin's soulful blues stylings. The band shot to national stardom with its performance in June 1968 at the Monterey Pop Festival. They followed up with their first major-label album, *Cheap Thrills,* which included such hits as "Piece of My Heart" and "Ball and Chain." The LP, decorated with quirky cover art by famous underground comic artist R. Crumb, hit the No. 1 spot on the U.S. albums chart in September 1968, a month after its release.

Abbie Hoffman is arrested as he arrives to testify at a HUAC meeting in Washington, D.C., on October 3, 1968. The leader of the Yippie Party pulled one of his classic guerrilla theater stunts when he showed up wearing an American flag shirt. He was arrested on charges of flag desecration. Active in the civil rights movement in the early 1960s, Hoffman by 1968 was devoting himself to shocking Americans into accepting the cultural revolution symbolized by the hippie movement. Wearing the flag shirt, as with his decision to shower the floor of the New York Stock Exchange with dollar bills in 1967, no doubt alienated more Americans than it entranced.

1968

October 2: An unending GOP fili-buster in the U.S. Senate prompts President Johnson to withdraw his nomination of Abe Fortas as chief justice of the Supreme Court. • Another clash, the bloodiest yet, takes place between troops and students in Mexico City.

October 4: Intense pressure from the USSR prompts the Czech government to abandon liberal policies and to allow Soviet and other Warsaw Pact troops to remain on Czech soil for an indeterminate period. *See* October 28, 1968.

October 5: Several hundred Catholic civil rights marchers in Londonderry, Northern Ireland, revolt against the ruling Protestants, who have in effect excluded Catholics from housing, jobs, and local government.

October 8: John Lennon and his girlfriend, Yoko Ono, are arrested in London for possession of marijuana. *See* October 9, 1968.

October 9: It is announced that John Lennon and Yoko Ono will be fea-tured on an album titled *Two Virgins*. The sleeve will feature frontal nude photos of Lennon and Ono.

October 11: Three U.S. astronauts aboard Apollo 7 make a successful launch from Cape Kennedy. *See* October 14, 1968.

October 12–27: The Summer Olympics are held in Mexico City. American highlights include Bob Beamon's smashing of the world long jump record, Al Oerter's fourth consecutive gold medal in the discus, and Dick Fosbury's innovative "Fos-bury Flop" in the high jump. The U.S. tops all countries in gold medals (45) and total medals (107). *See* October 16, 1968.

October 14: Television viewers wit-ness the first live network footage from inside a manned U.S. space capsule in orbit. ➤

George Wallace entered the 1968 presidential race determined to reclaim the blue-collar whites "forgotten" by the Democratic establishment. The former Alabama governor had first distinguished himself in 1963 as the South's most prominent defender of segregation. Five years later, he recognized the potential for capitaliz-ing on those disaffected by civil rights and social liberalism. Running as an inde-pendent on a platform of "law and order," Wallace chose outspoken retired General Curtis LeMay as his running mate. But LeMay's desire to "bomb the North Vietnamese back to the Stone Age" alienated voters. On election day, Wallace came in third with more than 13 percent of the vote.

A boy brandishes a toy gun at a 1968 civil rights demonstration in Londonderry, Northern Ireland (Ulster). For the previous 18 months, Ulster Catholics had been complaining about job and housing discrimination by majority Protestants, but to little effect. The Northern Ireland Civil Rights Association then planned a protest march on October 5, 1968. The Royal Ulster Constabulary blocked the march, then beat the peaceful demonstrators with batons—an event that marked the real beginning of the "Troubles" in Northern Ireland.

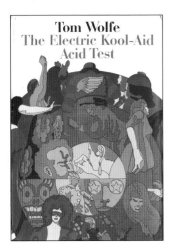

Jane Fonda starred in the 1968 science-fiction farce *Barbarella*. Fonda is the title character, a young space vixen seeking out the evil Duran Duran, who has invented a death ray that threatens her peaceful galaxy. Featuring skimpy clothing, flesh-eating dolls, and torture by a pleasure machine, the film became a cult classic. Ironically, the sexy and seemingly naive Fonda would become a leader in the radical wing of the anti-Vietnam War movement.

Uproar in Mexico City

" I DO NOT WANT to run on the blood of other people," asserted an Italian Olympian as the Summer Games opened in Mexico City in October 1968. From July to October, students from the National University of Mexico and the National Polytechnic Institute had clashed with police while protesting the policies of the Partido Revolucionario Institucional (PRI)—Mexico's ruling political party. Their chief complaint was that the government did little to alleviate social problems, such as widespread poverty, underemployment, corruption, and police brutality.

Worried that the demonstrations would interfere with the Olympics, President Díaz Ordaz eventually ordered in the army. Ordaz's heavy-handed tactics alarmed many observers, including one foreign diplomat who remarked "the PRI doesn't know how to bend.... [W]hen it encounters an obstacle it engulfs it, like an amoeba with a piece of food."

On October 2, 10 days before the Games' opening ceremony, federal troops opened fire on the unarmed students. Hundreds lay dead or wounded. Though the protests simmered down in the following weeks, American medalists Tommie Smith and John Carlos stirred controversy within the Games when they gave the Black Power salute on the medal podium. The events reinforced the fact that, in 1968, political dissension was international in scope.

In the 1968 book *The Electric Kool-Aid Acid Test*, author Tom Wolfe chronicled the trippy journey of Ken Kesey and his Merry Pranksters. In 1964 Kesey, the author of *One Flew Over the Cuckoo's Nest*, had used his royalties to buy a 1939 International Harvester bus; he loaded it with friends and hangers-on for a cross-country adventure. Wolfe's own manic style matches the feverish nature of the journey, as we meet such 1960s characters as Owsley, the world's premier LSD manufacturer; Timothy Leary, the drug's celebrated advocate; and a Prankster stalwart named Mountain Girl. Wolfe's frenetic account of the trip and its "trips" became a cult classic.

Mexico City police beating a student protester in September

1968

Heavyweight boxer George Foreman proudly waves an American flag after winning a gold medal in the 1968 Olympic Games. In stark contrast to the Black Power salutes offered by U.S. track stars John Carlos and Tommie Smith, Foreman's patriotic stand was condemned by black militants as Uncle Tomism. Those who knew Foreman simply considered him a nice guy. After all, he claimed that he didn't knock out his Soviet opponent since, as he put it, "My mother was watching on television, and she doesn't want me to hurt anyone."

Tommie Smith (*center*) and John Carlos (*right*) give a Black Power salute at the 1968 Summer Olympic Games in Mexico City. The American sprinters had earned the gold and bronze medals in the 200-meter run. But to protest what they saw as continuing racial oppression in the United States, they mounted the victory platform without shoes and gave their salute during "The Star-Spangled Banner." After the International Olympic Committee condemned the action, the U.S. Organizing Committee ordered the two speedsters to vacate the Olympic Village for violating the principle that politics should play no part in the Games. Interestingly, when a Communist bloc swimmer bowed her head in protest at the playing of the Soviet national anthem, there was no official condemnation.

American long jumper Bob Beamon breaks the world record for the event at the 1968 Mexico City Olympics. Considered by many the most amazing record-breaking performance in sports history, Beamon soared 29 feet, 2½ inches, stretching the record by almost two feet. His main competitor, Russian Igor Ter-Ovanesyan, marveled, "Compared to this jump, we are as children."

By the late 1960s dissent among the ranks of American soldiers grew more pronounced and organized. Here, on October 14, 1968, soldiers at the Presidio Stockade in San Francisco sing antiwar songs while an officer reads them the Army's Mutiny Act. Similar rebellions took place throughout the country, including one at Fort Jackson, South Carolina, where soldiers conducting a political discussion physically defied officers. At Fort Ord in California, more than 300 GIs rioted over conditions in the stockade there. Such protests raised questions about freedom of speech and freedom of protest among soldiers. The Supreme Court would rule that off-duty GIs out of uniform were indeed protected.

With a nod to the ancient Greek play *Lysistrata,* folk singer and peace activist Joan Baez (*left*) posed with her sisters Pauline Marden (*center*) and Mimi Farina for this poster. The message was meant to prod hormone-driven adolescent males into thinking twice before agreeing to enlist in the military. Some feminists decried the objectifying of women, but Baez insisted it was tongue-in-cheek.

Steve McQueen (*top and bottom right*) starred as the title character in the 1968 film *Bullitt.* In a convoluted plot, Bullitt, a San Francisco police detective, tries to track down hit men who killed a Mafia snitch he was supposed to protect. Director Peter Yates strove for absolute authenticity, as is evidenced by the classic car chase through the hilly streets of the city by the bay. (The sequence earned the film an Oscar for editing.) McQueen was perfectly cast as the tenacious but cool cop.

Twenty years after *The Naked and the Dead* introduced him to readers, writer Norman Mailer penned *The Armies of the Night,* a novelistic memoir of his role in marching on the Pentagon in protest of the Vietnam War. Though risking nothing of value himself (his arrest, as he anticipated, could only enhance his activist credentials), Mailer's third-person account of the event and a night in jail provides a glimpse into the world of the antiwar protester. The book earned Mailer a Pulitzer Prize.

1968

October 16: At the Summer Olympics in Mexico City, American sprinters Tommie Smith and John Carlos give a Black Power salute on the medal podium during the playing of the American national anthem. They will be suspended from the U.S. team and banned from the Olympic Village.

October 17: President Johnson signs the largest appropriations bill ever for defense: $71.9 billion.

October 20: Jackie Kennedy marries Greek shipping magnate Aristotle Onassis on Skorpios Island, Greece.

October 27: The streets of London fill with 50,000 antiwar demonstrators.

October 28: The 50th anniversary of the Czech Republic is marked by anti-Soviet street demonstrations.

November: Stuart Brand begins publishing the *Whole Earth Catalog,* which will become popular among the radical set. • More than 200 women from the U.S. and Canada convene in Chicago for the first national Women's Liberation Conference.

November 1: The Motion Picture Association of America announces that each new movie will be given one of the following ratings: G (general audiences), M (mature audiences), R (restricted audiences), and X (no one under 17 allowed).

November 5: Richard Nixon is elected as the 37th president of the United States with a hefty electoral-vote margin but a very close popular-vote edge over Hubert Humphrey. Democrats retain control of the House and Senate. • Shirley Chisholm (D–NY) becomes the first African-American woman elected to the U.S. Congress.

November 6: A student strike, led by the Third World Liberation Front (a coalition of minority campus groups), is conducted at San Francisco State University. The strike will last for 134 days.

Jacqueline Kennedy smiles after her wedding to Greek shipping magnate Aristotle Onassis on October 20, 1968. Jackie married in part for security, but according to historian Norma Noonan, "the marriage was not happy" as the couple "lived apart more than together." Onassis had become a billionaire, largely through a strategic marriage to the daughter of another Greek shipping tycoon. During his marriage to Jackie, the couple spent an extravagant amount of money.

Shirley Chisholm flashes a victory sign on November 6, 1968, after becoming the first African-American woman elected to Congress. A teacher and political activist in Brooklyn, Chisholm had been elected to the New York State Assembly in 1964. As a congresswoman, she sponsored legislation designed to help minority students and domestic workers. In 1972 she became the first black woman to campaign for the Democratic presidential nomination.

President-elect Richard Nixon—pictured with future son-in-law David Eisenhower, daughters Julie (*left*) and Tricia, and wife Pat—greets supporters following his win over Democratic candidate Hubert Humphrey. Campaigning on a platform of "law and order" (echoing Independent candidate George Wallace), Nixon successfully held his conservative base while reaching out to southern voters who traditionally went Democratic. He also promised a "secret plan" to end the war in Vietnam, throwing just enough doubt on the ongoing Paris Peace talks to pull some votes away from Humphrey. While the popular vote was close, Nixon's southern strategy won him a comfortable electoral margin. His empathy with the "silent majority" would remain his strong suit during a time of ongoing social upheaval.

In the early 1960s, longtime Marvel Comics writer and editor Stan Lee revolutionized the medium with Spider-Man, a superhero who learned that extraordinary powers didn't relieve him of debt, girl trouble, or anything else that bothered ordinary people. By 1968 Lee's "Marvel Revolution" had become increasingly preoccupied with events in the real world; hence, this "Crisis on Campus!" issue. The story line isn't as radical as John Romita's cover may suggest, for the students are agitating merely for a new dorm building. However, the signs partially hidden by Spidey's left foot read "DOW," which might have been a slap at Dow Chemical, manufacturer of napalm, the jellied gasoline used by U.S. forces in Vietnam.

In the 1968 film *The Producers,* scheming Broadway producer Max Bialystock (played by Zero Mostel, *right*) tries to corrupt his timid auditor, Leo Bloom (played by Gene Wilder). Masterful comic performances and Mel Brooks's sure-handed direction mark this show business satire, as Max tries to get out of debt by selling backers more than 100 percent of a play he is sure will fail. When his production of *Springtime for Hitler,* a lighthearted romantic musical about the regime of *Der Führer,* is a surprise hit, Max and Leo are in deep trouble.

Beverly Sills was probably the most famous and skilled American coloratura soprano of the 1960s, and a mainstay of the New York City Opera, the city's "second" opera company. She toured the world in the late 1960s and made her Metropolitan Opera debut in 1975 (earning an 18-minute standing ovation at the end). But her heart was with the New York City Opera; she retired from singing to manage that company in 1980.

1968

November 14: National Turn in Your Draft Card Day is celebrated with the burning of draft cards and war protest rallies on numerous U.S. campuses.

November 22: A federal district court rules that Title VII of the 1964 Civil Rights Act supersedes California protective labor laws that restrict women from working overtime and from lifting weights in excess of prescribed limits.

November 26: Halfback O. J. Simpson of the University of Southern California wins the Heisman Trophy.

November 27: President-elect Nixon asks Harvard professor Henry Kissinger to be his national security adviser. Kissinger will accept.

December: A pandemic of the Hong Kong flu begins to peak in the U.S. From September 1968 to March 1969, approximately 33,800 Americans will die from the flu.

December 1: A report issued by the National Commission on the Causes and Prevention of Violence is highly critical of the conduct of Chicago police during the 1968 Democratic National Convention.

December 3: Elvis Presley makes his first television appearance in eight years in an hour-long NBC-TV special.

December 20: Famed American author John Steinbeck dies at 66.

December 22: North Korea releases 82 crew members of the USS *Pueblo*, a U.S. surveillance ship captured off the North Korean coast on January 23, 1968, after the U.S. signs a document confirming that the ship had been in North Korean waters. • Julie Nixon, daughter of the president-elect, marries Dwight David Eisenhower II, grandson of former President Eisenhower.

December 24: Apollo 8 astronauts become the first humans to orbit the moon.

December 27: Red China resumes nuclear testing.

This split image illustrates one of the most famous gaffes in television sports history—the "Heidi Game." In a pro football contest on November 17, 1968, the New York Jets led the Oakland Raiders 32–29 with a minute left in the fourth quarter. NBC left the game in the eastern and central time zones because of a contractual obligation to show a film special based on the beloved children's story, *Heidi*. Football couch potatoes in the East and Midwest were outraged when they learned that they had missed two Oakland touchdowns in a stunning comeback during that final minute. A torrent of angry calls led to an abject apology from NBC President Julian Goodman the next day.

Police battle demonstrators at San Francisco State University in the fall of 1968. A coalition of students representing African-American, Latino, and Asian-American student organizations stopped classes and struggled with police in what became the longest student strike in the 1960s, lasting from November 1968 to March 1969. The strike was finally broken by the determined action of acting President S. I. Hayakawa, who became something of a hero to conservative critics of student activism. Ultimately, however, the students achieved their central goal—the creation of America's first College of Ethnic Studies.

Artist Wes Wilson, with wife Eva, poses in front of his work. While working for concert promoter Bill Graham, Wilson virtually single-handedly invented psychedelic poster art. He began producing posters for shows at the Avalon and Fillmore West venues in San Francisco in early 1966. Soon, his use of LSD-influenced imagery and idiosyncratic lettering that filled every bit of space began to attract notice. His genre-defining work became widely imitated by other artists.

Actor Jack Lemmon (as Felix Unger) points accusingly at Walter Matthau (as Oscar Madison) in the 1968 film *The Odd Couple*. Based on Neil Simon's hit play (and later to become a popular television series), this film brought together for the first time the immense comedic talents of Lemmon and Matthau. It chronicles the adventures of a divorced sportswriter (Matthau) rooming with a friend (Lemmon) who has been tossed out by his wife. Oscar is the inveterate slob, while Felix is the ultimate in prissy neatness. The writing is sharp and witty, and the chemistry between the actors is superb.

Elvis Presley entertains fans during his hour-long NBC special on December 3, 1968. Elvis, who had been making films almost nonstop during the 1960s, feared he was losing his fan base to newer, more socially conscious rockers. His live NBC show marked the beginning of his comeback. The King went on to record 21 songs in 1969, including the hit "In the Ghetto." His album *From Elvis to Memphis* reached No. 8 in the U.S. and No. 2 in Britain.

A victim of the Hong Kong flu looks quizzically at his bottle of medicine as he takes his temperature. This variant of the Asian flu, which struck in 1957, hit the United States in September 1968 and peaked in December. The Hong Kong flu killed 33,800 people, mostly elderly, in the United States. Upwards of 700,000 people worldwide succumbed to the virus.

New & Notable

Books

Airport by Arthur Hailey
The Armies of the Night
   by Norman Mailer
Couples by John Updike
The Electric Kool-Aid Acid Test
   by Tom Wolfe
Myra Breckinridge by Gore Vidal
Slouching Toward Bethlehem
   by Joan Didion
Soul on Ice by Eldridge Cleaver

Movies

Barbarella
Bullitt
Night of the Living Dead
The Odd Couple
Once Upon a Time in the West
Planet of the Apes
The Producers
Rosemary's Baby
2001: A Space Odyssey
Vixen
Wild in the Streets
Yellow Submarine

Songs

"Born to Be Wild" by Steppenwolf
"Elenore" by the Turtles
"Harper Valley P.T.A."
   by Jeannie C. Riley
"Hey Jude" by the Beatles
"Mrs. Robinson"
   by Simon and Garfunkel
"(Sittin' on) The Dock of the Bay"
   by Otis Redding
"Tiptoe Through the Tulips"
   by Tiny Tim
"White Room" by Cream

Television

Adam-12
Hawaii Five-0
Julia
Land of the Giants
The Mod Squad
60 Minutes

Theater

Hair
The Happy Time
Plaza Suite
The Prime of Miss Jean Brodie
Promises, Promises

The 1968 Beatles film *Yellow Submarine* was the only non-Disney, animated, full-length movie in the 1960s to achieve popular and critical success. The unique film mixes Art Nouveau with Surrealism and features such bizarre villains as the Blue Meanies and the Snapping Turtle Turks. The plot is pretty light, and clearly subordinate to the stylized visuals. And, of course, there is the music, which represents "the boys" at their zenith. The film features songs from *Rubber Soul, Revolver,* and *Sgt. Pepper's Lonely Hearts Club Band.* As reviewer Sam Sutherland wrote, the viewer is submerged "blissfully in the sights and sounds of this . . . treat."

U.S. Marines greet each other with the Black Power salute in Con Thien, South Vietnam, in December 1968. Martin Luther King's assassination earlier that year fueled an increasing black militancy, especially among those of draft age. African-Americans also were upset with "Project 100,000." The U.S. Defense Department had launched the project in 1966 partly to pull so-called black troublemakers off the streets. The department lowered the standards for draft requirements, making an estimated 100,000 former "rejects" acceptable for induction. The project resulted in a disproportionate number of black soldiers being sent to the front lines.

Although a combination of style and function, the average American living room of 1968 was a diluted reinterpretation of more exciting design trends available only to those with the means to afford them. Middle-class suburban families were less adventurous, and tended to fuse styles and mix many colors. Color schemes in the suburban home during the late 1960s often featured deep browns and avocado greens. Typical furniture included traditional low-slung couches and chairs with short, tapered legs. Eastern-influenced basket-style chairs also were popular.

Regrouping after a year spent largely in court or in jail (due to drug busts), the Rolling Stones in 1968 renounced their psychedelic dabbling to return to their country-blues roots. Stung by the nearly universal whipping they had received over *Their Satanic Majesties Request,* the new effort was consciously pared down, as the Stones ditched exotic trappings for acoustic guitars and crude ambience. What resulted was *Beggar's Banquet,* arguably their first masterpiece. Two tracks drew special notice: "Street Fighting Man," banned in Chicago on the basis of its title, and "Sympathy for the Devil," an enumeration of mankind's blackest moments. The album was the Stones' last with drummer Brian Jones, who drowned in 1969.

This spectacular photograph shows the rising Earth that greeted Apollo 8 astronauts as they came from behind the moon on December 29, 1968. This was the first manned spacecraft to successfully leave Earth's gravity and orbit the moon. The mission was designed to evaluate crew performance and test systems in preparation for a moon landing in 1969. Perhaps the mission's most memorable moment came on Christmas Eve, when members of the three-man crew, led by Commander Frank Borman, read passages from the Book of Genesis on live television.

1969
Shooting for the Moon

HALF A MILLION AMERICANS, young and old, of all races and ethnicities, made their way to southwest Florida in July 1969. A mule-cart procession from the Poor People's March arrived; so did Hollywood celebrities, United Nations diplomats, and Nobel Prize winners. They were joined by hundreds of reporters and television camera crews from around the world. All came to watch three men take off in a rocket ship from Cape Kennedy for a voyage to the moon.

On July 19, the Apollo 11 spacecraft achieved lunar orbit. The next day the lunar landing module, the spidery-shaped "Eagle," gently pulled away from the Apollo 11 craft and made its way cautiously to the moon's surface. Once the Eagle was safely stabilized on the moon's Sea of Tranquility, astronaut Neil Armstrong opened the craft's hatch and descended the nine-rung ladder. Just before he reached the ground, he pulled a protruding handle that turned on an RCA-built black-and-white television camera. The whole world watched and listened as Armstrong became the first man to walk on the moon. "That's one small step for man," he said, "one giant leap for mankind."

While television viewers watched Armstrong and then Buzz Aldrin gleefully bounce around the lunar surface in their spacesuits, President Richard Nixon appeared on their TV sets as a split-screen image, broadcast live from the Oval Office in the White House. After chatting with the astronauts, the President read a statement: "Because of what you have done, the heavens have become a part of man's world. And as you talk to us from the Sea of Tran-

"Here men from the planet Earth first set foot on the Moon, July 1969 A.D. We came in peace for all mankind."

—INSCRIPTION ON A PLAQUE THE APOLLO 11 ASTRONAUTS LEFT ON THE MOON

Apollo 11 astronaut Edwin "Buzz" Aldrin stands firmly planted on the surface of the moon on July 19, 1969. Visible in his faceplate is part of the lunar lander as well as Neil Armstrong, the first human being to set foot on an interplanetary body. The landing, and the astronauts' safe return, fulfilled a Cold War promise made by President Kennedy in 1961.

quility, it requires us to redouble our efforts to bring peace and tranquility to Earth. For one priceless moment in the whole history of man, all the people on this Earth are truly one—one in their pride in what you have done and one in our prayers that you will return safely to Earth."

The moon landing fulfilled a promise that President John F. Kennedy had made to the American people in May 1961. He had told them that the United States would beat the Soviet Union in the space race and that, "before the decade is out," America would put a man on the moon.

The space race had not been cheap. From May 1961 to July 1969, the United States government spent $33 billion on the space program. A few Americans, including Reverend Ralph Abernathy—who led the Poor People's Campaign mule-cart procession to Cape Canaveral—protested that the costs exceeded the benefits. However, when Neil Armstrong and Buzz Aldrin planted a nylon American flag on the moon's surface, held erect by an aluminum rod so it appeared to be blowing in a stiff wind, millions of Americans—even most of the mission's skeptics—marveled at the awesome sight.

Air and other environmental pollution had been serious problems in America for most of the 20th century, and by the close of the 1960s no American with eyes and a nose could ignore them. Business and industry had to be prodded into action by legislation, and the early cleanup campaign was slow. This smoky tableau of open hearth and blast furnaces, operated by U.S. Steel, was snapped in Gary, Indiana.

Still, almost as soon as the Apollo team landed its space capsule safely in the Pacific Ocean, the apparent unity that the moon walk had offered began to unravel. Nobel Prize winner Harold C. Urey worried that the whole affair was a bizarre act of hubris, "something like the building of the pyramids or the Parthenon." Lewis Mumford, one of the era's reigning intellectuals and social critics, characterized the landing as a symbolic act of aggression tantamount to what Mumford felt was the hypocrisy of the Air Force slogan, "Peace is Our Profession."

By the end of the 1960s, no consensus existed in the United States about the meaning of the Apollo space program or just about anything else. In particular, the belief in scientific and technological "progress" was under fire by an increasing number of Americans. Fueling much of the doubt and anxiety was a new ecological consciousness made relevant by a series of public environmental catastrophes.

In January and February 1969, an off-shore Union Oil rig line ruptured near Santa Barbara, California, spilling millions of gallons of crude oil that befouled 40 miles of California coastline and killed thousands of sea birds and other aquatic creatures. A few months later, in Cleveland, people were stunned when officials warned that the sludge-brown water of the Cuyahoga

River was so coated with chemical toxins and petroleum products that it was a fire hazard. (On June 22, it did indeed catch fire!) Moreover, scientists declared nearby Lake Erie a "dying sinkhole" polluted by a daily dose of 11 million pounds of chlorides and sulfates.

Other reports barraged the public: Scientists warned that the insecticide and likely carcinogen DDT was being found in dangerously high levels in mothers' breast milk. Even more harrowing, biologist Paul Ehrlich declared in the best-selling book *The Population Bomb* that the world's burgeoning population would soon devour all the Earth's natural resources.

In late 1969 Wisconsin Senator Gaylord Nelson proposed that college students needed to wake up the rest of the nation to environmental dangers by holding a nationwide teach-in, just as some of them had done four years earlier when they had launched the Vietnam War teach-in movement. After months of energetic organizing, Earth Day took place in April 1970. More than 10,000 schools took part and some 20 million people participated.

By the end of the 1960s, even as Americans cheered their nation's victory in space, tens of millions feared that an ethos that promoted—above all other considerations—economic growth based on technological advancement might actually threaten humankind's quality of life. They worried that the world was turning into a perilously overcrowded, resource-starved, toxic planet.

Uncertainty about the environment wasn't the only anxiety affecting the American people in 1969. The Vietnam War continued to tear apart the nation. Richard Nixon had run for the presidency promising to end the war by bringing "peace with honor." Once in office, Nixon did announce plans to "Vietnamize" the war by decreasing American ground troops and increasing aid to the Army of the Republic of Vietnam. But throughout 1969, the Vietnam War seemed to continue much as it had before. More than 9,000 American soldiers were killed in Vietnam during the year.

In May, soldiers of the 101st Airborne were ordered to assault a heavily fortified North Vietnam Army position on Dong Ap Bia Mountain. After 10 horrific days of combat that resulted in 56 Americans killed in action and some 400 wounded, the troops took the position, which they renamed Hamburger Hill to commemorate the carnage. Immediately after winning the objective, the men were told to move on and search out more enemy troops. The battle seemed to serve no purpose.

Members of the 101st Airborne Division fire into a North Vietnamese bunker on Ap Bia Mountain on May 20, 1969. That day, Communist forces retreated following a grinding 10-day battle in which 56 Americans and about 600 North Vietnamese troops were killed (420 Americans were wounded). Once taken, the mountain—dubbed "Hamburger Hill" by cynical American GIs—was abandoned to the Communists.

The American troops themselves were turning against the war in increasing numbers. Many serving in Vietnam viewed the conflict as an enormous gopher hole into which the U.S. had fallen. They could see no end in sight, and no sensible rationale for the fighting, either, since it looked as if the people of South Vietnam were being harmed more than they were being helped. Some GIs felt that to take the chance of getting killed in such a war just wasn't worth it. Vietnam vet and historian Terry Anderson wrote: "By the end of 1969 in some units, during 1970 in others, the army stopped fighting—and began surviving—in Vietnam."

At home, millions protested the war. Antiwar activists formed the Vietnam Moratorium Committee to launch a national teach-in. On October 15, as many as 10 million Americans participated, taking the day off from work or school to discuss how to end the war. It was considered the largest public protest ever held in the United States. Even some soldiers in Vietnam participated, wearing black armbands.

About 250,000 Americans, including this group near the Washington Monument, took part in War Moratorium activities in Washington, D.C., on November 15, 1969. General Earle Wheeler, chairman of the Joint Chiefs of Staff, dismissed Moratorium participants as "interminably vocal youngsters, strangers alike to soap and reason."

President Nixon was furious with the protesters. Not long after the moratorium, he went on national television to blast antiwar activists as traitors. He called on his supporters to stand up against the dissidents: "To you, the great silent majority of my fellow Americans, I ask for your support.... North Vietnam cannot defeat ... the United States. Only Americans can do that."

Public opinion polls taken after the speech revealed that the American people were, in fact, deeply polarized by the war. About half of all Americans told pollsters that they thought the war was "morally indefensible." About 60 percent called it a "mistake," and 80 percent were "fed up and tired of the war." Despite Americans' increasing rejection of the war and the mounting casualties, no progress was being made toward either victory or "peace with honor" as 1969 drew to a close.

Americans were distraught for other reasons in 1969. African-American student militants made headlines by taking over university buildings and even shutting down campuses. At Cornell University, about 100 black students armed with shotguns and rifles occupied the student union and demanded that the administration fund a black studies center. At San Francisco State, black students who had felt the sting of disenfranchisement called for "Third World revolution." They were joined by white radicals and other students of color in a strike that lasted 134 days.

Similar actions occurred at the University of Texas, University of California at San Diego, Rutgers University, and elsewhere. Largely inspired by such actions, Chicano activists in the Southwest also became far more militant. At the Chicano Youth Liberation Conference in Denver, activist Alberto Alurista outlined a new separatist agenda, calling for "the independence of our mestizo Nation." In November, Native Americans seized control of Alcatraz Island in San Francisco Bay as a protest for Indian rights.

Moreover, a faction of the primarily white student New Left was turning toward a revolutionary ideology. At a June 1969 national convention, the Students for a Democratic Society splintered ideologically. Out of the organizational rubble came the Weather Underground, which vowed to work with Third World revolutionaries both in the United States and abroad in overthrowing the American government. President Nixon responded to this radical turn by urging the FBI and the Justice Department to crack down everywhere on political dissidence.

At the local level, reaction was even stronger. On December 4, Chicago police raided the apartment of local Black Panthers leader Fred Hampton and, apparently without provocation, executed him and a fellow Panther, Mark Clark. Throughout 1969, the forces of law and order, led by President Nixon, and an increasingly militant antiwar and social justice movement angrily squared off against one another. In August, 400,000 young people retreated to Bethel, New York, near Woodstock, for a pot-smoking, acid-dropping, rock 'n' roll party. For most of them, it was merely a three-day respite from what they felt was a stifling society.

At the beginning of the 1960s, President Kennedy had promised Americans a man on the moon, a hard struggle against Soviet communism, and new domestic policies to ease racial inequality and economic inequity. Apollo 11 made good on the first pledge, but for most Americans the Vietnam War had demonstrated that something was wrong with the Cold War verities that had for so long governed the United States. Not surprisingly, even as monumental civil rights victories had been won by the end of the 1960s, Americans continued to fight over how to end widespread discrimination and to create greater economic equity.

In ways President Kennedy never could have imagined, new freedoms and new forms of cultural expression rocked American society in the 1960s, creating an era of experimentation that challenged almost every facet of conventional morality. By the end of 1969, whether they liked it or not, Americans were well aware that they had experienced a decade of extraordinary social and political turmoil.

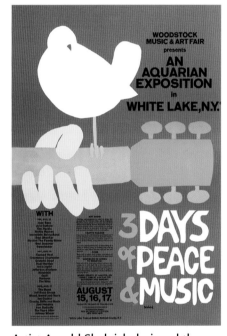

Artist Arnold Skolnick designed the catbird-and-guitar poster that promoted the Woodstock Music & Art Fair of August 15–17, 1969. Put together by four young entrepreneurs, the festival was held on 600 rented acres in rural Bethel, New York, near White Lake. At least 400,000 people jammed highways and roads to enjoy the Jefferson Airplane, Jimi Hendrix, the Who, Janis Joplin, and other top rock acts.

1969

1969: Former child star Shirley Temple Black is appointed to the U.S. delegation to the United Nations General Assembly. • Baseball's American League and National League each expand from 10 to 12 teams and divide into two six-team divisions. Division winners square off in five-game playoff series prior to the World Series. • Al Goldstein, publisher of *Screw* magazine, initiates publication of *Gay,* New York's first tabloid aimed at the gay community.

Early 1969: University of California academic Arthur Jensen, in an article in the February 1969 issue of the *Harvard Educational Review,* states that low test scores by African-Americans on standardized tests is indicative of their supposed genetic inferiority.

January: Sixteen percent of the U.S. budget submitted to Congress by the outgoing Johnson Administration is to fund military activities in Vietnam and elsewhere in Southeast Asia. • Following a drill malfunction, up to 200,000 gallons of crude oil are released into the Santa Barbara Channel off the coast of Southern California. Beaches on the California mainland and on nearby islands are contaminated. Restoration will be delayed by months of intensive cleanup. • Newark police seize 30,000 copies of John Lennon and Yoko Ono's *Two Virgins* album because of the nude images of the pair on the album's sleeve. Sale of the album will be prohibited in Cleveland. • The first national conference on abortion laws convenes in Chicago and establishes the National Association for the Repeal of Abortion Laws (NARAL). • Unofficial government studies suggest that as many as 50 percent of American troops in Vietnam have used heroin, opium, and/or marijuana, all easily obtainable in Saigon.

January 1: Ohio State beats No. 2 Southern California 27–16 in the Rose Bowl to finish as an undefeated national champion.

From the ashes of the British Invasion-era Yardbirds, guitarist Jimmy Page formed a new band, steeped in the blues but sonically heavier than anything that had come before. Joined by fellow studio veteran John Paul Jones, Page enlisted the talents of bombastic drummer John Bonham and vocalist Robert Plant to form the New Yardbirds, who became known as Led Zeppelin by the time their first album (*pictured*) was released in January 1969. Though regarded with ambivalence by most critics, the band's assault on listeners' senses found a ready audience among those who liked their rock raunchy, textured, and loud. An era of heavy-metal rock had begun.

On January 20, 1969, Richard Nixon was inaugurated as the 37th president of the United States, ending the turbulent, five-year reign of Lyndon Johnson. Despite the dismal weather and the voices of protesters nearby, Nixon did his best to articulate his inaugural theme to "bring us together again." Flanked by Johnson (*far left*) and Vice President Spiro Agnew (*near right*), Nixon appealed to his "silent majority," saying that his government would listen to the "voices of quiet anguish." "For all of our people," the law-and-order president said, "we will set as our goal the decent order that makes progress possible and our lives secure."

The Paris Peace Talks began in 1968, partially in reaction to the Tet Offensive, which increased political pressure to withdraw American troops. But negotiations quickly stalled over procedure, including what shape the conference table should be. Once in office in 1969, President Nixon appointed Henry Cabot Lodge as chief U.S. negotiator. Little was accomplished in the public talks that year, as both sides were stalemated over central issues. The United States wanted both sides to withdraw from South Vietnam before a negotiated settlement, and North Vietnam wanted total U.S. withdrawal and a coalition government to replace the Thieu regime. Behind the scenes, however, Henry Kissinger began meeting with Hanoi representatives in secret meetings that eventually would lead to peace in the 1970s.

In January and February 1969, thick, black crude oil began to wash up on the 35-mile coastline of wealthy and middle-class beach communities near Santa Barbara, California. One of the many nearby offshore oil rigs had sprung a leak, contaminating the water. The thick ooze covered ducks and other sea birds to the point that they couldn't move. Horrified residents nearby attempted to clean the birds. For many, the event accentuated the dark side of prosperity. Along with the Cuyahoga River fire in Cleveland the same year, the Santa Barbara oil spill helped to spur anti-pollution movements and the creation of Earth Day.

Broadway Joe

IN 1967 THE FIRST AFL–NFL championship game, called the Super Bowl, was played in a stadium only two-thirds full. By 1969, the big game's ascent to quasi-holiday status had begun, aided by the star quality of the New York Jets' upstart quarterback, "Broadway" Joe Namath.

Neither the Jets nor the AFL were given much respect, and New York went into the game against the Baltimore Colts as an 18-point underdog. Namath challenged the belittling three days before the contest when he responded to a heckler by saying, "We're gonna win the game. I guarantee it." Brash and cocky, Namath contrasted starkly with the Colts' longtime mainstay, Johnny Unitas. Although Unitas had spent the season on the bench, nursing an injured elbow, the press nevertheless relished the notion of the crew-cut veteran pitted against the shaggy-haired rebel.

At game time, the Colts quarterback was not Unitas but the merely competent Earl Morrall. His presence threatened to sap some of the energy from the contest, but Namath sparked the event by outwitting the vaunted Baltimore defense. He completed 17 of 28 passes for 206 yards. Morrall, for his part, was intercepted three times, overlooked a wide-open receiver in the end zone, and was replaced in the final minutes of the third quarter by Unitas. The veteran got the Colts on the board, but the Jets won the game 16–7. The upset made Namath a household name while simultaneously transforming the Super Bowl into a highly anticipated annual event.

1969

January 5: Dr. Benjamin Spock is indicted for "conspiracy to aid, counsel, and abet" young American men to violate Selective Service laws.

January 7: Fed up with campus unrest at California state universities and colleges, Governor Ronald Reagan asks the state legislature to "drive criminal anarchists and latter-day Fascists off the campuses."

January 12: The New York Jets win Super Bowl III 16–7 over the Baltimore Colts. Jets quarterback Joe Namath had "guaranteed" the upset victory.

January 14: The flight and hangar decks of the nuclear-powered U.S. Navy aircraft carrier USS *Enterprise* are engulfed by fire; 27 crewmen die and approximately 100 are injured.

January 16: The first-ever transfer of men from one space vehicle to another is achieved by Soviet cosmonauts when two Soyuz spacecraft dock.

January 17: Los Angeles Black Panther Party leaders Alprentice Carter and Jon Huggins are shot and killed by members of the United Slaves black power group. The confrontation probably was triggered by anti-Panther propaganda forged by the FBI's COINTELPRO intelligence unit.

January 18: At the Paris Peace Talks, U.S. and North Vietnamese negotiators are joined by representatives from South Vietnam and the pro-Communist National Liberation Front (NLF).

January 18–26: Torrential rain over Southern California leaves at least 100 people dead and 9,000 homes destroyed.

January 20: Richard M. Nixon is inaugurated as the 37th president of the United States. • Academic and political theorist Henry Kissinger assumes duties as national security adviser to President Nixon.

January 21: Navajo Community College, the first Indian tribal college, opens in Many Farms, Arizona.

In the months after Soviet tanks rolled into Czechoslovakia in August 1968, tensions ran high, as protesters continued to resist the Soviet pressures for "normalization" in the country. In Prague during January, a young man named Jan Palach burned himself to death in an act of public protest. Several more suicides followed, and the public protest continued. On January 26 in Prague, three busloads of riot police armed with tear gas descended on a crowd of protesters (*pictured*). They had gathered to commemorate Palach's martyrdom and protest the occupation.

On February 11, 1969, a group of students broke into the computer center on the campus of Montreal's Sir George Williams University. The group of mostly West Indian students hoped to draw attention to charges of racism against faculty members. Students damaged the university's computer system, set papers on fire, and tossed computer punch cards from windows. Elsewhere in Canada in 1969, student unrest occurred at McGill University in Montreal. The uprisings drew Canada's attention to the mistreatment of ethnic minorities in the country's public schools and job market.

Flight attendant Roberta Truppman describes how she was held at gunpoint by hijackers who demanded to be flown to Cuba. The February 1969 incident was relatively unremarkable, with the occurrence of skyjackings to the island Communist nation having become routine after 1967 (about 20 took place in 1969 alone). Skyjackers were usually disillusioned Cuban exiles looking for a quick way home or U.S. criminals looking to escape to Cuba. Stricter security measures, sky marshals, and severe penalties—as well as the fact that a fed-up Cuban government finally initiated a policy of returning skyjackers to the States—helped bring the problem under control by 1973.

After the 1967 Arab–Israeli war, Iraq cut off diplomatic ties with the United States, and its leftist regime grew increasingly anti-American and anti-Israeli. Iraqi leaders also linked the Arab cause to what they viewed as other anticolonial movements, such as North Vietnam's war with the U.S. In this atmosphere, the Iraqi government in early 1969 held a series of public espionage trials and executions. They targeted Iraqi Jews and others suspected of spying for Israel and the CIA. Here, the bodies of two convicted spies hang from gallows in Liberation Square in Baghdad, where officials put the bodies of seven men on display on February 21.

After decades of churning out heavy, gas-guzzling cars of indifferent quality, Detroit automakers were blindsided by Japanese competitors in the late 1960s. Both Toyota (represented here by the Toyota Corolla) and Datsun made steady inroads into the American market. Though Toyota first entered the country in 1957, only with 1968's Corolla—low-priced and gas-efficient—was a foothold established. In 1969 U.S. sales of the Corolla skyrocketed to 130,000. Detroit automakers would scramble to produce inexpensive cars of their own in the 1970s, leading to such infamously substandard creations as the Gremlin, Vega, and Pinto.

1969

January 22: The U.S. Marines begin Operation Dewey Canyon in Vietnam to secure the A Shau area, a supply destination for the enemy. Marines eventually will capture tons of enemy supplies, including machine guns, tires, and rockets.

January 25: Great numbers of Czech students in Prague turn out for the funeral of Jan Palach, a student who protested Soviet occupation of Czechoslovakia by burning himself to death on January 16.

January 30: President Nixon instructs the Defense Department to develop a plan for an all-volunteer military that would allow the U.S. to do away with the draft. • The Beatles perform an impromptu concert on the roof of Apple Records in London.

January–March: Between 100,000 and 200,000 Soviet troops—eight to 10 divisions—are moved to Mongolia, as Sino–Soviet relations grow increasingly tense.

February 2: Boris Karloff, famed horror-film actor, dies at 81.

February 3: Yasir Arafat, leader of the radical Islamic group Al Fatah, is appointed leader of the Palestinian Liberation Organization (PLO).

February 5: The FCC announces its support of a ban on cigarette advertising on television.

February 9: NOW proclaims "Public Accommodations Week," and takes action at "men only" restaurants, bars, and other public places.

February 8–10: The East Coast is hit with a heavy snowfall, up to two feet in some areas, contributing to the deaths of 166 people.

February 14: Vito Genovese, dominant underworld "boss of all bosses," dies in prison at 71. • Professor Robert Edwards, an academic physiologist at Cambridge University, achieves the first human in vitro fertilization, paving the way for human "test-tube" babies.

President Nixon picked Spiro Agnew as his running mate for the 1968 election as part of his strategy to court votes in the South. Agnew, the son of Greek immigrants, had worked his way up through the ranks of the Republican Party to become the governor of Maryland in 1966. When riots erupted in his state, Agnew publicly berated black leaders. His outspoken performance made his appearance on the ticket appealing to southern voters and to the country's "silent majority." A perfect attack dog for Nixon, Agnew criticized the media, intellectuals, and especially antiwar protesters, saying it was "time to sweep that kind of garbage out of our society." Agnew would resign in 1973 during an investigation of tax evasion.

Heeding lessons gleaned from his loss to John F. Kennedy in the 1960 presidential election, Richard Nixon attempted to soften his cold-blooded image by using televised photo ops and engaging those not among his natural constituency whenever possible. This cartoon by the *Atlanta Constitution*'s Baldy satirizes the transparent glad-handing Nixon engaged in—as well as the bad-guy role fulfilled by Vice President Spiro Agnew.

A product of the pop-psychology boom of the late 1960s, Dr. Thomas Harris's *I'm OK–You're OK* was based upon a reinterpretation of Freudian psychoanalytic methods. Written as a practical guide to understanding this new approach, referred to as transactional analysis, Harris argues that individuals are responsible for their own future regardless of their childhood experiences. One of the most sought-after self-help titles, *I'm OK–You're OK* went on to sell more than 15 million copies.

Yoko Ono, an artist connected to the avant-garde Fluxus movement, married John Lennon on March 20, 1969. The wedding was followed by an "open honeymoon" (*pictured*) at the Hilton in Amsterdam, where the couple invited reporters to visit. Soon after the honeymoon, they held their famous "bed-in" in a Toronto hotel room, where they sang "Give Peace a Chance" with Timothy Leary and other celebrities. Ono and Lennon had first met in 1966, and they eventually divorced their spouses and became inseparable. The intense personal and artistic relationship between the two helped to contribute to tensions among the Beatles in the period before the group's breakup.

Nixon and De-escalation

WHEN RICHARD NIXON CAMPAIGNED for the presidency in 1968, he pledged that if elected he would achieve "peace with honor" in Vietnam. By the time he took office, he well understood how unpopular the war had become with the public. In 1969 he moved to create the public appearance that he was de-escalating the war—while simultaneously expanding the war in secret.

In his first year in office, Nixon announced the first American troop withdrawals of the war: 60,000 in two phases by the end of the year. These withdrawals, the President said, constituted the first step in a process of "Vietnamizing" the war—that is, turning over the responsibilities for fighting the ground war, in particular, to the Army of the Republic of Vietnam (South Vietnam).

In addition, Nixon reformed the Selective Service System by introducing a random selection process. This draft lottery eliminated most of the draft deferments that had previously guaranteed that disproportionate numbers of poor, working-class, and minority men fought and died in Vietnam.

At the same time that Nixon seemed to be de-escalating the ground war, however, he took steps to expand and intensify the air war. Six weeks into his presidency, he authorized the so-called "Menu" bombings, a 14-month assault that involved more than 3,600 sorties and dropped about 150,000 tons of bombs on targets in Cambodia. The bombings were kept secret by having the pilots keep two flight logs—one with details of the real mission and another with details of a phantom mission that did not leave South Vietnam airspace. In May 1970 Nixon would send ground troops into Cambodia.

In May 1969 *The New York Times* broke the news of the secret bombings, prompting Nixon to order wiretaps on reporters' phones. This began a pattern of illegal behavior that would lead directly to the Watergate affair, which destroyed Nixon's presidency.

In 1969 tensions ran high between China and the Soviet Union, as a series of border clashes brought longstanding animosities between the Communist powers into the open. Here, Soviet soldiers defend an island on the Ussuri River, a border between the two countries. One skirmish on a contested island near the Ussuri resulted in the deaths of a Soviet photographer and at least 31 Soviet border guards. The violence raised fears of war between the two countries, and the nations exchanged heated rhetoric. The New China News Agency announced that if the Soviets had the "audacity to continue attacking China," they would be "crushed to pieces by the iron fists of the 700 million Chinese people."

1969

February 16: Some 20,000 people demonstrate in Istanbul, Turkey, in response to a stopover visit by the U.S. Sixth Fleet.

February 27: Police at California–Berkeley charge student picket lines and club and arrest two Chicano student leaders.

March: Soviet and Chinese forces exchange fire along the Ussuri River on the Sino–Soviet border.

March 1: New Orleans businessman Clay Shaw is acquitted of charges of conspiracy in the death of President John F. Kennedy.

March 2–4: National Guardsmen are called to the University of Illinois at Champaign to quell a violent student protest set off by on-campus recruitment by General Electric, General Motors, Dow Chemical, Lockheed, U.S. Steel, and Standard Oil.

March 5: Israeli Defense Minister Moshe Dayan calls for Israeli settlements on the West Bank of occupied Arab territory. He also calls for Israeli law to supersede Jordanian and United Arab Republic law as it pertains to occupation.

March 10: In Memphis, James Earl Ray pleads guilty to the murder of Martin Luther King, Jr., and is sentenced to 99 years in prison.

March 17: Golda Meir is sworn in as prime minister of Israel. • President Nixon authorizes secret B-52 bombings of Cambodia in "Operation Menu," which targets North Vietnamese supply sanctuaries located along the Cambodia–Vietnam border.

March 20: John Lennon marries artist Yoko Ono in Gibraltar.

March 22: Antiwar activists break into the Washington, D.C., office of Dow Chemical. They splash blood and destroy files to protest Dow's manufacture of napalm, a weapon used in Vietnam. *See* November 7, 1969. • UCLA wins its fifth NCAA men's basketball title in six years.

Lew Alcindor pronounces his team No. 1 after UCLA's 92–72 triumph over Purdue in the 1969 NCAA basketball championship game in Louisville, Kentucky. From 1964 through 1975, UCLA forged the greatest hoops dynasty in history, winning 10 national championships. In the 1969 title game, Alcindor (who would change his name to Kareem Abdul-Jabbar) amassed 37 points and 20 rebounds to win his third national title in a row. He also captured his third consecutive Final Four Most Outstanding Player Award.

After a series of heart attacks, Dwight D. Eisenhower—the five-star general, supreme allied commander during World War II, and popular president—died at age 78 in Washington, D.C., on March 28, 1969. "Ike," as the public fondly referred to him, symbolized the golfing, barbecuing, easygoing affluence of postwar life to which many Americans aspired—and that many in the 1960s disdained. President Nixon proclaimed a day of mourning for the former president, whom he said "spoke with a moral authority seldom equaled in American public life." Eisenhower's body lay in state at the National Cathedral and at the Capitol before a formal funeral was held at the National Cathedral. Friends and family accompanied his casket by train to Abilene, Kansas, Eisenhower's hometown, where he was buried.

With their matching blazers, short haircuts, and repertoire of acoustic folk ballads, it would have been easy to mistake the Smothers brothers as relatively innocuous. But Tom Smothers (*left*) and Dick Smothers (*right*) proved to be subversives in Establishment clothing, as CBS executives discovered to their regret. Conceived as a hip alternative to *Bonanza,* their variety show, *The Smothers Brothers Comedy Hour,* became increasingly controversial, openly criticizing America's war policy. Despite high ratings, the Smothers brothers battled endlessly with CBS executives until the network canceled the show in spring 1969. In an April news conference, the brothers accused CBS of censorship.

Unlike other elite universities during the war, Harvard was comparatively untouched by the militant protests of the era. But on a pleasant afternoon on April 9, 1969, a militant SDS faction seized the main administration building on Harvard's campus. At least 300 students moved on the building to protest the college's ROTC program as well as university housing rents. Here, Assistant Dean Archie Epps is escorted from the building by students, who in some cases dragged or carried resistant administrators from behind their desks. The next day, 400 police officers in riot gear ended the occupation.

Ed Whitefield (*right*) and several well-armed black students leave Straight Hall on the Cornell University campus in Ithaca, New York, on April 20, 1969, after barricading themselves in for 36 hours. An Associated Press photographer gasped, "Oh, my God, look at those goddamn guns!" The school administration was impressed, too, and gave in to the group's demand for a degree-granting Afro-American studies program. Whitefield and his fellow protesters believed that education about the history and conditions of African-Americans was a crucial aspect of the struggle for black liberation. The administration agreed to drop all charges against the group and moved quickly to create the program.

413

March 28: Former President Dwight D. Eisenhower, 78, dies in Washington, D.C.

March 29: A Detroit police officer is killed in a shootout with a black separatist group called the Republic of New Africa. • In Chicago, antiwar activists Rennie Davis, David Dellinger, John Froines, Tom Hayden, Abbie Hoffman, Jerry Rubin, Lee Weiner, and Black Panther cofounder Bobby Seale—the "Chicago Eight"—are indicted on federal charges of conspiring to cross state lines with intent to incite violence (at the 1968 Democratic National Convention). A week earlier, the same grand jury indicted eight Chicago police officers for civil rights violations against demonstrators and reporters at the convention. *See* September 24, 1969.

April: Students, including members of the SDS, riot at Harvard University. Following the arrest of more than 100 students, the general student population begins a three-day strike at the university. *See* April 22, 1969.

April 4: CBS cancels *The Smothers Brothers Comedy Hour* because the network did not receive a show in time for pre-screening and possible censorship. The action prompts a suit against the network from producers/stars Tom and Dick Smothers.

April 15: A U.S. EC-121 spy plane carrying 31 crew members is shot down by a pair of North Korean MiGs off the Korean coast. President Nixon elects to continue the overflights, but does not retaliate.

April 17: Sirhan Sirhan is convicted of the 1968 murder of Senator Robert Kennedy. • Northern Ireland nationalist Bernadette Devlin is elected to the British House of Commons.

April 19: About 80 armed African-American students take over the main administration building at Cornell University in Ithaca, New York, protesting racism on campus and demanding a black studies program.

In April and May 1969, students on the City College of New York campus protested in an effort to convince the Board of Higher Education to create black and Puerto Rican studies programs. They also wanted a curriculum and admissions policy that would more closely reflect the needs of New York's neighborhoods. In a culmination of weeks of protest and repeated class cancellations, more than 300 protesters clashed with police and at least 400 counter-protesters. During the turmoil and violence, protesters set several fires. Soon after the protests, the Board of Higher Education made substantial changes, including the introduction of Puerto Rican and Afro-American history classes.

Members of the National Organization for Women (NOW) picket the White House during "Freedom for Women Week" on May 8, 1969. NOW, which had helped to ignite the women's movement in the mid-1960s, hoped to pressure passage of the proposed Equal Rights Amendment (ERA) to the Constitution. Seeking equality within the existing system, NOW hoped that lobbying and the enforcement of legislation would curtail sex discrimination. The organization later would be criticized by radical feminists, who sought a revolution rather than reform. The ERA, which stated "equality of rights shall not be denied or abridged by the United States or any state on account of sex," was never passed.

Former SNCC organizer James Forman stood in front of Riverside Church in New York City on May 4, 1969, to read his "Black Manifesto," which insisted on reparations for African-Americans. The manifesto demanded $500 million from churches and synagogues for their roles in perpetuating and profiting from slavery. Forman warned that the patience of black activists was waning quickly, and that time was short. The idea of reparations was widely rejected, although it continued to be advocated by various African-American groups well into the 21st century.

After University of California–Berkeley officials tore down a group of buildings on campus, the university let the lot sit idle long enough for activists to imagine the space as a public park—"People's Park." Students even rolled out fresh turf and planted trees and a vegetable garden. However, the university planned to build a dormitory on the lot, and police arrived on May 15, 1969, to close off the park. The crowd attacked the police with rocks and bottles, and the cops fired back with buckshot, killing a bystander named James Rector and injuring 50. As skirmishes continued during the week, Governor Ronald Reagan called in the National Guard (*pictured*). On May 20, soldiers in helicopters sprayed tear gas on protesters, causing them to vomit and their eyes to burn. Street fighting continued for more than two weeks. All told, some 1,000 people were arrested and 200 were charged with felonies.

An American infantryman attempts to alleviate heatstroke near the Vietnam–Cambodia border. In March 1969, President Nixon ordered carpet bombing of targets in Cambodia in an attempt to wipe out enemy supply depots. "Operation Menu" widened the war into officially neutral territory, at the cost of nearly half a million civilian lives. The action, kept secret from Nixon's closest advisers and the public alike, was revealed by *The New York Times* in May 1969. To uncover the leak, Nixon ordered wiretaps of several reporters and administration officials. The following year's full-scale invasion of Cambodia triggered widespread protests throughout the country. Cambodian Prince Sihanouk, viewed as an unreliable ally, was deposed with tacit U.S. approval in favor of dictator Lon Nol, paving the way for the Khmer Rouge takeover and subsequent Cambodian genocide.

April 22: Following student unrest earlier in the month, the Harvard faculty votes to create a black studies program and give students a vote in selection of its faculty. *See* May 5, 1969. • Black and Puerto Rican students at City College of New York lock themselves inside campus buildings after requesting greater minority enrollment. The college is temporarily closed.

April 28: French President Charles de Gaulle resigns following defeat of a national referendum on regionalization reform of the French Senate. • An "Okinawa Day" student march in Tokyo to protest the 17th anniversary of the U.S. occupation leads to a stoppage of public transportation and about 800 arrests.

April 30: American troop levels in Vietnam peak at 543,400. So far, more than 36,000 Americans have been killed, more than in the entire Korean conflict.

May: *The New York Times* reveals the secret U.S. bombing of Cambodia. President Nixon wants to determine the source of the news leak, and orders FBI wiretaps on the telephones of four journalists and 13 government officials.

May 4: Sunday services at Riverside Church in New York City are interrupted by James Forman, a former organizer of SNCC, who presents the "Black Manifesto." He demands reparations for slavery, to be paid by whites and churches.

May 5: A fire damages the ROTC building at Harvard University. It will be ruled an arson.

May 11: North Vietnamese forces launch the heaviest offensive against the South since the Tet campaign.

May 13: Malaysia is rocked by racial violence that kills 196, most of whom are Chinese. More than 430 people are injured and about 40 disappear.

At a time when Nixon was pushing for the "Vietnamization" of the war, the battle at "Hamburger Hill" seemed to epitomize the "senseless and irresponsible" strategy of the war to such critics as Senator Ted Kennedy. The battle for Ap Bia Mountain near the border with Laos was particularly bloody. As U.S. soldiers climbed their way up the peak, the North Vietnamese Army greeted them by rolling hand grenades down the slope from above.

Fire, Smoke, and Tears on Hamburger Hill

THEN WE CALLED IN NAPALM on the enemy…these human beings.…Incredible.…It burned them up really bad. I was trying to take care of Cliff. We didn't have any medics any more. I was bandaging him. Then we called in the napalm, and it hit so close it singed off our faces. The North Vietnamese came out of their bunker and charged us. They were all wobbly and really hurt—but they opened up and charged us. The most frightening thing was the way they looked—the way the whole thing happened. We went crazy. We got enraged. Cliff was screaming things at them like, "YOU KILLED NICHOLAS!" Then it was over. The company commander lined all the rest of the company along the side of the hill. They threw smoke grenades down and enveloped us all in smoke…and we ran back up the hill…and picked up bodies. I don't remember doing that. We medivacked Cliff. He had to go out with the dead bodies. I was so sad. I couldn't believe the stuff I had lived through. I was really sad. I hid and cried. That was the only time I cried in Vietnam. I knew I was in trouble…because my system of numbing wasn't working anymore. I was really sad.

—U.S. ARMY SOLDIER STEVE TICE, RECALLING THE SCENE AT AP BIA MOUNTAIN (HAMBURGER HILL)

Hamburger Hill

FROM MAY 11 TO 20, 1969, the 101st Airborne Division fought one of the bloodiest battles of the Vietnam War on Ap Bia Mountain near the Laotian border. There, American forces encountered a large contingent of North Vietnamese regulars, who, contrary to their traditional tactic of evading direct frontal assaults by the enemy, battled the Americans head-on. Characterizing the often brutal, hand-to-hand combat as a "meat-grinder," the soldiers nicknamed Ap Bia "Hamburger Hill."

On May 20, after 10 previous attempts, and following an air assault that dropped more than a million pounds of bombs (including 152,000 pounds of napalm), the Americans took the mountain. The North Vietnamese retreated into Laos. Fifty-six American soldiers were killed, and 420 were wounded. An estimated 630 North Vietnamese were killed.

When American forces abandoned the hill eight days after the fighting ended, and the enemy reclaimed it, critics at home decried the senseless waste of American lives. The public outcry contributed to President Richard Nixon's

Wounded U.S. paratrooper near Ap Bia Mountain

decision to turn over most of the ground combat to the South Vietnamese—a process he called "Vietnamization"—and to begin withdrawing American troops.

Apollo 9 and 10 were crucial test flights in preparation for a lunar landing. During Apollo 9's mission in March, astronauts practiced maneuvers with the bug-like landing craft, including rocket tests and important rendezvous link-up procedures necessary for a successful landing and return trip. Apollo 10 soon followed in May with its orbit of the moon, during which astronauts practiced separating the lunar module from the command module. As Apollo 10, nicknamed "Charlie Brown," rounded the dark side of the moon, the crew photographed that area (*pictured*) and sent a live color television feed of the Earth to viewers. Apollo 10 marked the final rehearsal for Apollo 11.

On May 25, 1969, Norwegian adventurer and writer Thor Heyerdahl set sail from Safi, Morocco, on a 12-ton papyrus-reed boat he dubbed *Ra* after the ancient Egyptian sun god. Accompanied by reporters, Heyerdahl hoped to support his hypothesis that ancient Egyptians could have migrated to South America on similar craft. The *Ra,* however, soon became waterlogged in stormy seas, and Heyerdahl's rescue ended the experiment on July 22. He defended his idea of early Egyptian mariners, claiming he had proved it was possible for them to make the journey.

May 15: Supreme Court Associate Justice Abe Fortas resigns because of controversy over his financial dealings. • The California–Berkeley campus is struck by the "Peoples Park" riot, sparked by use of land purchased by the university. James Rector, 25, observing the riot from a rooftop, is killed by police gunfire. Governor Ronald Reagan declares a state of emergency in the area. More than 1,000 people are arrested.

May 19: Jazz saxophonist Coleman Hawkins dies at 64.

May 20: On their 11th try, U.S. and South Vietnamese troops capture a Communist stronghold at Ap Bia Mountain, popularly known as Hamburger Hill. Massachusetts Senator Ted Kennedy calls the campaign "senseless and irresponsible." *See* May 28, 1969. • Six hundred "1-A" draft files are stolen from a Pasadena, California, Selective Service office, then burned in a nearby field.

May 21: Antiwar activists break into Selective Service offices in Silver Spring, Maryland, throwing paint on files and destroying equipment. • President Nixon nominates Judge Warren Earl Burger as the 15th chief justice of the U.S. Supreme Court, succeeding Earl Warren.

May 22: Apollo 10 astronauts bring their lunar lander within 9.4 miles of the moon's surface before returning to the orbiting command module. • The Canadian government announces it will admit deserters from the U.S. military on the same basis as other immigrants.

May 25: A draft board on Chicago's South Side is broken into by antiwar activists, who stack files on a fire escape and burn them. • Adventurer and ethnologist Thor Heyerdahl launches the *Ra,* a 45-foot boat made of Ethiopian papyrus (bulrush), to demonstrate that sailors from Ancient Egypt could have crossed the Atlantic. The *Ra* will sail for two months and 2,600 miles before being abandoned.

President Nixon and longtime FBI Director J. Edgar Hoover shared a mutual hatred of political dissidents. Believing the country was under siege from internal threats during the 1960s, Nixon ordered the FBI to spy on numerous organizations, including the SDS, Black Panther Party, and American Indian Movement (AIM) as well as church and peace groups. The FBI's infamous COINTELPRO program utilized up to 2,000 agents to infiltrate such groups, spreading lies and promoting division and disarray. Nixon also ordered the FBI to conduct illegal wiretapping and surveillance of various musicians, journalists, and members of the peace movement.

"Nothing new to report again today, Mr. Hoover. . . ." Cartoonist Paul Conrad lampoons FBI Director J. Edgar Hoover's obsessive wiretapping campaign against groups and individuals Hoover termed "subversive," including Martin Luther King, Jr. The bureau's extralegal activities, which extended to infiltration, disinformation, and even criminal acts, eventually became public knowledge by the early 1970s, resulting in COINTELPRO's dismantling.

Dr. Mary Calderone, founder and director of the Sex Information and Education Council of the United States, holds examples of her organization's information pamphlets. Calderone encouraged informed sex education in public schools, an effort that about 70 percent of Americans favored. But in 1969 the issue of sex education inflamed religious groups and the John Birch Society, who viewed such efforts as at best the spread of immorality and at worst a Communist plot. Such groups disrupted PTA meetings throughout the country, and the controversy dominated many state assemblies during the year. Argued Calderone in *Time* magazine, "Sex is so intrusive and our culture is so permeated with sexual messages that planned and relevant sex-education programs are vital now."

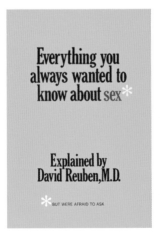

One of the most read and famous of all books on human sexuality, *Everything You Always Wanted to Know About Sex but Were Afraid to Ask* went on to become a bestseller in more than 50 countries. Written in a simple question-and-answer format, the book is based on author Dr. David Reuben's notion that the more knowledgeable people are about sex, the more enjoyable it can be. The book succeeds by lightheartedly relaying the information necessary to have a more fulfilling sex life and demystifying scientific and medical data. However, Reuben was roundly criticized for the false and degrading statements he made about homosexuals.

In 1967 India began an ambitious program to curb the country's birthrate. Through nationwide sterilization programs, and billboards such as this—which encourages couples to use a "loop" (contraceptive device)—Indian officials attempted to reduce births in a country that swelled to 533 million people by 1969. Despite the enthusiastic start to voluntary sterilization programs, government planners became discouraged by 1969. Interest in the program had slowed, and educating illiterate rural families had become too difficult. By 1999, India's population would surpass a billion.

A former radio DJ, Sylvester Stewart (*standing, second from left*) used his nickname, Sly, in the name of the band he formed in 1967. Sly and the Family Stone, according to Stewart, produced "psychedelic soul" music, earning Stewart comparisons to Jimi Hendrix. The group scored a hit in 1968 with "Everyday People," one of the cuts on their popular 1969 album *Stand*. The song, like the integrated band itself, promoted racial tolerance during turbulent times.

1969

May 28: U.S. troops in South Vietnam abandon Ap Bia Mountain (Hamburger Hill). *See* June 17, 1969.

May 30: Mario Andretti wins the Indianapolis 500 with a record average speed of 156.867 mph.

June: *Oh! Calcutta!,* by Kenneth Tynan, opens off-Broadway. The controversial play features an often nude cast and material by Samuel Beckett, Jules Feiffer, and John Lennon. The show's box-office success will establish the commercial viability of off-Broadway productions. • At Brown University's commencement ceremony, graduating students wearing black robes and white armbands stand and turn their backs on the featured speaker, Henry Kissinger.

June 1: John Lennon and Yoko Ono conduct a bed-in for peace at Montreal's Queen Elizabeth Hotel.

June 8: Following a meeting with South Vietnamese President Nguyen Van Thieu, President Nixon announces that 25,000 U.S. troops will be withdrawn from Vietnam by August 31.

June 17: The U.S. announces that North Vietnamese forces have reoccupied Ap Bia Mountain (Hamburger Hill).

Mid-June: The Students for a Democratic Society (SDS) holds its national convention in Chicago. The organization splits into at least two factions, including the Progressive Labor Party and the Revolutionary Youth Movement.

Summer: Sections of the northeastern U.S. experience periodic "brownouts" because of record-high air conditioner use that overwhelms power systems awaiting completion of nuclear powerplants.

June 22: Singer and actress Judy Garland dies at 47. • The chemically polluted Cuyahoga River in Cleveland catches fire. The incident serves as a wake-up call to legislators nationwide to deal with the problem of pollution.

When it first appeared on American screens in 1969, *Midnight Cowboy,* directed by Britain's John Schlesinger, was given an X rating. The film followed Joe Buck (played by Jon Voight, *right*), a naive country boy in search of fortune as a hustler, and Ratzo Rizzo (Dustin Hoffman, *left*), a pathetic petty thief. The story explored the seedy side of New York life and frank themes about homosexuality. Realistic but harsh, disturbing and undeniably touching, the film had a profound impact on audiences and Hollywood. *Midnight Cowboy* won an Academy Award for best picture.

Urban warfare continued to rage in northern cities during 1969, as black activists and citizens clashed with police. In Indianapolis, Indiana, a city with a long history of racial animosity and Ku Klux Klan activity, a black sniper injured six people, including a policeman, in consecutive nights of violence in early June. The subsequent uprising left windows shattered and fires burning throughout the predominantly African-American neighborhood. During the violence, police arrested more than 70 African-Americans, including at least 30 who were present near the Black Panthers headquarters where a white police lieutenant had been beaten.

Laugh-In

JUST BEFORE THE 1968 presidential election, the frenetic comedy show *Rowan and Martin's Laugh-In* invited both front-running candidates to appear and deliver one of its trademark punch lines. Hubert Humphrey refused, but a staid Richard Nixon showed up and uttered solemnly, "Sock it to *me*?"

Yet, as with many of the surrealistic show's zany bits, viewers had to keep their eyes peeled or risk missing the joke—because *Laugh-In* was quite literally the fastest comedy show in America, with "sketches" rarely lasting more than 30 seconds. That the high-adrenalin show captured the zeitgeist of the era is borne out by the ratings. Designed as a one-time special in 1967, *Laugh-In* proved so popular that it became the No. 1 show on television from 1968 to 1970.

Moderated officiously by prankster ringleaders Dan Rowan and Dick Martin, *Laugh-In* sneaked in jokes about pot, Vietnam, and the Sexual Revolution between standard shticks that included the show-ending "joke wall" and the "party," in which cast members—including the perpetually giggly Goldie Hawn—stopped dancing just long enough to utter zesty non sequiturs. *Laugh-In* lasted until 1973, but it gradually lost steam once key cast members left to pursue greater fame—or oblivion.

Dan Rowan and Dick Martin

A hippie passes time in Golden Gate Park on a foggy day in San Francisco. In the mid-1960s, hippies had espoused communal values, peace, love, and understanding. Their movement seemed fresh and promising at the time, but the luster faded as the decade wore on. Over time, opportunists, "plastic hippies," and runaways from America's suburbs abused the hippie culture's drugs and uninhibited lifestyle. In the late '60s, many flower children faced the harsh realities of poverty and drug addiction.

The belief that anyone unlucky enough to fall into Cleveland's Cuyahoga River wouldn't drown but merely decay gained credence when a surface chemical and oil slick caught fire on June 22, 1969. The mishap drew national attention to the river and the "dead" Lake Erie, long receptacles for industrial pollution that had killed off marine life. Massive cleanup efforts and strict enforcement of environmental codes eventually would restore Erie's status as a "great" lake, while the Cuyahoga also would be cleaned up considerably. Moreover, the attention that the flaming river received helped fuel the nationwide environmental movement.

June 27: Police raid the Stonewall Inn, a gay bar in Greenwich Village, New York, resulting in 13 arrests and four injured police officers. Violent confrontations at the bar will continue over the next three nights. • *Life* magazine runs portrait photos of all 242 Americans killed in Vietnam during the previous week, setting off reaction around the nation.

July: President Nixon sends a secret letter to Ho Chi Minh. He urges him to settle the war and threatens to resume bombing if peace talks are still stalled on November 1. • Elvis Presley returns to live performance with an extended gig in Las Vegas. He is a smash, redeeming himself for his failure in the gambling town more than a decade earlier.

July 1: Prince Charles is invested as Prince of Wales and Earl of Chester in a ceremony at Caernarfon Castle, Wales.

July 3: Brian Jones, drummer for the Rolling Stones, dies from drowning at age 27.

July 4: Maggie Geddes and other antiwar activists break into a draft board office in Rockefeller Center in New York City and shred 6,500 "1-A" files. They also destroy reference books and the office's "1" and "A" typewriter keys.

July 8: The first U.S. troops withdrawn from Vietnam fly back to the States.

July 9: The school boards of Chicago and the state of Georgia are warned by the U.S. Justice Department that they must address racial imbalances in their schools. *See* July 14, 1969.

July 14: The U.S. Justice Department orders 25 Alabama school districts to hasten desegregation.

July 16: Apollo 11 is launched from Cape Kennedy carrying Edwin "Buzz" Aldrin, Michael Collins, and Neil Armstrong. They are attempting to become the first humans to land on the moon. *See* July 20, 1969. ➤

"They were throwing more than lace hankies. I was almost decapitated by a slab of thick glass. It was thrown like a discus and just missed my throat by inches. The beer can didn't miss, though. It hit me right above the temple."

—Police officer describing rioting at the Stonewall Inn; *New York Daily News*, July 6, 1969

The Stonewall Rebellion

THE POLICE CHOSE THE WRONG NIGHT to raid the Stonewall Inn, a Mob-run bar in Manhattan's West Village. Gay icon Judy Garland was buried that day, and Stonewall's regulars of drag queens, gays, and lesbians were in a decidedly angry and downbeat mood.

When the police busted the club on June 27, 1969, as part of a routine practice of shaking down Mob joints for "protection money," the patrons responded not with compliance but with rage. On the first night, 13 people were arrested and four policemen injured. The riots escalated over the next three nights, as growing numbers of protesters chanted "Gay Power!" They emblazoned the Stonewall with graffiti that read "Legalize gay bars!" and "I'm a faggot and proud of it!"

Gay counterculture bard Allen Ginsberg, who partook in the insurrection, extolled the new mood of gay defiance. "You know," he said, "the guys there were so beautiful—they've lost that wounded look that fags all had 10 years ago."

The Stonewall riots triggered the gay liberation movement, which swept the nation during the 1970s. On a more fundamental level, however, Stonewall was about the right to party. In the wake of this cultural watershed, gay men seized control of several Mob-run bars and discotheques to create a distinctively gay club culture.

Michael Giammetta, a bona fide Stonewaller, called Stonewall a "turning point" that inspired him to launch his own gay club guide, *Michael's Thing*, which furthered gay men's quest for an above-ground, legitimate social life. The summer uprising, originally named "Gay Freedom Day," since has been commemorated annually during "Gay Pride" festivities nationwide.

Gay pride demonstration in New York on the first anniversary of the Stonewall riot

The Wild Bunch, directed by famous western filmmaker Sam Peckinpah, took movie violence to a new level. Seen by many as an allegory for the war-torn 1960s, The Wild Bunch premiered not long after Bonnie and Clyde, another movie that celebrated outlaw culture. The Wild Bunch starred Ben Johnson, Warren Oates, William Holden, and Ernest Borgnine (left to right) as aging gunfighters during the twilight years of the Old West. The movie arrived at a time when westerns were on the wane, but the film was a hit and is considered a masterpiece today.

After the success of Hair on Broadway, and in an atmosphere of experimental theater, Oh! Calcutta! pushed sexual themes to a new level for hip audiences. Oh! Calcutta!, which premiered off-Broadway in 1969, was comprised of short sketches that explored various erotic fantasies. It included not only full nudity but simulated sex acts as well. The hit play, made more popular by contributions from John Lennon, Samuel Beckett, and other luminaries, ran for more than 1,300 performances in New York.

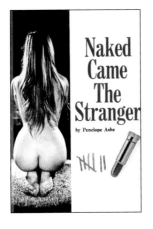

Intended as a hoax, Naked Came the Stranger became a literary phenomenon in 1969. The book was conceived by Newsday columnist Mike McGrady, who wanted to test his theory that well-packaged sexy trash would fly off the shelves. McGrady enlisted 24 Newsday colleagues to crank out a chapter each, with page after page of breathless sexual escapades. He even coaxed his sister-in-law, Billie Cook, to pretend to be the sole author, "Penelope Ashe." Sure enough, Stranger became a huge hit that showed up on The New York Times bestseller list for 25 weeks.

On July 10, 1969, the 814 men of the 9th Division's 3rd Battalion, 60th Infantry parade through the rain in downtown Seattle before a crowd of onlookers. The group was the first to be shipped home after President Nixon had announced that 25,000 troops would be withdrawn from Vietnam. The parade rolled past well-wishers and protesters, one of whom toted a sign that read, "Welcome Home. Now Help Us Bring Them All Home."

1969

Director of Flight Crew Operations Donald K. Slayton described what NASA looked for in selecting its moon-destined astronauts: "They've got to be good stick and rudder men, and also real smart." Neil Armstrong, Michael Collins, and Edwin "Buzz" Aldrin (*left to right*) fit the bill. The men who would journey to the moon were veterans of the Gemini missions, and each had proven himself in maneuvering space capsules.

Eleven days before they rode a Saturn 5 rocket into space, astronauts of the Apollo 11 mission appeared calm during a press conference. When asked at the conference if he had given thought to the historic words he might utter when he set foot on the moon, Neil Armstrong answered, "No, I haven't." By July 12, the astronauts tapered off their training and began resting in preparation. At the last minute, NASA's medical team even canceled President Nixon's planned dinner with the astronauts on the eve of the expedition. Meanwhile, as the countdown clock ticked away at 9:32 A.M. (EDT) on July 16, an estimated one million people gathered on nearby beaches to watch the spectacle at Cape Kennedy.

Apollo: "That Saturn gave us a magnificent ride." Houston: "Roger, 11. We'll pass that on, and it certainly looks like you're well on your way now." Once the Saturn 5 rocket blasted Apollo 11 off the launchpad at Cape Canaveral, the men in the Mission Operations Control Room at the Manned Spacecraft Center in Houston became the lifeline for the astronauts on their 238,857-mile journey. The technicians in Mission Control coached the astronauts through each of the intricate operations for landing the module on the lunar surface. Here, Mission Control receives a color television transmission of Neil Armstrong from Apollo 11, 130,000 nautical miles from Earth.

At 10:56 P.M. EDT on July 20, 1969, Neil Armstrong placed his size 9½ boot firmly on the surface of the moon. After a brief moment, the world's rapt television viewers and radio listeners alike heard the astronaut's words crackling over a quarter-million miles of space: "That's one small step for man, one giant leap for mankind." In an event that unified the world, 600 million people watched in awe. "It's different," Armstrong informed them, "but it's very pretty out here."

"This is the America we love," said a Czech broadcaster to a *New York Times* reporter, "one so totally different from the America that fights in Vietnam." That was the sentiment of many European observers (including Italians, *pictured*) who watched the Apollo 11 astronauts' moon walk. The universal human endeavor seemed for a moment to improve the tarnished image of the U.S. during the Vietnam War. British papers included colorful diagrams of the spaceships, and French newspapers circulated extra editions with facts about the voyage. Italian magazines featured interviews with Rocco Petrone, the Italian-American director of launching operations for Apollo 11. Although many Europeans were awed by the technological prowess of the U.S., others criticized the effort as a waste of money.

As the world watched, Buzz Aldrin and Neil Armstrong tested the low gravity on the moon, bouncing playfully on the lunar surface. They then planted an American flag, held erect by an aluminum rod. The astronauts prepared scientific devices, including a solar wind experiment, a seismometer, and a reflector to help measure distances with lasers. They also scooped up more than 60 pounds of moon rocks and dust for later testing. After a brief long-distance call from President Nixon, Aldrin and Armstrong packed up their gear and climbed back into the Eagle Lander.

An Astronaut's Perspective

DURING THE FLIGHT of Apollo 11, in the constant sunlight between the Earth and the moon, it was necessary for us to control the temperature of our spacecraft by a slow rotation not unlike that of a chicken on a barbecue spit. As we turned, the Earth and the moon alternately appeared in our windows. We had our choice. We could look toward the moon, toward Mars, toward our future in space—toward the new Indies—or we could look back toward the Earth, our home, with its problems spawned over more than a millennium of human occupancy.

We looked both ways. We saw both, and I think that is what our nation must do.

—APOLLO 11 ASTRONAUT MICHAEL COLLINS

July 19: Massachusetts Senator Ted Kennedy tells Edgartown, Massachusetts, police that he drove his car off a narrow bridge into water at Chappaquiddick Island more than nine hours earlier and left behind a passenger, a 28-year-old political worker named Mary Jo Kopechne. The woman's body is subsequently recovered from the automobile. *See* July 25, 1969.

July 20: The Apollo 11 lunar lander touches down on the surface of the moon. Astronaut Neil Armstrong becomes the first human to set foot on the lunar surface; he is followed by Buzz Aldrin. Together, they undertake a 2¼-hour exploratory and scientific walk while Michael Collins orbits overhead in the command module.

July 24: The Gay Liberation Front (GLF) is formed in New York City under the rallying cry "Homosexuals Are Coming Together at Last."

July 25: Senator Ted Kennedy pleads guilty to leaving the scene of a fatal accident that claimed the life of Mary Jo Kopechne. Kennedy receives a two-month suspended sentence. • The public gets its first glimpse of the "Nixon Doctrine," which advocates U.S. military and economic assistance to nations struggling against communism. Military self-sufficiency is emphasized.

July 30: President Nixon flies to Saigon for a short visit with American troops and talks with South Vietnamese President Nguyen Van Thieu.

July–November: Student radicals perpetrate bombings of numerous Manhattan businesses, including the Marine Midland Grace Trust Co., the Armed Forces Induction Center, the Federal Office Building, Macy's department store, a United Fruit Company pier, the RCA Building, and the Chase Manhattan Building. One suspect, 22-year-old Swarthmore student Jane Lauren Alpert, forfeits the $20,000 bond posted by her parents and disappears.

On July 24, the Apollo astronauts' space capsule, charred and peeling from its reentry into the Earth's atmosphere, dangled from parachutes in the air over the Pacific Ocean. At 12:50 P.M. EDT, it splashed into the water. The three astronauts, donning their special quarantine suits, climbed out the door and breathed fresh air for the first time in eight days. They bobbed for a short time on the waves in a raft beside the capsule, 11 miles from the USS *Hornet* and 900 miles southwest of Hawaii. There, they waited for the helicopters that would transport them back to civilization.

On August 13, 1969, an estimated four million people in New York lined lower Broadway and beyond to catch a glimpse of their heroes—the first men to walk on the moon. Remarked astronaut Buzz Aldrin, "I have never been so moved by anything in my entire life." The astronauts proceeded across the country in a series of parades. But before leaving New York, Neil Armstrong addressed the United Nations, where he told the assembly, "We citizens of Earth, who can solve the problems of leaving Earth, can also solve the problems of staying on it."

Chappaquiddick

ALTHOUGH MASSACHUSETTS SENATOR Edward "Teddy" Kennedy resisted heavy pressure in 1968 to take up the standard borne by his slain brother, Robert, no one doubted Kennedy's designs for a 1972 White House run. But a night of revelry in 1969 irrevocably ruined his chances.

On July 18, Teddy joined a group of RFK campaign workers for a reunion at a secluded rental cottage on Chappaquiddick Island near Martha's Vineyard, Massachusetts. Among the young "Boiler Room Girls" in attendance was 28-year-old Mary Jo Kopechne. Though commonly described as a secretary, she had been one of Bobby's most trusted aides.

A short drive away from the festivities, a primitive bridge crossed a tidal pool. On the morning of July 19, a pair of fishermen spotted a car lying inverted in the water. The plates were registered to Senator Kennedy, who was nowhere in sight. But crouched in an air pocket near the car's back seat was the body of Kopechne, dead for hours. Kennedy appeared in town shortly after with a story that, in his own words, "made no sense to me at all."

Kennedy said that while giving Kopechne a lift to the ferry the previous night, he became confused in the darkness and made a wrong turn onto the bridge road. Before he could get his bearings, the car plunged into the water. Dis-

The car driven by Kennedy

oriented and in shock after repeatedly diving for Kopechne, Kennedy swam to shore and collapsed in his room. But his failure to notify authorities immediately could not be adequately explained. Suspicions of drunkenness and infidelity dogged him.

Recognizing his political peril, the senator issued a televised mea culpa, asking for the public's support. He was convicted of leaving the scene of an accident—not manslaughter—and his sentence was suspended. Kennedy would retain his job as senator, but Chappaquiddick would doom his presidential aspirations forever after.

Richard Nixon became the first American president to visit Saigon, the capital of South Vietnam. On July 30, 1969, he touched down briefly in the city to confer with President Nguyen Van Thieu about impending troop withdrawals and changes in military strategy. Soon after the meeting, Nixon traveled north 12 miles to meet troops at a military base, where he shook hands, discussed sports, and commended the soldiers before ending his risky visit to the country. Describing his recent efforts to create peace, including the stoppage of bombing in the north, Nixon said during the visit, "We have gone as far now as we can or should go in opening the door to peace, and now it is time for the other side to respond."

1969

August 2: Belfast, Northern Ireland, is struck by violent clashes between Protestants, Catholics, and police.

August 4: Evidence of a March 1968 U.S. Army massacre of Vietnamese civilians at My Lai is turned over to the provost marshal general and the Pentagon. *See* September 5, 1969.
• Henry Kissinger conducts the first of many secret meetings in Paris with representatives from Hanoi.

August 8: President Nixon issues Executive Order 11478 requiring affirmative-action programs in federal employment.

August 9: Starlet Sharon Tate (wife of film director Roman Polanski) and four others are brutally murdered in a mansion in the Benedict Canyon area of the Hollywood Hills in California. The perpetrators are male and female acolytes of career criminal Charles Manson. *See* August 10, 1969.

August 10: Followers of Charles Manson murder Leno and Rosemary LaBianca in the victims' mansion in the Los Feliz section of Los Angeles.

August 12: The most intense Communist attacks in months are mounted across South Vietnam.

August 15–18: An enormous outdoor music festival is held at Max Yasgur's 600-acre farm in Bethel, New York, near Woodstock. The festival attracts more than 400,000 people and many of the top rock and folk acts of the day. The event's organizers and promoters are Michael Lang, 25; John Roberts, 26; Joel Rosenman, 24; and Artie Kornfeld, 25.

August 17–18: The Mississippi Gulf Coast is ravaged by Hurricane Camille, the strongest U.S. storm since 1935.

August 24: A U.S. infantry company in South Vietnam refuses an order to make a sixth attempt in as many days to reach a downed American helicopter. ➤

So-called liberation schools operated by the Black Panthers in the San Francisco Bay area in the late 1960s were a short-lived effort to teach black children what the Panthers regarded as true black history, and the African-American role in contemporary society. Taking an educational approach that would later be termed Afrocentric, the schools emphasized black resistance to white authority, and black heroes; images of Malcolm X and Panther leader Bobby Seale adorn the wall of the liberation school lunchroom (*above*), and the students give enthusiastic Black Power salutes.

This drawing appeared in the *Black Panthers Coloring Book,* accompanied by the caption "THE PIG IS AFRAID OF THE BLACK CHILDREN BECAUSE THEY ARE BRAVE WARRIORS." The Panthers created important community programs, such as free health clinics, but with such slogans as "off the pigs" (kill the police) and frequent cries for violent black revolution, the Panthers scared many whites. And the group often moved beyond rhetoric, committing several murders and dealing drugs. Several chapters set up bloody protection rackets. All of this gave the FBI and other law enforcement officials incentive to crack down hard on party members.

On August 12, 1969, Catholics in Derry, Northern Ireland, marched through the center of town in protest of anti-Catholic discrimination. Things turned violent when Protestant Nationalists held their own counter-protest. Within a short time, Catholic youths spread out through the community. As the Royal Ulster Constabulary moved in to quell the violence, Catholic rebels threw firebombs and bricks at police from rooftop perches. The British police finally moved in to restore order, but the troubles in Northern Ireland were just beginning.

Romanian President Nicolae Ceausescu and the people of Bucharest warmly greet President Richard Nixon on his arrival to the Communist nation in August 1969. Nixon made the precedent-breaking trip in response to Ceausescu's calculated distancing of Romania from Soviet foreign policy—in particular Romania's condemnation of the 1968 Soviet invasion of Czechoslovakia. In this, the first visit by an American head of state to a Communist country since 1945, Nixon was able to successfully open a back door to secret negotiations with the Chinese. The increasingly repressive Ceausescu regime would extend to 1989, when a popular uprising led to the arrest and public execution of the dictator and his wife, Elena.

On August 17 and 18, 1969, Hurricane Camille pummeled Mississippi, Alabama, and Louisiana with winds exceeding 190 mph, making it the second most powerful hurricane in United States history at the time. The storm left thousands of people homeless and killed at least 250. Much of the Gulf Coast went without gas, water, and electricity for days afterward. President Nixon declared much of Mississippi a disaster area.

In 1968 and 1969, Yasir Arafat's *Fatah* movement, one of many Palestinian guerrilla organizations, seized power within the Palestinian Liberation Organization (PLO). Often wearing dark sunglasses and a commando uniform, an automatic weapon slung over his shoulder, Arafat inspired the youthful element of the Palestinian cause during the 1960s. As PLO chairman, Arafat used the armed core of his movement to assert pressure on Israel, committing acts of terror and other intimidation. Arafat remained PLO chairman well into the 21st century.

1969

Woodstock

THE WOODSTOCK MUSIC & ART FAIR was conceived by four young entrepreneurs—Michael Lang, John Roberts, Joel Rosenman, and Artie Kornfeld—eager to exploit the counterculture. Their plan, to offer rock's biggest names in a bucolic New York setting (a weekend pass for $18), promised "three days of peace and music"— a boast largely kept. Thrown into the mix, however, would be logistical nightmares: inadequate sanitation, traffic back-ups 20 miles long, too many hungry kids, and cloudbursts that turned the site into a mud bowl. Spontaneous nudity was applauded by most, but casual drug use was cause for concern.

Some of the biggest names in rock music entertained the 400,000-plus visitors from August 15 to 18, 1969. Santana, Jimi Hendrix, Janis Joplin, Joe Cocker, and others secured their renown. Melanie was one newcomer who would enjoy a measure of fame later. Others, like Quill and Sweetwater, rode their star turns back into obscurity.

Like many of the weekend's musical performances, organization for the festival was largely improvised. Denied a site permit by the town of Wallkill, which feared invasive hordes of hippies, the event was relocated outside Bethel, New York, on land owned by 49-year-old dairy farmer Max Yasgur. Among the unforeseen contingencies was a shakedown by Yippie leader Abbie Hoffman, who demanded (and got) $10,000 not to disrupt the proceedings. He nevertheless mounted the stage during the Who's set and launched into a political rant that was cut short by a blow to the head from Pete Townshend's guitar.

Some booked artists, including Iron Butterfly and Jeff Beck, failed to make the gig. Others, such as Joni Mitchell, were kept away by transportation difficulties. Many acts, including the Grateful Dead and Creedence Clearwater Revival, escaped documentation in the widely seen concert film taken that weekend. The event's ethereal qualities were recognized almost immediately, but they were quickly mythologized out of proportion.

Still, that nearly a half-million young people could assemble peaceably while sharing a generation-defining experience helped enhance the public's perception of the youth culture. Some cynics, however, refused to embrace the experience—Townshend for one. When pressed to explain Woodstock's meaning, he declared, "Well, it changed me—I hated it!"

Jefferson Airplane performs before a sea of humanity at Woodstock. The concert promoters had expected about 100,000 people, but as the first day of the event grew closer, it seemed that every young person in America was journeying to Max Yasgur's farm. The New York Thruway became so clogged with VW microbuses and other vehicles that police closed it down. Hippies got out of their cars and began hiking toward the music. Faced with the massive crowd, the promoters had to let everyone in for free. The crowds overwhelmed the sanitation facilities, and supplies of food and drinking water. Despite predictions of chaos and destruction, no fights were reported and few police were needed.

With crowds exceeding promoters' expectations and preparedness, living conditions during the three-day Woodstock festival were often dismal. Overflowing toilets and a shortage of hot dogs and hamburgers after the first day were capped by thunderstorms that turned the trampled farm fields into a slippery mud pit. The crowd made do by bathing in nearby lakes and attempting to eat corn from nearby fields. Thankfully, townspeople around the concert venue took pity on the flower children, providing food and water and even medical assistance.

Because Jimi Hendrix played late on the last day of Woodstock, most people already had gone home. But his rendition of "The Star-Spangled Banner" wowed the dwindled crowd. Moving between crystal-clear notes of the melody and screeching distortion mimicking the horrors of war, Hendrix articulated the clash between the country's greatest ideals and the ongoing compromise of those ideals in Vietnam. Other famous counterculture celebrities—notably Santana, Joe Cocker, the Who, and Sly and the Family Stone—dazzled the crowd with standout performances. But with his guitar virtuosity and depth of feeling, Hendrix left a lasting statement.

Considered one of the most powerful antiwar books ever written, Kurt Vonnegut's *Slaughterhouse-Five* is a surreal combination of fact and science fiction. Based in part upon his own experience as an American POW in Germany during World War II, Vonnegut catapults the main character, Billy Pilgrim, through the Allied bombings of Dresden to circa 1976, where he is gunned down by an assassin's bullet. The book deals with issues vital to the late 1960s, including war, violence, and consumerism.

Dancing in the Mud

THE MUSIC OF WOODSTOCK is legendary, but so is the rain. Some acts played, some stopped playing. Performance times were lost in the Sargasso of mud and grass and water that covered the ground like the scribbles of a giant palette knife. Surrounding the main stage, a rain-soaked amphitheater carved out by Mother Nature was populated by an undulating sea of wet, half-naked bodies, and covered in a haze of second-hand marijuana smoke. Helicopters dropped bundles of dry clothes and showered us with pinwheeling daisies. So we danced and chanted and surfed in the mud, trapped happily at the center of our own counterculture universe, in the uncomplicated Land of One Thing Follows Another.

Sometimes I can still hear Jimi Hendrix's "Star Spangled Banner" blasting from the Woodstock sound towers, reimagined for a generation of disillusioned young Americans weary of war and prejudicial politics. And I'll always remember that beautiful, brownie-mix mud—the cosmic paste that bonded 400,000 of us together, at least for a few days, with renewed hope for a better tomorrow.

—MICHAEL STEIN, WOODSTOCK FESTIVALGOER

Troubadour and raconteur Arlo Guthrie (*left*) starred in the 1969 film *Alice's Restaurant,* based on his popular underground song. Guthrie's 18-minute opus, "Alice's Restaurant Massacree," told the story of how a petty arrest for a good deed led to his draft deferment. The song was fleshed out into a film by Arthur Penn, the director of *Bonnie and Clyde.* Guthrie, the son of folk icon Woody Guthrie, became a fixture of the counterculture and gave a notable performance at Woodstock.

August 25: Construction sites in Pittsburgh are shut down by civil rights activists protesting discriminatory hiring.

August 26: The FBI reports a 98 percent increase in marijuana arrests from 1966 to 1968.

August 29–31: A quarter-million rock fans attend a music festival on the Isle of Wight. The lineup includes Bob Dylan, who uses the occasion to return to live performance.

August 31: Retired, undefeated American heavyweight boxing champion Rocky Marciano, 45, dies in a plane crash.

September: The first American edition of publisher Bob Guccione's *Penthouse* is published. From the start, it will exploit frank nudity to challenge the leading men's magazine of the day, Hugh Hefner's *Playboy*. • Following the Woodstock music festival, the local Roman Catholic diocese runs a two-page ad in the *Seattle Post-Intelligencer* calling for criminal prosecution of rock musicians, and for bans against rock festivals and their culture of sex and drugs. • Rod Laver of Australia wins the U.S. Open to capture tennis's Grand Slam.

September 1: A military coalition led by Colonel Muhammad al-Khadafy overthrows the Libyan monarchy and establishes a republic.

September 3: North Vietnamese leader Ho Chi Minh, who led his people in nationalistic struggles against the Japanese, the French, and the United States, dies in Hanoi at 79.

September 5: U.S. military authorities accuse Army Lieutenant William Calley of killing 109 Vietnamese civilians. He will be convicted in 1971 of 22 murders and sentenced to life in prison. The sentence will be commuted by President Nixon.

Woody Allen began writing and directing his own films in the late 1960s. In *Take the Money and Run*, Allen starred as an inept, small-time crook named Virgil Starkwell. The film made playful parody of the true-crime docudrama genre, complete with an earnest voice-over narrator (Jackson Beck) telling the story of the antihero's difficult childhood and inevitable turn to crime. The silly celebration of outlaw culture and life on the run affirmed one of the era's most popular themes, found in such movies as *Bonnie and Clyde*. In this scene, Starkwell works in the prison laundry, where he inexplicably finds a bra in the wash.

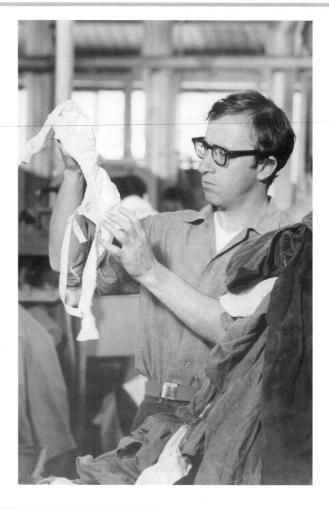

By the 1960s Shirley Temple Black, the former child actress famous for singing "The Good Ship Lollipop," had become hawkish about the Vietnam War and a conservative Republican. Like George Murphy and Ronald Reagan, two other famous California actors turned politicians, Black entered California Republican politics and ran unsuccessfully in the 1967 primary for a congressional seat. Black was rewarded for her party work by President Nixon, who appointed her to the five-person U.S. delegation to the United Nations in 1969.

At a memorial service in Hanoi seven days after Ho Chi Minh's death on September 3, 1969, a section of his will was read aloud. "We are sure to win total victory," Ho had written. "This is an absolute certainty." The North Vietnamese leader never did see total victory in the long independence struggle he helped lead against successive colonial powers. As Hanoi mourned its 79-year-old leader's passing, North Vietnamese forces adhered to a 72-hour cease-fire, and the U.S. backed off from the fighting. But the lull in the warfare that the U.S. leadership hoped might lead to a permanent cease-fire was soon shattered by a resumed Vietcong offensive. The U.S. followed with B-52 strikes.

During a press conference on September 17, 1969, Secretary of Defense Melvin Laird stands among charts meant to illustrate what *The New York Times* described as a "somewhat confusing arithmetic of Vietnam reduction." Using such military language as "manpower authorization ceilings" and "authorized space reductions," Laird described what would be a substantial troop reduction in Vietnam, particularly among Marines. Nixon hoped to placate critics and take the wind out of campus protests by approving sharp reductions of troops.

The Manson Murders

"A VALLEY OF THOUSANDS of plump white rabbits surrounded by wounded coyotes" was how counterculture activist Ed Sanders described the many kids who descended on Haight-Ashbury to partake in the Summer of Love, only to encounter vile exploitation instead. The most wounded animal of all was Charles Manson, who made his way to Haight-Ashbury in fall 1967 at age 32 after spending more than half of his life behind bars. Surrounded in the Haight by young and impressionable female runaways, Manson refashioned himself as an "acid fascist" guru. He entranced his disciples with visions of—not peace and love—but apocalyptic race war.

The "Manson Family" soon mutated into a notorious hippie murder cult. Their first victim was musician Gary Hinman, killed on July 31, 1969. On August 9, 1969, the Manson Family broke into the secluded home of actress Sharon Tate, best known for her starring role in the 1967 hit *Valley of the Dolls*. She was eight months pregnant with director Roman Polanski's baby. The Manson Family brutally massacred the young starlet and her four guests.

The following night, the Family savagely claimed the lives of businessman Leno LaBianca and his wife, Rosemary, who was stabbed 41 times. On the refrigerator read a blood-scrawled message: "Healther [sic] Skelter," a reference to a track from Manson's beloved Beatles' *White Album*. Apart from portending the death of the hippie "peace and love" ethos, the Manson murders fueled widespread paranoia in the Hollywood film community. Sales of guns skyrocketed.

Manson and his cohorts were arrested in late 1969 and convicted. Manson received the death penalty for first-degree murder, but the sentence was commuted to life imprisonment after the California Supreme Court abolished the death penalty in 1972.

Charles Manson

September 11: Air attacks by the United Arab Republic, mounted in reprisal for a September 9 Israeli raid on the Gulf of Suez, are disastrous for Arab forces. They lose seven MiG-21 fighters, three Su-7 fighter bombers, and one MiG-17 fighter. Arab pilots are apparently unprepared for Israel's Phantom F-4 fighter-bombers, which were delivered to Israel by the U.S.

September 12: The U.S. Commission on Civil Rights criticizes the Nixon Administration for policies that repress school desegregation.

September 19: President Nixon announces that, for the remainder of 1969, 50,000 fewer men than had been anticipated will be drafted. • As a result of her social activism and her membership in the Communist Party, philosophy professor Angela Davis is fired by UCLA.

September 20: Landing approaches at Da Nang Air Base in South Vietnam end disastrously when a Vietnamese DC-4 commercial jet collides with a USAF F-4 Phantom fighter-bomber. The Phantom crewmen escape injury but the DC-4 plummets to the earth, killing 74 on board as well as two people on the ground.

September 21: Operation Intercept, a U.S. campaign to halt drug flow from Mexico, goes into effect.

September 24: The "Chicago Eight," accused of conspiracy to incite a riot during the 1968 Democratic National Convention in Chicago, go on trial in that city. *See* October 8, 1969.

September 26: In *Bowe v. Colgate–Palmolive,* the U.S. Supreme Court rules that women who meet physical requirements can work at any job that had been reserved for men only, if seniority applies.

September 27: South Vietnamese President Nguyen Van Thieu announces that because his country has "no ambition" to prosecute the war alone, the withdrawal of U.S. forces will take "years and years."

In the late 1960s, Monty Python's Flying Circus became Britain's comedic equivalent of the Beatles. Pictured are group members Eric Idle, Graham Chapman, Michael Palin, John Cleese, Terry Jones, and Terry Gilliam (*left to right*). With a television show that premiered in Britain in 1969, Monty Python showed off its brand of comic anarchy with such classics as "The Parrot Sketch," "Spam," and the "Lumberjack Song." The series, crafted with absurdist logic, complete irreverence, and much cross-dressing, eventually led to feature films. By the mid-1970s, Monty Python's presence on American television and in movies made their humor ubiquitous.

In their first film together, Paul Newman (*left*) and Robert Redford (*right*) portrayed western outlaws in 1969's *Butch Cassidy and the Sundance Kid*— characters based loosely on the historical figures from the Hole in the Wall Gang. The anti-authoritarian theme of the film appealed to Sixties audiences, who enjoyed the tale of two train robbers on the run. The two actors had obvious chemistry and charmed audiences with their humor and good looks.

The Weathermen

THE NEW LEFT, embodied by the Students for a Democratic Society (SDS), grew increasingly fragmented in the months following the 1968 Democratic National Convention. At issue was the struggle for control between the Progressive Labor faction of the SDS, which favored educating the public, and the more strident voices arguing that passivity was useless.

The SDS party convention, held in June 1969, ended in disintegration. Emerging from the chaos was a group espousing violent revolution, aligned with Communist and Third World struggles. Taking their name from a line in the Bob Dylan song "Subterranean Homesick Blues," they called themselves the Weathermen.

Fiercely idealistic yet politically naive, the Weathermen were driven by deep frustration and anger about the Vietnam War. Although their Third World model had no hope of succeeding in the United States, the Weathermen were nevertheless convinced that a small group could inspire radical change and even revolution. Weathermen attempts to forge alliances with the Black Panthers and lower-middle-class youths were not fruitful. Many Weathermen were middle class, and even children of privilege, so common ground was lacking. Would-be allies may also have been wary of the Weathermen's very real fury and singleminded, high-profile devotion to their cause.

A wanted member of the Weathermen

In their manifesto, the Weathermen sought to "bring the war home" via a series of October confrontations in Chicago to be called "Days of Rage." A rally in Lincoln Park led to the bombing of a statue, rock-throwing, broken glass, and many arrests.

Despite their revolutionary fervor, the Weathermen struggled to be perceived as something more than dangerous curiosities. Ultimately, the only casualties of their "war" would be three of their own, who were accidentally blown up while building bombs at a safe house in New York City.

"Their adrenalin rose at the forbidden, musical sound of breaking glass: ten plate-glass windows in a bank went crumbling, a Rolls Royce had every window in it shattered, on one block every parked car got hit...."

—WRITER KIRKPATRICK SALE, IN THE BOOK *SDS*, DESCRIBING THE ACTIONS OF THE WEATHERMEN IN CHICAGO ON OCTOBER 8, 1969

Hundreds of Weathermen cross the Chicago River Bridge to "bring the war home" to America's streets. On October 8, 1969, demonstrators initiated a window-smashing spree in Chicago's wealthy Gold Coast district as police battled to contain the damage. The episode resulted in six participants shot (none fatally) and dozens of arrests. Perpetrating vandalism upon cars and buildings endeared Weathermen to no one, and their violence estranged even would-be allies. Chicago Black Panther leader Fred Hampton called their tactics "Custeristic."

1969

October: Rumors fly that Beatle Paul McCartney is dead.

October 7–8: A strike by Montreal police leads to looting and other unrest: Ten banks are robbed, a taxi drivers riot leaves three dead, and downtown stores are smashed and looted by hundreds of young people.

October 8: The radical left-wing Weathermen, an offshoot of the SDS, breaks windows in Chicago during the conspiracy trial of the "Chicago Eight" antiwar activists.

October 12: Responding to weeks of unrest, England sends 600 troops to Northern Ireland.

October 13: President Nixon declares that his Vietnam policy will not be swayed by street demonstrations.

October 15: In a nationwide moratorium staged by antiwar activists, millions of Americans take the day off from work and school to discuss how to end the war. • In a public letter to America's antiwar movement, North Vietnam Prime Minister Pham Van Dong states, "[M]ay your fall offensive succeed splendidly." American conservatives are infuriated.

October 16: The New York "Miracle" Mets defeat the Baltimore Orioles in Game 5 to win the World Series.

October 19: Vice President Spiro Agnew describes organizers of antiwar demonstrators as "an effete corps of impudent snobs."

October 21: More than 70,000 Japanese riot police are called out to quell violent political demonstrations. • American "beat" writer Jack Kerouac, author of *On the Road,* dies at 47.

October 29: In a unanimous ruling, the U.S. Supreme Court holds that 30 Mississippi school districts must integrate at once. • After "Chicago Eight" defendant Bobby Seale repeatedly challenges District Court Judge Julius Hoffman, the judge has him handcuffed to a chair and gagged. *See* November 5, 1969. ➤

Rejecting the sensory and technological overload of 20th-century life, many Americans in the 1960s sought an alternative lifestyle in an attempt to get "back to the garden." Communes mushroomed around the country, drawing those seeking a purer, nonmaterialistic way of life. Armed with the highest of ideals—community sharing of responsibilities and extension of family beyond "oppressive" conventions—unforeseen contingencies nonetheless often doomed such efforts. The dynamics of partner-sharing and the need for individual space were elements that often sowed considerable conflict.

In the late 1960s, saffron-robed Hare Krishnas were a regular feature of the street scene near universities and in counterculture enclaves. Shaved-headed adherents danced and whirled down sidewalks, drumming and chanting "Hare Krishna." As more American youths sought authentic and exotic alternatives to mainstream religions in the 1960s, many turned to Eastern religions. A man named A. C. Bhaktivedanta had founded the International Society for Krishna Consciousness in New York in 1965 in an effort to spread the teachings of the Hindu deity Krishna. The lifestyle of Hare Krishnas appealed to many in the counterculture but disturbed many mainstream Americans, some of whom viewed the religion as a cult.

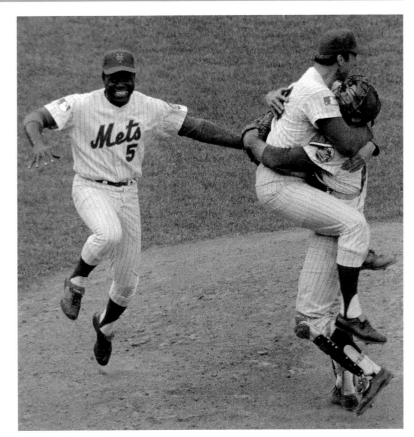

On October 15, 1969, millions around the world turned out in force to demand an immediate end to hostilities in Vietnam. In Washington, D.C., alone, a quarter-million people gathered to voice their disgust with the war. Sporting black armbands of mourning, many Americans skipped work and school that day to protest the ongoing conflict. The magnitude of the resistance compelled President Nixon to consider floating a story that he was considering the use of nuclear weapons in the conflict. No such claim was ever made, but Nixon continued to ponder ways to intimidate North Vietnam.

After never finishing better than ninth place in their previous seven seasons, the New York Mets won the World Series in 1969—a feat that many cynics considered more astonishing than the moon landing. Led by pitching phenom Tom "Terrific" Seaver (25–7), the Mets had closed the season strong to surge past the fading Chicago Cubs. They then swept the Atlanta Braves in the first-ever National League Championship Series before downing the heavily favored Baltimore Orioles in the World Series, four games to one. Fans at Shea Stadium went wild, ripping out pieces of the field as souvenirs. Office workers on Broad Street and Wall Street celebrated by heaving reams of paper and punch cards from their windows.

A bizarre footnote to the Beatles' final year, 1969, came with word that Paul McCartney had been dead since 1966, replaced by a look-alike in time for the *Sgt. Pepper* release in 1967. American disc jockeys propagated the myth, citing a host of "clues" revealed in the band's music and on the artwork of the 1969 album, *Abbey Road*. While the fully alive Paul was enjoying a lower profile than usual, the Beatles' record company did little to dispel concerns, as sales of back-catalog Beatles albums soared. Magazines such as this one were gobbled up by fans, who scoured the text for confirmation of the death rumor.

During the Vietnam War, both sides relied heavily on propaganda. The National Liberation Front (NLF), a North Vietnamese guerrilla organization, attempted to sow dissent among the enemy ranks. The NLF tried to inflame racial tension, persuade soldiers that they were merely serving corporate interests, and remind troops of the holiday activities that they were missing. Some pamphlets featured antiwar quotes from prominent Americans, planting doubts among the soldiers about the justness of their cause.

"Conspiracy? Hell, we couldn't agree on lunch."

—ABBIE HOFFMAN

The Chicago Seven

DUBBED BY *Newsweek* as "a combination of the Scopes Trial, revolution in the streets, the Woodstock Festival, and People's Park all rolled into one," the trial of the "Chicago Seven" became one of the most famous court cases of the 20th century.

The defendants—David Dellinger, Tom Hayden, Rennie Davis, Abbie Hoffman, Jerry Rubin, John Froines, Lee Weiner, and Bobby Seale—were a mélange of peace-loving pacifists, militant radicals, and Yippie pranksters. Together, they were accused of conspiring to incite the riot at the 1968 Democratic National Convention. (Seale was ultimately treated separately, hence the "Chicago Seven" rather than the "Chicago Eight.")

The incoming Nixon Administration sought to undercut the antiwar movement by prosecuting "hardcore" leaders, despite the fact that government reports placed the blame for the riots squarely on Chicago Mayor Richard Daley and the city's police department. When the trial commenced in September 1969, Yippies Abbie Hoffman and Jerry Rubin quickly transformed it into a theatrical farce. "'The World Series of Injustice,' I called it," recalled Hoffman in his autobiography. "We brainstormed a baseball program (we called it 'the official pogrom') and even got the cartoonist who does the Mets' scorecard to design the cover—the Chicago Conspiracy versus the Washington Kangaroos."

The Yippies called in a parade of poets, musicians, playwrights, and comedians as key witnesses. Folk singer Judy

Clockwise, left to right: Rubin, Hoffman, Hayden, Davis, Dellinger, Froines, Weiner, Seale

Collins interrupted her testimony to break into an impromptu version of "Where Have All the Flowers Gone?" The jury eventually found each of the defendants, as well as their lawyers, guilty of contempt of court. Black Panther Bobby Seale, who was chained and gagged after calling the judge a "blatant racist," was handed a four-year prison term. Dellinger, Hoffman, Rubin, Hayden, and Davis were sentenced to five years for inciting the Chicago riot. In 1972 a federal appeals court overturned the lower court's verdicts, asserting that the defendants had not received a fair trial.

The "Chicago Eight" trial was often unruly, but when Black Panther leader Bobby Seale repeatedly interrupted, accusing Judge Julius Hoffman of racism and demanding to represent himself, the proceedings turned nasty. On Hoffman's orders, marshals forcefully removed Seale from the courtroom. He was returned with a cloth gag around his mouth. The marshals used handcuffs to bind his hands and leg irons to attach his legs to his chair. Despite the effort to silence him, Seale managed to shout through the gag, "You fascist dogs!" Seale was sentenced to four years in prison for contempt of court, although the conviction would be overturned in 1971.

The Public Broadcasting Act of 1967 led to the establishment of the Corporation for Public Broadcasting, which provided funds for a noncommercial network of television and radio broadcasting. The Public Broadcasting System (television's PBS) and National Public Radio (NPR) resulted from this new arrangement. Meanwhile, New York's WNET (whose emblem is pictured) on Channel 13 was a pioneer in noncommercial television. Its innovative Children's Television Workshop, funded in part by the Carnegie Endowment, launched the groundbreaking children's educational program *Sesame Street* in 1969.

Haskell Wexler's *Medium Cool* (1969) follows reporter John Cassellis (played by Robert Forster) as he films the social unrest and street demonstrations of the 1968 Democratic National Convention in Chicago. Setting the tone for the film is this opening shot, in which reporters stumble upon a terrible car wreck (*pictured*) and proceed to film it without offering assistance to an injured victim. This emotional distance is pervasive until the last scene, when the lines of reality and fiction are crossed as riots unfold during the convention. Slick camerawork coupled with a politically charged backdrop provide a hauntingly real portrayal of the volatile late 1960s.

Ordained Presbyterian minister Fred Rogers was a comforting presence for multiple generations of young children. *Mr. Rogers' Neighborhood* began on Canadian TV in 1963, was picked up by NET in 1967, and premiered on PBS two years later. Rogers gently stressed neighborly virtues and the beauty of each day. He made a ritual of changing into sneakers and a cardigan at the beginning of each show, before leadings his viewers in song or taking them by trolley into the "Land of Make Believe," where he talked to puppets King Friday and Lady Elaine. To the delight of children and parents, *Mr. Rogers' Neighborhood* remained on the air well into the 21st century.

Big Bird was one of the many lovable Jim Henson Muppets who populated the television series *Sesame Street,* which premiered on public television in 1969. Big Bird's friends included odd couple Ernie and Bert, Oscar the Grouch, and the

always-ravenous Cookie Monster. The Children's Television Workshop, which produced the educational show, was a not-for-profit company funded by private foundations and the federal government. *Sesame Street* mixed the live action of the Muppets with real people who inhabited a staged inner-city neighborhood. The producers created an innovative and entertaining way to help two- to five-year-olds make the transition from home to school.

October 31: Selective Service records are shredded at 44 Selective Service offices in Indianapolis. An antiwar group that calls itself Beaver 55 claims credit.

November: Several Black Panther women are jailed in Connecticut on charges of murder and conspiracy. The arrests are part of the FBI's COINTELPRO "dirty tricks" campaign designed to harass and destroy the Panthers. The women are Frances Carter, Maude Francis, Peggy Hudgins, Erica Huggins, Rose Smith, and Jean Wilson.

November 3: President Nixon announces that he plans to withdraw American troops from Vietnam on a secret timetable. His "Vietnamization" plan calls for continued training of South Vietnamese troops to take over the fighting from American forces, and development of the Saigon government so that it can rule effectively. • In a televised speech, President Nixon asks the "great silent majority of my fellow Americans" to support his Vietnam strategy, and suggests that most Americans already stand with him.

November 5: In Chicago, Black Panther leader Bobby Seale is sentenced to four years in prison for contempt of court.

November 7: The Washington, D.C., offices of Dow Chemical are vandalized by antiwar protesters. Activists also break into a Dow Chemical data center at Midland, Michigan, where they erase magnetic tape carrying chemical and biological research. • In Boston, antiwar activists break into four offices that hold Selective Service files and splash the room with ink and chemicals.

November 11: The UN rejects, for the 20th time, a motion to seat Red China.

The former Vera von Lehndorff of Germany burst upon the international modeling scene as "Veruschka" in the mid-1960s. Notable for her long, lithe body and cat-like grace, her image graced the covers of the top fashion magazines of the day. She even posed while clad only in body paint. Veruschka made an unforgettable appearance as herself in Michelangelo Antonioni's avant-garde 1966 film *Blowup*.

A product of the Sixties' sexual revolution, Philip Roth's novel *Portnoy's Complaint* is a carnal journey into the psychology of protagonist Alexander Portnoy and his unappeasable sexual desires. Written as a narrative between the main character and his therapist, this brash and laugh-out-loud story examines the nagging sense of guilt that afflicts Portnoy when his fantasies get the best of him. Portnoy's complaint is ultimately based upon the relationship he has with his overprotective mother and how his Jewish upbringing has shaped his identity.

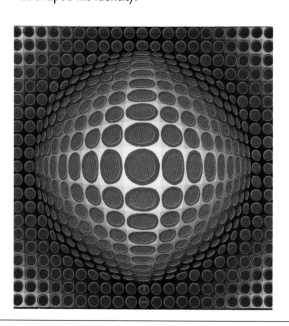

Hungarian-born artist Victor Vasarely's *Vega-Tek* is an example of the Op Art movement that came into prominence in the 1960s. The genre was typified by its "kineticism," or movement, which was distinct from the static nature of conventional renderings. Op (for optical) Art relied on illusion of depth or changing perspective, inviting the observer to interpret images freely. Along with British artist Bridget Riley, Vasarely deserves credit for making Op Art a signature style of the decade.

On November 15, 1969, throngs of peaceful protesters, hailing from the far corners of the nation, converged on the streets of Washington, D.C., demanding that the United States withdraw from the war in Vietnam. All told, the crowd swelled to at least a quarter-million people. The massive protest, organized by the New Mobilization Committee

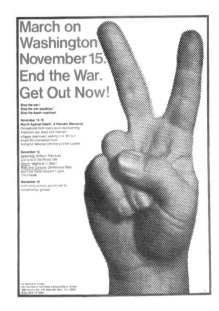

to End the War in Vietnam (MOBE), capped three days of organized protests in Washington and throughout the country.

After World War II, the U.S. government made efforts to relocate Native Americans from reservation lands to cities. As the population of urban Indians increased by the 1960s, and as civil rights preoccupied a generation, urban Native Americans in such cities as San Francisco began to agitate for Indian rights. Alcatraz, a former prison standing idle in San Francisco Bay, became a potent symbol in this fight for native rights in 1969. That year, a group of Bay Area Indians decided to bring attention to the problems of discrimination and ongoing treaty disputes. Beginning in November, about 100 Native Americans took "the rock," claiming the federally owned island as liberated land for an Indian cultural center. Though they never got their cultural center, the occupation became a symbolic rallying point for the growing American Indian Movement.

The protesters who took over the streets of Washington, D.C., on November 15 were predominantly students, arriving on buses and trains from around the country. They flew flags and carried signs with such slogans as "Tyranny has always depended on a silent majority" and "Vietnam: Love it or leave it." Many politicians and celebrities also showed up. Black activists Dick Gregory and Coretta Scott King marched, as did senators Eugene McCarthy and George McGovern. Conductor Leonard Bernstein viewed the sea of humanity that he addressed during the protest and said, "I'm with you. You're beautiful."

1969

November 13: Some 46,000 demonstrators parade past the White House with names of U.S. soldiers killed in Vietnam. • Vice President Spiro Agnew accuses the three major television networks of irresponsible news coverage.

November 15: In Washington, D.C., approximately 250,000 people march down Pennsylvania Avenue and sing for peace at the foot of the Washington Monument. It is the largest antiwar demonstration in the nation's history.

November 17: The first Strategic Arms Limitation Talks (SALT I) between the United States and the Soviet Union begin in Helsinki, Finland.

November 18: Joseph Kennedy, patriarch of the Massachusetts Kennedy clan, dies at 81.

November 19: Apollo 12 astronauts Charles Conrad and Alan Bean walk on the moon while command module pilot Richard Gordon orbits overhead.

November 20: American Indian activists seize control of Alcatraz Island in San Francisco Bay, ostensibly to gain what they claim to be rightful title to the island, but more broadly as a way to make Americans aware of Indian issues and grievances. The island will be occupied for 19 months. • The Nixon Administration orders a halt to the use of the pesticide DDT in residential areas within 30 days. • Henry Cabot Lodge, chief U.S. peace negotiator in Paris, resigns.

November 25: President Nixon orders that stores of germ warfare agents in the U.S. be destroyed.

November 26: President Nixon signs a bill providing for a draft lottery.

On December 1, 1969, nervous young men and their families tuned in to watch Paul M. Murray of the Selective Service reach into a hopper filled with 366 blue plastic capsules, each one representing a day of the year. The first draft lottery held in the United States in a generation resembled a gloomy sweepstakes. The government had initiated the system after widespread student protest and criticism of the overall inequity of the draft. By selecting random birth dates, it was thought, the system could not be accused of inequity. For this lottery,

men born from 1944 through 1950 were eligible, and the drawing set the order of call-ups for 1970. The first date drawn was September 14. The drawing continued until all days of the year had been paired with sequence numbers.

The peace sign painted on the front of this armored vehicle near Con Thien, South Vietnam, was an indication that morale and discipline among soldiers—especially involuntary draftees—had begun to diminish. Like their peers back home, many soldiers questioned the war, listened to protest music on radios, and indulged in drugs. In fact, nearly 50 percent of GIs experimented with opium, pot, and other drugs that were easily available on the streets of Saigon. U.S. Army hospitals were increasingly deluged with drug-related casualties.

Unjustifiable Homicide

ALTHOUGH MANY BLACK PANTHERS were preoccupied with violent reaction against authority, others had higher goals. Young Fred Hampton, who founded the Chicago chapter of the Black Panther Party in 1968, was one of the party's leading lights. He established a community service program that provided a free medical clinic and free breakfasts for black schoolchildren. He also persuaded Chicago's most powerful street gangs to stop fighting each other.

Fearful of the power such a leader could wield, federal agents working for J. Edgar Hoover's infamous COINTELPRO program targeted Hampton. This extralegal FBI operation sought to destroy and undermine any group deemed "radical" by the bureau, including civil rights and antiwar organizations.

A federal informant who had infiltrated the Chicago Panthers provided police with a detailed map of the party's communal apartment, in which Hampton lived. In the early morning hours of December 4, more than a dozen police officers stormed the residence, spraying the occupants with automatic weapons fire. Hampton, who had been drugged and was sleeping beside his pregnant fiancée, was riddled

Fred Hampton

with 44 bullets. Twenty-two-year-old Mark Clark, leader of the Panther's Peoria chapter, also was killed.

In due time, the transparently false police account of the events unraveled. Although the city settled with survivors of the raid and families of the deceased in 1982, no one ever was charged in the deaths.

"We told the cops how bad these guys were, that the cops had better look out or their wives were going to be widows.... We set up the police to go in there and kill the whole lot."

—CHICAGO-BASED FBI AGENT ON THE KILLING OF FRED HAMPTON, AS RECALLED BY FELLOW FBI AGENT WESLEY SWEARINGEN

Chicago police officers smile as they carry the body of local Black Panther Party leader Fred Hampton from his apartment after police shot more than 90 bullets into the party's Chicago headquarters. The attack took place not long after the riots at the Democratic convention and the Chicago Seven trial. The event illustrated the escalating level of violence and paranoia that gripped radicals, who threatened to "off the pigs," and American police departments, which reacted with overwhelming force.

1969

December: An underground abortion referral service called Jane, which helps women obtain safe and affordable abortions, becomes active in Chicago.

December 1: The Selective Service conducts the first draft lottery since World War II. Each day of the year is pulled at random and assigned a sequential number. Draft-eligible men whose birthdays match the first-selected dates will be the first men drafted.

December 2: Nearly 200 members of the press get a preview flight in Boeing's new 747 jumbo jet. Participants are astonished that a craft as large as the 747 can fly.

December 4: Two Black Panthers, including Chicago Panther leader Fred Hampton, are killed by Chicago police in an early-morning ambush raid. *See* December 12, 1969.

December 6: A free rock concert at Altamont Raceway in northern California, organized and headlined by the Rolling Stones, gets out of hand when the expected crowd of 10,000 swells to 300,000. Four people die during the mayhem.

December 12: The U.S. Justice Department announces its intention to investigate the December 4 killing of two Black Panthers by Chicago police.

December 15: The ultraconservative John Birch Society calls for a national campaign to oppose sex education in America's public schools.

December 17: *The Tonight Show* wedding of singer Tiny Tim and Miss Vicky (Budinger) draws the highest-ever late-night television ratings.

December 31: During the year, America's fighting strength in Vietnam is reduced by 115,000 men. The overall number of troops killed rises to 40,024.

Chief Warrant Officer Hugh Thompson talks with reporters after testifying before the My Lai inquiry on December 4, 1969. Thompson's heroism had saved some villagers from the slaughter by U.S. soldiers during the My Lai massacre. Although the atrocity, in which more than 300 civilians were killed, had occurred on March 16, 1968, it remained a secret until GI Ron Ridenhour sent letters to Army brass and members of Congress beginning in March 1969. Reporter Seymour Hersh went public with the news in November 1969. Many Americans, in a state of denial, believed false reports that the American soldiers had been under attack at the time.

In September 1969, U.S. military authorities accused Army Lieutenant William Calley of murdering 109 Vietnamese civilians. In taking the fall for the My Lai massacre, Calley—in many minds—was being scapegoated for the wrongs of his superiors. His murder conviction and sentence to life at hard labor in March 1971 was quickly commuted by President Nixon to house arrest during the appeal process. By November 1974, Calley was a free man.

Called the "White Lady of Soul," Dusty Springfield began her music career as part of a folk group called the Springfields in her home country of England. During the mid-1960s she developed a love for soul music, and with her sultry voice she won over fans. By 1969 Springfield had produced many popular songs, including "Wishin and Hopin," and that year she recorded the album *Dusty in Memphis,* which featured "Son of a Preacher Man." The album and the song became international hits.

On December 6, 1969, the Rolling Stones held a free concert at the Altamont Raceway near Livermore, California. It was a total disaster. The event became synonymous with drugs and violence, marking the end of hopeful youth culture. The Stones played the Altamont festival along with such Bay Area rock bands as Santana and Jefferson Airplane. The Stones made the big mistake of hiring the Hell's Angels as security for their show, paying them with $500 in beer. During the concert, as the crowd pushed against the too-low stage, the Angels beat spectators with pool cues and pelted them with full beer cans. At the height of the violence, members of the motorcycle club beat and stabbed to death a black man named Meredith Hunter. Three other people died at the festival.

When *Time* magazine remarked on the ubiquitous new pantsuit in 1969, it noted that the outfits could be seen, in fabrics casual or elegant, at student demonstrations, hippie love fests, and even the office. More than 45 million pantsuits were sold that year. From the height of couture fashion (they were popularized by designer Yves Saint Laurent) to the masses, pantsuits became an expression of feminist consciousness and relaxed style. "By the year 2000," designer Geoffrey Beene predicted, "women will be wearing only pants."

Musical performer Tiny Tim (Herbert Buckingham Khaury) and "Miss Vicky" (Victoria May Budinger) verge on a kiss during their wedding on NBC's *The Tonight Show* on December 17, 1969. The appearance broke late-night ratings, as Americans could not wait to see the eccentric performer's nuptials. With his ukulele, falsetto voice, and odd appearance, Tiny Tim had made a name for himself in the folk clubs of Greenwich Village in the early 1960s as a novelty act. In 1968 he produced his only hit single, "Tiptoe Through the Tulips." His marriage to a fan, Budinger, on Johnny Carson's popular show marked the apex of his fame.

New & Notable

Books

Everything You've Always Wanted to Know About Sex But Were Afraid to Ask by Dr. David Reuben
The Godfather by Mario Puzo
The Kingdom and the Power by Gay Talese
Naked Came the Stranger by Penelope Ashe
The Peter Principle by Laurence J. Peter and Raymond Hull
Portnoy's Complaint by Philip Roth
The Promise by Chaim Potok
The Sensuous Woman by "J"
Slaughterhouse-Five by Kurt Vonnegut, Jr.
The Spook Who Sat by the Door by Sam Greenlee

Movies

Butch Cassidy and the Sundance Kid
Easy Rider
The Love Bug
Medium Cool
Midnight Cowboy
Take the Money and Run
True Grit

Songs

"Aquarius/Let the Sunshine In" by the Fifth Dimension
"Bad Moon Rising" by Creedence Clearwater Revival
"A Boy Named Sue" by Johnny Cash
"Everyday People" by Sly and the Family Stone
"Get Back" by the Beatles
"Get Together" by the Youngbloods
"Honky Tonk Woman" by the Rolling Stones
"Lay Lady Lay" by Bob Dylan
"Suspicious Minds" by Elvis Presley

Television

The Brady Bunch
Love, American Style
Marcus Welby, M.D.
Room 222
Sesame Street

Theater

Butterflies Are Free
Coco
Last of the Red Hot Lovers
Oh! Calcutta!
1776

Linda Kasabian (*foreground*) and Leslie Van Houten, two members of the Manson family cult, are escorted by police from a Los Angeles courtroom after a December 22, 1969, hearing on the multiple murder charges against them. With a combination of charisma, drugs, and spiritual rhetoric, Charles Manson had wooed troubled young people, especially young women, into his "family" in the desert near L.A. In August 1969, his followers committed several shocking murders at his bidding. During their trial, most of them sought to take the blame and protect Manson from prosecution. Kasabian later received immunity for testifying against Manson and against those who committed the murders.

By the end of the 1960s, Robert Crumb and other leading lights of the underground comix movement satirized not just the depredations of the establishment, but the pretensions of activists. This 1969 issue of *Motor City Comics* is an all-Crumb effort that skewers what the artist/writer viewed as loudmouthed, naively militant feminists. In true superhero style, Lenore Goldberg and her Girl Commandos outfight and outfox the dreary, sexually repressed middle-aged power brokers who oppose them. But problems arise when one of the Commandos turns out to be an informant for "the Man." Crumb's point was that activists are as prone as anybody else to misjudgment and overconfidence.

Most young American men who made a point to avoid induction into the armed services during the Vietnam War remained in the States, but Canada became home to thousands of draft dodgers, deserters, and conscientious objectors who felt safest beyond U.S. borders. Many of the "refugees" worked to help settle others who had made the journey. Here, the Montreal American Deserters Committee holds a Christmas celebration in December 1969. Some who fled were well educated and had little difficulty supporting themselves, but most had had modest schooling, little hope of wrangling deferments at home, and dim prospects for work in Canada. Some of the expatriates elected to remain in Canada and seek Canadian citizenship. In the 1970s, after the war, presidents Gerald Ford and Jimmy Carter offered amnesty for draft-related offenses—an offer that was accepted by many.

In 1969, a year they devoted to peace and love, the recently married John Lennon and Yoko Ono held their "bed-in" for peace in a Canadian hotel room and recorded the single "Give Peace a Chance." For Christmas 1969, the couple rented billboard space in major cities throughout the world to advertise their holiday message, which was taken from lyrics to "Happy Christmas," a song later released by the Plastic Ono Band. This billboard in Times Square in New York City reads, "WAR IS OVER! If you want it. Happy Christmas from John & Yoko."

A nun passes the body of a North Vietnamese soldier killed in Dong Lach, South Vietnam. Through 1969 the United States had expended a total of 8,061,000 metric tons of munitions in the air and on the ground in Vietnam. The decade of warfare resulted in the deaths of 40,024 U.S. troops, including 9,414 in 1969 alone. Despite the loss of 109,465 North Vietnamese soldiers during the war and the death of their leader, Ho Chi Minh, the North continued its strategy of protracted war. Peace talks with the U.S. remained stalemated, as President Nixon continued to pursue an honorable settlement and a policy of "Vietnamization" of the war, slowly withdrawing troops from the country.

Epilogue

Echoes of an Era

THE DRAMATIC EVENTS and movements associated with the 1960s did not end with its chronological close. The rights revolution launched by African-Americans continued to evolve well after the 1960s had officially ended. New Frontier and Great Society programs, forged by Democratic presidents John F. Kennedy and Lyndon Johnson, respectively, endured through the subsequent decades, even as conservatives gained hold of the White House and Congress. The cultural experimentation that shocked so many during the Summer of Love became a part of the nation's mainstream. The movement mantra, "question authority," became conventional wisdom due to the Watergate scandal. Even the 1991 collapse of the Soviet Union, which ended the Cold War, did not completely erase the East–West tensions that had defined much of the 1960s. And for millions of Baby Boomers, the Sixties era would forever represent their coming of age, a time when their generation was, in so many ways, not just living through historical changes but actually making history.

Some aspects of the 1960s, it should be noted, withered away. The Cold War certainties emphatically pronounced by President Kennedy at the beginning of the 1960s dissolved in the bloody quagmire of Vietnam. The cocky post-World War II optimism that had allowed President Johnson to declare a "war on poverty" was gone as well. Some pundits, noting that many of Johnson's policies had failed, declared that poverty had won the war. And as the nation suffered through a series of economic shocks, the exuberant prosperity that had undergirded Sixties cultural and political experimentation and risk-taking was replaced by a general malaise and a "crisis of confidence," to use President Jimmy Carter's memorable phrase. The nation was in a very differ-

> *"Having had intimate contact with some of the most violent of our universities during the days of antiwar... demonstrations, it's a joy to be invited to a campus today. The students are courteous to visitors, aware of world happenings, and have inquiring not closed minds."*
>
> —RONALD REAGAN, RADIO ADDRESS, APRIL 3, 1978

The Cold War, the underpinning of so many social and political currents of the 1960s, was drawing to a close in 1987, when President Reagan spoke in front of the Berlin Wall at the Brandenburg Gate. Longtime U.S. policies of containment and military buildup initiated during the Truman Administration climaxed with the 1991 dissolution of the Soviet Union. But other echoes of the Sixties remained.

Epilogue

ent place in 1978 than it had been in 1968, even as the legacies of the 1960s continued to shape American society.

The most enduring political legacy of the 1960s was, undoubtedly, the rights revolution launched by African-American civil rights advocates and made law of the land under presidents Kennedy and Johnson. While some outspoken conservatives, including Ronald Reagan, had opposed such measures in the 1960s, a decade later almost no mainstream politician advocated rolling back basic civil rights laws. Instead, the African-American civil rights movement inspired numerous other subordinated groups to demand equality before the law.

A group commemorating the 50th anniversary of women's suffrage marches in St. Louis in 1970. Despite the eventual defeat of the Equal Rights Amendment and imbalances that persist to this day, contemporary women find many more opportunities in the workplace than women did a generation ago.

In the 1970s the women's movement, which had caught fire in the late 1960s, successfully overturned myriad state laws that discriminated against women. Feminists made freedom from sexual harassment at the workplace a legal right, and women's rights lawyers won a Supreme Court decision, *Roe v. Wade* (1973), that made a pregnant woman's decision to have an abortion a constitutionally protected right.

Chicanos fought throughout the Southwest and in the nation's capital for equal protection under the law, including the right to bilingual education and freedom from housing discrimination. Native Americans, in a different vein, fought throughout the 1970s and beyond for greater sovereignty on their reservations and redress for a century of broken treaties.

By the late 1970s, the rights revolution had led to the politicization of gays and lesbians, disabled people, and other groups that had long been victims of discrimination and even public contempt. While some policies aimed at redressing past wrongs—such as affirmative action—were and are controversial, the Sixties-era rights revolution had made an indelible mark on American politics.

Similarly, the smorgasbord of liberal policies and programs instigated by Kennedy and Johnson have, by and large, continued to shape life in the United States. Decades after Kennedy first promoted the idea, young people still join the Peace Corps. Johnson's idealistic belief that poor preschool children deserved a Head Start has become an enduring American institution. The 1965 national health insurance programs for low-income people (Medicaid) and the elderly (Medicare) are even more well-entrenched government policies.

While some parts of the liberal government-established safety net, especially public-housing programs, were torn away by conservative politicians and a more parsimonious electorate, a great deal of New Frontier and Great Society ideas developed into widely popular programs. And it is worth underlining that Republican President Richard Nixon, with an eye on the political mainstream, began the 1970s by creating the Environmental Protection Agency and maintaining the Johnson Administration's commitment to strong antipollution measures. Sixties-era liberal policies that called on the federal government to regulate the marketplace, subsidize human services, and support Americans through hard times continue to touch the lives of virtually every American citizen.

Improper disposal of toxic waste resulted in scenes like this one in Oswego, New York. One of the Sixties' lasting legacies was the creation of the Environmental Protection Agency in 1970. That federal body set pollution standards while mandating clean-ups and punishing violators. Discernable progress was made, despite the constant threat of rollbacks from industrial lobbyists.

Sixties-era political programs are easy to list; harder to describe is the cultural shift that the Sixties generation bequeathed to society. Everything from the popularity of yoga and other forms of eastern spirituality to the omnipresence of sexually explicit movies and music can be connected to the rebellious culture of the 1960s. In the 1950s, situation comedies wouldn't even show a married couple in the same bed. Today, satellite television airs X-rated films while broadcast TV titillates its audience with glimpses of sex and nudity. The line from *Leave It to Beaver* to *Sex in the City* runs straight through the 1960s, an era in which the U.S. Supreme Court outlawed most obscenity and censorship laws.

Drug use in the 1960s moved from the far margins of society to somewhere in the center, where it has stayed today even as substances such as marijuana, amphetamines, and cocaine have remained illegal. Americans have become far more tolerant and even curious about formerly exotic beliefs, foods, dress, and sexual orientation. In a suburban-school celebration of an African-American hero, in a middle-class family's dinner at a vegetarian Thai restaurant, in a "soccer mom's" delivery of her daughters to afternoon practice, in the welcome the extended family gives cousin Robert and his partner Bill at the big Easter dinner, the anti-establishment Sixties live on. Aspects of the Sixties counterculture that challenged so many traditional verities have become, for many people, the new American common sense.

A neighborhood in the Bronx, New York, resembles a war zone. President Lyndon Johnson's "war on poverty" was doomed by under-funding followed by cutbacks under subsequent administrations. As policy shifted toward promoting private-sector economic growth, it became clear that "poverty had won the war."

While the Sixties gave shape to the decades that followed, aspects of the era fell away as times changed and as a popular conservative countermovement sprang up to challenge liberal policies and cultural attitudes. Ronald Reagan made the conservative political argument against the expansive liberal

Epilogue

Travelers at Washington National Airport read of President Nixon's impending resignation in August 1974. Two years earlier, Nixon had attempted to obstruct justice to cover up a break-in at the Democrats' Watergate headquarters. Investigations detailing the President's foul play became public knowledge. With certain impeachment looming, Nixon resigned.

American involvement in the Vietnam War ended on the rooftop of the U.S. Embassy in Saigon in late April 1975, as military helicopters evacuated American personnel. The peace agreement signed in Paris in 1973 had marked the beginning of the United States' withdrawal from hostilities.

agenda of the Sixties when he was inaugurated as president in 1981: "Government is not the solution," he said. "It is the problem." Under Reagan's leadership, welfare payments were cut and food stamp benefits were reduced. Federal antipollution regulations were rolled back, key industries were deregulated, and a host of other government measures were attacked as a waste of taxpayers' money and as a hindrance to economic growth. Over time, many Americans accepted conservatives' belief that people should put their hopes for a more equitable and just society not in government reform but in the job- and wealth-producing power of the economic marketplace.

Reagan's successful attack on liberal big government probably could not have succeeded without the economic shocks of the 1970s. Much of the government experimentation of the Sixties era had been based on the economic success of the post-World War II years that had lifted family income not just for the wealthy but for working-class Americans as well. Economically comfortable, Americans in the 1960s were willing to attempt the war on poverty that President Johnson supported.

In the 1970s international competition, led by America's onetime enemies, Japan and Germany, began to drag down such core American industries as automobiles, steel, and electronics. Foreign manufacturers undercut American companies on price, and for the first time since the late 19th century, the U.S. began to import more than it exported. At the same time, a shrewd cartel of oil-producing nations, led by Saudi Arabia, Iran, Iraq, and Kuwait, drastically increased the cost of oil. In the economic chaos of the 1970s, unemployment rose while American productivity slumped. An inflationary spiral began forcing Americans to pay more for everything from hamburger meat to gasoline. In such an economic climate, fewer Americans wanted to send a substantial percentage of their dwindling paychecks to Washington, D.C., to support government spending on the indigent. The economic boom years of the 1960s ended in the early 1970s, and the mood of the country shifted.

This apparent malaise also was shaped by a domestic political scandal as well as by international events. Beginning shortly after Richard Nixon was inaugurated for his second presidential term in January 1973, investigative newspaper reporting and congressional hearings began to tighten a noose around the Nixon White House. The President and his most senior advisers had known about a politically motivated break-in at the Democratic National Committee headquarters at the Watergate office complex. They then fabricated a complex cover-up that included bribery, obstruction of justice, and perjury. The nation reeled as the truth emerged.

Finally, congressional investigators discovered that President Nixon had tape-recorded Oval Office conversations with his staff. These revealed that Nixon was fully implicated in the Watergate scandal. In August 1974, facing sure impeachment, Nixon became the first president to resign from office. Americans were forced to wonder what had gone wrong in the long journey from John Kennedy's buoyant Camelot to Richard Nixon's fallen White House.

Less than a year later, on April 30, 1975, the whole world watched as victorious Communist troops took control of Saigon. After a 30-year war, Vietnam was a unified, independent, Communist nation. American troops had been gone for about two years, but the last United States officials were forced to flee the U.S. Embassy by helicopter. Thousands of terrified Vietnamese who had worked for the Americans were left behind to the uncertain mercies of the Communists. It was an ignominious end to a Cold War foreign policy that had begun some 30 years earlier as an idealistic adventure in nation-building. President Gerald Ford called it "one of the saddest days of my life." The American "victory culture" that had been bred in World War II was in shambles.

In 1984 civil rights activist Jesse Jackson became the first African-American to make a serious run for president. A protégé of Martin Luther King, Jr., Jackson and his Rainbow Coalition drew disaffected voters from all races into a formidable movement. Possessing spellbinding rhetorical skills as well as a knack for self-promotion, Jackson ensured his influence within the Democratic Party for years to come.

In the final tragedy of Vietnam, the Watergate debacle, and the economic slump of the 1970s, the great dreams of the 1960s faded away. A new, more conservative political establishment emerged. All the while, a culture war broke out between those who wanted to build on the legacy of the Sixties and those who wanted to retreat to an idealized version of the Eisenhower years.

Despite the altered national landscape, the Sixties became forever woven into the national fabric. Equal opportunity became the law of the land. National diversity became widely accepted and even celebrated. A citizenry more skeptical and challenging of authority became empowered. Today, some Americans claim that such changes did society more harm than good and pray that the controversial Sixties era will lose its grip on the American imagination. Others, who see in the Sixties a rare era of progressive change, say only: Dream on.

Index

Righteous Brothers, 201, *201*
    Springfield, 444, *444*
    sweatshirts, 102
    Warwick, 182, *182*
    Woodstock Festival, 329, 405, *405*, 428, 430–431, *430–431*
    See also rock 'n' roll/rock music.
Muskie, Edmund, 382, 385, *385*
Mustang (car), 184, *184*
My Fair Lady, 209, *209*
My Lai massacre, 362–363, *362–363*, 364, 428, 432, 444

N

Nader, Ralph, 231, *231*, 246
Naked Came the Stranger (McGrady, *et al.*), 423, *423*
Naked Lunch (Burroughs), 128
Namath, Joe, 218, *218*, 407, *407*, 408
Napalm, 224, 267, *267*, 334, 412
Nashville, Tennessee, 30, 34
Nasser, Gamal Abdul, 38, 317, 318, 320
Nathanson, Bernard, 352
National Abortion Rights Action League (NARAL), 352, 406
National Advisory Commission on Civil Disorders, 325, 326, 360
National Association for the Advancement of Colored People (NAACP), 17, 77, 186
National Commission on the Causes and Prevention of Violence, 396
National Committee for Sane Nuclear Policy (SANE), 56, 101
National Conference for a New Politics, 330
National Coordinating Committee to End the War in Vietnam, 269
National Council of Churches, 70
National Farm Workers Association (NFWA), 120, 243, *243*, 264
National Liberation Front (FLN) (Algeria), 112
National Liberation Front (NLF). *See* Vietcong.

National Organization for Women (NOW)
    Equal Rights Amendment and, 256, 414, *414*
    founded, 254, 256, 276
    job discrimination and, 330, 340, 378
    media and, 259
    Miss America Beauty Pageant and, 382
    Public Accommodations Week, 410
    strategy, 257
National Public Radio (NPR), 439
National Review, 111
National Student Association (NSA), 45, 304
National Traffic and Motor Safety Act, 231
National Turn in Your Draft Card Day, 396
National Welfare Rights Organization, 260
National Wilderness Preservation System, 194
Nation of Islam (NOI), 40
    Malcolm X and, 68, 186, 190, *190*, 219
    Muhammad Ali and, 178, 180, 311
Nation of Sheep, A, (Lederer), 73, *73*
Native Americans
    Alcatraz takeover, 405, 441, *441*, 442
    American Indian Movement, 378, 405
    fish-ins, 180
    legacy of Sixties for, 450
    Navajo Community College, 408
    reservation snowed in, 340
Natural disasters
    earthquakes, 36, *36*, 181, *181*, 182, 382
    floods, 30, 288, 290, *290*
    hurricanes, 42, 80, 428, 429, *429*
    rains, 408
    snowstorms, 128, 340, 410
    tornadoes, 226, *226*, 228, 370
    wildfires, 86, 93, *93*
Navajo Community College, 408
Nedelya, 167, *167*
Negro American Labor Council, 34
Negroes with Guns (Williams), 77
Nehru, Indira, 186

Nehru, Jawaharlal, 89, 122, 186, *186*
Nelson, Ed, 209, *209*
Nelson, Gaylord, 403
Nesmith, Michael, 292, *292*
Nevins, Al, 127
Newark, New Jersey, 322, 325, *325*, 326, 358
New Buffalo Commune, 318
Newell, Amelia, 102
Newfield, Jack, 384
New Frontier. *See* Kennedy, John Fitzgerald.
New Guard, 45
New Hampshire, 144
Newhart, Bob, 26
New Haven, Connecticut, 328
New Jersey, 192, 194, 278, 322, 325, *325*, 326
    See also specific cities.
New Journalism, 245
New Left, 217
    See also Students for a Democratic Society (SDS).
New Left Notes, 257
Newman, Paul, 340, *340*, 434, *434*
New Orleans, 54, *54*
New Right. *See* conservative movement.
Newspapers
    alternative, 299
    gay and lesbian, 326
    New York Mirror, 160
    underground, 186, 218, 234, 286, 385, *385*
Newsweek, 204
Newton, Huey
    Black Panther Party, 286, 314, *314*
    murder conviction, 334
    sentenced, 386
New York. *See specific cities.*
New York City
    antiwar protests, 230, 310, 371, *371*
    City College of, 414, *414*, 416
    counterculture movement in, 318
    draft protests, 343
    garbage strike, 356
    Greenwich Village, 15, 38
    Lincoln Center, 284
    Lindsay elected, 246
    race riots, 190, 193, *193*
    Transport Workers Union strike, 260
    World's Fair, 181, *181*, 184, 193, *193*, 240
    World Trade Center, 280, 284, *284*

New York Mets, 117, *117*, 120, 437, *437*
New York Mirror, 160
New York Radical Women, 338
New York Stock Exchange, 110, 330, 389, *389*
New York Times, The, 119, 191, 199, 232, 244, 259, 268, 312, 317, 330, 360, 361, 378, 411, 415, 416, 433
New York Yankees, 122
Nhan Dan, 324
Nicaragua, 41, 304
Nichols, Mike, 44, 52
Nicklaus, Jack, 110
Nico, 262, *262*
Nidetch, Jean, 43, 82, *82*
Nigeria, 272, 318, 341
Night of the Living Dead, 389, *389*
Nike-Zeus anti-missile missiles, 88
Nimoy, Leonard, 285, *285*
Nixon, Julie, *395*, 396
Nixon, Pat, *395*
Nixon, Richard, *22*
    background of, 127
    California gubernatorial defeat, 124, 127, *127*
    civil rights and, 180, 428, 434
    election of 1960, 22–23
        loss, 50
        nominated, 40
        television debates, 44, 46, 47, *47*, 50
    election of 1968, 350, 356
        campaign, 387, 388, *388*, 395, 421
        nominated, 380
        television, 386
        victory, 351, 394, 395, *395*
    environment and, 451
    FBI spying and, 418, *418*
    foreign policy, 426, 429, *429*
    Hoffa and, 195
    image of, 353, *353*, 410, *410*
    inaugurated, 406, *406*, 408
    popularity of, 388
    resignation, *452*, 452–453
    space exploration and, 400, 402
    Vietnam War and, 403
        antiwar movement and, 310, 404
        bombing of Cambodia, 411, 412, 415
        Calley and, 362, 432, 444

Acknowledgments

All included material by Dr. Martin Luther King, Jr., reprinted by arrangement with the Estate of Martin Luther King, Jr., c/o Writers House as agent for the proprietor, New York, New York. All material copyright © Dr. Martin Luther King, Jr. All material renewed by The Estate of Martin Luther King, Jr.

Pages 32, 120, 272, 276, 327, 353, and 380: Editorial cartoons by Herb Block. Taken from *Straight Herblock,* Simon & Schuster. Reprinted with permission from The Herb Block Foundation, Washington, D.C.

Page 43: Metrecal ad reprinted with permission from Mead Johnson Nutritionals, Bristol-Myers Squibb Company.

Pages 69, 73, 194, 222, and 410: Clifford H. "Baldy" Baldowski editorial cartoons (chb 272, 238, 287, 1846, and 161), *Atlanta Constitution.* Courtesy of the Richard B. Russell Library for Political Research and Studies, University of Georgia Libraries. Reprinted with permission.

Pages 99 and 131: Excerpts from the SDS Port Huron Statement by Tom Hayden. Reprinted with permission from Tom Hayden.

Page 100: Cover of *Eros* magazine, summer 1962 issue. Copyright © Ralph Ginzburg. Reprinted with permission.

Page 113: "Campbell's Soup Can, 19¢" by Andy Warhol, 1962. Copyright © 2004 Andy Warhol Foundation for the Visual Arts/ARS, New York. TM Licensed by Campbell's Soup Co. Reprinted with permission. All rights reserved.

Page 132: Passage by Fannie Lou Hamer, cofounder of the Mississippi Freedom Democratic Party, from a June 1, 1964, article in *The Nation,* by Jerry DeMuth. Reprinted with permission from Jerry DeMuth.

Page 159: "Two Cheeseburgers, With Everything (Dual Hamburgers)" by Claes Oldenburg, 1962. Copyright © Claes Oldenburg and Coosje van Bruggen. Reprinted with permission.

Page 168: Quote by Jacqueline Kennedy taken from *Look* magazine, November 17, 1964, issue. Reprinted with permission from Hobby-Catto Properties, LLC.

Page 207: "Think Small" Volkswagen ad. Courtesy of the Corporate History Department, Volkswagen AG. Reprinted with permission.

Page 261: "They won't get *us* to the conference table . . . will they?" Editorial cartoon by Pat Oliphant, 1966. Reprinted with permission of the Universal Press Syndicate, Andrews McMeel Universal.

Page 277: "Love" by Robert Indiana. Copyright © 1999 Morgan Art Foundation, Ltd./Artists Rights Society (ARS), New York. Reprinted with permission.

Page 313: Promotional poster from *The Last Redwoods and the Parklands of Redwood Creek,* by François Leydet and James D. Rose. Copyright © 1969 by the Sierra Club. Reprinted with permission of Sierra Club Books.

Page 418: "Nothing new to report again today, Mr. Hoover." Editorial cartoon by Paul Conrad, April–October 1969. Reproduced with permission of the Huntington Library, San Marino, California.

Page 440: "Vega-Tek" by Victor Vasarely, 1969. Copyright © 2004 Artists Rights Society (ARS), New York/ADAGP, Paris. Reprinted with permission.

Photo Credits

Front cover: **AP/World Wide Photos** (top center & top right); **© Corbis** (bottom right); Bettmann (top left & bottom left); **Robert Altman Photography** (bottom center).

Back cover: **Jo Freeman** (top left, left center, right center & bottom right); **PIL Collection** (top right & bottom left).

Advertising Club of New York: 207 (bottom right); **The Albert and Shirley Small Special Collections Library University of Virginia Library:** 261 (top right), 385 (bottom left); **AP/World Wide Photos:** Contents, 22, 25 (bottom), 26 (bottom), 27 (bottom), 29 (top), 30 (top), 31 (top right & bottom), 33 (bottom left), 35 (bottom left & bottom right), 36 (top), 37 (bottom), 38 (bottom), 39 (top & bottom right), 40 (top), 41 (top & bottom), 43 (top right), 44 (bottom), 45 (top left), 48 (bottom), 49 (bottom), 50 (bottom), 51 (bottom left), 55 (top right), 56 (top), 57 (top), 64, 66 (top), 67 (left center & center), 68 (top), 70 (bottom), 75, 77 (bottom), 80, 81 (bottom right), 82 (top), 83 (bottom right), 84 (top), 86 (top), 87 (bottom left & bottom right), 89 (top right), 91 (top right & bottom right), 92 (left center & bottom right), 93 (top left), 98 (top), 99, 102 (top & center), 103, 104 (bottom), 105, 106 (bottom), 107, 109 (right center), 111 (top), 113 (top), 114 (bottom), 115 (top left), 116 (bottom right), 120 (bottom), 121 (top right), 124 (top), 125 (bottom), 129 (top & bottom right), 137, 141 (bottom), 144, 145 (top left & bottom), 147 (top), 148 (top & bottom right), 151, 152 (bottom), 156 (left), 157 (top right & bottom), 159 (left center), 161 (top), 165, 166, 167 (top right & bottom left), 169 (top & bottom right), 171, 172 (bottom), 178 (top), 179 (top), 180 (bottom), 181 (bottom right), 183 (top), 184 (top), 193 (bottom right), 197 (top left), 201 (top left & bottom left), 203 (bottom), 204 (left center), 206 (bottom), 214, 216, 218 (top), 220 (top), 225 (bottom right), 229 (bottom), 231 (top), 235 (top left & top right), 236 (center), 238 (top right), 239 (bottom left), 240 (bottom), 243 (top left & top right), 245 (top right), 247 (bottom right), 248 (top left), 249 (top right), 253 (bottom right), 260 (top), 264 (top), 265 (bottom left), 266, 267, 269 (bottom), 271 (bottom right), 272 (center), 274, 275 (bottom), 277 (top right), 278 (bottom), 280 (bottom), 281 (top left & right), 282, 283 (bottom), 284 (bottom), 288, 290 (top), 293 (right), 294, 295 (bottom left), 303 (top), 304 (top), 305 (center), 307 (bottom), 311 (top), 312 (top), 313 (bottom), 314 (top), 315 (top left), 325 (bottom), 327 (bottom), 329 (top right), 336 (bottom left & bottom right), 337 (bottom left & bottom right), 340 (top), 345 (bottom), 348, 351, 354 (top), 356 (top), 357 (right center), 361 (top right), 364 (bottom), 365 (bottom), 366 (bottom), 368 (bottom), 369 (bottom), 371 (top left), 373 (top), 374 (top), 376 (right), 377, 378 (bottom), 379 (top & bottom left), 380 (top), 381 (bottom), 382 (bottom), 384, 385 (top & bottom right), 387 (bottom), 388 (top left & bottom right), 389 (bottom right), 391 (bottom right), 392 (top left & top right), 394, 398 (bottom), 399 (bottom), 406 (bottom), 407 (bottom right), 410 (top), 411 (top), 413 (bottom), 417 (top & bottom left), 419 (top left & top right), 421 (bottom left), 423 (top left & bottom right), 424 (left), 425 (top right), 427 (bottom), 428 (bottom), 429 (bottom right), 433 (top), 439 (bottom right), 441 (top right), 442 (bottom), 443, 444 (top & center), 445, 446 (top), 449; **Art Resource:** 440 (bottom); The Andy Warhol Foundation, Inc.: 113 (bottom); Digital Image © The Museum of Modern Art/Licensed by SCALA: 141 (top right), 159 (top); Tate Gallery, London: 323 (bottom); **Bert Babcock:** 29 (bottom left); **Tom Barbaruolo:** 250 (bottom); **Brown Brothers:** 117 (bottom left), 121 (bottom right), 186 (top); **CBS/Landov:** 51 (bottom right); **Civil Defense Museum:** 23 (top), 109 (top); **Cleveland Public Library Photograph Collection:** 421 (bottom right); **Collection International Institute of Social History, Amsterdam:** 162 (bottom left), 309 (top left); **Concordia University Archives:** 408 (bottom); **© Corbis:** 15 (top), 42 (bottom left), 44 (top), 57 (bottom), 58 (bottom), 65 (top), 67 (top), 79 (top), 83 (bottom left & top right), 84 (bottom), 85 (bottom), 89 (top left & bottom), 90 (top), 91 (top left), 93 (top right), 101 (bottom left), 104 (top), 111 (bottom right), 122, 125 (top left), 138 (top), 152 (top), 163 (bottom right), 164 (bottom), 180 (top), 185 (bottom), 190 (top), 193 (bottom left), 194 (top), 195 (top), 205 (top right), 210 (top), 215 (bottom), 218 (bottom), 220 (bottom), 228 (top), 230 (bottom), 238 (top

DOUGLAS GAINES Jr · CHARLES M THOMPSON
EDDIE RAY KELLEY · RALPH W KUCHCINSKI · LOWELL
JAMES R MILLER · WILLIAM J MOORE · CLYDE E MO
ANCE McDONALD · WILLIAM J OSKILANEC · NORMA
HARRY E RIVERS · JOSEPH F ROBLE · JOSE MAN
D STANTON Jr · SAMUEL R SUMMERFIELD · DONA
WILLIAM H WHITE · JOHNNY BEE WILLIAMS · ARNO
NEAL G BOLLINGER · SAMUEL BRYANT · ROBE
BERNARD J COOK · DEWAYNE C CORBITT · EDGAR
KEVIN H DUGAN · DAVID EISENBRAUN · RA
KEVIN C HANLEY · WILLIE C HARDY · RA
REX M HOOVER · MICHAEL W ISSENMANN · G B
LEON E KIZZIE · GEORGE LEE Jr · LIONEL MALDO
GARY HILL · WAYNE E MONISMITH · GREG
ARLES E OWENS · WILLIAM PARK · RONALD J P
WILLIAM T PRATT · PAUL M RESSER · THOMAS
LARRY E RICHARDSON · WILLIAM A RIDENOUR
ORGE SANDOVAL · GEORGE D SHANNON · ALBERT W
LLOYD H SMITH · WARREN A SMITH · DARNE
PHILIP E ZELESKI · RONALD W ZYDEL
JOSEPH S BRAVI · RONALD L BROWN · GARY L BRO
ALBERT J DA · GILFORD F DASHNER · STEVEN
WALTER H FENNEL · CHARLES L FREEMAN · JAMES O
ROBERT E GRAY · RALPH L GREEN · WAYN
FREDDIE L LOWERY · CHRISTOPHER D LUCCI · GILBE
STEVEN M ORT · WILLIAM D ROBINSON · JOSE